Guide to
THE BEST
BUSINESS SCHOOLS

SEVENTH EDITION

Kellogg
Harvard
Stanford
UCLA
Wharton
Tuck
Cornell

Guide to
THE BEST
BUSINESS SCHOOLS

SEVENTH EDITION

Betsy Gruber

Margaret Littman

Jennifer Merritt

Management Education Editor, BusinessWeek

with a team of
BusinessWeek Editors

McGraw-Hill
New York   Chicago   San Francisco
Lisbon   London   Madrid   Mexico City
Milan   New Delhi   San Juan   Seoul
Singapore   Sydney   Toronto

Library of Congress Cataloging-in-Publication Data

Gruber, Betsy.
    BusinessWeek guide to the best business schools / Betsy Gruber, Margaret Littman,
Jennifer Merritt.—7th ed.
        p. cm.
    First-5th ed. by John A. Byrne; 6th ed. (not yet in LC) by Cynthia Green.
    Includes index.
    ISBN 0-07-137824-3
    1. Business schools—United States—Evaluation.   2. College choice—United
States—Handbooks, manuals, etc.   3. Master of business administration degree—
United States—Handbooks, manuals, etc.   I. Title: BusinessWeek guide to the best
business schools.   II. Littman, Margaret.   III. Merritt, Jennifer.   IV. Byrne, John
A. BusinessWeek guide to the best business schools.   V. Title.

HF1131 .B95   2001
650'.071'173—dc21   2001032695

McGraw-Hill

A Division of The **McGraw·Hill** Companies

This book was set in Minion by North Market Street Graphics.

Printed and bound by R. R. Donnelley & Sons Company.

 This book is printed on recycled, acid-free paper containing a
minimum of 50% recycled, de-inked fiber.

BusinessWeek

CONTENTS

PREFACE

Scratching your head trying to figure out whether or not to get an MBA—and where to get one if the answer sounds like a yes? You've come to the right place. You are now reading the seventh and most comprehensive edition of a book that is considered the bible for all students and observers of graduate schools of business. Hundreds of thousands of applicants have relied on earlier versions of this book for its wealth of unvarnished, tell-it-like-it-is information and analysis of the top MBA programs. Deans and recruiters also use this guide as a benchmark of how well they've put their ideas and strategies into place.

For this guide, BusinessWeek magazine used the thousands of surveys of graduates and corporate recruiters that it collected for its most recent ranking of business schools as primary research material. That was just the beginning. Next, the staff interviewed hundreds of students, alumni, recruiters, faculty members, and deans to gain an even better understanding of the strengths and weaknesses of the top schools. The result is this book—a product that reveals far more information and insights on the best B-schools than exist anywhere else.

This guidebook is an outgrowth of BusinessWeek's biennial ranking of the best business schools, a project first tackled in 1988. Since then, the magazine has carved out management education as an important and critical area of coverage. It's a mission that extends far beyond the pages of the magazine. BusinessWeek Online, for example, has an extensive site devoted to the best business schools. It includes lengthy profiles of the 82 schools surveyed by BusinessWeek in 2000, featuring helpful statistics, links to schools' Web sites, and dozens of student comments from the survey. And this year, there are even more profiles on nonranked schools—more than 220 total B-schools, divided by geographic region. There's a return-on-investment calculator that helps you determine the true costs of any one program and a host of transcripts of chats with students at the top schools. And something more—there are dozens of video interviews with B-school deans, admissions officers, and placement directors. You can download the transcripts of online conferences with admissions and placement professionals, read the journals of current and recently graduated MBA students, and post a question on a variety of message boards to be answered by BusinessWeek staffers or other visitors to the site. You can access the site at www.businessweek.com/bschools/ or by going to keyword "BW" on America Online.

The authors for the seventh edition were Betsy Gruber, Margaret Littman, and BUSINESSWEEK management education editor Jennifer Merritt. Gruber, a New York City–based freelance writer, is a contributor and former editor for *Chicago Social* and *Angeleno* magazines. Littman, a Chicago-based freelance writer, has been published in numerous national magazines. Merritt, based in New York, is responsible for BUSINESSWEEK's coverage of management education and directed the 2000 rankings project. The format for this book follows that used by BUSINESSWEEK Senior Writer John A. Byrne, who authored the first five editions and created the BUSINESSWEEK ranking of the top schools back in 1988.

Making significant contributions to this book were freelancer and former BUSINESSWEEK editor Cynthia Green, who co-authored the sixth edition of this book; BUSINESSWEEK Online reporter Mica Schneider, who assisted in the research and prepared several pieces for the book; and Francesca Di Meglio, a former BUSINESSWEEK intern and assistant on the rankings project who wrote several of the school profiles. BUSINESSWEEK intern Eric Dash also wrote several school profiles. Both Di Meglio and Dash assisted in research and survey response gathering for the rankings project. Frederick Jespersen served as our number-crunching guru and provided invaluable survey analysis. Cambria Consulting created and managed the online portion of the survey. BUSINESSWEEK Online reporter Schneider, producer Jessica Loudon, and technical guru Joshua Tanzer managed the flow of information to the Web site. Assistant Managing Editor Joyce Barnathan and Managing Editor Mark Morrison supervised the project.

WHY GO FOR THE MBA?

After years of sustained economic growth, the early 2000s have made way for what looks like a slowdown—and if history is any indicator, securing a spot in business school over the next two years could be more competitive than ever. In the boom times, applications at top B-schools fell, some as much as 23 percent. But by the end of application season 2001, those numbers are well on the plus side. And why not? What other degree than the MBA can pack an education into two years, and land grads with starting pay packages that are often double their pay before getting the degree? Moreover, as companies—Old Economy and New Economy—face the challenges of management and corporate growth chock full of e-commerce initiatives and ever-changing technology, the demand for skilled managers is bigger than ever. And having an MBA can open the door to a challenging job with lots of responsibility and ample payback.

Getting an MBA is anything but a move away from the real world. It's a combination of technical and practical skills, a sometimes brutal two-year boot camp in which you learn to deconstruct a balance sheet, negotiate a raise, and make buddies and business contacts everywhere on the planet. Says Donald P. Jacobs, retiring dean of Northwestern University's Kellogg Graduate School of Management: "Twenty-five years ago, the degree was something that mimicked best practices. Since then, it's become a research-based curriculum that is really at the frontier. It gives you the ability to have life-long education."

As we enter the new millennium, the MBA is unquestionably the hottest degree you can hold, particularly from an elite school. The stats prove it: At virtually all of the best schools, GMAT scores and starting pay packages are setting records. Applications are too, although a large part of the boom is coming from overseas. Domestic applications have been relatively flat, in part because so many Americans didn't want to miss out on the thriving economy. The 82 U.S., Canadian, and European schools surveyed by BUSINESSWEEK for its 2000 rankings waded through nearly 140,000 applications for the Class of 2002, and the average GMAT score was 672 for those attending the Top 30 schools, up from 667 just two years earlier.

> These days, the MBA is the hottest degree you can hold.

The boom has been all the more surprising because in past decades, MBA education was a countercyclical phenomenon, something you did when the job market was shaky and you wanted to stand out when people were hiring again. "The economy has been strong since 1992, but demand in terms of applications and enrollment has been strong too," says Charles W. Hickman, director for projects and services at the AACSB—International Association for Management Education and the principal MBA accreditation agency. Today, the MBA is on its way to becoming a requirement for anyone who hopes to build a career in Corporate America, and, indeed, much of the world. "Probably our number-one social contribution is compiling great talent," says retiring Dean B. Joseph White of the University of Michigan Business School.

Certainly, it's true that corporate recruiters can't seem to hire enough MBAs these days. The 247 recruiters who participated in BUSINESSWEEK's 2000 survey of the best business schools hired 15,558 MBAs in total, a significant rise from 1998, when 247 recruiters hired 10,348 MBAs. And they would have hired even more if they could have: Grads of the Top 30 business schools averaged 3.2 job offers each, and compensation exploded. The median pay package (salary, bonus, and extras such as stock options or moving expenses) at the Top 30 hit $126,930, up 14 percent from just two years ago. Another telling figure: Median pay topped $100,000 at 28 of our Top 30—versus 5 two years ago. "The competition for MBAs has definitely quickened," says David L. Reed, director of global recruiting at Accenture. "It's as fierce as I've ever seen it."

Those numbers come from the top of the heap. For the last four years, grads of the very best B-schools were able to hold all the cards in the recruiting game, playing offers off of one another and not being afraid to turn down what in years past would have been a dream job. Even for those coming out of second- and third-tier schools, however, the sizzling economy had them in the catbird seat as well. Despite the dot-com shake-out of 1999, 2000 was a good year to get an MBA; most experts expect the gap between the top echelon and the rest to widen despite the steady demand for employees. Middle-of-the-road schools have a unique opportunity to wow recruiters who have given their grads a chance in the last few years.

The main reason for the MBA's current success is that the degree has changed significantly over the last decade or so. B-schools have listened to their customers—their students and the

> MBAs are always in demand in the corporate world.

recruiters who hire them—and reinvented themselves as a learning laboratory where, once they get their sheepskins in hand, students can immediately add value to their place of work. The first and most radical change is the injection of real-world experience into the degree program itself, something occurring more and more since the mid-1990s. Although you may imagine B-school as a quiet, contemplative experience full of sweater-clad, staid, pipe-smoking profs, think again: B-school is fast-moving, exciting, and more relevant than it's ever been.

Start with your physical surroundings, which are likely to be a lot more comfortable—and more high tech—than you probably could have imagined. Any schools in the Top 30 that don't already have a new facility are likely building or planning one. And expanding technological capabilities remains a top priority. Deans now spend a large part of their time on the road, raising millions so that they can offer their students glistening new buildings (some including everything from showers to a concierge desk to burrito joints), comfy placement facilities, and the best in technology. Indeed, if you haven't been working in Silicon Valley or Seattle, you might think about B-school as a way to catch up with the real world rather than as a way to check out of it. At Cornell's Johnson Graduate School of Management, for example, the Parker Center offers a simulated trading floor with the same analyst software used by the most tech-savvy professionals.

It's not simply the physical plant. Today, not only do professors spend a lot of their time consulting with companies, but students do too. At more and more schools, tackling a real-time project for a real-life company—in which a student may have to present his or her findings to the senior management team—is part of the degree. At Washington University's John M. Olin B-school, for example, four-student teams spend a full semester working with client companies such as Monsanto or Apple Computer, and the companies pay the school for the services of its "consultants"—who also can make up to $1200, depending on performance. And with executive education booming on the same campuses that offer the full-time programs, both students and faculty are interacting on a regular basis with working executives. Schools are also grasping the fact that leadership skills and teamwork, ignored in the past by both academic institutions and companies alike, make as much of a difference to a company's ultimate success or failure as a sound financial strategy does.

Tackling a real-time project may be part of the degree.

Another trend that companies are applauding is the slow but gradual move to change the way students learn. Although you are still likely to take a finance course, an accounting course, and a marketing course at different times and with different professors, most schools are putting pressure on their faculties to break down the professional silos and recognize that the real world has very few subject-specific problems. At the University of Virginia's Darden Graduate School of Business Administration, all of the faculty work together to create a truly integrated group of courses. You may spend two weeks learning finance before you stop to integrate a section on commodity trading in different parts of the world. Then you might return to finance to work on both the micro and macro levels of a metals company's capital-raising options, with both professors guiding you. Additionally, some schools are moving the basics of finance and accounting to pre-term online formats, taken before you arrive for classes.

> More students are able to tailor their own programs.

This breakdown of standard procedure means that more and more students are able to tailor their own programs to personal career goals and interests. It also means, however, that companies play a greater role in this academic arena than ever before—for better and for worse. One somewhat disturbing example is the growing tendency of schools to allow students to take electives earlier and earlier, sometimes before they've had the chance to comprehend the basics relevant to that subject. It's done primarily so that students can show some level of specialization before they leave for their summer internships. The intended result? The student outshines his or her colleagues and gets the final job offer. The responsiveness to customers is a good thing, but some worry that the pendulum is swinging too far away from academic pursuits. "I've always felt that professional schools of business must not allow themselves to become simply a farm system for industries," says Rex D. Adams, dean of the Fuqua School of Business at Duke University. "I think we should have the courage of our convictions."

Cynicism aside, it's hard to find a graduate from one of the top schools who doesn't now think his or her investment was worth it. They describe their two years of graduate study as one of the high points of their lives: meeting bright new friends, sharing new experiences, discovering horizons and careers they never knew existed. The skills and knowledge you accumulate in a good MBA program teach you to think and analyze complicated business problems. They open doors to some of the world's great organizations, including the highest-paying public and private corporations, consulting firms, and investment banks. Yet because some prospective students fail to do their homework, they end up wasting a lot of time and money. They don't find out what an MBA can and can't do for them. They fail to properly evaluate a particular school or program to discover what it can deliver. The upshot: Some people find the rewards of their degree elusive. Much to their chagrin, it fails to deliver on a better job, a bigger salary, and a quick climb up the corporate ladder.

You can avoid that disappointment, however, if you take the MBA quest seriously. You are now holding the best possible guide to help take the guesswork out of one of the most important career decisions you'll ever make. Not merely an uninformed ranking or a series of flimsy profiles written by public relations folks employed by the schools, this guide is a tell-it-like-it-is scouting report on the best of the bunch. For years, as many as 50 schools claimed they were among the top schools, and well over 100 institutions told prospective applicants that they were in the Top 50. We chose the 67 schools we felt were the best in the United States and 15 in Canada and Europe, surveyed nearly 16,500 of their grads (of whom 10,039 responded), and then got feedback from 247 important corporate recruiters. The result: The Top 50 B-schools profiled in this book. You can get information about more than 150 other schools, too, by going to our Web site (www.businessweek.com/bschools/). There you will also find profiles for more than 250 part-time programs.

WHAT ARE MBA STUDENTS LIKE?

In the 1990s, business school emerged as the top draw for the best and the brightest young people—those that might in other eras have become teachers, politicians, or doctors but have chosen business because of its influence and relevance. In this century, the trend is continuing. We are living in an era when, for better or worse, everyone seems to have come down with the capitalist bug and many see the MBA as a way to go from a touch of business fever to a full-blown upward jolt, be it in traditional consulting or investment banking fields or with start-ups and New Economy ventures. What that means is that there's no longer much stereotyping when it comes to the typical MBA student. Of course, you can still find a group of narrow-minded, competitive folks uninterested in much beyond the almighty dollar. But there are fewer and fewer of them these days, and, indeed, admissions officers aren't very interested in that stereotype.

What the admissions folks prefer—and what those at the best schools have the luxury to choose—are true all-arounders, diverse and fascinating members of society who want an MBA for a multitude of reasons, whether it be to start a lightbulb company or to wow Silicon Valley with the next success or to find a way to make charities more efficient. Although many have known exactly what they wanted to do since they were six, just as many others are career changers, those who never really planned a career in business and grew unhappy with what they were doing for a living. Still others have been bitten by the entrepreneurial bug. That doesn't mean they're shiftless, however. You can expect to find some of the most focused individuals you've ever met.

More and more, MBA students are not likely to be corporate drones—although you won't see many pierced tongues, either—and many more intend to start their own businesses, if not immediately after school, then a few years later, after they've paid off some of that hefty debt. Schools have responded to the calls of these students for entrepreneurial training with a bevy of courses, majors, and, occasionally, complete programs in the subject. If you go to a Top 50 school, you should be able to count on such offerings as how to assemble a business plan; raise money from venture capitalists and other investors; incorporate your business; and produce, market, and sell a product. There should be plenty of outside speakers and potential money sources brought in to network with you on a regular basis.

Your fellow students are also likely to be social types who like to let their hair down occasionally. Remember that B-school, unlike other academic experiences you may have had, places nearly as much emphasis on socializing and building teamwork and communication skills these days as it does on your classroom performance. At many schools, such as Kellogg, you won't be admitted unless you show that you can handle a social situation as well as an intricate analytical problem. Says Kellogg's Dean Jacobs: "It's the raw material we start with. We turn down two-thirds of people over 700. It's not just GMATs. What else have you got?"

There is an upside, however—more fun than you probably ever expected to have at B-school. Charity events, salsa parties, international political meetings, hockey or Frisbee games, and formal balls are part of the MBA experience, and some say that the

> There should be plenty of opportunities to network with alumni and outside speakers.

most tiring thing is making a choice about which gatherings to attend. Oh yeah, and despite the reputation of MBAs as being overly concerned with money and not much else, a large part of the socializing is done to support nonprofit charities or other good works. At Notre Dame, for example, the incredible popularity of the university's football team provides opportunities for students to get to know recruiters out of the sterile cocktail party setting. Before every fall game, the school's MBA association holds a tail-gate party in the courtyard of the building and gets a prominent company to sponsor the event.

ALL MBAs ARE NOT CREATED EQUAL

The increased value placed on the MBA by Corporate America has led to an explosion of MBA programs, be they full-time, part-time, or evening and weekend programs for executives. Many schools are relying on these programs to subsidize a slew of other degrees that are losing funding or are not able to support themselves. Indeed, there are now more than 850 MBA programs in the United States that require the GMAT, and dozens more around the world. Some 50,000 or more students started full-time two-year programs in 2000.

Yet although the MBA has become the graduate degree of choice among the corporate elite, emblazoning those initials on your résumé doesn't guarantee you stardom on Wall Street or in Silicon Valley, or anywhere else for that matter. Although many MBA programs appear similar at first glance—all offering accounting, finance, etc.—they're not. The quality of the faculty, the fellow students, the buildings, and the level of technology all have a dramatic impact on your education. Also important is how that degree is perceived by the outside world. If your dream company doesn't even know that your program exists, you'll have a really tough time getting a job there. It's not impossible, of course, but you'll have to get hired on your own, rather than using the connections and the historic relationship developed by other schools' placement offices.

The upshot: Little-known institutions with small MBA programs that lack accreditation aren't likely to give you either a quality business education or a hefty starting salary. It's tougher to get those from some part-time evening MBA programs, too, where the dropout rates are high and you don't get to move through the classes with a cohort of bright students. Certainly many part-time

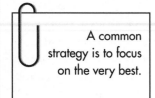

A common strategy is to focus on the very best.

programs are exceptional, but to succeed in them, you need to be incredibly self-disciplined, even more so than those embarking on a full-time MBA plan.

If you want a worthwhile MBA, you need to get it from a school with prestige and a reputation for quality—whether it's known worldwide, throughout the United States, or regionally, depending upon your career goals. Says Meyer Feldberg, dean of Columbia Business School: "The top-ranked MBA programs all share something in common—an outstanding research-based faculty that is not only creating knowledge but able to carry that into the classroom." It's also the students, he says. "You're going to learn a great deal from the faculty, but you'll learn the same amount or more from each other. My advice would be always to go for the quality. You want to be surrounded by people who are going to be as successful as you, if not more successful than you, because it creates the network you will need for so many years."

BUSINESSWEEK customer satisfaction surveys of graduates have found that the greater the reputation of the school, the more likely you are to be happy with your results. Still, you might consider ignoring the big national schools if your goal is to take over the family business or simply to gain basic business know-how. In some cases, an MBA from a local school could be more valuable than one from Wharton, because the relevant business and government contacts to help you in your career would be nearby. It's likely to cost a lot less, too.

When should you think about business school, and where should you go? As flip as it sounds, the answer to the first question is when you've got enough experience under your belt to get into a school that's good enough to have a real impact on you and your career. Although years ago most applicants applied to a huge range of schools, from "safeties" to the truly elite, today a common strategy is to focus only on the very best. If you don't make it the first time, simply reapply. Many schools will meet with rejected students to explain why they didn't make the cut and what they might do differently next time. At Wharton, for example, Robert J. Alig, director of admissions and financial aid, conducted about 1100 "why deny" meetings in 1999–2000.

There is no perfect time for B-school, although applicants are getting older, averaging 27 to 28 years of age when they start school, according to the Graduate Management Admission Council. That's partly due to career changers, who see a pot of gold at the end of the MBA rainbow. But it's also because companies prefer to hire MBAs who already have some work experience and will be able to jump right into a management position as soon as they get out of school. Corporations are giving more responsibility to MBA hires right from the start, say employment experts, a shift from the pre- to mid-1990s when MBA hires were given light loads and gradually advanced up the responsibility ladder. Although it is still possible to get into a good school without much work experience, it's becoming tougher and tougher. At most top B-schools fewer than 2 to 3 percent of the incoming Class of 2002 have less than two years of work experience. At the elite schools, admissions officers are asking for at least two and often three or four years of work experience, although they will make exceptions for truly outstanding candidates. Because so much of your education comes from other students with different backgrounds, it's nice to be able to contribute to the discussion with an example from the workplace. If all of your examples are straight out of your undergrad economics class, your classmates may not be too pleased. That said, you'll get more out of the program if you've already tried to tackle an organizational behavior problem or financial conundrum before going to school. Many MBAs who went directly to B-school from undergrad say they regret not having waited a few years first.

A TOP MBA DEGREE RARELY COMES CHEAP

Like most things valued and coveted by many people, the MBA degree isn't cheap and probably won't ever be. Other than buying a house, going to graduate school is probably the single largest investment a twenty- or thirty-something will make. Think about it: In addition to spending more than $50,000 for two years of tuition and another $20,000 in room and board at many top schools, you're likely to give up twice as much in lost earnings from the job you would have held. Indeed, you could practically start a business on what it costs to get through business school today. The average total investment (two years of tuition plus 18 months of forgone earnings) for graduates of BUSINESSWEEK's 67 surveyed U.S. schools was $126,700, with the costliest total investment the incredible $192,500 spent by members of Harvard Business School's Class of 2000. That helps put into context the fact that those graduates were able to snag the highest median total pay package of all B-schools surveyed by BUSINESSWEEK when they finished—$145,000, including salary, bonus, and such extra perks as moving expenses, stock options, and computers.

That's quite a pretty penny for a business education and a piece of parchment, isn't it? The exorbitant cost of the MBA helps explain why so many grads flock to the best-paid sectors—management consulting, investment banking, and marketing. Of the 2000 graduates from the Top 30 B-schools 74 percent chose one of those three areas, even if they had plans to strike out on their own later on. Ironically, despite the entrepreneurship craze sweeping through business schools over the last four years, fewer than 8 percent of 2000 grads chose to work in a start-up straight out of school. Perhaps they thought they'd do better if they got a few years of more general experience and paid off some of that debt first. (The average 2000 grad owed more than $20,600 coming out of school.)

Yet all of that expense seems to pay off, both in the long run and—until recently, at least—the short run. According to an analysis done for BUSINESSWEEK by Jens Stephan, academic director of MBA programs at the University of Cincinnati, the Class of 2000 will take between 2.8 and 6.3 years (including the 2 years of school) to pay back its investment—down from the 5 to 8 years projected in 1996. That class got a running start on the payback this year, with 2000 grads of the Top 50 schools earning a median salary and bonus of $75,900. Offering the fastest return was Brigham Young University's Marriott School, where students landed jobs with a median salary of $67,000, a 120 percent increase over their pre-MBA salaries. The tuition: $7000 per year. That means grads will pay back their investment of $70,900, including lost wages, in about 3.5 years, compared with an average of 5.2 years for the 67 U.S. B-schools surveyed by BUSINESSWEEK. The slowest return? George Washington University's business school. With a total investment of $125,800 and an average salary increase of 67 percent, it will take about 6.3 years for students to break even.

Some top B-schools are now offering, in addition to their two-year flagship degree, the compressed MBA, in which students with lots of prior business experience can get their degrees in one year or less. Now available in some form at eight of the Top 30 B-schools, it's often one-third the price and gets you out into the workplace quicker. The downside: Less opportunity to network,

---

The MBA is expensive—but seems to pay off.

and no summer internship opportunity for those who aren't 100 percent certain of their career goals.

There are other ways to limit the degree's cost. If you're an entrepreneur, Cornell's Johnson School now offers fellowships that help pay off debt incurred in school. And at Vanderbilt University's Owen School, a certain number of top applicants are offered full fellowships and living stipends. Although many public B-schools are moving to boost their tuition to private-school rates so that they can be self-sufficient and break free of many of their parent university's restrictions, there are still deals to be had. If you're a Texas resident, for example, you can get a two-year MBA at the University of Texas at Austin's No. 17 ranked B-school for about $21,000. Even if you're not a resident, you can get a better deal than you would at a place like Columbia, where the annual tuition—not to mention New York City living expenses—will run you over $30,000.

Although that's a pretty compelling argument in favor of the public university, keep in mind that one reason people agree to pay inflated tuitions is that they sometimes lead to inflated salaries. Those 2000 Columbia grads, for example, took home a median pay package of $142,500, while Michigan State MBAs received just $93,000. Not included in the return-on-investment calculations are intangibles such as the added confidence and psychological comfort you get from having the MBA under your belt, not to mention the all-important alumni network—cited by many students at schools such as Harvard, Stanford, and Dartmouth's Amos Tuck B-school as the best reason for going there. Good connections can help you get your first job, but they can also help you make the transition to a better gig years down the road. Cost, then, is certainly one criterion in deciding whether you should go for an MBA and where you should go. But it shouldn't be the only consideration.

SEEK A
SCHOOL THAT
MATCHES
YOUR
INTERESTS

As tempting as it is to choose a school on the basis of the BUSINESSWEEK rankings alone, you should resist doing so. The rankings are a wonderful tool, perhaps the best one available, for those considering a Top 50 program. But not every school is right for every person, and you should study the culture and strengths of each school to determine what best fits your needs. That means that a school ranked No. 12 may, for you, be a better choice than No. 6.

Are you the type of person who needs the buzz and bustle of the big city to be happy? You'd probably do better at Columbia or

NYU's Stern B-school than in a wooded, secluded setting like that of Dartmouth's Tuck B-school in Hanover, New Hampshire. By contrast, if you like an intimate, close-knit community with great access to the great outdoors, Tuck's the place for you. If you're a Type A person who thrives on a pressured, individualized, highly competitive atmosphere, the University of Chicago may be your call. But if you want to spend most of your time working in small groups, you might prefer a Kellogg or a Duke, both of whose grads gave their schools stellar marks in the teamwork department. (See Chapter 3 for BUSINESSWEEK's survey of top graduates and what they say about their schools.)

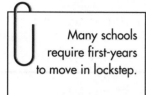

Many schools require first-years to move in lockstep.

Certainly, most B-schools offer the same basic curriculum—a group of core requirements with the option to choose your own electives—but there are plenty of variations to pick from. At the University of Chicago, for example, there are no mandatory classes except for a special orientation program. Students are encouraged to branch out on their own, pursuing advanced topics in finance or accounting if they already know the basics. But the flexible curriculum is fairly unconventional these days at B-schools; many schools require the first-year students to move in lockstep through their core courses, and students at schools that offer flexible programs can often feel alone in their MBA program. The rationale for cohesive cohorts? The CPA in the class will learn more about management and teamwork from helping his or her classmates to grasp basic concepts than he or she loses by repeating material already known cold. That's the idea at North Carolina's Kenan-Flagler school, where students must work with a single team for the entire first year, and everyone must take the requirements—no substitutions allowed.

Areas of specialty are another important consideration in your decision-making process. Some schools, such as Harvard or Virginia's Darden school, are focused on teaching general management and tend to send forth graduates who work well in areas of general expertise such as consulting rather than narrow technical specialties. Other schools pride themselves on their niche programs, attracting students who know exactly what they want. The University of Texas is now offering a specialization in energy finance, sponsored by Enron Corp. Wisconsin has risk management/insurance and real estate and urban land economics; Babson is world-famous for entrepreneurship and now offers a second-year program designed to launch a business; Vanderbilt has an exciting specialization in e-commerce; and Michigan State emphasizes its supply chain management training. Cornell has put into place a unique immersion course in manufacturing, offered in the second semester of the first year. It's the only course of the semester, and you spend much of your time out of the classroom, visiting manufacturing plants, studying live cases, and working on your final presentation.

Before applying to any school, do your homework. Go beyond the slick brochures, Web sites, and promises made by the marketing staffs of these schools. Read the extended profiles in this book, and check out the MBA journals, student survey comments, links to hundreds of school profiles, and everything else that's available on BUSINESSWEEK's Best Business Schools Web site (www. businessweek.com/bschools/). Treat it the way an MBA would in a typical case study. "You should gather all the information about placement, the quality of the school, and do an analysis of it," suggests Robert L. Virgil, former dean of Washington University's Olin B-school. "If you're investing two years of your life and a lot of money, I think you should visit the school when it's in session. Attend a class or two, talk to the students, grab a recruiter during a coffee break to find out what he or she thinks the place is like. Then look at yourself in the mirror and see if you really match up with the school." Most schools—with enough notice—will accommodate such visits.

It's not a bad idea to speak with recent graduates of the programs that you're interested in—keeping in mind, of course, that things are changing so quickly in the B-school world that the experience they've had may be radically different from the journey you're about to embark on. If you already have your heart set on becoming a consultant at McKinsey & Co., it would be wise to find a McKinsey staffer who is an alumnus of the school you want to attend. Most alumni and/or admissions departments will help you find recent grads, and some, like Wharton, go so far as to send all applicants a directory of alumni who have volunteered to share their firsthand knowledge of Wharton by telephone. What's more, once students are admitted to Wharton, they gain access to a recent addition—E-talk—that lets incoming students get to know one another online even before they arrive on campus.

> It's not a bad idea to speak with graduates.

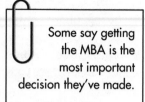

Some say getting the MBA is the most important decision they've made.

In general, you're not likely to find too many terribly disappointed people. MBAs from top schools generally give positive endorsements of the experience, whether they are recent graduates or not. Most have little doubt that the time and expense of getting the degree were well worth it. They say they forged friendships and contacts that will endure for a lifetime, and they linked up with new jobs that paid better and offered greater opportunities for advancement than the positions they left. Some consider it the most important and formative decision they've made in their lifetimes.

HOW TO GET INTO ONE OF THE BEST B-SCHOOLS

I f you've got your sights set on business school, expect plenty of company. Although the early 1990s witnessed a cooling off in MBA applications, today's market is still red hot. In fact, despite a slight decline during the dot-com boom, most of the schools in the Top 30 have seen an increase in applications overall in the last four years.

Dartmouth's Tuck School received 18 applications for every one of its 190 class spots. The Wharton School garnered just over 8300 applications—the highest number ever received by a single B-school and a 90 percent increase from its 1993 total. And Stanford's Graduate School of Business turned away 6560 of its 7052 aspirants—a paltry 7 percent acceptance rate, for those of you doing the math. *The upshot:* Getting into B-school is more competitive than ever. And the prospects of an economic downturn aren't going to slow the frenzied pace much since B-school applications tend to rise when the economy looks less stable.

So what does an MBA wannabe have to do to get inside the hallowed halls of a good B-school? First and foremost, don't rush. Give yourself enough time to become an informed consumer. Some admissions directors suggest starting the process a full year before actually applying to carefully gauge one's fit with a program. That may be a touch unrealistic, but you should give yourself at least a full year to do your homework before enrolling in B-school. Read the school profiles in this book. Check out the admissions director Q&As on the BUSINESSWEEK Best Business Schools Web site (www.businessweek.com/bschools/). Surf the Web sites of the schools in which you're interested. Send away for literature. Swap stories and advice with fellow applicants on various online message boards. And attend an MBA Forum, a GMAC-sponsored event that connects prospective students with over 100 school admissions officers. Held worldwide in 16 cities—8 international and 8 in the United States—the forums provide an informal venue for applicants to converse one on one with school officials. They are held at different times in different cities between September and January. You can check the GMAT Web site (www.gmat.org) for a calendar of events.

The major factors B-schools consider when evaluating applications are your undergraduate grades, GMAT score, and work expe-

> Become an informed consumer.

rience—called the Big Three by many admissions folks. In recent years work experience has grown in importance; most schools now require their students to have at least two years' worth, while the average work experience of those attending BUSINESSWEEK's Top 50 programs is closer to 4.5 years. That's a direct result of schools' growing selectivity, as well as a response to recruiters' desire to hire MBAs who are already familiar with the work world. "You have a much savvier individual, with more maturity and more experience," says Maury Hanigan, CEO of Hanigan Consulting Group in New York, who helps companies recruit MBAs.

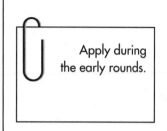

Apply during the early rounds.

There are, of course, other factors on which admissions committees base their decisions other than the Big Three, including leadership ability, special talents, background characteristics, motivation, emotional intelligence, and career interest. Although these factors are less tangible, and it's harder to predict how they'll be weighed, they do help admissions directors determine whether you can add to the diversity they're trying to create. "We are looking for people who are going to change the world," says Kirsten Moss, admissions director at Harvard Business School. That means folks with a variety of interests and demonstrated leadership capability have a leg up at most schools.

Above all, hedge your bets by applying to half a dozen or so schools—the norm for today's applicants. And try to apply as early as possible. Although most schools list their final deadlines for applications between March 1 and June 1 (some even later, depending on their rolling admissions process), ignore them; the later your application arrives, the more you put yourself at a disadvantage. Most programs now have their first deadline scheduled for as early as November. Ideally, you should get your application in no later than early January for fall admission. And although the earlier applicants tend to have higher credentials, an application that doesn't make it in the first round will usually be dropped into the next round for further consideration.

It might help you to organize your plan of attack by creating a calendar. It'll put you on a defined schedule and make it easier for you to meet critical deadlines. Here's a loose outline:

Spring or Early Summer: Narrow down schools, check out Web sites, request program literature and applications, chat with other aspirants on message boards, and set up on-campus visits for the early fall.

August: Enroll in six-week GMAT prep course or set aside two months to practice the test at home.

September: Begin to visit campuses, attend classes, and chat with current students and faculty. Attend an MBA Forum, if there is one in a nearby city. Do an admissions interview, if allowed before you file an official application.

October: Take the GMAT. Begin the application process by filling out the forms, requesting undergraduate transcripts, creating a personal marketing plan for yourself, crafting answers to essay questions, choosing recommenders.

November: Visit more campuses. Retake the GMAT if dissatisfied with your score (anything less than a 600 will put you at a big disadvantage for the best schools). Schedule the bulk of your personal interviews. Begin to file your applications with schools. First complete the applications for schools that are not at the very top of your list. Save the best for last, when you can approach them having had more practice. In almost all cases, it's better to file early—never in the last round.

December: Finish up the rest of your applications. Ask for personal interviews at schools that refused to do an interview before an application was filed. Cross your fingers!

ZIPPING THROUGH THE APPLICATION

As you might expect, one of the most time-consuming tasks in the entire B-school process is the application itself. Although technology has shortened the time it takes to complete each mind-numbing, head-scratching, 15-page application, the typical MBA candidate still can expect to spend a good 40 hours slogging away at it. Fortunately, that slogging can be focused on the truly difficult parts, since a host of new products has made filling in your demographic information (i.e., name, birthplace, Social Security number, job history, etc.) a relatively painless process.

For example, there's multiple application software, which allows you to enter those pesky vitals each school demands in one fell swoop—and for as many schools as you like. The most popular application software product on the market is called MCS Multi-App. The $59 program allows you to apply to more than 60

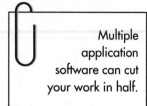

Multiple application software can cut your work in half.

of the best schools, most of which are profiled in this guidebook. And while it's quickly become the standard for MBA wannabes, many schools now have downloadable applications on their Web sites as well. The program can be downloaded via the Web (www.multi-app.com) or ordered by phone. To contact the firm, call 800-516-2227. Other Web sites, like embark.com, also offer easy-to-use application links and devices.

How does the multiple application software work? After you mark the schools to which you are applying, a screen prompts you to begin answering a set of "core questions"—the common information required in each application. You'll start by entering simple data, like your name and address, and move on to work experience and academic records. Once you've filled it all in (it takes about 45 minutes), the software neatly distributes the information to each application you've selected. When you open each application on your desktop, you'll find that core info already entered.

Next, you'll have to tackle the school-specific questions on the application, including the dreaded essays. Here, Multi-App serves up a dangerous little option: With a keystroke, you can copy an essay written for one school to any application. You'll then have to customize the essay manually for each school. But at a time when most B-schools hear from far more qualified applicants than they can accept, it's a better idea to tailor your essays to each individual school to which you're applying. After carefully checking your forms, print out your masterpiece, and presto! Your finished product looks almost exactly like the paper versions put out by the schools. Schools not offering Multi-App applications will often offer an electronic version themselves.

If you want to cut even more toil and cost out of your life, hop on the Internet and apply online. Cyber-vendors use the "core questions" function of multiple application software while also sending users e-mail reminders about deadlines or missing application data. They allow applicants to save partly finished applications through any computer that has access to the Internet and send everything but recommendations and academic transcripts electronically. That means your forms reach admissions offices almost immediately, cutting out Federal Express charges. It's particularly helpful for international applicants, many of whom must contend with antiquated postal systems.

Though online applications are still young—the oldest major vendor has been working with B-school applications only since 1997—a paperless application process is on the horizon. Some schools don't even take paper applications. Many of the top B-schools have signed on with at least one online application vendor in the last year, and on August 1, 1998, MIT's Sloan School of Management became the first school to require its candidates to apply online. Several others followed suit.

The two best online application vendors currently available are relative old-timer Embark and GradAdvantage, the product of a partnership between GMAC, ETS, and Peterson's that hit the scene in August 1998. Similar in many ways, the two services are inexpensive—costing $10 and $12 per application, respectively—and are rapidly expanding their networks of participating schools. GradAdvantage (www.gradadvantage.org) has agreements with about 30 MBA programs. Embark (www.embark.com) provides applications to more than 100 MBA programs and is signing up several new members a month. Most of the schools currently online are part of BUSINESSWEEK's Top 50.

To apply online, you'll first have to create secure user IDs and passwords. (If you forget your password, you'll have to answer a personalized question or two correctly before they e-mail it to you again.) Embark then prompts you to enter your personal information into two quick forms—taking 5 to 10 minutes total—that are then filtered into all of your chosen applications, much like Multi-App. GradAdvantage does the same thing by embedding "standard" questions into the first application you fill out. While Embark creates replicas of school applications, GradAdvantage creates a standard application based on feedback from over 100 schools, then tacks on school-specific questions.

Both services provide ample space for school-specific questions, particularly the essays, which can be written entirely online in one or several sittings (though there is no spell checker). You can also cut and paste your essays if you prefer to use a desktop word processing program. Be sure to save early and often: Both services are vulnerable to abrupt Internet connection failure. As a reminder, both programs have save buttons prominently displayed on their browsers, and Embark requires its users to save their work at the end of each application page before continuing.

Both companies do a good job of helping users keep track of the progress of their applications. Upon re-entry to either site, users receive an overall view of the applications they've submitted and the ones they're still working on. GradAdvantage lets you know

Be sure to save your work often.

how many days you have left until the application deadline arrives and whether you've received any feedback from a school. Embark, meanwhile, offers a checklist function that essentially reminds you what remains to be done. Once you've finished up an application, both services also inspect your work to make sure all of the proper fields have been filled out, providing a direct link to the area in question if there's not enough information in that section. Finally, you enter a credit card number, and with a click of a button, your application flies cyberstyle to the school of choice, although you can print it out and mail it in if you prefer. GradAdvantage even lets customers bundle GMAT scores with the online application. "I see some real customer benefits by going online for both the applicant and the schools," says Linda Meehan, assistant dean for admissions and financial aid at Columbia Business School. "It will have a dramatic effect on the processing of applications." Indeed, admissions directors at the elite B-schools expect online applications to make up between 25 and 50 percent of their overall applicant pools, and several will require online applications within the next three years.

PREPARING FOR THE GMAT

No matter how you slice it, your chances of getting into a good school depend in large part on how well you score on the Graduate Management Admissions Test (GMAT)—long viewed by admissions officers as one of the best predictors of academic success. Now the test has gone digital. Since October 1997, it has been administered only via computer, forever altering the landscape for the 210,000 people who sign up for it each year. For one thing, scheduling the new test, called the CAT (computer-adaptive test), is definitely a lot easier than it was in the paper-based days, when the GMAT was offered only four times a year at 970 different locations. Now test takers can choose to take the exam any one of 250 days of the year—during the first three weeks of every month—as long as they schedule in advance.

The CAT is similar in content to the old test, with verbal and math sections and two essays. But the computerized test has different ground rules, the most important of which is that it is adaptive. Unlike the paper version, how well you do on early questions determines how hard the questions that follow will be. What's more, the difficulty of the questions, not just the number you get right, affects your final score. "The larger number of difficult questions you answer, the higher score you receive. By the CAT's end,

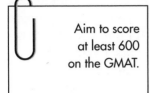

Aim to score at least 600 on the GMAT.

you come to a point where you are consistently getting the same level of questions correct, and your score reflects that," says Fred McHale, a vice president at GMAC and the lead developer of the CAT. What this means is that questions must be answered in order; you can't jump to the no-brainers and save the puzzlers for later, as you could with the paper-based version. You're also penalized for not finishing all the sections. So guessing—and knowing how to eliminate incorrect answers—is more important than ever. Adding to the pressure of taking the test, the CAT requires that you decide before you leave the test center whether you want to cancel your score. Otherwise, you get the multiple-choice results immediately, tattooing an official score on your academic file for the next five years. On the old paper test, a test taker had one week to cancel and didn't find out the grade for more than a month.

While you do still have to wait for your essay grades, they don't contribute to the main score. Every accredited B-school requires the GMAT, and admissions officers typically give anywhere from a 20 percent to a 40 percent weight to the score alone. If you manage to eke out only the average score of 531 for all test takers (that's within a range from 200 to 800), your chances of making it into a top school are pretty slim. You really need to score above 600 to seriously entertain the idea of making it into a Top 30 school, where students entering in the fall of 2000 averaged a score of 672. And you probably need to score no less than 600 to walk through the door of one of BUSINESSWEEK's Runners-Up; their members of the Class of 2002 averaged a score of 639.

Although you want to score as well as you can, admissions directors do say there's a lot more to getting into a top school than the GMAT alone. If your test score doesn't quite measure up, don't surrender just yet. It's possible that you could be rejected from one school based on your GMAT score and be accepted by a Top 30 school with the same score. Why? Some schools, feverishly working to boost their reputations by appearing selective, will simply toss you out of their admit pool for a subpar score. They are using GMAT averages as a marketing tool to attract better candidates. Other schools, already assured of their quality reputation, might pay more attention to other parts of your application: work experience, essays, personal interviews, and undergraduate grades.

If you feel your score is really too low, however, then retaking the test might be your best plan of action. But that doesn't mean you should retake it half a dozen times just to raise your score a few points. While admissions directors will take only your highest score into consideration, they might question the goal of someone who has taken the test three or four times, only to boost his or her score by a tiny amount each time. The CAT's average change in score from one test to the next is about 30 points, and most admissions directors won't attach much value to your second go-round if you fall within that range.

Before taking the new test, it's imperative to gain familiarity with its structure. There is one verbal and one quantitative section, as well as two essay questions. The verbal section has 41 questions, the quant 37, and you are given 75 minutes for each—nearly twice the average amount of time per question as in the previous test—with 30 minutes for each essay. The verbal questions measure your ability to understand and evaluate what you read, while the quant questions test basic math skills (tougher than your old SATs) as well as your ability to solve quantitative problems and interpret data in graphs, charts, and tables. It's a good idea to brush up on algebra and geometry.

Since 1994, GMAC has also required two essays to measure how well you present logical arguments and express ideas that are "correct, concise, and persuasive." Called the AWA, or analytical writing assessment, the section is also an easy way to expose applicants with weak English skills. You can cut and paste your essays on the screen—but there's no spell checker, so be careful. The first question asks you to analyze a given issue by presenting a statement followed by a series of questions. Here's an example:

> Ask most older people to identify the key to success, and they are likely to reply "hard work." Yet I would tell people starting off in a career that work in itself is not the key. In fact, you have to approach work cautiously—too much or too little can be self-defeating.

After reading the statement, you'll be asked the following:

> To what extent do you agree or disagree with this view of work? Develop your position by using reasons and/or examples from your reading, experience, or observations.

The second essay question requires you to analyze an argument, also using a statement followed by several questions. Example:

Familiarize yourself with the GMAT CAT.

In a recent citywide poll, 15 percent more residents said that they watch television programs about the visual arts than was the case in a poll conducted five years ago. During these past five years, the number of people visiting our city's art museums has increased by a similar percentage. Since the corporate funding that supports public television, where most of the visual arts programs appear, is now being threatened with severe cuts, we can expect that attendance at our city's art museums will also start to decrease. Thus, some of the city's funds for supporting the arts should be reallocated to public television.

After reading and digesting this bit of esotericism, you'll be asked to assess the validity of this argument. You'll want to "analyze the line of reasoning and the use of evidence" and suggest ways to strengthen or refute the argument using examples. If you'd like to practice answering a few of the AWA questions, you can download for free a complete listing of actual writing topics used in the CAT at GMAC's Web site (www.gmat.org/mbastore.html). You'll need Acrobat Reader software to view this listing (which you can also download). Or, if you want to shell out a few bucks, you'll also find the topics included in *The Official Guide for GMAT Review*. The essay section is graded separately from the others, with scores ranging from zero (unscorable because the test taker failed to write on the assigned topic) to six (outstanding). Two people score each essay, and you'll get an average of their scores.

Still feeling nervous about the CAT? GMAC has a customer service line (609-771-7330) as well as an e-mail address (gmat@ets. org) to field questions about anything from a test score to a situation at a test center.

SHOULD YOU TAKE A GMAT PREP COURSE?

The GMAT CAT has been the first time many Generation Xers (and late-blooming baby boomers, for that matter) have had to take an exam on a PC. So it's not surprising that applicants are clamoring for help from test preparation services. Indeed, enrollment in the test-prep classes run by Princeton Review and Kaplan Educational Centers has boomed in the years since the GMAT went digital. Kaplan, the nation's largest coaching service, offers an 11-session course. Meanwhile, Princeton Review's GMAT enrollment increased 20 percent for its 10-session course. "People want to prepare more for a test that's in a format they are not used to," says Cathryn Still, managing director of GMAT programs for Princeton Review.

One thing you can expect from a prep course is plenty of practice GMAT tests (at least three, plus as many as you like on your own). You'll begin by taking a paper-based GMAT to diagnose your strengths and weaknesses. Instructors will then analyze which mistakes tend to be made frequently, and then work those areas to death. If you're weak in algebra, expect to get drilled in the subject. If it's reading comprehension that throws you off, get ready for a customized lesson. After the first diagnostic test, the rest of the exams will be administered on the computer to make you more comfortable with the medium of the CAT.

Is a prep course worth it? It depends. If you study well on your own and have a good grasp of the concepts you might find in a store-bought test-preparation book, an $800+ course might not be worth it.

But, a Kaplan or Princeton course may be right for some applicants, especially those lacking self-discipline. If you want to review specific subject matter or discuss test-taking strategy, the classes can be valuable. If you're worried about taking the test on a computer, it will give you familiarity with the format. And if nothing else, paying the steep fee ($895–$1000) inspires applicants to prepare more rigorously. Moreover, going to a classroom on a regular basis with other MBA hopefuls can help to keep you motivated.

Your payment includes 10 computer practice tests at Kaplan and 5 practice CATs downloadable via the Net at Princeton— along with 25 to 40 hours of class time. Both services provide financial aid to offset the cost, although you must fill out a financial aid form in order to be eligible. Kaplan offers tuition assistance covering up to 50 percent of the cost for those earning less than $18,000 a year, while the Review discounts its classes up to $350 for those who prove financial hardship.

So which course should you take? It's a tough call, since so much depends on the individual instructor and how well he or she motivates you. The best strategy overall is to compare both services to see which curriculum better meets your needs. Princeton, for example, caps its classes at 15 students, compared with 25 at Kaplan. Princeton also wins kudos for requiring the teacher to

> If you lack self-discipline, take a prep course.

schedule one-on-one sessions as often as students request. Kaplan offers extra-help sessions but not always with the same person, though it does offer its own computer labs in which to practice the CAT. To get more information on the Review courses, call 800-2-REVIEW or check their Web site at www.review.com. To obtain more information on the Kaplan courses, call 800-KAP-TEST or check their Web site at www.kaplan.com.

There's another, less expensive option: Simply buy a workbook for around $20 and use the sample tests in it for practice. To gain a true sense for how the CAT works, pick up GMAC's review guide and POWERPREP software (about $70 for both), which includes two complete tests. You can order the package from www.gmat.org, where you can also download a list of essay topics for free. The Princeton Review site offers a book and CD-ROM with four practice tests, and Kaplan sells software review packages.

If you do decide to enroll in one of the prep courses, do so no more than two months before you sit down for the real deal. Preparing for the GMAT is the equivalent of training for a race. You don't stop two months before the starting gun is set to go off. It also helps to start preparing for the test before classes begin. Get Kaplan or Princeton Review to give you the study materials a few weeks before you start so you have the time to familiarize yourself with them. There are usually so many books and tests that it's virtually impossible to get through all of them during the course.

CREATING A PERSONAL MARKETING STRATEGY

As you've probably figured out by now, you've really got to make yourself stand out in order to successfully clear the admissions hurdles at the top business schools. Don't expect to be a shoo-in if all you've got are a solid GMAT score and a 4.0 grade-point average. Whether you have those qualifications or not, the one thing you need in this incredibly competitive environment is a strategy with which to market yourself; it's a concept they'll soon be teaching you at B-school. It will help guide you through your admissions interview and your application—particularly your answers to essay questions and your choice of recommenders. More importantly, though, it will convey a clear picture of who you are to the admissions committee.

Consider the strategy of Phil Carpenter, a Stanford MBA: "When I was applying to business school, I developed a positioning strategy based on what I thought made myself unique. I was a liberal arts major, yet had plunged into the fray of Silicon Valley and over the course of three years had become fairly technical. I therefore positioned myself as the liberal arts guy with a technical twist, and provided evidence to show just how my combination of strong written and verbal skills, plus a solid technology background, made me not only a unique candidate but one who had been very successful in my chosen field of high-tech marketing."

Carpenter, who has gone on to co-author the superb *Marketing Yourself to the Top Business Schools,* reinforced this image of himself through his selection of recommenders. One of them was the chief executive of the start-up company he worked for before business school. Another recommender was an art history professor whom he got to know during his undergraduate studies. Yet another was a Stanford Law School professor who had known him since he was a child. Together, they helped to position him as the "liberal arts guy" with a technical bent.

The bottom line is that admissions officers are looking for diverse and interesting people who will contribute something to the general educational process, not just a group of successful analysts who know how to pick a stock. That's why a typical elite B-school class these days might include such varied types as an Olympic runner, a venture capitalist, a Navy SEAL, and a ballerina. Put yourself in the admissions director's shoes and envision the type of person to whom you would want to give the nod. You should express "tangible examples of you in the workplace, the community, and leadership from your college days," says Sally Lannin, president of MBA Strategies. Temper your accomplishments at work—which are important, but often tend to look like those of many aspirants with similar employment backgrounds—with anecdotes that display your unique characteristics. That means discussing the confidence and conviction you learned as editor of a newspaper you started in college, analyzing your failed attempt to start an e-business Web site, or the maturity and compassion you developed while working with your city's leading homeless services organization, where you did everything from hanging fliers to serving meals to counseling the less fortunate.

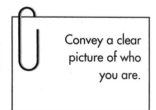

Convey a clear picture of who you are.

Don't sell yourself short—let admissions folks know how special you really are, even if it seems unconventional.

CRAFTING THE PERFECT B-SCHOOL ESSAY

The B-school essay questions are your single best opportunity to make yourself really shine for an admissions staff. Yet they can just as easily be your downfall if you drown your responses in clichés and bland, nonspecific examples, says Jon Megibow, admissions director at the University of Virginia's Darden Graduate School of Business Administration. "Getting four essays that deal with nothing but platitudes and content that answers what we want to hear is counterproductive. The essays are an opportunity to display the different facets of the applicant's character."

Start with a little self-reflection. Ask yourself, "Who am I, and how can I convey my essence in writing?" In doing so, you should be bold and incisive, explaining through relevant, colorful examples why you want to earn an MBA and what you'd like to accomplish with it. Draw from unique, personal experiences: the more detail, the better. Most B-school applications will hit you with about four mandatory essay questions, with an optional fifth that invites you to explain any potential shortfall in your application. That's not an absolute, however. The University of Texas Graduate School of Business has only two mandatory essays with an optional third, while Harvard Business School requires its applicants to answer seven. You should use the optional essay if you feel there's something you haven't yet explained, or if you feel that the admissions officers might see a problem with your application. It's the perfect place to explain, for example, that your low GPA is partly the result of taking on a 35-hour-per-week job to pay for school or to deal with a medical situation that at one point hurt your professional performance.

What will the essays ask? Many schools pose the same question, phrased slightly differently: If accepted, how would you add to this class? MBA programs are trying to understand what makes you tick, and which leadership positions, jobs, and responsibilities make you a winner. Look at a few of Harvard Business School's previous essay questions: "While recognizing that no day is typical, please describe a representative work day"; "What specifically have you done to help a group or organization change?"; "Describe your three most substantial accomplishments and explain why you view them as such"; and "What are your career aspirations and why? How will you get there?" These queries are pretty straightforward, broad, and potentially dangerous to the applicant because they are so similar to essay questions on other schools' applications. Don't surrender to the temptation of writing a one-size-fits-all essay. It may come off as unfeeling and vapid, and, more importantly, it will miss the subtle nuances a school uses to figure out whether you're really the right fit. (Plus you risk accidentally writing the wrong school name on the form.)

That's not to say that all essay questions conform to a specific formula. Some schools seem to delight in thinking up unusual questions. One recently asked potential students to write a succinct description of how they handled real-life ethical challenges. Another asked applicants to describe the details behind the failures in their careers. As part of their applications, candidates to Northwestern's Kellogg B-school face the unusual task of responding in short answers to three of six questions or statements. The novel ones include: "Outside of work I enjoy . . ."; "Describe a situation that forced you to re-evaluate a personal belief"; "Be your own career counselor. What aspects of your personality or background present the greatest obstacle(s) to achieving your goals?"; "I wish the Admissions Committee had asked me. . . ."

Remember, when answering the essay questions, be sure to emphasize how different you are, not only how great you are. To stand apart from the all-quite-capable masses, write about how you have tutored underprivileged children. Discuss the influence your father or other family members have had on you, or your role as a neighborhood activist working to combat crime, or what it's like to play lead guitar in a budding rock band. "Don't view your essay as an academic article or a business memo, but as a human interest story about yourself," advises Linda Abraham, a consultant who guides applicants through the essay process. "Use anecdotes and analysis." And don't embellish—be honest.

Keep in mind that schools also use the essays to assess your personal goals and values so that they can create a class of interesting people. Try to blend those goals and values together in your essays by discussing an accomplishment in terms of the obstacles you overcame to achieve it. It's not enough to write about leading a project team or managing people of diverse backgrounds; you also need to discuss how you dealt with someone who didn't accept or respect you. Use personal experiences that reveal strength of char-

> View your essay as a human interest story.

acter, leadership qualities, and integrity. Too frequent use of the word "I" and too rare use of the word "we" in recording your accomplishments can put off some B-school admissions officers. Sensitive to criticisms that MBAs are too self-centered, many schools today emphasize teamwork and read essays with an eye toward ferreting out the egomaniacs. Says Donald P. Jacobs, dean of Kellogg: "We don't want loners with sharp elbows."

Of course, crafting well-thought-out, creative essays that articulate your vision can't be accomplished overnight. Expect to spend between 20 and 40 hours thinking, organizing, drafting, and polishing each set. For each individual essay, be sure that you stick to the point you want to make and that your point addresses the question being posed. Besides typos and grammatical errors, not answering the question asked is the single greatest mistake admissions directors say they come across. Also, be succinct. Most schools ask for responses of about 500 to 750 words, which works out to be about two pages, printed and double-spaced, and admissions staff, weary from reading through thousands of applications, favor quality over quantity. Though, for example, Berkeley's Haas School has a minimum length required for its essays, that's not an open invitation to submit a 20-page tome.

If you're having trouble putting pen to paper or, more aptly, saving type to diskette, you may consider contacting a B-school consultant for help with the application process. For a few hundred to several thousand dollars, consultants offer you inside connections from their previous jobs at B-schools, tips on interviewing, and, sometimes, essay critiques. MBA Strategies (www.mbastrategies.com) is one of the largest domestic consulting firms, with 200 clients. At upwards of $150 an hour, President Sally Lannin, a former placement officer at Stanford University, says her company sometimes helps clients brainstorm on essay topics, although it doesn't edit essays for ethical reasons. The drill is similar at Kaplan Educational Centers, which opened an admissions consulting arm in 1996. The program tries to match applicants with consultants who once worked at their chosen schools to increase knowledge exchange. If you're looking for help that runs a lot cheaper, $50 will buy you a package of about 40 essays written by applicants who have been accepted by your preferred school from an online service named IvyEssays (www.ivyessays.com). The essays should be used as examples only.

Yet such services, which might seem to encourage cheating,

> Stay within 10 percent of the upper word limit.

could backfire. "If the school feels any part of the application is not the student's own work, they are immediately disqualified," says Robert Alig, Wharton's director of admissions and financial aid. Alig's comment underscores a simple and very important point: Above all, honesty is vital. Certainly emphasize everything you've done, but don't cross the line by lying or padding your accomplishments. Admissions staff aren't likely to check your facts, but they've read through so many applications that they can sense when something doesn't quite add up.

If you know a graduate of the school, ask him or her to read over your essays before you turn them in. As far as gimmicks go, don't get too carried away. Writing your responses in crayon, or submitting videotapes or CD-ROMs to accompany your essays, can be both clever and cute, helping to differentiate you from the crowd, but they can also flop. Says Shannon Dahill, admissions director at the University of Washington Graduate School of Business Administration, "We had a candidate who wrote his essay on creative problem solving and included an LP record of an Elvis single called 'Are You Lonesome Tonight?' The flipside had 'I Gotta Know' on it." [He got in.] But, Dahill cautions, "It wasn't that the application stood on Elvis alone. The Elvis song . . . helped to flesh out the candidate's essay." Translation: Don't go overboard unless you've got a lot of substance to begin with.

PREPARING FOR THE INTERVIEW

With selectivity on the rise, the personal interview has gone from being simply an extra to an integral part of the application process. Kellogg, the first B-school to interview every applicant to its full-time program, did nearly 7000 of them in 2000 in one-hour sessions in places as far-flung as Tokyo and Kuala Lumpur. "The interview is important for two reasons," says Michele Rogers, Kellogg's director of admissions. "First, it answers the question: Can the candidate effectively present himself or herself to another person? But it's also a chance for the student to learn about our programs from someone who knows what we really offer." Kellogg officials don't think you can assess a person's composure, ability to articulate his or her ideas, or leadership ability from test scores or past grades alone. And many observers believe that one reason Kellogg's corporate recruiters continually rank the school high—placing its 2000 grads in the Top 10 for general management, marketing, finance, and technology skills—is because it prescreens its candidates so well.

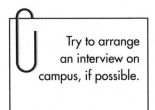

Try to arrange an interview on campus, if possible.

Today, the interview is required or encouraged at many top MBA programs. Michigan and Wharton claim to have interviewed over 90 percent of their entire 2000 applicant pools, and a growing number of schools, including NYU, Chicago, Harvard, and MIT, say that most of the applicants who ended up being accepted did have an interview. In order to speak with more potential students, schools are asking current students to conduct campus interviews and alumni to file interview reports on candidates living in remote parts of the world. There's also an increasing emphasis on telephone interviews, which are required for international applicants at Washington University's Olin school, for example, and on using other events such as the MBA Forums as a place for admissions officers to set up sessions.

What all of this means is that it's probably in your best interest to try to arrange an interview—especially if you're articulate and think you can demonstrate some leadership skills. It's always helpful for admissions officers to put a face to an application, and it's another opportunity for you to fill in some of the gray areas that might be putting your acceptance at risk. If you feel you're not likely to do well in an interview, however—especially if your English skills aren't up to snuff—you might consider trying to avoid it gracefully, since a lousy showing can torpedo your chances. That won't be easy to do, however, since so many schools are paying more attention to the interview than ever before. Some may interpret declining the interview as a lack of interest. Your best bet: Practice what you'd like to say in advance—and stay calm.

Don't fret if you can't spend the money on an on-campus interview; schools say that alumni and student interviews are just as worthwhile. "There's no difference in weight if you are interviewed by an alum, student, or admissions officer, but candidates never want to believe that," says one admissions director. "It's true though, I swear!" But there is a reason to spend the cash if you can; it gives you a chance to interview the school as well and make sure that the flavor and culture of the place are right for you. If you do have a face-to-face sit-down, treat it as if it were a job interview: Be punctual, dress professionally—no sandals, jeans, T-shirts, or sweats—and remember to write a thank-you note afterward.

What is a personal interview like? In general, interviewers want to evaluate leadership and communication skills. For non-native English speakers, it's also a way to assess English proficiency. "We've told our interviewees that this is a conversation, not an interrogation," says Donald Martin, director of admissions at the University of Chicago Graduate School of Business. "We want to create an environment where applicants are able to express themselves in a way that an application can't." Most interviews are behavioral; the questions asked have no right or wrong answers. They usually begin with broad questions and then hone in on the individual's particular interests and characteristics. For instance, at Washington University, the interview starts with why applicants are interested in an MBA program and in Olin in particular. Then it moves on to what they think they can add both in and out of the classroom, and what type of community involvement they've had. At the end, they're asked if there's anything they'd like to add that wasn't brought up earlier. Sometimes, interviews will be conducted in groups. MIT, for example, does this with its foreign applicants to get a sense of how much a candidate will participate in a discussion. No matter what the setting, however, the keys to success are the same: Try to relax, don't be afraid to talk or ask questions, be sure to answer a question directly without waffling, and—above all—be yourself.

MANAGING YOUR RECOM- MENDERS

Choosing the right people to recommend you is one of the most important parts of the application process, and most applicants don't spend enough time doing it. If possible, start with successful alums of your target school—but ask them only if they really know you and can write eloquently on your behalf. Advises Judith Goodman, assistant dean of admissions at the University of Michigan Business School: "An applicant is wise to ask people to recommend somebody who knows him or her well and is wise to think of people who will speak well of them but speak honestly. Hopefully, they will provide enough info to impart details about the candidate; just to say that Jon Doe is a wonderful person doesn't say anything." Don't choose a big-name CEO, government official, or celebrity to write about you unless they really know who you are. Big names do not impress admissions officers nor do they improve your chances of acceptance if they refer to you in broad platitudes.

Most schools require two to three recommendations, usually from folks whose experience with you has been professional. Approaching a professor who knows you well is also appropriate. Do not, however, ask a family member to extol your virtues unless you work in a family-run business. Admissions directors will assume bias and probably not attach any weight to such a recommendation. Although this may seem obvious, make sure you pick someone on whom you can rely to write you a good recommendation—and who won't forget to send it in on time. Remember, writing recommendations can be hard work. At Harvard, for example, recommenders must rate you on a scale from "outstanding (top 5 percent)" to "below average (bottom third)" on such characteristics as integrity, sensitivity to others, personal and professional maturity, intellectual ability, and imagination. Be sure to prepare recommenders for their assignment by providing them with background material on you, including your résumé. Consider sharing completed parts of your application, and, at the very least, put together a quick memo outlining why you feel you need to pursue the MBA and what it will do to help further your goals.

HOW TO GET A SCHOOL TO FOOT PART OF THE TUITION BILL

Getting accepted to B-school is a great achievement. Now you've got a new challenge: finding a way to pay for the two years of education. That's no small feat if you're aiming for one of BUSINESS-WEEK's Top 30 programs, where the average annual tuition tops $25,000. That works out to roughly $50,000 over two years, not including room and board, or the amount of payola you're forgoing by going to school rather than working. The MBA programs at Columbia, NYU, and MIT now clear the $28,000 tuition barrier, with Wharton, Chicago, Harvard, and Dartmouth not far behind. It's not surprising, then, that the average investment by a 2000 graduate of one of BUSINESSWEEK's Top 30 schools was a stunning $144,930.

Scholarships and financial aid can help you cope with the staggering costs of an MBA degree—but that money doesn't exactly grow on trees. You'll have to do your homework. That means searching for both public and private scholarships, applying for need-based and merit-based financial aid, and playing up the different aspects of your background if they can help you qualify for a special deal. The best way to get financial help is to ask for it, and ask early. That means your aid application should arrive at the admissions office on the first day possible. Ask the admissions staff and student aid office what's available. Most schools offer merit scholarships that cover part of the cost of

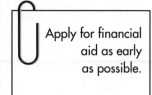

Apply for financial aid as early as possible.

tuition and set specific early deadlines for consideration. Also, find out whether work-study or graduate research and/or teaching assistantships are available. Although assistantships aren't used as much by business schools as they are by other types of graduate programs, they are an option at some schools. At Purdue's Krannert School of Management, for instance, B-school students can put a dent in their already-cheap tuition with graduate assistantships or jobs as residential advisers for the 30,000 Purdue undergraduates.

Most scholarships are based on either merit or need, so you have to prove one or the other—and it's nice if you can prove both. Consider, too, that a top applicant may be offered better financial aid packages from a second-tier school than a brand-name one; only a handful of Top 30 schools offer full rides to more than a few students. New York University's Stern School, for example, started offering Dean's Scholarships in 1993, which cover full tuition for 10 to 20 students with "outstanding abilities and exceptional potential for management." "You need to compete in a lot of ways, and we've learned that people are sensitive to price and to the personal attention they get," says George Daly, dean of Stern. Another innovative plan—the Park Leadership Fellows program—comes from Cornell's Johnson School. Funded by a foundation named after the late media entrepreneur Roy Park, the program brings 30 top MBA applicants with identifiable leadership potential to Cornell by awarding them two full years of tuition plus living expenses. The idea behind the fellowship is to allow Cornell to compete more aggressively for the best students. Vanderbilt has a similar program, offering grants to cover tuition and living costs for 25 students.

Most schools offer merit-based financial assistance to 20 to 35 percent of their students. At Northwestern's Kellogg School, 20 to 25 percent of the class gets scholarship money, while Indiana's Kelley School says 35 percent of its MBAs get a boost. That's pretty slim pickings overall, slimmer if you're not a member of a minority group, whose students tend to get the few full scholarships available. There is, however, no shortage of companies willing to loan money to MBA wannabes who are considered good credit risks by most banks. One option: The "MBA Loans" program run by the Graduate Management Admission Council (GMAC). The program ties together federal, need-based loans and private loans in a one-stop-shopping approach. Students who apply for help under this program are simultaneously considered for all federal loan programs as well as private loans, eliminating the need to fill out numerous applications. For more information on the program, call 1-888-440-4MBA, or visit the GMAC Web site (http://www.gmat.org/financing_frames.html). It's also a good move to surf the Web for ideas and resources. One notable site is called FinAid: The Financial Aid Information Page. Sponsored by the National Association of Student Financial Aid Administrators, FinAid (www.finaid.org) provides a slew of links to Web sites containing scholarship information for all students, not just B-schoolers. It's broken down by special interest (i.e., minority, female, disabled), offers tools such as a calculator projecting loan payback, and provides text of the latest government legislation on financial aid.

Minority students looking for help have another resource— The Consortium for Graduate Study in Management (CGSM), a 12-school alliance, 11 of which are in BUSINESSWEEK's Top 30. The Consortium's goal is to propel people of African-American, Hispanic-American, and Native American descent into managerial positions, and it offers 350 students per year fellowships covering full tuition and fees at 1 of the 12 schools. Those odds aren't too shabby, since only about 1000 individuals apply for admission to the schools directly through the Consortium and are eligible for the aid. Applicants rank their desired schools in order of preference, and the Consortium uses the ranking to determine how to extend its fellowships, although admission to B-school through the Consortium doesn't guarantee a fellowship. It does provide access to a network of more than 4000 alumni and 140 corporations—all committed to diversity. To learn more, visit the organization's Web page (www.cgsm.org).

The financial aid situation is far grimmer for international students, who must rely primarily on merit-based aid because virtually no federally based aid is available to them. Adding to the problem is the dearth of loans offered by U.S. banks, which fear a higher rate of default from students returning to home countries where they can't be as easily tracked or the economic situation is relatively unstable. Although they can apply through the GMAC "MBA Loans" program, they must have a U.S. citizen co-signer. There is some good news, however, if you're a Harvard B-school

> Surf the Web for ideas and financial resources.

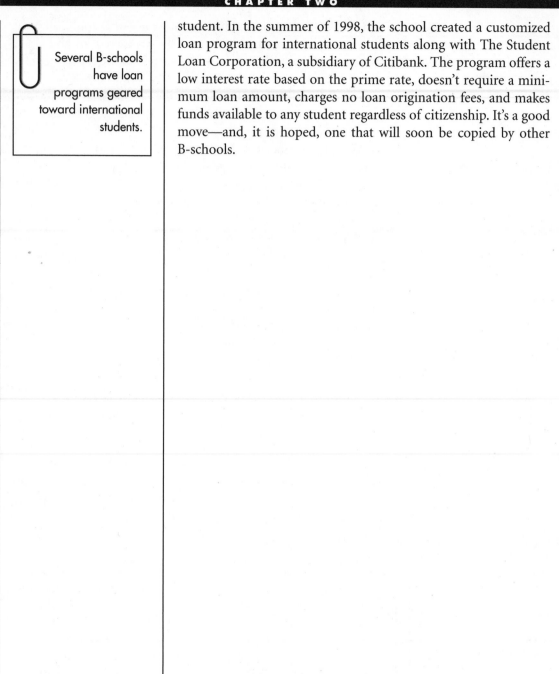

Several B-schools have loan programs geared toward international students.

student. In the summer of 1998, the school created a customized loan program for international students along with The Student Loan Corporation, a subsidiary of Citibank. The program offers a low interest rate based on the prime rate, doesn't require a minimum loan amount, charges no loan origination fees, and makes funds available to any student regardless of citizenship. It's a good move—and, it is hoped, one that will soon be copied by other B-schools.

RANKING THE B-SCHOOLS

Rankings. The word alone makes some people break into a sweat. Controversial by definition, rankings are loved by those that top the charts and dismissed as biased and irrelevant by those that don't. This is true of beauty pageants, consumer products such as cars, and stockbrokers. And it's very true of business schools, many of which believe that their reputations rest entirely on how they do in the two most widely followed rankings, both done by magazines: the biennial BUSINESSWEEK list and the *U.S. News and World Report* project.

Although the rankings presented by both magazines are taken seriously, the approaches they use are entirely different—as are the results. BUSINESSWEEK uses extensive surveys of graduates and corporate recruiters to come up with its ranking. By contrast, *U.S. News* determines much of its list through admissions and placement data, including average GMAT scores and starting salaries of MBAs. Most of this data comes directly from the schools, whereas BUSINESSWEEK's ranking data comes only from the schools' customers—the graduates and the recruiters who hire these graduates.

This attention to customer satisfaction may seem somewhat obvious at a time when everyone's favorite mantra is "the customer is always right." But that was not always the case—especially at B-school. In fact, until BUSINESSWEEK began to rate the schools on customer satisfaction in 1988, most rankings were based on the reputation of the schools and their professors. B-school deans and/or faculty were usually asked to list their top schools in order of personal preference. That meant that a school's academic prestige and reputation for academic research usually had a great impact on the ratings. Although it's clear that research is vital both to a school and to American business—and BUSINESSWEEK has added such a measure to its methodology—those surveys didn't take into account how this knowledge was conveyed to the students. They ignored such key attributes of a B-school as teaching excellence, the quality of the curriculum, and the value of a school's graduates to the world's business leaders.

We think that the people in the best position to call it like they see it are the graduates, who pay a small fortune to go to B-school, and the recruiters, who must live with the results once they've hired them to work at their companies. So those are the folks whose input counts

BUSINESSWEEK measures graduate and recruiter satisfaction for its rankings.

for 90 percent of the BUSINESSWEEK rankings. The 2000 graduate poll, consisting of 45 questions, was e-mailed to 16,843 newly minted MBAs from 82 of the best schools in the United States, Canada, and Europe, and we heard back from 10,039 of them, a response rate of 60 percent. We then added the views of the Class of 2000 to those we gathered in 1998 and 1996 to create our graduate ranking. The corporate poll was mailed to 419 companies that actively recruit MBAs from the campuses of the best B-schools. Our surveys were filled out by 247 companies, which together hired 15,558 MBAs in 1999 and 2000 alone, for a response rate of 59 percent. The results follow.

The BUSINESSWEEK results are very different from the 2000 rankings posted by *U.S. News and World Report*, which listed the top 30 schools as follows: (1) Harvard, Stanford (tied); (3) Wharton; (4) MIT; (5) Kellogg; (6) Chicago, Columbia (tied); (8) Duke; (9) Michigan; (10) Berkeley; (11) Dartmouth, UCLA, Virginia (tied); (14) NYU; (15) Cornell; (16) Texas, Yale (tied); (18) UNC; (19) Carnegie Mellon; (20) Indiana; (21) Emory; (22) USC; (23) Purdue; (24) Vanderbilt; (25) Ohio State, Rochester, Washington University (tied); (28) Minnesota; (29) Georgetown; (30) Michigan State.

Why the discrepancy? It's all about methodologies. The *U.S. News* ranking relies mostly on numerical data: Placement success counts for 35 percent, and student selectivity (starting salaries, the percentage of students employed three months after graduation, and the number of firms recruiting per student) makes up another 25 percent. The remaining 40 percent comes from a reputational survey of recruiters (15 percent) and of B-school deans and MBA program directors (25 percent). However, a closer look shows that at the end of the day, the BW rankings have much more in common with the *U.S. News* rankings than you might think. Both rankings really help a potential student to identify the superior business programs in the country.

BUSINESSWEEK's rankings have far more detailed information on the strengths and weaknesses of one program over another. If you're the type of person who favors teamwork and cooperation, you'd probably do best at Duke or Kellogg. On the other hand, if you thrive on competing with your teammates, you might consider Harvard or Chicago. Need a school where technology flows through the classroom? Try Carnegie Mellon or MIT. Prefer an environment in which faculty members are at the leading edge of their research areas? Think about Chicago, Cornell, or Rochester. This information and lots more can be found on the following

> Over 10,000 graduates of 82 business schools answered a satisfaction survey in 2000.

pages, which give a question-by-question breakdown of the student survey, along with a list of the top and bottom schools for each question out of the Top 50 schools we surveyed. If you're interested in a school that doesn't appear, you can assume that the school got average marks—neither excellent nor poor.

BusinessWeek's TOP 30 BUSINESS SCHOOLS

OVERALL RANKING	1998 RANKING	CORPORATE RANKING	GRADUATE RANKING	INTELLECTUAL CAPITAL RANKING	GRADS EARNING OVER $100,000	AVERAGE JOB OFFERS
1. Wharton	1	1	3	8	89%	3.6
2. Kellogg	2	2	1	15	83	3.5
3. Harvard	5	3	4	13	89	4.1
4. MIT	15	7	7	2	88	3.9
5. Duke	7	8	10	1	80	3.1
6. Michigan	4	6	5	12	81	3.3
7. Columbia	6	5	17	6	85	3.1
8. Cornell	8	10	8	4	82	3.2
9. Virginia	11	9	2	16	84	3.4
10. Chicago	3	4	24	7	86	3.1
11. Stanford	9	12	15	3	80	3.8
12. UCLA	12	13	6	10	68	2.8
13. NYU	13	11	16	23	77	2.8
14. Carnegie Mellon	14	14	13	22	70	3.1
15. UNC	19	16	11	21	68	0.3
16. Dartmouth	10	17	12	14	85	2.8
17. Texas—Austin	18	18	21	20	58	2.9
18. UC Berkeley	16	22	14	38	68	3.1
19. Yale	20	23	22	5	75	2.7
20. Indiana	21	20	20	36	58	2.9
21. Rochester	na	29	18	11	52	2.8
22. Vanderbilt	na	24	23	9	55	2.6
23. Washington U.	17	37	9	31	45	2.9
24. USC	25	25	19	39	38	2.7
25. Purdue	24	19	28	17	46	3.5
26. Georgetown	na	21	27	26	51	2.9
27. Maryland	22	28	25	33	33	2.4
28. Emory	na	34	26	25	48	2.6
29. Michigan State	na	26	29	27	14	3.3
30. Georgia Tech	na	15	39	32	40	2.9

1. To what extent did your MBA experience meet your expectations of what a good program should be?

The Class of 2000, faced with a booming economy, gave up a lot when they decided to trade in their suits and corporate credit cards for backpacks. And they paid a lot of money for the privilege. So which schools were best able to meet the very high expectations of their students? Virginia (Darden), Rochester (Simon), Washington (Olin), Northwestern (Kellogg), Harvard, Cornell (Johnson), MIT (Sloan), Indiana (Kelley), North Carolina (Kenan-Flagler), and Stanford. On the bottom end of the scale: Syracuse, George Washington, SUNY—Buffalo, Miami, Tulane (Freeman), Clark Atlanta, South Carolina (Darla Moore), William and Mary, Howard, and Tennessee—Knoxville.

2. Do you believe your MBA was worth its total cost in time, tuition, and lost earnings?

For most potential MBA students, the amount of money they plunk down for B-school may be the largest purchase they have ever made—not to mention the decent salary given up to do so. But with an average of three well-paying job offers per person for the taking, most students in the Class of 2000 felt they got an excellent return on their investment in B-school. Which students reported the best return? Virginia (Darden), Michigan State (Broad), Washington (Olin), MIT (Sloan), North Carolina (Kenan-Flagler), Cornell (Johnson), Tennessee—Knoxville, Brigham Young (Marriott), UC Davis, and Texas—Austin. The least obvious payback: Miami, Syracuse, George Washington, Tulane (Freeman), Thunderbird, SUNY—Buffalo, Boston University, American University, William and Mary, and South Carolina (Darla Moore).

3. Would you urge friends and colleagues to take the same MBA program at the school?

It's the ultimate recommendation: Would you wish your experience on your best buddy, or your spouse? Would you do it all over again? In a year like 2000, many students said they'd happily do so. The most enthusiastic: Northwestern (Kellogg), Harvard, Stanford, Virginia (Darden), Duke (Fuqua), North Carolina (Kenan-Flagler), Cornell (Johnson), UCLA (Anderson), Pennsylvania (Wharton), and Michigan. Less enthusiastic were grads from Syracuse, Miami, George Washington, Tulane (Freeman), SUNY—Buffalo, William and Mary, Tennessee—Knoxville, Pittsburgh (Katz), South Carolina (Darla Moore), and Illinois at Urbana-Champaign.

It's a good sign when grads say they'd recommend their school to friends.

4. How would you rate the quality of teaching in core courses?

Virtually everyone at B-school takes a version of the following fundamentals: accounting, finance, marketing, statistics, organizational behavior, and economics. But not every school does a good job of getting the basics across. The best: Virginia (Darden), Indiana (Kelley), Rochester (Simon), Washington (Olin), North Carolina (Kenan-Flagler), Carnegie Mellon, Cornell (Johnson), Northwestern (Kellogg), Penn State (Smeal), and Florida (Warrington). The worst: Syracuse, Tulane (Freeman), George Washington, SUNY—Buffalo, Clark Atlanta, Ohio State (Fisher), Miami, Howard, Tennessee—Knoxville, and Stanford.

5. How would you rate the quality of the teaching in elective courses?

Once you've covered the common territory, it's time to specialize in an area that you can tailor to your own specific career goals, be they in the fast-paced world of investment banking or in starting your own company. Here's the Class of 2000's perspective on the best and worst schools for electives. Best: Rochester (Simon), Virginia (Darden), MIT (Sloan), Harvard, North Carolina (Kenan-Flagler), Cornell (Johnson), Stanford, Northwestern (Kellogg), Washington (Olin), and NYU (Stern). Worst: SUNY—Buffalo, Clark Atlanta, Syracuse, William and Mary, George Washington, Tennessee—Knoxville, Miami, Arizona (Eller), Arizona State, and University of Washington.

6. Overall, how did the quality of teachers compare with others you have had in the past?

Going to an elite B-school should be an eye-popping intellectual experience, one that surpasses those overcrowded, boring lecture courses in college taught by teaching assistants barely out of school. But B-school profs are under tremendous pressure these days to teach not only in MBA programs but also in executive education classes and outside consulting gigs. Leading the pack here: Virginia (Darden), Rochester (Simon), Indiana (Kelley), Cornell (Johnson), Harvard, Northwestern (Kellogg), North Carolina (Kenan-Flagler), Washington (Olin), Michigan, and MIT (Sloan). The laggards: Syracuse, SUNY—Buffalo, Clark Atlanta, George Washington, Miami, Tulane (Freeman), Georgia Tech (DuPree), Tennessee—Knoxville, Pittsburgh (Katz), and Arizona State.

7. Were your teachers at the leading edge of knowledge in their fields?

Although students are thrilled to have full-time corporate warriors in the classroom telling them what things are really like, it's also important for schools to give their students teachers who are at the cutting edge of thinking in such subjects as marketing, finance, and entrepreneurship. Students said the most advanced thinkers were found at MIT (Sloan), Rochester (Simon), Chicago, Harvard, Indiana (Kelley), Cornell (Johnson), Carnegie Mellon, Stanford, Texas—Austin, and Pennsylvania (Wharton). Those least likely to lead the way: Syracuse, Clark Atlanta, SUNY—Buffalo, Miami, Tulane (Freeman), George Washington, Ten-

Don't underestimate the value of good teaching when choosing a school.

nessee—Knoxville, Pittsburgh (Katz), Georgia Tech (DuPree), and Wake Forest (Babcock).

8. Were the faculty available for informal discussion when classes were not in session?

Learning is never confined to the classroom, and students know it. But many professors, constrained by consulting deals, research, and exec ed requirements, can't seem to make extra time to help students through a challenging assignment. Others, however, go out of their way to be around at any time of the day or night. Most available: Virginia (Darden), Dartmouth (Tuck), Cornell (Johnson), Washington (Olin), Purdue (Krannert), North Carolina (Kenan-Flagler), Wake Forest (Babcock), Indiana (Kelley), Rice (Jones), and Georgetown (McDonough). Least available: George Washington, SUNY—Buffalo, Chicago, Tennessee—Knoxville, Syracuse, Miami, Rutgers, Thunderbird, Arizona State, and Brigham Young (Marriott).

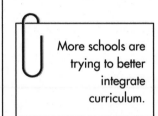

More schools are trying to better integrate curriculum.

9. To what extent were faculty aware of the material other faculty members would cover?

Although faculty members specialize in one discipline, they should certainly have an understanding of what their counterparts are teaching. It's frustrating for students to begin to cover a concept in one class and then find out that another professor thinks they know it cold—and assigns work based on that assumption. Which schools' faculties do the best job of communicating? Rochester (Simon), Virginia (Darden), Indiana (Kelley), Washington (Olin), Dartmouth (Tuck), Carnegie Mellon, Penn State (Smeal), Illinois at Urbana-Champaign, Cornell (Johnson), and Babson (Olin). Worst: Clark Atlanta, George Washington, SUNY—Buffalo, Tennessee—Knoxville, Rutgers, Miami, Georgia (Terry), Notre Dame (Mendoza), Arizona (Eller), and South Carolina (Darla Moore).

10. To what extent was the coursework integrated as opposed to being taught as a cluster of loosely related topics?

In the real world, you don't have an accounting problem or a finance problem. Usually, it's a combination of both. That's why many schools are trying to better integrate their curricula and to redesign programs to combine these topics rather than keeping them in separate silos. The most integrated: Virginia (Darden), Rochester (Simon), Babson (Olin), Wake Forest (Babcock), Indiana (Kelley), Georgetown (McDonough), Illinois at Urbana-Champaign, Penn State (Smeal), Cornell (Johnson), and Carnegie Mellon. The least integrated: Clark Atlanta, Syracuse, SUNY—Buffalo, George Washington, Tulane (Freeman), Georgia (Terry), Miami, Ohio State (Fisher), University of Washington, and Notre Dame (Mendoza).

11. Were the school's most prominent academics actively involved in teaching in the MBA program?

B-schoolers are paying big bucks to get the best education—and they expect some of that to be provided by the marquis names the schools tout in their view books and marketing material. Which schools have the big names in the classroom? Virginia (Darden), Dartmouth (Tuck), Indiana (Kelley), Cornell (Johnson), Washington (Olin), Yale, Rochester (Simon), NYU (Stern), Northwestern (Kellogg), and UC Davis. And those that don't? Syracuse, George Washington, Texas A&M (Mays), Clark Atlanta, Miami, University of Washington, SUNY—Buffalo, Arizona (Eller), UC Irvine, and Boston University.

12. Do you believe the faculty compromised teaching in order to pursue their own research?

The balance between teaching and research is a tough one for professors. On the one hand, many tenure decisions are made strictly on the basis of publication in scholarly journals. On the other hand, students expect their professors to be prepared for every class and able to communicate their ideas. Grads say the schools that get this right are Virginia (Darden), Washington (Olin), Indiana (Kelley), Cornell (Johnson), Dartmouth (Tuck), Yale, Texas A&M (Mays), Wake Forest (Babcock), Notre Dame (Mendoza), and UC Davis. Those that struggle: SUNY—Buffalo, Georgia Tech (DuPree), Thunderbird, Tulane (Freeman), Tennessee—Knoxville, Syracuse, Georgia (Terry), George Washington, Ohio State (Fisher), and Boston University.

13. How often was the material/research presented in class for discussion and review current?

With the business world changing faster than anyone could ever have anticipated, it's important that professors be able to place their research in a contemporary context. Students who must learn from out-of-date material often feel they're not as well prepared as their colleagues at other schools. Most current: MIT (Sloan), Rochester (Simon), Cornell (Johnson), Harvard, Indiana (Kelley), Texas—Austin, North Carolina (Kenan-Flagler), Florida (Warrington), Northwestern (Kellogg), and Howard. Least current: Syracuse, SUNY—Buffalo, Tulane (Freeman), Dartmouth (Tuck), Tennessee—Knoxville, Miami, Clark Atlanta, Arizona (Eller), George Washington, and Wake Forest (Babcock).

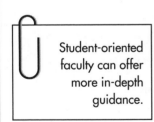

Student-oriented faculty can offer more in-depth guidance.

14. Did you receive information during the program that will be useful on the job?

B-school, unlike other academic disciplines, is as much about the real world as it is about theory. So the job of a professor is to get esoteric ideas across but also to make sure students have some street-smarts. Best in this category: Washington (Olin), Rochester (Simon), Cornell (Johnson), MIT (Sloan), Texas—Austin, Indiana (Kelley), Northwestern (Kellogg), Virginia (Darden), Carnegie Mellon, and Harvard. And bringing up the rear: Syracuse, SUNY—Buffalo, George Washington, Miami, Tulane (Freeman), Pittsburgh (Katz), South Carolina (Darla Moore), Georgia Tech (DuPree), Thunderbird, and Tennessee—Knoxville.

15. Was the amount of assigned work and reading either too little or so excessive that it impeded learning?

B-schoolers expect to work their collective tails off. But if the workload is too intense, they're unable to absorb everything. Conversely, if it's too much of a party atmosphere, they've gotten a piece of paper but little else they can use when they enter the workforce. Schools with the best balance were: Miami, Clark Atlanta, Stanford, UC Irvine, Tennessee—Knoxville, Georgia (Terry), Washington (Olin), Florida (Warrington), and Michigan State (Broad). And those that are struggling: Dartmouth (Tuck), Carnegie Mellon, Rice (Jones), William and Mary, Babson (Olin), Indiana (Kelley), USC (Marshall), Syracuse, Georgetown (McDonough), and Thunderbird.

16. To what extent did your school weave e-business topics throughout the curriculum?

It's all the rage—electronic commerce, dot-com mania, and everything e-business. And despite the volatility of the market, even the most traditional of Old Economy companies has an e-commerce effort underway or around the bend. And MBAs need to know how to manage these ventures and their specific challenges. Which schools do the best without going overboard or underplaying? USC (Marshall), Cornell (Johnson), Illinois at Urbana-Champaign, UCLA (Anderson), Texas A&M (Mays), Rochester (Simon), Case Western Reserve (Weatherhead), Virginia (Darden), Duke (Fuqua), and Indiana (Kelley). And those still looking for the right recipe? UC Irvine, Carnegie Mellon, Maryland (Smith), Vanderbilt (Owen), American (Kogod), Georgia Tech (DuPree), Tulane (Freeman), Syracuse, South Carolina (Darla Moore), SUNY—Buffalo, and Clark Atlanta.

17. To what extent were interpersonal skills stressed in the curriculum?

Touchy-feely things may not get respect from the number-crunchers, but it's a fact that those who can't communicate or manage well won't go far—no matter how smart they are. Who does the best job in this category? Harvard, Pittsburgh (Katz), UC Irvine, UCLA (Anderson), Rochester (Simon), Stanford, Texas—Austin, Pennsylvania (Wharton), Yale, and NYU (Stern). And those that miss? Case Western Reserve (Weatherhead), Penn State (Smeal), Thunderbird, Texas A&M (Mays),

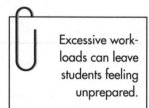

Excessive workloads can leave students feeling unprepared.

Babson (Olin), Ohio State (Fisher), Chicago, Rice (Jones), and William and Mary.

18. Did your school provide you with enough information to make you feel confident starting your own business?

If you ask a class of first-year MBA students to raise their hands if they ever hope to start their own businesses, you can be sure that about half the class will extend their arms. Even though that dream isn't always realized, skills learned in B-school can give an MBA the confidence to take that hope and turn it into a reality. So which schools provide the necessary tools? Babson (Olin), Texas—Austin, Virginia (Darden), MIT (Sloan), Carnegie Mellon, Stanford, UCLA (Anderson), Northwestern (Kellogg), UC Berkeley (Haas), and Harvard. And those that leave grads jelly-legged? SUNY—Buffalo, Syracuse, Arizona State, Miami, Ohio State (Fisher), South Carolina (Darla Moore), Tulane (Freeman), Pittsburgh (Katz), Tennessee—Knoxville, and George Washington.

19. How useful do you think the computer skills and analytical tools taught at your school will be in your work as a manager?

More and more, technical knowledge and analytical models are key to getting an edge in the workplace. Many B-schools have gotten on the ball, teaching more relevant and up-to-date computer and analytical models. Those that have done the best: Indiana (Kelley), Texas-Austin, Carnegie Mellon, Duke (Fuqua), Virginia (Darden), Rochester (Simon), Northwestern (Kellogg), MIT (Sloan), Purdue (Krannert), and Arizona (Eller). And those that trail: Syracuse, Clark Atlanta, South Carolina (Darla Moore), Tulane (Freeman), SUNY—Buffalo, Howard, Notre Dame (Mendoza), George Washington, Miami, and UC Berkeley.

20. To what extent was the learning environment enhanced by the use of technology? Who's got the most wired study rooms? The best simulated trading areas? The most up-to-date intranet?

Students say it's UC Irvine, Queens University, Virginia (Darden), North Carolina (Kenan-Flagler), Texas—Austin, Emory (Goizueta), MIT (Sloan), Carnegie Mellon, Indiana (Kelley), Northwestern (Kellogg), and Iowa (Tippie). Less tech-savvy: Clark Atlanta, South Carolina (Darla Moore), University of Washington, Howard, Chicago, Tulane (Freeman), Syracuse, George Washington, Michigan, and UC Davis.

21. To what extent did technological tools (Internet, advanced computer simulations, interactive learning, etc.) become a part of the curriculum?

Face it, those things will be everywhere in the workplace, and the more experience B-school students have with these tech-tools, the better pre-

Technology and technological tools are becoming more important at B-schools.

pared they'll be for managing them and using them in their jobs. So who's getting it right? Carnegie Mellon, UC Irvine, Indiana (Kelley), Texas—Austin, Virginia (Darden), Duke (Fuqua), North Carolina (Kenan-Flagler), Iowa (Tippie), MIT (Sloan), and Emory (Goizueta). And who's playing catch-up? South Carolina (Darla Moore), Clark Atlanta, University of Washington, Syracuse, Chicago, Tulane (Freeman), Rice (Jones), Brigham Young (Marriott), Yale, and SUNY—Buffalo.

22. To what extent were analytical skills stressed in the curriculum?
Some schools are famous for their quantitative offerings, while others don't get much beyond the basics and spend much more time focusing on softer skills. Who does the analytics right? Michigan, Stanford, UC Berkeley (Haas), UCLA (Anderson), Harvard, Northwestern (Kellogg), Minnesota (Carlson), Arizona State, UC Davis, and Boston College (Carroll). Those that stress it too much or not enough: Carnegie Mellon, Purdue (Krannert), Clark Atlanta, Chicago, William and Mary, Iowa (Tippie), Indiana (Kelley), MIT (Sloan), Howard, and Rutgers.

23. How would you judge the school's performance in providing you with numerous ways of thinking about or approaching problems that will serve you well over the long haul?
It's not just what you learn, it's how well you can apply it—and that's just another part of the B-school education. So whose students feel like they've got it? Virginia (Darden), Rochester (Simon), Harvard, Northwestern (Kellogg), Indiana (Kelley), Stanford, Washington (Olin), MIT (Sloan), Chicago, and Texas—Austin. Those who feel a little shaky? Syracuse, George Washington, SUNY—Buffalo, Tulane (Freeman), Miami, Clark Atlanta, South Carolina (Darla Moore), Pittsburgh (Katz), Tennessee—Knoxville, and Boston University.

24. Do you feel your classmates emphasized individual achievement at the expense of teamwork?
B-school is not the cutthroat place it once was, with many schools eschewing grades altogether (or at least avoiding releasing them to recruiters). Yet there are still some places where being top dog really means something and other places where classmates would happily give others the shirts off their backs—or at least their notes. Increasingly, the workplace has moved to a team-style management approach that MBAs need to be well versed in. The best at teamwork: Yale, Stanford, Northwestern (Kellogg), UC Berkeley, UC Davis, UCLA, Duke (Fuqua), Indiana (Kelley), Dartmouth (Tuck), and Virginia (Darden). The most competitive: Clark Atlanta, Chicago, Thunderbird, Boston University, Syracuse, Pittsburgh (Katz), George Washington, Tulane (Freeman), Georgia Tech (DuPree), and Howard.

A school should help you hone your analytical and thinking skills.

25. Did the caliber of your classmates impede or advance the learning process?

Having smart colleagues often raises the bar in the classroom. Conversely, if you're the only one to grasp a concept, there may be many frustrating hours in your future. Because MBAs spend so much time in teams, they learn as much from one another as they do from teachers. Those with the most stellar classmates: Stanford, MIT (Sloan), Virginia (Darden), Harvard, Yale, Northwestern (Kellogg), UC Davis, UC Berkeley (Haas), Dartmouth (Tuck), and Michigan. The least: SUNY—Buffalo, Syracuse, George Washington, Pittsburgh (Katz), Miami, Tulane (Freeman), Clark Atlanta, Tennessee—Knoxville, Arizona State, and South Carolina (Darla Moore).

26. How would you judge the responsiveness of the faculty and administration to students' concerns and opinions?

Some schools bend over backward to listen and respond to their students—most of whom have definite ideas on things that might be improved on and off campus. Others still ignore them, preferring to rule by fiat instead. The most responsive teachers and staffers are found at Cornell (Johnson), Northwestern (Kellogg), Duke (Fuqua), North Carolina (Kenan-Flagler), UC Davis, Emory (Goizueta), Virginia (Darden), Michigan, Georgetown (McDonough), and Pennsylvania (Wharton). The least: Syracuse, George Washington, South Carolina (Darla Moore), Clark Atlanta, Tennessee—Knoxville, Miami, Pittsburgh (Katz), Georgia Tech (DuPree), Illinois at Champaign-Urbana, and Stanford.

27. How would you assess the responsiveness of the school in meeting the demand for popular electives?

If you've spent an entire year waiting for the opportunity to get into that Nobel Prize winner's corporate finance course and it ends up being oversubscribed every time, you may not feel you got your money's worth. That wasn't the case at some schools, which worked to create new sections and tried to meet the needs of every student. The most responsive: Washington (Olin), Cornell (Johnson), Indiana (Kelley), Northwestern (Kellogg), Duke (Fuqua), Rochester (Simon), Dartmouth (Tuck), North Carolina (Kenan-Flagler), Ohio State (Fisher), and Emory (Goizueta). The least: Syracuse, Clark Atlanta, George Washington, SUNY—Buffalo, Howard, Tennessee—Knoxville, Miami, Arizona (Eller), Thunderbird, and Pittsburgh (Katz).

Administrative and faculty responsiveness is key to a good B-school experience.

28. How would you judge the school's efforts—either in class or in extracurricular activities—to nurture and improve your skills in leading others?

B-schools are, it is said, the incubators for the future leaders of Corporate America and the entire world. But not every school takes that statement as seriously as it might by teaching leadership skills. The best, say the students, are Northwestern (Kellogg), Virginia (Darden), Washington (Olin), SMU (Cox), Cornell (Johnson), Duke (Fuqua), Case Western Reserve (Weatherhead), Indiana (Kelley), Michigan, and Emory (Goizueta). And the worst: Syracuse, George Washington, South Carolina (Darla Moore), Clark Atlanta, Miami, Arizona State, Pittsburgh (Katz), Howard, Georgia Tech (DuPree), and Boston University.

29. To what extent did your school foster interaction between the various ethnic and national groups in your class?

It's not enough to have a class full of diverse students from all sorts of backgrounds and countries. A B-school has to make strides to get folks together—much like the real world of multinational corporations and deals. Do it too much and it'll feel forced. Those doing a good job, say students, are Cornell (Johnson), Texas—Austin, UCLA (Anderson), Brigham Young (Marriott), Yale, Wake Forest (Babcock), UC Berkeley, Tulane (Freeman), Michigan, and Minnesota (Carlson). And those that aren't there yet: Ohio State (Fisher), SMU (Cox), Chicago, UC Davis, Rice (Jones), Thunderbird, Case Western Reserve (Weatherhead), William and Mary, Howard, and Syracuse.

30. How would you appraise your school's efforts to bring you into contact with practicing professionals in the business community?

Hard as it may be to admit, a large part of B-school has to do with schmoozing for a job. Some schools have excellent connections with real-world professionals—and exploit them—while others are happy to remain ivory-tower bastions and rarely bring in big shots. Still others bring in so many professionals that education falls by the wayside. The 10 schools best able to balance this: Columbia, SMU (Cox), Emory (Goizueta), NYU (Stern), Texas—Austin, Pennsylvania (Wharton), Harvard, Washington (Olin), Northwestern (Kellogg), and Minnesota (Carlson). And the least: Syracuse, George Washington, South Carolina (Darla Moore), Tulane (Freeman), Tennessee—Knoxville, Miami, Rutgers, Florida (Warrington), SUNY—Buffalo, and Georgia (Terry).

31. How would you judge the school's network and connections that can help you throughout your career?

As suggested by the previous question, networking can make a world of difference for a student hoping for start-up financing for her backpack company or one who needs an extra helping hand before his job interview. Having a strong alumni base works to the advantage of schools like Harvard, Stanford, Dartmouth (Tuck), USC (Marshall), Columbia, Pennsylvania (Wharton), Notre Dame (Mendoza), Northwestern (Kellogg), Virginia (Darden), and Howard. Others don't offer such a strong

> Schools with strong alumni networks can serve grads well throughout a career.

base, like Tulane (Freeman), George Washington, South Carolina (Darla Moore), William and Mary, Miami, Georgia (Terry), Boston University, Wake Forest (Babcock), Pittsburgh (Katz), and Tennessee—Knoxville.

32. How would you judge the aggressiveness of the school in helping you with summer job placement or a summer internship?

Getting a summer job after your first year is more important than it's ever been, because recruiters are focusing their efforts on first-years in hopes of building company loyalty early on. The schools putting forward the most outstanding summer placement efforts were Duke (Fuqua), Columbia, Michigan State (Broad), Harvard, Stanford, MIT (Sloan), Michigan, Howard, NYU (Stern), and Northwestern (Kellogg). And those that need to step up: Syracuse, George Washington, Tulane (Freeman), William and Mary, Boston University, Georgia (Terry), Miami, Thunderbird, Illinois at Urbana-Champaign, and Notre Dame (Mendoza).

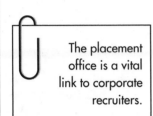

The placement office is a vital link to corporate recruiters.

33. How would you characterize the school's performance in helping you find a job before graduation?

Students know from their own marketing coursework that you need to sell a product, no matter how good it is. Some schools have brought in human resources executives from major companies as placement officers and completely revamped their offices after benchmarking companies as well as other schools. The schools getting kudos from students for their efforts are Duke (Fuqua), Michigan State (Broad), Michigan, Columbia, MIT (Sloan), Harvard, Northwestern (Kellogg), Dartmouth (Tuck), Washington (Olin), and NYU (Stern). And those getting panned: Syracuse, George Washington, Tulane (Freeman), William and Mary, Thunderbird, Notre Dame (Mendoza), Rutgers, Arizona (Eller), Wisconsin—Madison, and Ohio State (Fisher).

34. How would you characterize the number, diversity, and quality of firms recruiting on your campus?

The on-campus interview experience can leave much to be desired if all the interviewers are from the same industry or the firms aren't desirable places to work. Moreover, if there aren't many recruiters coming to campus, finding a job can be frustrating. Which schools have quality recruiters aplenty from all sorts of industries? Harvard, Duke (Fuqua), Pennsylvania (Wharton), Northwestern (Kellogg), Michigan, Columbia, Stanford, MIT (Sloan), Texas—Austin, and Chicago. Those that leave something to be desired: Syracuse, Tulane (Freeman), George Washington, William and Mary, Georgia (Terry), Wake Forest (Babcock), SUNY—Buffalo, Notre Dame (Mendoza), Pittsburgh (Katz), and Miami.

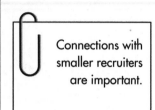

Connections with smaller recruiters are important.

35. If the organizations you targeted for employment did not recruit on your campus, how would you assess your school's assistance in supporting your independent search for a job?

While on-campus recruiting remains a core of most MBA job searches, many students want more than what the campus can offer. The schools that are best at supporting these searches, says students, are MIT (Sloan), Duke (Fuqua), Columbia, Michigan, Northwestern (Kellogg), Howard, Chicago, Michigan State (Broad), Virginia (Darden), and Pennsylvania (Wharton). Those that leave students hanging: South Carolina (Darla Moore), Tulane (Freeman), Syracuse, George Washington, William and Mary, Miami, Notre Dame (Mendoza), Wake Forest (Babcock), Thunderbird, and Georgia (Terry).

36. How would you characterize your school's assistance in connecting you with nontraditional or smaller recruiters?

MBAs want to make a difference, and that can sometimes be hard in a big company. B-schools that realize this are helping their students find that niche where they'll fit best. Those that lend an assist: Duke (Fuqua), Michigan State (Broad), Northwestern (Kellogg), Michigan, Columbia, Chicago, Emory (Goizueta), Stanford, Pennsylvania (Wharton), and North Carolina (Kenan-Flagler). And those that don't do as much: Tulane (Freeman), South Carolina (Darla Moore), Syracuse, William and Mary, Miami, Thunderbird, Georgia (Terry), Pittsburgh (Katz), Boston University, and Arizona State.

37. How would you appraise the placement office's help with matters such as interview training, negotiating strategy, résumés, etc.?

The placement office must make connections and market the students as the cream of the crop. But once an interview begins, it's the student who's completely in control of his or her own destiny. Schools can help make sure that students are polished, well-spoken, and don't throw away the chance at a better salary than they asked for. Best at helping to prep students: Duke (Fuqua), Michigan State (Broad), Washington (Olin), UCLA (Anderson), Michigan, Columbia, Indiana (Kelley), Stanford, NYU (Stern), and MIT (Sloan). Those that aren't: Georgia (Terry), Syracuse, Tulane (Freeman), South Carolina (Darla Moore), William and Mary, George Washington, Clark Atlanta, Tennessee—Knoxville, Georgia Tech (Dupree), and Notre Dame (Mendoza).

38. Based on your level of satisfaction, please appraise your school's efforts to include international business in the MBA program.

Globalization has become so overused as to appear clichéd these days, even in B-school. Yet there are some schools that students think do a great job of exposing them to other cultures and management styles. Topping the list: Thunderbird, Georgetown (McDonough), Columbia, MIT (Sloan), Pennsylvania (Wharton), USC (Marshall), Rochester (Simon), NYU (Stern), UC Berkeley, and Harvard. Schools that haven't quite gotten it yet: Tennessee—Knoxville, Arizona (Eller), SUNY—Buffalo, Arizona State, Rice (Jones), Howard, Syracuse, William and Mary, Pittsburgh (Katz), and Clark Atlanta.

39. Based on your level of satisfaction, please appraise your school's efforts to include ethics in the MBA program.

Although only a handful of schools require a business ethics course in order to graduate, the debate continues on how best to teach ethical behavior in an industry periodically plagued with violations. The schools singled out by grads as best in the area: Virginia (Darden), Notre Dame (Mendoza), Brigham Young (Marriott), North Carolina (Kenan-Flagler), Northwestern (Kellogg), Georgetown (McDonough), Washington (Olin), Harvard, Case Western Reserve (Weatherhead), and Pennsylvania (Wharton). The laggards: Clark Atlanta, Tulane (Freeman), Syracuse, Tennessee—Knoxville, Arizona (Eller), SUNY—Buffalo, Boston University, Ohio State (Fisher), UC Irvine, and Babson (Olin).

40. Based on your level of satisfaction, please appraise your school's efforts to include leadership in the MBA program.

Weaving leadership skills throughout the curriculum is not an easy thing to do, and making them stick until graduates get an opportunity to put them into action is even tougher. Best in this category, according to grads: Harvard, Virginia (Darden), Northwestern (Kellogg), Michigan, SMU (Cox), Cornell (Johnson), Stanford, Washington (Olin), Indiana (Kelley), and Pennsylvania (Wharton). Falling behind: Syracuse, George Washington, Tulane (Freeman), Arizona State, Miami, South Carolina (Darla Moore), UC Irvine, Clark Atlanta, Georgia Tech (DuPree), and Pittsburgh (Katz).

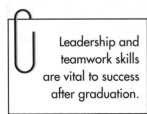

Leadership and teamwork skills are vital to success after graduation.

41. Based on your level of satisfaction, please appraise your school's efforts to include teamwork in the MBA program.

A skill more immediately relevant to recent grads than leadership is teamwork. Without it, you'll be a disaster in the workplace, since few projects are undertaken by a solo flier. Schools that lead the teamwork pack are Northwestern (Kellogg), Duke (Fuqua), Virginia (Darden) North Carolina (Kenan-Flagler), Dartmouth (Tuck), Michigan, UCLA (Anderson), Indiana (Kelley), Babson (Olin), and Stanford. Those that need to focus more on teamwork: Clark Atlanta, George Washington, Syracuse, Tulane (Freeman), Miami, Wisconsin—Madison, Arizona State, Harvard, Chicago, and Brigham Young (Marriott).

42. Based on your level of satisfaction, please appraise your school's efforts to include entrepreneurship in the MBA program.

Although only 8 percent of the students at the surveyed 67 U.S. schools chose to go into business for themselves, the level of interest in the topic has exploded, and nearly every school now offers a variety of courses or a concentration in the area. But there's a big difference between lip service and the kind of training that really helps launch a start-up, and the grads at the following schools say they got the latter: Texas—Austin, UCLA (Anderson), Babson (Olin), Stanford, MIT (Sloan), UC Berkeley, Harvard, Northwestern (Kellogg), USC (Marshall), and University of Washington. Grads were most disappointed by the entrepreneurship offerings at these schools: SUNY—Buffalo, Arizona State, Clark Atlanta, William and Mary, Ohio State (Fisher), Tennessee—Knoxville, South Carolina (Darla Moore), Miami, Purdue (Krannert), and Tulane (Freeman).

43. Based on your level of satisfaction, please appraise your school's efforts to include diversity in the MBA program.

Nearly all B-schools have made a big push to include a large proportion of students from other countries in their programs. Not all have done the same with women and domestic minorities, who remain largely underrepresented in B-school. Overall, however, the faces in the crowd look a lot more varied than they have in the past, especially at these schools: Thunderbird, Rochester (Simon), Case Western Reserve (Weatherhead), MIT (Sloan), Columbia, NYU (Stern), Michigan, UC Berkeley, Duke (Fuqua), and Pennsylvania (Wharton). Getting the lowest marks in this area: Brigham Young (Marriott), University of Washington, Wake Forest (Babcock), Clark Atlanta, Rice (Jones), Dartmouth (Tuck), Notre Dame (Mendoza), SMU (Cox), Tennessee—Knoxville, and Ohio State (Fisher).

44. Based on your level of satisfaction, please appraise your school's efforts to include information technology in the MBA program.

Depending on your career objectives, you may happily wear the "quant geek" label or reject it. But at B-school, having access to and superior training in info tech can make all the difference in your career, whether or not you choose to work at a tech firm. Grads were happiest with the info-tech offerings at MIT (Sloan), Texas—Austin, UC Irvine, Maryland (Smith), Carnegie Mellon, American (Kogod), North Carolina (Kenan-Flagler), Northwestern (Kellogg), Vanderbilt (Owen), and Harvard. They were unimpressed at Clark Atlanta, Syracuse, Tulane (Freeman), South Carolina (Darla Moore), Notre Dame (Mendoza), Tennessee—Knoxville, UC Davis, Rice (Jones), SMU (Cox), and Georgetown (McDonough).

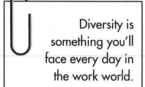

Diversity is something you'll face every day in the work world.

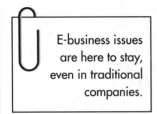

E-business issues are here to stay, even in traditional companies.

45. Based on your level of satisfaction, please appraise your school's efforts to include e-business in the MBA program.

Face it, e-business is where all business is going. Even Old Economy stalwarts have e-commerce efforts. And B-schools are following suit. Those that do a good job are MIT (Sloan), Vanderbilt (Owen), Texas—Austin, Stanford, Northwestern (Kellogg), Maryland (Smith), UC Berkeley, Harvard, Carnegie Mellon, and UC Irvine. Those that aren't: Clark Atlanta, Syracuse, SUNY—Buffalo, Howard, South Carolina (Darla Moore), Wake Forest (Babcock), Tulane (Freeman), Tennessee—Knoxville, Iowa (Tippie), and Notre Dame (Mendoza).

B-SCHOOLS BY THE NUMBERS

These numbers let the reader make direct comparisons among schools.

There are many ways to select a business school and just as many ways to look at one. Here we use numbers and statistics to provide a snapshot of the 50 best schools. Some of this data was provided by the schools themselves. They routinely publish tons of information. But you won't find a lot of what's available here elsewhere; it was gathered specifically for this project by BUSINESS-WEEK from the surveys of the latest crop of MBA graduates. What also makes these numbers valuable is that they let the reader make direct comparisons among the best schools. Rather than looking at a GMAT average or selectivity measure in isolation, you can see exactly how a school you're interested in compares with its peers.

You'll find a wealth of data in these pages. You'll discover which of the top schools are the most selective and, therefore, the toughest to get into. You'll find out which schools boast the largest enrollments and the highest and lowest percentages of international students, women, or minorities. You'll find out how much money an MBA graduate from each of these schools is likely to command in the job market. And you'll discover which schools' graduates leave campus with the largest debt burdens hanging over their heads.

None of this information constitutes a ranking, nor is any of this data used by BUSINESSWEEK to compile its own ranking of the top schools. But it may help you put the schools you're thinking about into a broader context.

GMAT SCORES

One of the most anxiety-filled parts of the admissions process is the Graduate Management Admission Test, taken by more than 210,000 people each year. Now computerized, it's required by some 850 business schools worldwide—including the 50 schools listed here. Although it's hardly perfect, the test is one of the only consistent yardsticks used to measure student quality, and it usually counts for some 20 to 40 percent of an application's overall weight. Scores continue to climb, with the largest jump over the past two years occurring at Washington University, where average scores rose 37 points to 661. Here are the numbers for the Class of 2002.

TOP 30 SCHOOL	AVERAGE GMAT	RUNNERS-UP SCHOOL	AVERAGE GMAT
Stanford	722	UC Davis	673
Columbia	706	UC Irvine	670
UCLA	698	Notre Dame	659
Dartmouth	692	Ohio State	645
Kellogg	690	U. of Florida	645
MIT	690	U. of Georgia	645
Harvard	689	Wake Forest	645
Texas	686	Arizona State	644
Yale	686	SMU	644
Wharton	685	Minnesota	640
Chicago	684	Rice	640
Duke	683	Babson	638
U. of Michigan	677	Iowa	638
Virginia	676	Wisconsin	635
NYU	675	William & Mary	629
UC Berkeley	674	Boston U.	628
Cornell	673	Illinois	621
USC	670	Pittsburgh	620
UNC	667	Penn State	616
Washington U.	661	Thunderbird	611
Carnegie Mellon	660		
Georgetown	657		
Maryland	653		
Emory	650		
Michigan State	650		
Indiana	646		
Rochester	646		
Purdue	644		
Vanderbilt	640		
Georgia Tech	635		

B-SCHOOL SELECTIVITY

Another critical indicator of a business school's quality is the number of applicants it accepts and rejects. As it has for the past several years, Stanford remains the most selective school, rejecting an amazing 92 percent of applicants for the Class of 2002. With MBAs more in demand than ever, it has gotten even tougher to get into a Top 50 school. Although top-ranked Wharton accepted 23 percent of its applicants in 1994, today it allows in just 14 percent.

TOP 30 SCHOOL	APPLICANTS ACCEPTED	RUNNERS-UP SCHOOL	APPLICANTS ACCEPTED
Stanford	8%	Penn State	15%
Columbia	12	U. of Florida	22
Harvard	13	Wisconsin	26
Wharton	14	U. of Georgia	28
Dartmouth	14	Notre Dame	29
Berkeley	14	Ohio State	29
UCLA	15	UC Davis	31
MIT	17	Minnesota	33
Yale	17	SMU	33
Kellogg	18	UC Irvine	33
Duke	19	Arizona State	35
Virginia	19	Iowa	38
Georgetown	19	Rice	39
U. of Michigan	21	Babson	40
NYU	22	Illinois	41
UNC	22	Boston U.	43
Purdue	23	Pittsburgh	43
Maryland	23	William and Mary	49
Cornell	25	Wake Forest	51
Chicago	25	Thunderbird	76
Texas	25		
Michigan State	26		
USC	27		
Washington U.	29		
Rochester	30		
Carnegie Mellon	31		
Indiana	33		
Emory	34		
Georgia Tech	35		
Vanderbilt	38		

FULL-TIME ENROLLMENTS

The size of an MBA program is an important attribute of a school's culture and a key element in choosing your ideal program. Do you like the big-city buzz and the chance to meet more people than you ever imagined? You might do well at Harvard, Wharton, or Columbia. Do you prefer a more secluded, intimate environment? Dartmouth or Iowa might make a better fit. Although enrollments have remained more or less steady, some smaller schools have added to their rosters. These figures are the total full-time enrollments for the combined Classes of 2001 and 2002.

TOP 30 SCHOOL	FULL-TIME ENROLLMENT	RUNNERS-UP SCHOOL	FULL-TIME ENROLLMENT
Harvard	1742	Thunderbird	1400
Wharton	1566	Boston U.	636
Kellogg	1200	Wisconsin	467
Columbia	1155	Arizona State	424
Chicago	1016	Illinois	379
U. of Michigan	874	U. of Florida	356
NYU	840	Babson	337
Texas	808	Notre Dame	325
Stanford	730	Rice	307
MIT	717	UC Irvine	290
Rochester	677	Ohio State	286
UCLA	655	U. of Georgia	256
USC	599	Minnesota	250
Cornell	568	SMU	236
Indiana	566	Wake Forest	221
UNC	543	Penn State	209
Georgetown	520	William and Mary	196
Virginia	488	Pittsburgh	170
Berkeley	484	Iowa	165
Maryland	470	UC Davis	139
Vanderbilt	458		
Carnegie Mellon	442		
Yale	420		
Dartmouth	398		
Emory	360		
Duke	335		
Purdue	320		
Washington U.	298		
Michigan State	246		
Georgia Tech	195		

INTER-NATIONAL ENROLLMENTS

Global is one of the most overused buzzwords in B-school these days. Yet some schools have been more receptive to large numbers of non-U.S. students than others. In the Top 30 schools, Rochester leads the way with 50 percent of their students coming from outside the United States. Thunderbird tops the Runners-Up list with 67 percent. The greatest rise in MBA applications has come from international students seeking an American MBA.

TOP 30 SCHOOL	INTERNATIONAL STUDENTS	RUNNERS-UP SCHOOL	INTERNATIONAL STUDENTS
Rochester	50%	Thunderbird	67%
Purdue	41	Illinois	52
Wharton	39	Iowa	47
Georgetown	38	Boston U.	41
MIT	37	Wisconsin	38
Carnegie Mellon	37	Babson	37
Michigan State	36	Notre Dame	35
NYU	35	Penn State	35
Maryland	35	Arizona State	33
Washington U.	33	William and Mary	33
Kellogg	32	Minnesota	32
Harvard	32	UC Irvine	31
Dartmouth	32	SMU	30
Berkeley	32	Ohio State	29
Yale	32	Wake Forest	29
Emory	32	UC Davis	22
U. of Michigan	31	U. of Florida	22
Chicago	31	U. of Georgia	21
Stanford	31	Rice	20
Indiana	31	Pittsburgh	NA
Cornell	30		
UNC	29		
Georgia Tech	29		
Duke	28		
Columbia	28		
Vanderbilt	28		
UCLA	26		
Texas	26		
Virginia	25		
USC	23		

WOMEN MBA ENROLLMENTS

Although women now make up a good half of all medical and law school students, you won't see the same statistics for the Top 50 business schools, where women made up just 29 percent of the total for the graduating Class of 2000—virtually unchanged from 1988. The percentage of women varies widely in the Top 30, from a high of 39 percent at NYU to a low of 21 percent at Purdue. These figures represent the combined Classes of 1999 and 2000.

TOP 30 SCHOOL	WOMEN STUDENTS	RUNNERS-UP SCHOOL	WOMEN STUDENTS
NYU	39%	UC Davis	37%
Duke	38	Babson	36
Columbia	37	SMU	36
Georgetown	36	Illinois	36
Stanford	35	William and Mary	36
Maryland	35	Boston U.	35
Berkeley	34	Notre Dame	33
USC	33	Pittsburgh	30
Dartmouth	32	Rice	30
Kellogg	31	Ohio State	30
Harvard	31	Wisconsin	30
UNC	31	Arizona State	29
Yale	30	Iowa	28
Emory	30	Thunderbird	26
Wharton	29	U. of Georgia	26
Georgia Tech	29	Minnesota	25
U. of Michigan	28	Penn State	25
Virginia	28	UC Irvine	23
UCLA	28	Wake Forest	23
Michigan State	28	U. of Florida	12
MIT	27		
Cornell	27		
Vanderbilt	27		
Carnegie Mellon	26		
Washington U.	25		
Texas	24		
Indiana	24		
Rochester	24		
Chicago	23		
Purdue	21		

MINORITY ENROLLMENTS

Underrepresented minorities still make up a relatively small percentage of business school enrollments, although some schools have been more successful at wooing them than others. The following percentages—from the Class of 2002—are for African-American, Hispanic-American, and Native American students from the United States. Among the Top 30 schools, Rochester has the largest percentage, at 17 percent, while Cornell, Carnegie Mellon, Texas, and Vanderbilt, by contrast, have just 5 percent. For the Runners-Up, SMU leads the way with 13 percent.

TOP 30 SCHOOL	MINORITY STUDENTS	RUNNERS-UP SCHOOL	MINORITY STUDENTS
Rochester	17%	SMU	13%
Duke	16	Arizona State	12
Kellogg	14	Illinois	12
Harvard	14	Rice	12
Virginia	14	Ohio State	12
Columbia	13	Penn State	11
U. of Michigan	12	Notre Dame	10
Georgia Tech	12	Thunderbird	10
MIT	11	Minnesota	9
UNC	11	Wake Forest	9
USC	11	Wisconsin	9
Stanford	10	UC Davis	6
Maryland	10	Babson	5
NYU	9	Boston U.	5
Dartmouth	9	William and Mary	5
Indiana	9	U. of Georgia	5
Washington U.	9	Iowa	3
Purdue	9	UC Irvine	2
Wharton	8	U. of Florida	2
UCLA	8	Pittsburgh	NA
Georgetown	8		
Emory	8		
Michigan State	8		
Chicago	7		
Berkeley	7		
Yale	6		
Cornell	5		
Carnegie Mellon	5		
Texas	5		
Vanderbilt	5		

PRE-MBA SALARIES

Schools tend to focus on GMAT scores and essays as indicators of applicant quality. But another important—yet seldom analyzed—measure is the salaries applicants earn before deciding to go back to school. The larger the salary, the more likely it is that the candidate left a meaningful job in a demanding environment. The following figures are median salaries for the members of the Class of 2000 before they got their degrees.

TOP 30 SCHOOL	PRE-MBA SALARY	RUNNERS-UP SCHOOL	PRE-MBA SALARY
Harvard	$65,000	UC Irvine	$44,500
Stanford	65,000	UC Davis	44,000
Wharton	60,000	Rice	42,000
Kellogg	56,000	SMU	42,000
UCLA	55,000	Ohio State	41,000
Chicago	55,000	U. of Florida	40,000
MIT	55,000	U. of Georgia	40,000
Berkeley	50,000	William and Mary	40,000
U. of Michigan	50,000	Babson	40,000
Virginia	50,000	Boston U.	40,000
Columbia	50,000	Notre Dame	40,000
Cornell	50,000	Thunderbird	40,000
Dartmouth	50,000	Pittsburgh	39,000
Duke	49,000	Wisconsin	39,000
UNC	48,000	Arizona State	38,000
Texas	45,000	Wake Forest	35,500
Carnegie Mellon	45,000	Minnesota	35,000
Emory	45,000	Penn State	34,000
Georgetown	45,000	Illinois	31,500
NYU	45,000	Iowa	31,000
USC	45,000		
Yale	45,000		
Vanderbilt	43,000		
Indiana	42,000		
Washington U.	42,000		
Maryland	40,000		
Rochester	40,000		
Michigan State	36,000		
Georgia Tech	35,000		
Purdue	35,000		

STARTING PAY PACKAGES

Take a look at these breathtaking numbers and you'll know right away why so many people are getting their MBAs. For the Class of 2000, the median starting pay package at the Top 50 schools hit a whopping $97,100. For the Top 30, the total hit $111,420, up 19 percent from 1998. And salary was only part of the equation. Thanks to a brutally competitive environment in which MBAs held the cards in the recruiting game, newly minted MBAs could also expect hefty sign-on bonuses, along with benefits and perks—all of which BW includes in the total pay package. That's why these figures, which come directly from student surveys, tend to be higher than those reported by the schools.

TOP 30 SCHOOL	TOTAL PAY	RUNNERS-UP SCHOOL	TOTAL PAY
Stanford	$165,500	UC Davis	$103,000
Harvard	160,000	Rice	96,000
Wharton	156,000	SMU	93,000
Dartmouth	149,500	Wake Forest	89,000
MIT	149,000	William and Mary	88,000
Columbia	142,500	Iowa	87,000
Kellogg	142,000	Boston U.	87,000
Chicago	140,000	Wisconsin	86,000
NYU	140,000	Penn State	86,000
UCLA	136,500	Ohio State	85,000
Cornell	135,000	Arizona State	85,000
Virginia	135,000	Notre Dame	84,000
Berkeley	135,000	Babson	84,000
Michigan	131,000	Minnesota	83,000
Yale	130,000	Illinois	83,000
Duke	128,500	Thunderbird	82,000
Carnegie Mellon	125,000	U. of Georgia	82,000
UNC	125,000	UC Irvine	79,000
Georgetown	116,000	U. of Florida	71,000
Vanderbilt	115,000	Pittsburgh	68,000
Indiana	114,000		
USC	112,000		
Rochester	110,000		
Washington U.	109,000		
Texas	107,000		
Maryland	105,000		
Emory	105,000		
Purdue	101,500		
Georgia Tech	95,000		
Michigan State	93,000		

TOTAL MBA INVESTMENT

Sure, you're likely to boost your standard of living significantly by getting an MBA from a good school. But more likely than not this will come with a hefty price tag—which most people finance by borrowing money. These numbers reflect the average outstanding loans for the graduates of the Class of 2000, and the debt load can be staggering. At public universities, the pressure isn't quite as great as at private institutions, where debt can total $60,000 or more.

TOP 30 SCHOOL	MEDIAN TOTAL INVESTMENT*	RUNNERS-UP SCHOOL	MEDIAN TOTAL INVESTMENT*
Harvard	$192,500	SMU	$136,600
Stanford	179,300	UC Irvine	133,400
Wharton	175,400	Boston U.	133,200
MIT	170,000	Babson	132,500
Kellogg	167,800	Thunderbird	129,700
Chicago	167,500	Notre Dame	129,500
Columbia	164,200	UC Davis	129,200
Dartmouth	159,100	Wake Forest	119,000
U. of Michigan	156,200	Rice	118,500
Duke	154,900	William and Mary	112,700
NYU	154,700	Wisconsin	112,600
Cornell	153,800	Ohio State	110,600
Georgetown	149,900	Illinois	105,500
UCLA	149,800	Minnesota	105,200
Yale	148,600	U. of Florida	100,000
Emory	145,300	U. of Georgia	97,800
Carnegie Mellon	145,100	Penn State	97,100
Virginia	144,800	Arizona State	94,000
USC	144,600	Iowa	83,400
Vanderbilt	142,300	Pittsburgh	82,600
Washington U.	139,800		
Berkeley	139,600		
Rochester	137,000		
UNC	132,100		
Texas	118,600		
Indiana	118,500		
Maryland	106,200		
Purdue	102,600		
Michigan State	94,200		
Georgia Tech	93,500		

*Including lost wages.

THE TOP 30

The business schools that make up the BUSINESSWEEK Top 30 list offer the highest quality MBA education you can find in the United States, and perhaps the world over. And while many schools have moved toward similar styles of teaching and curriculum, the schools on this list all have their own distinct personalities, environments, and cultures. Each has strengths and weaknesses, differing curriculum styles, experiential learning opportunities, and more. And each school will offer a different education and experience.

So which school is the best fit for you? Read through the following profiles and you'll be well on your way to figuring that out. Each profile starts with a snapshot view providing information about a school's size, diversity, costs, selectivity, standing with the corporate recruiters, graduate and intellectual capital polls, and—the big question for many prospective MBA students—starting pay packages of graduates. Near the end of each profile, we identify the companies that hire the most graduates of each school; the most outstanding faculty, as identified by the Class of 2000; tips for applicants; and candid comments on the schools from graduates of the Class of 2000.

There are other interesting tidbits in each profile, too. For example, did you know that more than 600 students gather each Thanksgiving for dinner at Northwestern University's Kellogg Graduate School of Management—a tradition started by the dean more than 20 years ago? Or, did you know that Stanford, the most selective of all the B-schools, accepts only 8 percent of applicants—and of those, more than 80 percent enroll at the school?

All of these figures, except for the enrollment percentages, apply to the class that entered in the fall of 2000. Enrollment percentages are based on a two-year compilation to give a better view of the total number of women, international, and minority students enrolled at a school. The intellectual capital rating measures a school's influence and prominence in the realm of ideas. The list of each school's outstanding professors is based on the results of the magazine's graduate survey. Information about GMAT scores, selectivity, and diversity is provided by the school, while salary figures are provided by the graduates of the Class of 2000 who answered the magazine survey.

> Which of the top schools is best for you? Read these profiles and find out.

**1.
UNIVERSITY
OF
PENNSYLVANIA**

UNIVERSITY OF PENNSYLVANIA

The Wharton School
104 Vance Hall
Philadelphia, Pennsylvania 19104
E-mail address: mba.admissions@wharton.upenn.edu
Web site address: http://www.wharton.upenn.edu

Corporate ranking: 1	Graduate ranking: 3
Enrollment: 1566	Annual tuition & fees: $27,170
Women: 28%	Room and board: $12,500
Non-U.S.: 39%	Average GMAT score: 700
Minority: 7%	Average years of work exp.: 6
Part-time: 0	Accepted applicants enrolled: 73%
Average age: 29	Intellectual capital: 8
Applicants accepted: 14%	
Median starting pay: $156,000	

Teaching methods: Lecture, 55%   Case study, 30%
 Experiential learning, 15%

The University of Pennsylvania's Wharton School is putting on a different face—from its facilities to its leadership, the buzzword on campus could very well be "new." Since 1998, a new dean has taken the reins, plans for a new building have turned into poured foundations, and the career center has been reborn. Despite the transitions, Wharton came out on top for the sixth consecutive BUSINESSWEEK Business School Rankings. This time around, Wharton shares some of the limelight with Northwestern's Kellogg School, which is knocking on the door to number one. But for now, Wharton hangs on to the top spot by clinching kudos from corporate recruiters, who say the Wharton MBA is a dynamic program that produces the highest-quality graduates.

New dean Patrick T. Harker is demanding that the Wharton MBA program maintain its reputation as a leader and an innovator in the B-school arena. Harker is himself a leader, and he's certainly no stranger to the University of Pennsylvania. He received a bachelor's and master's degree in civil and urban engineering there in 1981. And in 1983, he earned a University of Pennsylvania master's degree in economics and a Ph.D. in civil engineering. In 1984, he joined the Wharton faculty as the Stephen M. Peck Term Assistant Professor of Decision Sciences, which was followed by a promotion to associate professor in 1987. By 1991, he secured a spot as the UPS Transportation Professor for the Private Sector. "I loved teaching," Harker says. "I still view myself first and foremost as a professor." For many students, it is that connection to the faculty that gives Harker an extra bit of appeal. And perhaps

Contact:
Rosemaria Martinelli
Director of Admissions
and Financial Aid
215-898-3430
Application deadline:
April 10

a bit unlike many of his colleagues, Harker was named a White House fellow in the early nineties.

Nowadays, Harker can be thankful for the school's long-lasting tradition of success, which can be measured in myriad ways: A Wharton MBA practically guarantees an array of job offers from the world's most prestigious investment banks, accounting firms, and consulting companies. Money appears to grow on trees for Wharton grads, with the median starting pay at $156,000—one of the highest in the Top 30. The school itself is profiting as well; Wharton's endowment, as of June 30, 2000, reached nearly $340 million. And with 73,375 alumni in more than 131 countries, students can find an ally in almost any company—something no perspective MBA can dismiss. The Wharton network serves its alumni well—and is a strength of the urban school.

Success sure can be sweet, but even the most well-oiled machines have a few squeaks. Though the job offers keep flowing and recruiters applaud students, the career services office made a less than stellar showing in the 2000 rankings. Indeed, recruiters ranked the placement office second worst in the Top 30, behind only Stanford University. Students agreed and question the school's aggressiveness when it comes to job searches, some worrying that the placement office may have been resting on its laurels. One recent graduate, James Newsome, notes the number of opportunities the career center offers a Wharton student, but advises the school to remember that in the emerging global market, the office needs to come up with ways to find international job options in traditional MBA fields. Not that the complaints have fallen on deaf ears—placement officials say they've moved quickly to assuage some of the problems, and future alumni may very well benefit from a more aggressive and knowledgeable placement staff.

Wharton students are an exacting bunch who appreciate what is overwhelmingly right with the school (the school ranked No. 3 in BUSI-NESSWEEK's graduate satisfaction survey) but aren't shy about pointing out things that need fixing. At the top of the student hit list: academics. Wharton was the only school in the top five to score less than an A for curriculum. The school earned a meager C, which marred the otherwise pristine report card of one of the oldest B-schools. Not everyone agreed that the curriculum was suffering. "I can think of no other place that so completely educates and develops an individual as the Wharton School," says one 2000 grad. "The school's approach struck an excellent balance between the concrete issues of business such as finance and the more nebulous but equally important concerns of ethics, leadership, and interpersonal skills. In every aspect, my education has been transforming."

However, other students gave teachers below-average ratings for being inaccessible and for compromising teaching in favor of research. Additionally, graduates complained that the first-year curriculum tends to be repetitive. But Harker has at least a partial answer—he plans to leverage the praise the school received for its global scope by emphasizing international initiatives and thinking of new approaches to teaching. Globalization is on the top of Harker's priority list. "Globalization isn't only a nice thing to do, it's reality," he says. Partnerships, such as a technology-enhanced joint program with INSEAD, are an example of Harker's vision. He believes B-schools must look at distance learning and other types of technology and find ways for students to learn "twenty-four, seven." This is the future—and it's a future that is quickly coming to Wharton. Year 2000 graduates note the wealth of new courses, all in line with the changing business world, available each year.

Of course, Wharton students do have access to some of the top thinkers in the business world, practically a who's who with names like Jeremy Seigel, famous market guru. His classes are standing room only as he does the morning stock market report. Indeed, Wharton professors published more journal articles and books than any other faculty—and although their minds might not be as accessible as students would like, their thinking translates into classroom instruction. For certain, their experience and caliber would be hard to match anywhere else.

Students have other gripes with the academic realm at Wharton. Some criticize a nondisclosure grading policy instituted in 1999. This policy no longer allows the grades of Wharton students to be disclosed to recruiters or fellow students. "The grade nondisclosure policy will slowly erode this program if they don't get rid of it soon," says a 2000 graduate. "It results in adverse selection of people who would rather not have to try too hard." It could be a catch-22 for the school: Some students say the nondisclosure grading allows them to concentrate more on their areas of interest, but others point out that students can end up not pulling their weight in some classes in favor of others—a potential problem in an environment that emphasizes teamwork.

Students here are full partners in the constant massaging of the MBA program—what Wharton dubs its "co-production" learning model. Courses and teaching styles are continuously retooled during each term according to student feedback gathered through frequent "stakeholder surveys" and "quality circle" meetings with individual professors. Indeed, students formed a group to come up with ways to make the first-year curriculum more relevant. And a panel of students even directs an annual reinvention of the school's intranet.

As recently as 1998, the intranet was not the buzz in West Philly. Instead, students criticized Wharton's insufficient electronic facilities—the computer labs were poor, they said, and there were few places to hook up a laptop. However, the administration kept its promise to respond to student concerns and broke ground on the impressive Jon M. Huntsman Hall, a 300,000-square-foot academic building. After gathering extensive input from faculty and students, Kohn Pedersen Fox Associates PC designed the building, which is expected to open sometime in 2002. Huntsman Hall will fill the void along 38th Street from Walnut Street to Locust Walk, where the old university bookstore was once housed. More than 50 group study rooms, equipped with the latest technology in audio and video conferencing and video production and editing, are intended to serve as mini-labs for student research. The Colloquium, located at the top of the building, will serve as a conference area. The main presentation room will seat 200 and can be used for laid-back luncheons or spiffy evening affairs. Huntsman Hall will house both Wharton undergraduates and MBAs. The MBA Café will be on the second floor, alongside an outdoor plaza that might be used for Wharton events and club gatherings.

The new facilities should serve as a nice complement to the administration's promise of an innovative and modern MBA education supported by a highly developed information technology infrastructure. Known affectionately as "Spike," the school's electronic communications suite isn't just a tool but has become an important part of the culture here. Even before you get to campus, you may already be well acquainted with some of your classmates through E-talk, an online forum that allows accepted applicants to communicate with one another, and with current students, as soon as they find out they've been admitted. An idea generated by the Wharton Graduate Association, E-talk provides bulletin-board forums for those who want to trade tips on what type of computer to purchase, for others seeking roommates, and for still others who want inside info on Philly nightlife.

Wharton's IT is designed to serve you from your first contact with the school until long after you've left campus. After exploring the school's smartly designed online catalog and asking questions of current students through the Student2Student chat line, you can submit your application via computer. (Wharton was the first B-school to offer that option, although almost all top-ranked schools do so these days.) Once you arrive, you'll find that materials for every MBA course are posted electronically—databases, notes, syllabi—along with bulletin boards for all 125 or so student clubs, the student directory, individual Web pages set up by most students, and continuously updated broadcasts of school news and announcements. You can bid for courses and set up interviews with job recruiters online. And after graduation, you'll have access to WAVE, a huge, searchable database of the school's 26,000-strong alumni network.

Incoming students arrive in early August, a full four weeks before the start of the fall term to ensure that students from diverse backgrounds begin on equal footing. Courses in basic accounting, microeconomics, and statistics bring liberal arts majors up to speed and, simultaneously, prepare those with business backgrounds for exams to waive several core courses. Classes in communications, computer skills, nine different languages, and a two-day leadership retreat, as well as tours of companies in Philadelphia, New York, and Washington, D.C., and plenty of barbecues, parties, and other social gatherings all get you ready to hit the ground running when the school year actually begins.

Your first year at Wharton is divided into four 6-week quarters. You'll move through your core courses as part of a 60-student cohort, with groups of three cohorts forming a cluster, a kind of class within a class. Each cluster shares the same team of core professors who work together to integrate the coursework and coordinate student workload, which helps to keep you from feeling too much at sea amid the enormous class size. (With some 1540 full-time students per year, Wharton is one of the biggest of the top-tier MBA programs. Add to that 2400 undergraduate business majors, several hundred evening, executive MBA and doctoral students, and about 8600 executive education partici-

pants moving through campus each year, and you can see how you might feel a bit lost in the shuffle.) In the first-semester Leadership course, you will work alone and in a five-person team on such soft skills as ethics, communications, managing diversity, and career development. In the second semester, your team will be assigned a 12-week-long field application project in which your analysis of a real-world problem will be presented to executives actively involved in the case. You'll also get to choose from a set of six-week "bracket courses" in such topics as information, entrepreneurship, geopolitics, crisis management, technology, or the environment.

Another option for first-year students is the Global Immersion Program, six weeks of introductory lectures on a country or region critical to the world economy, with a four-week overseas experience following final exams in which students meet corporate and government officials, tour, and attend cultural events in Southeast Asia, China, South America, or Eastern Europe. You'll be expected to submit a written assignment the next fall, and you'll have to pony up an additional $5000 or so beyond your already hefty tuition to pay for the trip. The global practicum is just one of a number of Wharton's international endeavors. The school's famous Lauder Institute, which offers an MBA/M.A. in international studies, is among the very best global management experiences anywhere, besting a degree from a top European B-school or any other U.S. school claiming to offer a truly international MBA. A joint venture between the B-school and the university's School of Arts and Sciences, this 24-month program allows students to specialize in a global region such as East Asia, Europe, Latin America, or North America (for non-U.S. natives). Students spend about 25 percent of their time abroad, including a cultural immersion program before the start of their Wharton classes and a summer internship with a multinational company that requires extensive use of a foreign language. There's also a joint MBA/MA program in international relations, in which Wharton joins forces with Johns Hopkins University's Nitze School of Advanced International Studies. Students spend about half the three-year program on the Wharton campus in Philadelphia and the other half at the Nitze School campus in Washington, D.C.

Even when pursuing a regular MBA degree, you can opt to spend a full semester abroad in one of 14 exchange programs with non-U.S. business schools in Italy, France, Spain, Japan, Hong Kong, Brazil, England, the Netherlands, Sweden, Australia, the Philippines, or Thailand. Or you can participate in the Multinational Marketing and Management Program, which partners Wharton with B-schools in Israel, Canada, and other locations to form multi-school MBA teams that design marketing strategies for companies hoping to enter the North American market.

In addition to the many international offerings, you'll find a dizzying selection of courses to choose from in your second year. Employers rank Wharton at or near the top in every bread-and-butter business discipline across the board, from finance to general management, marketing, and technology. The breadth of offerings beyond the basics is equally impressive: More than 140 electives and two dozen majors in everything from actuarial science to public and nonprofit management, including new concentrations in technological innovation and information and strategy. Don't find a major to your liking? Create your own, with faculty approval. Or join the three or four dozen Wharton students each year who pursue dual-degree programs with some of the Ivy League university's other world-class schools, including communication, law, medical sciences, nursing and health-care management, social work, and engineering.

Outside of class, students tend to scatter from this decidedly urban campus. Wharton has set aside a dozen floors of Grad Tower B for MBAs, and about 350 students, especially those among the international contingent, reside in the on-campus dormitory. Many MBAs opt to live in Center City, a 10-minute bike or bus ride from campus, because desirable housing is scarce in West Philadelphia, a rundown neighborhood that is gradually being swallowed by the ever-encroaching expansion of the university. Crime is an issue as well, with several highly publicized incidents taking place on campus in recent years. The most noteworthy involved a graduate student who, while working in a nearby office, was struck by a stray bullet from a fatal sidewalk shooting between two spectators at a sporting event at Penn's Palestra arena. The university has beefed up security, and administrators say safety hasn't been as much of an issue for the B-school as it has been for the undergraduate college, as MBA students tend to be older and more savvy about urban living.

For a school of this size and scope, Wharton does a surprisingly good job of holding down nasty competition among its highly ambitious and demanding students. Make no mistake: You won't find the cozy, cooperative atmosphere here that you'd find at Dartmouth, Virginia, or Northwestern, but it's no Harvard, either, according to BUSINESSWEEK's surveys. Students gravitate toward the serious-minded and business-oriented extracurricular activities, like the "It Adds Up" program that has student volunteers helping low-income families file their income tax returns. There's also the annual Christmas in April program that renovates housing for disadvantaged Philadelphians.

But there are ways to blow off steam, too. Philadelphia may not be New York, but it's a beautiful city with plenty to see and do—from the high culture of the world-class art museum and orchestra to historic sites such as the Liberty Bell and Independence Hall. The lower-brow bar scenes along South Street and the shores of the Delaware River give students a chance to unwind after a hard week's work. And no self-respecting Wharton student would miss the once-a-semester ritual known as "Walnut Walk"; after mid-terms, MBAs don a combination of formal attire and shorts and begin a bar crawl through as many as 20 local pubs, ending with a sobering 3 a.m. breakfast.

PLACEMENT DETAILS

Employment is not exactly a worry for Wharton grads; in fact, second-year students generally find themselves with an embarrassment of riches in the job search. What seems to attract companies the most is the well-rounded program that is strong in every key aspect of general management training. But the career placement office slipped in the ratings a bit. The number of companies recruiting on campus fell from 420 in 1998 to 254 in 2000. Some companies have resorted to posting jobs on the Internet instead of visiting campus. Others have simply abandoned campus visits for a variety of reasons. Now, the school is trying to bounce back by responding to the needs of consumers—both recruiters and students. Harker says the problems revolve around the mechanics of the career services office, a problem that will be alleviated when staff find a roomier home in Huntsman Hall. And the administration is investing in Web-based technology that will link recruiters and students regardless of whether the company actually sets foot on campus. Clearly, the Wharton brand name still brings in a number of employers who give glowing reports about grads. But the head honcho of B-schools does have some work to do in this area.

Despite the criticism, students still had successful job searches. They found themselves with an average of 3.6 job offers to consider as they received their degrees, and Wharton grads' median combined starting pay of $156,000 is up to par with the pay received by graduates of Harvard, Stanford, and MIT. Major management consulting firms led the pack of companies hauling away the most Wharton MBAs: McKinsey & Co. (61); Goldman Sachs & Co. (42); Bain & Co. (34); Boston Consulting Group (22); Merrill Lynch (17); Morgan Stanley Dean Witter (15); Donaldson Lufkin & Jenrette (14); Accenture (12); Deloitte Consulting (10); Booz-Allen & Hamilton (10).

OUTSTANDING FACULTY

Philip Berger (accounting); *Ian MacMillan* (entrepreneurship); *Franklin Allen* (finance); *Robert Inman* (finance); *Andrew Metrick* (finance); *Jeremy Siegel* (finance); *Richard Shell* (legal affairs); *William Tyson* (legal affairs); *Nicolaj Siggelkow* (management); *Michael Useem* (management); *George Day* (marketing); *Karl Ulrich* (operations and information management).

APPLICANT TIPS

If your heart is set on attending Wharton, be sure to get your application in early—at least if you are applying for the Class of 2003. The school operates on a rolling admissions basis, with applications starting to arrive as early as September for the following fall. Those who wait until March to apply are putting themselves in a predicament: Only 1 out of 50 who apply in April are accepted, compared with 1 out of 10 who apply by February. Don't fret if you are applying next year, however. Wharton saw an 11 percent decrease in the number of applications this year for the first time in recent history. As another victim of the booming economy and the pitter-patter of start-ups, the administration is retooling its admissions process, something they have considered for a long time. By the end of 2001, the school will shift to three deadlines and end the rolling admissions process. So, keep an eye on the Web site for the exact deadlines. The admissions office is also scheduling interviews by invitation only. Currently, more than

90 percent of admitted applicants are interviewed each year, and it's yet another venue in which you can attempt to distinguish yourself from the crowd. Rosemaria Martinelli, director of MBA Admissions and Financial Aid, warns that students should highlight personal contributions and be honest in the application. She also says that they should not settle for less-than-stellar GMAT scores or GPAs. "Take the GMAT again," Martinelli says. "Do it right." Applications are available through the school's Web site or by calling the admissions department, and can be submitted either electronically or by mail.

Contact: Rosemaria Martinelli
Director of Admissions and Financial Aid
215-898-3430
Application deadline: April 10

WHARTON MBAs SOUND OFF

Wharton is an outstanding choice if your goal is an MBA program that is international in scope and, arguably, offers the strongest array of functional departments available anywhere. Wharton will teach you how to put some quantitative rigor behind your gut instincts, and it will really force you to improve your teamwork and leadership skills. This, I believe, is more important than the academic learning that takes place. In the increasingly global economy, Wharton provides any aspiring MBA student with a platform for future success.

Wharton is a fantastic school. Its biggest handicap is location. For the best golf or mountain biking, I can't recommend West Philly. For the best education, however, there's no comparison.

Wharton has been an amazing, enriching experience—both from an academic and extracurricular perspective. I had originally had many hesitations about matriculating to Wharton because of its reputation as a "finance school." I was afraid that it would be a cutthroat environment with overrepresentation from a handful of industries such as banking and consulting. This was not the case at all and is one of the biggest myths about Wharton. I was very impressed with my marketing, e-commerce, and management classes at Wharton, and the students were extremely collaborative and diverse. My only concern is that this wonderful dynamic may change because of the new grading policy (the qualified credit, the equivalent of Low Pass, was added this year, in addition to another level of honors distinction). Students have been concerned that participation in clubs and activities has waned as a result of the increased academic pressure. I hope that the Wharton administration will continue to foster the vibrant student life outside the classroom— it's one of the critical elements that sets Wharton apart from the other top business schools.

The Wharton MBA Program is as incredible as I thought it would be. The finance department is exceptional. I would, however, warn anyone about the dual degree MBA/M.A. Lauder Institute Program. I did this, and it was the worst $20,000 I ever invested (because Lauder costs an additional 20K). The language training is laughable and the courses are of little real-world use. Another key point is that for every Lauder class you are taking you are paying an opportunity cost by missing a Wharton class.

The administration encourages creativity and leadership. Over a dozen new programs— charitable, athletic, professional, cultural— were all started by students in my class (including myself) and will continue long after we have moved on. The ability to have such an impact is truly remarkable.

2.
NORTHWESTERN UNIVERSITY

NORTHWESTERN UNIVERSITY

Kellogg Graduate School of Management

Leverone Hall

Evanston, Illinois 60208

E-mail address: kellogg-admissions@nwu.edu

Web site address: http://www.kellogg.nwu.edu

Corporate ranking: 2	Graduate ranking: 1
Enrollment: 2500	Annual tuition & fees: $28,677
Women: 31%	Room and board: $11,511
Non-U.S.: 32%	Average GMAT score: 690
Minority: 17%	Average years of work exp.: 4
Part-time: 1300	Accepted applicants enrolled: 61%
Average age: 27	Intellectual capital: 15
Applicants accepted: 18%	
Median starting pay: $142,000	

Teaching methods: Lecture, 33% Case study, 33%
Group projects, consulting reports, and
independent study, 34%

Contact:
Michele Rogers
Director of Admissions
and Financial Aid
847-491-3308
Application deadlines:
November 10
January 15
March 16

One fall term, about 20 years ago, 40 Kellogg MBA students were assigned to hand in a paper the Monday after Thanksgiving weekend. Dean Donald P. Jacobs was thoroughly annoyed by the professor's assignment, one that would keep those students from heading home for the holiday, but he could not persuade the professor to change the paper's due date. So the dean packed his own pots and pans, raided his refrigerator and pantry, and delivered himself—complete with all the Thanksgiving dinner trimmings—to the graduate dormitory—and cooked for everyone who couldn't make it home. The impromptu dinner became an annual event, and, in 2000, more than 800 MBA students, faculty, staff—and all their families—sat down in the school's executive education facility for a family feast.

So how is it possible that some 2500 people can be called a family with any legitimacy? Well, that's the Kellogg way—here, everyone is family. And it's not just a concept people talk about with a sneer. It's the foundation on which the Kellogg experience is built. Instituted by long-time dean Jacobs, the teamwork concept and family atmosphere have been in place at the school for more than 20 years. Many other B-school deans were skeptical when Jacobs pushed teamwork and team learning—one called it cheating. But the Jacobs way stuck, and even when he leaves at the end of the 2001 school year, the house he built will stand. One major reason: The MBA students who attend.

One example of this teamwork occurred in 1995. Four second-years had an idea: Instead of rushing off to a typical post-MBA celebratory vacation spent tanning themselves on a sunny beach or backpacking around Europe, why not take four or five weeks after graduation to give back some of their newfound knowledge to business ventures in developing communities around the world? So they went. Jacobs gave them the go-ahead to launch the Kellogg Corps. By the summer of 2000, 150 grads were splitting up into student-led teams that dispersed globally to consult on site—in 12 countries—with such diverse organizations as Haiti's Save the Children, which aims to improve children's living conditions; the government of the Altai Republic in southern Siberia, focusing on the region's fledgling ecotourism, herbal exports, and deer antler products; and Ghana's Progressive Women's Center, which conducts basic business training for female entrepreneurs in that African nation.

Around Kellogg, the ideas flow fast and furious, and whether you're an administrator, professor, or student there's an excellent chance your idea will quickly become a reality if you choose to pursue it. Ask the dean, "Why not?" and your answer is likely to be, "No reason, so go for it." Indeed, that's been Jacobs's attitude since taking the helm at the B-school all the way back in 1975. It's an attitude that has served both him and Kellogg well: He's outlasted the deans of every Top 30 school, and Kellogg's long-standing place among the world's very best business schools has once again been confirmed by its solid No. 2 ranking in BUSINESSWEEK's 1998 and 2000 polls.

Arguably the most successful B-school dean of this era, Jacobs established the model of the modern business school in the early 1980s. At the time, elite schools such as Harvard, Stanford, Chicago, and Wharton were content to ignore the demands for MBAs who could better lead and motivate others. Jacobs ignored tradition, building and nurturing a culture driven by cooperative learning and student empowerment. It worked like a charm. And Kellogg's rivals have since jumped on the bandwagon, overhauling their programs to be more responsive to their own MBAs and to Corporate America. It's no stretch to call Jacobs a revolutionary behind the last decade of widespread B-school reform. And while Kellogg will go on without him, his presence is deeply ingrained in the culture.

But when you start a trend, you can fall victim to the copiers, as Jacobs has discovered. Schools like Wharton, Michigan, and Harvard have hopped on the boat Jacobs pushed out to sea in the '80s, and now you'd be hard-pressed to find a top-tier B-school that doesn't boast of its team orientation, its well-rounded and involved student body, and its customer-oriented administration, all pioneered by Kellogg but now standard components of many MBA programs. The copycat factor was a major reason Kellogg slid in the BUSINESSWEEK ratings from No. 1, captured three times between 1988 and 1992, to its third-place ranking in 1996. With Jacobs leaving the helm, it will be time for another dean, perhaps at another school, to step into the leadership role among peer schools and deans.

So how does Kellogg distinguish itself from its rivals? One important area in which it continues to outshine the competition is teamwork—both students and the companies that hire them rank Kellogg the very best of all schools BUSINESSWEEK surveyed at turning out team players. "Teamwork is not just a motto here, it's almost a religion," says one grad. "Kellogg lives and dies by the teamwork structure." And while the school's curriculum plays a vital part in the development of this team mentality, so too does a culture that gives MBAs a huge measure of freedom—and responsibility—for shaping their program right from the get-go. Jacobs points to both the depth of student involvement in running the school and the speed of the school's response to marketplace trends and student interests as keys to its continued success. "It's easy to copy a strategy—what we've demonstrated is the ability to implement," he says. "I think we've got to continue to implement and change and evolve. And we've got to be able to trust our students, which other places don't. These are adults, with experience, who have a lot to contribute to this community. It would be silly not to take advantage of those abilities."

The uniqueness of the "Kellogg culture" starts to become apparent almost from the first day a student sets foot on the tree-covered campus in Evanston, a peaceful suburban town just north of Chicago on the shores of Lake Michigan. In 2000, more than 350 of the incoming 600-plus first-year MBAs arrived a week early to participate in Kellogg Outdoor Adventures, bonding trips in which groups of newcomers, led by 140 second-years, went backpacking in the Colorado Rockies, snorkeling in the Caribbean, or dog sledding in Alaska—among the 29 trips available to locations as exotic as Iceland and Hawaii. (The trips are a great way to meet classmates and get the inside scoop on Kellogg, but also lighten your wallet by up to $1500.) These voluntary expeditions precede CIM (Conceptual Issues in Management), a weeklong kickoff program organized and run entirely by second-years, which mixes business and pleasure with a business simulation game, sessions on cultural diversity and academic advising, community service, a beach party, and a trip to Wrigley Field for a Cubs game.

Kellogg classes, which meet twice a week for 1 hour and 40 minutes, are spread over three 11-week quarters each year. Cohorts formed during CIM week continue to take core classes together to a large extent, although some students waive out of basic classes and are free to sign up for more advanced ones. You need 23 courses to graduate, 9 required core courses and 14 others chosen from a long list of 166 electives. Jacobs

has aimed to keep the curriculum fresh by streamlining the course approval process, a cumbersome one- to two-year bureaucratic entanglement at most universities. Instead, Kellogg professors can offer any course they choose so long as at least 20 students are willing to enroll; in the past three years, 43 new courses have taken the place of staler offerings.

Most Kellogg MBAs (grads used to receive a master's of management, but the school joined the MBA crowd in 2000) major in 2 or 3 of 13 areas. Kellogg's reputation was built on its marketing program—it is, after all, named after the son of the breakfast cereal founder—and that hasn't changed. Employers in 2000 again ranked Kellogg grads' marketing skills above those from all other schools. But the largest portion of students these days is majoring in and eventually working in the field of finance: 27 percent versus 18 percent in marketing, and many students think the finance instructors are the best of all the teachers at the school. You can also opt for one of four professional program offerings: health services, public and nonprofit, transportation, or real estate management—or an interdisciplinary major such as international business or entrepreneurship.

Jacobs has pushed hard to globalize Kellogg in recent years. International students from some 60 countries compose 33 percent of the Class of 2002, a big improvement over the last decade, and in line with other top schools. Kellogg now operates three international executive MBA programs in France, Israel, and Hong Kong, which, along with an expanding alumni network abroad, helps familiarize potential MBA students from overseas with Kellogg.

Students may also opt to create specially designed, two-quarter international independent study courses called Global Initiatives in Management (GIM), focusing on a country of their choice. (It's a popular option: In 2000, 300 students studied 12 different regions.) For each of the geographic areas, students as a group arrange a syllabus, book guest speakers, determine research topics, and identify key issues facing local industries, all under the tutelage of a faculty sponsor. After coursework is completed during the winter quarter, students travel to the selected country over spring break for a two-week group consulting project and tour; results are presented to faculty and visiting executives in the spring. Jacobs says that international students who, for credit, can join groups studying their home countries are often able to provide valuable connections and insider knowledge that greatly enhance the trips. Students in the past have spent an entire day with Peruvian President Alberto Fujimori, helicoptering over the South American nation's towns and villages; those who visited South Africa in 1998 ended up running into President Clinton, who just happened to be meeting with that country's top officials on the same day. The First Lady even posed for photos in a Kellogg sweatshirt. Indeed, the program proved so successful that Kellogg modeled another course after GIM. TechVentures works in a similar fashion, only rather than studying ventures across the world, students study companies halfway across the country in Silicon Valley. The program, which was launched in 1999 with 80 students, has proved popular, growing to 160 students in 2000.

Another target of Jacobs's efforts of late has been advanced technology, an area in which Kellogg had been trailing its competitors. A $40 million renovation of Leverone and Andersen Halls, the heart of the B-school, was completed in 1995, opening up new computer-wired classrooms and group study rooms as well as a computer lab. News groups have been created on the school intranet for every course in the catalog, through which students can access course materials and share ideas and questions. Course bidding and student evaluations of faculty and courses are online, and "Kellogg Serial," the student Web page, offers a plethora of information about campus life and activities. In the spring, work finishes on the expanded Kellogg home—which nearly doubles the amount of space—

The Donald P. Jacobs–Kellogg Center. That three-building complex is also wired.

Students have been the driving force behind much of Kellogg's technological progress: In 2000, students and the Career Management Center started "Kellogg Tech Connection," an interviewing event on the West Coast, designed to bring employers and students together in the late spring, closer to the time when students are ready to take jobs. Another example: two members of the Class of '99 launched the school's first Silicon Valley Tech Venture (separate from TechVentures), a new addition to the curriculum in 1998 in which 46 students spent a semester intensively studying issues crucial to the information economy, then made on-site visits to 26 California high-tech firms, meeting with entrepreneurs and leaders in the field. The interest in IT dovetails with the increasing amount of attention entrepreneurship is receiving at Kellogg, as it is at many B-schools nationwide. Broadening interest in start-ups led Jacobs to add a sequence of courses and a major in entrepreneurship in 1993. Thirteen professors, 11 of them tenured, now teach the subject, up from 3 in 1994, and 80 percent of students now take at least one course in the department. Entrepreneurship Professor Steve Rogers, a former Bain & Co. consultant whose deal to purchase a lampshade company became a Harvard case study, was voted 1997 Teacher of the Year by students and one of the 12 best teachers of entrepreneurship in a 1996 BUSINESSWEEK survey. And since 1994, 10 Kellogg students have won the prestigious Kauffman entrepreneurial awards, tying Harvard for the most winners.

One of the biggest B-schools among the Top 30, some 600 students a year are enrolled in Kellogg's three full-time MBA programs. Most follow the traditional six-quarter schedule, with fall, winter, and spring classes followed by a summer internship and three more quarters during a second year in class. But students with undergraduate business degrees can finish in four consecutive quarters, starting in June and plowing through to graduate just a year later, as about 80 did in 2000. And some 60 aspiring gearheads each year sign up for the master of management in manufacturing degree, a six-quarter joint program with the university's McCormick School of Engineering. There's also a part-time evening MBA program, which meets in downtown Chicago; an executive MBA program, which meets on weekends at the Allen Center, a couple of blocks away from the B-school's main complex on campus in Evanston; and a very active executive education effort, which brings some 5000 execs to campus each year for short-term courses.

Although students have complained about space shortages, the new complex—including a $25 million addition of six floors to one side of the building—should bring relief. Jacobs also points out the advantages he believes synergy can bring to the MBA program: Keeping professors current with real-world business practices through their ongoing interaction with the full-time workers who make up executive education classes; drawing international faculty to Evanston through its links with schools overseas; and using executive education contacts with major corporations to keep the Kellogg name fresh on the minds of both deep-pocketed alums and the recruiters who will be hiring new grads.

Complaints aside, the overwhelmingly positive experience reported by most Kellogg grads—which led one wag to dub them the "shiny, happy MBAs"—can in large part be attributed to Jacobs's unflagging willingness to listen to his students. When students complained that they didn't like the MBA café, Jacobs wondered why. So he asked. Turned out that there weren't enough varieties of food that international students would like. Jacobs immediately had the food vendor contacted and the café fare diversified. Student fingerprints can be found on almost every one of the school's major innovations. Besides TEKcamp, the GIM trips, the Information Economy Task Force, and Silicon Valley TechVenture, student initiatives have

brought about LEAP—the Learning Through Experience in Action Program, a 10-week consulting assignment course with area corporations, which grew out of the interest in entrepreneurship—and Chicago Tours, a series of student-organized trips to Chicago businesses for observation and networking. Students, rather than paid consultants, designed the B-school Web site. The Graduate Management Association, the student government, is instrumental in school policymaking. Says Jacobs, "The size of the paid administration is drastically smaller at Kellogg than at most of our competitors because students take on so many duties and responsibilities." Now, with Jacobs leaving, the new dean will likely have to fill the ranks a bit in order to keep up the Jacobs tradition.

This outgoing bunch finds time for plenty of extracurricular activities, facilitated by a B-school schedule that holds no classes on Wednesdays. Business With a Heart, Kellogg's do-good MBA group, raised more than $160,000 in 2000 for charitable causes. Some built homes for low-income families, staffed homeless shelters, and collected and distributed clothing for the less fortunate. "Special K," Kellogg's follies production, draws some 100 participants each year and in 2000 traveled to San Francisco to perform the show. Married students, with and without children, are encouraged to be integrally involved in the B-school experience, starting with the fall beach luau for students and significant others behind the recreation center on the lake. The dean's assistants are generally spouses of students. Through the "Joint Ventures" program, many spouses say they made as many or more friends at Kellogg than the students. For singles, about a third are chosen by lottery for dorm rooms in the McManus Living-Learning Center on the southern edge of campus, jokingly dubbed the "loving and lusting center" by students. It's not that students here don't work hard—although Kellogg students do rate the workload on the lighter side compared with other top B-schools—but that they make it a point to make time for other things as well.

Every Friday afternoon in the atrium, the keg is tapped at 4:45 p.m. for the weekly TGIF session. With the icy winds whipping off the lake during the winter, no one's making a bee-line for the door. In the spring, the weekly ritual adjourns to Deering Meadow directly in front of the Jacobs Center, where Frisbee throwing and soccer are the sports of choice. Faculty and administrators, including the dean, often join the festivities; when students holding a "World Cup" soccer match once found the goalposts locked up, Jacobs himself went for the bolt cutters and snipped off the lock.

There are plenty of places to go for a beer or a good dinner in nearby Evanston or an elevated train ride away in Chicago neighborhoods like Lincoln Park, with its rhythm-and-blues clubs. Tommy Nevins and the Keg are popular Evanston hangouts, but beware, you might have to purchase food to buy beer. It's one of a number of strange Evanston laws, like the one that says you must bag your own food at Burger King. Evanston was a dry city until the early '80s; in fact, Prohibition got its start here, and the Women's Christian Temperance Union still has its national headquarters a few blocks from campus. Every year, undergrads hold a party in honor of the WCTU's Frances Willard—with lots of heavy drinking, of course. Downtown Evanston is a short walk from campus, and many students frequent the popular hamburger palace—Yesterday's—or catch some evening jazz at My Bar. In the warmer months, you may not even need to leave campus, what with the stunning fields and rocks that make up what students call the lakefill, where dogs romp, footballs soar, and studiers flock with their books.

PLACEMENT DETAILS

In 2000, 330 companies came on campus to recruit Kellogg grads. Although that's not as many firms as schools such as Harvard, Columbia, or Wharton attracted, those who came to Kellogg spent plenty of time here, conducting some 20,000 interviews—double the number of interviews at other B-school campuses. An additional 3120 jobs were posted electronically. Overall, Kellogg grads walked away with an average of 3.5 employment offers apiece—up from 3.39 in 1998. And grads garnered a median starting pay package of $142,000, near the top of the B-school pack. As at most schools, consulting continues to grow in popularity as a job choice, with about 40 percent of the Class of 2000 heading into that field. Dean Jacobs feels this is, surprisingly enough, consistent with the high interest in entrepreneurship: "You can work three to four years, with high current income to pay back your education debt, look broadly at different kinds of operations, make contacts, and look for potential ideas. The shift to start-ups will come 5 to 10 years down the road."

Top employers in 2000 included McKinsey & Co. (39), Boston Consulting Group (19), Bain & Company Inc. (18) Goldman Sachs (18), A.T. Kearney (17), Mercer Management Consulting (15), Booz-Allen & Hamilton (14), Lehman Brothers (13), Siebel Systems, Inc. (11), and Hewlett-Packard (7). Corporate recruiters say that, hands down Kellogg grads are well prepared for team management, and consensus-building. Says one recruiter, "You can usually spot the Kellogg MBAs because they're succeeding in the company, and helping their colleagues at the same time."

OUTSTANDING FACULTY

Scott McKeon (decision science); *Mohan Sawhney* (e-commerce/marketing); *Steven Rogers* (entrepreneurship/finance); *Mitchell Petersen* (finance); *Vefa Tarhan* (finance); *David Besanko* (management/strategy); *Daniel Diermeyer* (management); *Julie Hennessey* (marketing); *Martin Stoller* (organizational behavior).

APPLICANT TIPS

Kellogg was the first school to attempt to interview all of its applicants, and that's still the case: nearly 100 percent of the more than 6000 applicants to the Class of 2002 were interviewed, according to Michele Rogers, director of admissions and financial aid, who says the only exceptions were applicants from extremely remote geographic locations. If you aren't likely to come across well in a personal interview, your chances of getting in will be pretty slim. In other words, your GPA and GMAT alone—no matter how strong—won't get you in the door. That's especially true because Kellogg puts a lot of weight on your ability to communicate and get along with others. It's something to consider up front, because study groups are formed in almost every B-school class here, and you'll be graded on how well your team functions together. Like most top-tier schools, Kellogg places a high value on full-time work experience, with the average admitted student having spent at least four years on the job. And it's not just the quantity but the quality of your experiences inside and outside the workplace that counts, since the admissions committee evaluates your potential as a manager by reviewing your accomplishments at work, in the military, and in extracurricular activities. "We look for bright, active, caring people," says outgoing Dean Jacobs.

You can improve your odds of securing an invitation by applying early. Because applications are reviewed on a continuous basis, your chances of gaining acceptance and lining up financial aid and housing may fall if you wait until the last minute to apply. Rogers says merit-based scholarships—the highest being the Austin Scholar, which awards $10,000 a year to 20 lucky students—are most likely to go to those applying in the first two admissions rounds. Kellogg's application can be accessed through the school Web site. You can fill it out online and submit it electronically; download it and mail it in; or apply the old-fashioned way, by calling the admissions office and requesting an admissions packet to be mailed to you.

Contact: Michele Rogers
Director of Admissions and Financial Aid
847-491-3308
Application deadlines: November 10; January 15; March 16

KELLOGG MBAs SOUND OFF

Kellogg is an extremely well balanced program . . . it's not just a Marketing and Management school anymore. . . . Kellogg now has outstanding Finance and Operations departments and a fantastic newly developed Technology initiative (classes, conferences, and infrastructure).

Much of the buzz about e-commerce and the Internet is just that. I came from a background in high-tech and the Internet and I agree that there is much value in technology, but many students are too interested in classes that just teach them what they can learn in a magazine. Luckily, Kellogg held back and didn't give in completely. There are a couple of courses that are "current trend" related but much is focused on solid business concepts because at the end of the day, that is what differentiates a leader/manager. . . . the trends will always change . . . and the survey courses they have provide students with the opportunity to study areas of interest and work with/visit the companies.

It is difficult to fully explain the positive impact my two years at Kellogg has had. My mind has been opened to new concepts and fields that I never before thought about. I met and interacted with the best group of people, some of whom have become my closest friends and from all of whom I expect great things. As great as the two years have been, I am most excited to see what my colleagues will do with their lives in the future. For myself, this has been the most enriching two years of my life. I leave with more confidence in my abilities, more centered in what it is that I want to achieve in my life.

The Career Management Center has done an excellent job of organizing recruiting to meet the needs of students. It is particularly good at coaching and motivating career changers like me. Although I was initially intimidated at the prospect of competing against students with backgrounds in consulting, the Career Management Center gave me the tools to find and get the job I wanted.

Kellogg is a student-focused organization that understands the value of both teamwork and globalization—two of the key components to success in the business world.

Kellogg was everything I hoped it would be and more. My time at Kellogg has given me the skills and networks I need in order to make a run at the top of Wall Street. I've never had so much interaction with such motivated and accomplished individuals as I've had at Kellogg. The teachers and administration go to great lengths to encourage feedback from the students and work the suggestions into everyday life at the school.

3.
HARVARD UNIVERSITY

HARVARD UNIVERSITY

Graduate School of Business Administration
Soldiers Field
Boston, Massachusetts 02163
E-mail address: admissions@hbs.edu
Web site address: http://www.hbs.edu

Corporate ranking: 3	Graduate ranking: 4
Enrollment: 1742	Annual tuition & fees: $28,500
Women: 32%	Room and board: N/A
Non-U.S.: 33%	Average GMAT score: 701
Minority: 19%	Average years of work exp.: 4
Part-time: 0	Accepted applicants enrolled: N/A
Average age: 27	Intellectual capital: 13
Applicants accepted: 13%	
Median starting pay: $160,000	

Teaching methods: Lecture, 15%   Case study, 80%   Other, 5%

Contact:
Kirsten Moss
Director of Admissions
617-495-6127
Application deadlines:
November 4
January 16
March 2

Haah-vard. You can't help but sit up a little straighter at the mention of the name. Head honchos in the business world have been doing it since 1908, when HBS first opened its doors to fewer than 100 students. Perhaps it's the notion that this mega-MBA program, now with 900 students per class, was among the first of its kind. The nearly 39,000 alumni are living all over the world but are effortlessly linked through the school's electronic database. The 35-acre campus along Boston's Charles River encompasses more than 29 buildings and is still growing. And the endowment! Harvard's $1.4 billion figure towers over all the rest.

Recruiters are more than fond of the school. About 800 of them come to campus to recruit each year, and Harvard's 2000 grads received the highest average number of job offers: 4.1 each. Employers who responded to BUSINESSWEEK's biennial survey in 2000 named Harvard graduates No. 2 in general management and global skills and among the top five in marketing, finance, and technology skills. To sum up, as one student says gleefully, "You never have to make excuses for having gone to Harvard."

But, even this pillar of higher education has it weaknesses: Students gripe about the teaching quality in core courses ("inconsistent") and a lack of responsiveness from the administration: "They can't be bothered to solicit student input for regular operating decisions," says one graduate. Recruiters rank the Career Services office among the worst. But status does have its plus side—those very recruiters keep coming back, by the hundreds. Most students, too, say the school—

which advanced two notches in this year's BUSI-NESSWEEK Business School Rankings (from No. 5 to No. 3)—easily meets their expectations for an MBA. And those are some pretty high expectations, coming from a selective group of students (just 13 percent are admitted from the school's 8000-plus applicant pool). When all is said and done, it comes as no surprise that, after Kellogg students, Harvard's are the second most likely to urge their friends to enroll in the same program.

Much of this has to do with the initiatives put forth by Dean Kim B. Clark, a former HBS student and professor who, in his five years as dean, has focused on incorporating global issues and information technology into the program's content. Here you can do nearly anything and everything online, including finding materials for every course in the HBS catalog—syllabi, schedules, and assignments—all via the school intranet from the comfort of your apartment. And that's just a start. More than 90 percent of professors now give their exams by computer. Students in the Technology and Operations core course can participate in a "virtual" factory tour through two-way satellite communication, by observing their professor and a plant manager in one location and posing questions, in real-time, from behind their own desks. Another course, Developing, Managing, and Improving Operations, is entirely paperless. The professor, David M. Upton, is among the leaders of the school's technology initiative and the developer of Harvard's first electronic case study. Based on a Chinese sock-making factory, the case incorporates on-site video sequences of executives discussing the troubled company, with real-time Internet information and an online simulation that shows how changing production schedules will affect the plant's revenues, inventory, and costs. Faculty members continue to enhance a library of these electronic cases, and other business schools have been buying up copies.

Paper versions of cases have also been steadily increasing in number and scope as a result of new, internationally based facilities in Hong Kong and Buenos Aires, with a third planned for Europe. The centers—along with another in Silicon Valley—are used for faculty research and the development of cases, which form the basis of Harvard's curriculum (80 percent). Additional materials come from researchers and case writers with the Global Research Group, the latest addition to Harvard's research infrastructure.

Back at home in the bookish town of Cambridge, the student body comprises 32 percent international students, 14 percent minorities, and 31 percent women—more of a mix than at some of the other B-schools in Harvard's league. Professional backgrounds are just as varied, with students who have military or nonprofit training mixed with former consultants and investment bankers. The program is designed to be user-friendly for all.

But not that friendly; hard work is at the core of the HBS degree. Requirements begin prior to matriculation, with Internet-based courses in accounting, business writing, class presentation, computer skills, quantitative methods, and general business knowledge. Once school starts, you'll go through a three-week Foundations program that involves lectures, workshops, problem set reviews, case study discussions, and team projects. The courses here cover broad topics like applied personal skills, career development, and decision making. During term one of your first year, you'll also complete four required courses that hone in on internal business operations. Your five required courses in term two cover economic, governmental, and social environments. In all, over the two years, you'll master some 500 cases. If that doesn't sound rigorous enough, you should also know that classes are held on any of the five days of the workweek, with no free days designated for group meetings, study sessions, or job interviews, which many of HBS's peer programs offer. (Second-year students, though, reportedly have lighter loads on Mondays and Fridays.) Attendance is absolutely mandatory, too. "You don't miss class for any reason," admonishes one student. "That's the surest way to get into a ton of trouble."

Grades also can spell trouble. Calculated in each class on a forced curve, they can put students in a frenzy. The top 10 percent of the class earns the highest score, a "1," or a high pass. The majority, about 70 to 80 percent, fall somewhere in the middle with a pass, and the lowest group of 10 percent invariably receive the dreaded low passes. It's hard to believe such a daunting system began as a response to the concerns of students in the early '80s, who felt that grading was inconsistent among different professors. Today, class participation counts for 50 percent of a student's grade—meaning, you'd better come prepared to every class, and by all means, get over that fear of public speaking. Scary as it seems, most students appreciate the opportunity to rise to the challenge. "Having to concisely and persuasively argue a point in 10 seconds in front of 80 people was terrific," a recent grad insists. "I am much better prepared to be a strong contributor in my job."

Not surprisingly, some students have called the environment at HBS "cutthroat." But others say that, especially after the first semester, the term just doesn't fit. "The general attitude—aside from the small group of people who will kill themselves to be the best—is: 'We're all going to get passes anyway, so it doesn't matter,'" says Tom Arnold, a Class of '00 grad and associate with Booz-Allen & Hamilton. "A low pass can happen, but most likely it's just once in a while. If you put forth a normal amount of effort here, it's impossible to fail out—and you can't tell recruiters what your grades were anyway." That might not always add up to a score for the plus column if fellow students are lazy, but most grads say that's not common here.

Students have clamored for more team-oriented projects, and the administration is working on it. Already, the curriculum structure is set up for collaboration: Incoming students are assigned to an 80-person group with which they attend all first-year core courses. Very often the students who are more advanced in one area—accounting, for instance—will tutor others who don't have much experience with it. Aside from study sessions and team projects, the groups also serve a social purpose. Planned weekly activities like section pub nights are popular, continuing into the second year, and members of these groups form some of the strongest alumni bonds later.

HBS students take their academic obligations seriously and expect a great deal in return from administrators and faculty. The quality of teaching in core courses, once a major concern, is now just a mild complaint from students. Dean Clark chalks up any criticism to an unfair comparison: "Rookie" teachers in core courses can't possibly match the performances of other more experienced faculty who often teach subjects students find more dynamic. Some students cite a lack of availability of teachers outside of class, noting that only the most cunning and persistent scholars get their face time with the profs. To be fair, argues one student, these high-profile professors have extreme professional and academic demands on their time, and they wouldn't be such important advisers if this were otherwise. "You have to think of these people as CEOs of a big corporation whose time is really valuable." It's logical reasoning, but it does little to cheer the eager student who's paying $28,500 in tuition and simply wants an expert opinion on a business model. The good news is, if you do take the initiative to meet with a professor, students say, you won't find utter dismissiveness. In fact, some have had better than average experiences, going so far as to call professors "some of my greatest friends at HBS."

The teaching in the 68 elective courses plus 11 field study areas, on the other hand, is praised all around, with special kudos to the quality of professors and their ability to stay at the leading edge of knowledge in their fields. Courses are frequently revised and replaced to keep the offerings fresh (nearly one-third of electives course material is refreshed each year). Students can cross-register for up to two courses in other Harvard schools and departments, or at MIT's Sloan School of Business or Tufts University's Fletcher School of Law and Diplomacy. Those interested in public and nonprofit management can take part in the Initiative on Social Enterprise, a grouping of elective courses that also includes a pair of complementary class and field-based courses, extracurricular activities, assistance obtaining a summer internship, and a loan forgiveness program. More than 60 percent of Harvard's MBAs participate in a field-based project as part of a self-selected team of three or more students working with leaders at sponsoring a businesses or a nonprofit organization for a semester or an entire year. Projects can take the form of consultant-style organizational problem solving, an industry or country analysis, or development of a new-venture business plan.

Many who choose to develop their own business plans end up entering them in Harvard's Business Plan Contest, first held in 1996. The annual competition awards $10,000 in cash and $10,000 in professional services to the top winners; student victors in 2000 launched Bang Networks, which provides Internet companies with an advanced infrastructure network. It's one aspect of the school's enhanced studies in entrepreneurship, a subject that has compelled more than 95 percent of Harvard MBAs to take at least one course, and which now rivals finance in its range of offerings.

Nearly 50 percent of Harvard's faculty is tenured, which means that, at times, there's a distinct effort to bring in new hires. This is one of those times: In the past three years, 18 faculty members have come aboard in a variety of a subject fields. HBS has always made efforts to bring new teachers up to speed, and, lately, the school's intricate teacher training program has been admired and partially imitated by other B-schools in its league. Harvard's process includes a three-day start session, with assigned teaching groups and visits by senior faculty to observe and critique the new teacher's class. To help institutionalize these and other methods, the school is planning a new Teaching and Learning Center. Meanwhile, administrators also try to evenly distribute "rookie" teachers among the student sections so that every student has an equivalent experience.

If they're not satisfied with any aspect of the program, you can bet your Palm Pilot these MBAs will speak up about it. Dean Clark says the administration receives an astounding number of suggestions, inquiries, and criticisms from the student body, a reflection of both the large number of enrolled students and their enthusiastic, resolute nature. "Frankly, it's a challenge to deal with all of it," Clark says. "We do say 'no' to our students a fair amount of the time." But some students say it isn't the "no" answer that bugs them, rather a sometimes dismissive attitude from the administration. Hence, Harvard's next-to-last ranking in the area of responsiveness.

But this, too, is an area in flux. The HBS student government has recently teamed up with administrators to tackle some 25 to 30 prioritized initiatives gleaned from a campuswide call for suggestions. The concerns are wide-ranging, from recruiting issues (expanding the support for high-tech, international, and nontraditional recruitment experiences) to service at Shad, the school's fitness and recreational sports facility. For the latter, a state-of-the-art center with steam-room-equipped locker rooms and well-maintained sports facilities, the only issue is the operating hours—students want to add a few more. But no problem is too big or too small in Dean Clark's relatively new "open door" policy, and all concerns are being addressed, with one student leader and one faculty member heading a task force that considers costs, workforce, and other improvement factors.

One aspect HBS students never have to complain about is the school's connections to recruiters and alumni. MBAs can call on any of the more than 35,000 alumni career advisers for guidance within a particular industry or city. In addition to searching for more than 1000 recruiters by industry, location, or function online, students can also dig up recent news and analysis about specific firms here, get information on alumni and fellow students with experience in areas of interest, and apply for jobs or schedule interviews online. Calendars and schedules of events for the whole HBS community are online, and Harvard holds networking events to bring in companies that may not traditionally recruit at the school. The High Growth Career Fair targets high-tech, venture capital, retail, media, and health-care companies. Students can also reach out to Executive Education Mentorships for career advice, the WesTrek trip to Silicon Valley and other CareerTrek visits, and speakers and career fairs held by about 50 industry-specific on-campus clubs. "Pursuing interests in high-tech was very easy, with Harvard's high-tech treks and the large alumni network in high-tech and venture capital," says one satisfied student who accepted a job while participating in the Denver trek.

Other selling points are some of the new structural changes on campus, including the Spangler Center, a 121,050-square-foot campus center completed this January. Inside is space for student meetings, guest speakers, social events, and receptions, in addition to dining facilities, a bookstore, business and travel centers, a post office, and offices of MBA program staff. It's just one part of a major campus overhaul that includes the construction of Hawes Hall, a new building with eight classrooms; McArthur Hall, a new residential facility for exec ed participants; and Mellon Hall, completely renovated housing for MBAs as of January 2001.

Housing here can be a little less than accessible and border on expensive off campus, but is available on campus for singles; couples and families can reside off campus at Harvard-affiliated complexes such as Soldiers Field Park.

But because space is limited for both, if you're interested, be sure to have your application in by the January deadline.

When they're not flexing their job contacts or preparing for classes, Harvard students make time for any number of on-campus organizations, including student government or the European Club, High Tech and New Media Club, Volunteer Consulting Organization, and Women's Student Association. They'll also take advantage of recreation in their picturesque New England setting adjacent to the Charles River. Boating, bicycling, and running along its border are popular activities in warmer weather. Come winter, students take off for nearby ski resorts in New Hampshire and Vermont. The warmest months can be spent on the beaches of Cape Cod or along Maine's rocky coast, and anytime is good for browsing the cafés, shops, and bookstores just across the river in Harvard Square.

Nightlife in Cambridge affords many choices. Most often, evenings for HBS students entail a quick trip across the river to grab a few beers at Shay's or Grendel's, or an on-campus stop at Spangler's lounge. But students also frequently head into downtown Boston for trendy dinner spots in the North End or along Newbury Street, or dancing at a club like the Cantab Lounge. If you want to stick closer to home, visit Pho Pasteur for Vietnamese cuisine or Tommy's House of Pizza to top off a night of barhopping. Arguably the best burger can be found at (Mr. and Mrs.) Bartley's, a hole-in-the-wall joint with menu items named after politicos, like the Bob Dole burger topped with a pineapple slice. Students also attend a range of on-campus events, from high-powered conferences to black-tie galas. The Cyberposium, whose speakers have included Amazon.com CEO Jeff Bezos and CMGI CEO David Wetherell, is completely run by students, as is the Women's Student Association Conference, which recently featured iVillage CEO Candice Carpenter. HBS students also played hard last year at parties like

"Holli-dazzle," the winter ball, and an Austin Powers–themed cruise. A favorite every year is the Australian Club's Priscilla Ball, where you'll find about 500 of America's potential future business leaders dressed in drag. We hear it's a hoot.

PLACEMENT DETAILS

Even Harvard's much-griped-about Career Services office, which recruiters ranked next-to-last, can't keep the companies away. About 800 mainstream and nontraditional MBA recruiters came on campus last year to court HBS second-years, whom they find to be the best and the brightest MBAs.

Students also turn to an extensive alumni network totaling 28,974 for top-rate connections that can be easily accessed and identified by industry or location through an online database. Specialized career fairs and CareerTreks to Silicon Valley and other high-tech hotspots help cover all the bases. "I now have a more exciting job, I'm able to earn a lot more money, and I had companies fighting over my services," gushes one satisfied grad. As a whole, the HBS Class of '00 grads commanded an average median pay package of $160,000, highest of the 82 B-schools surveyed by BUSINESSWEEK. Harvard traditionally declines to name its employers, but if you want to know, just take a look at the types of recruiters who visit other top 10 B-schools—and perhaps enhance that list a bit. You get the idea.

OUTSTANDING FACULTY

David Moss (business government/international economy); *Debora Spar* (business government/international economy); *Richard Tedlow* (business history); *Joseph Lassiter* (entrepreneurial management); *William Sahlman* (entrepreneurial management); *Marc Bertoneche* (finance);

Benjamin Esty (finance); *Andre Perold* (finance); *Das Narayandas* (marketing); *Nitin Nohria* (organizational behavior).

APPLICANT TIPS

Among the most selective of the B-schools, Harvard admits just 13 percent of its 8000-plus applicant pool—and few turn down the offer.

So, more than anything, you've got to stand out. Director of Admissions Kirsten Moss suggests you first understand what the school is looking for, and then describe in your essays how you have demonstrated leadership ability. "We are looking for people who are going to change the world," says Moss. "Our mission is to develop outstanding leaders who will contribute to the well-being of society." One of the biggest mistakes Moss has noticed is applicants who write about generic work experiences without mentioning how they contributed to the project, the deal, or the launch of a product. You won't impress anyone if you can't convey the impact you've had as an individual.

You can also express these ideas in an interview, but Harvard doesn't extend the option to every applicant—only those who are close to being admitted. (So, if you are asked to have one, consider it a good sign.)

The one dramatic change for Harvard this year is that the school is actively encouraging people straight from college or just a few years out, in addition to traditional candidates, to think about applying—if not now, in a few years. Admissions officers are traveling to a handful of colleges to talk to sophomores and juniors about applying to business school. "People can apply here when they're ready," says Moss. "They don't necessarily have to wait four or five years."

Applicants can choose from among three deadlines, each of which is given equal consideration for admissions and financial aid. The application can be downloaded from the HBS

Web site, but must be mailed in. A paper copy can be requested from the admissions office. Prospective students are invited to visit campus and attend one of the HBS information sessions conducted daily by second-years. With advance notice, a class visit can be arranged as well.

Contact: Kirsten Moss
Director of Admissions
617-495-6127
Application deadlines: November 4; January 16; March 2

HARVARD MBAs SOUND OFF

Key factors that make this program great include the case study learning method; incredible access to professors; a diverse, motivated, and supportive student body; entrepreneurial spirit everywhere; the "small school" section experience (80-person groups) combined with a larger network of classmates and alumni; and the opportunity and support offered by everyone—students, teachers, administrators—to pursue your dreams.

One extraordinary thing about HBS is its ability to make change quickly and effectively. When criticized for not being entrepreneurial last year, this year it suddenly became "HBS dot-com."

I was nothing but impressed throughout my two years at Harvard Business School. The professors are all up to date on current materials, extremely knowledgeable in their respective areas, and very accessible. The school seems responsive to student requests and demands in altering and updating the curriculum. I would suggest more team activities during the first year as well as more analytical assignments.

In the case of the faculty, the responsiveness is outstanding. But I believe the administration view their role, in part, as guardians of the "HBS Brand." Although this is a proper role for the administration, they often appear to take it to extremes by disregarding student concerns. I have felt that they view any given group of students as transitory and therefore do not involve them in critical decisions that impact the program. The result is that the status quo changes either very slowly or with little or no student input.

HBS surprised me by teaching me things I didn't expect to learn. Rather than leaving with a set of tools and frameworks, I am leaving with a broad "business intuition." I am now more able to ask the right questions and to focus more quickly on key issues. I think this is more valuable than learning frameworks since, in four years, I won't remember how many of Porter's forces there are. . . .

4.
MASSACHUSETTS INSTITUTE OF TECHNOLOGY

MASSACHUSETTS INSTITUTE OF TECHNOLOGY

Sloan School of Management
50 Memorial Drive
Cambridge, Massachusetts 02142-1347
E-mail address: masters@sloan.mit.edu
Web site address: http://mitsloan.mit.edu

Corporate ranking: 7	Graduate ranking: 7
Enrollment: 717	Annual tuition & fees: $29,860
Women: 27%	Room and board: NA
Non-U.S.: 35%	Average GMAT score: 703
Minority: 8%	Average years of work exp.: 4.8
Part-time: N/A	Accepted applicants enrolled: 73%
Average age: 28	Intellectual capital: 2
Applicants accepted: 17%	
Median starting pay: $149,000	

Teaching methods: Lecture, 30%   Case study, 45%
Business projects, simulations, 25%

Contact:
Rod Garcia
Director of Admissions
617-253-3730
Application deadlines:
December 6
February 7

Stock market performance be damned. The proliferation of new tech companies and the country's technology renaissance has been very, very good to the Sloan School of Management at the Massachusetts Institute of Technology. And many say that's because Sloan itself is very, very good.

The most improved darling of the BUSINESSWEEK rankings this year, Sloan skyrocketed from No. 15 last year to become No. 4 in 2000. Over the last decade, Sloan has been working hard to shake those stereotypical techie images—you know, the quant jocks wearing too-starched white shirts and pocket protectors. It's been a gradual positioning into a larger, more diverse, and more flexible B-school. And as tech started to be sexy at the end of the twentieth century, Sloan began to look very seductive to recruiters and prospective MBAs alike.

The tweaking began by building on its widely recognized analytic and technical strengths. Then it raised the profile of its lesser known—albeit equally strong—tradition, entrenched throughout MIT, of serving as an incubator for budding entrepreneurs. For those interested in launching their own companies or working for start-ups—particularly those with an eye toward careers in the high-tech or manufacturing sectors—MIT has created one of the most vigorous entrepreneurship programs this side of the West Coast.

Students here are so eager to spread their entrepreneurial wings that they created a business plan competition just for fun. The MIT Sloan Challenge, now in its third year, raised $25,000 for City Year

Boston, a local charity. Some 13 teams of students, faculty, and executives from such companies as Diamond Technologies, Donaldson Lufkin & Jenrette, Polaroid, Siemens, Silverback and Turbolinux vied to come up with the best strategy for marketing a fictitious invention. This year's winner was a smart umbrella that is supposed to create a protective wind tunnel around the user, dry instantly, and then shrink down to pocket size.

The umbrella isn't the only thing that's weathering storms at Sloan. After a downward trend—Sloan dropped from 9th in 1996 to 15th in BUSINESSWEEK's 1998 overall ranking—the school seems to have emerged from the rain, now topping grads' and recruiters' best-of-the-best in several categories and garnering a spot in the top five. And few recruiters now see Sloan as a niche school because grads have more of a leadership-oriented, well-rounded persona then they appeared to even two years ago. "Sloan is really enjoying a renaissance for us," says Justin Kulo, recruiting manager for New York–based Broadview. "Every year we reassess the schools we go to. Sloan historically is not the easiest. We're an investment bank, and one of the three core competencies we require is boardroom presence. While Sloan students were technical and smart, we used to think that they were falling short on client interaction. That's not the case any longer."

The current high premium for technology recruits and Sloan's new emphasis on a well-rounded grad have certainly changed the world's impression of the school. In the BUSINESSWEEK survey of corporate recruiters, MIT climbed from No. 14 to No. 7 in two years, with corporate types putting MIT among the top 10 places to find finance, globally oriented, and, of course, technology grads. MIT also enjoyed the second-greatest leap in MBA satisfaction, as graded by students, following only the University of Virginia's Darden Graduate School of Business Administration.

Bringing the public up to date on what's happened at Sloan has been the major focus of the school's still relatively new leadership. After five years in the school's top job, Dean Glen Urban opted in June 1998 to return to teaching. His replacement, Richard Schmalensee, served as Urban's deputy for two years before being named interim dean upon Urban's departure—and then took over the top job permanently four months later. Coming from the faculty has given Schmalensee a much-needed leg up. He's been able to assess what Sloan needed to do to get a broader national reputation from the inside out, and he's proven that he could get it done.

First on his list was to hire someone to overhaul the three main components of MBA life: admissions, student services, and placement. Schmalensee's idea was to put one person in charge from start to finish. Margaret Andrews, a Sloan alum herself, was hired to do the job. She rebuilt all three departments by putting into practice what both students and alums want from the school, which includes better quality of life, more accessible services, and a more cohesive curriculum. The dramatic rise in satisfaction at Sloan has been a group effort, of course, but everyone, from Schmalensee to first-years, credits Andrews with the turnaround. "She forced people to change quickly and move quickly," says one 2000 grad.

Andrews signed on in August 1999, after initially intending to return to Sloan only to participate in the alumni gab sessions she now organizes. She joined Schmalensee and his team in time to redesign the core curriculum, in part to redress the reputation of Sloan as a place for techies only, and in part to soothe students, who in the past had said the workload was excessive, particularly during fall of the first year. But she didn't do it alone—she actively sought out students, faculty, and even alums to help guide the program and the changes. And dozens of 2000 grads have stressed that this effort wasn't a one-time-only effort. It reflects a real change of character at the school.

"We are a different kind of place," Andrews concedes. She says that it's not the intention of the administration to make Sloan into a clone of other top B-schools. "At MIT everyone takes academics very seriously. We needed to change our academics. But we will never get too soft. That could never happen at MIT. Academic rigor is part of this place." But the new core does address student concerns about the workload as well as charges that the coursework was not well integrated. Faculty, students, and alums were called in (including Andrews before she took the new job) to discuss how to approach the overhaul. "Faculty were really a big part of it. It used to be that each faculty member owned his or her own course and everybody had an assignment due the day before Thanksgiving," she says. "Now, we map out the semester to really manage it. We make sure that we don't have a week that is excessively heavy." On average, students in our survey now say they feel that faculty are aware of what their colleagues are assigning in other classes, and that the workload is not as oppressive as it has been in the past.

In addition to a look at the courses themselves, the administration decided to limit the number of first-year courses to no more than five to ensure that students could focus on their work. Sloan also upped its already heavy emphasis on working in teams—you'll work on 10 to 20 teams during your MIT tenure. The five to eight people with whom you are assigned to work during that first semester to tackle pre-term exercises in team building, leadership, organizational learning, diversity, and ethics will remain your team throughout, and you'll often be graded as a unit. To anticipate and alleviate teamwork pressure, Sloan instituted a first-year daylong break one month after classes start. You'll get the chance to look at team dynamics and explore why some teams are experiencing stress, Andrews explains.

That said, despite the extensive team-building exercises, graduates say Sloan doesn't do enough to cultivate interpersonal skills and other "soft-management" techniques. There are efforts afoot to improve this by admitting a more varied student body and incorporating interpersonal issues into the curriculum. Grads say the school puts a priority on analytical skills in the classroom and that Sloan professors almost always present material in a current and relevant format for class discussion.

In the spring, you can opt to design your own program or write a thesis, a Sloan graduation requirement before 1994, but now an option that earns you the designation of master of science in management and about one-sixth of the credits you need to get your diploma. One recent grad feels her thesis gave her exposure to job offers she would not have had otherwise, not to mention the start of a book she wants to write. You can enroll in one of seven of the current list of management tracks: new product and venture development, financial engineering, financial management, strategic management and consulting, information technology and business transformation, operations and manufacturing, and e-business and marketing—the newest offering. Each track consists of 8 to 10 courses, about half the elective requirements for graduation, plus a ProSeminar, in which outside practitioners lead discussion groups and field projects in their particular specialties.

In January 2000 Sloan and Arthur Andersen launched a five-year, $10 million research program called the New Economy Value Research Lab and started to perform research on what the rules are—and should be—in the new economy. There you'll explore such issues as how businesses are investing in different assets to create economic value, how the financial markets value businesses in the new economy, and risk management, performance measurement, and financial reporting of all assets.

Reports one recent grad: "The school academic program offers multiple options and is flexible enough to guarantee that each student will find the best subject alternatives depending on his or her needs and interests. I always got in the classes I wanted to take, and I had lots of options from which to choose." And that certainly can't be said of all B-schools. Indeed, in some cases, Sloan struggles to meet some elective demand: Grads say Sloan still needs to work on developing electives that are requested by students. Current students gush about how great it was to play an active role in the creation of the new first-year curriculum. About 21 percent of the 174 electives at Sloan were added between 1997 and 2000. You can also avail yourself of up to two courses in other MIT departments or at Harvard Business School, which has an exchange agreement with Sloan. "The several non-MBA programs offer amazing synergies in [the MBA's] educational development," says one student. "We regularly interact with and take classes with the Sloan Fellows, and Sloan Management of Technology students, the Leaders for Manufacturing students, and even undergrads, who keep us grounded in the perspectives of those straight out of college and remind us of the challenges of managing less-experienced people."

Of course, Sloan wouldn't be Sloan without the tech emphasis, and the school still has that in spades. Andrews describes the school philosophy as "the intersection of management and technology." That's why Robin Cahan, manager of college relations for Analog Devices, just added Sloan to her schedule. "We recruit special people. We need double ees [electrical engineers] with the broad business background. There aren't many places to find them." Not surprisingly, graduates rave about the use of technology in the classroom and give it high marks for weaving e-business issues into the core curriculum. If you've been heavily into science since your undergraduate years, you might want to consider MIT's elite Leaders for Manufactur-

ing Program. Each year 48 students enroll in an even more intense 24-month experience than the typical MBA, but come out with dual degrees in business and engineering. You have to have an undergraduate degree in science or engineering, experience in manufacturing or a related field, and acceptance by special application (note that the application deadline, January 4, is more than a month earlier than that for the regular MBA program), and a sense of humor about giving over two years of your life to work and study. On campus, LFMers are called "Jedi Knights" because of their intensity, but those who have been through it say it's worth the trial. LFM currently gives scholarships—basically full tuition. LFMers are sought after by tech and nontech firms alike that want managers who really understand operations.

"We had to find ways to attract students to go into manufacturing," says Donald B. Rosenfield, Director of the LFM fellows program. Rosenfield thinks the centerpiece of the program, a six-month management internship at 1 of 14 sponsoring U.S. manufacturers, which include Alcoa Inc., Boeing Co., Ford Motor Co., Motorola, and others, has done just that. Of course, the free ride doesn't hurt either. Started 12 years ago as a pet project of Lester Thurow's, MIT's favorite faculty member, the program's immodest mission was to help the United States recapture world leadership in manufacturing.

At the same time, however, entrepreneurship has become as much of a buzzword at Sloan as engineering. The fastest-growing managerial track is new product and venture development, and many students who choose a self-managed track are headed for entrepreneurial careers as well. Entrepreneurial fever runs at its highest each spring when the MIT $50K Entrepreneurship Competition swings into gear. In 2000, 206 entrants—a 145 percent increase from 1998—crafted business plans to capture $50,000 in seed money. One stipulation of winning is that the money must be used to transform your plan into a corporation. But you don't have to win to see your dream come to life: Since it was started in 1990 as a joint initiative of two student clubs, the contest has spawned the birth of more than 50 companies, many of them since gobbled up by info-tech giants such as Microsoft and Motorola. One recent grad cited the $50K competition as the highlight of his tenure at Sloan.

In all areas of study, both students and grads rave about Sloan's faculty. Although Thurow tops the list, across the board grads in our survey ranked Sloan first out of all B-schools for having teachers at the leading edge of their fields. Graduates also say the prominent academics at the school are highly involved in teaching in the program, although they say faculty members aren't always available for informal meetings. This is a big change from just six years ago when grads universally griped about poor instructors. Since then, full-time faculty at Sloan grew by about 35 members, to 94. Thurow, the popular economist and prolific writer, brought much attention to the school, hiring faculty experts in other cultures and countries and luring a greater percentage of non-U.S. students. In July, MIT showed its new practical side, too. It hired Gerhard Schulmeyer, the current president and CEO of New York–based Siemens Corp. Indeed, it is names like these that helped MIT garner the No. 2 spot in BUSINESSWEEK's first-ever ranking of intellectual capital and helped to move it up to No. 4 overall. "I was impressed to see Thurow in the news, then in class the next day. Same with Michael Cusumano: in the news about Microsoft, as they go to trial, then in class talking about strategy," says one alum. It's that kind of prominence—similar to that of Harvard and Wharton—that helps set Sloan apart.

A broader academic focus, interesting specialized programs, and first-rate faculty, though, can't distract students from their biggest gripe: the buildings that house all that brainpower. While they're prime real estate overlooking Boston on the Charles River, they're old and hardly state-of-the-art. By the 2006–2007 school year, Schmalensee hopes to have a complex that would link now disparate offices, classrooms, and social facilities. But the right site hasn't yet been found. And even a new B-school building won't alleviate the other Sloan frustration: finding a place to live. There's virtually no housing close to campus, so students live scattered throughout Cambridge and Boston—both of which are getting increasingly expensive.

Housing problems aside, graduates are glad to have gone to Sloan. Most say they'd recommend the school to friends and believe their degree was worth the time and money. An important contributor to that good will is Sloan's international flavor. Of the Class of 2001, more than a third of the students hailed from 67 countries outside the United States, and Sloanies say it's a more eclectic assortment than they had expected at B-school. A large contingent always comes from the Far East, especially Japan, where an MIT degree is a major status symbol. Chinese students are recruited with the China Management Education Project, a collection of several China-centric efforts. Sloan MBAs interact with MBAs from three Pacific Rim schools (not in an exchange mode, but rather, in a student-to-student information-sharing/cross-training mode): Fudan University of Shanghai; Tsinghua University of Beijing; and Lingnan (University) College of Zhongshan University in Guangzhou. Sloan offers foreign exchange programs with the London School of Business and IESE in Barcelona. Each year student groups also plan their own study tours around the globe, raising money, organizing pretrip seminars, arranging meetings with international executives, and enlisting faculty members to accompany them. Recent locations included Australia, New Zealand, Jordan, and Norway.

The international flavor spills over into Sloan's social scene. Throughout the year, students from various countries put on weeklong parties for the school called "C-functions"—at one time, Consumption Functions, but now renamed Cultural Functions—with lectures, decorations, sports and games, dance classes, and dinners offering indigenous food, drink, and music to share with their classmates. Beginning with the Fall Formal and winding up with the Sloan Follies variety show, students participate in activities ranging from the serious minded to the more lighthearted, such as Graduate Management Society–sponsored ski trips and cruises on the Charles. For less organized socializing, Sloanies unwind at the Muddy Charles, a bar located a couple of minutes away from campus, or head over the bridge to Boston's chic Beacon Hill neighborhood for drinks and dinner.

PLACEMENT DETAILS

Upon leaving Sloan, grads end up at companies around the world and, increasingly, at smaller firms that reflect student interest in entrepreneurship as well as the school's growing reputation as a leader in that area. In recent years the school has worked hard to connect with more small- to mid-sized companies, and recent grads in the BUSINESSWEEK survey say it shows. Of all B-schools, grads ranked Sloan first in assisting them with independent job searches and in helping them to connect with small or nontraditional company recruiters. In 2000, 20 percent of the companies recruiting on campus were small firms. There's also an aggressive program for summer jobs and internships.

Last year Sloan's Career Core for students was revamped. Now the school conducts four sessions instead of three, according to Jacqueline A. Wilbur, new director of the MBA Career Development Office. The first one is mandatory and gives an overview of the market factors as well as the different resources available through the career office. Some 200 alums also serve as mentors for first-years, and administrators from all parts of the MBA program participate in the Career Core.

Members of the Class of 2000 averaged 3.9 job offers upon graduation—more than at many other top schools. Despite the interest in start-ups, the employers who hired the most Sloan grads in 2000 were still the big consulting firms and I-banks, not to mention the tech firms: McKinsey & Co. (17); Goldman Sachs (12); Bain & Co. (11); Intel Corp. (10); Morgan Stanley Dean Witter (9); Boston Consulting Group (8); Diamond Technology Partners (7); and Booz-Allen & Hamilton (7).

OUTSTANDING FACULTY

Roberto Rigobon (economics); *Lester Thurow* (economics); *Simon Johnson* (entrepreneurship); *Paul Asquith* (finance); *Kevin Rock* (finance); *Barbara Bund* (marketing); *Rebecca Henderson* (strategy); *Michael Scott-Morton* (strategy); *John Sterman* (system dynamics).

APPLICANT TIPS

Starting with admissions for the Class of 2001, MIT became the first B-school to require online submission of applications—you can't mail in a paper copy even if you want to. The Sloan application utilizes a software program called GradAdvantage, now used by many other B-schools, which allows prospective students to fill out forms for multiple schools without retyping basic information. To apply, you'll need to open the GradAdvantage Web site, http://www.gradadvantage.org, and set up a user name and password. After you've begun filling out the information, you can save your work and keep coming back to it until you're finished and ready to submit it.

Despite the overall decline in MBA applicants, the competition to get into Sloan is still stiff. Applications have increased more than 70 percent since 1994, from 1671 to 2859, and only 17 percent of applicants to the Class of 2000 were admitted. MIT has one of the earliest final application deadlines of any of the top business schools, so if you're interested in applying, do so early. Applications received by the December deadline should get a response by late February. Those who wait until February don't get the nod until late April. Given the quantitative nature of the program, GMAT scores and undergraduate grades in math and science are weighted here more than they might be elsewhere.

But Andrews says Sloan is looking for students who are more than super-smart techno-geeks. "We would never want to admit people who could not make it here. Because we take a lot of smart motivated people, there is a lot going on on campus. The people who fit in here are very nice. They don't take themselves too seriously. They're the kind of people who are amazingly great to be around."

Interviews at Sloan are done by invitation only, with about half of those admitted in 2000 asked to come in for a chat with the admissions committee. It's meant to be a casual way for the staff to get to know candidates who have strong records but may not come across clearly on paper. If you'd like to learn more about the school, you can sign up for the Ambassadors Program, which arranges information sessions with current students and a chance to attend classes and get a feel for the place. Sloan's Web site has all you need to know about visiting the school.

Contact: Rod Garcia
Director of Admissions
617-253-3730
Application deadlines: December 6; February 7

SLOAN MBAs SOUND OFF

The Sloan School comprises a remarkable group of people. With a very diverse student body, learning at Sloan happens on many levels: academics, diverse cultures, leadership, and teamwork.

The school opened my opportunities to learn and access several fields in which I was extremely interested, such as entrepreneurship and technology. I believe that Sloan has a lot to say and contribute in the e-business world: its connections with the engineering school, the entrepreneurial environment, the outstanding faculty, and tech-savvy students.

MIT Sloan has cross-registration with the Harvard Business School. While I am very happy to have experienced HBS and enjoyed the classes there, in my mind, Sloan develops a much more rounded business professional with a stronger emphasis on meritocracy.

I was originally hesitant about attending Sloan due to the many stereotypes that circulate about MIT and its affiliates. But I found a unique community where diversity of background and experience is sought so as to enhance the overall community and learning experience. At the same time, never in my life, in one place, have I felt such a support network. The collaborative atmosphere of Sloan encouraged me to take courses that were outside of my usual realm because I knew that others would give me the extra time to help me through the difficulties of the course.

My experience at MIT Sloan has far exceeded my expectations. I could never have made the transition from being a journalist at CNN to a business development manager at Microsoft (last summer) without going to Sloan. Through various entrepreneurship courses and activities at MIT, I have become very interested in start-ups, which I did not anticipate when I began at Sloan. After graduation, I will be joining a start-up as director of business development.

The new Entrepreneurial Finance class was awesome. It was built around a simulation that included negotiation and strategy sessions between small student teams and local big name law firms in preparing for negotiations of term sheets with prominent VCs. Most of the learning took place in interactions between the small teams of students and the partner-level professionals in these firms that liberally donated their time to work with Sloan students.

**5.
DUKE
UNIVERSITY**

DUKE UNIVERSITY

The Fuqua School of Business
Durham, North Carolina 27708
E-mail address: fuqua-admissions@mail.duke.edu
Web site address: http://www.fuqua.duke.edu

Corporate ranking: 8	Graduate ranking: 10
Enrollment: 341	Annual tuition & fees: $28,910
Women: 41%	Room and board: N/A
Non-U.S.: 31%	Average GMAT score: 690
Minority: 20%	Average years of work exp.: 5
Part-time: 0	Accepted applicants enrolled: 54%
Average age: 28	Intellectual capital: 1
Applicants accepted: 19%	
Median starting pay: $128,500	

Teaching methods: Lecture, 45% Case study, 40%
Simulations, role plays, 15%

Contact:
Liz Riley
Director of Admissions
919-660-7705
Application deadlines:
November 2
December 9
January 25
March 15
April 26

Duke University's Fuqua School of Business is almost overshadowed by the lush green trees surrounding campus. The pictures in the catalog depict an unreal serenity, a more civilized air. And Dean Rex D. Adams, the former Mobil Oil vice president who became dean in 1996, calls Fuqua "a bit of the ol' South." Charm aside, this Southern school is making waves in the B-school world. In 2000, Fuqua leapt to No. 5 in BUSINESSWEEK's rankings, continuing its steady climb. Corporate recruiters ranked Fuqua the most improved program. When BUSINESS-WEEK conducted the last rankings in 1998, Adams told the world he wanted to claim a spot in the B-school big leagues. He was planning to conquer MBA programs by hiring 50 percent more faculty, expanding ties with corporate giants, and raising money for major facility face-lifts. The hard work appears to be paying off.

The career placement office contributed to the glory by again earning a spot among the top five career placement offices as ranked by recruiters. Not long after he became dean, Adams and Dan Nagy, assistant dean for MBA programs, sat down to figure out why Fuqua graduates had not effectively penetrated the elite consulting and investment-banking community that each spring culls the cream of the country's MBA crop. In addition, Nagy took a close look at the details that can make an employer's visit to campus successful—or downright miserable. To cut down on student no-shows at interviews, he began requiring those who missed an appointment to write a letter of apology to the slighted company before being allowed another interview through career services. A second no-show, and you're persona non grata ever after—no more interviews will be arranged for you by career services. He made loaner cell phones available to recruiters and started handing out free soft drinks and home-baked cookies every afternoon. The result: Fuqua followed up 1998 success with even more accolades. Graduates applauded the school's efforts to link them with nontraditional companies, for which Nagy credits student-run clubs. The venture capital and entrepreneur's organizations on campus are "driving this train," he says. In addition, prime traditional companies like Lehman Brothers and Goldman Sachs have begun to visit Fuqua as well.

High-caliber job placement didn't increase the 2000 applicant pool. Though admissions numbers were flat, Fuqua did comparatively well; some of their rivals saw as much as a 23 percent dip in applications. Much of Fuqua's success can be attributed to the administration's ability to roll with the punches. The folks at Fuqua realize that a hot economy makes potential students think twice about spending two whole years out of the workforce. Adams says he's going to respond to the new competition the only way he knows how—like a business-man. And every smart businessman knows how to cater to consumers. Hence, Adams developed the Duke MBA Cross-Continent, a program designed for "young guns" who simply cannot leave their jobs for the required two years of full-time MBA studies. The unique degree program, which was launched in August 2000, lasts for 20 months and combines online learning with face-to-face classes at Duke's Durham, North Carolina, campus and in Frankfurt, Germany. Adams says initiatives like this are part of the evolving MBA world, which now requires more flexibility than ever.

Students give high marks to Adams for his ability to respond quickly to their needs. In fact, students say he forges many personal relationships with students, distinguishing him from some of his figurehead counterparts at other schools. Student leader and 2000 graduate

Christian Ryan got to know Adams and his staff well during his tenure in various Fuqua clubs and activities. He calls the dean a "vibrant figure," who would have spent even more time with students if recent commitments didn't inhibit him. (The dean was busy opening up a school in Europe and tending to external relations.) Adams expresses his disappointment about not getting to allocate more time to current students. But he knows exactly how he feels about Fuqua students. "I love them, and I think they like me," Adams says. The likeable dean plans to leave Fuqua after the 2001 class graduates, and it may be hard to find someone to fill his shoes with a handful of deanships at top schools also needing to be filled.

Students give the school praise for smart, accessible faculty and relevant, team-oriented coursework. Many say they also like the balance the program strives for: a middle-of-the-road general management approach that doesn't emphasize one specialty over another (the school offers only one formal concentration, in health sector management) and a team orientation that includes plenty of work on leadership skills as well. In fact, team building and leadership are the focus of first-year orientation, the first of four required Integrative Learning Experiences that punctuate each semester with a group project intended to synthesize all you've been learning in your core and elective courses.

After arriving on campus, the incoming class of some 330 is divided into four groups that tackle outdoor teamwork exercises and a high ropes course in a sort of miniature Outward Bound in the piney woods outside Durham. Back in the classroom, more sessions on alliance building and leadership are followed by personal assessment exercises and career planning, with the aim of getting you to think deeply about what you want to achieve—not just at Fuqua, but in your career and your life.

The second integrative experience comes midway through the second semester, with a one-week computer simulation that pits eight teams of 40 students against one another in a competition to formulate and implement strategy for a global business. The exercise is designed to give students the opportunity to apply—in a cross-disciplinary, practical way—what they've been learning in the core. The third and fourth integrative experiences are more complicated. In recent years, faculty have begun to respond to student concerns that the last two projects, which used to have students focusing on real-world managerial problems, simply were not as successful as the first two. The curriculum committee continues struggling to create the best sort of program for the end of the MBA experience. The group toyed with allowing students a choice of weeklong workshops, including one with Chicago's powerhouse improvisational group, Second City. Like most aspects of Fuqua, it's something students take a big part in shaping.

The four integrative exercise weeks are woven into an intense, tightly compacted schedule in which terms last just seven weeks, with courses meeting twice a week for 2 hours and 15 minutes per session. First-years take four courses per term, second-years only three to allow more time for the job hunt, for a total of 28. In the first year, students move rapid-fire through their 14 functional core courses in sections that are further divided into study groups, project groups, and case teams—in fact, a good part of your grade in every course, core or elective, is based on team functioning. Each first-year class is divided into five sections of about 65 students each, with sections moving through core classes together; within each course, teams of four or five students are assigned as well. At the same time, many of the team projects come in the form of contests among teams, so there's an element of competition built in that you won't find at some team-happy schools. Though teams are far from the focal point at Fuqua, students say they are encouraged to help each other. For example, Ryan had been a high school teacher in his pre-MBA life. In a PowerPoint presentation about statistics he strutted his teaching skills and shared his knowledge with an impressed class gearing up for its first quiz. His peers applauded his efforts and asked him to help out the next time around. Soon he was a regular at review sessions. "One student told me, 'That's what Team Fuqua is all about,'" Ryan says.

First-years are immersed in the core curriculum. The courses give them a firm foundation in economics, quantitative analysis and statistics, accounting, finance, organizational behavior, marketing, and operations management. A series of management communications courses are integrated into the core curriculum to help develop communication, computer, and career planning skills. First-year students are divided into several sections that serve as study groups, project groups, and case teams. In the last term of the first year and throughout the second year, students can choose from a number of electives, including an ever-growing array of international courses. A popular option is one of the Global Academic Travel Experiences, with coursework on your region of choice—Asia, Latin America, Russia, South Africa, or the Middle East. It culminates in a two-week study tour of indigenous companies. In 2001, a GATE course to India will commence. Or you can spend a term or an entire semester abroad at one of many management schools in Australia, Europe, Asia, and Africa with which Fuqua has exchange agreements.

Adams has been working hard to bolster Fuqua's global orientation, putting on a major student recruitment push overseas that has resulted in an increase in international student enrollment from 25 percent in 1998 to 28 percent in 2000. Current international students and overseas alums have been drafted as "Fuqua Ambassadors" to publicize the school and identify potential students in their home countries. Specialized career counseling and job development are now available through career services for those seeking to work abroad after graduation. Adams's efforts gained further support in 1998 when J. B. Fuqua, the entrepreneur and philanthropist for whom the school is named, designated that half of a newly bestowed $20 million gift be earmarked for development of international initiatives. When it comes to diversity, students haven't exactly bought into the idea that Fuqua is a melting pot. "Yes, [Fuqua] offered diversity and propitiated minority participation," says Luis Capobianco, an international graduate from Venezuela. "My take, as a foreigner, is that it is a little bit forced, as it is in any other aspect of the American education and work environment." Capobianco, however, lauded efforts to promote international career fairs and to hire a career counselor solely for foreign Fuquans. But international students are just one part of a diverse student body that includes 20 percent minorities and 41 percent women. These numbers, which continue to grow since the school stepped up marketing efforts, place Fuqua among the more balanced, inclusive enrollments at top-tier B-schools.

In addition to attracting a more balanced student body, Fuqua continues to bolster on-campus technology. Students give high marks to the school's information technology efforts, which have received an infusion of $5.5 million in improvements in the past three years. Fuqua does benefit handsomely from its location in North Carolina's Research Triangle—the area bounded by Durham, Chapel Hill, and Raleigh that encompasses four major universities (the others are the University of North Carolina, North Carolina State University, and North Carolina Central University) and 100 major research companies, including GlaxoSmith-Kline, IBM, and CIBA-Geigy. A partnership with Bay Networks, Hewlett-Packard, and IBM allowed Fuqua to construct the largest local-access computer network in the state; up and running in 1998, "Fuqua World" incorporates calendars, course schedules and materials, stu-

dent and faculty profiles, and links to alumni. Through the partnership, students can sample even more advanced, emerging technologies at the nearby Bay Architecture Lab. Recruiters also give Fuquans' technology skills excellent ratings, along with marketing, finance, and global scope—all ranked in the top 10 in BUSINESS-WEEK's 2000 survey of employers.

Virtually everyone agrees that Durham is a nice place to spend two years. The mild climate, the relaxed yet intellectual atmosphere, and the Duke campus, with its towering faux-Gothic chapel and world-famous gardens, have powers to charm. Hop in a car, and you can be anywhere in the Triangle within half an hour. Like California's Silicon Valley and Massachusetts' Route 128, the area has leveraged its nearby academic resources to woo businesses. You'll never confuse the area for New York or Chicago, but you won't feel like you're in the middle of nowhere, either. Indeed, Durham is a nice compromise between the access a big city provides and the serenity that a tucked-away college town offers.

Fuqua is located on Duke's West Campus, its modern, concrete-and-glass complex boasting an airy, mall-like environment with trees, horseshoe-shaped classrooms, a 500-seat auditorium, two computer labs, and a library and student lounge that were renovated in 1997. The wings that house the MBA program were named in honor of Thomas F. Keller upon his retirement in 1996. (He became dean of the B-school just four years after its founding in 1970 and stayed for 22 years.) A bridge across a ravine connects with the R. David Thomas (that's right, "Dave" the Wendy's founder) executive-education center, built in 1989. These days, Fuqua is sporting a new look. In the spring of 2000, the administration dedicated the new five-story Wesley Alexander Magat Academic Center for faculty and Ph.D. students. By moving professors to their own complex, Fuqua made more room for students and corporate recruiters. It's a concept some schools reject, though, saying it separates student life too much from professors. The school has plans to expand deeper into campus with the addition of a new student center and a classroom building. Adams hopes the student center, which will include outdoor terraces, a glass roof and exterior designed to show off the surrounding woods, and an atrium, will be the centerpiece of the Fuqua campus.

There's no student housing on the construction schedule, so it looks like most MBAs will continue to live off campus in privately owned apartments just a walk or bike ride away from school. (Fewer than 1 percent of Fuquans live in university-owned housing.) It's good to be close by, because you'll probably spend most of your spare time in "Team Fuqua" activities—students play a very active role in running the school, serving on the curriculum committee, the MBA programs advisory committee, and even managing The Kiosk, Fuqua's snack bar and store. They also sponsor the highlight of the annual social season, the Fuqua-MBA Games, a series of wacky competitions held each spring to raise money for the North Carolina Special Olympics. Teams of students from 13 B-schools and Special Olympics athletes raise money from corporate sponsors by vying in events such as the Briefcase Toss, the Recruiting Obstacle Course, and the Corporate Swim"suit" Relay (swum, of course, in business attire). The 2000 games netted more than $175,000 for the charity. Another fund-raiser, the International Business School Rugby Tournament, hosted by Fuqua every April, pits student teams from 20 B-schools in the United States, Canada, Great Britain, and Australia against one another to benefit Habitat for Humanity.

These charitable folks have a creative flair as well. Students laugh at themselves every time Fuqua Vision, a student club that creates Saturday Night Live–type videotapes, airs an episode. The dean and other top administrators are known to participate in spoofs and the organization has become a major part of the end-of-the-semester traditions at Fuqua. In addition, Fuqua musicians can help raise funds for the MBA games by participating in an unplugged show and CD compilation. Duke basketball inspires more bonding moments for Fuqua students. Many MBAs pile into an RV and stay up all night just to score tickets to a home game.

PLACEMENT DETAILS

As befits a school with a strong team culture, Fuquans tend to help one another out in the job race. Through the Career Fellows Program, begun in 1995, second-year students counsel first-years on interview skills and job-hunting techniques. Every so often, the career placement office sends out an e-mail asking students which companies they would like to see on campus. In 2000, MBAs at Duke cashed in on the hot economy and took advantage of the links Fuqua gave them to nontraditional companies. "It's a great time to be a business student," says 2000 graduate Jason Covitz.

In 2000, 236 companies recruited on campus, with 97 percent of second-year students getting their first job offer by graduation. The Class of 2000 was responsible for launching three businesses, and 92 percent of them received signing bonuses. The 10 employers hiring the most 2000 grads were: Booz-Allen & Hamilton (10); PricewaterhouseCoopers (9); Deloitte & Touche LLP (8); Johnson & Johnson (8); McKinsey & Company Inc. (8); Dell Corporation (7); Lehman Brothers (7); Goldman Sachs (6); Morgan Stanley Dean Witter (6); Cap Gemini Ernst & Young (6). Although Fuquans averaged 3.1 job offers upon graduation, the median starting pay package of $128,500 lags behind a few other schools in the top 10, but not nearly as much as in the past. In the realm of recruiters, Duke is showing that it's an up and coming force to reckon with. Moreover, the school's diversity is a big attraction for recruiters.

OUTSTANDING FACULTY

Jennifer Francis (accounting); *C. J. Skender* (accounting); *Jim Smith* (decision sciences); *Michael Bradley* (finance); *Alon Brav* (finance); *John Graham* (finance); *Campbell Harvey* (finance); *John Lynch* (marketing); *Christine Moorman* (marketing); *Debu Purohit* (marketing); *Gerard Cachon* (operations).

APPLICANT TIPS

Fuqua's admissions office says it's looking for applicants with "innovation, vitality, and drive," who show a "spirit that is dynamic, team-oriented, and intellectually challenging." That means your grades and GMAT scores will be looked at closely, and you'll be well advised to display both leadership and team-player qualities through your professional and extracurricular activities.

Things have changed a bit in the admissions office. Technology has revolutionized the process at Fuqua. Director of Admissions Liz Riley says potential Fuquans still get personal attention but far more communication takes place via e-mail. She adds that online correspondence is changing the way she markets the Fuqua MBA. Online advancements make communication easier and more convenient for applicants and the school. If you're interested in Fuqua, heading for the home page is a safe bet.

Applicants are encouraged, but not required, to interview with admissions officers on campus; about 85 percent of the admitted applicants for the Class of 2000 did so. If you want an on-campus interview, you are urged to do so as early as possible in the admissions cycle; those who apply early have a better chance both of getting in and of getting scholarship money. Riley urges potential students to visit the campus and take a tour. "You should try to figure out the best fit for you," Riley says. She stresses that applicants should do extensive research on the various MBA programs before they apply to be sure their needs will be met.

Contact: Liz Riley
Director of Admissions
919-660-7705
Application deadlines: November 2; December 9; January 25; March 15; April 26

FUQUA MBAs SOUND OFF

The opportunities and learning that resulted from my taking two years out of my career path have exceeded expectations tenfold. I do not feel like I have wasted any time. On the contrary, I have been given the tools with which to access the highest echelons of any organization, though it is now up to me to use them to the best of my ability. I am ecstatic about my experience at Duke as I feel that I have learned valuable material that, judging from my internship successes, will remain pertinent for many years to come.

Fuqua is a very humane place, not filled with the cutthroat competition reported at other top business schools. Students are certainly competitive, but a team spirit and ethics take priority.

Fuqua, like every school, is not for everyone. The short terms can be very intense and very demanding. There is a huge emphasis on developing excellent teamwork and leadership skills. You cannot come in with a Lone Ranger–type attitude and expect to be happy here. If you don't know coming into the program how to work effectively on and/or lead a team, you will certainly learn by the time you're done. My undergraduate institution had an Honor Code that wasn't followed; I assumed that it would be the same here. It's not. Honesty, ethics, and adherence to the Honor Code are almost a religion here for most people. There's even a basket left out in the open in the Kiosk where students can just put the money they owe for food. Expect to work hard but also expect to become very involved in social activities. Do not expect to be pampered; you have to be willing to work and to ask for help when you need it. Students here will bend over backward to help other students when asked or when it's obvious that people need help. It's just part of the culture here to lend a helping hand. The only major downside of this culture is that people are sometimes too nice and not critical enough.

Duke's MBA program is excellent and gaining speed. I interned with Goldman Sachs' equities division, and from my observations, I would pit a Fuqua student against a Harvard or Wharton student any day. The school's limitations right now are physical (it's in the process of expanding its facilities) and temporal (more years needed to expand the relatively small network of alumni). With its key location in the heart of North Carolina's booming high-tech sector and its intense focus on expanding e-commerce courses, Fuqua is perfectly positioned to become a twenty-first-century B-school powerhouse.

6.
UNIVERSITY OF MICHIGAN

UNIVERSITY OF MICHIGAN

University of Michigan Business School
Ann Arbor, Michigan 48109
E-mail address: umbusmba@umich.edu
Web site address: http://www.bus.umich.edu

Corporate ranking: 6	Graduate ranking: 5
Enrollment: 1939	Annual tuition & fees:
Women: 27%	resident—$23,500
Non-U.S.: 32%	nonresident—$28,500
Minority: 11%	Room and board: $8190
Part-time: 1065	Average GMAT score: 677
Average age: 29	Average years of work exp.: 5.1
Applicants accepted: 21%	Accepted applicants enrolled: N/A
Median starting pay: $131,000	Intellectual capital: 12

Teaching methods: Lecture, 40%   Case study, 40%
Experiential learning, 20%

Contact:
Jeanne Wilt
Assistant Dean for
Admissions and Career
Development
313-763-5796
Application deadlines:
November 15
January 15
March 1
April 1

At the University of Michigan Business School, there's a mantra that echoes through the halls almost as loudly as the chants from the 110,900 Wolverine football fans who pack Michigan Stadium for home games each fall: "Think about it. Research it. Do it."

While other business schools boast that their students learn to combine classroom theory with actual practice, Michigan's experiential approach to management education ensures that MBAs actually get to "do it" before they graduate. In fact, every Michigan MBA must participate in at least one—and most likely several—hands-on assignments where they can test their business skills while solving real-world business problems alongside senior executives at Fortune 500 companies, New Economy start-ups, and everywhere else in between. The payoff can be enormous, as many corporate recruiters will attest: Michigan MBAs not only grasp the theory, they understand how to put the nuts and bolts together quickly to make a company run.

Sure, Michigan may not have the brand name cachet of some of the other elite B-schools, which have also topped the BUSINESSWEEK rankings for the past 12 years. It may even lose some more luster with students and recruiters after falling out of the top five and settling in at No. 6 in 2000. But there's no doubt that Michigan's trial-by-fire, down-and-dirty approach to management makes it an ideal training ground for budding Wall Street wizards and entrepreneurial hotshots alike.

Throw in world-class departments in general management, finance, and entrepreneurship—along with one of the more global orientations that you'll find at any top-tier B-school—and you should consider spending two years in Ann Arbor, one of America's premier college towns. And that's not to mention that you'll be surrounded by hundreds of down-to-earth Michigan students and an administration that rivals the best with its bend-over-backwards service.

Spurring it all along has been, perhaps, the B-school's greatest asset: Dean B. Joseph White. His can-do attitude and gutsy leadership have supplied the electricity for the University of Michigan to surge toward the top of BUSINESS-WEEK's rankings. Yet, White also might just be Michigan's greatest liability: After nearly a decade as dean, White recently announced that he'll step down as head of the school in June 2001, and a new dean has yet to be named.

Whoever that person is, though, will certainly have big shoes to fill. Since White signed on as dean in 1991, the former Cummins Engine Co. human resources executive moved determinedly to bolster the school's image, long considered lagging behind its academic excellence. More importantly, though, he's been equally adept at improving the school's content. For the past decade, Michigan has been at the forefront of school innovation through curriculum reform. Although students still gripe about poor teaching quality, particularly in electives, and the limited use of technology, recruiters considered Michigan's overall curriculum among the most innovative of all the schools surveyed by BUSINESSWEEK for the third time in a row. In the process, White has cultivated a world-class faculty that can rival Harvard in general management, Wharton in finance, and Northwestern in marketing. And the dean has recently strengthened the areas of entrepreneurship, operations, and e-business.

In addition, White has transferred Michigan's "put-it-in-practice" approach to the way the school's own administration does business. Consider this: Not only do Michigan students complete semester course evaluations and exit surveys, but just weeks into the fall semester this year, Dean White and the student government hosted an "Innovation Day" planning session. The marathon meeting put more than 900 ideas for new programs and improvements for the school on paper and White had at least a few "quick wins" for his students within a month, using a newly created "innovation endowment" to fund the new initiatives. As one 2000 alum put it: "Almost anything that Michigan students wanted to do, the B-school would back."

However, White's biggest contribution might be instituting the Multidisciplinary Action Project (MAP)—an intense, experiential learning program that has become the cornerstone of a Michigan business education. "A lot of other schools have a lot of elective courses that involve field work," he boasts of the program, now in its ninth year as of 2000–2001. "No other top business school has chosen to involve field work in its core." MAP is unique both for the depth of its integration of different subjects and for its use of real-time, real-world situations and teaching. In this shorter, business version of a medical-school residency—a requirement during the last seven weeks of the first year—students bid to work on projects in an industry that interests them, from financial services to information technology. Then, under the guidance of a cross-functional teaching team of Michigan faculty, groups of about six or seven MBAs work hand-in-hand on special projects with senior corporate managers from such companies as American Express, Boeing, Deloitte & Touche, Dell, Intel, Microsoft, and Oracle. But those aren't the only options available. MBAs with extensive business experience can waive out of MAP in favor of an international version of the course, placing them in the heart of an emerging economy. And starting in spring 2001, MBAs interested in entrepreneurship can get hands-on experience by participating in a new pilot version of the program called E-MAP, where the student teams will collaborate on projects with New Economy start-ups.

Indeed, the wide array of projects allows students to tailor their MAP experience to their interests. MBAs in 2000 consulted with Amazon.com management to improve its vendor relationships, developed a global marketing strategy for Citibank's business-to-business Internet service, and teamed up with senior managers at Tommy Hilfiger and a Web development firm to create a "Club Tommy" section of the tommy.com site as a way of building customer relationships. In fact, reflecting the New Economy, more than half of the projects were e-commerce strategy related. Students consistently rave about the experience, saying the trial-by-fire management exercise provides them with essentially a second internship and an opportunity to apply their skills. "It was a primary reason that Michigan was my first choice," says one recent grad. "It's a great opportunity to practice the skills we've been learning in class, and provides good experience working on teams—working with six other MBAs with no official leader can teach you a lot."

MAP is part of a core curriculum that accounts for a little more than half of the 60 credit hours required to graduate and takes up almost all of the first year's schedule. Students move through their required courses in 6 sections of 70 with each section assigned its own team of professors, which helps make the large aggregate of MBA faces seem a little more familiar. While a few core courses last 14 weeks (financial accounting, applied microeconomics, and marketing management), White has limited most to just 7 weeks in length, forcing professors to pare their material to the essentials. The shorter format also allows greater flexibility for introducing new electives, including those on very specialized topics, to follow the flow of the business world; some 20 percent of the 149 electives offered by the school have turned over in the past three years.

But whatever the course, Michigan MBAs know that it's bound to feature group projects, not unlike a mini-MAP. "I don't think I can remember doing a project by myself," recalls Marc Weiser, a 2000 grad. "I don't think they

exist." To coordinate team activities with busy schedules, students often meet daily at local coffee shops or in the living rooms of classmates' apartments. That type of interaction is one reason that Michigan students give their B-school high marks for its collaborative culture and friendly environment. One 2000 alum quipped that Michigan MBAs are so anticompetitive that it's not uncommon to see job-hungry students relaying interview tips to a classmate who has a later appointment—even if they are seeking the same position.

During the second year, MBAs are required to take courses in either ethics or business law. They also must fulfill a managerial writing requirement if they haven't passed a test to waive out. However, the rest of a second-year's schedule is left open for electives, a vast array of course offerings in more specialized business areas. And for those who haven't had their fill of business skills in their regular classes, several times a semester students can sign up for optional Executive Skills seminars. The daylong courses, held on Fridays, provide exec-ed training for MBAs on workplace topics such as managing diversity and negotiations.

Moreover, students are also able to take classes on relevant topics from the larger university. The school prides itself on its close connection with "Big Blue"—some 20 percent of the faculty have joint appointments with other university departments, and there are 18 joint degree programs in areas from architecture and Chinese studies to law, social work, and music. Two popular interdisciplinary programs are those in corporate environmental management, with the School of Natural Resources and Environment, and manufacturing management, with the engineering school.

Although Michigan has no majors, the school encourages students to pursue a track of courses that revolves around their career goals. For instance, a "fast-track" program in finance front-loads Wall Street wannabees with a quant-heavy curriculum that might provide an edge in securing that important summer internship. On the other hand, MBAs interested in supply chain management want to integrate specific electives in a variety of fields such as operations management, marketing, and entrepreneurship. And given student interest in New Economy start-ups, the school put together two highly popular tracks in e-commerce and entrepreneurship, which more formally assemble a list of suggested courses in those fields.

Moreover, Michigan recently devoted even more faculty and financial resources to the booming area. In 1999, the university established the Samuel Zell and Robert H. Lurie Institute for Entrepreneurial Studies with a $10 million gift from the real estate moguls, who, interestingly enough, built their fortunes from an Ann Arbor property rental business they ran as Michigan undergraduates. The Zell-Lurie Institute, headed by senior marketing professor Tom Kinnear—a successful entrepreneur himself who has served as adviser, investor, and board member for numerous start-ups—now oversees an "e-lab" business incubator. He recently revamped the B-school's entrepreneurship offerings—more than half of the Class of 2000 enrolled in at least one class.

Now, like the rest of the Michigan curriculum, entrepreneurship courses also link theory with Michigan's trademark on-the-ground experience. Take, for instance, the entrepreneurship elective "Idea to IPO in 14 Weeks," a semester-long course taught by assistant finance professor Joshua Coval. The seminar takes about 50 students through the steps of launching a dot-com, from writing the initial business plan to getting venture capital. Working in teams, the students consult other faculty members to develop their business concept and then have the opportunity to pitch their refined ideas to real VCs. Not only did the MBAs walk away with an appreciation for what it takes to succeed, a few student groups receive funding.

But Michigan MBAs also have the opportunity to sit at the other side of the VC table. In 1997, the school put up $250,000 to launch the Wolverine Venture Fund, in which a student committee joins a volunteer advisory board of venture capitalists, business leaders, and faculty members to identify and invest in promising start-ups. "Nothing can teach our students risk-taking better than sizing up a venture and then watching the results," explains White. They must be learning something: Over the past few years, a number of donations and even a few investment returns have propelled the fund to more than $3 million.

However, one of Michigan's most distinguishing features is the large menu of international business opportunities open to students. Paradoxically, many say they come to Ann Arbor in order to see the world. "We aim for a more substantive global experience for students—actually working in companies around the world, not just taking study tours," explains White. Through the 14-week Global Project Course elective, teams of five or six students work for multinationals such as AT&T, Lucent Technologies, and Motorola, or start-ups in Southeast Asia, Japan, China, Western Europe, and South America, and spend spring break on site at various overseas locations central to the work at hand. Recent groups of 2000 grads did a consumer behavior and product study for Procter & Gamble in Russia, traveled to Israel to set up an equity fund so that businesses in the West Bank and the Gaza Strip could have access to capital, and developed new business models for Dow Chemical in Argentina and Brazil. During any given spring, as many as half the second-year students may be outside the United States for part of the term working with pharmaceutical companies, automotive manufacturers, or indigenous firms in Thailand, the Czech Republic, China, Brazil, or Indonesia. (Many of the 250 or so first-year students who waive out of MAP each year even opt to complete two global projects, one in their first year and another in their second.)

The global options extend into the summer, when Michigan's William Davidson Institute, one of the world's foremost research organizations on emerging economies, offers paid internships for MBAs to spend three months working on what amount to advanced MAP projects in Central and Eastern Europe and Asia. For pharmaceutical giant Eli Lilly, an MBA intern team in 2000 traveled to Albania, Bulgaria, Hungary, and Romania to make recommendations for restructuring the company's organizational chart to improve its effectiveness in Central and Eastern Europe. In Argentina, another group of interns developed a merger-and-acquisitions strategy in the beer market for the country's largest beverage maker. In Brazil, a Michigan team did a market analysis for BCP, the country's second largest cellular operator, which was looking to enter a new higher-margin market space. Another group worked for a domestic bank in Ghana on introducing smart cards to a country where hyperinflation literally caused farmers to carry bushels of cash when selling their goods. Ninety to 100 students vie for the 40 to 50 spots available each year, with a few even opting to stay the summer after graduation to take advantage of the opportunity. The school's Center for International Business Education even provides financial support for living expenses and intensive preparation in 48 different languages as an additional lure. Don't want to give up your summer? During fall of your second year, you could sign up for one of the 15-credit, semester-long exchange programs offered at business schools in 14 locations around the world, from Austria to Singapore.

Michigan's international outreach is really part of a larger philosophy that aims to get B-school students out of the classroom. The push starts as soon as you show up for the Leadership Development Program, a weeklong orientation before classes begin. For a day, you and your 430 or so classmates will be shipped off to Detroit or the high-unemployment city of Benton Harbor to work alongside executives who have volunteered to roll up their sleeves and take a paintbrush to the walls and a broom to the floors of homeless shelters and job retraining centers. The week culminates with a lab that assesses your strengths and weaknesses as a manager. Throughout your Michigan career, you'll be encouraged to sign up for seminars in executive skills such as providing transformational leadership, managing workforce diversity, and balancing work and family. Although these activities are derided by some as superficial, White says he hopes he's planting seeds of social consciousness and sensitivity that Michigan grads will carry with them into the workforce.

To further that goal, White has publicly declared that he wants to make Michigan the business school of choice for women. That's why, in 1998, the school, along with the University's Center for the Education of Women and Catalyst, a New York–based organization whose research supports the advancement of women in business, embarked on a study, dubbed the Women's Initiative, to identify ways to make business school female-friendly. With major findings now in, the study will move into what White calls phase two: action based on insight. He'll meet with the leaders of 10 other top B-schools, including Wharton, Stanford, and MIT, and the CEOs of more than a dozen major corporations, including Citibank, Deloitte & Touche, and Procter & Gamble to work on combating the perception that business school is for the boys.

It's not surprising that the fruits of these efforts are already visible on the Ann Arbor campus. Although Michigan is still not split along gender lines 50/50, females do account for more than 27 percent of the Class of 2000—not as high as some schools, but respectable. In addition, White recently hired two women for key administrative positions: Assistant Dean Jeanne Wilt, in charge of admissions, student services, and career development, and Susan Ashford, associate dean for academic affairs. And he's had ongoing conversations with the Michigan Business Women Club's "here-and-now" committee to identify issues that enhanced or detracted from their student experiences.

The Women's Initiative mirrors a push to enroll minority students undertaken by Michigan during the early 1980s. As a result, the B-school's enrollment of African-American, Hispanic, and Native American students for the class entering in 2000 reached 11 percent. The Black Business Students Association and Hispanic Business Students Association together boast nearly 200 members, and *The Journal of Blacks in Higher Education* has deemed Michigan the best B-school for blacks. Both groups, as well as the international students who make up another 32 percent of the class, thrive on the open support they get from the entire student body.

Many of the school's extracurricular activities tend to have a socially conscious bent. Following orientation week, a number of students choose to join the Michigan Business Assistance Domestic Corps to perform optional yearlong consulting projects for nonprofit groups, whether it be developing a business plan for a United Way branch or helping tribal leaders create culturally appropriate enterprises for the Navajo Nation. A handful of students each year spend a summer month before or during their internships in Washington, learning about business and public policy. The school boasts one of the largest and most active chapters of Students for Responsible Business, which promotes corporate leadership in social and environmental issues.

None of the current activities your cup of tea? Then start your own—a student in the fall of 1999 launched the UMBS Women's Ice Hockey team, with funding from the Dean's office and the full support of the B-school behind them. Although about 90 percent of the team had never played hockey before and quite a few didn't know how to skate, by the end of the season, they were taking to the ice like semi-pros. Other students get involved with activities like case competitions and the annual MBA Olympics, in which student sections compete against one another in athletic contests. Still others organized a food drive that brought in $25,000 for charity.

But Michigan students also know how to have fun. The B-school gets high marks for lifestyle; Michigan doesn't hold classes on Fridays, so weekends start Thursday nights by sampling the six house-label beers at Grizzly Peak Brewing Co. or wolfing down pizza at Dominick's. Ann Arbor's charming downtown, which lays claim to more bookstores per capita than anywhere in the entire country, is chock full of entertainment options. Besides browsing along blocks lined with quaint boutiques and eclectic thrift shops, students often share a cup of coffee at local cafés and mingle at local bars and restaurants, which offer everything from Italian and Chinese to Mongolian and down-home barbecue. The town—and the B-school—goes a little nuts over the famed Wolverines sports teams, especially during home football and hockey games. Indeed, a favorite recruiting event is a company sponsored tailgate party outside Michigan Stadium.

Families are made more than welcome through the efforts of the SOS (Significant Others and Spouse) club, whose Baby MBA play group is a hit with B-schoolers who have small children. The only lifestyle-related complaints: the bitter cold winters, which can seem to go on forever; the housing crunch, which makes apartments hard to come by and nearly as expensive as in a bigger city; and the parking, which is virtually nonexistent on football weekends.

Although the school is experimenting with a number of high-tech initiatives—such as a new e-commerce course that uses videoconferencing and Internet technology to link Michigan MBAs with peers at Berkeley and the University of Virginia—overall, students say the school could do a better job integrating technology into the classroom. Still, with new consortium programs in the works and more than $6.8

million directed toward in-house technology upgrades and improvements, the situation is improving. Although not required, most Michigan MBAs now carry a laptop computer to class, taking advantage of a new wireless network that allows them to connect to the Internet from anywhere in the B-school complex. That has helped alleviate previous student complaints of long waits and often filled-to-capacity computer lab terminals, caused by the scarcity of outlets and modems in the older buildings. And with additional computer labs in nearby Sam Wyly Hall, a recently constructed $18 million executive education and residency complex, computer access should be less of a concern.

PLACEMENT DETAILS

While Michigan may not have the same name recognition as top East and West Coast schools among corporate recruiters from Wall Street or Silicon Valley, graduates from Ann Arbor are doing quite well for themselves. Michigan's 2000 median starting pay package of $131,000 ranks respectably with other B-schools—up considerably from a few years ago. Over 65 percent of Michigan students these days are entering into higher-paying careers in consulting and investment banking instead of the relatively lower-paying marketing and product management fields that used to draw the most Michigan grads. Another reason for the improved median starting salary is enterprising students and a responsive administration. A student-initiated Wall Street Forum held in New York for those focused on investment banking and mergers and acquisitions and, for the past five years, a similar dean-sponsored West Coast Forum held in California for those interested in high-tech careers have been pulling together alumni in those regions who can network with student job seekers and attracting a number of other firms which ordinarily wouldn't recruit in Ann Arbor. The results seem to be paying off: More than 15

percent of Michigan grads are heading west; that's up from 5 percent a few years ago.

Top hirers from among the 234 companies who conducted more than 5000 interviews on campus in 2000: McKinsey & Company (23), A.T. Kearney (14), Dell Computer Corp. (10), American Express (9), Diamond Technology Partners (9), Ford (9), and Chase Manhattan (8). And almost 2000 jobs also were posted electronically. Michigan grads walked away with an average of 3.3 job offers. Keep in mind that although Michigan is a public university, you'll be paying private-school-sized tuition, particularly if you're coming from out of state—so you may need that private-school-sized salary to pay off your post-MBA debt.

OUTSTANDING FACULTY

Richard Sloan (accounting); *Alan Afuah* (corporate strategy); *C. K. Prahalad* (corporate strategy); *Thomas Kinnear* (entrepreneurship/marketing); *M. P. Narayanan* (finance); *William Lovejoy* (operations); *Andy Andrews* (statistics).

APPLICANT TIPS

Most B-schools say they look for smart, well-rounded students. But at Michigan, the admissions committee has added a new wrinkle to the application game: They're looking for results-producing leaders who demonstrate "successful intelligence," a fiery mix of school and street smarts that make a person effective. In fact, the essay questions have recently been tweaked so that they now ask candidates to demonstrate their creativity and behavior rather than simply regurgitate a résumé. Those accepted usually boast a strong academic record, but also have a history of professional and personal achievements, solid interpersonal skills, community participation, and focus in their career goals. Although interviews are not mandatory, nearly

100 percent of admitted applicants in 2000 were interviewed. So it's a good idea to try to arrange to speak with someone on campus, at an MBA Forum, with an alum, or over the telephone. The admissions office is also looking for applicants who have done their homework and can show that they're specifically interested in the Michigan programs.

It's also wise to apply early if you can. If you get your application in by the November 1 early decision deadline, you'll get an answer by January 31. Applications can be downloaded from the school Web site as a Microsoft Word document, then filled out and submitted electronically in the same form. If you do get in, the admissions office will actually phone you with the good news—a personal touch that foreshadows the friendly, helpful environment you'll find if you take up their invitation.

Contact: Jeanne Wilt
Assistant Dean for Admissions and Career Development
313-763-5796
Application deadlines: November 1; January 15; March 1

MICHIGAN MBAs SOUND OFF

As one of my friends says, "What I love about Michigan is that we have some streetfighter in us." Amen. Michigan's students' and faculty's aggressive innovation continue to inspire and motivate everyone in our community. We dream up innovative ideas together and we make them happen—we do, we don't talk. And the deans fuel this fire—if someone thinks of a good idea, the deans say, "Do it!—and ask questions later!"

I feel strongly that Michigan's strengths are in the most high-impact areas: recruiting, teaching, and a diverse, team-oriented, and highly accomplished student body. So, overall I've been very satisfied with my experience here. My criticisms about the program are that it is notably weak in some less impactful areas: facilities and technology. Compared with other top-tier business schools, Michigan is lagging in these areas. Even though landscaping, building design, a dated student lounge, and a poorly organized computer lab (long, long lines) have not influenced the quality of the education and recruiting, they have added some frustrations that should be remedied.

The MAP project, though at times frustrating, was a very valuable learning experience. Working on real problems for real companies was a nice change from the classroom. Also, a student essentially comes away with two summer internships. I came to Michigan with seven years of experience in dental insurance as an actuary. In 20 months I added an MBA, a project with a Dow 30 diversified manufacturer, and an internship with a Dow 30 technology company.

UMBS is committed to developing strong leaders. The administration is happy to provide financial and other support to student-led initiatives. In fact the Dean believes in the presumption of yes. For instance, one student championed the creation of a women's club ice hockey team at UMBS. She generated interest among members of the business school community, organized team activities, and obtained funding from the Dean's office and other sources. Suffice it to say we had a great inaugural season of the UMBS Women's Ice Hockey Team with the full support of the school behind us. About 90 percent of the team members had never played hockey before and quite a few did not even know how to skate. This experience furthered our team skills, strengthened our friendships, and challenged us to be adventurous and unconventional. All things that will help us succeed in business.

Michigan has an excellent program and I would put it up against any other school's program. The only place that it is a little lacking is technology integration—laptops should be required and full classroom technology integration should be implemented.

One of the best things about Michigan is that the people here are not arrogant and/or conceited. There is a team quality. They are down-to-earth people who are able to get things done. The program here is excellent and the next best thing about Michigan is how responsive the school is to the students. When I got here, there weren't any e-business courses . . . since I've been here they've added at least 10. Students are empowered to a level that I've never seen anywhere.

7.
COLUMBIA UNIVERSITY

Contact:
Linda Meehan
Assistant Dean and
Executive Director of
Admissions and
Financial Aid
212-854-1961
Application deadlines:
Domestic—
October 1 (Spring)
April 20
International—
March 1 (Fall)

COLUMBIA UNIVERSITY

Graduate School of Business
216 Uris Hall
New York, New York 10027
E-mail address: apply@claven.gsb.columbia.edu
Web site address: http://www.gsb.columbia.edu

Corporate ranking: 5	Graduate ranking: 17
Enrollment: 1155	Annual tuition & fees: $30,548
Women: 37%	Room and board: N/A
Non-U.S.: 27%	Average GMAT score: 704
Minority: 12%	Average years of work exp.: 4
Part-time: 0	Accepted applicants enrolled: 69%
Average age: 27	Intellectual capital: 6
Applicants accepted: 12%	
Median starting pay: $142,500	

Teaching methods: Lecture, 40%   Case study, 40%
Group projects, 20%

When the chairman and CEO of Chase Manhattan Corporation, Bill Harrison, drops by to give a lecture (just after the bank's high-profile merger with J.P. Morgan, no less) you've got to expect a full house and rapt attention, especially where business types are concerned. Recently, the chairman's appearance at the Columbia Business School drew just such attention. There were, however, a few empty seats—much to the surprise of the school's charismatic dean of nearly 12 years, Meyer Feldberg, who had arranged the event.

The reason? The only conceivable one: competition from across the hall. Famed assets manager Mario Gabelli was speaking to Professor Bruce Greenwald's Value and Investing class. Win-win situations like these are more than familiar to students at Columbia, which regularly holds events and hosts an astounding assortment of leaders, from J.P. Morgan's Sandy Warner and Starbucks' chairman Howard Schultz to Martha Stewart and King Abdullah of Jordan. In fact, the school's overstuffed calendar reads like an activities board at a dream resort for business execs—seamlessly tying together, for example, a private equity conference, a lecture by Benjamin Netanyahu, and "Cigar School" at Club Macanudo, all in the course of a week.

It's one of the reasons prospective students are targeting Columbia in droves. Not bad for a once-faltering B-school that climbed the ranks from No. 14 in 1988 to No. 6 in 1998, and now holds fast to its No. 7 ranking. Over the past eight years applications surged 96 percent, and since 1996, the school has admitted just 12 percent of those applicants, compared with a full 47 percent in 1992.

They come for the distinguished contacts, but also for a program rich with top-notch academic offerings from many of the 121 full-time faculty members and 81 adjuncts who have made their mark in the Big Apple's business core. The school's 78-member Board of Overseers alone boasts such accomplished leaders as former White House Chief of Staff Erskine Bowles, Ogilvy & Mather Worldwide Chairman and CEO Shelly Lazarus, and Goldman Sachs International Managing Director Jean Luc Biamonti, all of whom at some point received their MBAs from Columbia. An Executive Leadership series—established in 1977 and still popular for its mentor-like approach—is team-taught by Dean Feldberg and executives-in-residence, corporate principals who are retired or have time to spare for would-be apprentices. The execs draw on their experiences and explore with students the idea of leadership, especially the differences between managing and leading. In 1999, McKinsey & Co. and the school introduced a new course, Management Consulting Roles and Relationships, to provide students with sample projects and mentoring from actual consultants. And, with Columbia's campus planted firmly in a sea of mega-corporations, students have ample opportunities to visit corporate giants like General Motors, Estee Lauder, and Pfizer through a first-term Operations Management core course. The possibilities, like the array of on-campus speakers and visitors, are seemingly endless. "You just wouldn't get these kinds of dignitaries, CEOs, and opportunities anywhere else," insists 2000 grad Loretta Cranbourne.

Since 1999, arriving students have also been pleased to find a new $42 million Business/Law Building that has added classrooms and study and event space to the existing areas in Uris Hall—the school's main building. The latter has been undergoing renovations during the past few summers, but students still don't consider it up to par with facilities at peer schools. "Recruiters understand that we're an urban school," counters one Columbia administrator, "and that we work with what we have." What they do have is resources. On any given day, you can find students in classrooms with snazzy features like high-resolution video document cameras, dual LCD projectors, and videoconferencing capabilities. All the media in classrooms can be coordinated through a media center to simulcast to other rooms, for example. Finance students, in particular, frequent the "virtual" financial markets laboratory, where they use data programs like BridgeFeed and Nexis to keep up with industry movements. You can find them in their apartments doing the same thing—these programs can also be accessed through their own notebook computers (a requirement for all MBAs here).

Traditionally, the school has adhered to a global emphasis and, as Feldberg terms it, a "heterogeneous" environment. The Class of 2002 comprises 37 percent women and 12 percent underrepresented minorities, many of whom have taken leadership roles within the B-school community as editors for the school paper, heads of student government, and the like. Feldberg is looking to boost those numbers higher. Twenty-seven percent of the students are from abroad, hailing from 60 countries, and more than half are fluent in languages other than English. Feldberg says he and the admissions team—like those at many other schools—make diversity a deliberate goal, with the intention of mirroring today's international business environment. This way, grads can feel comfortable taking a job or working with clients in any part of the world. "Our students tend to end up in any number of cities, usually ones that are money centers," says Feldberg. "They are 'global entrepreneurs.'"

When classes begin, these students with varying backgrounds—from ballerinas to ex-military officers to finance whizzes—ethnicities, and professional interests form assigned groups of 60, as part of a "cluster" system Feldberg implemented eight years ago. The clusters go through core courses together throughout the two terms of their first year, and are further divided into project groups of six to work on team assignments. The program is designed to leave students' competitive edges intact but also encourage collaboration; the teams, therefore, help to mitigate the effects of a strict grading curve that could otherwise deter students advanced in some areas from bringing others up to speed. Columbia students are not quite as cutthroat as this grading system, and their reputation, once led others to believe. "It was not nearly as competitive as I thought it would be, especially once we finished the first semester," Sharon Nevins, a recent graduate, concurs. Feldberg calls the school's environment "collaborative-competitive," and according to recruiters, who ranked Columbia fifth, the system appears to work.

Known as a "feeder" school to Wall Street, with about half its graduates landing jobs in finance each year, Columbia has shown consistent strength in this field. About 35 percent of applicants indicate an interest in finance on their application. And while recruiters consider Columbia students' skills among the top 10 in the areas of general management, marketing, and global competitiveness—as well as finance—some students complain that, without a finance background, you're at somewhat of a disadvantage. "The program just isn't designed for you," one student warns. "Finance and consulting types definitely dominate."

For students who are not mathematically proficient or up to date on the latest software packages, the school offers pre-term, noncredit courses in these subjects—otherwise known as math and computer camp—most of which are offered online. All students can attend seminars on presentation skills, team building, and writing proficiency in year one. And, with 13 areas of concentration and a choice of electives now numbering 160, plus nearly 90 on-campus clubs

and organizations in a range of fields, non-numbers types find more than enough areas to explore. In recent years, students have picked up more courses with a creative angle, like Professor John Whitney's In Search of the Perfect Prince, an exploration of leadership issues through the plays of William Shakespeare. Not surprisingly, students are also drawn to courses that address emerging industries like e-business—for instance, a class from Adam Dell (brother of Michael) called The Internet Economy, Venture Capital, and the Entrepreneurial Process: What It Takes to Win on the Net and Why.

The 13 required first-year core courses and half-courses—in such broad areas as economics, corporate finance, management, marketing, and accounting—draw praise for their overviews. But students' comments on teaching quality vary. "It was either very good or awful," admits one recent grad. "I had no average professors in any of those classes." Feldberg and his staff are trying to combat this sentiment by encouraging new Ph.D. professors to first observe an entire term of a class before starting up their own. Seven to 12 new faculty members have been hired each year for the past five years in all five of the school's divisions—Finance and Economics, Accounting, Management, Management Science, and Marketing—plus the Entrepreneurship and Real Estate programs. The aggressive hiring will continue, but student body numbers are expected to remain the same.

One aspect that won't soon change is the program's flexibility. You can exempt yourself from core courses by exam, and although you have to replace them with electives, you don't have to stick with the same subject areas. (All courses are obtained through a bidding system, where points are used to indicate preferred classes.) Students are encouraged to take advantage of the Ivy League quality of the larger university through any of 14 dual-degree programs, including architecture, engineering, international affairs, journalism, law, nursing, public health, social work, education, and the newest additions: Physicians and Surgeons (MBA/M.D.) and Dental (MBA/DDS). Even if you don't opt for a joint degree, you can take up to two courses in some of these other schools. Or, go beyond the university's immediate reach, as about 30 students do each year, by participating in one of 22 exchange programs offered in 20 different places, including Argentina, Brazil, West and South Africa, Central and Eastern Europe, China, India, and Japan.

The most recent batches of students are pleased to find increased offerings and updated facilities in some of the newer fields like entrepreneurship and technology. In late 2000, the school was given $6 million to open the Eugene M. Lang Center for Entrepreneurship, an extension of Columbia's effort to work with students aiming to launch new ventures. With the Lang Center as a focal point for entrepreneurship, the school has integrated the subject into five core courses: Financial Accounting, Marketing, Finance, Decision Models, and the Global Economic Environment. Electives like Managing the Value of Internet Firms and Technical Innovation venture into more specific areas. Selected students with business plans can gain funding for prelaunch expenses, access to experts in the field, and opportunities to present their concepts to investors through the Entrepreneurship Greenhouse Program, which acts as a lab and incubator. Last year, nearly half of the 19 plans created in the program were launched as businesses by graduation, and some are still on their way. Additionally, students can apply for funding from the Lang Fund, which invests selectively in student businesses in the amounts of $50,000 to $250,000. A key factor in the Lang Fund's success is its extensive mentoring process, which helps students develop high-quality business proposals. Students are matched with experienced, industry-appropriate financiers and other professionals who provide guidance and help shape the business concept and financial model.

Still, amid this new affection for emerging industries, traditional corporate recruiters remain a strength for Columbia. Of the nearly 600 firms that recruited on campus in 2000, the majority were companies in the investment banking and consulting fields. Career Services Director Regina Resnick notes that lately she's seen more and more students combining a range of interests by seeking employment with a traditional company that allows them to specialize in a newer area like media and entertainment or high-tech.

Students who don't go for the old standbys can reach out to smaller or more nontraditional recruiters through the school's Media, Entertainment, and Communications Program or high-tech offerings. On an annual trip with Dean Feldberg to Silicon Valley, more than 100 students meet on-site with recruiters from companies there. The school's Institute for Tele-Information, a research center, offers studies and information on strategy, management, and policy issues in telecommunications, computing, and mass media. And active student organizations like the Media Management Association, Internet Business Group, and High Tech Club provide networking opportunities, speaker series, and alumni events. All three clubs present one of the school's most successful on-campus conferences, Silicon Alley Uptown, which brings students face to face with venture capitalists and leaders in the new media field. Additionally, Media Networking, an annual media job fair, has counted more than 200 students and 40 recruiters (from such companies as MTV and Viacom) among its participants. And there's something for those interested in international business: Since 1996, study tours of about 25 students led by faculty members have visited corporations, factories, and cultural sites and met with company managers, government officials, and entrepreneurs at such far-reaching locations as Argentina, Brazil, West and South Africa, China, India, and Japan. Columbia is continuously pushing to improve opportunities for job recruitment outside the United States by hosting an annual conference with 95 participants from 63 schools from around the world to discuss issues in hiring.

Also available to students is the school's real estate program, which uses new case-study materials developed annually by industry professionals working in real estate finance and investment management in New York, a city undergoing constant development and redevelopment of its gold-standard square footage. Eleven new cases made their way into the curriculum last year. "The school is unsurpassed in its preparation of students for careers in real estate, whether it be in finance, development, asset management, or investment management," says Steven Shores, a recent grad now working in Denver. "The faculty is supported by a strong advisory board of leaders in the real estate industry, and the real estate alumni network is one of the strongest professional networks at the school." The school's nonprofit management program, too, continues to sustain itself with the help of $15,000 grants each year for one or more graduates working in that lower-paying business sector who are weighed down by student loans.

Global education has much to do with the Jerome A. Chazen Institute of International Business, where the school's exchange programs, research efforts, and international government and business outreach take place. For a fee of $300, students can take eight weeks of intensive three-hour classes in any of 12 languages here. Additionally, the school recently garnered press attention with the announcement of a new Executive MBA–Global MBA program in which students take courses at both CBS and the London Business School, earning degrees from both. All graduates have the chance to participate in the annual Pan-European Alumni Reunion, which has been known to draw more than 500 alumni from 25 or more countries for lectures and events, including a symposium on Technology and Business.

Alumni can play a large part in students' job search efforts, especially for those in New York, as more than half the graduates in each class remain in the Manhattan area. For all, an extensive alumni database managed by the career services office keeps track of more than 26,000 grads who can easily be accessed online, pinpointed by field or location. Career counselors are a good resource for students looking into smaller or lesser known companies that haven't traditionally recruited Columbia MBAs.

Fridays are reserved for study sessions, work on group projects, or interviews, as no classes are scheduled. Taking the time to travel is an option, and some say the school can take on a commuter feel once in a while, while others report that on-campus activities are well attended. Among the biggest and the best is the annual spring ball, held each year at a creative or ritzy location, such as the New York Public Library or Tavern on the Green in Central Park. Although some students do cite a lack of unity, or at least the feeling that social events take on more of a networking feel, true bonding opportunities are there for those who want them, Dean Feldberg insists. "My impression is that students live in this building," he says of Uris Hall. "If the school could have 10 percent of the money from pizza deliveries that come here after 8 p.m., we could all retire."

Students also regularly venture off campus to experience the array of cultural offerings, from Broadway productions and world-class museums to opera, ballet, and a bounty of fine restaurants (students loans allowing). "Don't discount the fun factor!" one recent grad implores. For housing, admitted applicants can apply to live on campus, and about 60 percent of those who apply receive it (preference goes to students coming from furthest away). But most MBAs live on the Upper West Side, where lively bars and restaurants pepper the neighborhood streets—and the obscene rental figures often reflect that. In any case, following happy hour in the Uris Deli on Thursdays, students head out to any number of neighborhoods, from the Village or Little Italy to the ultratrendy meatpacking district. There's much to see and do, but the urban locale isn't for every personality type. Warns Dean Feldberg: "If you're meek or tentative, even if you're very smart, this is just not the place for you. You have to have a strong sense of competition. Just crossing the street here, at 116th and Broadway, is a competitive event."

PLACEMENT DETAILS

It's clear that Columbia's Manhattan location gives the school an edge in recruitment performance. This year, a whopping 589 companies came to campus to recruit second-year students, who raked in a median pay of $142,500 and landed an average of 3.1 job offers. Not surprisingly, the majority of students land in investment banking or consulting, at 38 percent and 22 percent, respectively. The biggies: Goldman Sachs (46), Morgan Stanley Dean Witter (27), McKinsey & Co. (24), Lehman Brothers (20), American Express (18), Citigroup/Salomon Smith Barney (18), Booz-Allen & Hamilton (16), J.P. Morgan (16), and Merrill Lynch (16).

But interest in entrepreneurship and emerging fields like e-business is on the rise, and the school has made efforts to address this trend. A newly hired Manager of Outreach Services encourages companies that may not traditionally hire MBAs, like media and entertainment corporations, to come to campus to interview students or at least to submit job postings. Nearly 4000 listings have been posted electronically, and the school's new BANC system, an online database of alumni contacts that launched two years ago, now contains information on approximately 26,000 MBA graduates. Students also find networking opportunities in career fairs, trips with Dean Feldberg to companies in Silicon Valley and other high-tech hotspots, and the school's numerous formal and informal events with prominent business and government leaders.

Much of the job search process has taken the form of preparation, with a noncredit career services course, a mentor society, specialized workshops on etiquette or business attire, and a career discussion series among the offerings. The career placement office has grown especially strong in dealing with international issues, a result of the large percentage of students with varying citizenship status. "The international counselor was tremendous," one Filipino student recalls. "She was knowledgeable, caring, and very concerned—still to this day she remembers my situation and uses it to advise others."

No aspect of the job search process is more weighty than Columbia's ongoing close ties to accomplished professionals who happen to find the B-school's students among the best and the brightest. Keeping up these relationships is a priority for Dean Feldberg, and he does so in many ways, including a "Take a Student to Lunch Program" and by hosting nearly a dozen cocktail parties for students, alums, and members of the Board of Overseers each year. Moreover, in the summer, Feldberg makes personal visits to 35–40 recruiting companies to discuss their needs and how well Columbia grads fill them.

OUTSTANDING FACULTY

Deen Kemsley (accounting); *David Beim* (economics/finance); *Bruce Greenwald* (economics/finance); *Laurie Simon Hodrick* (economics/finance); *Michael Mauboussin* (economics/finance); *Michael Feiner* (management); *Sunil Gupta* (marketing).

APPLICANT TIPS

Columbia offers fewer than 500 spots for a class that begins in September and nearly 200 for the

January class, which usually attracts students who have significant work experience and aren't in need of a summer internship. Admissions are rolling for both, so getting your application in early helps your chances. If you want to apply for January admittance, you must turn in an application by October 1. For a September start, you have until April 20 (March 1 for non-U.S. residents).

The admissions staff says it looks for "leadership, bright applicants, interesting people, and commitment to something—a club they started, for instance." College students or applicants just one or two years out of school who have had significant leadership or entrepreneurial experience are also encouraged to apply. For the all-important essay questions, you should demonstrate the strengths and skills you've shown at a current job and indicate how those skills will help you achieve your goals after business school. "Sometimes there's no direct tie between the careers, but you have to market yourself to show some focus, initiative, and possibly a desire to give back to the community," says Director Linda Meehan, adding, "A sense of humor works sometimes, but only if it's natural, not forced."

About 90 percent of applicants are interviewed by invitation only after an application has been submitted. Interviews are conducted either by the admissions committee; a volunteer from the B-school's alumni network, which encompasses 150 cities and 48 countries worldwide; or by current students. Applicants are welcome to visit classes Monday through Thursday. Students who are wait-listed should take the opportunity to clarify anything vague in their application or submit more materials to support their presentation, but the school no longer offers feedback on applications that have been denied. You can download the application from the school's Web site, and you are encouraged to submit your completed application electronically.

Contact: Linda Meehan
Assistant Dean and Executive Director of Admissions and Financial Aid
212-854-1961
Application deadlines: Domestic—October 1 (Spring), April 20; International—March 1 (Fall)

COLUMBIA MBAs SOUND OFF

I would recommend Columbia to anyone who is serious about working in finance in New York. There really is no better place for access to companies and adjunct professors. Moreover, buyside and sellside research departments interview more here than at any other school. They're in the neighborhood, so they have no excuse not to.

The school's location in New York City gives it unrivaled access to business leaders. Most of these leaders, whether or not they're Columbia alumni, give graciously of their time to students, in the classroom or as professional mentors.

There is always a multitude of fantastic events to attend at CBS. The facilities are improving, yet there will always be limitations to the quality of life at a city school. The program would still benefit from more group study space, more student housing, and food service that's not inundated with undergrads! The biggest problem, though, is the broad range of quality among professors. Some are brilliant, current, dedicated, and good communicators. Most of the others are still brilliant and current, but too often fail to be dedicated and able communicators.

I made some great friends here. While everyone works hard, there was never a feeling of competition among students. We tutored each other, traded interview slots, and collaborated on just about everything. We even compared salary packages.

I chose to come here because Columbia has the best commitment to promoting women in business of all of the top business schools. Women are a powerful force here on campus, and I can't imagine having settled for something less than this at any other school. My mother graduated from Columbia Business School in 1965—there was only one other woman in her class.

The dean was simply amazing. Coming from the French education system, I was very impressed with the ability of Columbia's administration to solve problems. I already miss it.

Wonderful administration, excellent teachers, and, most important, fantastic classmates. My experience has been unbelievably valuable. It was also tremendously fun. The bonus: my salary has tripled.

8.
CORNELL UNIVERSITY

Contact:
Natalie Grinblatt
Director of Admissions
800-847-2082
Application deadlines:
November 15
January 15
March 15

CORNELL UNIVERSITY

Johnson Graduate School of Management
Sage Hall
Ithaca, New York 14853-6201
E-mail address: mba@johnson.cornell.edu
Web site address: http://www.johnson.cornell.edu

Corporate ranking: 10	Graduate ranking: 8
Enrollment: 568	Annual tuition & fees: $27,600
Women: 27%	Room and board: $7650
Non-U.S.: 30%	Average GMAT score: 673
Minority: 5%	Average years of work exp.: 4.8
Part-time: 0	Accepted applicants enrolled: 52%
Average age: 29	Intellectual capital: 4
Applicants accepted: 25%	
Median starting pay: $135,000	

Teaching methods: Lecture, 25%   Case study, 40%
                    Discussion, projects, 35%

Looking for strong academics? A spirited and supportive group of classmates? More accessibility to professors than you could ever take advantage of?

Spending two winters in sometimes-dreary upstate New York is a small price to pay for such indulgences—especially when you're talking about the Cornell campus, which really isn't so dreary, and the Johnson School of Management, one of the hottest tickets on the MBA scene. Cornell, a top 5 B-school when BUSINESSWEEK's first rankings were published in 1988, slipped over the next decade, reaching a low of 18th in 1996. Back then, students criticized both the placement office and technology as inadequate. Recruiters were not overly impressed. But what a difference a few years of hard work and effort can make. Recruiters now rate Cornell's placement office one of the top five. And a 1998 curriculum overhaul and the introduction of newer facilities on a grand scale have given Johnson students a new outlook, better academics, and upgraded services—with the resulting positive, forward-thinking environment serving as one of the school's chief selling points.

This is the program where, after all, you could be one of 30 students to get a free ride. Park Leadership Fellows—selected for having demonstrated exceptional leadership qualities, professional achievement, academic accomplishment, community service, and the drive to excel—are granted a full two-year scholarship with a stipend. In return, each is expected to work on a project that leaves something behind for the business school, Cornell University, or the Ithaca community. In 2000, as part of their project, former commercial investments manager Alexander Ivanov and ex-lawyer John Kyles left behind the first entirely student-run venture capital fund, now known as the Big Red Venture Capital Fund. A testament to its solely educational purposes is the fact that funds come from donations, not investments. The Fund currently serves as an incubator for student-conceived businesses, and what it was intended to be—a simple proposal—flourished in the supportive Cornell community with the help of administrators, professors, and alumni until it had become a full-fledged operation. Even before any capital had been raised, MBA interest was high; nearly 40 student-created proposals were submitted. But the greatest show of support came at graduation time, when the Class of 2000 presented their gift to the school: a $200,000 donation to the fund, which is now in the process of reviewing more than 70 plans.

The fund illustrates some of the Johnson School's best-loved features: a student-oriented system, a learning-by-doing emphasis, and a highly collaborative atmosphere. There's no question that the Park Leadership Fellows program is hugely popular. An average of 300 applicants each year vie for a chance to have specialized leadership training and rub shoulders with CEOs like Priceline.com founder and vice chairman Jay Walker and Motorola chairman Robert Galvin. But the school's focus on leadership and practical experience extends to the entire B-school student body. "We're like a laboratory," says Dean Robert J. Swieringa, a longtime Cornell professor who arrived back on campus in July 1997 after spending a decade as a member of the Financial Accounting Standards Board.

One important highlight is Cornell's "immersion learning" semester, in which approximately two-thirds of the B-school's population participate each year. Students take advanced courses in one of five disciplines—

Investment Banking, Manufacturing, Managerial Finance, Brand Management or, as of 2001, e-Business—and they have a chance to visit related work sites, meet with prospective employers in the field, and learn from among the best practitioners. All this, mind you, months before beginning their all-important summer internships. "It gives you confidence in analyzing business problems and presenting solutions," says Jeffrey Zivan, a 2000 grad who followed up his brand management immersion with a summer internship at McNeil Consumer Health Care (Johnson & Johnson). "Looking over cases, presenting to the class, and having your professor try to poke holes in your analysis helps you learn to ask yourself the right questions first, so you're prepared when your boss asks them."

By spring 2001, students should be better prepared to tackle the ever-changing e-business sector, thanks to a $1 million grant from Corning Inc. (The company helped launch Cornell's first semester in manufacturing in 1994.) Professors from both the Johnson School and Cornell's Computing and Information Science program will lead students in learning to execute e-business applications and work with strategies for different industries. Topics like one-to-one marketing and supply chain disintermediation in e-tailing first made their way into courses when, two years ago, the Class of 2000 wondered if they were "missing out on the whole e-business revolution." They don't wonder anymore, especially with the new e-business immersion in place, but some students do note weaknesses in the teaching in this arena—perhaps due, in part, to the newness and ever-changing material of the industry. In response, professors are increasingly in touch with outside practitioners and often call upon guest speakers or even experienced students who may have valuable input to contribute to the class.

Updated facilities have also made real-life experiences more attainable. In 1998 the school opened its newly renovated, $38 million home,

Sage Hall, a 120-year-old Venetian Gothic structure that was restored outside and completely gutted inside to provide 60 percent more space than its former, outdated digs in Malott Hall. Here you'll find students in eight amphitheater classrooms, with laptop connections at every seat. You can also conduct videoconferences, work in one of 32 team project rooms, and utilize a real-time replication of a Wall Street trading room, where classes are often taught "live" with the use of the Internet. There's a 100,000-volume management library and a multimedia computer lab with 56 well-equipped workstations. The school's executive education center, offices for faculty members, admissions and career services, dining areas, and student lounges are housed in Sage Hall as well. But most notable is a stunning, three-story glass-roofed atrium, where, "even when it's cold, it's beautiful when it's sunny out," one graduate notes. Not surprisingly, the atrium is the most popular meeting spot among the B-school crowd.

Finance students, in particular, benefit from high-end features like the Parker Center for Investment Research on Sage Hall's second floor. The full-scale trading room and research studio house $2 million worth of hardware and software and a back-wall electronic display of market happenings that's nearly identical to those on the stock exchanges. It is here that students take in the "Wall Street Wakeup Call," a weekly interactive broadcast from the New York Stock Exchange exclusively to the Johnson School. Some students are fortunate enough to try their fund-management skills through the new Cayuga MBA Fund, launched by the Class of 1998. The competitively chosen 20 MBAs conduct research, perform portfolio risk management and financial analysis, and make stock selections based on a two-thirds majority vote. The fund has been a success so far, outperforming the S&P 500 and garnering heady attention from dazzled recruiters. After all, the students are handling 20 accredited investors and managing more than $2.5 million. And although their environs have been spruced up, finance students by the dozens venture off campus regularly. Visits to New York City investment houses (scheduled on Fridays, when few or no classes are held) are a must for all finance-forward folk. "It's a 4½-hour drive down Route 17, but if you really want to work there," says one enterprising student, "you just have to do it."

Much as the finance features are top-rate, the Johnson School is, at its core, a general management program. And, as such, the retooled facilities and strong academics hit on a range of areas. Cornell ranks No. 4 in intellectual capital, and students laud the school's educational standards and rigor, as well as the extreme willingness of professors to hold discussions or provide guidance outside of class. High marks from students on these topics also landed Cornell at No. 4 for teaching quality, an honor that is largely a result of the 1998–1999 curriculum overhaul, which called for more case analysis and more attention to strategic and global issues. Since then, the first semester has been divided into two half-semesters, with three required core courses taken during each. Students work in teams on projects. But beforehand, during orientation, first-years go through leadership assessment exercises designed to enhance self-awareness, which, administrators say, can help with teamwork.

Although core courses remain a sore point for some, who find them "either very interesting or a bit dull," electives are plentiful (25 to 30 percent new as of 2000), and they've been considered well implemented. Rising interest in entrepreneurship is addressed with some of the more modern courses like Case Studies in Venture Investment and Management and Workshop: Internet Start-ups, in addition to revered professor David BenDaniel's standby, Entrepreneurship and Enterprise.

Professors, all around, are almost ubiquitously accessible, according to some students. "I was blown away when I noticed our two core statistics professors wandering through the atrium at 10 p.m. on a Sunday night to answer questions that groups might have been struggling with for an assignment due the next day," reports Peter Dukes, a recent graduate. Not only this, but they're increasing in number; eight were hired last year, and seven two years ago. And, while class size will remain the same (about 250), the school is attempting to increase the faculty tenfold in the next few years to accommodate new features like an executive MBA program in Westchester and the possibility of some distance learning programs.

Students here are pleased to find a sense of collaboration among professors, who aren't averse to rescheduling a test or two that conflict with other class work. They find that the integration of material among courses functions well, also. "The professors know what everyone else is teaching," remarks one recent graduate, "so you're never just taking tons of classes and running around in different directions."

Being one of the smaller graduate programs helps in this area. Because of its size, the Johnson School is able to shine in its responsiveness to students (duly noted by a No. 3 ranking in this area). Johnson MBAs, in turn, seem to show an intensified level of interest in identifying problems and helping to make improvements. Morning coffee breaks in Sage Hall have become a tradition, drawing each day an average of 150 students and administrators who talk shop in the three-story glass-enclosed atrium. "Very often, a student will bring something to my attention at the coffee break, I'll see a faculty member who can address it, and we'll discuss the situation right there," says Dean Swieringa. "The whole thing is resolved that day by 2 p.m." The administration's responsiveness can be so great that one recent graduate notes: "I'd sometimes want to tell them, 'Be careful! You listen to us so much—but what if we're wrong?'"

So far, so good, though, especially with a No. 8 ranking among graduates. The school's combination of an intimate program and broad

extension of the research-oriented university allows students, who are not required to declare a major, to "personalize" their MBAs. Up to 25 percent of the curriculum can be taken in other Cornell schools, and joint degrees with the School of Agriculture (producing environmental consultants) and the School of Hotel Administration are especially popular. Special one-day seminars from the Leadership Skills Program on subjects like business etiquette or time management help round out the education. To really extend your schooling, you can try out a second-year exchange program in any of 12 countries, including Sweden, Australia, Thailand, Italy, and Venezuela.

The options for outside exposure are rich, but a lack of diversity back on campus, where minorities comprise just 5 percent of the population, is a major source of contention. "It's definitely a huge focus for us right now," insists Swieringa, who has been working with the administration to conduct full-scale recruiting efforts and pushes to increase brand recognition for the school, especially in Europe, Latin America, and Asia. In addition to hosting targeted receptions and programs, the Johnson School is working on establishing relationships with institutions like historically black colleges and universities, the American Indian Higher Education Consortium, and the Hispanic Association of Colleges and Universities to increase interest among minority applicants. The Office for Minorities and Women in Business, launched in 1999 and headed by faculty member Angela Noble, is another improvement. "Having her at the school has made a difference to a number of people, including myself," one student raves. "She is not only an advocate for important causes, but also a support system that is often needed."

Another initiative is enhancing the recruitment experience. Cornell's remote location can be a challenge, but it's one that has become more manageable thanks to the school's devotion to service and an influx of top-rate recruiter facilities (like interview rooms with fax and Internet hookups in Sage Hall), which have made the time investments from companies more justifiable. About 180 recruiters made the trek in 1998, and although this year's crop was 30 fewer, the outcome was positive. Graduates in 2000 received an average of 3.1 job offers, many from firms in traditional fields like consulting (30 percent), financial services (30 percent), and marketing or brand management (about 30 percent). According to career placement figures, a once-booming interest in emerging sectors has diminished somewhat along with the euphoria for the stock market. But that's not to say students and start-ups have stopped pursuing each other here.

Cornell's Career Services office is focusing more on quality than quantity by specifically targeting companies proven to interest their students. Following survey results last year, student volunteers held cold-calling sessions to sell the school and encourage the companies most in demand to recruit at Cornell. As a result, companies like Dell and Genuity made their first appearances in 2000. Recruiters also take advantage of the option to reach Cornell students electronically, by submitting online job postings. The number of listings, which are easily accessed by students and alumni on Cornell's Web page, is said to be increasing steadily and is currently over 500.

On the other end, the Career Services office has been working closely with recruiters to tailor their presentations and functions so as to avoid disappointment. A smaller, lesser known company, for example, might be encouraged to attend a well-publicized career fair instead of risking an individual information session that may yield few participants because of other obligations on campus. "If it's not a marquee name, it's very easy to fall by the wayside since students have so much demand on their time," says John Nozell, a 1983 grad and former investment banker who is now in his second year with the Johnson School as Director of Career Services and Alumni Relations.

As Nozell's title indicates, alumni are an important part of the program, and keeping them updated with lectures and events in their areas is a priority. Most alumni settle outside the Ithaca area and may find it difficult to return regularly, but that doesn't mean the college town wasn't ideal for their two years of school; students who have prepared for a change of scenery consider the location a plus. It's a "town you can get your arms around," Dean Swieringa likes to say—and many students do make an impact on the community through any number of service projects. Athletic types take advantage of sporting options, from team sports like rugby, lacrosse, and volleyball to more individual pursuits like ice skating at the university's rink or cross-country or downhill skiing at nearby runs. A favorite annual event is the battle between the Frozen Assets, the female MBAs' hockey team, and a group of professors. And, pending any snowstorms, golf fanatics test their skills on the school's golf course, where, each spring, B-schools from all over the country send teams to participate in a tournament. When the weather turns warmer, MBAs make their way around Lake Cayuga in sailboats or rowing sculls.

Housing is available through the school for singles and families, including those with children, but in a town where "you can be any-where—*anywhere*—in under 10 minutes," it's easy to look beyond campus to settle into one of Ithaca's affordable rentals. A popular spot is Westview Apartments, the college town's nod to Melrose Place, where a large majority of residents are twenty- and thirty-something Johnson students. Second-year students often take over lakefront rented homes from their predecessors; one MBA reported that his four-bedroom, three-bathroom house with its own dock, which he shared with just one other student, rented for about $1600 a month.

Needless to say, parties at homes like these are popular, in addition to gatherings at some of Ithaca's cozy bars and happening restaurants— of which there's no shortage, given the large number of Hotel School grads who stay in town. The famed Moosewood Restaurant is a top choice for special occasions or when parents or long-distance significant others are visiting. The New Orleans Cajun–style Maxie's Supper Club is a favorite for seafood and grits and, true to its name, Thai Cuisine puts out standard Thai fare. Deep-dish pizza at the Nines in Collegetown is always a hit, and The Chapter House, a traditional pub, is good for a casual beer or two. The Royal Palm Tavern, a.k.a. The Palms, on the other hand, is deemed the best spot for loud music and strong drinks. On-campus options include the winter and spring formals, a Halloween party, and a Mardi Gras bash—and the standing Thursday afternoon happy hour is reportedly a must.

PLACEMENT DETAILS

Recruiters laud Cornell's Career Services office for its full-service accommodations and the personal attention they receive. This year, 150 came to campus to recruit ("a good number, vis-à-vis our capacity," says Director John Nozell). A large number submit job postings electronically, too; Cornell now boasts a database of more than 500 listings. The school also relies on alumni for career connections. From the school, alums get access to an online directory to keep tabs on each other, archived speakers via video through Cornell's Web site, and opportunities to attend functions with school officials who are visiting their area. Corporate partnerships with companies like Corning have become more of a priority, and the school is also focusing on technology to make their efforts more efficient. A new platform this year includes the CJ System, which tracks students from the time they apply to the program until their graduation. Students can upload their résumés, sign up for company presentations, bid on courses, and rearrange their schedules through this system online.

Long before students begin the recruitment process they have opportunities to learn about varying fields. A "Smarts Series" that began with second-year students informing first-years about investment banking positions now covers other industries like tech and brand management. And through the vital Career Trak program, a nine-session noncredit career planning course that meets about once a week, you can get overviews and specific information on networking, résumés, mock interviewing, and the like. Career Fairs and events organized by industry-specific clubs are well-attended, especially the Technology Management Club's tours to Silicon Valley, Boston, and New York sites, with attendance figures near 100.

The highest percentage of Cornell students go into consulting and financial services (nearly one-third of the class in each), and fields like marketing and brand management also continue to be popular. Some of the companies who most favor Cornell students for their collegial and teamwork-oriented traits include: PricewaterhouseCoopers (13); Salomon Smith Barney (9); Bain & Company (8); Hewlett-Packard (8); American Express (7); Accenture (6); McKinsey & Co. (6); and Warburg Dillon Read (6).

OUTSTANDING FACULTY

Charles M. C. Lee (accounting); *Mark W. Nelson* (accounting); *David J. BenDaniel* (entrepreneurship); *Warren B. Bailey* (finance); *Harold Bierman Jr.* (finance); *Bhaskaran Swaminathan* (finance); *L. Joseph Thomas* (operations); *Kathleen M. O'Connor* (organizational behavior).

APPLICANT TIPS

Director of Admissions Natalie Grinblatt is particularly proud of some of the traits that connect Johnson School students. "These are people who know what they want; they have a can-do attitude and will create or seize the opportunity to go forward," she says. No one particular background is an advantage, but you must show "lots and lots of passion." Work history is important, but you can't rely on that alone, of course, to convey who you are as an individual and how you have added value to the organization or the community. About half the applicants who are interviewed are accepted, and interviews are by invitation only. Should you receive one, make sure you're up to date on current business events, especially if you have a nonbusiness background.

Applications are examined in batches by deadline, with a designated number of spots available for each. That said, it is to your advantage to apply early so that you can get an earlier reply. (Apply for the final deadline and you won't hear until June, plus you'll miss out on the Welcome Weekend, offered only during the first two acceptance periods.) Deadlines for domestic and international students are November 15, January 15, and March 15. Applicants interested in the school's unique 12-month program for students with scientific or technology backgrounds must send in all materials by the January 15 deadline.

Contact: Natalie Grinblatt
Director of Admissions
800-847-2082
Application deadlines: November 15; January 15; March 15

JOHNSON MBAs SOUND OFF

JGSM is competitive, but not in the way a lot of other schools are. People want to do well, and work very hard to succeed, but they also want their classmates to do well. Students readily share their contacts, resources, research, and ideas, and many people have gotten great job offers through a contact of a classmate.

I could not have expected more from this program. Cornell really bends over backwards to do all it can for its students. The faculty members are outstanding and are available at all times. The small number of students at the school allows for small classes and let me develop close relationships with the faculty.

Perhaps the one aspect of the JGSM that I don't admire is the fact that many of my classmates were not accepted to any other top schools, and so they chose Cornell by default. I often wonder if the caliber of students at those other schools would have been dramatically different, and how that might have affected my education.

I had a wonderful experience at Cornell's Johnson School—it was much more challenging than I expected, yet in a good way, and I've made lasting friends and contacts. Students at the Johnson School tend to stay around campus during the week and on weekends, perhaps by nature of location—this promotes many opportunities for building friendships and participating in a multitude of activities, which people are very open to.

One improvement that I would like to see made to the Johnson School is the diversity of faculty members. I like and have confidence in the current faculty members, but I would like to see an African-American on staff.

The Johnson School in general, and Cornell University in particular, are profoundly altruistic in nurturing and inspiring their students. The tremendously "consumer-friendly" nature of the faculty and staff, I have found, which goes above and beyond expected levels of service to their students, is just one tribute to the generosity of this program. I can hardly imagine a different MBA program that would give as much.

The administration was extremely responsive to student concerns. When students last year approached the faculty with a request to create an e-business immersion, the administration quickly responded, creating an all-new curriculum by the next semester.

I have loved my two years at the Johnson Graduate School of Management. It is no coincidence that Cornell's Business School is known as the friendly school. While everyone here is intelligent, fascinating, and ambitious, there is general sense of helpfulness and caring that flows throughout the school. The faculty and administration work side by side with the students to continuously improve the school and to respond to our needs. There is always someone willing to help you out in tough times. The faculty love to teach and are *always* available and accessible to students.

9.
UNIVERSITY OF VIRGINIA

UNIVERSITY OF VIRGINIA

Darden Graduate School of Business Administration
P.O. Box 6550
Charlottesville, Virginia 22906-6550
E-mail address: darden@virginia.edu
Web site address: http://www.darden.virginia.edu

Corporate ranking: 9	Graduate ranking: 2
Enrollment: 488	Annual tuition & fees:
Women: 30%	resident—$19,208
Non-U.S.: 27%	nonresident—$24,208
Minority: 18%	Room and board: $8000
Part-time: 0	Average GMAT score: 676
Average age: 27	Average years of work exp.: 4
Applicants accepted: 19%	Accepted applicants enrolled: 52%
Median starting pay: $135,000	Intellectual capital: 16

Teaching methods: Lecture, 15% Case study, 70%
Business projects, simulations, 15%

Contact:
Dawna Clarke
Interim Director of
Admissions
800-UVA-MBA1
OR 804-924-7281
Application deadlines:
November 1
December 1
January 8
February 5
March 19
April 13

Now entering his third year on campus, Dean Edward A. Snyder still refers to himself as "the new dean." So do students and faculty. This is not because Snyder has kept his distance in getting to know the school. On the contrary, Snyder has immersed himself in the student body, resurrecting traditions in the spirit of Thomas Jefferson's original mission for the "academic village" he envisioned at the school that has turned into the University of Virginia.

Every morning students meet in Darden's foyer for "First Coffee," a tradition since the school's founding in 1955. Snyder joins the casual group whenever he's not on the road, using the time to get feedback on what needs to be tweaked in the MBA program and garner reactions to the changes he has made thus far. And Sunday through Thursday, when he's not off attending to school business elsewhere, Snyder meets with a rotating group of students for an even earlier breakfast. But perhaps the most coveted invitation—Sunday dinner at the dean's house—is extended to a different group of students almost every week. At Darden, the dean is not just a figurehead or money-raiser.

The close-knit Darden community may still think of him as "the new dean" because he continues to institute and evaluate substantive new changes that have helped the University of Virginia's Darden Graduate School of Business Administration rise two spots since last year's ranking, earning its way back into the top 10. The small Southern school's ranking moved up based on the favorable impressions held by grads and recruiters of the changes Snyder has implemented as well as on the way he has instituted mechanisms for continued feedback on the work that has been done and the work that is left to do.

Two years ago, Darden's rankings moved more dramatically in the other direction—dropping from 5th to 11th—in 1998, largely on the basis of student dissatisfaction. Snyder recalls that when he got the top job, the BUSINESSWEEK ranking that plucked the school out of the top 10 had just been released. He became what he now describes as "the world's expert on those issues at Darden." Within 100 days, he had memorized the comments and criticisms from the BUSINESSWEEK rankings and met with students and faculty to try to determine what wasn't working at one of the country's most elite B-schools—and he worked to create an action plan.

It's early, of course, but much of what he's done seems to work. You'll be hard-pressed to find students and grads who feel as strongly about their alma mater as Darden MBAs. In the BUSINESSWEEK survey, the school ranked second among graduates, placing only behind Northwestern's Kellogg School of Management. When asked about specific criteria, such as "Did the school meet your MBA expectations?" and "Was your degree worth the lost time and pay?" student replies ranked Darden highest of all 82 schools surveyed by BUSINESSWEEK. And grads with the UVA pedigree overwhelmingly say that they'd recommend the Darden experience to their friends. And this endorsement comes with an added bonus: As a public school, Darden is affordable, especially for Virginia residents.

If there is one thing recent graduates and those from two years ago agree on, it's that Darden is tough. The workload is formidable, the material challenging, and the expectations high. If you're headed to Darden, don't delude yourself into thinking that it'll be anything less than a two-year intensive intellectual experience. Sure, the school is just five miles from The Barracks, a horse stable that will provide you with entry into the Blue Ridge Mountains and Shenandoah Valley. But students rarely have time to take off like that. Darden's boot camp reputation isn't based on fiction—its program is designed to be rigorous.

In fact, in 1998 students chastised the school for piling on the work, with the law school–style Socratic method intimidating many. Snyder heard that particular complaint the most clearly. Balancing the workload while keeping Darden competitive became one of his most challenging tasks. And keeping the program on a serious and rigorous bent while lightening the excess workload became his goal.

His efforts seem to have been successful thus far, as today's grads now describe the amount of coursework as heavy but not onerous. Snyder made real changes to help temper the "boot camp" reputation of the MBA program just a tad, but students today still say rigorous academics are why they chose Darden. The hard work is considered worth it, even in terms of lost sleep and social lives.

"I have friends from Wharton, Harvard, Northwestern, and other B-schools," says one recent grad. "From them I know that most students at those schools don't study as hard as Darden students and their major goal is just finding a highly paid job no matter how much time (even class time) they need to spend on it." Others are more blunt: "I would not recommend the program to the faint of heart."

Snyder has one word to describe that tough-but-worth-it philosophy: purposeful. "We want to keep Darden intense, but make sure it is purposeful. We wanted to affirm the value system here. Students work hard and we take their investment of time seriously," he says.

One of his accomplishments was the integration of professional development and placement activities into the academic calendar. No longer would several big projects be due the same weekend as hundreds of pairs of moms and dads made their way to Charlottesville for Parents' Weekend. Professors' syllabi also take job interviews and placement center activities into consideration so that the "first-year 'ouch points' are eliminated."

Snyder encouraged faculty to integrate the first-year curriculum, so that the same case could be read and analyzed in different ways for different courses—without too much repetition. One class would look at operations, for example, while an Internet strategy class would examine the e-business potential of the same case.

Scott Balwinski, now a consultant at Diamond Technology Partners in Chicago, says his first-year curriculum was well connected. "I call it just-in-time learning. I'd get the basic finance fundamentals in one class and then use them in the next. More than once that I learned something in an accounting course and literally applied it the next day." There's still a bit of work to be done. The curriculum is not as integrated as recent grads might like it to be. Some say that professors weren't always aware of what other professors were teaching.

Part of the school's heavy workload may be tempered by the fact that it's not a lonely nose-in-the-books pursuit. Darden's emphasis on the case study method—the teaching method used 70 percent of the time—requires MBAs to work in so-called "learning teams." In fact, Snyder expects students to be with their study groups every school night, something he sometimes evaluates by looking at the cars in the various parking lots. "Students shouldn't be able to do the work on their own. If that were the case, that would be an indicator that we have gone too far [in lightening the workload]," he says. The number of required classes and cases has been reduced, and there are no longer classes, exams, or paper deadlines scheduled for Saturdays, as there were not too many years ago. Although Darden still has more classroom hours than any other leading business school, an effort has been made to make the workload more manageable. The school often schedules only two classes on Wednesdays for first-year students, with day-long programs on specific issues regularly inter-

spersed throughout the year in lieu of regular classes, and more travel days for second-years. Currently, at least 98 percent of those who enroll at Darden end up with degrees in their hands.

The heavy emphasis on case study has not shifted in recent years, and most grads say they're glad to see that. Balwinski describes himself as the case study method's "leading evangelist." "I can understand why people don't like it. If you don't have the patience, it can feel frustrating. But once you are done, the learning is a lot longer lasting," he says. In fact, if you've kept up with reading—which you must do in order to participate in class discussions—you'll be well prepared for the exams.

The first-year class, totaling an intimate 240, at least until 2002, is divided into 60-student sections, which are then split further into six-person learning teams assigned by the school to foster diversity. Teams meet each night to review cases and form topics for discussion for the next day's classes. With class discussion accounting for as much as 50 percent of your grade, you'll need to be ready to answer questions and offer thoughtful comments. And you'll find yourself depending heavily on the other members of your team to help you. On your first day, second-years guide group discussions of case studies to show you how it is done.

Dean Snyder's efforts don't stop with academic issues. Perhaps his most ambitious effort thus far has been to expand the MBA program by 25 percent—adding one new section—in 2002, the result of a 10-month discussion among administrators, alumni, students, and faculty. For the last quarter century, Darden has had four sections of 60 students each, a tradition that has contributed to the small-school atmosphere and one of the things alums consistently mention as one of Darden's strengths. The know-everyone atmosphere may help contribute to the loyalty they feel, as evidenced by the fact that Darden has the highest ratio of endowment per alumnus of any B-school. The we're-all-in-this-together camaraderie permeates almost every aspect of Darden life. During finals, for example, students send out mass schoolwide e-mails with their notes for classes, encouraged by the fact that there's no forced grading curve.

Teamwork and respect for others are aspects of a larger focus on ethics you'll find here. Darden is clearly a pioneer in the field. Many other B-schools are still grappling with how to incorporate ethics into their programs. MBAs here are required to take a graded, 20-session class in ethics as part of first-year requirements, and the subject is blended into courses in accounting, marketing, and operations as well. The 20-year-old Olsson Center for Applied Ethics creates teaching materials, tracks scholarship in business ethics, and sponsors seminars on the subject for executives.

Part of Darden's success and appeal is its small-school atmosphere—it's what makes the study groups work and gives grads the feeling they've had the same kind of bonding with their classmates as their predecessors have. Adding 60 students over a three-year period is a slow enough pace that the school shouldn't be in danger of losing that appeal. "The philosophy here is simple: each person matters. Even as we're aimed at transformational tasks, we'll remember that. We will make sure that our graduates do well, right after they graduate and life-long," says Snyder.

In addition, the school will get a boost as it increases its faculty roster by 10 percent to accommodate the student body growth. This will give Darden the chance to up the school's number of well-known and leading-edge thinkers, though Snyder insists the school has plenty of those already and instead is working on letting outsiders know about the quality of thinkers the school presently has. As was the case in 1998, in the BUSINESSWEEK poll of recent graduates, the same faculty members who receive praise for their dedication in the classroom and availability outside class—both in core and elective classes—are criticized for not being as cut-

ting-edge as professors at more research-oriented schools. The lack of such big names notched Darden down in the overall 2000 rankings, as BUSINESSWEEK added intellectual capital to its formula. However, students appreciate the faculty who are at the school. Darden grads benefit from the close-knit atmosphere, with the school's most prominent academics actively involved in teaching in the MBA program and almost always available for informal, out-of-class discussions. Indeed, you won't have to go too far to hear a story about a professor who came to campus on a Sunday to help a student or about informal, impromptu faculty–student lunches. Overall, the quality of teaching and personal relationships students have with professors might be Darden's biggest strengths.

Going forward, Snyder and his staff will work to strengthen Darden's relationship with the rest of the University of Virginia. More UVA law, medicine, engineering, architecture, and arts and sciences students will work with Darden MBAs in the school's Progressive Incubator. Darden faculty member Professor Wendell E. Dunn III is leading the effort to strengthen this partnership.

Darden sponsors the University's Black Leadership Project, a historical retrospective of the *Brown vs. Board of Education* U.S. Supreme Court decision of 1954. Darden students will be more involved in looking at the development of leadership during this formative period of American history, Snyder says.

The business school has also added a new faculty member in the first move to increase its rolls: William McDonough, former dean of UVA's School of Architecture will develop curriculum on sustainability.

But some suggest Darden, like many other B-schools, has still another area on which to focus its efforts. True, the face of Darden has changed in recent years, with the number of international students and minorities both increased since 1998, from 21 percent to 27 percent and 11 percent to 18 percent, respectively—

but it's an area where many top schools still need some work. Some, like alum Stephen Stalker, now in a finance rotation at GlaxoSmithKline in North Carolina, describe the reputation Darden has had as a place without a lot of diversity as a "complete misperception." "In terms of student body, there has been a move toward a more internationally based student body. Because you are divided in learning teams, you get to be good friends with people from all over the world," he says.

One added bonus: scholarship funds increased by 64 percent this year, a move that attracted more students from diverse backgrounds. And the continued presence of the Graduate Women in Business national headquarters at Darden helps make the place female-friendly. Currently, Darden students participate in over 30 professional and social organizations. There's even a cohesive and active spouses' group, called the Darden Partners Association, which, thanks to thrice-weekly events, often knows what's going on at Darden before some current students do.

The school's current efforts in this area follow on those of Leo I. Higdon Jr., Snyder's predecessor. Before exiting to take over the presidency at Babson College in Massachusetts, Higdon and staff took head-on the complaints that the school's environment was less than welcoming to women and minorities. Since then, the criticism about minority comfort levels at the school has waned, but no one is confident that the issue is gone for good.

And while students remain happy with the quality of teaching and the use of technology in coursework, they worry that Darden is leaving them on an analog track in a digital world. When Snyder was the senior associate dean at the University of Michigan, he founded the William Davidson Institute, one of the world's foremost research organizations dealing with emerging economies, and instituted an international consulting project requirement in the MBA program. Now he's charged with bringing that kind of innovation to both international and e-business studies at Darden. He's revamped the Darden Business Project, now a second-year elective in which small groups of students consult for outside companies or draw up their own business plans, with many of those ideas focused abroad. But don't expect Darden to open campuses across the world like University of Pennsylvania's Wharton School or University of Chicago's Graduate School of Business. Course offerings in global business will continue to grow, but Darden itself will stay contained in Charlottesville.

One area expected to continue to blossom: the school's newly developing entrepreneurial orientation. The Batten Institute, named for Frank Batten Sr., chairman of the Norfolk, Virginia communications company that spawned the cable TV Weather Channel and the father of two Darden alums, was formed with a $60 million endowment. The center provides assistance to start-ups in central and northern Virginia, where a pocket of high-tech companies is forming, as well as resources for the burgeoning segment of MBA students and faculty who are interested in studying entrepreneurship. In 2000, graduates of the class started nine new companies.

All this takes place in the Charlottesville area—a truly breathtaking place in its own right. Within view of campus is Jefferson's hilltop Monticello, a classic architectural masterpiece that lent its distinctive red-brick, Roman-Neoclassical style to most of the university buildings, including Darden Grounds, completed in 1996. Three handsome main buildings—one for classrooms, one for faculty offices, and a third serving as commons—surround a manicured courtyard, where cricket is often played between classes, with a separate building for student services and another serving the 4000 or so executive education students who come to campus each year.

Most MBAs live in private housing within walking distance of the university, largely because Darden lacks sufficient dormitory facilities. Although growing fast, Charlottesville retains a small-town, slow-paced, Southern feel, and you can still rent a spacious two-bedroom apartment for as little as $600 a month, an attractive perk for MBAs with families. If your significant other works, however, he or she may find job-hunting rough going, as there simply aren't the career opportunities available here that you'd find in New York, L.A., or Chicago. Even so, many students say the tradeoff for two years is worth it—a greater sense of camaraderie among students, spouses, and faculty than is possible at a large urban school. Professors and students team up to play pick-up basketball games. Every weekend UVA students congregate at The Corner, a strip of main street with music, beer, and the chance to unwind. There's an annual Chili Cook-Off, the Birdwood Picnics, the 25-year-old Foxfield Races, a local steeplechase, the Holiday Ball, and the Darden Follies—all provide a bit of release and relief from the hard work.

PLACEMENT DETAILS

In 1998 students griped that Darden's placement services weren't helpful enough with their employment searches; students ranked the school dead last among the Top 25 in terms of aggressiveness in helping students find both summer internships and jobs after graduation. In 2000, though, four out of five student internships resulted in job offers, and grads in our survey cited the placement center as another one of Snyder's quick turn-arounds. Students were happy with the way the school helped them conduct independent job searches. But those who want the big-name corner offices still say the Darden community lacks connections to influential names in the national business community, perhaps because of its small alumni body.

Students remain positive about the selection of recruiters with whom they were able to

interview on campus: Some 191 companies conducted interviews with second-years while another 135 showed up for first-year internship recruiting. That's a respectable showing considering the effort recruiters have to make to travel to out-of-the-way Charlottesville, as opposed to New York, Boston, Chicago, or San Francisco. The school's attempts at improving the quality of the recruiting pool has paid off, with a stellar roster of consulting and accounting firms, investment banks, and manufacturers snatching up the most graduates in 2000, not to mention a good showing of tech firms: Diamond Technology Partners (10); PricewaterhouseCoopers (8); Boston Consulting Group (8); Ernst & Young LLP (7); Goldman Sachs & Co. (6); Merrill Lynch (6); McKinsey (5); Morgan Stanley Dean Witter (5); A.T. Kearney (4); Booz-Allen & Hamilton (4); Deloitte Consulting (4). Graduates of the Class of 2000 pulled down a median starting pay package of $80,000, and 83 percent received signing bonuses averaging $20,000. The class averaged 2 job offers apiece. Eleven percent of the Class of 2000 went to work at a start-up.

OUTSTANDING FACULTY

Luann Lynch (accounting); *S. Venkataraman* (entrepreneurship/strategy); *Ed Freeman* (ethics); *Bob Bruner* (finance); *Susan Chaplinsky* (finance); *Bob Conroy* (finance); *Paul Farris* (marketing); *Ed Davis* (operations); *Jeanne Liedtka* (strategy); *John Colley* (strategy/operations).

APPLICANT TIPS

In 2000, Darden received 2510 applications, less than it did in 1998 (thanks to the general decline in applicants during a strong economy), but few would say that translates into a less selective admissions process or a less accomplished student body. The number of applicants is up 20 percent over 1994 applications and just 19 percent of those who applied were accepted.

Interim Director of Admissions Dawna Clarke says she is "really proud of the fact that the admissions process is not at all formulaic." Of course the stats matter. In 2000 the average GMAT score was 676, fairly steady with 1998's 685. But Clarke says work experience, evidence of leadership skills, and overall academics are heavily weighted. The ideal Darden student will have work experience from any number of a diverse cross-section of industries but will also evidence a progression of responsibility, and leadership and management skills. Letters of recommendation are read carefully to get a sense of what a prospective student's "future potential is for leadership and management."

Those are factors that don't often come across on the written application. As a result, Darden strongly encourages all applicants to have a personal interview, and the admissions team has retooled itself to make sure that's possible.

On campus Clarke added more interviews, more slots for interviews, and more opportunities to sit in on a class and experience Darden while you're there. Clarke herself conducts more informational sessions and more prospective students are taking her up on suggestions to have lunch and see the school. On-campus interviews skyrocketed 46 percent as a result.

The interview scenario for overseas students has changed as well. International applicants are still not expected to make the trip to Virginia, although they are welcome, but the admissions staff is visiting foreign countries more often to conduct the one-on-ones. Clarke says Darden administrators used to go overseas only in the fall to drum up interest in the school. Now they book a follow-up trip to Latin America and Asia in March to interview candidates there.

The in-person interview also allows the admissions staff to assess a prospective student's ability to excel at the Darden case study approach. Confidence in body language, flexibility in terms of responses to different kinds of questions, and attentive listening skills are all part of the assessment. Interviews are done "blind," Clarke explains. Her staff doesn't know anything about the candidates' backgrounds going in, so that there aren't any biases. Because of that, she feels interviews can't hurt applicants, but can help push them into the admitted column.

Applications are considered in rounds, with deadlines each month between November 1 and the final deadline of April 13, with a certain number of slots set for each deadline. However, Clarke believes that there are advantages to applying early. "I think it is easier for a candidate to be distinctive earlier." Plus, she notes, students who apply earlier are notified earlier and have a head start in looking for housing and applying for financial aid, and the admissions office has more time to answer questions and help candidates decide if Darden is right for them in November than in April.

You can submit your application on paper through the mail, but candidates are encouraged to apply online, through the Darden Web site. About 60 percent of candidates do so.

Contact: Dawna Clarke
Interim Director of Admissions
800-UVA-MBA1
OR 804-924-7281
Application deadlines: November 1; December 1; January 8; February 5; March 19; April 13

DARDEN MBAs SOUND OFF

I can't imagine attending another school. To be exposed to the areas of business in which I had no particular strength coming in was fantastic. There were times when I was humbled by the knowledge in the class or by an exam grade. But here, you have to get back on your feet fast just to withstand the next challenge.

Darden is not a school for everyone, especially not for people who think of an MBA program as a two-year vacation. But, for people who look to challenge themselves beyond what they have had in their past, academically and personally, for people who want to explore a lot of things in a friendly environment, Darden is a 10-plus.

Darden's program is undeniably tough, but I cannot think of any other experience I have had that has been so rewarding and fulfilling. I can honestly say I have learned more in two years here than in any other four years of my life. My classmates continue to astound me in their raw intellectual ability as well as in their continually supportive, giving, caring manner. Rather than becoming detrimentally competitive in this intense environment, Darden students tend to form very tight bonds with one another, taking turns helping along those classmates who are struggling.

The school has unquestionable strengths in terms of the teaching method, the quality of the faculty, and technological resources. The school has been improving significantly in terms of becoming a more international program. Additionally, Darden offers a level of academic intensity and teamwork dynamic that is unmatched and those are aspects that becoming more and more valuable.

Because of the school's out-of-the-way location, Darden has not been a cutting-edge hub for entrepreneurship. Thankfully, this is changing very rapidly. Dean Snyder has done an exceptional job bringing in funding ($60 million for the Batten Institute) and launching several initiatives in northern Virginia. The administration and faculty's responsiveness and willingness to adapt to changing student needs continues to impress me.

While I was skeptical about starting an MBA, my experience at Darden was better than I ever could have imagined business school to be. As a liberal arts undergrad major, the well-rounded first-year curriculum was a good foundation for me. The quality of teaching and the quality of my fellow classmates was absolutely top notch. I loved Charlottesville, in the heart of the Blue Ridge mountains.

Darden had been criticized in the past for an excessively heavy workload. The school has made what I believe are very positive steps to reduce the caseload while preserving the integrity of the curriculum. Many changes occurred between my first and second years, almost all of which I feel very positively about. Our dean took a much more active role in interacting with the students—including individual meetings, opening his house on the main lawn for students to use as was done in Jefferson's day, becoming more directly involved with student conferences and activities.

While at times I felt that the content of [e-business] courses was still a little weak, the opportunities to get involved with faculty on business issues, research, and class projects more than made up for the catching up that Darden needed to do in e-business. For example, my second-year business project with a small producer of fiber optics was integral in my obtaining my future job.

10.
UNIVERSITY OF CHICAGO

UNIVERSITY OF CHICAGO

Graduate School of Business
1101 East 58 Street
Chicago, Illinois 60637
E-mail address: admissions@gsb.uchicago.edu
Web site address: http://gsb.uchicago.edu

Corporate ranking: 4	Graduate ranking: 24
Enrollment: 2372	Annual tuition & fees: $29,231
Women: 26%	Room and board: $10,800
Non-U.S.: 31%	Average GMAT score: 684
Minority: 8%	Average years of work exp.: 4.7
Part-time: 1356	Accepted applicants enrolled: 59%
Average age: 28	Intellectual capital: 7
Applicants accepted: 25%	
Median starting pay: $140,000	

Teaching methods: Lecture, 50%   Case study, 25%
Laboratories, simulations, projects, discussion, 25%

Contact:
Carol Swanberg
Director of Admissions
and Financial Aid
773-702-7369
Application deadlines:
November 3
January 5
March 9

The University of Chicago Graduate School of Business had much to celebrate when the 1998 BUSINESSWEEK rankings were released. The students, faculty, and administrators still had the sweet taste of champagne in their mouths after honoring 100 years of business education on the shores of Lake Michigan. The good times got even better when Chicago found itself ranked third in BUSINESSWEEK's 1998 B-school rankings, overcoming low marks in 1996. But in 2000, the party is over. Chicago dropped with a resounding thud from No. 3 to No. 10. In fact, the GSB is the school with the greatest decrease in student satisfaction, falling from 9 in 1998 to 24 in 2000. Students say Chicago fails to produce a strong sense of community, a key part of any educational experience, and that professors are unavailable.

And now, that community is being shaken even further, with the abrupt, day-before-Thanksgiving announcement by Dean Robert S. Hamada that he will step down in June 2001. Hamada says he will stay until August if the search committee fails to choose a replacement on time, a task that in recent years has proven quite difficult for schools like Vanderbilt and Wharton—both of which ended up with deans from within their own walls. His reason for leaving: "I believe strongly that this job now requires a younger person infused with fresh energy to balance the interests of all the Chicago GSB constituents—faculty, current and prospective students, alumni, corporate community, media, donors, the University's central administration, and non-GSB faculty and students at the University—while adhering to the historical culture and traditions of the GSB that made us great and world-renowned."

Whoever takes the reins will have to deal with a somewhat frustrated student body. Some students diagnose the detached community as a function of location; the B-school is located in Hyde Park, on the south side of Chicago, and campus is surrounded by poverty-stricken neighborhoods. First-years usually live in the apartment building called Regents Park. But second-years disperse and often move to the north side of town. "When you end up commuting, that means the nature of the community changes quite a bit," says 2000 graduate Richard J. Boubelik, who remained near campus both years. But Boubelik adds that the surrounding community prompts conversations about poverty and crime—topics B-school students are often criticized for ignoring. Professors often commute as well, leaving them homeward bound shortly after class ends. Chicago is making an effort to address student concerns about the less-than-tight community. Deputy Dean Mark Zmjewski has open forums, and administrators extend an open invitation to students for lunch once a month. Other students say Chicago offers a more personalized course load in which students choose their own paths and classes instead of being grouped into a series of classes with a cohort of students. This personalized program exaggerates the less-than-social atmosphere. Dean Hamada admits the student gripes are justified, but says change takes time. His replacement will be left with the task of making that change. In the meantime, community bonds aren't the only problems Chicago needs to address.

In addition to the dying school spirit, students rated Chicago faculty the least accessible of any in the Top 30. And while Chicago students gave professors a gold star in 1998, in 2000, graduates gave lower scores for core courses and elective teaching. (In '98, teachers were ranked No. 1 for core teaching, but in 2000 core teachers were ranked 15th of the 82 schools surveyed by BUSINESSWEEK.) Chicago is no place for students who want their hands held; a proactive, aggressive student fits the Chicago mold much better.

Curriculum at the school, though, remains quite strong despite other pitfalls. The finance department continues to get top billing from students and recruiters. In fact, recruiters place Chicago students second, behind only Wharton, for their finance skills. But make no mistake: Chicago has no intention of providing the cozy, glued-at-the-hip feel students get at such teamwork-obsessed schools as Kellogg, Dartmouth, or Virginia. Back in 1998, one student referred to Chicago as a "haven for the academically superior and socially inept." Even current students say the school gets a somewhat deserved reputation for the competitive nature among classmates. They say the competition is friendly but that Chicago is an intense place to study. Some students say the fact that grades are disclosed to recruiters might give the impression of an overly competitive environment but most students say back stabbing and cutthroat tactics are not the norm. John O'Brien, an investment banker from the Class of 2000, says Chicago is only as competitive as an individual makes it. "Chicago mirrors real life in so many ways," O'Brien says.

The rigorous academic adventure begins with the mandatory LEAD (Leadership Effectiveness and Development) program. Newcomers are divided into 12 cohorts of 50 students, each of whom is assigned eight second-year facilitators who underwent an intensive 12-week training program the previous spring. A faculty member oversees the entire operation. Before your other classes begin, you'll be offered the chance to spend three days camping at various sites outside Chicago. There, you'll negotiate ropes courses and try your hand at a 40-foot climbing wall with other members of your assigned team; then you'll head back to Hyde

Park for 12 more days of outdoor team-building exercises and seminars on leadership communication skills, academic planning, and career management. The orientation culminates in a two-day Dean's Challenge, in which teams of eight students scramble to come up with plans to attack a business problem or opportunity; after all the plans are presented to a panel of alums for judging, prizes are awarded at a Saturday-night gala.

LEAD no longer ends with the start of the first quarter, however. To foster community ties, cohorts can continue to meet every Tuesday and Thursday from 2 to 5 p.m. throughout the fall to cover material on diversity, leadership, problem solving, ethics, and career skills such as self-marketing and negotiation. There are even two evening social events built into the schedule and an October sports competition pitting cohorts against one another in volleyball and miniature golf. There is a November awards ceremony where prizes are given for student-produced videos made earlier in the quarter. Students also take LEAD and one or two other first-year courses (microeconomics, financial accounting, or managing in organizations) in a cohort of about 50.

In addition to LEAD, you have to complete 20 courses to graduate: 3 foundations courses in microeconomics, financial accounting, and statistics; courses in 4 of 6 "breadth requirements," which include financial management, human resources management, macroeconomics, managerial accounting, marketing management, and production management; 2 general management courses; and 11 electives, selected from 128 GSB offerings from the university's giant catalog (6 of the 11 can be taken outside the GSB). For any of the requirements, you can skip the basic-level course and substitute a higher-level one if you can show that you've mastered the material elsewhere.

If you wish, you can choose 1 or 2 of 13 different subject areas as concentrations, with requirements varying from one concentration to the next. Most of the concentrations reflect Chicago's strong tradition as a quantitative powerhouse; indeed, recruiters say no other school's MBAs can match the finance, accounting, or analytic skills of GSB grads. But tracks established in entrepreneurship, general management, strategic management, and managerial and organizational behavior reflect Chicago's growing breadth. For those interested in even more intensive study of specific disciplines, joint degrees are available in international relations, law, medicine, physical sciences, public policy, social services administration, or a number of geographic-area studies.

One area in which the GSB's presence is being increasingly felt is that of international studies. About 60 students a year enroll in the two-year international MBA program, which combines traditional MBA courses with special courses on global business. In addition to completing all the regular MBA requirements, students in this program must also take four international business classes and spend at least three months studying or working outside their home country. The GSB has affiliations with 29 different management schools in Europe, Asia, Australia, and Central and South America, which students in the regular MBA program can utilize through a traditional exchange program. Students in the international MBA program must also become fluent in at least one non-native language before graduation. The program includes a summer Global Study Tour. Students who went on the 2000 trip went to Budapest and London, where they met with corporate executives, attended corporate receptions, and went sightseeing. In September 2000, GSB enhanced its global initiatives by opening a campus in Singapore, making it the first B-school with permanent campuses on three continents. The Singapore campus opened its doors for the Executive MBA Program Asia course in September 2000. In addition to Singapore and the U.S. campus, executive MBAs who want a Chicago degree can also study in Barcelona, Spain.

Unfortunately, for those who stay on the Hyde Park campus for their two years, the experience will be far less culturally diverse. Although enrollment of international students increased to 31 percent in 2000 from 23 percent two years ago, Chicago lags far behind most other top B-schools in its recruitment of women and minorities, who make up 26 percent and 8 percent of the student body, respectively. Chicago did respond to earlier complaints about faltering diversity initiatives. Hamada launched a task force to tackle the problem and come up with ways to attract women and minorities. Students say an increased international population was a move in the right direction but does not entirely make up for the poor showing of women and minority students. The folks in the admissions office think the problem is that minorities and women are unaware of what Chicago can offer them. As a result of the task force, the admissions office launched a marketing effort to seek potential minority and women applicants and then to undo the stereotypes about Chicago's program. "The perception is that we're not a minority- or women-friendly school—a reputation is a hard thing to overcome," says Director of Admissions and Financial Aid Carol Swanberg. As a result, Chicago is calling on women and minority alumni to meet with potential students and speak up about how Chicago can meet their specific needs.

Chicago has always had some difficulty attracting a balanced student body. Hamada believes financial aid issues and the availability of a high-quality MBA education in Chicago's part-time program have helped keep the minority population low in the full-time program. It has been suggested that women were scared off by the school's quant-jock image and perceptions of the urban Hyde Park neighborhood as unsafe. (In truth, Hyde Park itself experiences much less crime than most neighborhoods in the Windy City, and a large number of faculty reside there, but nearby neighborhoods are indeed deemed much less safe.) In 1996, Hamada hired Monique Vernoudy to fill the post of director of diversity relations; her charge was to recruit women and minority students, monitor their experience while at Chicago to offer extra tutoring, counseling, or placement help if needed, and to strengthen the school's small minority alumni network. By 2000, Vernoudy had left GSB and was replaced by Janice Robinson.

Hamada also recognizes the need to continue work on the school's aging infrastructure. Perhaps he will stress these concerns to his successor. Despite renovations in Edelstone Center and the GSB's other two classic buildings, which are linked together on the southeast edge of the university's 172-acre campus, the facilities are badly out of date, particularly when compared with the sparkling, modern Gleacher Center downtown, where part-timers take evening classes. Hamada launched a money-raising campaign for the construction of a 300,000-square-foot state-of-the-art integrated campus to replace the school's four buildings on the Hyde Park campus. There's been some internal, university bickering over where the building will go, but the project has been cleared. The infrastructure will include technologically advanced classrooms, group study rooms, informal gathering space, a student lounge, winter garden, and outdoor courtyard. In addition, career services, admissions, and other administrative offices will be under one roof. Hamada also put a 400-bed GSB residence facility into the mix. The administration says the mission of this $125 million campus is to address the lack of community by trying to implement cohesiveness through infrastructure. It'll be a while before the results will be seen, though. The building may not open for five years.

The new building won't change the fact that you know you're on an urban campus here—which has both advantages and disadvantages. A short ride north on the el (elevated train), and you're in the Loop, where you'll find a world-class symphony orchestra and art museum, as well as a lively nightlife along Rush Street. Head a little farther north, and you end up in Lincoln Park, with its blues bars, trendy restaurants, and cute zoo. It's one neighborhood where a fair number of GSB students end up living, since housing at International House, the university dorm, and in apartments and homes in Hyde Park is limited.

In good weather, students spend time after class flipping Frisbees or tossing softballs around on the Midway, a field that cuts through the GSB campus and stretches down to the lake. The really smart ones also spend some time at Medici's, a neighborhood restaurant where, for a few bucks each morning, you can get a tasty breakfast, read the papers, and drink your fill of orange juice—as long as you squeeze it yourself.

Students do tend to disperse after class, but most wouldn't miss TNDC, the Thursday night drinking club, which roams to pubs throughout the city and lets everybody know where to gather via e-mail. Most also participate in at least one of the GSB's 27 extracurricular clubs, which tend to be serious and career-related—witness the "Competitive Intelligence Group," a club which organizes speakers and workshops on analytic skills. Most popular, however, is the Bowling Club, started in 1997 and encompassing much more than just a toss at the pins—in fact, you don't even have to bowl to be a member. Besides holding regular charity bowling tournaments with corporate sponsors such as Boston Consulting Group, the club's 300 members meet each Friday afternoon in Cox Lounge for "beer pong," a ping-pong game in which you aim to hit a cup filled with beer at your opponent's end of the table; if successful, your competitor must drink it. There's even an Aerospace Division of the club, which launches solid-fuel rockets at the start of each week's festivities.

PLACEMENT DETAILS

Chicago's career center overhauled services between 1996 and 1998, and the changes continue to surface even now. The school remained among the top five favorites of recruiters for its placement office. Chicago students walked away in 2000 with an average of 3.1 job offers at graduation. Their median starting pay package of $140,000 was not up to the level of Harvard, Stanford, MIT, or Kellogg, but near the top of the B-school pack nonetheless. Top employers for the Class of 2000 were McKinsey & Co. (31); Lehman Brothers (20); Booz-Allen & Hamilton (16); Goldman Sachs & Co. (15); Merrill Lynch (14); Accenture (13); Chase (13); The Boston Consulting Group (13); Bain & Co., Inc. (12); Salomon Smith Barney (10). Ninety percent of the job-seeking members of the Class of 2000 were employed by graduation.

The newly reorganized career services office was taken over in the fall of 1998 by Glenn Sykes, former associate director of MBA career development and placement at Wharton and a former Citibank vice president. The office is spending more time than ever engendering a "career management" mentality in students, rather than simply assisting in one-time job searches. The office staff increased by two-thirds since 1998, and the new group emphasized job search skills. Staffers helped students get the most out of Web searches and offered advice on finding the best resources to suit their career desires.

OUTSTANDING FACULTY

Merle Erickson (accounting); *Austan Goolsbee* (economics); *Steven Kaplan* (entrepreneurship/finance); *James Schrager* (entrepreneurship/strategy); *Anthony Marciano* (finance); *Robert Vishny* (finance); *Sanjay Dhar* (marketing); *Ann McGill* (marketing/behavioral science); *Toby Stuart* (strategy/organizations).

APPLICANT TIPS

Following the publicity surrounding Chicago's difficulties over the past couple of years, the number of applications has dipped 23 percent since 1998. Like its counterparts, Chicago suffered some from hot economy syndrome and lost potential students who were making too much money to leave work for two years. Administrators are hoping to target more women and minorities to increase both diversity and the number of applications coming through the admissions office. That doesn't change the school's quantitative persona. In other words, GMAT scores get considerable weight in consideration of applicants. In recent years, though, the school has begun to interview nearly all its applicants to assess their interpersonal abilities. Be sure to schedule your interview at least a month before the application deadline you wish to meet. You can download and submit your application by computer or on paper. Improve your odds by applying early, and if you're looking to get financial aid or want to start in the summer quarter, you've got to apply by the January deadline.

Chicago has also begun putting a lot of effort into getting its name before the public, so it wouldn't be surprising to find the school becoming significantly more selective in coming years (in 2000, Chicago admitted about 25 percent of those who applied). Marketing was among the skills stressed when the school announced the appointment of Carol Swanberg, who moved over from the admissions office at the University of Pittsburgh's B-school to become admissions director in 1998. The school holds Super Saturday sessions on campus the Saturday after each application deadline, where 100 to 150 candidates are interviewed by alumni and have Q&A sessions over lunch with current students. There's also a Fall Preview weekend each fall for prospective applicants and an Admit Weekend in the spring for those already admitted who want to learn more about the school.

Contact: Carol Swanberg
Director of Admissions and Financial Aid
773-702-7369
Application deadlines: November 3; January 5; March 9

CHICAGO MBAs SOUND OFF

I feel that Chicago is working hard to improve the sense of community at the school. Every year, the school brings in students who are more committed to making the two years an enjoyable group experience. As the students have become more community focused, the cutthroat reputation of Chicago has melted away. That being said, it seems that the school has more of an individualistic focus than a school like Kellogg or Harvard.

The University of Chicago lives up to its reputation 100 percent. In terms of pure skills and analytic ability, no MBA program could come close. I suspect Chicago MBAs come out of their program armed with a larger business skill set than any of their fellow MBAs from other programs. However, Chicago does not emphasize the "softer" managerial skills. Chicago MBAs are the highly trained financial and strategic technicians of the business world and not necessarily the captains. Chicago does not produce CEOs—it produces consultants, investment bankers, and advisers who tell the CEOs what to do. This is not a weakness, although every now and then the Chicago administration gets confused and acts as if it is. Chicago shouldn't try to be a CEO-prep school like Harvard or Stanford; it should be a place where corporate strategists and financial engineers can learn their trade from the best. It fulfills that function better than any other university in the world.

The business school at the University of Chicago is a machine for pumping out investment bankers and consultants. If you don't fit that mold, it's not a good place for you. Though the administration has added a few e-commerce classes to the curriculum, this misses the point that a good business education should extend beyond a narrow-minded collection of analytical tools. There is no focus on building leadership skills or fostering a sense of community within the school, and the student body is dismally homogeneous. Granted, most business schools are not noted for their diversity, but the University of Chicago is horrible in this aspect. To make the University of Chicago's lack of diversity even worse, the campus is surrounded by some of the poorest neighborhoods in the entire country, and the school pretends those neighborhoods don't exist.

Chicago was a fantastic MBA program if you knew what you wanted to get out of it. Those that were not focused on their future coming in at the beginning often had a challenge in figuring out the system. Excellent place for me, albeit not for everyone.

As a woman entering the GSB, I was concerned that the heavy-quant, majority male environment would be rough. First quarter was very competitive for grades to use in internship recruiting. Once people get their summer jobs, however, the grade frenzy cools down. I found the environment to be great and completely manageable. One advantage of the small percentage of women is that we all know each other.

**11.
STANFORD
UNIVERSITY**

STANFORD UNIVERSITY

Graduate School of Business

518 Memorial Way

Stanford, California 94305-5015

E-mail address: MBAinquiries@gsb.stanford.edu

Web site address: http://www.gsb.stanford.edu

Corporate ranking: 12	Graduate ranking: 15
Enrollment: 730	Annual tuition & fees: $28,896
Women: 40%	Room and board: $12,626
Non-U.S.: 28%	Average GMAT score: 727
Minority: 10%	Average years of work exp.: 4.3
Part-time: 0	Accepted applicants enrolled: 82%
Average age: 27	Intellectual capital: 3
Applicants accepted: 8%	
Median starting pay: $165,500	

Teaching methods: Lecture, 30%   Case study, 55%
                                   Simulations, projects, 15%

Contact:

Marie M. Mookini

Director of Admissions

415-723-2766

Application deadlines:

November 1

January 4

March 21

The big news for this management-program monolith should be the fact that, a little over a year ago, the school got a new dean: banker and Stanford alum Robert Joss. The former principal with Australia's Westpac Banking Corporation is also a 20-year-plus veteran of San Francisco–based Wells Fargo Bank, where he rose through the ranks to become vice chairman. Selected from an applicant pool of more than 100 qualified candidates, Joss replaced former Dean A. Michael Spence, who had quite capably served the Stanford Graduate School of Business for about a decade. The community at the long-revered B-school has been buzzing about it, but something else that's undoubtedly on their minds is the program's slip in this year's BUSINESSWEEK rankings. For the first time since the survey's inception, the school landed just outside the hallowed top 10.

Dean Joss expressed his concern in a schoolwide e-mail. "We wondered what was behind [the ratings]," he says now, "and how the whole thing worked." Administrators who point to the students' exceptionally, but justifiably, high expectations as part of the explanation make the claim that, in the survey, Stanford MBAs judge the school according to their own elevated standards, not compared with other competing B-schools. Adds Associate Dean and Professor George Parker: "I find it hard to believe that our students are the least happy in any area." Indeed, there aren't too many people turning down Stanford when accepted.

Stanford's admissions situation certainly hasn't registered any problems. Historically among the most selective of B-schools, it's kept an edge in attracting new students. What may be changing, perhaps, is the type of student who is attracted to the elite school. For the Class of 2002, just 8 percent of a 5400-plus applicant pool were admitted, and a full 82 percent of those students enrolled. "If you're admitted, you come," says Dean Joss. And it may be that basis—the elite status of the school—that has led to a lower satisfaction level among students and recruiters.

Still, the school's academic environment remains solid. The campus is spectacular, dotted with red-tiled Spanish mission-style buildings still referred to by many as "The Farm," a throwback to the late nineteenth century, when Leland Stanford still farmed and bred racehorses on the site. And with the added benefit of a mild northern California climate, it's no wonder heaps of students each year clamor to be among the elite 360 or so chosen to study amid the redwoods and palm trees, rolling hills, and views of San Francisco Bay. Being perched in the middle of Silicon Valley gives the school both an edge and a handicap when it comes to opportunity—fewer that one-third of its graduates leave California and recruiters are well aware of that fact. Not that Stanford grads have any problem landing a job.

But is there something to the criticisms? GSB students gave such low ratings to the school's level of responsiveness from the faculty and administration that Stanford was among the worst of the 82 schools surveyed by BUSINESS-WEEK in this area. The quality of teaching in core courses also came in near the bottom of the Top 30, and recruiters took their shots at the school's Career Management Center. But despite the fact that some companies have called Stanford's career services office the least effective of any school's, employers last year bestowed GSB grads with a median pay package of $165,500—the highest of any school surveyed. So are there, or are there not, grave problems here?

To find out, Dean Joss has been holding small-group and town hall–style meetings with students and faculty more often. He has also established a "complete access" approach by implementing an open-door policy and encouraging steady e-mail interaction.

When the dean first arrived, he hired 10 faculty members and a Chief Operating Officer, and these days, along with the efforts to heighten student–administration interaction, he and his staff are moving forward by raising funds and working toward new initiatives. Global awareness is one of those initiatives. Dean Joss hopes to further integrate a global aspect into the school's content and overall impact. This has entailed diversifying the student body to a greater extent—a goal he and the admissions staff have been working on double-time by increasing the number and scope of recruitment efforts. Female students are currently more plentiful here than at most other schools—a full 35 percent. International students make up 31 percent of the MBA population, but minorities have leveled off at about 10 percent, the same as in 1998. Stanford seeks to encourage diversity through programs like the Toigo Foundation, which awards top minority MBA candidates pursuing careers in financial services with financial and career support. Additionally, through the Stanford Business School Charles P. Bonini Partnership for Diversity Fellowship Program, exceptional students from a variety of racial, cultural, and professional backgrounds are selected to receive a full-tuition scholarship for their two years at Stanford after completing a 9- to 12-month internship with a Corporate Partner. (The most recent participants include Goldman Sachs, GlaxoSmith-Kline, and Sun Microsystems.) Unlike other corporate sponsorships, where a student's place of employment might pay for one or two years of school in return for a prearranged commitment, there is no obligation for Stanford's Bonini Fellows to resume employment with their corporate sponsors.

Curriculum-wise, a global focus is being worked into nearly all classes, with international cases being used more and more as standard course material. (Cases in general make up a little more than half the school's teaching methods; lectures and other means, like simulations or projects, make up the rest of the curriculum.) Students who participate in the global management certificate program by taking a sequence of planned courses with an international angle are trained to handle management issues and strategies in a global environment.

Like every B-school dean these days, Joss also wants to regularly reshape the curriculum to keep the program current on New Economy issues. But this is especially important here, given Stanford's home in Silicon Valley and the large number of incoming MBAs with high-tech experience or an interest in dot-coms and start-ups. Within the school's Center for Electronic Business and Commerce, faculty members conduct research and work on course development, and relevant speakers and conferences are arranged. The Principal Investment Conference—sponsored by the Venture Capital, Merchant Banking, and Finance and Investment clubs—also brings in speakers to discuss the issues of private equity investing. Students gain hands-on business development experience as part of the Entrepreneurship: Formation and New Ventures course, taught by Management Professor Charles Holloway and John Morgridge, chairman of Cisco Systems and a lecturer in management. As a project for the class, MBAs can write business plans with assistance from venture capitalists and then pitch their ideas to a panel of leaders in the related industries. An additional eChallenge event brings local venture capital firms to campus to review business plans and help students through the launching process.

Stanford may have been quick to build up its entrepreneurial and e-business resources, but it's not so fast to give up its general management label. There's an array of about 100 wide-ranging electives here, plus a solid base of core courses that cover plenty of ground. And,

despite the school's reputation as a feeder to Silicon Valley start-ups, its students do take jobs in varying industries in different parts of the country and world—49 industries and 118 cities among last year's grads, to be exact. "A lot of people think they'll come to Stanford and it will be this entrepreneurial bazaar or something, with a bunch of people in tents," muses Parker. "A hell of a lot of our graduates do become entrepreneurs, but not because we pushed it." But some faculty members say the draw of Silicon Valley means students attend class less, and some students complain that their counterparts don't put enough effort into their studies because of the draw of all that's around them.

Of the electives, about 40 percent are new in the past three years, and many of those do focus on e-business or entrepreneurship, reflecting market trends. The Entrepreneur and the Investment Climate in Emerging Nations, Public Policy Issues in e-Commerce, and Environmental Entrepreneurship are among the recent e-themed debuts. But if you're looking for variety, there are Foreign Ventures and Alliances: Strategies and Pitfalls; Europe, the EU, and the World Economy; and Topics in Human Resource Management, which were also recently introduced. Each year, about a dozen new courses are added, albeit carefully and with much thought. "The Stanford way is evolutionary rather than revolutionary," explains Parker. It's also pretty flexible. MBAs do not have to declare a major or a concentration here, and although core required classes, as always, cover such standard areas as finance, marketing, management, and operations, you can exempt out of some of them by exam, as long as you replace them with electives.

To combine another major interest with B-school, you can take on one of Stanford's dual-degree programs, such as the MBA/A.M. (Education), the MBA/MSE (Engineering), and the J.D./MBA (Law). Some subjects naturally draw a mix of graduate students, like health-care management, which unites business and medical scholars. And joint-taught classes like Strategy and Action in the Information Processing Industry, with Professor Robert Burgelman and lecturer and Intel Corp. chairman Andrew Grove are popular for providing varied perspectives. A class taught by Management Professor Seenu Srinivasan and School of Engineering Professor David Beach—Integrated Design for Manufacturing and Marketability—gives students from the two schools solid real-world experience: In teams, they design a prototype product, build a working model, and compete for simulated sales and profitability. And, you'll always learn from classmates. Prior to enrolling, more than a few of Stanford's recent MBAs already held master's degrees in communication, Latin American studies, East Asian studies, and industrial engineering—enough to add a new dimension to the base of a B-school curriculum.

Aside from some inventive options, one reliable stalwart is the 26-year-old Public Management program, designed to prepare students to take on leadership roles in public service and to help public-sector and nonprofit organizations run more effectively. MBAs who complete a designated set of courses in this area receive a certificate, but many others also take part in study trips and case studies that fall under the program's auspices. Each year, PMP students select one major public policy topic or social problem to highlight by organizing a series of programs on the subject, with speakers, site visits, panel discussions, workshops, case studies, and community service projects. Recent themes include Investing in Social Change; Public/Private Partnerships; and Global Sustainability: Business, the Environment, and Responsible Development. If you fear the choice of a fulfilling work experience over financial rewards, you'll find solace in the Stanford Management Internship Fund, which offers financial support for students who spend their summer internships in a low-paying nonprofit or public-sector job.

Stanford grads on any career path turn to the Management Communications program at some point in their two years here. Most, if not all, have taken at least one of its noncredit courses, which cover such all-important practical subjects as media training, persuasive presentations, improving interview skills, and effective listening. Aside from those, the school's array of online resources makes it easier to find jobs, schedule classes, and handle a mountain of other tasks, including downloading class assignments and accessing research information. About 450,000 books and serials can be found in the Rosenberg Corporate Research Center; targeted databases are continuously updated; and a Traders' Pit offers online corporate information services like Bloomberg and The Bridge.

When it's time to find employment, Stanford MBAs historically have their pick of positions, although some major corporations have sworn off the school of late. This is undoubtedly a response to disappointing turnouts at corporate presentations and in their recruitment numbers, and a growing sentiment that Stanford harbors a "You need us a lot more than we need you" mentality. About 270 companies did come to campus to recruit second-years in 2000 and, after MIT's grads, Stanford MBAs reaped the second highest average number of job offers (3.8). GSB students typically develop connections and create ample opportunities for themselves with some of the local start-up companies; in 2000, 5 percent took jobs with start-ups, most often with local firms. Stanford's network and alumni connections are perhaps one of the most valuable tools of the MBA program. Nine percent of 2000 grads started their own businesses. This die-hard interest in high-tech endeavors has been a sore point among some of the more traditional or non-Valleycentric recruiters, who have been grumbling about a Stanford crop of students that are there just to get rich quick and bring that attitude to interviews. After all, nearly two-thirds of the Class of 2000 settled in the tech-charged area, so the intensity is a bit difficult to escape. But Parker insists that Stanford is still a national and international school. "We are not the Stanford Business School of Silicon Valley," he proclaims. "Our location does afford us extraordinary job opportunities for graduates, but we also have a commitment to training people for the entire nation and world."

Also playing a part in students' job searches are alumni, and the 50 alumni clubs established in different parts of the world are a help. Given Stanford's small size (classes of about 360 each), experiences here tend to be intimate and cooperative, and alumni relations follow in that vein. "There's a tighter connection here between students and alumni," says Acting Director of Career Services Uta Kramer. "Our alumni have also been very good about giving back to the school in terms of their expertise." Current and former students alike can search an online database for contacts according to a particular industry or location, and high-profile alums such as Hewlett-Packard's Ann Livermore (MBA '82) and eBay's Jeff Skoll (MBA '95) are frequent speakers on campus. Alumni looking for career guidance can also work with a counselor by phone or in person through the Career Management Center and utilize most, if not all, of the resources available to current MBA students.

Other sources for job leads and networking opportunities can be found in Stanford's conference offerings, which also help familiarize students with specific fields or industry issues. Some, like an annual women's conference, are planned by the school and/or the alumni association. Others are assembled by leaders from some of the more than 60 on-campus clubs, which range from ethnic-specific organizations like the Asia Forum, Hispanic Business Students Association, and Black Business Students Association to career-oriented groups like the Sports Management Club, Consulting Club, and Arts, Media, and Entertainment Club. There are also organized groups for nearly every diversion, including the rough-and-tumble Rugby Club, the Ski Club, and the popular Wine Circle. Many students take time to give back to the community through events like the well-attended Challenge for Charity, in which West Coast B-schools take part in friendly athletic competition and social events to raise funds for the Special Olympics.

Stanford's facilities, quite simply, are top-notch. The B-school's modern, four-story headquarters, an anomaly amid the stucco and tile buildings that dominate much of the university's charming 8200-acre campus, was joined in 1998 by the colorfully painted, Mexican-influenced Schwab Residential Center, housing 220 MBAs and 60 executive education participants a few blocks from campus. (Other on-campus apartments are reserved for married couples and families with children.) Faculty offices and classrooms are found in the school's other main building, Littlefield Hall, while the Dean's offices and administrative offices, plus more faculty offices and meeting rooms, are contained in the 1999-dedicated Knight Building. Improvements to the computer network capacity have been made on an ongoing basis, thanks to an investment of $10 million over the last five years.

Stanford is a school where the students cherish team players in class and, likewise, team outings on the social front. At the end of each week, everyone heads outdoors for an LPF ("Liquidity Preference Function") party. On Tuesday nights, MBAs shun the yuppie bars in Palo Alto and instead take over The Old Pro, a place where windows are covered with black plywood to protect the glass from unruly customers and barstools are patched with silver duct tape. Those most dedicated to the ritual call themselves FOAM (Friends of Arjay Miller, a former dean and head of Ford Motor Co.) and pay about $60 up front in September to drink free beer for the rest of the year. It's just one of the quirky differences Stanford students embrace.

PLACEMENT DETAILS

Despite the fact that recruiters designated Stanford's career services office the least effective of any school's, GSB students continue to fare extremely well in the job market. About 270 companies recruited second-year students for full-time jobs and internships on campus in 2000, and 850 opportunities were posted electronically. Not too shabby for a school with an enrollment of just 730. And that's not all. The median pay package of $165,500 was the highest of all 82 schools surveyed by BUSINESSWEEK in 2000, and new grads walked away with an average of 3.8 job offers apiece.

Just two years ago top hirers consisted largely of consulting firms, but the companies hiring Class of 2000 MBAs varied greatly among investment banking, consulting, and high-tech firms: McKinsey & Co. (20); Goldman Sachs (13); Bain & Co. (6); Intuit (6); Siebel Systems (6); Boston Consulting Group (6); Loudcloud (5); Morgan Stanley (4); Cyclone Commerce (3); Deloitte Consulting (3); and Yahoo! (3). The change reflects a growing interest among Stanford's students in high-tech start-ups, but the trend's future, at the mercy of market factors, is hazy. For now, the school's alumni connections and guest speakers in high-tech industries are most in demand, while the more old-school members of the recruiting circle have been caught a bit off-guard by a decrease in student interest. Director Sherrie Taguchi and her staff are making continuous efforts to manage recruiters' expectations through new innovations, like a Web site just for potential employers that provides information on students' preferences (type of industry, job function, location of workplace, size of company, and more). A greater number of international companies have, in fact, recently come on board—and the total number of recruiters for full-time jobs, 117, shows a 34 percent increase from 1999. But as those traditional companies face more disappointing student turnouts at corporate presentations, significantly less fruitful recruiting results than in other years, and high-and-mighty attitudes from some Stanford students who have come to expect an over-stuffed wallet, recruiters who used to be regulars, like Toys R Us and Dell, are temporarily bidding the career services office adieu. With persistence in its efforts and the inevitable influence of market fluctuations, however, Stanford is hoping they'll be back soon—and, reportedly, are working to ensure it.

OUTSTANDING FACULTY

Paul Romer (economics); *Irv Grousbeck* (entrepreneurship); *Peter Wendell* (entrepreneurship); *James Van Horne* (finance); *Edward Lazear* (human resources); *James Patell* (operations); *Jefferey Pfeffer* (organizational behavior); *Robert Burgleman* (strategic management); *Garth Saloner* (strategic management).

APPLICANT TIPS

What's the secret to getting into a school where just 8 percent of applicants were accepted in 2000? Aside from a touch of luck (you're one of more than 5400 applicants, after all), you should have a strong academic and professional record, demonstrated management potential, and a unique perspective to bring to the school. Stanford maintains it has no minimum GPA or GMAT requirements, but to give you an idea, the average GMAT score for the Class of 2000 came in at 727. Stanford doesn't conduct evaluative personal interviews, so your application essays are your chief means of distinguishing yourself. To do so, avoid what Admissions Director Marie Mookini points out as four main mistakes applicants make in tackling the essay: not answering the question; writing what they think the school wants to hear instead of what they really believe; trying too hard to market themselves; and believing that they have to present a unique or glamorous image. "You don't have to do something sexy or wild," assures Mookini. "It's more important that you've processed what you've actually done, and that you can convey it."

You'll want to apply early, before the first or second admissions deadlines. With Stanford's high yield, there aren't many spaces left by the third round. The sooner your application's in, the more quickly you'll get a reply: Those who make the November 1 deadline should get an answer within 7 or 8 weeks, whereas applicants for the March 21 deadline may have to wait 10 weeks or more. You can fill out your application online and submit it electronically, download it and mail it in, or request a paper copy and do things the old-fashioned way. If you're one of the chosen few, you may not have to wait for the thick envelope; you'll probably get a phone call from Mookini herself, who reaches at least 90 percent of admitted students for a personal congratulations before letters of acceptance are mailed.

Contact: Marie M. Mookini
Director of Admissions
415-723-2766
Application deadlines: November 1; January 4; March 21

STANFORD MBAs SOUND OFF

I've never been so proud of my affiliation with an institution. The GSB is at the epicenter of the new economy. The school's culture emphasizes cooperation—the program is extremely collegial. My classmates were extraordinarily bright, and brought with them a breadth of experience that opened my eyes to a number of opportunities. The relationship between Stanford and Silicon Valley cannot be overemphasized. John Doerr audited my econ class. I was able to see practically every tech visionary over my two years at the school.

Certainly, there are a few professors that are not spectacular. However, on balance the teaching is excellent. Furthermore, there is an incredible opportunity to apply classroom learning to real-world Valley businesses. In conjunction with the classroom, I worked with four different start-ups to help them formulate their business strategies/plans. Two were with entrepreneurs and two were spin-offs of a major corporation. Three of the four have been subsequently funded. I think it would have been hard to get this level of classroom-plus-business-world experience (and access) at some of the other schools I was considering attending.

Aside from the occasional lame teacher in the core, the faculty at Stanford are largely excellent. I've had some of the best professors I have ever had, here. The administration, on the other hand, leaves a lot to be desired. Time and again they treat the students like children, fail to engage the student body in meaningful dialogue before taking actions that directly impact the students, and generally show little respect for this important constituency.

It's hard to believe another business school provides as much to its students as the Stanford GSB. The students and overall experience are utterly outstanding, and the value of the Stanford MBA is hard to overestimate. Being from Stanford provides unparalleled access to opportunities. They seem almost limitless.

Attending the Stanford Graduate Business was the best experience of my life. My classmates were exceptional, the faculty and curriculum were extraordinary, and the network is unrivaled. No other business school can come close to providing the depth and breath of interpersonal and professional value that the GSB provides.

[Stanford] is a place where no one talks about grades, everyone is willing to help each other out, and you end up making some of the best friends you'll ever have. The complaints about teaching are in my opinion blown way out of proportion—some students come to the GSB as the top school of business in the country and have unrealistic expectations. They expect every class to be the best they've had, and every instructor to be infinitely insightful, engaging, and humorous (and many are). Unfortunately a few sub-par junior professors give the good ones a bad rap. Recruiters rank us low because it's a small class and people here aren't impressed by the Goldman Sachs and McKinseys of the world, like at other top schools. And I love it because of that.

Stanford was awesome! The quality of the professors and the teaching, the experience and motivation of my fellow students were all very impressive. The opportunities for experiential learning classes such as Interpersonal Dynamics, Negotiations, and IDMM were also wonderful.

One of Stanford's problems is its lack of responsiveness to students, both in regard to administrative and academic issues: Not enough sections of the popular classes are made available, and policies are often decided without regard to student's wishes.

**12.
UNIVERSITY OF
CALIFORNIA AT
LOS ANGELES**

UNIVERSITY OF CALIFORNIA AT LOS ANGELES

John E. Anderson Graduate School of Management
110 Westwood Plaza
Los Angeles, California 90095-1481
E-mail address: mba.admissions@anderson.ucla.edu
Web site address: http://www.anderson.ucla.edu

Corporate ranking: 13	Graduate ranking: 6
Enrollment: 1263	Annual tuition & fees:
Women: 28%	resident—$10,991
Non-U.S.: 26%	nonresident—$21,235
Minority: 8%	Room and board: $9297
Part-time: 608	Average GMAT score: 698
Average age: 28	Average years work exp.: 4.3
Applicants accepted: 15%	Accepted applicants enrolled: 48%
Median starting pay: $136,500	Intellectual capital: 10

Teaching methods: Lecture, 50%   Case study, 30%
Field study, 20%

Contact:
Linda Baldwin
Director of Admissions
310-825-6944
Application deadlines:
November 6
December 29
January 29
March 30

Los Angeles, the city of angels. It's a metropolis that attracts hopeful actors, sun-kissed beach goers, surfers, and more. These days, it attracts others with stars in their eyes, too: Internet entrepreneurs. They're drawn to the access to new media outlets and the pulse of the New Economy. Those are some of the same reasons that as many as 325 full-time students descend on a business school just 10 miles from the beach every September. The students pile into lecture halls to study the ins and outs of business—the things that make companies as successful and trendy as the some of the hot communities around Los Angeles. They are the MBAs at the John. E. Anderson Graduate School of Management.

Lifestyle is one of the top attractions to this Top 30 school. You'd be hard-pressed to find a more beautiful B-school, where the sun shines 334 days out of the year. It's a place where spreadsheets and financial models come together, and golf handicaps improve at the same time. But once you look beyond the school's palm-tree-lined walkways and rollerblading paths, you'll discover a superior business school with several assets besides the weather. Indeed, Anderson will appeal to even the most serious high-rise-confined analysts looking to break from work to brush up on management skills.

The 65-year-old B-school has been sitting pretty as BUSINESSWEEK's No. 12 business school in the United States since 1996, when it fell from its highest perch yet at No. 9. In 2000, Anderson's grads remained happy overall, with strong leanings in entrepreneurship—a topic that's been a gem at the school for close to a decade. Grads say information technology and e-business take second rank. So it makes sense that the MBAs would also tag their favorite elective Financing the Emerging Enterprise and praise the school for its teaching in elective courses, where they can dive into subjects besides the core finance, operations and technology management, human resources, and others. Another plus: Anderson's employment of technology in the classroom. Combine those strengths with the weather, a wired B-school building, and access to the rich and famous, and Anderson could be a good bet if you're looking to settle in southern California. Of course, that SoCal appeal also hits the school hard, with nearly two-thirds of 2000 grads staying in the state. Such has been the trend at Anderson and other California schools, keeping some East Coast, Midwest, and Southeastern recruiters away.

The sunshine can cast shadows in L.A., too. Recent graduates question the adequacy of the administration's responsiveness to student concerns and opinions and say the school needs to add more sections of popular electives to the roster. And with a class that includes 27 percent women and just 8 percent minorities, grads worry that Anderson's efforts to foster interaction among various ethnic groups is just not adequate.

That may change now that the school's new dean has gotten his feet wet. Bruce Willison is the seventh dean at Anderson, and the first to come to the school from the rat race—he spent 26 years in the banking industry at places like Home Savings of America and H.F. Ahmanson & Co., and, most recently, Bank of America and First Interstate Bancorp. His arrival in 1999 seems to have dried up past graduates' qualms about a dearth of leadership at the school after Dean William Pierkalla left the job in 1997 to return to teach operations and technology management at Anderson. Now, Willison says, it's the "appropriate time for business schools to redefine management education." For him—

and Anderson—that means the constant production of new knowledge that stretches across academic fields. Lucky for him and all Anderson MBAs, the school has six centers where that's the name of the game: The Price Center for Entrepreneurial Studies, the Center for International Business Education and Research, the Center for Communication Policy, the Center for Real Estate, the Center for Management in the Information Economy (one year old), and the UCLA Anderson Forecast. "We'd better focus on things that make us world class," he says. Willison still has tasks before him. He needs to attract some $70 million to the school as part of Campaign UCLA. The school has collected over $40 million, but in his annual letter Willison says that the school is "way behind schedule." That means other improvements to the school's facilities and departments may be slow-going.

Still, students at Anderson can be sure they'll get an interesting courseload. The curriculum requires students to take eight core courses, allowing time in the first year to enroll in some of its 140 elective courses. The long-standing favorite is professor William Cockrum's Managing Finance and Financing the Emerging Enterprise. "Wild Bill," as he's known by his students, has become something of a legend for his relentless cold-calling in this case-study course in finance. He says to the students, "I'm teaching you this so you can one day be clipping coupons on the beach." The core was revised in 1998 and consists of classes in human resources, statistics, financial accounting, managerial economics and finance, operations and technology management, and marketing. The classes are tackled in 60-student sections, which are reshuffled after each of the three 10-week quarters that make up the first year. (Students who pass exams can waive core courses, but the credits must be replaced with more advanced classes.) Teamwork is the mantra at Anderson. And most graduates will also add that without their classmates, Anderson wouldn't be Anderson. "I learned as much from my peers as I did from the professors," says one Anderson MBA turned entrepreneur.

The teams don't break down after the first year. A 35-year-old required capstone field study spans the last one or two quarters, depending on the scope of the project. Teams of three to five students put on their consulting hats with a sponsoring "client" company and its managers, working on substantive issues and problems in real time. Ultimately, students take the analytical and theoretical lessons learned in the classroom to the highway for a test drive. Sure, a lot of B-schools consider such projects a given these days, but Anderson MBAs have a chance to work with clients such as Microsoft, DreamWorks Studios, and Los Angeles Center for Community and Family Services. And perhaps the nicest perk for the MBAs approaching the tail ends of their loans before graduation is that the two best field studies are each awarded cash prizes of $4000—thanks to a Deloitte & Touche sponsorship—to be split among team members. Anderson requires 14 additional courses for graduation, 11 of which are chosen from among the B-school's 140-elective catalog. Students may concentrate in 1 of 14 traditional functional areas, ranging from entertainment management and high technology to information systems and marketing, or they can craft their own.

But as many entrepreneurs say, you can only learn so much in the classroom. The Harold Price Center for Entrepreneurial Studies, the student-run Entrepreneur Association (EA), with 500 members, and the High Tech Business Association (HTBA), with 262 members, tap into the local venture capital, high-tech, and entertainment communities for assistance often. In 1999, those clubs and others attracted keynotes such as Al Berkeley, president of the Nasdaq; Sky Dayton, founder of Earthlink; Dr. Susan Love; Jimmy Carter; and Los Angeles Mayor Richard Riordan. If that's not enough practice, the school has a student investment fund of $2 million to be managed. Another program matches local entrepreneurs with students. And over 75 speakers visit campus to tell tales from the front lines. The Wolfen Fund helps students trying to start their own companies by providing them with cash to live on as they're writing their business plans.

There's plenty of room for anyone who doesn't have an itch to own his or her own company, too. And would-be business owners may feel the need to get their feet wet in more established companies before giving it a try on their own. To that end, finance and marketing also remain strong at Anderson. The school is a great jumping-off point for those interested in real estate or entertainment management, both interdisciplinary offerings and the latter placing MBAs in classes with aspiring actors, directors, and producers in UCLA's department of film and television. (Where else can you leave class and grab an espresso with a Hollywood mogul?)

Although global management isn't one of Anderson's strengths, the school has recently made strides. About 100 students apply every year for the international management fellows program and the school accepts 25 to 30 of those applicants. The 24-month program at Anderson is called International Management Fellows program in Mandarin Chinese, Japanese, or Spanish. The summer before the beginning of the MBA program, participants take intensive classes in language and culture. One year later, they head off to a foreign country for nine months of internship, work at a local company, and study everything from political economy to history and, of course, business at a local university before returning to finish up their last two quarters. For those who prefer a traditional exchange program, UCLA has pacts with 38 different schools in Australia, Europe, Central and South America, Asia, and South Africa. Back at home, the newly reduced core allows students to take up to three courses in the larger university's extensive offerings; joint degrees can be taken in law, computer science, Latin American studies, library and information science, nursing, urban planning, public health, and medicine.

No matter what you choose, you'll have to have the school's required laptop computers. Anderson says it's spent $500,000 on technology over the past three years. Every seat in every classroom, office, study room, and library is wired for access to the computer network, 2900 ports in all. Of course materials are posted on the school's intranet (with plans to post 100 percent by 2002), along with faculty and student directories, student Web pages and résumés, course bidding and registration, and job search resources. Multimedia presentation equipment, videoconferencing capabilities, laser printers, and other high-tech gadgetry are at student disposal as well.

You need a car to survive anywhere in L.A., but remember to pack your patience before trying to park at UCLA. Even prospective Anderson MBAs quip that if you're driving to your interview at Anderson, give yourself an extra hour and bring your parking angel to find a spot. On campus, many end up taking the bus. But once students are settled into life at Anderson, they can't help but relax. They've got an on-site café, souped-up lecture halls to study in, venture capital competitions to test their business plans in, and plenty of MBA nights to enjoy.

PLACEMENT DETAILS

Students and corporate recruiters alike hand top marks to Anderson's Parker MBA Career Management Center, which brought 143 companies to campus to recruit for summer interns and 196 companies to recruit for permanent placements in 2000. (That's a 35 percent increase over the prior year for second-year recruiting.) The companies held 187 presentations before conducting 7951 interviews in 2000. The office is working hard to convince students from outside of the United States that they've got options after graduation. Alysa Polkes, the career office's director, has a team set up to work with non-U.S. students. For three days before classes start, the

non-U.S. MBAs meet to bring their CVs and résumés up to a U.S. standard, experience a day on the job, and practice convincing U.S. employers to take the time to consider them for employment—if they want to land a job on U.S. soil. After all, 12.9 percent of Anderson grads took jobs outside of the United States in Asia, Latin America, and Europe. To help all Anderson students, the office wired its resource library and remodeled its interview rooms. The Anderson office is also making strides to meet the needs of its fully employed MBA students who are studying part-time. Since more are interested in changing careers with their MBAs, Polkes has career programs specifically geared to them. Indeed, the school lets FEMBAs in their last year of study interview alongside the full-time MBAs.

But don't start thinking that UCLA's career office is cutthroat among the various MBAs. Students say it's pretty relaxed. Those with a dot-com leaning say that once the "suited" MBAs are done interviewing for their I-banking (I-banks attracted 31 percent more Anderson grads in 2000 than in 1999) and consulting jobs in the fall, the office becomes even more relaxed. Grads in 2000 reaped the benefits of a still-sizzling economy with job options aplenty and compensation to match. The high-tech industry enticed the largest number of Anderson grads—29 percent. In 2000, grads secured total compensation packages that averaged $110,000. Over half of the grads who took jobs in the high-tech sector landed at Internet services.

In the end, nearly 70 percent of grads stayed in California in 2000, and just 10 percent packed for New York City, proving that sunshine and Hollywood rule at the end of a work day, too. Top hires: Intel Corporation (8); Goldman Sachs (7); Lehman Brothers (7); Morgan Stanley Dean Witter (7); Robertson Stephens (7); McKinsey & Co. (6); Salomon Smith Barney (6); Diamond Technology Partners (now Diamond Cluster International) (5); Banc of America Securities (4); Digital Coast Partners (4); Mattel, Inc. (4).

OUTSTANDING FACULTY

Eric Sussman (accounting); *Antonio Bernardo* (economics); *Victor Tabbush* (economics); *Al Osborne* (entrepreneurship); *Bill Cockrum* (entrepreneurship/finance); *Mathias Kahl* (finance); *Randy Bucklin* (marketing).

APPLICANT TIPS

Qualified minority candidates are bound to merit a second look from the admissions staff at UCLA because Proposition 209, the 1997 California statute barring preferential treatment of minority students in higher education, resulted in a decrease in African-American, Hispanic-American, and Native American students from 10 percent in 1996 to 8 percent in 2000. That's in spite of Anderson's best efforts to build minority enrollment through its Riordan Programs, designed to encourage promising disadvantaged high school and college students to pursue higher education in management and careers in business. Linda Baldwin, director of Anderson's admissions office, says: "We have to demonstrate how Anderson is a place where students of color participate in the widest range of leadership roles, and moreover that it is a place where there are fellowships and resources that they can access even in a [Proposition] 209 climate."

That doesn't make it any easier to make the cut in Anderson's admissions. Baldwin's team accepted 15 percent of its 4563 applicants in 2000 for 330 spots. The average GMAT for the Class of 2002 was 698—two points shy of Wharton's average GMAT.

Applications can be filled out online, downloaded from the Web, or requested and submitted on paper, though fewer people are doing so these days. Applicants face the usual batch of requirements, such as recommendations, taking the GMAT, writing essays, and the like, but the whole package should be into the office as early as possible. Don't wait for the March 30 deadline to file your applications. Since Anderson has rolling admissions, the class can fill up quickly. Interviews aren't required, but encouraged, and the school warns that interview slots fill up quickly. There are, of course, options. Applicants can interview in select cities when Anderson visits, at forums, or with alumni of the school. The school says that no one interview holds more weight than the next.

Linda Baldwin has made a concerted effort to attract younger and more diverse students to the program lately. In the fall of 2000, she visited undergraduate students with other top B-schools to tell them that it is okay to apply as a 24-year-old despite an average age of 28. If you make the cut, don't plan on deferring to hold on to your job. Anderson doesn't grant deferrals. They do, however, hold on to applications for two years, so even if you miss the cut one year, you can renew your application two years later.

Contact: Linda Baldwin
Director of Admissions
310-825-6944
Application deadlines: November 6; December 29; January 29; March 30

ANDERSON MBAs SOUND OFF

I cannot imagine any other program in the country offering a better experience for students interested in entrepreneurship or the entertainment business than the Anderson School. The Price Center for Entrepreneurial Studies offers the students academic and nonacademic programs alike that distinguish this institution even among the best business schools in the world. Additionally, being involved in the rapidly growing Los Angeles technology community at the earlier stages of its development offered unparalleled access to community and business leaders as they were building this burgeoning community. Going to Anderson was one of the best decisions of my life.

Two key strengths of the Anderson School at UCLA are its finance and entrepreneurial programs. As an aspiring entrepreneur, I found the strong entrepreneurial program of UCLA and the progressive, creative nature of Los Angeles to be a great combination to foster innovation. Also, the addition of Dean Willison this year has provided new-found leadership. And, what most people forget is the very attractive return on investment at Anderson—tuition is significantly lower than that of other private schools. Finally, the quality of life here is excellent—I only wish I moved here sooner.

I chose Anderson over Wharton, Chicago, and Michigan. I am very glad I made that choice.

Coming from the East Coast, I originally had no idea what a great MBA program was offered at the Anderson School. Had I been admitted to Harvard, I probably would have gone there. In hindsight, not getting into Harvard was probably the best thing that could have happened to me. Anderson has provided me with an equally great academic experience, a very team-friendly learning environment, significant leadership opportunities, and a lot of great friends (not to mention a serious reduction in my golf handicap).

I am pursuing a nontraditional career in the television industry. Although I have had to conduct a self-directed job search, the school offered several educational and networking advantages, such as electives in the entertainment-management field; an opportunity to take electives at UCLA's graduate School of Film & Television; a very strong student organization, the Entertainment Management Association; a speaker series arranged by UCLA's Center for Communication Policy that brings in top level entertainment executives such as Frank Biondi and Sandy Grushow on a regular basis; a Los Angeles location that has allowed me to intern part time during the school year and to set up frequent informational meetings with entertainment executives; and, finally, an active, accessible network of alumni working in the entertainment industry.

I believe that although assessing the quality of teaching and course content is important in evaluating an MBA program, the most valuable long-term takeaways of an MBA education—judgment, leadership, effective communication, and organizational skills— are developed experientially through the extracurricular culture of the program. In this regard, I believe that the Anderson School fostered an excellent learning environment.

13.
NEW YORK
UNIVERSITY

NEW YORK UNIVERSITY

Leonard N. Stern School of Business
Henry Kaufman Management Center
44 West 4th Street
New York, New York 10012
E-mail address: sternmba@stern.nyu.edu
Web site address: http://www.stern.nyu.edu

Corporate ranking: 11
Enrollment: 2740
Women: 36%
Non-U.S.: 34%
Minority: 8%
Part-time: 1900
Average age: 27
Applicants accepted: 22%
Median starting pay: $140,000

Graduate ranking: 16
Annual tuition & fees: $29,956
Room and board: $13,397
Average GMAT score: 686
Average years of work exp.: 4.5
Accepted applicants enrolled: 50%
Intellectual capital: 23

Teaching methods: Lecture, 38%   Case study, 37%
                       Presentations, consulting, 25%

Contact:
John Lyon
Director of MBA
Admissions
212-998-0600
Application deadlines:
December 1
January 15
March 15

In 1998, New York University's Leonard N. Stern School of Business was sitting pretty. The school, after continuing its rise in BUSINESS-WEEK's rankings, had just received a $10 million gift from Henry Kaufman, an economist and chairman of the Stern Board of Overseers. The money helped pay for the addition of 60,000 square feet to the education center, making room for classrooms, study lounges, and reception areas.

From the glass windows of the recently renamed Henry Kaufman Management Center, students see a pavement piazza bustling with all New York's charm—an eccentric artist beating a bongo drum, a dreadlocked hot dog vendor, and beatniks selling books on the corner. "We're in New York," Dean George G. Daly says. "You can't tell where the city ends and NYU begins." Mere moments away from Wall Street, Stern appears to have it all. The Class of 2000 seemed to think so, inching Stern from No. 20 to No. 16 in the graduate satisfaction poll and recruiters rank it slightly higher. For now, Stern is stuck in the 13th spot overall, where it has lingered since the mid-1990s. Why the plateau?

For starters, Stern faces an obstacle plaguing many top B-schools in these booming economic times. Like its counterparts in Silicon Valley, Stern experienced a 17 percent falloff in the number of applications since 1998. One reason for the drop: New York, referred to as Silicon Alley, tempted some young hotshots to attempt to strike it rich with start-ups and defer B-school. In addition, other traditional economic opportunities were just too good for potential MBAs to pass up. This phenomenon has Stern on alert and was an impetus for the admissions office to take a different approach. Enter John Lyon, director of MBA Admissions and Student Services. These days he is the one with the answers, fulfilling the role of admissions officer and counselor. Admitted applicants can talk options with the man in charge. Attention to candidates is the key, and Stern is making an effort to offer the personal touch after applications dropped. One example: Lyon found himself advising a Los Angeles applicant, who was admitted to the Stern School in 2000. She had a counteroffer from her employer, who was trying to keep her from leaving for B-school in the Big Apple. Lyon was torn. He wanted her to see the long-term value of a graduate degree, but knew today's financial opportunities are hard to resist. In the end, Lyon won the woman over, and she's attending Stern.

Recruiters remain satisfied with the school's grads for the most part. But, although corporations say they benefit from the finance skills Stern MBAs possess, the school loses points with recruiters for what was perceived as a lack of innovation, and some recruiters worry that Stern students lack technology skills in comparison to their peers at other top B-schools. That might change if the latest crop of MBAs take more advantage of sleek, new Bloomberg terminals and enhanced videoconferencing. In addition, the Digital Economy Initiative, a group of core courses focused on e-commerce and related fields, is allowing Stern to jump on the high-tech bandwagon more immediately, rather than waiting to offer students an e-commerce major. Students have raved about the quick response and the link to Silicon Alley superstars. Seth Godin of Yahoo, for example, taught an Internet marketing course. 2000 graduate Susanne Mei, who took a job at a dot-com in San Francisco after graduation, says her participation in the Digital Economy Initiative kept her on the cutting edge of industry and gave her plenty to talk about when she was interviewed by potential employers.

Although praise for tech initiatives is nice, Stern won't rest on its laurels. Progress has become a hallmark of the school. Back in the late 1980s—the last time the school made heads turn—the administration had Leonard N. Stern to thank for his $30 million donation. Those funds revolutionized the B-school, helping to put NYU on the management education map. During the next decade, under the leadership of Dean Richard R. West, who left in 1993, and Daly, his successor, Stern has pushed to shake its image as a "night school." The image, which is a result of its 1916 roots as a satellite campus on Trinity Place designed for Wall Streeters who walked to class after work, is certainly fading. Although such students still account for a large part of the MBA enrollment, the school continues to shrink its part-time population. It's down to to 1900 part-timers in the Class of 2002. But, those part-timers serve as a valuable asset to full-time students. Evening classes are often a mix of full- and part-time students, giving full-time MBAs the advantage of more experienced counterparts in class.

Despite a decrease in applications, the caliber of Stern students continues to improve as the administration aggressively recruits a diverse student body. GPAs and GMAT scores of admitted applicants rose slightly in 2000 from two years earlier. But alumni have noticed the difference in the quality of students. "You find you're not as smart as you think you are, or there are others as smart as you," says 2000 graduate Justin M. Ziegler of his initial encounters with classmates.

In addition, NYU continues to attract more women and international students than some other top programs. Stern remains one of the few schools able to attract females, with women accounting for 35 percent of the student body. The urban B-school also has become the hot spot for international students, with foreigners making up about 34 percent of the total enrollment. "The business model was born here," says Nicola Bonelli, a self-proclaimed promoter of the Stern experience and 2000 graduate originally from Naples, Italy. NYU's vicinity to the trading floors made the school the only choice for her, Bonelli says.

Stern has one of the finest finance programs in the world—recruiters rated it ninth of 82 schools surveyed by BUSINESSWEEK in 2000—and students find themselves frequently rubbing elbows with wizards from the corporate and entertainment worlds. In recent years, guest speakers have included MTV's Vice President of Consumer Marketing David Cohn, Bravo Networks President Kathy Dore, and CEO of Credit Suisse First Boston Allen Wheat.

Teaching at Stern isn't too shabby either. The 200-member faculty is supplemented by a star-studded cast of 100 adjunct professors. Former Federal Reserve Chairman Paul A. Volcker, for example, signed on in 1998 to guest lecture a number of finance and economics courses. Also, students call Professor of Finance Aswath Damodaran a dynamo, citing his accessibility and vast knowledge.

In 1998, Daly tried to jumpstart the school again with a brand new curriculum and an emphasis on team projects. This program called for faculty to introduce more advanced material in basic-level courses, and the dean severely restricted waivers for students attempting to place out of core requirements. The idea was to create small learning communities that provide students with plenty of practice in teamwork and communication skills.

The results: Students gave middle-of-the-road ratings to Stern faculty and course work, with teaching in core classes receiving particularly low marks. But students say they were thrilled to see additional elective courses and improved career counseling. Steve Boscoe, a 2000 graduate, says the availability of guest lecturers from Wall Street and local industries both helped and hindered. Courses that require concrete knowledge can suffer from the slew of guest lecturers coming in and out, occasionally leaving graduates feeling a few knowledge gaps.

Students begin the Stern journey with a two-week pre-term that levels the playing field with required sessions in computer proficiency, ethics, management communication, case analysis techniques, and diversity; those who need extra help with accounting, mathematics, or statistics can sign up for optional workshops in those subjects as well. Social activities and free time allow students to meet classmates and find adventures on the streets of New York before plunging into first-year classes.

During pre-term, students are divided into groups of about 65 with which they will take most first-year classes and interact often throughout the second year. The core curriculum is made up of integrated courses like business strategy analysis, foundation classes like financial accounting, and breadth courses like marketing. Incoming MBAs can choose among eight majors, two co-majors, and numerous concentrations when developing specialties.

To major in a traditional field, students must take at least 12 of the 61 course units required for graduation in that area, or they can combine these majors with further concentrations in such areas as entertainment, media and technology, law and business, and real estate finance. Co-majors include international business and entrepreneurship and innovation, a program created about two years ago to respond to growing interest in start-ups. In an effort to give students a multitude of choices and a breadth of knowledge, the administration offers formal joint-degree programs as well. Students can opt for joint degrees in law, French studies, creative arts, politics, and statistics and operations research.

Though recruiters snub Stern for lack of innovation, students cheer about the responsiveness of the administration to student needs and desires. Indeed, students have begun their reign at Stern. Recently, the administration even had three students interview Assistant Dean

Gary Fraser, who heads the career placement office, before hiring him. Fraser, a Stern alumnus, says he thought the students were his toughest and most important audience. Nowadays, more than anything else, students need space. Like many B-school administrators, Daly finds himself constantly searching for available classrooms, lounges, and reception areas. The Kaufman donation relieved some pressure by giving Stern students more room to move. The Legacy Campaign, for which graduating students collect and donate money, also enhanced the quality of student space. A student lounge, which was built with legacy money, looks like something out of MTV's *Real World*. Additional construction this year is intended to please students and recruiters alike, including the renovation of reception areas. Though campus is looking spiffy, housing in New York's trendy Greenwich Village remains an obstacle for Stern MBAs. In addition to renovating academic areas, NYU administrators are having a new dormitory built on 14th Street between Third and Fourth Avenues. The dorm, which is being constructed on the site of the defunct Palladium nightclub, will include about 120 rooms for B-school students. All of the rooms will be singles, and each of the four MBA floors will include a meeting area and separate computer lounge equipped with PCs. Those who opt for city living often do so as roommates, since even a small studio apartment near campus can cost upwards of $1600 month.

Regardless of where Stern MBAs hang their hats, these students have their eyes on the world. And Stern's optimal location makes it a mecca for students with a keen global perspective on business. The centerpiece for international business students is a global exchange program, which sends 50 to 60 MBAs each year to study at one of 33 management schools in Australia, Europe, South America, Asia, and Africa with which Stern has reciprocal agreements. Students may also earn certification in European Management Studies by working in Europe for a summer and tacking on a postgraduate semester studying at a European business school.

Those who stay in the United States all four semesters need not miss out on the global experience. About three dozen each year sign up for the Global Business Consulting Program, which sends students to emerging markets in Asia during January break to work on projects for paying clients such as Royal Dutch Shell, J.P. Morgan, MasterCard, and IBM.

Just going to school in New York City can be an international experience, considering the community is composed of an array of ethnic backgrounds. Students flaunt their heritage at International Passport Day, a Stern tradition. At the last passport day, students, who donned Brazilian soccer jerseys, danced to ethnic music and aired a slide show featuring highlights from their homeland, Brazil. In addition to campus events, Stern students can eat their way through New York, while developing an acute sense of culture, with Turkish, Korean, Russian, and Middle Eastern restaurants (just to name a few) mere blocks from campus.

Stern students demolish stereotypes of stuffy MBAs. These folks say they know how to party and unwind. Take Thursday nights for example—when students gather for what's basically a night of subsidized drinking. And how could you not be social, given the hundreds of bars, restaurants, and clubs within walking distance of the school? Traditionally, first-year MBAs send graduating classmates off with a stylish shindig. In 2000, first-year students held a "Party for Departing Parties" at No Idea, a bar in the Grammercy Park area.

And despite maintaining close ties with students, Dean Daly refrains from partying like a New York City rock star. "I don't want to run around with a Stern T-shirt and get drunk with [students] or anything," he says. "But they are why I do this job." While students probably won't find themselves grabbing a brew with the dean, they certainly might get a few laughs at his expense at the Stern Follies, a ritual for MBAs.

At the annual show, the dean appears in a quasi-humiliating skit. But when the fun is over, the Stern community gets back to business. And work is no laughing matter for these urbanites.

PLACEMENT DETAILS

With the majority of Stern students going into finance, it's not surprising that as Wall Street turns, so do the fortunes of Stern grads. And, in recent years, those fortunes have certainly been on the upturn. In 2000, Stern graduates garnered an average of 2.8 job offers apiece and a median starting pay package of $140,000—toward the top of the B-school list. Top employers were Lehman Brothers (17); J.P. Morgan (15); Chase Manhattan (14); Deutsche Bank (12); McKinsey & Company (11); Salomon Smith Barney (10); American Express (9); Bear Sterns (9); Goldman Sachs (9); Merrill Lynch (8).

In 2000, 133 companies recruited on campus, with 90 percent of second-year students receiving their first job offer before graduation. Despite the convenience of studying in Silicon Alley, only about 4 percent of graduates took a job at a start-up. For the most part, NYU is sticking to its finance roots. The second largest group of employers of Stern grads included Booz-Allen & Hamilton, Credit Suisse First Boston, and Deloitte and Touche.

The placement office experienced some changes after Gary Fraser took over. He has made new efforts to market Stern. Fraser plans to maintain Stern links to Old Economy favorites, but he also wants to look into partnering with companies beyond mere recruiting, perhaps bringing companies into the classroom for special projects and programs. Of course, Fraser also expects to take advantage of Stern's prime location by enhancing relationships with recruiters in the entertainment and new media industries.

OUTSTANDING FACULTY

Aswath Damodaran (finance); *William Silber* (finance); *David Yermack* (finance); *Richard Freedman* (management); *Christopher Tucci* (management); *John Czepiel* (marketing); *Michael Darling* (marketing).

APPLICANT TIPS

The admissions office accepted 22 percent of applicants in 2000, compared with 18 percent in 1998. However, quality is still the priority with GMAT scores and GPA remaining high. Administrators will closely examine test scores and the quality of your undergraduate program, according to the admissions office—which means that a 4.0 at a community college is not going to give you an edge over a lower GPA at an Ivy League school. Interviews at Stern are done by invitation only, and because the school now interviews virtually all students who are eventually admitted, consider an invite to come to campus a positive sign.

Lyon says today's applicants are educated about the school and make knowledgeable decisions about where to apply. He encourages students who might be lured by the hot economy to look at the big picture and note the future value of attaining an MBA. Honesty is the best policy, if you ask Lyon. He says potential students should be truthful in the application and, especially, in the essay. Taking time with the essay is a necessity because Lyon says it can reveal elements of an applicant that no other part of the application addresses. But be sure to answer all the questions posed in the essay section—and answer them fully. Lyon says the biggest mistake people make is partially addressing a question. Also, remember slow and steady wins the race and there is no need to rush. Pace yourself and edit, edit, edit. But keep in mind that while Stern has two admissions rounds, if you want scholarship consideration, you must apply by the January deadline.

Contact: John Lyon
Director of MBA Admissions
212-998-0600
Application deadlines: December 1;
January 15; March 15

STERN MBAs SOUND OFF

Stern had it all. I have heard the school maligned as being successful because of its proximity to so many recruiters in New York. But to view this as anything but an asset is, frankly, sour grapes. My decision to go to Stern was based on two goals: learn finance and management, two topics that I needed a strong foundation in for my career and to find a job in finance (in sales and trading). To the extent that Stern met those two goals, I cannot possibly complain.

Coming from a nonprofit background, I had my reservations going into school. I was worried that I would find my classmates' politics objectionable and that I would become personally corrupted by the "capitalist pig" experience. I am happy to report that I found just the opposite. Students at B-school never ever talk politics, and on the whole, I found the ones at Stern to be a great bunch. Regarding how my own politics have changed, I feel that the experience has opened me up to another perspective and given me a deeper understanding of the issues that I had before taken for granted. Anyway, I now recommend the B-school thing (and Stern in particular) to all my lefty friends.

A drawback to Stern is the lack of social interaction with the other professional and graduate students at the university.

I came into Stern thinking that it would be full of students only from the metropolitan New York area, and came to be pleasantly surprised at the geographic diversity of the student population. Also, the school lived up to its promotional materials in the view books. The school has some well-regarded academics who actually care about the students learning the material and express interest in them. The same can be said for some of the high-profile visiting lecturers such as Paul Volcker and John Bogle, whom I had the chance to hear speak on numerous occasions and ask them questions as well. Overall, the school exceeded my expectations.

14. CARNEGIE MELLON UNIVERSITY

CARNEGIE MELLON UNIVERSITY

Graduate School of Industrial Administration
Schenley Park
Pittsburgh, Pennsylvania 15213-3890
E-mail address: gsia-admissions@andrew.cmu.edu
Web site address: http://www.gsia.cmu.edu

Corporate ranking: 14	Graduate ranking: 13
Enrollment: 649	Annual tuition & fees: $26,750
Women: 28%	Room and board: $9800
Non-U.S.: 41%	Average GMAT score: 660
Minority: 5%	Average years of work exp.: 5.4
Part-time: 192	Accepted applicants enrolled: 61%
Average age: 28	Intellectual capital: 22
Applicants accepted: 31%	
Median starting pay: $125,000	

Teaching methods: Lecture, 60%   Case study, 30%   Other, 10%

A lot of top B-schools like to boast that they are *wired* for the twenty-first century. But even though Carnegie Mellon was recently heralded as Yahoo!'s "Most Wired University for 2000," administrators and students at the Graduate School of Industrial Association might dispute that claim. After all, the university is not really wired at all—the entire campus is *wireless*.

Since the summer of 2000, Carnegie Mellon students with the right Ethernet card installed in their laptops have been logging on to the university's network from virtually anywhere on campus, from the classrooms and library to the parking lots. Need to check a stock quote while en route to finance class? No problem—just log on to the network while standing in the hall. Feel like catching some sun on grassy Flagstaff Hill outside the GSIA building while catching up on that flood of e-mails? Just click. Even most of the B-school's exams are now given via computer, and a laptop is required for nearly every class.

Indeed, the Wireless Andrew network is just the latest in a long line of technologies to appear at GSIA. It's been that way since the 1950s, when GSIA became the first B-school to install one on campus. And it's still that way: In 2000, recent graduates rated the information technology and technological tools among the top of the heap of all 82 schools surveyed by BUSINESSWEEK, and corporate recruiters once again ranked GSIA No. 2 in the nation in information technology, just behind MIT. Computer access practically borders on obsession here, with over $4.3 million pumped into technology improvements since 1995. The school's seven computer labs boast 600 personal computers—nearly

Contact:
Laurie Stewart
Director of Admissions
and Financial Aid
412-268-2272
Application deadlines:
November 17
January 31
March 23

four times the number you'd find at Harvard, which has three times as many students. And that's in addition to the laptops all GSIA students are now required to own.

In a world moving at Internet speed, Dean Douglas M. Dunn argues that students' familiarity with technology gives Carnegie Mellon's alums a competitive edge over grads from other top B-schools. "Technology is moving so quickly that in order to make the bets as a manager, you need to understand how it is evolving," he says. "That will allow (managers) to pick solutions that work."

So does that mean GSIA classes are filled with row upon row of green-eyeshaded geeks? Not exactly. More and more GSIA students are, in fact, coming from diverse, liberal arts–type backgrounds, the result of an administrative initiative to "put more balance in terms of the students we matriculate," according to Dunn. Recent classes have included archaeologists and aerospace engineers, prize-winning violinists and professional golfers, off-track betting directors and naval officers. Over the past two years, Dunn, a former AT&T vice president who in 1996 became GSIA's first-ever dean hired from the corporate world, has launched a number of initiatives to improve his MBA's "soft skills." GSIA started its own case competition, evaluated by a panel of print and television journalists and faculty members who judge contestants' writing and speaking abilities. The B-school now provides each MBA a free subscription to *The Wall Street Journal,* encouraging students to meet and mingle over the day's business news. And on weekends, interested students are welcome to attend public speaking workshops from the GSIA chapter of Toastmaster's International. Even the diplomas will now de-emphasize GSIA's technical tradition. Starting in 2000, Carnegie Mellon stopped conferring a Master of Science in Industrial Administration degree that confused recruiters and prospective students, and now awards a standard MBA diploma instead.

Underneath this new schoolwide countenance still beats the heart of a quant jock. Before spending 26 years in telecommunications, Dunn himself earned a doctorate in business statistics, so he's no stranger to the fundamental mission that underpins everything GSIA does— "to develop the scientific principles that underlie business management," as the school's Web site proclaims. And despite the growing diversity, up to 60 percent of entering students have technical backgrounds, in engineering, physics, mathematics, or computer science. Those who don't generally have come to Carnegie Mellon precisely because of its emphasis on quantitative thinking, to acquire the solid grounding in computers, operations, and finance that will complement their other skills and which two years at GSIA virtually guarantees. It's a core competency Dunn, for one, recognizes and hopes to preserve as his legacy when he retires as dean at the end of 2002. "We know what our comparative advantage is," he says. "We're not looking to change what we're doing—just to add to our strengths."

Those strengths include nurturing some of the skills employers value most right now, such as thinking analytically and being able to back up your ideas with hard data—skills that have enabled GSIA to settle in at No. 14 in BUSINESS-WEEK's rankings for the third time in a row. Two years at GSIA, and you can't help but be comfortable with high-powered number-crunching; you'll be able to read a balance sheet like it was a dime-store novel. Computers and other cutting-edge telecommunications tools will be second nature to you. And you'll find no shortage of companies willing to pay handsomely for your proficiencies: In 2000, GSIA graduates drew an average of 3.1 job offers apiece, on target with other top B-schools, and nailed a median starting pay package of $125,000, on par with what most B-school grads from Top 30 schools can expect.

By accounts of recent grads, however, those skills aren't acquired easily. Surpassing almost every other school, including University of Virginia's Darden—known for its boot camp work atmosphere—in 2000 only Dartmouth College's Tuck School was rated by students to have a heavier workload than GSIA among the Top 30, with "rigorous" and "difficult" among the more polite ways of describing a grueling first year that tackles the bulk of its core requirements before January. The emphasis on mathematics and quantitative methods can make the burden even more staggering, with some students complaining that the more than 40 hours they spend completing homework problems each week make the job search incredibly challenging. Even courses that are not usually laden with lots of quant work, such as microeconomics, have a heavily mathematical bent here. Teamwork is fostered as a means of making it through this boot camp, and the quick and daunting pace teaches at least one critical lesson: the interdependence of the group and the need to prioritize everything. Yet, GSIA students report they lack a sense of camaraderie with their classmates. "There is not a great esprit de corps among our class," notes 2000 alum Daniel Crouse. "The workload is high enough that people feel more relieved to get out than appreciative that they were here. It's a major problem." Another grad puts it even more bluntly: "GSIA is not for the faint of heart or the undirected. MBA wannabes who know what they want and are willing to work hard for it are well served, but if you're coming to graduate school to 'find yourself,' my advice is to go elsewhere."

For those who are looking to prove themselves in the dot-com world, GSIA launched a one-year Master's in e-Commerce program in spring 1999 that might be an even tougher crucible. The fast-track program for about 60 students—ranging from Wall Street warriors to a dentist with relatively little business or computer knowledge—features an intense courseload. Starting in May, students must take 24 required courses split between learning the technical ropes of e-commerce from Carnegie Mellon's top-ranked computer science faculty and sharpening their business acumen at GSIA. The degree program ends with a capstone project that allows students to apply their new skills for a real, high-tech client. Carnegie Mellon also offers a rigorous one-year degree program that confers a Master's in Computational Finance.

Whatever track you choose, if you're looking for a touchy-feely, people-focused B-school experience, you might want to go elsewhere. Although the curriculum doesn't ignore this area completely—business communications has been a required course for over 10 years, and a new oral communications workshop was added in 1999—it's more on a value-added basis than a central concern. GSIA students rate their training in interpersonal and leadership skills among the lowest of the Top 30, and corporate recruiters are far more enthusiastic about graduates' analytical and technological talents than their abilities in communications, teamwork, and marketing. That said, recruiters in 2000 called the school one of the most innovative and improved, and lauded graduates' ability to compete globally—and grads have slowly climbed the ranks in general management skills in the last four years.

But while recruiters have been happier with graduates, the grads themselves have given the school lower marks in 2000. In 1998, Carnegie Mellon finished 5th overall in BUSINESSWEEK's poll of graduates, but in 2000, grads rated the school 13th overall—pinpointing a lack of responsiveness on the part of the administration when it comes to student concerns. Still, grads like the program's relatively small size, pragmatic approach to management, and distinct international flavor—more than 37 percent of the student body comes from outside the United States, one of the highest proportions among the Top 30. (The school is considerably less diverse when it comes to underrepresented U.S. minorities, who make up only 5 percent of current enrollment—the lowest proportion in the Top 30, and barely an improvement over the meager 3 percent minority presence two years ago.) Grads still laud the school's ability to meet demand for popular electives and the flexibility they have in scheduling required courses, both of which can be attributed to Carnegie's mini-semester system—one of a number of innovations pioneered at GSIA and later adopted by other B-schools.

Most courses, core and elective, are seven weeks long; over the course of eight mini-semesters, students may take as many as 18 electives without overloading their schedules. That's almost as many electives as some schools require in total courses to graduate. The compressed schedule means you have the opportunity to take several electives during your first year, and having already mastered advanced material can be a definite advantage when you get to your summer internship. (A very small minority, about 15 percent a year, waive out of enough courses to finish their degrees in 16 months, and a slightly larger number choose to spread their classes over three years as part-timers.) On the other hand, within three and a half weeks of arriving on campus, you'll be sitting down for midterm exams. Study groups convene until 2 or 3 a.m. as panicked students attempt to slog through the incredible amount of work GSIA profs pack into a single mini. There's something of a badge of honor about having survived the core intact: "The first three mini-semesters are extremely busy and there is an enormous amount of work," says 2000 grad Jeffrey Briglia. "More than anything else, it gave us all the ability to manage time on a tight schedule."

Still, many students feel that 30 to 40 hours of homework each week is often overkill—especially during the time-intensive job-hunt. And more often than not, they place the blame squarely on administrators' shoulders, finding them among the least responsive to student needs in the 2000 BUSINESSWEEK student survey. However, after all those years of student lobbying, the GSIA administration seems to be taking the hint: Officials say that GSIA will overhaul its core courses and streamline its curriculum,

already among the most innovative, by the fall of 2001. Administrators hope to improve the classroom experience and reduce the overall workload, allowing students to pass out of some core requirements if they have extensive work experience. They also plan to better integrate core classes, for instance, combining lessons in managerial economics with those in managerial accounting. And the new curriculum will also allow students to tailor their courses to their interests, encouraging MBAs to follow elective tracks grouped by career skills—not academic disciplines.

Yet, the centerpiece of GSIA's program, The Management Game, will be left unchanged. The computer simulation was pioneered by Carnegie Mellon in the 1950s, and is yet another aspect of the experience here that many other B-schools are only now putting into their revamped programs. Beginning in the last mini-semester of the first year and extending over the summer into the first mini-semester of the second year, the game pits teams of five to seven students in a race to dominate the worldwide wristwatch industry over a two-year business cycle. The game has been retooled so that the MBAs simultaneously compete against more than 80 teams at B-schools in Japan, India, Mexico, Sweden, and the Ukraine. Thus, GSIA students find themselves in a truly global competition. Students even have to negotiate a labor agreement with local union leaders, acquire financing through area banks, and glean legal advice from law students next door at the University of Pittsburgh. And each team has to overcome a crisis—whether charges of price-fixing, employee discrimination, or toxic-waste dumping—by, among other things, meeting with local reporters.

Each team reports to a board of directors made up of faculty members and senior executives from some of Pittsburgh's leading corporations, such as Alcoa, H.J. Heinz, and PNC Bank. During meetings in the companies' actual plush and well-appointed boardrooms, the board can be tough and demanding. "You're desperately trying to please your board," recalls one graduate, who reported to an unusually hard-to-please chairman. "He'd look at every move we made with a microscope, and continually say, 'It hasn't been like this in the past. I'm not sure you're sticking to the strategy. We have to crush the competition.' We had the dominant market share, but he still wasn't satisfied. We nicknamed him Mr. Marketshare."

If the game helps to prepare students for general management assignments, Wall Street–bound students gain invaluable insights into today's global financial markets through the school's Financial Analysis and Security Trading (FAST) program. The cornerstone of the program is the FAST trading room, a multi-million-dollar facility that replicates the computer workstations, live international data feeds, and sophisticated software of Wall Street's top trading firms. GSIA students interact and trade in real time with B-school students in other locations around the world, and some get the opportunity to work with investment-house research teams who, along with GSIA profs, use the room as a laboratory to explore key issues in computer trading and financial engineering.

According to the 2000 BUSINESSWEEK recruiter survey, Carnegie Mellon had the third most innovative curriculum and also showed some of the most significant signs of improvement among all B-schools. Of the 115 electives offered in any given year, among the most popular are the so-called "project courses" in operations and marketing, in which students consult with real-world companies to develop information systems for Westinghouse, General Electric, and Mitsubishi, to refine inventory control for Heinz, or to devise a marketing plan for the Pittsburgh Pirates baseball club, all recent student projects guided by GSIA faculty. An international project course was launched in which students analyzed companies from different countries in the same industry—for that year, it was printer-copier manufacturing—and then traveled to Canon and Xerox facilities in Japan, Mexico, and the United States for on-site observation.

More than 27 percent of GSIA students are enrolled in the school's growing entrepreneurship track, supported by the Donald H. Jones Center for Entrepreneurship. While other schools have only recently jumped on the bandwagon, GSIA's entrepreneurship program has been in place for nearly a quarter of a century, and a number of ventures have grown out of school projects. These include a software firm that helps physicians manage their businesses (Class of '78); a company that performs oceanographic surveys for the government and private sectors (Class of '81); manufacturers of high-tech scientific instruments (Class of '82) and sun-protection products (Class of '86); and a chain of day-care centers (Class of '97). However, Dunn is not content to rest on past success. He recently hired S. Thomas Emerson, a successful entrepreneur who developed and launched three high-tech start-ups before entering the ivory tower, as the Jones Center's new director. He spearheaded the creation of more than 20 new electives over the past three years, many of them related to e-commerce strategy and entrepreneurship. And Dunn recently established a satellite site for GSIA in Silicon Valley, located in NASA's Maffett Field research park, which will serve as a base for faculty research and executive education while bolstering Carnegie Mellon's West Coast presence with companies and alumni.

For students interested in an international experience, GSIA offers French, German, and Japanese business language courses for credit, as well as a semester abroad at one of seven exchange-partner management schools in Europe, Japan, and Mexico. It has also set up what Dunn calls "satellite campuses" for the computational finance degree program in New York City, Bangalore, Frankfurt, and London, as the school looks to take advantage of distance education technology. Ties with the larger university and community are also well utilized. Witness the "business acting" course offered in conjunction with Carnegie Mellon's acclaimed arts school, or the joint degrees available with the engineering school, the Heinz School of Public Policy, or Pitt's law school. The B-school's 10 research centers, in everything from information networking to "green design," or environmentally conscious engineering, fuel rapid turnover among an elective catalog full of up-to-the-minute courses developed by professors on the leading edge of knowledge in their fields. Indeed, over the past two decades, GSIA has spawned four Nobel laureates.

If you still think of Pittsburgh as a polluted, smokestack-filled steel town, you're way behind the times. It's an attractive city of ethnic neighborhoods, heading lists of most-livable cities nationwide for the past two decades and home to some two dozen major corporate headquarters, from old industrial powerhouses like PPG Industries to New Economy players such as Freemarkets, Inc. and Redleaf. Carnegie Mellon is located in hilly Oakland, alongside the University of Pittsburgh. There's no dorm life at GSIA; students instead look for private housing in the nearby Shadyside and Squirrel Hill neighborhoods, preferably within walking or biking distance of campus since parking is scarce.

Once on campus, students tend to stay holed up in Hunt Library, the university library next to the B-school, or walking and studying in neighboring Schenley Park, Pittsburgh's version of New York's Central Park. Since 1993, they've also spent more time hanging around Posner Hall, GSIA's modern, $14 million building, whose high-tech classrooms, state-of-the-art computing facilities, comfy student lounge, and social activity areas were a welcome replacement to the aging, yellow brick structure that had been home to the B-school for 40 years. The school recently completed renovations to the third floor of Posner, supplying more space for executive education classrooms, seminar and team meeting rooms, as well as the admissions and placement offices.

When they're not slaving away at the books, GSIA students and faculty stop off for Friday Beers, served up at the end of each week in the B-school courtyard or lobby. Some then head down the street to swim or work out at the university's sparkling Student Center, which opened in 1996 and also houses a food court and several retail stores. Monday Night Bowling and the Tuesday Bar Crawl, an imbibing adventure at the week's pub of choice, also draw folks away from the library. (First-years with perfect Bar Crawl attendance are tapped to become members of the elite "selection committee," which gets to decide which establishments to frequent during their second year.) Doc's in Shadyside, C.J. Barney's, and Silky's are some of GSIA's favorite haunts, great places to take in a Pirates baseball, Steelers football, or Penguins hockey game on the tube if the game's sold out. On the more serious side, students belong to 23 different extracurricular clubs, most of them career-oriented but including service projects such as the I Have a Dream Foundation, through which the GSIA "adopted" a local elementary school class.

PLACEMENT DETAILS

Dean Dunn's administration has worked hard to improve ties with companies over the past couple of years, establishing a Business Advisory Council (which includes such corporate heavyweights as PNC Bank CEO James Rohr and Xerox CEO Paul Allaire), hiring a new director of corporate relations activities, and marketing Carnegie Mellon through a "quarterly report" publication sent out four times a year to let firms know what's happening on campus. The school has also tapped alumni by starting a mentorship program and asking alums to conduct mock interviews and review résumés for students. With more than 27 percent of the student body heading to the West Coast, GSIA, like many of its peers, now hosts a "Go West!" Silicon Valley road show to aid students in the job search over spring break. And for 2000, it is planning a similar "Go East!" event in New York. Moreover, GSIA recently joined forces with the larger university to host a major technology conference in the spring called Interface, which brings in leading academics, executives, and recruiters for industry discussions, lectures, and a career fair. The effort shows in GSIA's steady rise in the esteem of corporate recruiters, who ranked the school 14th in 2000, up from 26th four years earlier. By industry, most students are heading for jobs in either manufacturing or consulting (especially in information technology) as well as a number of small start-ups. In 2000, consulting drew 32 percent of the grads; financial services drew another 15.5 percent; and e-commerce and high-tech firms drew roughly 30.7 percent of the graduating class.

Some 200-plus companies recruited on campus in 2000, conducting more than 2500 interviews; nearly 4000 additional jobs were posted electronically. Hiring the largest batches of GSIA grads in 2000 were Diamond Technology Partners (11); Intel (11); PRTM (8); Citibank (8); Siebel Systems (7); Booz-Allen & Hamilton (6); Corning (6); Deloitte Consulting (6); Ford Motor Co. (6).

OUTSTANDING FACULTY

Kathryn Shaw (economics); *Robert Dammon* (finance); *Bryan Routledge* (finance); *Duane Seppi* (finance); *John Mather* (marketing); *Shridar Tayur* (operations); *Peter Roberts* (strategy).

APPLICANT TIPS

Minority applicants should take an extra-long look at Carnegie Mellon, since they may have an important advantage here—or may feel entirely isolated. The reason: Of all the Top 30 B-schools, GSIA is dead last in the number of minorities enrolled in its master's program. Although the percentage of full-time African-American, Hispanic-American, or Native American students has doubled since 1998, minorities still make up just over 5 percent of the Class of 2002—despite Dunn's efforts to build relationships with traditionally black universities and the availability of special scholarship monies for minority students. The dean says he hopes to enlist industry's help by figuring out ways to pre-admit minority students straight from undergraduate programs who would then work at firms for a period of time to build experience before arriving at GSIA. Moreover, Carnegie Mellon now holds a "Minority Challenge Weekend" each January to provide information to prospective minority students about the GSIA program, and B-school life in general.

Dunn has had better luck attracting women, upping the female enrollment from a paltry 19 percent in 1996 to a more respectable 28 percent in 2000. Students pitched in as well, with the Graduate Women in Business Network establishing an outreach program to contact all women admitted into GSIA to answer questions about the program and student life. "Our women graduates have been very successful, and in fact our top student awards for two of the last three years have gone to women," Dunn says.

The school says it seeks "highly motivated individuals with superior intellectual capabilities," and applicants are advised up front to keep GSIA's quantitative focus in mind: "The rigorous curriculum at GSIA will challenge you, push you, and help you to achieve more than you ever thought possible." Translation: Be prepared to work your butt off. A demonstrated capacity for mathematics is essential; students are required to have completed not one, but two, semesters of calculus before enrolling—if not by application time. Applications are considered in three decision periods, with replies anticipated about a month after each deadline; after March 12, applications continue to be accepted and reviewed on a rolling basis until the class is filled. The application can be mailed in on paper or filled out and submitted via computer by linking to the school Web site.

Interviews are strongly recommended and can be conducted by admissions officers on campus and at candidate forums held in selected cities across the United States, Europe, Asia, and Latin America throughout the fall. If you come to campus, you can be paired up with a student host who will give you a tour, buy you lunch, and escort you to a class. International applicants who may be nervous about attending school in the United States should be aware that Carnegie Mellon offers a Summer Institute before first-year classes start to ease the cultural and academic transition, with intensive classes in communications and presentation skills, teamwork, and classroom interaction. Students also analyze a case, participate in a mini-simulation game, take classes in accounting, organizational behavior, and financial and strategic decisions, and make company visits.

Contact: Laurie Stewart
Director of Admissions and Financial Aid
412-268-2272
Application deadlines: November 17; January 31; March 23

CARNEGIE MELLON MBAs SOUND OFF

The capstone required course at GSIA is Management Game, a computer-run simulated business environment in which teams compete against each other for sales and product positioning. The course includes meetings with the corporate board (composed of executives from the Pittsburgh area and GSIA alumni who often fly in for meetings). I believe that this experience afforded us the opportunity to practice what we had been taught—analytics, communication, teamwork, problem solving, and strategy—and receive valuable feedback from business leaders. As president of one of the teams, I learned much about leadership, management, and teamwork in a challenging environment. I chose GSIA over a higher-ranked school and could not be happier with my decision. The administration at GSIA (although they have some problems) are extremely responsive to the demands of the students. Based on requests from students they moved almost all of the administrative paperwork online, and added four or five classes during my two years here. The faculty here is also very impressive and seems to be on the cutting edge of research. The biggest problem with this school is that it does a poor job of marketing the quality of the education and students. For example, during my two years here we placed first and second in two finance case competitions, beating 5 other top 10 schools, however the school did not publicize this and our Finance program remains undervalued.

GSIA is a great school. It has made great steps to embrace the e-economy as well as remain fundamentally sound in core business skills.

The school seems to be trying to address student concerns, but its efforts are insufficient. I believe the lack of interpersonal skills shown by our students is disheartening. While over half the class show quite good interpersonal skills, probably 20 percent just don't know how to communicate effectively. The single most critical factor contributing to this problem is input control. We accept students who clearly have little or no interpersonal skills or social graces. The administration is still concentrating on quantitative skills and, for the most part, forgoing leadership, strategic, and interpersonal skills.

Overall I have been very impressed with the caliber of the students and faculty, and in my view this institution attracts the brightest in the country and abroad. Finance courses rock at this school. Recruitment is fantastic. I had seven job offers by the end of December—mostly high-tech companies. Pittsburgh, Carnegie Mellon University, and GSIA are hotbeds for entrepreneurship. Anyone interested in starting their own business or understanding the venture capital process would be well advised to investigate GSIA.

The myth that Carnegie Mellon students are just a bunch of quant jocks is just that, a myth. I am proud to be friends with an amazingly diverse, intelligent, fun group of people who can compete head to head with any top business school. The one area the school truly needs is marketing. Not enough people know how great the school is.

The professors here exemplify the school's culture. They are never satisfied with "good enough." They constantly push to improve their lectures and course materials—and most of them would gladly grab a drink, go to a hockey game, or play basketball with their students after class.

15. UNIVERSITY OF NORTH CAROLINA

UNIVERSITY OF NORTH CAROLINA

Kenan-Flagler Business School
McColl Building, CB #3490
Chapel Hill, North Carolina 27599-3490
E-mail address: mba_info@unc.edu
Web site address: http://www.Kenan-Flagler.unc.edu

Corporate ranking: 16	Graduate ranking: 11
Enrollment: 543	Annual tuition & fees:
Women: 33%	resident—$9154
Non-U.S.: 30%	nonresident—$21,110
Minority: 12%	Room and board: $8453
Part-time: 0	Average GMAT score: 667
Average age: 27	Average years of work exp.: 5
Applicants accepted: 22%	Accepted applicants enrolled: 46%
Median starting pay: $125,000	Intellectual capital: 21

Teaching methods: Lecture, 35%   Case study, 40%
                    Immersions, simulations, 25%

Contact:
Sherry Wallace
Director of Admissions
919-962-3655
Application deadlines:
October 27
November 27
January 12
March 9

By the time Dean Robert S. Sullivan arrived at the University of North Carolina's Kenan-Flagler Business School in January 1998, he had already engineered a major turnaround in the early '90s at Carnegie Mellon. In fact, Sullivan came to Chapel Hill armed with an extensive background in academia as well as nonprofit service. For nearly 10 years he had toiled in Ethiopia as a Peace Corps volunteer and as a teacher at the famine-stricken country's national university. And following his stint at Carnegie Mellon, he served as director of the University of Texas's Innovation and Creativity Institute.

Perhaps that is what left Sullivan poised for his next task—propelling a solid Top 30 B-school into the upper echelon of rankings. But, in an opening move more typical of Corporate America than his former educational arenas, he ordered a sweeping overhaul of the school's top leadership, asking all existing academic program heads and area chairs to step down in June 1998 and replacing them with fresh faces. "It wasn't an easy thing to do," admits Sullivan, "but we needed it to achieve some of our aspirations."

And achieve they have. Many of the initiatives introduced in the first two years under Sullivan's management have resulted in recognizable improvements. The application pool has increased 52 percent—83 percent among prospective international students. Selectivity in admissions has inched up slightly; average GMAT scores are 26 points higher. The faculty has been bolstered with a new batch of about two dozen members in the past few years—among them, some award-winning professors from top schools like Wharton, Chicago, Duke, and USC's e-commerce department, all of whom Sullivan successfully hired away. Most noticeable, perhaps, is the way in which the makeup of a once rather homogeneous student body, where minority students made up just 9 percent of the population in 1998, has changed for the better—to 12 percent in 2000. And diversity continues to be an initiative. Grads say the school is above par when it comes to responding to student concerns and engaging students in decisions on the program. The changes at Kenan-Flagler's led to a significant greatest rise in MBA satisfaction in 2000. No longer just a "safe bet" for an MBA (a long-time attribute based on the school's strong program and bargain-basement tuition rates, even for out-of-state students), UNC–Chapel Hill now stands out at No. 15 in BUSINESSWEEK's rankings, having scooted up four notches in the past two years.

Those two years have been productive ones, certainly, for a school that once resembled a "solid B student." No longer. "We're not content to be good, or even very good anymore," insists Sullivan. "The expectation from our school and our community is that we have to be excellent at everything we do." The slew of new, talented, and experienced administrators helps. Senior Associate Dean Julie Collins, Admissions Director Sherry Wallace, and Career Services Director Mindy Storrie all were either Kenan-Flagler alums or veterans of the school's administration prior to accepting their roles. From the outside, Sullivan brought in James W. Dean Jr., a former quality guru for the National Science Foundation and a longtime senior examiner for the Malcolm Baldrige quality awards. Shortly after being tapped as associate dean, Dean used the Baldrige criteria to assess the MBA program and then worked with teams of faculty, staff, and students to establish priorities for the highly anticipated change. Today, students, faculty, and the general public can keep track of the school's ongoing progress by visiting the "MBA scorecard" Web site, www.MBAScorecard.unc.edu, where the initiatives, strategies, and accomplishments to date are published for public use.

One of the first orders of business in the new academic era was revamping the MBA curriculum of a school largely known for its general management focus. Ten "career tracks" from 1998 have been transformed into eight career concentrations and two enrichment concentrations. Each second-year career concentration encompasses a carefully planned sequence of elective courses that give students in-depth instruction in a specific area they might target as a career—including finance, customer and product management, e-business, entrepreneurship and venture development, global supply chain management, investment management, management consulting, and real estate. "The career concentrations have deepened our strength in fundamental areas," explains Associate Dean James Dean. "We've essentially placed bets on what's important here." The school's two enrichment concentrations, sustainable enterprise and international business, are not so closely aligned with specific job targets, but their sequences of coursework also provide detailed instruction and learning opportunities. In sustainable enterprise, students explore issues like urban reinvestment, minority economic development, social marketing, and life cycle management.

With these changes among the 100 or so electives came another addition: the creation of corporate advisory boards, one for each concentration. Industry experts in specific areas like consulting or corporate finance serve as board members and advise faculty on ways to modify their curriculum to accommodate changes or modern movements in their fields. The board members become important resources for students eager to find related jobs—and the students, for them, are highly prized protégés. "There's a shortage of good people in most areas these days," says Dean. "Companies are trying to hire the best students and this is one way we can help prepare them."

Not to be outdone, the first-year core program also underwent reshaping. What was once a flatter sequence of courses, covering just the business fundamentals, is now a more focused, leadership-oriented experience. The newer first-year program consists of 17 courses divided among four modules, which correspond to the curriculum's four themes: analyzing capabilities and resources; monitoring the marketplace and external environment; formulating strategy; and implementing strategy and assessing firm performance. Throughout the modules, students complete a valuation exercise, a business plan exercise, and a business simulation to learn the intricacies of starting a new business. With teamwork a part of Kenan-Flagler's MBA program for more than two decades, programs like the leadership development one conducted at the start of orientation hold an important place in the school's framework. All students are assigned to a five- or six-person "non-negotiable" study group that participates in management skills workshops and team-building exercises and stays together throughout the first year's nonwaivable core courses in accounting, finance, strategy, operations, marketing, quantitative methods, international business, management skills, and ethics. There's no switching among teams for any reason; personality conflicts and ineffectual relationships must be addressed up front, mirroring the reality of the actual business world.

On top of the group experience, all students are now required to take a Leading and Managing course taught in two parts, at the beginning and at the end of the first year, to assess students' progress on their self-development plans. Prior to the start of school, students are required to have their bosses, peers, and subordinates at their former jobs fill out a "360-degree" personal evaluation to help determine areas they can improve upon to become better leaders.

Each then creates a personal leadership development plan to work on throughout the year.

Some of the of greatest strengths of Kenan-Flagler repeatedly mentioned by students are faculty- or teaching-related. Of the 82 schools surveyed by BusinessWeek, UNC came in fifth for the proficiency of teaching in both core courses and electives. "High quality teaching clearly is the top priority at Chapel Hill," affirms one recent grad. "Academic research among professors is certainly stressed as well, but it does not water down the key ingredient—top-notch instruction—which is the school's 'bread and butter.'" Graduates also laud the level of responsiveness from faculty and the administration. While some Kenan-Flagler MBAs hesitate to describe their professors as being at the leading edge of knowledge in their fields, there is a general appreciation for the preparation and personal attention that go into the coursework, as well as the ease with which you can track down a professor outside of class.

In line with this student-satisfaction focus, Kenan-Flagler has made advances in incorporating technology into the MBA program. An e-commerce course is now a requirement for all first year students, and the McColl Building, which opened about four years ago, is equipped with more than 2800 Internet connections. And that's not all. "We'll be a wireless complex within the next year," promises Dean Sullivan. "Students will be able to connect to our network from any location." For now, the Wall Street set favors the state-of-the-art Trading Room. There, students in the Applied Investment Management course try their hands at managing an equity fund with a charity feature: Part of the Cherry Hills Investment Fund's income supports community outreach activities for children's needs and education. The students, using the same software, databases, online information, and teleconferencing tools trading professionals use, are tasked with generating regular reports to a board of advisors hailing from the local, regional, and national investment communities. On the whole, McColl houses 19 classrooms, a large auditorium, study rooms, and a dining hall—all with up-to-the-minute videoconferencing and multimedia presentation capabilities. The school's newest building, dedicated in September 2000 and about a five-minute drive from McColl, is The Paul J. Rizzo Center at Meadowmont, a cyber-community for executive education, corporate board meetings, and retreat planning. The Rizzo Center's McLean Hall residence building boasts 56 guest rooms, six study rooms, and two multipurpose seminar rooms. Loudermilk Hall, the "brain center" of the conference facility, is equipped with high-speed Internet access and advanced instructional technologies among its two 65-seat tiered classrooms and 14 breakout rooms. Adding to that is the 15,800-square-foot DuBose House, a 1933 Georgian Revival home that was renovated to become a social and dining center.

While technology appears to be on target, the lack of diversity on campus is being addressed. Both students and employers have complained about it in the past, and rightly so. For one thing, in 1998, Kenan-Flagler had the third smallest population of international students among the top B-schools, a mere 21 percent. But a recent wave of energetic recruiting overseas has increased the proportion of non-U.S. students, who now number 29 percent—achieving a goal previously set by Sullivan that he and the admissions staff are now looking to surpass. One major source of global networking is the school's alliance with one of Latin America's top-ranked business schools, the Monterrey Institute of Technology in Mexico (ITESM); the two academic institutions are taking advantage of technological facilities to create an "extended campus" in which speakers at either school can give their presentations and lectures abroad by way of compressed video or teleconferencing. Faculty from both programs have

already developed four new courses covering service marketing, Internet marketing, global supply chain management, and service strategy that are to be shared among both sets of students. Tests for the curriculum and distance delivery methods are currently underway, and additional cross-border courses are in development. On the career front, students interested in jobs in Latin America can receive leads and assistance throughout ITESM, and UNC itself receives help from the Institute in attracting international applicants.

For other global opportunities, students turn to the Office of International Programs, which helps in planning trips abroad. The Frank Hawkins Kenan Institute of Enterprise also offers international immersion electives that combine classroom study with visits to foreign countries, where students participate in executive and government briefings and attend lectures at some of the countries' top-ranked schools. One example for 2001: Information Technology and e-Commerce (ITEC) Professor Arv Malhotra has planned a global immersion elective for spring—"Exploring the Wireless Society"—which means a trip to Helsinki, Stockholm, and Warsaw, with about 25 students selected as participants based on their backgrounds and future plans. More than 40 percent of the school's MBA and EMBA students take one of these global immersion electives, and that number should increase with the introduction of the Global Immersion Elective on Sustainable Enterprise, planned to debut in May 2001, with travels to Ho Chi Minh City, Singapore, and Bangkok. The travel portion of a new GIE planned for March 2001 features Delhi, Bangalore, and Mumbai (Bombay). Others focus on South America, Northeast Asia, or Africa.

Students find adventure and fulfillment in the MBA Enterprise Corps, a program modeled after the Peace Corps, which sends MBAs from Kenan-Flagler and other top B-schools on one-to-two-year assignments assisting newly privatized businesses and start-ups in the emerging markets of Eastern Europe, Asia, and Africa. A steady stream of international speakers also provides networking opportunities. And a six-year-old international lunch series sponsored by Mobil Corp. and coordinated by Finance Professor Marc Zenner brings together students, faculty, and guests each Tuesday to discuss global business issues over the meal. Americans looking to brush up on their Spanish—or learn the language entirely—should check out the Working Spanish course, which prepares MBAs to work in a Spanish-speaking environment. The course combines classroom and computer-based language learning with a weeklong cross-cultural immersion experience and, based on its success, it's likely that courses in Portuguese, Mandarin Chinese, and Thai will soon follow. Additionally, nearly 10 percent of Kenan-Flagler's MBAs participate in an exchange program with 1 of the 40 foreign B-schools that partner with UNC.

Like pretty much every other B-school in the United States, Kenan-Flagler is seeking a presence in entrepreneurship education. The school's Center for Entrepreneurship and Technology Venturing has designed a series of electives that walk students through the life cycle of a start-up, from concept to initial public offering. The annual venture capital competition is a big draw, pitting teams of MBAs from Kenan-Flagler and three other B-schools against each other to match wits over investment pitches from real-life start-up companies. The MBAs present a panel of judges with their strategies for deciding which companies should receive funding from a $5 million mock capital pool. The results are fourfold: students get a hands-on learning experience; companies receive intensive feedback on their plans; and VC firms glimpse the work of promising start-ups and scout new hires for their firms. New in terms of coursework is a capstone course for the Entrepreneurship and New Venture Development concentration, which will be taught by Dean Sullivan and titled Launching the Company. Admission to the two phases of the course is by competitive application and students are expected to have developed a refined business concept prior to enrolling. They'll then have access to resources and expertise to help them conceptualize, formulate, and implement an entrepreneurial start-up using advanced technology and the Internet. At the end of the course, teams of students working to launch their plans will have an opportunity to compete for early-stage capital with a panel of venture financing sources. The school's entrepreneurship support and offerings appear to have had a special effect on at least five Class of 2000 MBAs, who started their own companies upon graduation. A handful of others have taken time off in the past two years to launch their endeavors, with an option to return to Kenan-Flagler at a later point to complete their degrees.

The entrepreneurship program takes on a civic-minded focus through the Kenan Institute's Urban Enterprise Corps, which took off in 1998 under the direction of Professor Jim Johnson. As the MBA Enterprise Corps does overseas, the Urban Enterprise Corps taps newly minted MBA grads from Kenan-Flagler and other schools to work in inner cities in North Carolina to help create seed capital and businesses run largely by minorities and women. Also administered by the Institute is the Durham Scholars Program, which organizes Kenan-Flagler MBAs to tutor inner-city Durham students in grades six through nine. Last year about 80 MBAs and 100 Durham youths participated and, with a supportive $1.3 million grant from the Z. Smith Reynolds Foundation, the program will soon expand into four other North Carolina communities.

In recent years an e-business emphasis has brought greater attention to the school, especially with its proximity to the highly regarded Research Triangle Park, well known as one of the world's top high-tech hubs. With UNC, North Carolina State, and Duke University making up the three points of the triangle, the zone is an effective spot for generating high-tech business ideas and obtaining funding and resources to back them. The park encompasses more than 130 organizations, about 20 biotech and biopharmaceutical companies, 22 software companies, and a handful of others, including Cisco and Nortel. All Kenan-Flagler students take a first-year required core course in information technology, and during their second year, they can choose from electives in Internet marketing, IT strategy, data mining, intellectual property, global supply chain management, designing an online customer experience, and technology commercialization.

Beyond coursework, Kenan-Flagler's attention to the dot-com world resulted in the recent addition of eLauncher, a business innovation center in McColl's basement that provides students with support and guidance from tech-savvy faculty. The school is well-connected with such industry gurus as Joseph Galli (BSBA '80), former president and COO at Amazon.com; Matt Szulick, Red Hat Inc. president; and Michael Dell, chairman and CEO of Dell Computer, all of whom speak regularly at Kenan-Flagler. Some indications of the strong MBA interests in e-business and entrepreneurship are the MBA Entrepreneurship Club's nearly 200 members and the fact that more than 40 students accepted entrepreneurial jobs or internships last summer with high-tech heavies like BuildNet, BusinessModel.com, and Fusion Ventures. (Additionally, six students took jobs with VC companies.) The university's connection with pharmaceutical companies like DuPont and Eastman Chemical has also brought about an interesting partnership. By donating some of the patents and disclosures they're not able to address themselves, these companies get tax credit while students in the chemistry and business school work in teams to evaluate the poten-

tial products' market value. The students have further opportunities to set up real companies around the intellectual property contributed as well—and the school takes equity. The theory here is that a success for one benefits the entire academic community.

Not only has the school focused on innovative education, but there has also been a recent push for the career services office to achieve better workplace results. About half of Kenan-Flagler's MBAs said that school-facilitated activities were responsible for leading them to the job offer they accepted, while smaller percentages credited internships or student-facilitated activities. Management Professor Daniel M. Cable has taken Kenan-Flagler's customization tactics to the extreme by offering an evaluation of students' personal values and qualifications to determine the type of working culture that would be a good fit for each. A whopping 258 students responded to the offer. "It took a while," says Cable—but he delivered.

For further help with job searches and transitioning to new fields, the school has made it a priority to keep up relationships with alumni, or "stakeholders in the school," as Dean calls them. But they're also valued for their help in admissions efforts, both in recruiting and interviewing. High-profile alums of the larger university, like Chase's Bill Harrison and Hewlett-Packard's Ann Livermore, are popular guests for the school's speaker series, which holds events about once or twice a month.

How could they resist returning to UNC's picturesque Chapel Hill campus? Life here is pretty much centered around the university, with hordes of bright young students carrying on intellectual discussions in coffeehouses, independent bookstores, and vegetarian restaurants. The climate is mild most of the year, making this a great town for families as well as singles. Don't expect to find housing on campus—the waiting list for UNC married student housing is nearly a year long—but check out the abundant, rustic-named apartment complexes near the school, including Poplar Place, Sterling Brook, Autumn Woods, and Alta Springs, where MBAs tend to congregate. Although the MBA program is fairly demanding, especially in the first year, students manage to squeeze in time to participate in one of the 30-some Kenan-Flagler clubs, committees, and advisory boards that govern the school or are dedicated to professional or extracurricular interests. Not surprisingly, few miss out on a chance to head next door to McColl to the "Dean Dome," the UNC basketball arena, to see the top-rated Tar Heels—led by new coach Matt Doherty, a graduate of UNC's undergraduate business program—trounce their competitors.

PLACEMENT DETAILS

In 2000, recruiters who came to campus increased by 21 percent, leaving Kenan-Flagler grads with an average of 3 job offers each—just about comparable to schools like Duke and Columbia. It's a clear improvement, and Career Services Director Mindy Storrie is intent on keeping the momentum going. Her office is taking steps to establish deeper relationships with long-term recruiters by encouraging them to hire students in a broader range of areas. Many students have expressed an interest in working on the West Coast or abroad, and Storrie and her staff have been working steadily to provide those opportunities. International students get special service, including extra training and workshops to address their hiring issues and a list of employers targeting them, so they can streamline their job search efforts. The dot-com trend hasn't gone unnoticed (nearly 20 percent of 2000 grads went to high-tech companies) and many students take advantage of the school's connections with local start-ups, corporate advisory board members in entrepreneurship, or other subjects, to secure employment.

Median pay packages for Kenan-Flagler graduates in 2000 were around $125,000, just about average for the top B-schools surveyed by BUSINESSWEEK. Top employers in 2000 were IBM (10); Dell Computer Corporation (8); Deloitte Consulting (8); Chase Bank (7); First Union (7); Citibank (6); Eli Lilly & Company (6); McKinsey & Company, Inc. (6); and Intel (5).

OUTSTANDING FACULTY

Joe Bylinski (accounting); *Ed Maydew* (accounting); *Al Segars* (e-commerce); *Rollie Tillman* (entrepreneurship); *David Ravenscraft* (finance); *Richard Rendleman* (finance); *Marc Zenner* (finance); *Jay Klompmaker* (marketing); *Valarie Zeithaml* (marketing); *David Hartzell* (real estate).

APPLICANT TIPS

The qualities a top MBA candidate possesses, according to Kenan-Flagler, are: "analytical and organizational abilities, communication skills, motivation, and leadership that indicate strong potential for success in business." Since you can probably paint a better picture of yourself in a personal interview, it's a good idea to schedule one as early as possible if you can travel to Chapel Hill. Otherwise, you will submit your application without one, and there will not be any effect on the admissions decision—but in this case you should be especially certain to use the essays to express your ideas as clearly as possible. If your written package is deemed among the most competitive in the pool, however, you will be contacted by an admissions officer to arrange an interview prior to the final decision. Even though many college-age students have had entrepreneurial or significant leadership experiences these days, for the most part, only candidates with at least two years of full-time work experience are considered competitive for admission by UNC.

Kenan-Flagler's application consists of two parts, and getting it in by the October, November, and January deadlines is a good idea, not only because you'll hear sooner, but also because applicants for the March deadline are not considered for any of the school's merit-based fellowships. You can expect a reply within eight weeks after the deadline you meet.

Contact: Sherry Wallace
Director of Admissions
919-962-3655
Application deadlines: October 27; November 27; January 12; March 9

KENAN-FLAGLER MBAs SOUND OFF

What sets Kenan-Flagler apart [from other top B-schools] is an environment that takes a holistic approach to developing people that will not only contribute to society as business leaders, but as quality people.

In an age where the use of words like "family" and "team" has become clichéd, KFBS has managed to maintain an environment where faculty, administration, and students take an active interest in each other's lives beyond that found in the vast majority of programs. The end result is that we as graduates come away having received far more than just a diploma and a big paycheck, and as such realize the importance of giving back to society, both professionally and personally.

At KFBS, I enjoyed that small, community feel—i.e., the professors invite you to receptions at their houses. Yet, thanks to the resources of UNC-CH you also had access to speakers, recruiters, and technology of a large university. I feel confident that our rankings will only continue to ascend as more people understand this neat combination.

Kenan-Flagler is a great school, and it is headed in the right direction. The administration of the school is now strong and stable, and taking the school in the right direction in terms of curriculum development, career services, and admissions.

The admissions office has done a tremendous job in bringing together a very diverse class in a friendly, collegiate, but professional environment. The new building affords an excellent, cutting-edge work environment and the faculty, while not always at the forefront of their fields, are truly excellent educators.

Kenan-Flagler was truly a great experience, but does not get much attention because of poor external relations (PR) and this tends to hurt the school. It is top quality!

My business school experience at Kenan-Flagler was outstanding. Our Dean of Students (Jim Dean) was extremely supportive of student activities and continuously reached out for student input. A great majority of our students were well-rounded, outgoing leaders that will certainly positively impact the business community. Our infrastructure is lacking nothing but a large library.

The workload during the first year is extremely heavy, making teamwork essential to completing all the necessary assignments. This fosters a very cooperative atmosphere at the school which will be beneficial to all Kenan-Flagler graduates in the workplace. The school's utilization of technology and curriculum was excellent and will give most Kenan-Flagler graduates an edge over students graduating from other top business schools around the country.

KFBS team focus is outstanding. It enhances the learning experience by simulating a real work environment, in which you have to deal with the same group of people over a long period of time. It not only helps to improve your teamwork skills but to know yourself. When you compare the total package, including cost, quality of life, and the quality of people you will be working with, Carolina is the best two-year MBA experience available.

**16.
DARTMOUTH
COLLEGE**

DARTMOUTH COLLEGE

Tuck School of Business Administration
Hanover, New Hampshire 03755-0900
E-mail address: tuck.admissions@dartmouth.edu
Web site address: http://www.tuck.dartmouth.edu

Corporate ranking: 17	Graduate ranking: 12
Enrollment: 398	Annual tuition & fees: $28,740
Women: 32%	Room and board: $11,000
Non-U.S.: 32%	Average GMAT score: 692
Minority: 11%	Average years of work exp.: 5
Part-time: 0	Accepted applicants enrolled: 52%
Average age: 28	Intellectual capital: 14
Applicants accepted: 14%	
Median starting pay: $149,500	

Teaching methods: Lecture, 30%   Case study, 40%
                              Field studies, action learning, simulations, 30%

Contact:
Sally Jaeger
Director of Admissions
603-646-3162
Application deadlines:
December 4
January 19
February 20
April 16

Tradition both spurned and aided recent graduates of the Tuck School of Business at Dartmouth University. On the one hand, the small B-school set in charming Hanover, New Hampshire has 100 years of history and the honor of being the first MBA program behind it, as well as a cozy community that ensures loyal alum who support fellow Tuck grads. On the other hand, getting stuck in the glory days of yesteryear prohibits innovation. And the Class of 2000 has let administrators know it's time for a change—evident in the school's belly-flop from No. 10 in 1998 to No. 16 in the 2000 BUSINESSWEEK rankings of the top B-schools.

Tuck dropped four spots with recruiters and five places with students. In other words, complacency won't cut it anymore. Tuck Dean Paul Danos knows student satisfaction must become a priority. "We've got to solve this problem," he says. As the centennial celebration winds down, the administration is responding to low marks by shaking up tradition a bit.

Well, you say you want a revolution? Step one: change the curriculum. Everyone noticed that old-hat Dartmouth business courses were stale. After all, the year 2000 marked the first curriculum overhaul in more than half a century. But change doesn't happen all at once. Therefore, the revamped curriculum is initially getting phased into the first-year course of study. Administrators still are unsure how they will adjust second-year schedules. The administration launched the curriculum changes in fall 2000. "This curriculum combines Tuck's century-old tradition of rigorous coverage of basic fundamental practices with an unprecedented degree of choice—including electives—for today's students, who have more work experience and are entering different types of businesses than students of years ago," according to a brochure for the Class of 2002.

But what will the fancy title, Tuck General Management Forum, and the ambitious hopes actually mean for first-year students? The new coursework occurs at the start of the student schedule. In the early fall, incoming students will take a class called Analysis for General Managers, intended to teach students how to identify business opportunities and take advantage of them. As part of this class, students will learn the fine art of developing a complete business plan. In the late fall, a course called Management Communication is intended to teach students how to express their ideas to a variety of audiences. This course ends with a project proposal. Projects can range from the development of a new business to assigned, sponsored teams which work on existing plans. The winter term relies on execution of the project. Students will have the opportunity to meet with faculty and even corporate sponsors about any obstacles they face in devising their businesses. In spring, students are asked to integrate all their coursework through a competitive business simulation. They present their completed projects to Tuck faculty, alumni, and venture capitalists.

Those courses take care of the entrepreneurial aspect of the new curriculum. In addition, first-year students take the year to complete typical core requirements and now have the freedom to take two electives. On top of all that, Tuck created the Industry Knowledge series. Students are required to attend at least six of these programs, which are designed to "introduce students to passionate executives who dramatically changed their industry," says Steven Lubrano, assistant dean of Career Services and The Forum. Through this series, students already have spent the day with Phil Murphy of Goldman Sachs, among others. Meg Whitman,

CEO of eBay, even informed Tuckees that she spent 13 nights on a cot in the office when the server went down. Now that's insider information!

In fall term A, speakers are varied and include Corporate America's head honchos. But in fall term B, the seminars are practical and functional. The speakers are industry leaders, and they are prepped with information about specific student projects. For example, a public relations guru might advise a group about how to market their invented product or service. The guru can also help the team devise a memorable logo. The best part of the series of encounters with bigwigs is the easy access students are promised. The school's small size—only about 400 students are enrolled in the MBA program—makes it possible for all interested parties to get a word in.

The curriculum wasn't the only gripe the Class of 2000 had with Tuck academics. Lackluster faculty ratings also marred the school's longtime good record. Though students say professors are often available for informal discussions, they also ranked Tuck faculty last among the Top 30 schools for failing to be at the leading edge of knowledge in their field. The school's faculty also received below average marks for core and elective course teaching, which is unusual for the B-school pioneer. One other consistent problem Tuck faces is its remote location. Don't kid yourself—recruiters might find the campus charming, but the trek to Hanover is daunting, especially with such a small pool of students. The school lost some on-campus recruiters, falling from 175 companies in 1998 to 137 in 2000. New programs like the Industry Knowledge seminars might reverse the trend by attracting companies to campus for things other than recruiting. But the location will always be an obstacle. That doesn't mean Hanover is without beauty. Far from it.

If you love the great outdoors, if you enjoy the slow, quiet rhythms of small-town living, if you thrive on togetherness and crave the comfort of a place where everybody knows your name, Tuck might be your version of Nirvana. Only propeller planes can fly into the tiny airport in West Lebanon, six miles south of Hanover. When the weather turns bad, you face a white-knuckle flight onto the short landing strip that's carved into a mountainside. Boston, the closest major city, is a two-hour drive away. And sleepy Hanover rolls up the sidewalks fairly early. The only time people are out late is when they're coming out of the Nugget Theatre along the main street's collection of brick-façade shops, cozy restaurants, and colonial homes, or attending an event at the Hop, the college's impressive performing arts center.

Things are getting even more impressive as the school invests in construction to improve its infrastructure. In January 2001, Whittemore Hall, which will house about 60 students, will open. The $15 million residence hall will include an exercise room, meeting room, and courtyard in addition to private beds and bathrooms for MBAs residing there. Most Tuckees live on campus, especially in the first year, and this hall is the first in a series of new amenities coming to campus. The already existing surroundings have charm too. The B-school sits on the edge of the Dartmouth campus, bordering the Connecticut River. The cluster of five brick Georgian buildings and two contemporary structures that make up the school resembles a private 13-acre encampment and is at the end of a private road appropriately named Tuck Drive. Underground tunnels and glass-enclosed halls—dubbed "Habitrails"—connect all the buildings, so students needn't venture outside to attend class during the bitterly cold winter months. You could trek from your Woodbury House dorm (that's an existing hall that fits about 75 residents) to a class at Tuck Hall in your slippers.

But while fully intending to preserve the insular atmosphere so cherished by students, faculty, and administrators, Danos is opening Tuck up somewhat to the world at large. His foremost tool: technology. In the last three years, Tuck has invested a bit of money—$2.6 million to be exact—in technology on campus. Every student is required to have a super-powerful laptop bought at his or her own expense. Some of the improvements are appearing in the extracurricular options. In the fall of 2000, the school opened the Glassmeyer/McNamee Center for Digital Strategies, which aims to bring cutting-edge information into Tuck. The center includes a laboratory for students to investigate entrepreneurial ideas. Director Phil Anderson is at the helm, and Danos says this has the potential to serve as a sort of incubator. In addition, students who use the center will also work hand-in-hand with the Foster Center for Private Equity, an existing Tuck institution that brings venture capitalists into the school. Ultimately, student business ideas could become reality if Danos's vision comes to life.

Though Danos clearly is looking to the future, the year 2000 was spent reflecting on the past. The school's celebration of its 100 years enhanced the tight community by uniting faculty, students, and alumni for lectures, symposiums, and regional parties. Celebrations were held in San Francisco, New York, London, Boston, and Chicago. The Tuck Centennial Fund raised $36 million by November 1999, almost reaching the goal of $40 million a year before the close. In addition to all the hoopla, Wayne G. Broehl, Jr., the Benjamin Ames Kimball Professor of the Science of Administration Emeritus, wrote a book transcribing the history of the world's first graduate business school. In the book, Groehl reminds readers of the vision Dartmouth President William Jewett Tucker and the business school founder Edward Tuck had 100 years ago. "The needed education . . . must be an immersion in business thinking, where students learn from leading scholars and from each other; it must be broad-based; and it must have a global perspective, with inputs from diverse cultures," Groehl recounts. Perhaps Danos and company have those words in mind as they try to improve and grow the program.

Don't be mistaken—the party is not over just because Tuck is past the 100-mark or because it's tucked away in New Hampshire. Students always have known how to bring small-town Hanover to life. Every Thursday, they gather at Café Buon Gustaio for Pub Night, which also might include fine Italian dining if you're game. Tuckees also can be found at the Hopkins Center for performing arts, and in the winter they might be studying cozily by the fireplace in Stell Hall. Director of Admissions Sally Jaeger found the perfect description for a two-year stint in Hanover—a sweet "respite from the city."

PLACEMENT DETAILS

In 2000, 137 companies recruited on campus at Tuck. That's not nearly as many as you'd find at the large powerhouses such as Wharton or Columbia. But Tuck grads are pulling down salaries to match the biggest names in B-schools—in 2000, the median starting pay package of $149,500 for Tuck students was higher than Kellogg and Chicago, bested only by Wharton, Harvard, and Stanford—largely because of the graduates' consulting and investment banking bent. At graduation, students averaged 2.8 job offers apiece. Hiring the most Tuck MBAs were: Bain & Co. (13); McKinsey & Co. (10); Goldman Sachs & Co. (8); Mercer Management Consulting (7); Accenture (6); Bowstreet (6); Booz-Allen & Hamilton (5); Wheelhouse (5); Boston Consulting (5); The Parthenon Group (4); Credit Suisse First Boston (3); Deloitte Consulting (3); Lehman Brothers (3); Morgan Stanley Dean Witter (3); Gen 3 (3). Tuck students managed to snag spots with some nontraditional employers, too, which isn't too shabby considering the school's location and size.

Tuck's success is partially attributable to its alumni network, about which students rave.

Even though the school has just 7341 living alumni, they are amazingly supportive. About 63 percent give money to the school every year—the highest contribution rate of any graduate B-school. They're supportive in other ways, as well, providing invaluable connections that offset some of Tuck's inherent placement disadvantages. Devin Mathews, a 2000 graduate, says Tuck alumni formed the foundation of the job search. "I went to undergrad at a big state school, and while I expected the Tuck network to be more personal and loyal than my college alumni, I never expected them to be so happy to talk, help, advise, and reminisce," Mathews says. "Almost all of my job leads and interviews were through Tuck contacts. I plan to pay back the favor in a big way with future Tuck grads."

OUTSTANDING FACULTY

Clyde Stickney (accounting); *John Shank* (accounting); *Michael Knetter* (economics); *Stephen Powell* (management science); *David Pyke* (operations); *John Vogel* (real estate); *Vijay Govindarajan* (strategy); *Phil Anderson* (technology).

APPLICANT TIPS

The Tuck School seeks applicants with five key attributes: You need to demonstrate that you are creative, cooperative, humane, have leadership ability, and view your career as your central—but not your only—focus. Both your interview and application materials should reflect how you portray these characteristics. Interviews are encouraged but not required, and can take place either on campus or in city locales visited by admissions officers or alumni interviewers each year. (About 96 percent of those admitted in 2000 were interviewed.) Be sure to call six to eight weeks in advance if you'd like an on-campus interview; the school will set up an entire day's itinerary for you, including attendance of one or two classes, lunch with first-year students, and a campus tour led by second-years. The main purpose of the interview is to ascertain your "fit" with the unique Tuck culture, says Sally Jaeger, director of admissions.

Jaeger says the administration is planning to expand to 240 students per class but that will come in time—over the next decade or so. Tuck also took the initiative to enroll a more diverse student body by joining the Consortium for Graduate Study and Management. They joined 13 other business schools in the consortium, including Michigan, Haas, Darden, and the University of Texas. As a member, a school accepts minority fellows. Tuck has taken in nine fellows from underrepresented minorities so far.

Tuck was behind on getting an online application. By visiting the Web site, you can request an application to be sent to them via snail mail.

Contact: Sally Jaeger
Director of Admissions
603-646-3162
Application deadlines: December 4; January 19; February 20; April 16

TUCK MBAs SOUND OFF

The small size and location of Tuck provide a special MBA experience. Some outsiders mistakenly think that these attributes detract from the learning experience. I believe that they enhance the learning experience. The professors always have time to talk with you after class if you have questions or a problem. Fellow classmates also are willing to help each other. Not only do you get to know your entire class on a first-name basis, but the professors and administrative staff also know every student by their first name. One thing about a Tuck MBA is that it is not an anonymous experience. For those students simply seeking an MBA diploma, Tuck is not the

place to be. Professors like to cold call and there is pressure to get involved with the school outside of the classroom.

Although I was accepted into programs with higher rankings and greater brand recognition than Tuck, I am thrilled with the quality of my education, the job I received upon graduation, and the friendships I formed with my classmates. Admittedly, Tuck is not for everyone. The small-town atmosphere and the close-knit class make it a self-selecting environment; however, it is a very special place to spend two years, and I would encourage everyone to give Tuck a very serious look. I'm leaving Tuck with some great friends and a great job. Looking back, if I had to decide among business schools again, I'd choose Tuck in a heartbeat.

Tuck's facilities are truly remarkable and one of the best-kept secrets about the school. The classrooms are beyond my wildest expectations. Two exceptions exist to this: climate control and the parking lot. The heat/air never come on at the right times. It's always too cold or hot in class. And the parking lot (actually it's more like a bombing range) is about a 1000-foot climb from the school, and it keeps getting worse. The entrance keeps moving uphill. The parking lot, for lack of a better term, is full. What's more, they seem to be making up the rules as they go, so students all get lots of tickets. The new technology initiative, Tuckstreams, stinks—slooooooow, unreliable, useless information, poorly organized, too much clutter. The faculty and students alike openly mock Tuckstreams in class. The school was way ahead in the technology game until they shoved that thing down our throats. The Career Center is the best run part of the school—significantly exceeding expectations. Overall, the community is very open and supportive. It is also much more diverse than I expected. Teachers are generally great, and I believe that my MBA was well worth it. I also have little doubt that Tuck was the right school.

Everyone at Tuck is very bright and deserves to be here. That said, the school still needs to cultivate an environment that is more diverse. Despite that, the small size of the school is conducive to lasting relationships.

Tuck was my first choice. I turned down a $56,000 scholarship to another top 10 school to attend the Tuck School. Some of my criteria when selecting an MBA program were:

1. Attain and be prepared for a job at a top Wall Street firm (I start at Goldman in July); 2. Meet diverse and interesting people (my closest friends here have incredible and completely different backgrounds); 3. Become part of an institution that sincerely cares about its members (goes without saying). Tuck has provided me with opportunities and skills that will allow me to pursue my career ambitions. For that, I plan to continue the steep tradition of alumni support. Consider this particular question . . . Knowing what you know now, would you have gone anywhere else? My answer is a loud and boisterous NO.

UNIVERSITY OF TEXAS–AUSTIN

The McCombs School of Business
Austin, Texas 78712
E-mail address: texasmba@bus.utexas.edu
Web site address: http://www.bus.utexas.edu

Corporate ranking: 18	Graduate ranking: 21
Enrollment: 868	Annual tuition & fees:
Women: 22%	resident—$10,438
Non-U.S.: 28%	nonresident—$16,063
Minority: 5%	Room and board: $10,500
Part-time: 60	Average GMAT score: 687
Average age: 29	Average years of work exp.: 5
Applicants accepted: 25%	Accepted applicants enrolled: 61%
Median starting pay: $149,500	Intellectual capital: 20

Teaching methods: Lecture, 45%   Case study, 35%
                      Simulations, projects, 20%

Contact:
Carl Harris
Director of Admissions
512-471-7612
Application deadlines:
January 1 (early)
February 1 (int'l)
April 15 (final)

In Texas, as they say, bigger is better. Perhaps that's what local business-man Red McCombs was thinking when he pledged a $50 million naming gift—the University of Texas–Austin's largest donation to date—to the B-school at the University of Texas–Austin in May 2000. Now, says Dean Robert G. May, the McCombs School of Business is better positioned to expand its educational offerings by building a stable of top-rate faculty, continuing the advancement of technology in classrooms, augmenting faculty research and support, offering more student scholarships, and adding to the facilities.

On top of this most recent and most generous of improvements, it was just two years ago that Texas unveiled a grand, new $1.2 million placement center with a sprawling, semicircular, glassed-in reception foyer. There's multi-toned paneling, upholstered chairs, and thick carpet within . . . not to mention a true stamp of Texas: an enormous, backlit, wooden Lone Star sprawled across the middle of the ceiling. Interview rooms contain phone and modem access, and with six people on staff devoted to employer service, the accommodations, food and drink provisions, and personal touches for recruiters are exemplary. The employer pool had continued to build all through the '90s, even before the new facility's existence, in part because of masterful marketing by both students and administrators as well as a schoolwide commitment to corporate partnership, along with a new interest in Texas MBAs from recruiters. So the updated career services office, then, would seem to have cemented a place for Texas in the forefront of recruiter seriousness—were it not for what some companies have come to consider a lack of efficiency within the well-appointed office.

Of the Top 30 B-schools ranked by BUSI-NESSWEEK, the McCombs School was ranked the third worst by recruiters, just after Stanford and Wharton. Potential employers criticize the mechanics of the place, but praise the graduates. Never fear, though—officials are working on it, polling recruiters and making changes. But even amid this recruiter dissatisfaction, students don't find the placement office to be as much of a problem for them. They continue to laud the number and diversity of potential employers who come to campus. With an additional few thousand jobs posted electronically, 2000 grads were able to land an average of 2.9 job offers each. Although some students do find fault with the school's efforts to connect with smaller or less traditional firms, administrators have marked this an initiative, and with the school's location in the start-up-happy town of Austin, improvements should come fast and furiously. The career services office also arranges job treks to the West Coast, and they've recently streamlined procedures for applying for overseas positions. Students now have access to a database with information on hundreds of companies all over the world, with contact names and descriptions of hiring practices. Because the McCombs School attracts and maintains a good number of international students (the Class of 2002 has 28 percent) the career services office has some unique hiring issues to consider. Recently the staff created a task force of about 10 international students to serve as advocates to the school's international student body as a whole. These liaisons convey important information on companies' hiring practices for non-U.S. citizens as well as basic instructions, such as how to use the career services office. So far the system's been branded a success.

The career services staff has also shown concern for the larger, more traditional companies. To help alleviate some of the mainstay recruiters'—like consulting firms and invest-ment banks—disappointing results compared with past years' recruiting efforts, the office is now working more closely with these companies to rethink hiring strategies and job offers. Eleven percent of the McCombs grads in 2000 went to work for start-ups. More than half received the trendy stock options concession as part of their pay packages—though it's tough to say if many have realized their rewards. Students are still interested in exploring opportunities with the more traditional firms, according to Career Services Director Sharon Lutz, but they're increasingly looking for a high-tech emphasis integrated throughout the company and the rampant use of technology—not to mention greater compensation, bonus incentives, and stock options. "In general, schools are having a harder time all around keeping these traditional recruiters happy," says Associate Dean Philip Zerrillo, who is also director of the MBA program. "They're just not getting the results they've come to expect from past experiences." All recruiters also have the opportunity to view the school's recruiting schedule online, so they can steer around their competitors when planning events.

The career services office may be mired in the mending of these ways, but as a whole, the McCombs School has much cause for celebration. Aside from the newly inflated endowment, there has been a round of genuine improvement, culminating in the school's one-notch gain in BUSINESSWEEK's 2000 rankings. Many of the areas perceived as weaknesses just two years ago, from teaching quality to faculty and administrative responsiveness, are now regarded as fair or even very good by McCombs MBAs. "The University of Texas has done an outstanding job of addressing student concerns," concurs one recent grad, "not only about previously missing pieces of the MBA curriculum but also enhancing the learning environment through technology." The progress didn't happen by chance. Plagued by discontent from students in the past, the school has made efforts to monitor customer satisfaction. Associate Dean Zerrillo gathers evaluative information from students just a few weeks into the first semester of their first year, as they're taking core courses—rather than solely from the more formal end-of-semester evaluation—so that any problems are now addressed as they're taking place. Many find it's made a difference. "The University of Texas is making a huge commitment to offer an even better graduate business institution," gushes another grad. "It's apparent in many ways, but most of all, the administration is listening to the students."

Although there's this new attention to core courses, they've actually been pared down, to just one-third of the credits required for graduation. This means more room for electives (including three during the first year), so students can better prepare themselves before their crucial summer internships. McCombs students are among the oldest compared with those at peer schools; Class of 2000 MBAs averaged 29 years old upon entering the program, making them the third oldest in our survey. Incoming students boast an average of five years of work experience as well. Associate Dean Zerrillo placed confidence in these factors when revising the curriculum, reasoning that students at this stage in their lives can make their own decisions about how to build their portfolios.

The core course program now consists of five required courses in the first semester and a choice of two management courses not taken in the fall semester, in the areas of operations, marketing, or finance, to be taken during the spring semester of the first year. Financial accounting, statistics, information technology management, and managerial economics are all covered in the first wave. You can't exempt yourself by exam or other means from any required or core courses, but with room for three electives in the spring semester, you are able to customize your degree, starting in your first year. McCombs MBAs don't have to major or concentrate in any one area—but many do, since there are 16 to choose

from. The modern basics are all there, from corporate and real estate finance to operations management. Newer selections include entrepreneurship, human resources management, investments, and even customer insight, which focuses on the use of technology in meeting customer needs and is supported by research partners Accenture, 3M, Dell, and Intelliquest. Students leaning toward the consulting field, service-based businesses, or strategic alliance and development groups take a special interest in it. Energy finance, another concentration that's new in the past three years, is backed by a research center and funded by industry giant Enron. With a requirement of just 15 hours of coursework in the discipline of your choice, most MBAs pick up at least one concentration during their time at Texas.

First-years are assigned to cohorts of 60 students with whom they are supposed to take all these required courses. But the emphasis on more individual choice in the curriculum can detract from group cohesiveness, which some consider a plus and others a minus when evaluating the program. There is such a focus on customization that within the 16 formal concentrations are some 20 optional specialties. In information management alone, there are tracks for technology strategies, managing intensive business change, financial information management, health care management, systems management, controls and assurance, and risk management and insurance. Students can custom-design their own concentrations, or just sample what they please from the array of about 80 elective courses offered by the B-school.

Texas was, until recently, probably best known for its highly regarded accounting program; about a fifth of the school's tenure-track faculty teach in the subject. But information management has also taken the school by storm. It would have been surprising had it not happened at this school planted squarely in the high-tech boom town of Austin, home of Dell Computers and more semiconductor producers than any other city in the nation. Each year Texas spawns 150 so-called "techno-MBAs"—those who take one of the info-tech concentrations—and more of the B-school's faculty teach in this area than any other (about a quarter of those on the tenure track). Administrators recently introduced a new, three-hour required information management course to give students a basic degree of technical proficiency so they'll know how to create a database or post a Web site, for example. The school's info-tech program has traditionally been ranked among the best in BUSINESSWEEK's surveys. In the program's current form, students have exclusive use of a state-of-the-art information management laboratory, where advanced technology shows up first before being incorporated into the rest of the school's computer arsenal. All classrooms are equipped with Ethernet ports and power at each seat, and the school provides nearly 900 workstations in seven computer labs. Maintaining interaction through technology is clearly a focus, too. As part of a "laptop initiative," students must all come equipped with the same portable computer so that they have use of standardized technology and, therefore, a common platform for communicating within a group. Students obtain information on classes, events, and recruiter schedules through the school's intranet system, Texas Nexus—and, from on campus or around the world, they can quickly access data sources like the school's alumni database.

Entrepreneurship is another area drawing attention here, especially as it increasingly goes hand-in-hand with IT. The school offers electives on entrepreneurial growth, marketing, and processes, and the MOOT CORP business plan competition each May draws would-be entrepreneurs from some two dozen B-schools around the world. Along with presentations over three days, participants have their business plans judged by a panel of venture capitalists and start-up artists who award the winning team with a $15,000 prize. Students interested in learning to launch a business can also connect with an Austin technology incubator with which the school has an ongoing relationship, and they can gain access to the university's IC^2 Institute, a world-renowned creativity and innovation think tank. Austin Power, a new nonprofit organization launched in 2000 by a group of Texas MBAs, matches local high-tech companies with B-school students seeking related internships or full-time jobs. The Entrepreneur Society and e-commerce club also bring in successful contacts, and the school holds start-up-heavy career fairs from time to time.

Less acknowledged is the well-received area of study in finance, made even more popular recently with the addition of the energy finance concentration. About one-third of Texas MBAs specialize in the subject each year. Much of the department's focus has centered on an MBA-managed investment fund in which 25 students each year are selected to handle $14 million for 50 accredited investors—as well as an $8.5 million Wall Street–style financial trading room, which opened in 1995. In the past, students have argued that those two programs serve a relatively small number of students, while the most desired finance electives are limited to one or two sections. But perhaps the addition of energy finance, "an area of need in the Texas economy"—and the possibility of other new options like it—can accommodate a broader range of finance-focused students in the future.

Dean May has also directed a fair amount of effort toward bulking up the B-school's international business program, which already benefits from the school's strong relations with Latin America. Texas has formed alliances with half a dozen top management schools in that region, offering exchange semesters and dual degrees that require a full year of foreign study at schools in Mexico, Brazil, or Chile. Double degrees are also available in conjunction with schools in Germany and France, and an additional 21 exchange programs take place in either

Europe, Australia, or Asia. Back home, students can take a three-course Spanish-language track, which consists of a summer of intensive cultural and language study before entering the MBA program, a course in commercial Spanish, another business elective taught entirely in Spanish, and the possibility of a follow-up internship or overseas study in Mexico, Chile, Venezuela, or Peru. Texas has also pushed to increase its international enrollment, which grew in the past two years from 22 to 28 percent, with at least half of those students hailing from Latin America. The B-school has a full-time career adviser who helps with overseas job placement, and the recently dispatched international student task force represents a global spectrum.

Although international enrollment has increased, however, the McCombs School remains on the low end for a Top 30 program in terms of underrepresented minorities; just 5 percent of the incoming Class of 2002 were of either African-American, Hispanic-American, or Native American descent. A large part of the problem is the federal court decision barring public institutions of higher education from practicing affirmative action—a decision that has affected not only the University of Texas as a whole, but also other public schools in the U.S. Fifth Circuit region, such as the University of North Carolina. The B-school has reacted by changing its recruiting strategies to increase diversity, with targeted mailings to bulk up the applicant pool among specific ethnic groups, for example—and by offering student scholarships through a consortium of schools. The McCombs gift will likely create more. The school has also been building relationships with minority Chamber of Commerce groups throughout Texas and has hired an admissions officer to work with corporations to identify potential students and support their education.

The school's strong network of corporate relationships provides a number of learning opportunities, both in and out of the classroom.

The marketing department has teamed with Procter & Gamble, 3M, and Motorola to provide about five summer internships each to students, who follow up their stint on the job with a symposium in which executives of the three firms discuss current cases in the field of customer business development. Annual corporate-sponsored academic challenges in accounting, consulting, entrepreneurship, finance, and marketing offer student teams the opportunity to work on simulated cases and then make analytical presentations to executives from sponsoring firms. The student-run Quality Management Consortia, co-sponsored by the College of Engineering, hires some 20 students a year to work for pay with local client companies seeking advice in implementing total quality programs.

Student organizations are plentiful here, ranging from the Graduate Business Council student government to career-related clubs, and especially community service groups. The Central Charity Challenge, launched by a group of Texas MBA students in 1996, engages several B-schools in the central United States in a friendly competition to rack up service hours and fundraising dollars for local and national charities. Charity begins at home, as well—the Class of 2000 raised more than $115,000 as a class gift to support the refurbishing of an area in the B-school that will serve as the MBA lounge.

The B-school's six-story, modern glass-and-concrete headquarters, with its mall-like atrium and spacious hallways, is located on the south end of the university's 300-acre campus in this lively state capital. Nestled along the Colorado River at the edge of Central Texas Hill Country, Austin is a fulfilling place to spend two years—and, some would argue, a decent place to groom a President. It's the intellectual and political capital of the nation's second most populous state, with students numbering nearly 50,000, and there has never been a scarcity of fun here. Many students unwind on Sixth Street, Austin's entertainment corridor, where an eclectic menu of live music from rock and blues to country and Tejano can be had any night of the week. As far as housing is concerned, some MBAs shack up in the loud, bustling West Campus neighborhood favored by undergraduate Greeks. But most prefer the quieter environs of eclectic, trendy Hyde Park north of campus; the inexpensive and convenient, but not always safe, Riverside area; or the quiet, family-oriented, but less accessible, Far West neighborhood.

PLACEMENT DETAILS

Like many top B-schools these days, McCombs finds among its main concerns the ability to connect with smaller recruiters to meet students' expectations. In addition to ongoing treks to the West Coast to seek such opportunities, the school has increased its focus on local start-up activity and has held more small gatherings to encourage interaction among students and area business leaders. Working with the more traditional recruiters to manage *their* expectations is another priority. "It's a challenge for the larger recruiters to effectively compete," says Career Services Director Sharon Lutz. "Students are still interested in exploring opportunities with them, but these larger companies have to rethink their strategies and their offers to lure employees. They haven't been getting the numbers of students they were used to getting."

But McCombs students, meanwhile, are faring fine. Despite the recruiter dissatisfaction that placed the McCombs' career services offices among the top five worst in BUSINESSWEEK's survey, the number of these potential employers coming to campus has increased from past years. The fairly new facility, opened in 1998, offers some consolation, with its top-notch amenities, fairly large staff devoted to service, and four account representatives handling specific industries and helping to strategically coordinate schedules. McCombs MBAs in 2000 received an average of 2.9 job offers, and while 11 percent did take work with start-up companies, the majority

landed in larger firms. Top employers included: Dell (28); Deloitte Consulting (10); Cisco (9); PricewaterhouseCoopers (8); McKinsey & Co. (7); Motorola (7); Diamond Technology Partners (6); Intel (6); Agilent (5); American Airlines (5); American Management Systems (5); A.T. Kearney (5); Enron (5); and Ford Motors (5).

OUTSTANDING FACULTY

Steven Tomlinson (economics); *Jeff Sandefer* (entrepreneurship/management); *James Nolen* (finance); *Andres Almazan* (finance); *Robert Parrino* (finance); *Gautam Ahuja* (management); *John Doggett* (management); *Britt Freund* (management).

APPLICANT TIPS

The McCombs School provides a great MBA bargain, with its 2000–2001 out-of-state tuition of $16,063 the lowest among the Top 30 B-schools (in-state students pay just $10,438). About 400 accepted students get to take advantage of it each year. Admissions officers look for basic criteria, like two to four years of work experience and a solid academic background; the Class of 2002 averaged a 3.4 GPA and a 687 GMAT score. But these aren't set standards, and the subjective part of the application process is substantial as well.

Applicants should be as communicative and as creative as possible in expressing defined career goals and ways in which they have excelled or shown leadership. Aside from the essays, you can use interviews to make your case for acceptance. Conducted on campus by student members of an admissions committee or in other locations by volunteer alums, interviews were offered starting last year and are suggested but not required. If you would like to come to campus, you can call the admissions office to set up an interview and reserve a space for an information session (held every Friday during the school year at 1 p.m. in the Office of the Graduate Business Dean). You can also arrange to visit a class and take one of the school tours, which begin at 11:30 a.m. Monday through Thursday. Apply early if you can, since acceptances are made on a rolling basis, with application reviews beginning in mid-December. About half the class is filled by mid-March, and the entire class is usually in place by the beginning of May, so waiting until the April 15 final deadline is not recommended.

Contact: Carl Harris
Director of Admissions
512-471-7612
Application deadlines: January 1 (early); February 1 (international); April 15 (final)

McCOMBS MBAs SOUND OFF

UT was an ideal MBA program. The students are not only bright and motivated, but are also committed to enhancing other students' learning experiences as well. Students are eager to assist others even given the time constraints each managed. The student population is diverse, yet seems to be drawn together by these differing backgrounds and experiences. The administration is especially responsive to student needs. In the time I have studied here, they have wired substantial portions of the business school for Internet access (classrooms, study areas, and common areas), refurbished a large independent study area, and built MBA-only group study rooms. The interviewing and changing rooms are first-rate, and the library is remarkable. Much of the bureaucracy one would associate with a school as large as UT is refreshingly absent.

The Texas MBA Program's best asset is its student body. My peers had depth and diversity in their professional experiences. They were also friendly and collaborative individuals with a sense of perspective. We work hard together yet still have fun. This program develops a very well-bonded community.

I thought the Austin location was great. The city provides numerous activities available outside of class. This really helped to bring my life into a balance between work and relaxation. I think the students at UT are top notch and I made many lifelong friendships with people from my study groups and cohort.

I believe that the strength of the Texas MBA is in its teamwork orientation. In addition to theory, the program teaches us how to leverage social, informal, and professional networks to successfully execute management decisions in the workplace. I interned for Intel Corporation last summer and was told by many of my colleagues that they would prefer to work with UT MBAs who are willing to "get their hands dirty" as opposed to some MBAs from the other top programs who are more concerned about position and image.

Going to Texas was one of the best decisions I've ever made in my career. While the "depth on the bench" of student/course quality may not be the same as a Harvard or a Wharton, make no mistake—the top third of this program contains faculty and students that are easily on a par with the best of any other school. Add to that the wealth of contacts in venture capital, high-tech, and the Austin location, and UT represents a huge winner in MBA programs.

The Entrepreneurship program at UT is world class. Outstanding lecturers come from a broad spectrum of entrepreneurial pursuits. The program holds both professors and students to incredibly high levels of effort and achievement. I would have no trouble telling someone who was accepted into both Harvard and UT and is interested in entrepreneurship to come to UT.

UT benefits greatly from its location. Austin is a beautiful, fun city. The diversity of opportunities is almost overwhelming. Huge companies like Dell, Intel, IBM, 3M, etc. are complemented by a large and rapidly growing start-up community. The biggest difference between my expectation and experience at UT is the level of companies that recruit here. I was surprised at the number and quality of the firms.

18.
UNIVERSITY OF CALIFORNIA AT BERKELEY

UNIVERSITY OF CALIFORNIA AT BERKELEY

Haas School of Business
440 Student Services Building #1902
Berkeley, California 94720-1902
E-mail address: mbaadms@haas.berkeley.edu
Web site address: http://www.haas.berkeley.edu

Corporate ranking: 22
Enrollment: 836
Women: 31%
Non-U.S.: 31%
Minority: 4%
Part-time: 352
Average age: 28
Applicants accepted: 14%
Median starting pay: $135,000

Graduate ranking: 14
Annual tuition & fees:
   resident—$10,458
   nonresident—$20,702
Room and board: $10,586
Average GMAT score: 684
Average years of work exp.: 5.6
Accepted applicants enrolled: 56%
Intellectual capital: 38

Teaching methods: Lecture, 30%   Case study, 50%
   Group projects, 20%

Contact:
Ilse Evans
Director, Career
Services and
Admissions
510-642-1405
Application deadlines:
November 1
January 16
March 16 (domestic
and international)

It's hard to say whether or not an applicant is a good fit for the Haas School. That's because there really is no such thing. At this top graduate program at the University of California at Berkeley, students move to the beat of a different drummer almost as if it is a part of their education. They come from a variety of industries and locales. Many Haas MBAs have a background influenced by socially responsible business leadership, having done public policy, nonprofit, or environmental work—or they aspire to incorporate social issues into their careers. "People in the program are very interested in learning how to do good business and how to be responsible to the environment, the world, and mostly to other people, like employees," says Jerry Millendorf, a recent grad.

Even so, the student body is consistently divided in terms of backgrounds and interests. Of last year's graduates, about 26 percent ended up in consulting jobs, 19 percent landed in investment banking or brokerage positions, and a full 38 percent dove into the high-tech or Internet industries. A handful started companies. Their bountiful interests and experiences make even more sense when you consider that last year's graduates were the among the oldest (averaging about 29 years), compared with students from other top B-schools.

A majority of students actively participate in the dozens of wide-ranging clubs and organizations on campus, from the Berkeley Real Estate Club and MBA Association to Redwoods@Haas and the Wine Industry Club. The Haas Visitation Program for prospective students has current MBAs perpetuating the "active engagement" credo by helping to recruit like-minded applicants during the admissions process. They may have their differences, but all Haas students follow a much-loved tradition of teamwork, a practice facilitated by the intimacy resulting from the school's small size. The total enrollment is 484 full-time MBAs. One student, having most enjoyed working with Haas graduates at his former place of employment, cites their influence as the main reason he applied. "The Haas MBAs were so friendly and easy to work with, and they got a lot done because everyone really wanted to be staffed on their projects," says the former investment banker. "They signified the type of person I wanted to be as a businessman and as an individual." Others at this team-oriented B-school blessed with mild weather and the excitement of nearby Silicon Valley share this sentiment.

The uniqueness of Haas's students and setting is perhaps best enhanced by the school's dean, Laura D'Andrea Tyson, who became the first woman to head a top-ranked B-school when she was appointed to the role in July 1998. Tyson's impressive record in public affairs and economics preceded her: The highest-ranking woman in the White House from 1995 to 1996, she served as National Economic Advisor to President Clinton and as sixteenth chairman of the White House Council of Economic Advisors. Prior to her work in government, Tyson spent two decades as a highly respected professor and researcher in the male-dominated field of economics—and with regard to her latest role in academia, she calls herself "more of a reflection" of the culture than a creation of it. "If you had asked me, 'What is a major business school most likely to appoint the first woman dean?' I would have definitely listed Berkeley among the top five," she says.

The high-profile dean has been well received by students and faculty alike. Most praised are her efforts to gain greater independence for the business school from its larger university, which have allowed for greater flexibility in raising funds from alumni and donors. The money has gone, most recently, toward establishing salaries and services that are competitive with other top B-schools. Tyson is also credited by some with shaping the administration for success. "She's brought a terrific group on board," says Ilse Evans, former career placement maven at MIT's Sloan School and Haas's Director of Admissions and Career Placement as of October 1999. "They're open-minded people with an eagerness to try new ideas, and to learn if they fail." Tyson also brought aboard two assistant deans.

Indeed, there has been some adjustment to change here. Haas has historically attracted and nurtured a well-rounded student body, but since 1998, the number of minority students (African-Americans, Native Americans, and Hispanics, primarily) has dropped significantly, to a current low of just 4 percent. The shift is due, in part, to a change in California law that now forbids ethnicity to play any role in admissions decisions. Haas no longer has control over the makeup of the student body, and potential applicants from minority populations have begun to feel unwanted at the university—based on the dwindling numbers, some say. The admissions team has stepped up efforts to increase recruiting activity among these groups, and the school participates in a number of programs that create and encourage minority scholarships and incentives, including the Consortium for Graduate Study in Management and the Robert Tioga Foundation. But while the school's Minority Affairs Liaison, Karese Young, dispenses advise to minority applicants on applying to and attending Haas, attracting interest from underrepresented minorities in the first place proves to be an ongoing challenge.

The student body at Haas, nevertheless, continues to represent varying international origins, professional experience, and aspirations, at the very least. But much as student interests are far-reaching, the school's curriculum is grounded by three main themes—entrepreneurship and innovation, global management, and management of technology—which, administrators note, were in place *before* achieving trend status within the New Economy. Certificates are offered in each. At the Lester Center, which was created with an initial endowment gift by W. Howard Lester, chairman and CEO of Williams-Sonoma, course development, research, outreach activities, and public programs take place with respect to entrepreneurship and innovation. Each year the Center awards two $5000 Price Institute Fellowship awards to eligible students angling for an entrepreneurial career. Since 1997, the Center has also sponsored a program that arranges three-month summer internships with venture capital firms for students to gain experience in investments, capital management, and operating. Haas MBAs are matched with the firms, which may then place the intern within their own offices or with a portfolio company upon graduation.

Consultant types, too, can gain experience with small local businesses through the Berkeley Solutions Group, a student-run program that sets up Haas MBAs to advise local new enterprises, small businesses, and nonprofit organizations that can't afford professional consulting fees. The student consultants might focus on market research, financial analysis, or human resource organization; a recent project helped launch a handful of Internet companies' new product ideas online. To get a foot in the door of one of the region's many high-growth, high-tech start-ups, a number of students also pounce on internship opportunities presented by the Partners for Entrepreneurial Leadership organization. The projects, which range from business and financial planning to the development of new computer systems, often carry over into the students' second year. If you don't want to invest in the internship but you're networking savvy (or aspire to be), you can also make an appearance at the monthly Berkeley Entrepreneurs Forum, which draws industry bigwigs from nearby Silicon Valley.

The Management of Technology theme fuses contributions from the College of Engineering and School of Information Management and Systems in a joint program designed to guide students in the procedures and strategies for bringing high-tech products to market. Highly interested students can work toward a certificate in this subject by following a set of requirements. Your two core courses could be Internet Strategy and Managing Innovation and Change, for example; you'll also select two related courses from a list that includes Global Supply Chain Management, Precision Manufacturing, Project Risk Management, and Entrepreneurship. "It's terrific for someone without a technology background who wants the experience," says David Downes, the director of the Haas MBA program.

The International Business Development course, a part of the school's global management theme, is considered a "big draw" by the admissions office. The course has full-time Haas MBAs preparing for an international consulting project in the spring, and when summer comes, they are sent on assignment to a foreign destination. Teams of about a dozen students each year work on business plans, feasibility studies, or market analyses with organizations like Ford Motor Company and Lucent Technologies in such remote locations as Costa Rica and Ghana. International-minded students who don't take the course still have an opportunity to go abroad, by participating in a semester-long exchange program with one of six international business schools.

Semesters at Haas are 15 weeks long, and incoming students attend a one-week orientation program at the start of school that's designed and run almost entirely by second-years, with mainly a social (as in, get-to-know-each-other) focus. Some of the 13 required core courses have recently been dismantled or reshaped, including a professional skills core course, which has become a more comprehensive management development program with four modules. Taken for pass/fail credit only by first-years (just after orientation in the fall semester), the program covers speaking, writing, strategic business interactions, and career planning. "We're teaching students to market themselves here," notes one administrator, Ilse Evans. "Networking is the No. 1 tool. They also learn to research the job market and have a positioning strategy so they can show companies what makes them different." An information technology core course was recently canceled, but students cover technology topics in many of their electives. The school's emphasis on careers is reflected in a pre-midterm intra-session period set aside to help prepare students for their job search efforts. During the three-day "break," students conduct mock interviews, attend presentations on résumé development, and learn strategies for negotiation. It's a wonder to the career management office that, even with such an arrangement, students continue to give their services dismal marks, concluding that the assistance in securing summer jobs or internships, as well as employment prior to graduation, is inadequate. Dean Tyson has said Haas students don't like too much handholding, but clearly the objective is to find some middle ground.

Elective courses run the gamut, with popular favorites like Competitive and Corporate Strategy, New Venture Strategy, High Technology Marketing, and Internet Strategy taking center stage. New additions joining their ranks include Contemporary Philanthropy; Implementing Mergers, Acquisitions, and Joint Ventures in the Internet Economy; Introduction to the Health Care System; and Law and Strategy of e-Commerce. It's not necessary to declare a major or a concentration during your two years at Haas, but many students do choose to participate in one of the school's four certificate programs. The fourth, in addition to the three main themes of entrepreneurship and innovation, global management, and management of technology, is a new business and financial engineering offering. Targeted to students with superior quantitative skills, the new MFE/MBA degree is mainly for those planning to enter the computational finance field. MFE students can take a one-year intensive program that runs from April through March, and applicants who are admitted to Berkeley's MBA and MFE programs can complete a two-year concurrent degree, which is, in effect, two degrees. If you're looking at a career in risk management, investment banking, asset management, derivative trading, or specialized securities, this program could be a smart option.

Techie types and others with a bent for innovation have a unique opportunity to take part in an experimental joint program with Michigan and Darden. A professor from one school conducts class live and via a videoconferencing system for groups of students at all three schools. The fall 2000 Darden-taught class on e-business innovations was the first, and all concentrate on e-business, including a course on financial issues in the Internet sector taught by Haas faculty and one on the strategic applications of Internet technologies taught by Michigan faculty. Speaking of technology, in general, it's up to date at Haas. Nearly everything school-related can be accessed online, from the handbook and materials for classes to students' entire recruiting schedules. The school's three interconnected buildings with 21 classrooms contain 450 laptop docking stations, 55 videoconference locations, and 30 broadcast origination sites. There's also a computer center with modern resources and a financial engineering lab, plus a business economics library stocked with 130,000 bound volumes, more than 300 network ports, and all-important research services like Dow Jones Interactive, Lexis-Nexis Universe, and Datastream. Be warned, though, you might need a map to figure your way through the winding corridors. Administrators say they're working on better signage.

Haas also has a history of innovation. In 1997 the B-school became one of the first to offer an incubator, which presently has room for seven ventures at a time. The forward-looking focus is alive and well today, mainly in the school's entrepreneurial forte. A full 30 percent of last year's graduates took risks in working for start-ups, and 37 percent received stock options as part of their pay packages. Funded with donations from advisers and friends of the Lester Center, the Berkeley Business Incubator provides office space and advanced telecommunications capabilities to new ventures that are deemed promising and have progressed beyond initial planning. Students leading these ventures get guidance and support from the school's network of venture capitalists, attorneys, accountants, and consultants—not a bad position to be in, and probably part of the reason 14 graduates from the Class of 2000 were successful in launching their own companies. Many more were involved in the UC Berkeley Business Plan Competition, in which about 60 Silicon Valley VCs serve as judges tasked with awarding a grand prize of $50,000. Past winning teams have gone on to gain further funding, including Skyflow, a provider of wireless hands- and eyes-free information ($3.5 million); GetRelevant, a direct marketing network for Internet retailers ($4.85 million); and ZipRealty, possibly the first fully online real estate service ($27.7 million).

Entrepreneurs interested in social or environmental issues get to showcase their ideas through the Haas Social Venture Business Plan Competition, which calls for business plans with not just a positive financial bottom line, but also a social or environmental one. Launched last spring, the competition is hosted by Haas and open to teams from other top B-schools like Harvard, Wharton, Kellogg, and UCLA. Haas extends its entrepreneurial focus beyond the school through the Young Entrepreneurs at Haas (YEAH), a group of Berkeley MBAs and undergrads that helps more than 170 disadvantaged students from local high schools and middle schools develop their ideas for new businesses and learn effective study habits.

The concepts of helping and teamwork carry over into most areas of the Haas experience, especially with an end-of-the-fall-term capstone project, in which groups of five choose one of three established companies (in 2000, the contenders were Chevron, QRS, and Southwest Airlines) to place a value on the firm. The valuation must be backed up with information gathered through the accounting, finance, organizational behavior, data analysis, and communication skills acquired during your first semester core courses.

In general, the level of student participation on campus—in events, clubs, and organizations—has made an impression on the faculty. "It's hard for Haas students to hide," says full-time MBA Program Director David Downes, referring to the program's small size. "And it's the students who put pressure on themselves to get involved; we don't at all." Downes's history with the program began in the early '80s, when the place was more of a "commuter" school, and he has since noted a significant change. Today's Haas students stay after class to hold discussions or hang out, even as the numerous outside distractions of the cosmopolitan Bay Area beckon. Student-run conferences like Women in Leadership and Leading Edge Technology are popular and expanding. In addition, the school is among the smallest to produce a weekly student-run paper, *Haas Week*—published in print and, of course, online.

The recruiting experience at Haas, though fruitful, is yet to be considered a strength in the eyes of all students. Recent graduates who responded to BUSINESSWEEK's 2000 survey rated career services at Haas as mediocre compared with other Top 30 schools, citing their disappointment with the number and quality of firms that came to campus and the need for more assistance in landing summer internships and jobs before graduation. It's a tricky situation here. So many of Berkeley's students, enticed by the excitement of the growing Bay Area, are set on attaching themselves to one of the local start-ups, which, very often, have yet to achieve visibility. Finding the ones most likely to be successful can be a challenge for career counselors. The office maintains a database of electronic listings, holds seminars and conferences, and conducts its own outreach—but it's hard to keep up with a market in which things change so suddenly, at the whim of a venture capitalist or with the mood of the stock market, for instance. "It's a different way of recruiting," admits Tyson. "Getting jobs requires much more from the students." Hence, their possible reluctance to give high marks to an office that may not have helped them as much as they had expected or wanted.

Another difficulty for placement officials has been managing the expectations of traditional recruiters losing students to these New Economy opportunities. Of a recent class of Haas MBAs, more than half planted themselves in the Bay Area upon graduation, another aspect bound to concern companies that have been coming to campus from afar. But aside from the obstacles, many recruiters say they'll come back because they like Haas students and the placement office is accommodating, despite the low yields. And Haas's recruiting numbers are steady. The improved quality and diversity of on-campus recruiters is a relief to career counselors tasked with satisfying Haas students, who are almost evenly distributed among their chosen fields, be it consulting, investment banking, or high-tech and Internet work. More international opportunities have opened up here, thanks to targeted efforts by the career services office. Many of the improvements and ongoing initiatives can be credited to Tyson's addition of Ilse Evans, a former marketing whiz in the high-tech consumer electronics industry, as director of both Career Services and Admissions. The duality should serve the school well.

Both the career services and admissions departments have also augmented their efforts to connect with alumni, whom they look to for help in corralling the best and brightest students and providing important career opportunities for new grads. "They're the only way we can deal with smaller high-tech firms," Evans notes, adding that alumni connections with more traditional recruiters are invaluable as well. Alumni, in return, can utilize Haas's resources, such as phone or in-person interviews with a career services adviser, career seminars, and access to online directories with searchable alumni contact information, as well as 500 to 600 electronic postings each year.

But what really maintains the connection with alumni is the lasting goodwill found on campus and among Haas grads after their schooling. The attitude is one of sharing, from collaboration in class to the sliding-scale child-care the university offers staff, faculty, and students. (In true communal '60s spirit, parents are expected to work at the child-care center two hours a week.) The Long Term Assets club—which says it "focuses on critically important long-term investments in the MBA portfolio: spouses, families, and significant others"—shares a job database, babysitter list, and doctor and dental recommendations with newcomers, and arranges picnics, zoo trips, and viewings of the "Nutcracker" ballet at holiday time. Members also share tips about house-hunting, a difficult prospect in the Berkeley area, where housing is scarce and expensive. University housing is available for singles and married couples but it's extremely limited; about 600 graduate students from all Berkeley departments, half of them from the United States and half from overseas, manage to secure spots each year in the International House dormitory.

It's a good thing, then, that Haas's management complex offers such a homey, stay-a-while, residential look and feel. The main building, which opened in 1995, anchors the B-school and "mini-campus" at the eastern edge of the Berkeley campus near California Memorial Stadium. It connects by bridge with two other buildings and surrounds a courtyard where students congregate to talk, read, and catch sun. And, it's a short walk from Berkeley's tranquil redwood garden—a collection of the stately trees set beside a meadow. Inside, you'll find the library, research centers, computer labs, faculty offices, and executive programs. MBAs gather here every other Friday for schoolwide "Consumption Functions," then fan out to parties at students' apartments or nearby eateries for Thai food at Plearn, Ethiopian at Blue Nile, or Indian at Ajanta, or to Kip's or Bear's Lair for more mundane burgers and pizza. The Bay Area's proximity to the wineries of the Napa and Sonoma Valleys appeals to wine lovers, but local residents and MBAs are also beer and ale connoisseurs. Triple Rock, which serves beer brewed on the premises, is a favorite. The town of Berkeley is a quick walk—and the sidewalks there are often crowded with street vendors and people. Undoubtedly, a beautiful setting in which to spend two years.

PLACEMENT DETAILS

Establishing its own career center was one of Haas's first acts of independence from the larger university, and Tyson has since added Ilse Evans to head the place. With three account managers to help, they've significantly stepped up the recruiting machine. First-years kick off the fall semester with a management development curriculum that covers the art of self-marketing, using speech, writing, and negotiation skills. During a three-day intrasession, they also focus on career-oriented activities, including workshops for self-directed job searches, networking groups for those seeking employment in the high-tech, health-care/nonprofit, or finance/venture capital fields, and workshops for students with low-tech backgrounds who want to switch into the high-tech arena. Students at all levels are encouraged to do a substantial amount of research in the job market so they can differentiate themselves from other candidates when applying for a position. Haas goes the extra mile in some ways, like flying students with an interest in Wall Street to New York for a couple of days to meet with recruiters. But applicants should be advised that, generally, they're expected to do a fair amount of the job-search work on their own.

Even without the handholding, Haas students do fine for themselves. Last year's crop of graduates scored an average of 3.1 job offers and a median pay package of $135,000. Despite all the talk about a high-tech start-up craze, in 2000, Haas's top employers were largely made up of biggies from the investment banking and consulting industries: McKinsey & Co. (9); Charles Schwab (8); Goldman Sachs (7); Pittiglio Rabin Todd & McGrath (6); Siebel Systems (5); Hewlett-Packard Companies (4); A.T. Kearney (3); Accenture (3); Arthur D. Little (3); Bain & Company (3); and Clorox Company (3).

OUTSTANDING FACULTY

Brett Trueman (accounting); *Jonathan Leonard* (economics); *Andrew Rose* (economics); *Peter DeMarzo* (finance); *Richard Lyons* (finance); *Rashi Glazer* (marketing); *Peter Wilton* (marketing); *Paul Tiffany* (strategy).

APPLICANT TIPS

Haas, like nearly all B-schools these days, is looking for a good mix of students—but top credentials are important. A strong undergraduate record is a must and high GMATs are helpful; about 85 percent of the 2000–2001 incoming class came in at a range of 620 to 750. The type of work experience you've had isn't as important as the impact you've had within the company; you should be clear in your essay when you describe how you've shown leadership. The school likes to see some sort of interesting experience, such as a global one outside the United States, and an entrepreneurial venture that went sour is not necessarily a bad thing. "Those are some of our ideal students," remarks Admissions Director Ilse Evans. "They believe that an MBA can make your life easier, and they understand the value of the degree." In the past, Haas has admittedly been "too enamored with work experience," but the school now finds three years to be an acceptable average. Despite the fact that some of the other top schools are targeting applicants directly out of college or with one or two years of experience, Haas will only rarely consider such an individual for acceptance to the MBA program.

Students are expected to demonstrate computer proficiency before arriving on campus and are asked to submit two letters of recommendation, with at least one being from a current employer. Academic recommendations are definitely frowned upon.

Applications can be filled out on paper, on a disk supplied by the admissions office, in a computer file downloaded from the school Web site, or entirely online. Completed applications can either be mailed in or submitted electronically, depending on the format you choose. Evaluative interviews are not required, but applicants can schedule one from mid-September through mid-December and late January through the end of March by calling the admissions office. The school also offers drop-in information sessions run by second-year students Monday through Friday at 1 p.m. from September through mid-May; the staff will coordinate class visits and lunch with current students if you so desire (be advised that no classes are held on Mondays, however). If you can't make it to campus, you can take an interactive, virtual tour via the school Web site.

Contact: Ilse Evans
Director, Career Services and Admissions
510-642-1405
Application deadlines: November 1; January 16; March 16 (domestic and international)

HAAS MBAs SOUND OFF

Haas's recruiting process has much improved since the hiring of Laura Tyson as dean. I noticed a dramatic improvement in recruiting between my first and second year in terms of the diversity and caliber of firms that were coming here. Despite efforts to increase the number of large banking and consulting firms that come to recruit, the school still actively promotes recruiting by small high-technology companies. Therefore, the recruiting process continues to appease the desire by many Haas students to join small, entrepreneurial companies.

At Haas, I had two of the best years of my life, met a lot of fun and talented people, expanded my knowledge, created a wide network of contacts in the finance world in the Silicon Valley, and spent a fair amount of my time skiing in Lake Tahoe and surfing at the Berkeley Marina. In fact, I liked it so much here that I have accepted an offer to work in San Francisco after I graduate.

The entire community at Haas gave me the most valuable two years of my life. Not only did I not expect such an unbelievable spirit of teamwork and willingness to help in any aspects, but also a professional experience (including the part-time work opportunities in the Bay Area) which I will draw upon over my entire life.

That we are situated at the nexus of entrepreneurial business, internationalism, and high tech is remarkable. But the beauty of attending Haas is that when graduation comes, the students who don't move to Asia, Europe, or South America after graduation remain, in large part, in the Bay Area. The regionalism that worried me when I applied to Haas over two years ago has become a competitive advantage in this "new" economy. I remember a conversation with a friend from another B-school two years ago, the day she was moving out of her apartment after completing her MBA—her classmates experienced total diaspora. That doesn't happen after your graduation here; we're already planning the BBQs, monthly meetings, and intranet that will help keep us collaborating professionally and strengthening our friendships well into the future.

Haas's biggest problem is all the restrictions placed on it by the university bureaucracy. The dean and the administration have been very successful at convincing the university to lift many of its restrictions and grant Haas more autonomy, and the result so far has been significant improvements in the Haas program. Haas is definitely an up-and-coming program, and it gets visibly better every year. I'm a bit sorry that I won't be around to take advantage of the initiatives they have planned for next year.

Geography is one of Haas's great strengths. Once people are exposed to the Bay Area, they don't want to leave. Even many foreign students from my class have decided to stay. The economy is booming, and the quality of life is excellent. But unfortunately, in many rankings systems, this shows up as a weakness in recruiting. In reality, there are many more good job openings available through the Haas career center than there are grads to fill them. Even for people who have postponed job searches to travel or work on business plans (like me), they are confident that they can find jobs whenever they decide to start looking.

**19.
YALE
UNIVERSITY**

YALE UNIVERSITY

School of Management
Box 208200
New Haven, Connecticut 06520-8200
E-mail address: som.admissions@yale.edu
Web site address: http://mba.yale.edu

Corporate ranking: 23

Graduate ranking: 22

Enrollment: 420

Annual tuition & fees: $27,680

Women: 28%

Room and board: $9055

Non-U.S.: 33%

Average GMAT score: 687

Minority: 5%

Average years of work exp.: 5

Part-time: 0

Accepted applicants enrolled: 48%

Average age: 28

Intellectual capital: 5

Applicants accepted: 17%

Median starting pay: $130,000

Teaching methods: Lecture, 60%   Case study, 35%
Experiential, 5%

Contact:
James R. Stevens
Director of Admissions
203-432-5932
Application deadlines:
November 1
January 2
March 15

For nearly 25 years, one of the most distinctive and widely copied features of Yale University's School of Management was also one of its biggest liabilities. When the school was founded in 1974, university officials explicitly said they didn't want another Harvard Business School on the Yale campus. They envisioned instead a cross between a business school and a school of public policy that awarded a unique Master's in Public and Private Management degree to graduates destined to bring business savvy to the government and nonprofit sectors. Indeed, that hybrid image has been what has brought SOM its largest measure of notice, with top-tier B-schools such as Stanford, Kellogg, Wharton, Columbia, and, yes, Harvard jumping on the bandwagon to launch similar programs.

At the same time, SOM has struggled to attract the same level of acclaim for its other programs. Even its excellent offerings in finance and general management continue to escape the attention of enough potential students and corporate recruiters to boost Yale into the uppermost B-school ranks. Retaining the aura of an "alternative" program, SOM remains one of only two schools in the university not considered among the very best in the country (the divinity school is the other).

But since taking over the dean's office in 1995, Jeffrey Garten, a former investment banker who also served in the Clinton Administration, has gradually been moving SOM in a more mainstream direction—forging stronger ties with Corporate America and directing the bulk of the school's resources at training for private-sector careers, which is where virtually every member of the Class of 2000 ended up after graduation anyway. In the fall of 1998, Garten won a symbolic victory for his efforts by gaining faculty approval to change the degree awarded by the B-school from the MPPM to the traditional MBA—a change students had been lobbying for for years and which Garten had tried, but failed, to have implemented immediately on his arrival in New Haven.

By more substantive measures, Garten's strategy also seems to be succeeding, with Yale pushing up a spot in BUSINESSWEEK's 2000 overall rankings to No. 19, largely on the strength of enthusiastic graduates who rave about the B-school's close-knit community and say they are pleased with the direction Garten is taking the school. While many other B-schools have seen application level off during this boom economy, interest in SOM's program is soaring, with applications up 29 percent in 2000, and nearly 75 percent from when Garten signed on as dean. Moreover, Garten has been delivering on plans to increase dramatically the number of senior faculty while holding the size of the student body constant at 400. Since 1998, the number of the SOM senior faculty has grown by over 41 percent, and Garten has plans to recruit a few more professors over the next few years. Alums seem pleased with the school's performance, too, backing their sentiments with cold, hard cash: Alumni giving, with a 52 percent participation level, was among the highest of the schools surveyed by BUSINESSWEEK—even though, as the newest B-school on the list, Yale's alumni base is still quite small, at 3928. The handsome rewards Yale business grads draw from employers may also have something to do with their high level of satisfaction: The Class of 2000's median starting salary-and-bonus package of $135,000 is also among highest of the schools polled.

Although he is certainly making a strong start, Garten's job is far from finished. Even if a handful of recruiters consider SOM the most improved program, placing its program in the top tier of BUSINESSWEEK's 2000 corporate poll, students say that Yale's small size simply does not attract enough of them to campus. The number of companies recruiting on campus has increased a whopping 87 percent since 1996, but the total of about 110 who stopped at New Haven in 2000 compares poorly with other, higher-ranked B-schools with similarly small enrollments, such as Dartmouth's Tuck School, which drew more than 150 firms—and it's a lot harder to persuade recruiters to trek to Charlottesville, Virginia, or Hanover, New Hampshire, than to a school sitting smack dab in the middle of the Northeast Corridor. Although Yale has attempted to beef up its offerings in entrepreneurship and information technology, graduates and recruiters are slow to be impressed by the school's offerings in those areas.

Nevertheless, SOM does appear to have a positive momentum going, with plenty of good news to share. Since taking the reins, Garten has stressed that managers in today's economy need strong quantitative skills and has pushed hard to make Yale a leading center for financial research. To that end, Yale launched an interdisciplinary, campus think tank called the International Center for Finance in 1999. The new center taps into the larger university, bringing together prominent scholars from the law school and the economics and mathematics departments. Housed in a sprawling university-owned mansion next door to the existing business classroom and administrative building, the ICF has added 30 percent more square footage to a B-school already squeezed for space and has been instrumental in luring new faculty to New Haven. It's also brought more visibility to the SOM program thanks to the "Smart Investor" National Public Radio talk show. The weekly program features several ICF fellows, including best-selling author and Yale economist Robert Schiller, who banter about financial issues and dish out investment advice.

But perhaps most importantly, the center's cutting-edge research often trickles into the MBA curriculum. For example, in finance professor William Goetzmann's popular investment management course, students were asked to evaluate the risk of hedge funds based on data sets he was studying as director of the ICF. By the end of the project, Goetzmann boasts, "our students knew as much about the fund and its analysis as the fund manager himself." That's no small task, of course, because the hedge fund manager to whom Goetzmann was referring was none other than George Soros.

Moreover, the dean's office has finally achieved some stability after a period of turmoil and turnover in the early '90s. Garten, who arrived at Yale after stints as a banker with Lehman Brothers and as President Clinton's Undersecretary of Commerce, spent his first months in office jump-starting the career development office, hiring Mark Case from the University of Michigan as director. Since then, the staff has been reorganized and multiplied threefold, and space dedicated solely to recruiting has been renovated and upgraded.

In 1997, Garten formed a high-profile advisory board, chaired by William H. Donaldson, SOM's founding dean and co-founder of Donaldson, Lufkin & Jenrette, and including such corporate and Wall Street luminaries as AT&T Chairman C. Michael Armstrong, American Airlines CEO Robert Crandall, New York Stock Exchange Chairman Richard A. Grasso, and Dow Jones CEO Peter R. Kann. The board's 23 members meet as a group twice yearly, as well as individually with the dean two more times a year. Besides heartily endorsing Garten's aim to focus on general management and leadership rather than any highly specialized programs, they've given Yale a pipeline to potential employers.

Garten has also turned his attention to internal relations, making himself widely available to students to discuss their concerns. He began writing a monthly open letter to students to keep them up to date on administrative happenings, and he personally exit-interviews every one of the members of the graduating class, acting quickly to fulfill such suggestions as refurbishing the computer lab, making alumni more accessible for job advice, and reviewing the curriculum, both core courses and electives, to incorporate student input. Even when he's on the road, students aren't far from Garten's mind—he often carries a portfolio of résumés with him when he travels the country to talk with alumni and potential employers. "Both the students and alumni are incredibly demanding about the school and the direction of SOM," says 2000 grad Emily Bremner Forbes. "He did a pretty good job of working with students, faculty, and alumni to bring cohesion."

One of the biggest concerns Garten found in talking with students is that SOM maintain its culture as an intimate, supportive community that has been steeped in teamwork since its inception and welcomes applicants from a broad range of backgrounds, including those with only government or nonprofit experience and little in the way of technical expertise. "Everyone I interviewed said the best part of their [Yale] experience had been the student body and the incredible educational experience of being in class with people of such different backgrounds, as well as the access to faculty who know the names of every student and a campus where everything is within 100 yards of everything else," Garten says. The dean assured them he has no desire to tamper with this formula, one of the school's biggest strengths. Although the grading system, previously pass/fail, was shifted in 1996 to a more evaluative categorization that rates students on four tiers of achievement—Distinction, Proficient, Pass, and Fail—more closely resembling an A-through-F structure, there are still no grading curves and no class ranks, and students still rate themselves among the most noncompetitive at any B-school.

Courses have as many as 70 students in the core survey courses to as few as 10 in some specialized electives. Students are primarily taught in lectures (60 percent), combined with case studies and a few "real-world" projects. But whatever you take, you can probably bet that a professor's scholarly research will be infused somewhere into the syllabus, providing a high-level of intellectual rigor that faculty and students consider to be the trademark of a Yale MBA. "It's not just about learning the right tools," says 2000 grad Brian Upbin. "It's about thinking in different ways."

Students say they find the quality of teaching in their core classes to be hit-or-miss, depending on the professor. But elective teaching fared much better. Grads were extremely pleased how good the school is at meeting the demand for popular electives, especially given its small size. And unlike many other top B-schools, grads said the faculty was often available for discussion outside of class. In the first year, students take 10 required core courses, 5 in each 13-week semester (you may waive out of any core class by passing an exam). Among the requirements are classes in accounting, statistics, economic and decision analysis, strategy, leadership and team-building, and organizational behavior; students may choose two among three courses in marketing, operations, and finance.

Students here do not take all their core courses with the same section or cohort, so class composition varies from course to course. Nevertheless, teamwork is the norm, with assigned and student-generated groups tackling projects and study time together in almost every class. In addition, first-years must complete a two-semester sequence called Perspectives on Organization and Management, which brings in business executives and consultants to put a real-life spin on the theoretical foundation being laid down in the core courses. And that's not mentioning the star-studded line-up of former execs who teach electives. For instance, in 1999–2000, former Procter & Gamble CEO John Pepper taught a course in global leadership, and Reed Hundt, former head of the FCC,

taught a course on regulation and strategy in the television industry.

Throughout the school year, Garten taps his broad network of contacts to bring in a supplementary stream of high-wattage speakers from the private, public, and government sectors, with distinguished guests in '99–'00 including Ford Motor Company Chairman William Clay Ford Jr., Dell Computer founder Michael Dell, America Online CEO Stephen Case, and Fannie Mae Chairman and CEO Franklin Raines. Students can also sign up for daylong field trips to companies like Lehman Brothers, Amtrak, DuPont, Xerox, and the Ford Foundation.

Second-year students are asked to choose one area of interest for either a two-course "in-depth training sequence" in any of a broad range of advanced management topics such as international finance, corporate finance, policy analysis, or consumer behavior, or a three-course concentration in finance, marketing, strategy, operations management, public management, or nonprofit management. Then you're free to choose from among the 70 electives offered by SOM, including about 40 percent of courses that were entirely new in 2000.

Driven by student interest, Yale has increased the number of courses it offers in entrepreneurship, especially those such as venture capital and private equity that harness its faculty's strength in finance. The B-school recently sponsored a highly selective summer internship program in entrepreneurship led by professor David Cromwell, who headed J.P. Morgan's Capital Corporation for more than 30 years before coming to Yale. Under Cromwell's guidance, six MBA interns spent the summer working on several major projects for local entrepreneurial high-tech ventures. The experience paid off big-time: Not only did the student group quickly learn the tricks-of-the-trade, the management of one firm hired the team back to actually run the company after graduation.

Garten's overriding goal has been promoting the B-school's ties with the rest of Yale, and it shows: A course on high-tech start-ups is offered jointly to business, law, and medical students; another in product design for entrepreneurial teams combines business and engineering students; one on business and regulation in the information age taps both law and business students; and a real estate course teams up architecture and business students. Full-fledged joint degrees are available with Yale's schools of architecture, divinity, drama, public health, forestry and environmental studies, law, nursing, and a number of study areas in the School of Arts and Sciences, including East Asian or Russian and Eastern European studies, international relations, and international development economics.

SOM's international offerings are stronger than one might suspect simply from perusing the course catalog. Students say global content is infused throughout the curriculum of pretty much every B-school course, and the school draws nearly a third of its students each year from outside the United States. These students contribute firsthand knowledge and experience to class discussions. In addition, students have put together spring break educational trips to get a taste of other cultures. For example, about 25 MBAs and faculty members headed to Cuba in 1999 to get a sense of the business climate and potential opportunities directly from business leaders and government officials. For those who want more depth from taking formal classes, a new Emerging Markets Program offers an interesting sampling of courses on China, Latin America, Russia, and the legal and financial intricacies of economies in transition; the SOM's palette of half a dozen additional international courses is supplemented by other university offerings in law, politics, economics, history, international relations, environmental studies, sociology, and a number of foreign languages.

Less impressive is the school's information technology program, although Garten has begun to work on improving this critical area. Over the past three years, he has bolstered SOM's IT operating budget by 28 percent, doubled the size of its staff, and improved the B-school's computer facilities to increase network reliability, capacity, and speed. Most recently, SOM created a state-of-the-art interactive multimedia computer lab that is the most sophisticated of its kind at Yale.

Despite the overall change in focus, Yale has not forgotten its dual public-private mission. In almost every class, students gain perspective in both areas, with case studies carefully culled from public and nonprofit institutions. SOM professors believe SOM graduates switch back and forth between sectors more often than other MBAs, and the program is designed to provide them with the training they'll need should they decide to do so. In that respect, Garten himself is an excellent role model, having moved among the highest levels of government, Wall Street, and the nonprofit world. The school boasts a substantial internship fund to underwrite roughly a dozen SOM students who forgo lucrative positions in investment banks or consulting firms to spend their summers doing low-paying work with charities or in Third World countries. The entire student body pitches in to support the effort, donating a portion of their own internship earnings and organizing fund-raising activities throughout the year, including a student-run eatery called Food For Thought, a Valentine's Day flower sale, and an auction in which the B-school community bids for goods and services donated by one another. (Dean Garten once forked over $600 for a personalized song written by a musically inclined SOM student.) There's also a loan forgiveness program for graduates who head for the public sector on a more permanent basis.

Indeed, many students emphasize the close-knit, "nice" atmosphere that permeates Yale. That's particularly striking considering that SOM students are among the most qualified MBA candidates anywhere, with an average GMAT score—682 for the Class of 2000—well above that of other similarly ranked schools.

About a third of each class is made up of women, and female students and alumni are quite active in recruiting applicants and making them feel comfortable at Yale. The same can't be said for underrepresented minorities, however—with just over 5 percent of the Class of 2000 made up of African-Americans, Hispanic-Americans, and Native Americans, SOM ranks among the least diverse B-schools in that respect. More than 30 "Student Interest Groups" reflect a wide range of personal and professional concerns, from sports and service projects to industry-specific clubs.

Every Thursday night—there are no classes on Fridays—a keg party kicks off the extended weekend for most students. Bars of choice include Bar and Archie Moore's, the latter conveniently located for the majority of students who live in the Grad Student Ghetto, a somewhat yuppified section of New Haven consisting of gracious Victorians that have long since split up into student apartments. It's a good place to look for housing, because you'll find hardly any available on campus. The neighborhood is dotted with gourmet grocery stores and coffee bars, about a 15-minute walk from campus, and a noticeable contrast to the surrounding areas of New Haven, which tend toward the down-at-heel.

The School of Management buildings are set apart from those of the undergraduate campus, the law school, and the medical school. So there isn't much mixing among schools during the day. One place you'll be sure to find undergrads and other grad students is Donaldson Commons, the SOM dining facility across the street from the B-school and named for SOM founder Donaldson. It's widely considered the crown jewel of the university's otherwise grim food offerings. Another place the Yale community comes together is at Payne Whitney Gymnasium, the centerpiece of the university's fine athletic facilities, which include an ice rink, tennis courts, riding facilities, a yacht club, and one of the best rated golf courses in the country that is open to students for just $18. An annual sporting highlight is the "Garstka Cup" hockey game, named for former acting dean and accounting Professor Stanley Garstka, which pits first-year skaters against second-years.

PLACEMENT DETAILS

Consensus among faculty and students is that SOM's career development office is vastly improved over its sorry state only a few years back. One high point is the two-year Professional Strategies Program, started in 1996, a required series of career-related workshops that begins during orientation and continues right through second year. The first-year portion is particularly intensive, with seven weeks of lectures and group projects on topics such as developing a personal marketing plan, researching industries, crafting a résumé, writing cover letters, networking, and generating and carrying out effective interviews. Because so many of their students come from non-business backgrounds and are looking to change careers, SOM strongly encourages students to take summer internships, and, in fact, has created some of its own. Besides the summer entrepreneurship program, SOM also offers a unique program that puts about a half-dozen MBAs to work in Yale's Investment Office. Their job: Oversee the university's $10 billion endowment. Besides gaining firsthand money management experience and making important contacts with institutional investors, these MBAs also helped their alma mater reap big rewards: In 2000, Yale's endowment soared 41 percent.

To aid students in their full-time job search, the Career Development office established its New Economy Series last year. With programs in both New Haven and Silicon Valley, the series provides SOM students with real-world insight into New Economy careers through panel discussions, guest lectures, and job fairs.

Top employers of SOM grads in 2000 were Booz-Allen & Hamilton (10); Lehman Bros. (6);

Intel Corp. (6); marchFIRST (5); McKinsey & Co. (5); Donaldson, Lufkin & Jenrette (4); Fleet Financial Services (4); Goldman Sachs (4); ING Barings (4); Merrill Lynch (4). The 100-plus companies that visited campus generated nearly 1500 interviews, with an additional 2000-plus jobs posted electronically. Yale students garnered an average of 3.1 job offers apiece.

OUTSTANDING FACULTY

Sharon Oster (economics/strategy); *David Cromwell* (finance); *Roger Ibbotson* (finance); *Jon Ingersoll* (finance); *Ravi Dhar* (marketing); *Arthur Swersey* (operations); *David Collis* (strategy).

APPLICANT TIPS

As you might have guessed from both the high quality of Yale students and the B-school's historic mission and new direction, admissions criteria are threefold. Applicants should demonstrate "capacity and motivation for academic achievement and intellectual performance"; "motivation and ability to cope with the practical problems of organizations, to influence the outcome of events, and to work effectively with others"; and "commitment to effective management as a socially useful activity." The emphasis is on both the academic and experiential aspects of a candidate's background; you are expected to submit letters of recommendation from both school- and work-related references. Students here tend to be older and more experienced than most schools, but that experience doesn't have to come from the business world—Yale is one place you'll have a decent shot even if you've only worked in government or nonprofits.

Yale groups applicants into three separate rounds. The first are those whose paperwork is in by November; a second round comes in January; and a third in March. You can expect a reply roughly two months after you apply. Due to the surging interest, Yale now strongly encourages an interview—a significant shift from a few years ago when just over a third of students arranged for meetings. Administrators also revised the essay questions to force prospective candidates to articulate why they need the MBA and how their past experience relates to their future plans.

Campus visits can be arranged by calling the admissions office. Group information sessions are held on Mondays and Thursdays at 11:30 a.m. and can be followed up with student meetings, campus tours, and class attendance. In addition, SOM has partnered with a number of schools to conduct information sessions geared to women and minority applicants in several cities, including New York, Miami, Washington, D.C., and Atlanta. Applications can be completed online, downloaded from the school Web site and then mailed in after completion, or a paper copy can be requested from the admissions office.

Contact: James R. Stevens
Director of Admissions
203-432-5932
Admission deadlines: November 1; January 2; March 15

YALE MBAs SOUND OFF

Yale has been trying for the last several years to become a more traditional MBA program. In the two years I have been here, the change has been remarkable. Everything from the professors to the curriculum to the career development office has been upgraded.

Yale is an incredible place because of the students, the administration, and the faculty and the interactions among these groups. My sense is that the intellectual focus of Yale and the students that select the program is quite unique and the value of which I will discover increasingly over many years to come. These two years were challenging and fulfilling. Not only were we taught specific skills but we were taught and sometimes forced to think and consider how our skills will fit into the greater landscape of business and society. I was consistently struck over my second year by how far my classmates and I have come from when we arrived. I have met the smartest individuals that I will ever have the honor of working with again. As you can see, I will miss Yale SOM.

Because of this diverse student body, it is often difficult to teach and keep everyone—with varying experience levels with the material—interested. SOM works hard at being able to do that well, and it is evident. What is perhaps best about the school is how much the administration, the faculty, and the students want SOM to be of the quality that they expect from a Yale graduate school. And when they feel it misses, they change and make visible improvements.

One of the advantages of Yale SOM is the diversity of student backgrounds. I remember during the first semester being continuously amazed at all the different—and fascinating—things that my classmates had done prior to coming to Yale. I feel that this greatly enhanced the learning environment, as everyone brought a slightly different perspective to the table.

I believe our career office has made tremendous strides but still can improve. I never felt any of their advice or "expertise" was particularly useful, insightful, or consistent with reality for that matter. I felt that more attention was paid to helping students secure jobs with more traditional I-banking and consulting firms than with new economy employers.

This school has continued to grow and make great strides in all areas since I arrived, and Dean Garten has pushed forward on a number of initiatives, which will improve the school for future classes. For example, SOM has added at least 10 new faculty members as part of Dean Garten's plan to increase tenured faculty by 60 percent, while at the same time maintaining current enrollment. Dean Garten has attracted great business leaders to teach/speak at the school. This semester former P&G CEO John Pepper taught a course in leadership, and Reed Hundt, former head of the FCC and current adviser to McKinsey & Co, taught a course on regulation and strategy in the television industry. This year, SOM also opened the International Center for Finance to bring thought leaders from industry, SOM, Yale Law, and Economics together under one roof to foster cutting-edge research in all areas of Finance.

20.
INDIANA UNIVERSITY

INDIANA UNIVERSITY

Kelley School of Business
1309 East Tenth Street
Room 254
Bloomington, Indiana 47405-1701
E-mail address: mbaoffice@indiana.edu
Web site address: http://www.bus.indiana.edu

Corporate ranking: 20	Graduate ranking: 20
Enrollment: 566	Annual tuition & fees:
Women: 20%	resident—$9908
Non-U.S.: 37%	nonresident—$19,258
Minority: 8%	Room and board: $6292
Part-time: 0	Average GMAT score: 646
Average age: 28	Average years of work exp.: 5
Applicants accepted: 32%	Accepted applicants enrolled: 51%
Median starting pay: $114,000	Intellectual capital: 36

Teaching methods: Lecture, 30%   Case study, 40%
                   Group projects, 30%

Contact:
James Holmen
Director of Admissions
812-855-8006
Application deadlines:
December 1
January 15
March 1
April 15

Indiana University's MBA program has run into the age-old problem of many mid-top-tier schools: Its programs are good, its students are relatively satisfied, and its recruiters continue to visit campus, but, unlike some movers and shakers, this middle-of-the-nation B-school has had trouble getting others to see what it does—the Kelley School is a school on the rise. After several years of a free fall in stature, the school has righted itself. Once steady member of BUSINESSWEEK's top 10—lauded for a straightforward, integrated curriculum—the Kelley School of Business seemed destined to become an also-ran. Plagued by weak international programs, behind-the-times technology, and a sub-par placement center, not to mention that very un–Wall Street location of Bloomington, some had written the B-school off. But administrators are determined to move Kelley up the ladder once again.

After four years of sliding, Kelley's move from No. 21 to No. 20 is evidence that Dean Dan Dalton and MBA Program Chair Dan Smith took the recent concerns of students and recruiters to heart and have set about completely rebuilding the school's curriculum, orientation program, and career center as part of an effort to bring Kelley back to where it once was. No one expects the climb to be as rapid as the decline was, but as far as students are concerned, the changes are noticeable. In the 2000 BUSINESSWEEK survey, Kelley ranked second highest at responding to student concerns among grads.

Quips a 2000 grad, "To go along with its similar colors, IU has adopted the Avis Rent-A-Car motto, 'We try harder.' There have been serious problems at the business school here regarding placement services and classroom facilities, [and] IU's administrators were aware of these issues." As a B-school faculty member, Dalton himself observed Kelley's ups and downs for 20 years before replacing outgoing dean John Rau in 1997. As a result he had the combination of historical perspective and new enthusiasm that was necessary to reevaluate and rework the school from top to bottom. One of his first moves in 1998 was to recruit Smith, a popular marketing professor, to help lead the MBA program. Together, the team tackled the two most pressing problems at Kelley: student satisfaction, or dissatisfaction as it were, and a poorly performing career services center.

Many of the Class of 2000 wax enthusiastic about the progress that has been made: "This year has seen the true coming-of-age of Team Kelley," says one. It's a real live lesson in organizational change. From a new Graduate Career Services office to a multitude of student-driven initiatives including a new study abroad opportunity, a new Health Care Academy, and several new recruiting tools, the school has accomplished a lot, and quickly. Says one grad, "The real success story, though, is how these changes have occurred. Administration, faculty, students, and staff have all created an environment where management and change are practiced, not just taught, and teamwork is the status quo." The new curriculum divides the first year into three blocks, giving you a "big picture" look at the fundamentals of leadership and management—and returning a former Indiana moniker of the early 1990s: innovative.

Indeed, even in the program's recruiting materials the school concedes, "Every top-ranked MBA program has a solid, substantial, well-regarded curriculum. Maybe that's not enough for the blink speed of business today."

The school's new curriculum is meant to "break rules." The new coursework is what the school calls a problem-based core, starting with two weeks of orientation (up from 10 days previously), the second of which includes a Leadership Development Institute. After orientation, you'll have a nine-week block focused on Foundation of Management and Decision Making with courses on quantitative tools, economic analysis, understanding financial statements, critical thinking, the function of markets, information technology, and creating and leading high performance teams. Four or five faculty members work with one problem so that you'll be exposed to how different people from different disciplinary functions would approach the same problems.

The middle five weeks are based around Identifying, Evaluating, and Capitalizing on New Business Opportunities, including project implementation and management, new product development, and getting your ideas funded. You'll be prepared for a final venture capital project. In upcoming years, Smith hopes this block will be infused with a more entrepreneurial focus. The third block, Profitably Managing Ongoing Operations, includes pieces on margin management, assessing recent performance, demand, and market share. After the blocks, there is an eight-week period when you can start taking electives in the first year, although some students complain that this isn't really enough time to get into any material as deeply as they might like.

During your second year, you will select a specific discipline in which to concentrate, and you'll have more flexibility than you would have had a few years ago. Smith says that previously 75 percent of the second year was "required," a factor that made students frustrated and led to an "enormous amount of redundancy" with the first year. Concentrations added in the last three years include: e-business, economic consulting, decision support modeling, and strategic management consulting.

Also new is a major in e-commerce that is a pilot program which will offer an MBA online to executives. Dalton concedes that distance learning is a risky proposition that creates a good deal of skepticism. Dalton has been proactive in preventing the problems he sees occurring at other schools that are launching e-learning programs.

With the coursework now on its way back to where it was, Dalton is also concentrating on remedying that other Kelley complaint: physical space. Over the last four years he has raised more than $100 million and is close to naming a new B-school building in honor of a benefactor. The new building, scheduled to open in 2001, will accommodate class size increases from 265 to 300, have better interviewing rooms for recruiters, and make more technology, like videoconferencing, available to students and faculty. The MBA-only building will have open meeting rooms, laptop hookups, and other tech perks available at most top-tier schools.

The Kelley program is ranked third by graduates for having the best teachers. Students say the faculty at Kelley is a clear strength of the school, with professors always available outside of class, often giving out home phone numbers and scheduling weekend meetings and house calls to students. It's not uncommon to find Kelley professors at MBA social events or hosting students at their homes on a regular basis.

Not holding classes on Fridays perpetuates that B-school tradition of Thursday nights out. But here, faculty will often join you at The Bluebird, Kilroy's, and Nick's, Bloomington's oldest bar and an IU institution. And during the week, Smith is known for buying you coffee at midnight to help you get through a grueling study session.

Faculty—119 full-timers in 2000 and 47 visiting professors—also offer themselves up in the spring faculty auction, with home-cooked meals, picnics, and hikes.

Surprisingly, the one thing that you might think would be the downside to life at Kelley is one of its strongest selling points: Bloomington. One recent alum who had gone to New York University as an undergraduate and had grown up in Manhattan was leery about leaving the big city for Indiana. But, with a good music program and strong drama department, he says IU brings in better traveling shows then he ever saw in New York, and at a fraction of the price. Black Crows, Cowboy Junkies, the Dalai Lama, Bill Gates, and Les Miserables are just some of the concerts, speeches, and shows he saw when he was there.

Says another: "Bloomington is a wonderful town to get an MBA in because it's small enough not to have too many attractions, but big enough to have something to do."

And others dispel any myths that Middle America is all white bread: "I am a lesbian who moved to Bloomington from the New York area and found the MBA program here wonderfully inviting and diverse. The program is great for students with partners, spouses, and families." Not to mention that you'll enjoy telling your friends in the big city that rent on your three-bedroom house is about what they're paying for a studio without a parking space. And if you're expecting Indiana to be rows of cornfields, fuggetaboutit: Bloomington is home to gently rolling hills, perfect for biking and with easy access to hiking.

PLACEMENT DETAILS

"We built this thing from scratch," says Dick McCracken, director of graduate career services of the new graduate-focused MBA placement office that was born of the student and recruiter complaints that plagued Kelley from 1996 to 1998. Current and future MBAs as well as faculty supported the changes, McCracken says, which started by splitting the career services office into undergraduate and graduate placement efforts. McCracken, an Indiana B-school alum, heads the grad effort, and, under his watch, the program has managed to hang on to existing recruiters while luring new firms.

Neal Kinney, manager of staffing and recruiting at Cinergy Corp. in Cincinnati, which just began recruiting at Kelley in 1998, says McCracken is one of the clearest advantages of the school's recruiting program.

The number of companies that the school attracts has never been a problem. In 2000 the placement office brought in a respectable 144 firms, decent for a school of its size, especially away from the East and West Coasts. The real difficulty has been attracting the kinds of firms that Kelley students want to work for.

"There is a tremendous interest in technology, such as students going into marketing and consulting in the tech field, but they are not big on start-ups," says McCracken. He estimates just 2 percent of graduates go to work at start-ups, and Kelley has not seen the boom in entrepreneurship that other MBA programs report.

To address these concerns, Kelley has hosted recent employer receptions in the Silicon Valley. More than 30 companies showed up to offer students advice on how to secure jobs in the Bay Area and to give them contacts so that they'll avoid that cold call with résumé in hand approach.

In addition, the office hired a staffer to specifically address the job placement needs of international students. Because many employers have run into brick walls when it comes to hiring international students, the office is now more focused on helping those students conduct independent searches. The effort has been noticed, with more than one recent grad citing the willingness of the career staff to work 60 to 70 hours per week to help students make that right first impression. But others say there is still more to be done. "The graduate career service was established to serve the Kelley MBAs. As the school has made great progress in this manner, they must continue to develop the strength of the office and attract a broader range of companies to the school."

Top hirers in 2000 were Pricewaterhouse-Coopers (14); Ford Motor Co. (12); Procter & Gamble (11); Eli Lilly & Co. (9); Hewlett-Packard (8); Intel (8); BP Amoco (6); Bank of America (4); Cummins, Inc. (4); Kraft (4).

OUTSTANDING FACULTY

Walter Blacconiere (accounting); *James Whalen* (accounting); *Wayne Winston* (decision science/operations); *John Boquist* (finance); *Scott Smart* (finance); *Anne Massey* (information systems); *Idie Kesner* (management/strategy); *Dan Smith* (marketing).

APPLICANT TIPS

Kelley continues to aggressively recruit women to its program. And not a moment too soon. Indeed, the percentage of women in the program dropped from 28 percent in 1998 to 20 percent in 2000. These percentages are indicative of a trend true of both the U.S. and international students, and the school is trying targeted mailings as well as looking for female role models already at the school to attract more women students.

Overall, applications were up 3 percent in 2000, despite declines at many schools. Most of that jump is from international applications because the school's tuition costs make it a good value for those who are dealing with a strong dollar and fluctuating exchange rates. The decline among domestic students has been due to an increase of those who are deferring after acceptance, having been offered promotions that were too good to pass up, according to Director of Admissions and Financial Aid James Holmen. International students' applications are not accepted for the final April 15 deadline available to U.S. candidates. The school lifted its cap on the number of international students in 1999, and this is one of the reasons the percentage of foreign students jumped from 19 to 37 percent in two years.

Despite Kelley's rating roller coaster, it isn't a safety school. The percentage of accepted applicants actually decreased 7 percent between 1998 and 2000. Holmen offers some basic, but tried-and-true tips for getting into that one-third: "Don't try too hard to write what we want to hear. Be honest. Help us get to know you. After we read an essay, we ask, 'Do I know anything about this applicant?'"

Basic writing tricks such as giving yourself time to edit and not turning in an application until it is completed may help you against the other 1817 filling out the forms. You're encouraged to come to campus and have an in-person interview. Kelley does not conduct any telephone interviews, and only about 50 percent of applicants make the effort to do the face-to-face. Some road interviews can be arranged if you cannot make it to Bloomington.

Contact: James Holmen
Director of Admissions
812-855-8006
Application deadlines: December 1; January 15; March 1; April 15

KELLEY MBAs SOUND OFF

To be honest, the Kelley School of Business has needed a wake-up call during the last few years. I believe the school strayed from the core values and philosophy that brought success (at least in the rankings) during the early to mid '90s. Innovation has been a fundamental aspect of the school's success. I think the current administration is aware of this and has taken significant steps to correct the problems (complacency) of the past few years.

My interactions over the summer with students from other top schools only highlighted the benefits of the Kelley program, namely the outstanding coursework, caring faculty, and emphasis on interpersonal skills. In terms of coursework and interpersonal skill development, my performance this past summer proved Kelley's value to me.

I have always been able to approach our administration with ideas or requests. In 1999, I wanted to attend the Gay and Lesbian MBA conference in Boston, so I approached our MBA office, which worked it out with no problem. They sent three Kelley MBAs to the conference. We were the only students at the conference (consisting of only Top 30 programs) whose school had sponsored us. All of the other students had paid out of pocket. We, the Kelley MBA students, are treated fairly as adults and as the No. 1 customers of the program.

I joined the Investment Management Academy, which proved to be my single best decision. We brought in speakers from all over the country to talk about their experiences and views of the business. It was a tremendous networking opportunity as well as a chance to narrow down what I specifically wanted to do with my life. I contacted many alumni from the Academy, all of whom went out of their way to talk with me and help in any way they could. Because it is harder for a person coming from a Midwest school to break into the business, Indiana alumni feel a special bond and loyalty to help each other. I feel that this is a huge advantage for students coming out of the Kelley School of Business.

The whole two years was worth it, every minute, even the painful moments. After the 1998 BUSINESSWEEK rankings, I questioned my decision to attend Kelley. It was a low moment, but we pulled together as a class and worked hard in conjunction with the faculty to make great things happen and happen quickly.

If you are seeking a down-to-earth student body with the drive to succeed, if you are looking for a talented faculty who loves to teach, if you are looking for a career office that is driven by student input, look no further than Kelley.

I am continuously overwhelmed by the accessibility and personal attention that the professors and administration pay to the students. Faculty were consistently engaging students in conversations in the hallways, in the lounges, and outside of the academic environment. Faculty provided their home phone numbers and at times shared their personal time with students to make the atmosphere more collegial and, at times, to aid in the learning process.

Above all else, the Kelley School is a constructive, supportive, and dynamic environment. I believe we are a unique student body. To a person, each one of us wants to succeed and achieve a high level of success, both personally and professionally. However, I firmly believe that 99.9 percent of the student body would not sacrifice a fellow student for personal gain. While this may not seem common in today's business environment, I believe it accurately demonstrates the ethics, business prowess, and leadership inherent in the Kelley student.

Whether it's from hurt ego or fear of losing their jobs, the business school administrators have gone to Warp 9 to try to fix the leaks. They tried some immediate reorganization, such as gutting and revising the placement office. That has had some short-term pluses (getting a new face out there to recruiters) which will likely be a great help starting next year (new recruiters on campus, other companies more receptive to an IU MBA). Other problems are being taken care of with long-term projects (a new grad-student-only building, a curriculum based on problem solving, not individual academic topics).

21.
UNIVERSITY
OF
ROCHESTER

UNIVERSITY OF ROCHESTER

William E. Simon Graduate School of Business Administration
Rochester, New York 14627-0107
E-mail address: mbaadm@simon.rochester.edu
Web site address: http://www.simon.rochester.edu

Corporate ranking: 29
Enrollment: 677
Women: 24%
Non-U.S.: 50%
Minority: 17%
Part-time: 235
Average age: 29
Applicants accepted: 30%
Median starting pay: $110,000

Graduate ranking: 18
Annual tuition & fees: $26,460
Room and board: $7695
Average GMAT score: 646
Average years work exp.: 6
Accepted applicants enrolled: 39%
Intellectual capital: 11

Teaching methods: Lecture, 50%   Case study, 30%
Team projects, 20%

Contact:
Pamela A. Black-Colton
Assistant Dean for
MBA Admissions and
Administration
716-275-3533
Application deadlines:
November 15
(January entry)
December 15
February 1
April 1
May 1
(September entry)

The University of Rochester's William E. Simon School is, as they say, back in the game. It was just two years ago that the upstate New York institution, whose microeconomics emphasis permeates the program, was knocked out of the Top 30 as the marketplace clamored for more global- or tech-oriented innovation. These days, Dean Charles I. Plosser—a former Rochester professor—is at the helm, and the school has reacted and recovered to regain the top-tier status it held in 1996.

The finance-focused school and a team of outside consultants did a careful analysis after the slip to address concerns of students, faculty, and potential MBA employers. They determined that, among other things, students were looking for greater flexibility from the relatively rigid core curriculum and more guidance in successfully maneuvering the recruiting process. The school responded in small ways like cutting the statistics requirement from two courses to one, and also in larger ways. For one, the entire first-year curriculum was revamped to create room for students to take elective courses in their second term, before obtaining an internship. Now students have access to more specialized academics and training to help them land the summer position of their choice and excel at it.

Companies who had employed Rochester MBAs found Simon students to be strong team players but weak in their ability to sell their ideas and themselves. In particular, employers were looking for more professional polish. The school's overburdened career services staff gained more members and responded to both student and recruiter concerns by taking on a larger role in the education process. A new Pre-term Program was designed to help groom students not only in job-hunting finesse but also for their overall careers. The two-week session has students conducting self-evaluations and performing goal assessment exercises to help pinpoint their professional goals. Career counselors here have traditionally provided one-on-one guidance sessions throughout students' two years in the program. But some of these newer steps toward more comprehensive training—plus the construction of a more modern facility opening July 2001—are sure to add even more to the career services experience at the Simon School.

The overall curriculum, including both career-building skills and general academics, continues to command much of the attention of the administrators, who take pride in the school's consistently top-notch teaching quality (rated so highly by Class of 2000 grads that the school landed at No. 2 in this area of all 82 schools surveyed). The quality of teaching among professors puts Rochester near the top of the heap as far as grads are concerned—and in the leagues of other teaching powerhouses like University of Virginia's Darden School and Indiana University's Kelley School. At Simon, students will find the coursework well integrated. This is not surprising, as professors in a small program (especially one without an undergraduate business component) find it convenient to regularly powwow about their MBA classes. "We're not departmentalized," explains Associate Dean for MBA Programs Stacy Kole. "People from different areas do research together; cases are taught across courses. At the lunch table we often talk about curriculum."

The collaborative attitude is widespread among the student body, too, where entering MBAs are assigned to Blue, Gold, Green, or Purple 40- to 50-person cohorts they stick with throughout their nine core courses. Subjects range from corporate financial accounting and managerial economics to operations management, the economic theory of organizations,

and management communication. The composition of the cohorts reflects the diversity of this internationally packed program, with the highest number of international students, 50 percent, among the Top 30 schools (and the largest contingent hailing from the People's Republic of China). International students arrive earlier, to acclimate themselves through their own one-day orientation. For a fee, they can also take an eight-week "pre Pre-term" session, called English Language and U.S. Culture, which focuses on improving English language skills and addressing cultural differences in the business world and beyond. Throughout the school year, international students have the opportunity to educate their classmates about their backgrounds by giving presentations on their homeland's economy, culture, politics, and business protocols over lunches featuring indigenous cuisine. Even the school's founding father is not excluded from these events: Students often dress his statue—located in the current main classroom building, Schlegel Hall—in clothing worn in the countries being featured. It's the ultimate in global bonding. For longer-term connections with foreign cultures, each year some Simon students—both U.S. and international—also participate in one of eight exchange programs with B-schools in Europe, Asia, South America, and Australia.

Within the cohorts, more intimate study teams of five students each work on class assignments and prepare for exams for their nine courses in the first year of the program. But the teamwork element shows up as early as orientation for students in both the September and January start dates. In the Simon Games, first-year MBAs from more than 50 countries unite in competition through games of flag football, soccer, and volleyball. There's also the VISION program, a series of 16 corporate-sponsored seminars and group exercises that encourage students to delve into topics like career exploration, creativity, ethics, communication in a diverse environment, and leadership. Each module has a student leader, a faculty adviser, and one or more executives from a sponsoring company. A newer coach-mentor program, implemented in 1998 with financial support from General Electric in the form of a $219,000 grant, matches about 25 percent of each second-year class—specially selected and trained by the school—with first-year teams for guidance in resolving conflicts, selecting courses, and securing internships. The coaches report on team progress, and first-years have a chance to evaluate their coach and each other. Coaches also offer their team members ongoing counsel on getting acclimated to Rochester and searching for a job. "The role for coaches has become than we originally intended," confirms Kole. The second-year participants receive no credit and are paid minimally—but what they don't make in money, they pick up in valuable skills like providing feedback, delivering a tough message, and helping a team effort succeed.

Simon students consider their teachers at the leading edge of knowledge in their fields, and it's no wonder. These are, after all, profs who edit top academic publications like the *Journal of Financial Economics,* the *Journal of Monetary Economics,* and the *Journal of Accounting and Economics.* But many of these same students also find fault with faculty members who compromise teaching to pursue their own research or consulting projects, something that can be more prevalent at research-focused institutions. "If our professors don't do research today, what will they teach five years from now?" counters Dean Plosser. "This research is complementary to the high quality of teaching we get here. We have a responsibility to future generations. We have to look down the road."

Divided opinions come up in other areas at Rochester as well. Simon students, for the most part, say that their business school experience met their expectations—more than students at most other Top 30 schools. The MBAs at Simon say one key to this is that faculty members are nearly always available for discussion outside of class. But contrary to these accolades, grads have criticized the responsiveness of these same professors and the administration, saying that the powers that be don't always listen seriously to student concerns. The inconsistencies may reflect the transitional state of Simon, a school trying to care for as many "consumers" as possible. But Dean Plosser is the first to admit: "You can't be all things to all people." So, while the school continues to work toward some long-term plans, like a $15 million James S. Gleason Hall capital campaign and a faculty expansion of 10 to 15 percent, administrators are striving to better express their goals and expectations to the Simon community. "Organizational changes come about more gradually," says Kole. "We haven't done a good enough job communicating the time it takes to make these changes."

Since Dean Plosser took over in 1992, when a new dean resigned after eight months on the job because of a funding dispute with the university president, the Simon School has caught up to, or surpassed, its peer schools in some ways. The menu of concentrations now boasts 14 subjects, including Accounting and Information Systems, Business Environment and Public Policy, Competitive and Organizational Strategy, Operations Management (Manufacturing or Services), Marketing, Health Care Management, and that old standby, Finance. Introduced in September 1999 was a new Electronic Commerce concentration that exposes students to the marketing, logistical, financial, and service delivery aspects of doing business online. Classes within the concentration give students the opportunity to create, manage, direct, and analyze e-commerce initiatives. Students can find e-business work experiences the same way they seek out other opportunities, through the career services office or a more formal setup, the Kaufmann Internship Program, which helps place students with internships in various areas.

Still, the vast array of hands-on e-commerce, high-tech, or nontraditional work experiences and partnerships so many other schools gleefully promote seem to be missing here. And while the student-run High-Tech Management League (HTML) club does its share of bringing in relevant speakers and coordinating recruiting trips, one of the chief complaints Simon students have against the school is the absence of relationships with smaller or less traditional companies, thus creating a bit of a dichotomy between the school's ample teachings and its follow-through in bringing those industries to campus. In general Rochester's recruiter roster is in flux. Two years ago the school had nearly 100 recruiters come to campus to meet with second-years compared to 76 in 2000. It's not for lack of trying. The school consistently targets its alumni network for recruiting leads and career advice for the MBAs, but with such a high number of international grads, maintaining contact across geographical divides can be a daunting challenge. On-campus recruiters from U.S. companies, also, are often disappointed to discover a large portion of the school's international students seeking employment only within their home countries or at other foreign locations. To ingratiate themselves with existing recruiters, Rochester's career services staff members go to endearing extremes, such as providing complimentary limousine service to and from the airport and dispensing "comfort kits" containing useful items like pantyhose and nail files for women, and shoe polish and mints for men. The recruiting period in 2000, nonetheless, resulted in an average of 2.9 job offers for each student—similar to offers at peer programs like the University of Texas–Austin McCombs School and Carnegie Mellon University. Just 37 companies came to campus to recruit first-year students for summer internships, and after students completed their summer jobs, only 14 percent of them then received permanent job offers from the companies. Students have indicated that the problems stem from Simon's lagging outreach efforts, job interview and negotiations training, and the maintenance of

recruiter relationships. But, the school is making headway, working to catch up.

Some promise for the future lies within the new career services facility, which is currently underway and will encompass almost the entire second floor of the James S. Gleason Hall. It debuts in 2002. The eight private interview rooms will have phone and modem hookups with landline and cell phones available, a larger kitchen area, and a concierge to arrange breakfast, lunch, and snacks. The school is also looking into videoconferencing capabilities to reach those potential employers who can't make the trip to Rochester. A 200-seat classroom will hold nearly all of a class's students for one session at the same time. An enhanced career resources center will be 30 to 35 percent larger than the current library, and students with interviews will be able to make use of an isolated waiting area beforehand. In addition, part of the Class of 2000's departing gift—changing facilities—will prevent students from having to wear their suits all day. This new 38,000-square-foot addition to Schlegel Hall is more than just an upgrade for the career services department. Because there's no undergraduate business program at Rochester, most of the resources here can be lavished on the MBAs and the doctoral program candidates. Once completed, Gleason Hall will increase Simon's space for teaching, admissions, and corporate partnership activities by about 64 percent. Five new classrooms will be housed here, and students will also have the use of 16 new study rooms—a boon, indeed, for the quiet, upstate New York campus.

In many ways Rochester is a company town, home to Eastman Kodak and Bausch & Lomb, two major supporters of the B-school. It's located on the University of Rochester's River Campus, on the banks of the Genesee River three miles from downtown. You'll be pleased to find low rates and high availability in Rochester's housing market. Most married couples live in apartments or townhouses in Whipple Park or University Park, each just a short distance from campus. Unmarried students can live in the university-owned Goler House's one- or two-bedroom apartments, also nearby, but because applications exceed capacity, the decision is made by lottery system. Other options include buildings in the Park Avenue area of Rochester and surrounding areas of Brighton and Henrietta.

On campus, Schlegel Hall is the most active spot, but students also venture out to socialize at popular local haunts like The Distillery and The Elmwood. The Empire Brewing Company is always good for a few rounds of beer. Planned social events are popular, too, from the Blackjack Ball and Night at the Eastman Theatre to outdoor activities like Ski Day and the Fall and Spring picnics. At the Annual Roast, faculty, staff members, and students are made fun of through a variety of humorous sketches and songs, and intellectual endeavors like the annual Faculty-Student Debate are another source of diversion. Here, two teams of students led by a faculty member debate a business-related topic (such as "Are Internet Stocks Overvalued?") in front of a Simon audience. Charitable organizations and activities also benefit from the time and efforts of Rochester MBAs. The students, faculty, and staff involved with Simon Volunteers work with groups like the Ronald McDonald House, Habitat for Humanity, Volunteers of America, Open Door Mission, and the Y.M.C.A. to help improve the community. One of the most popular events takes place during the holiday season, when student participants in the Simon Secret Santa Program raise money to purchase and wrap Christmas gifts specifically requested by disadvantaged children in the Rochester area.

PLACEMENT DETAILS

Simon students have done fine for themselves in terms of employment; Class of 2000 grads enjoyed a median pay package of $110,000, and they scored about 2.9 job offers each. But concerns from both students and recruiters have demonstrated room for improvement, and just as the Simon School as a whole is in transition, the career services department on its own has morphed as well. The specific curriculum has become more skill-based, most notably through a new six-phased model that takes students from a self-assessment period through the job offer and negotiation. Career Services Director Lisa McGurn reports that recruiters are seeing an improvement in the preparation and confidence of Rochester MBAs. And students themselves seem pleased. "The reorganization of career services between my first and second year greatly enhanced the ability of the program to meet our needs," one recent grad gushed. Said another: "During the time I was there, the career services office at Simon improved by leaps and bounds."

The school has also stepped up its efforts to bring in new recruiters by conducting more outbound phone calls and outreach procedures. Even so, the number of companies recruiting second-year students did drop from 98 two years ago to just 76 in 2000. The task of Simon's placement office to attract new companies to campus is difficult for a couple of reasons. Rochester's location on the eastern shore of Lake Ontario is off the beaten path for employers making the rounds of B-schools along the Northeast Corridor. Some are reluctant to make a special trip to interview a relatively small pool of prospective employees—a pool made even smaller by the large number of international students, many of whom return to their homelands to seek employment. The harsh winters of the Great Lakes snow belt don't help either—it's not exactly like trying to lure recruiters to, say, Los Angeles or Dallas in January.

In addition to the companies that did come to campus in 2000, some 627 jobs were posted electronically. Financial services claimed about 47 percent of the Class of '00, including those who took jobs in accounting and investment commercial banking. Consulting drew 22 percent, and manufacturing another 27 percent. Top employers were Citibank (8); American Management Systems (8); Deloitte & Touche (6); Chase Securities (5); Pricewaterhouse-Coopers (4); Salomon Smith Barney (4); U.S. Bancorp (4); M & T Bank Corp. (4); and Johnson & Johnson (4).

OUTSTANDING FACULTY

Andrew Leone (accounting); *Gregg Jarrell* (economics/finance); *Michael Barclay* (finance); *Gregory Bauer* (finance); *Clifford Smith* (finance); *Greg Shaffer* (marketing/strategy); *Robert Shumsky* (operations); *Ronald Schmidt* (strategy).

APPLICANT TIPS

Prospective students have two choices for admittance: the mainstream 22-month program which begins each September and holds 170 students, or the 18-month accelerated MBA option that 60 to 70 students enter in January each year. Those in the January program complete two quarters of core courses and then have three choices: taking a full schedule of coursework during the summer before joining the regular schedule of classes for the second year; taking a part-time load of summer classes in the evening while working at an internship in the Rochester area, then taking one extra course during the second year; or pursuing a regular summer internship away from school and then finishing up the first-year requirements on top of the regular second-year schedule, which means handling two extra courses. For the September option, applications are accepted up to May 1, but March 1 is the deadline for those seeking financial aid consideration. Prospective January entrants have a November 15 deadline.

The Simon School considers applicants mainly in terms of how they might contribute to the program and to the global business community. The admissions committee considers a set of criteria that includes evidence of leadership and initiative; the nature and scope of prior work experience; teamwork and communication skills; career focus; recommendations; and, of course, undergraduate GPA and GMAT scores. (In fact, the school waives the $75 application fee for applicants who score well on the GMAT—roughly 600 or above.) Interviews, though not required, are strongly encouraged; everybody who ends up being admitted has had one, according to Assistant Dean for MBA Admissions and Administration Pamela Black-Colton, who also encourages prospective students to visit the campus. The admissions office can arrange for a student ambassador to give you a tour, escort you to a class, treat you to lunch, and chat with you about the Simon experience.

Contact: Pamela A. Black-Colton
Assistant Dean for MBA Admissions and Administration
716-275-3533
Application deadlines: November 15 (January entry); December 15; February 1; April 1; May 1 (September entry)

SIMON MBAs SOUND OFF

The Simon School has entered a period of dramatic transformation. The school has made great strides to fine-tune and improve the program, both academically and from a student services standpoint. The program is vastly underrated, but the quality of the education, especially from a finance perspective, was quite outstanding. Nearly everyone I know, myself included, has gotten his or her dream job. Most are headed to NYC, but quite a few are off to Silicon Valley. For someone looking to spend two rigorous years of total academic immersion, the Simon School is the place to be.

The Simon School deserves to be in the very elite group of B-schools. It is definitely one of the top three finance schools in the country—only Chicago and UCLA even come close to teaching corporate financial skills at the level they are taught at Simon. The faculty and the school are small, which gives it a very special and unique feeling of community, and the professors are always accessible outside of class to discuss current issues. I had never heard of Simon until I started researching B-schools and now I am extremely happy I decided to attend. It is definitely the best-kept secret in business schools, and this hurts it because it is not so widely known as its peer schools. But I have no doubt that I received the best business education available in the world.

The William E. Simon School of Graduate Business Administration did an outstanding job of providing opportunities and preparing me to succeed. I took a job off the usual MBA path. Though the position I took was the lowest paying of my offers by a significant margin, the career services counselor I worked with (Angela Petrucco) encouraged me to make the right choice for me—not the right one to help Simon's placement statistics. Angela and her peers knew me and worked to help me achieve my goals. This type of personalized service is a benefit of a smaller program and one of the hallmarks of a Simon education.

The finance faculty is world-renowned and certainly underrated. The e-commerce curriculum is innovative. The biggest drawback of the school is location. Move the school to New York City and it is arguably a top 10 school.

The best part of the Simon experience is the relentless pursuit of problem solving from several different approaches. All my classes have been woven together to enable me to attack business problems with much more assertion than I previously could have prior to B-school. However, the program is very quantitative and extremely competitive, so be prepared for a rigorous two years.

The Simon School went through a painful soul-searching process after falling off the BUSINESSWEEK rankings. It was, however, one of the best things that could have happened to the school because it forced the students, faculty, and staff to define what was important, devise a plan to meet newly identified goals, and begin implementing that plan. I am happy to have been a part of the process, and I am sure that the Simon School is a much better place for our efforts. I am also sure that the education I received at the Simon School was as good as they come, and that I can compete with MBAs from any other school. I have full faith and confidence that the tools I have been given are the tools that will lead to a successful career in business and in life.

Simon helped me to develop into the manager that I wanted to be. They did not try to mold me into the manager that they wanted me to be. I don't think that any individual can truly reach his or her potential unless allowed to mature in his or her own way and provided an opportunity to develop ideas and creativity. This is what Simon did for me.

Overall, the academic rigor of the Simon School is especially high. In my talks with other B-school students, I have learned that many other schools in the Top 30 do not work as hard as we do on our academics. Although I might argue that, on average, students entering top 5 or top 10 programs are "better" statistically than those students entering Simon, I am not convinced that they are always better when the program is complete.

22.
VANDERBILT UNIVERSITY

VANDERBILT UNIVERSITY

Owen Graduate School of Management

401 21st Avenue South

Nashville, Tennessee 37203

E-mail address: owenadms@ctrvax.vanderbilt.edu

Web site address: http://www.mba.vanderbilt.edu

Corporate ranking: 23	Graduate ranking: 24
Enrollment: 458	Annual tuition & fees: $26,300
Women: 27%	Room and board: $9350
Non-U.S.: 28%	Average GMAT score: 640
Minority: 5%	Average years of work exp.: 4.5
Part-time: 0	Accepted applicants enrolled: 45%
Average age: 28	Intellectual capital: 9
Applicants accepted: 38%	
Median starting pay: $115,000	

Teaching methods: Lecture, 50%   Case study, 30%

                             Projects, 20%

Contact:
Todd Reale
Director of MBA
Program and
Admissions
615-322-6469
Application deadlines:
November 30
January 31
March 15

The Owen Graduate School of Management at Vanderbilt University has a new dean who fashions himself after Lucy from the Peanuts cartoon—at least on Mondays from 5 to 6 p.m. That's when you'll find Dean William G. Christie with an old-school metal mug and a sign announcing that the "Dean Is In," just like Charlie Brown's pal Lucy. The mug serves as a makeshift collection plate. "I have informed the students that compliments are free, factual questions cost them a dime, and if they want to abuse me, it costs a quarter," Christie says. "I seem to be running ahead by about $5 per week." This outlandish but purposeful gesture is the symbol of a new dawn at Owen. Christie took the helm in July 2000 after an unsuccessful 17-month search for the successor to Martin S. Geisel. Christie, who remains a top-notch Owen finance professor, was part of the search committee. Though he was not the first or obvious choice, Christie has committed himself to engaging students and increasing the visibility of Owen in the public arena. "I want to let everyone know there's some blood flowing in the dean's office," he says. But Christie has much work to do.

Vanderbilt faced a harrowing two years since the last BUSINESS-WEEK rankings. First, Geisel passed away from complications after a heart attack, which left students and faculty in despair and without a leader. Longtime professor of management Joseph Blackburn stepped up to the plate as interim dean. All the while, Christie and others supported him and searched for a permanent replacement. (Blackburn turned down an offer for the position, saying, "It was not a job I aspired to.") When Geisel died, loyal faculty left Owen, leaving at least nine faculty slots empty. In addition, the career placement director left. But the solid few who stuck around must have made all the difference; somehow Vanderbilt redeemed itself from a less-than-stellar showing in 1998 by garnering the No. 22 spot on the 2000 BUSINESSWEEK rankings. Two years ago, the school failed to reach the Top 25 and fell into the second tier. The revival "shows we worked really hard in the midst of adversity to make sure everything got covered," Christie says. And some things never change.

Christie continues to make sure everything is getting covered. In addition to being dean, Christie is teaching four finance classes in the MBA and Executive MBA programs to make up for faculty who have not yet been replaced. He also plans to maintain extracurricular activities like researching and serving on a slew of boards and committees. Christie, who gained notoriety for initiating an investigation into NASDAQ that proved market makers manipulated pricing, is publishing two papers in addition to all his other duties. That's dedication. "I don't know anyone who gets as excited as Bill," says Aaron Bickford, a 2000 graduate who lauded the decision to hand the reigns over to an Owen insider. Students seem to have envisioned this promotion before everyone else. Christie was a great choice because he developed relationships with students and always maintained an open door policy, says 2000 grad Matt King. Students consistently ranked Christie among Owen's top professors in the BUSINESSWEEK rankings. Perhaps that is why Christie has unparalleled devotion to students. Christie's first goal is to improve student satisfaction by enhancing the dean's relationship with the student body.

But he says one thing he won't touch is the curriculum. "We got that right," he says. Geisel, who has a Ph.D. from the University of Chicago, overhauled the curriculum in 1996 by convert-

ing from a semester system to one that features courses in four 7-week modules per year. All required courses are completed before the end of the first year, with room for four electives before heading for your summer internship. And core courses make up 40 percent of graduation requirements as opposed to the 60 percent required under the old system.

Students start the program in August with an orientation that includes review classes in statistics and calculus. During the first semester, they are limited to lecture-heavy requirements, with the first seven weeks dedicated to accounting, macroeconomics, statistics, and a course in leading teams and organizations. The second module covers additional accounting, finance, operations, and marketing. After winter break, aspiring MBAs take macroeconomics in the third module and strategy in the fourth module; required courses in communications and human relations and organization management can be taken in either module. You'll fill out your first-year schedule with electives, for a total of four courses per second-semester module. Core exemptions have been reduced to a bare minimum, with waivers by examination allowed only in accounting, statistics, and economics; any exempted courses must be replaced by an elective—so no early graduations are allowed.

The system allows students to fit in more than one concentration or to combine a concentration with an "emphasis" (Owen's term for a minor, which requires about four courses). Concentrations include finance, marketing, operations, accounting, human relations management, organization management, telecommunications and electronic commerce, and a customized major in general management. Among the complementary emphases are international, service, e-commerce, environmental management, entrepreneurship, and health care. Besides info tech and e-commerce, the school's strongest areas are finance, marketing, and operations. The entrepreneurship track is still in its infancy and seems to be lagging behind other top B-schools. And Christie says this area will have to wait again because, in light of the recent changes, other things need tending to first. In other words, potential students with visions of start-up grandeur might want to head elsewhere.

Many of the electives include teamwork and hands-on training, although MBAs are not formally assigned to cohorts and team assignments are made on a class-by-class basis. Students are also encouraged to utilize the many and varied courses available through the larger university; up to 15 credits can be taken outside the B-school. Dual degrees are offered in law, engineering, nursing, and Latin American studies. The B-school also has exchange agreements with 14 management schools outside the United States, enabling MBAs to spend a semester in Europe, South Africa, or Latin America. Don't want to spend 14 weeks away from campus? There's an International Management Seminar that divides students into teams that take classes on the language, business culture, economics, and politics of an overseas region, then travel there during spring break for a firsthand look at what they've learned in theory. In the past, MBAs have trekked to Japan, Mexico, Europe, Brazil, and the Philippines—at an extra cost averaging around $1500 above what is already a fairly pricey annual tuition.

These global initiatives are finding their way onto campus as well. The admissions office is interested in candidates who have an avowed interest in the cultures of the world and have demonstrated their fascination with study-abroad endeavors or foreign language studies. Todd Reale, director of MBA Program and Admissions, says Owen is trying to reach a more diverse audience, but one that will contribute to the community. In fact, student-run organizations like the Owen Black Students Association initiate on-campus events, with corporate sponsors and alum, intended to promote the school to potential minority students. The same thing is being done about the short-

age of women on campus. This year, Reale says he hopes to inaugurate Diversity Weekend, which will include events for current and prospective students and will highlight the potential for multiculturalism and gender diversity at Owen. In addition, special scholarships are awarded to outstanding minority and women applicants.

But Scholar's Weekend is quickly becoming the most coveted prize. The administration invites undecided candidates with the most sought-after credentials for an expenses-paid weekend in Nashville. From their arrival, potential students are wooed with luncheons, dinners, lectures, one-on-one encounters with faculty and enrolled students, and the list goes on. The Vanderbilt staff rolls out the red carpet for these top-notch applicants and then distinguishes a select few for the honor of Dean's Scholar. Candidates awarded this title receive a $10,000 stipend in addition to already-doled out merit scholarships.

Although diversity is among the top concerns, Owen must also retool career services. In November 1999, Peter Veruki, the former director of career services, left the hallowed halls of Owen for those of Rice University's MBA program. In a bind, the interim administration named a temporary replacement, who hung around until the end of August 2000 while the administration searched for the perfect replacement. The solution: Stephen Johansson, assistant dean for Career Services and Corporate Relations. Johansson took over on August 21, 2000. With only a few months under his belt, he already has high aspirations. He says his number one priority is making sure various constituencies look at Owen as an "A-one service provider." He also wants to help students better prepare for interviews and help them meet individual goals. He promises personalized service.

Though Owen is trying to reach corporate recruiters far and wide, students share some good times right on the Nashville campus. The MBA action centers around Management Hall, a modern red-brick and plate-glass structure merged with the historic architecture of Old Mechanical, a vintage 1880s building that is one of the oldest structures on the 300-acre Vanderbilt campus. Potential MBAs often overlook Vanderbilt because of its Nashville location. But there's lots more to this city than country music and the Grand Ole Opry, although it's not exactly a corporate mecca. The few nationally known companies that call it home include Columbia/HCA, Genesco, and Aladdin Industries. Recent grads say Nashville is a stellar place to relocate for a couple of years. Jennifer Herbert, a 2000 grad, says she never intended to go to Vanderbilt, but after she visited, she was hooked. Herbert and her classmates gathered for Kegs in the Courtyard Thursdays at 5 p.m. The Capitalists Ball, a charity formal in the spring, is a much-anticipated event. Under new management, the Owen School is trying to show that life in Nashville can be a ball.

PLACEMENT DETAILS

Johansson has a big job to do. In addition to re-creating a permanent career service strategy and joining the rest of the Owen crew in turning a new leaf after Geisel's passing, Johansson is hiring a director of corporate relations to reach recruiters in more creative ways. Though the placement office was in transition while the Class of 2000 was searching for jobs, students still managed to fare well. Sixty companies came to the Nashville campus, which Johansson says is becoming more accessible. He also lauds the sunny skies for attracting top recruiters. Though marketing must remain a priority, students snagged an average of 2.6 job offers before graduation, which is slightly lower than most of the Top 30 but is nothing to sneeze at either. Median starting pay packages hit $115,000, which matches most of Vanderbilt's counterparts.

The companies who hired the most Owen graduates include: PricewaterhouseCoopers (9); First Union (8); Dell (6); Goldman Sachs (4); Deloitte Consulting (4); KPMG (3); Mastrapasqua & Associates (3); MSDW (3); Johnson & Johnson (3); Arthur Andersen (2). Johansson and Christie have already begun spending a few weeks touring the country for alumni receptions, trying to make inroads with Owen graduates at top-notch companies. They are using these receptions as a way to develop relationships with the nontraditional sector as well. Johansson says they will leverage Owen's impressive e-commerce program and help place interested students in start-ups or on teams that launch New Economy initiatives in Old Economy firms. Johansson promises that students are "only limited by their energy and their own creativity." The new career services office is simply another part of Owen's effort to redefine itself in the aftermath of tragedy.

OUTSTANDING FACULTY

Luke Froeb (economics); *Bill Christie* (finance); *Amar Gande* (finance); *Craig Lewis* (finance); *David Rados* (marketing); *David Owens* (organizational management); *Amit Basu* (telecommunications/e-commerce).

APPLICANT TIPS

While other schools lost applicants because of economic highs and start-up frenzy, 8 percent more applications passed across the Owen admissions desk. Christie is taking a personal stake in the continued success of the admissions office. If you tour campus nowadays, don't be surprised if you get to shake hands with the dean. Among his other goals, Christie hopes to usher in a more hands-on approach with applicants. He spent some of his time as a professor catering to requests by the admissions office to meet with potential students; as dean, he plans to do the same.

Before you whisk into Nashville, pay attention to the Owen admissions staff. Todd Reale expects applicants to do their homework and weigh their numerous options before submitting an application and certainly before interviewing with someone at Owen. Owen requires applicant interviews. But these days, they are prescreening applicants and inviting them to interview, as opposed to the old system where anyone could snag a one-on-one. You can get around this if you absolutely must have an interview; if you visit campus before actually submitting an application, the admissions office still will have someone sit down and chat with you. They figure you are pretty interested if you traveled all the way to Nashville to come face-to-face with the Owen experience. Another useful reminder: Be sure to write meaningful essays that describe what you can contribute to the Owen environment and tell Reale how you will fit into Owen's distinct culture. If you want scholarship consideration, apply by the first two deadlines.

Contact: Todd Reale
Director of MBA Program and Admissions
615-322-6469
Application deadlines: November 30; January 31; March 15

OWEN MBAs SOUND OFF

Considering all of the challenges that Owen has encountered during the past two years, the school has done remarkably well. The core of the school's faculty and administration have all stepped up and worked harder. The faculty defections, while undesirable, included mostly individuals who tended to be less skillful and interested in teaching than in research and publishing. The school is poised in an excellent position for the arrival of a new dean to lead the school into the future.

I would like to give kudos to the administration of Owen for their honest and forthcoming communication regarding our school's dean search, as well as other school issues. With the death of Geisel in my first year of school, our class experienced a transition at Owen; yet one that has been immensely helped by the support and leadership of our acting administration. Also, judging from our Class of 2001 and having a peek at 2002 admits, it appears we're on track to continuous improvement in the quality of our students, which has already left me with a great deal of pride. Last, I'd like to applaud (interim) Dean Blackburn's recent statement that the next year will be some of the most active in recruiting superior faculty to our school. It's been an intense two years, but two that I consider contribute the most to my future career development.

My largest complaint is that there is much overlap between courses (this may only apply to finance courses). This could be a result of the "mod" system, which was intended to give courseload flexibility. Unfortunately, subjects are compressed into seven-week sessions, the first couple of weeks of which often consist of "reviewing," because students end up enrolling in no logical sequence. I really felt cheated in some cases; some basic topics were re-taught to me two or three times. Courses in general seem like watered-down overviews. There is little in-depth examination of issues, striking de-emphasis on quantitative aspects.

My Owen experience was two forever memorable years in an environment where it was safe to make mistakes and a blast to chalk up successes. I did a lot of both and learned a ton as a result. The most valuable tools I carry forward from Owen are belief in my insight, courage to implement change, the humility to accept and learn from mistakes, and the love of myself and those around me that makes it all worthwhile.

With Dean Geisel's illness and death last year, this has been a challenging time for Owen.

Nevertheless, this experience has been great. I expected great things from this school, and I haven't been let down. The doors are always open on the third floor (faculty offices) and the quality of the teaching remains excellent.

**23.
WASHINGTON
UNIVERSITY**

WASHINGTON UNIVERSITY

John M. Olin School of Business

Campus Box 1133

One Brookings Drive

St. Louis, Missouri 63130

E-mail address: mba@olin.wustl.edu

Web site address: http://www.olin.wustl.edu

Corporate ranking: 37	Graduate ranking: 9
Enrollment: 664	Annual tuition & fees: $27,140
Women: 25%	Room and board: $10,089
Non-U.S.: 32%	Average GMAT score: 661
Minority: 10%	Average years of work exp.: 5
Part-time: 366	Accepted applicants enrolled: 44%
Average age: 28	Intellectual capital: 31
Applicants accepted: 29%	
Median starting pay: $109,000	

Teaching methods: Lecture, 25%   Case study, 45%
Experiential learning projects, simulations,
group projects, 30%

Contact:

Pamela K. Wiese

Director of MBA

Admissions and

Financial Aid

314-935-7301

Application deadlines:

December 14

January 16

February 12

March 26

April 30

Stop off any weekend at Simon Hall, the main building at Washington University's John M. Olin School of Business, and you'll find him there, wandering the corridors. Hapless MBAs who cross his path will soon find themselves deep in conversation about the ongoing job hunt: Who are their contacts at company X? What strategies are they using to snag an interview? Or he'll corral them into an impromptu brainstorming session on ways to improve life at Olin: What did you think of last night's speaker? Having any trouble finding a port to plug in your laptop? Not that many students mind being grilled by Dean Stuart I. Greenbaum—in fact, most describe him as one of the program's greatest assets.

No one familiar with Greenbaum's background would be surprised to learn that he's inordinately concerned about what his students think—after all, he learned the fine art of giving the customer what he wants at the feet of a master, Dean Donald P. Jacobs of Northwestern's Kellogg Graduate School of Management. Back in the 1980s, Jacobs, Greenbaum—then a banking professor at Kellogg—and a few colleagues regularly spent hours at a Russian steam bath in Chicago. Their sweat-soaked bull sessions covered politics, baseball, and, above all, ways to help Jacobs turn Kellogg into one of the nation's best B-schools. All that perspiration apparently paid off: Kellogg emerged from the relative obscurity of its regional school status and is now one of a handful of the most high-profile MBA programs in the world. And one of the most distinctive hallmarks of Jacobs's administration has been student empowerment. Greenbaum is trying to follow Jacobs's lead. "I believe in Woody Allan's dictum: 'I show up,'" Greenbaum says.

But success stories like Kellogg's don't happen overnight, as Greenbaum has discovered since packing his bags in 1995 and heading down Interstate 55 to St. Louis, where he took the helm at Olin. Greenbaum and Olin were not an obvious fit at first—a relatively liberal, opera-loving son of a New York butcher, with the accent to prove it, is not the most likely leader for a Midwestern school surrounded by a conservative business community—but the dean has gradually become as comfortable here as any Show-Me State native. In the three years since his arrival, Greenbaum has also made headway in establishing Olin firmly in the Top 30 by overhauling the curriculum, recruiting a crop of vibrant young professors, planning a new executive education building, and, most importantly, listening to his students. Many of the initiatives have been borrowed directly from Greenbaum's two-decade Kellogg sojourn.

Students showed their appreciation for Greenbaum's approach in the 2000 BUSINESS-WEEK rankings; Olin rose from 16 to 9 in the graduate poll. However, recruiters told a different story. Olin witnessed a dramatic drop in the recruiter poll, slipping from 19 in 1998 to 37 in 2000. As a result, Olin lost its place in the top 20. The school is already on the road to recovery with a remodeled strategy in the career placement office. Greenbaum and his staff say the problem is getting the message out that Olin students match the quality of the other Top 30 schools. And he might be right, given the strength of the school's curriculum and the satisfaction of its students. To solve this problem, the career services office has begun mailing

postcards to recruiters and others about the skills of individual Olin students. The postcards feature a classic comic book graphic on the front with a photo and bio of a student on the back. For example, one card features a rocket speeding away from a burning meteor. The title of the psuedo-comic book cover is "Olin School of Business: Fantastic Adventure," which is written in funky bubble letters. Below in the right corner, made to look like a comic book teaser, recruiters read, "Adriana Rueda: Out-of-this-world Financial Skills." On the back, potential recruiters see a smiling Adriana alongside a quick bio and description of why she would make a fabulous employee. The postcards come with accompanying posters that feature the cartoon graphics and the latest school motto, which happens to match the quirky Martian characters on the cards: "Olin interns and graduates are out of this world." The question will be whether this colorful marketing scheme will actually produce results. It will likely take more than this—like a concerted effort among alumni, students, and the administration to market students' talents and skills and play up the many strengths of the Olin program.

These unusual cards were created under the leadership of new associate dean Gregory J. Hutchings. Hutchings joined the Olin administration in 1999 after a career in investment banking. Students are thrilled with his arrival. "When the director . . . left last year, [Greenbaum] seemed to want to move someone in A.S.A.P. to fill the gap, but students asked him to ensure that an appropriate search was done while preferring that someone was brought in from outside," one recent graduate recounts. "Despite his initial reservations, Stuart listened to students and spent a great deal of effort and money to hire [Gregory J. Hutchings] as the new associate dean, and this decision has probably been the most positive impact of my entire MBA experience." Hutchings says he always had a serious interest in recruiting and his position at Olin is an extension of that pursuit. The comic book marketing strategy is a way for students to build their own brand image, Hutchings says. "It is the day of the self-directed job search," he says. This approach has students, ultimately, marketing themselves to Corporate America as though they were a product.

The next obstacle Hutchings will tackle is getting nontraditional companies out to St. Louis—unless he can get the students out to those companies. For now, the career center is offering four road shows in Silicon Valley, Chicago, Boston, and New York. He says off-campus recruiting is the wave of the future and claims Olin will lead the pack. In addition to road shows, Olin is attracting nontraditional recruiters by hosting venture capital conferences and other informal networking opportunities. For instance, in April 2000, Olin launched Techportal, a monthly series of events designed to join students with local technology industry leaders. The goal is to position St. Louis as a national high-tech powerhouse by leveraging the smarts of Olin students and the community-at-large. For now, Washington University MBA students made a good showing, garnering 2.9 job offers on average and receiving a median starting pay of $109,000. But the school still lags behind B-school authorities like Wharton, Harvard, and—you guessed it—Kellogg.

Though Olin is still steps behind the folks at the top of the BUSINESSWEEK rankings, the recent changes have been a hit with Olin students, whose boundless enthusiasm for their school echoes Greenbaum's. However, passion will only take you so far. What Olin needs most now is focus, and Greenbaum believes he's hit on a mission that will help set his school apart from the crowd. While other schools have headed in a similar direction, Olin just may have a better chance of succeeding because of its size. With a full-time enrollment of only 298, it is one of the smallest in the top tier—an advantage when it comes to focus, and perhaps a slight dis-

advantage when it comes to luring more recruiters. But Olin can count on the support of some deep pockets—its $174 million endowment is significantly larger than a number of its peer schools, including Duke's Fuqua and Dartmouth's Tuck. St. Louis's corporate community, which includes such major companies as Ralston Purina, Monsanto, and Anheuser-Busch, also supports the school in many ways.

In line with Olin's goal of personalizing its program as much as possible, students embark shortly after arrival on a required self-assessment of interpersonal, teamwork, negotiation, and communications skills as well as potential career interests. Based on the test results, MBA candidates design their courses of study under the guidance of faculty advisers. By 1998–1999, the MBA curriculum committee had established a stripped-down core that is nearly complete by the end of the first semester, with eight courses in such basics as strategy, economics, statistics, accounting, finance, marketing, operations, and organizational behavior shoehorned into two 7-week mini-semesters. With this schedule, students can take as many as seven electives in advanced or specialized topics before their summer internships, a valuable selling point with some employers. In keeping with the idea of ultimate flexibility, no majors are offered, freeing students to specialize in traditional disciplines such as accounting, marketing, or finance, or to devise a concentration in any interdisciplinary combination they dream up. Flexibility is a strength of the program.

Of course, the compressed schedule also creates a hefty workload, which students discovered, to their dismay, when the mini-semester system was first introduced in 1997 and they found themselves cramming for exams every eight weeks. The solution: Switching to a modified pass/fail grading system intended to lower the pressure, minimize competition, and make learning a reward unto itself. Students can still distinguish themselves by earning a "high pass" for outstanding performance, but such a designation is limited to just 20 percent of each class.

Real-world programs, designed to simulate management decision making, highlight the Olin curriculum. In mid-December, first-year students appropriately gear up for ICE Week, otherwise called the Integrating Case Experience. During a period of four days, students receive four cases and analyze each within 24 hours. Each team presents a formal analysis of one case and turns in write-ups of the remaining three. The fall core faculty, along with Olin staff, second-year students, and members of the business community evaluate each team's efforts and declare one group victorious. Later, you'll choose from the 48 seven-week and 39 fourteen-week electives, which are heavily slanted toward experiential learning. You'd be hard pressed to find an Olin graduate who hasn't been involved in at least one of the school's real-world projects, and most students manage to work in two of these time-and-energy-intensive courses by the time they get their diplomas. One popular offering is the Practicum, in which teams of four students, under the tutelage of a faculty adviser, are paired for a full semester with client companies such as PricewaterhouseCoopers, MasterCard International, Ralston Purina, and Sprint PCS.

While Practicum projects generally focus on general management skills, other experiential learning courses are more specialized. Budding entrepreneurs might take a look at the Hatchery, launched in 1996, in which student teams create business plans either for emerging companies or based on their own ideas. Those with a bent toward community service should check out the Total Quality Schools project, where students use quality management principles to assist St. Louis public schools struggling with attendance, scheduling, communication, or activities issues. The Taylor Community Consulting Program, a one-week mini-course offered during the winter break in which Ernst & Young consultants pair with Olin students to offer expertise to local nonprofits, is another opportunity to help the community while getting educated. In addition to the real-world applications, up to 15 credits toward the MBA degree, or three full-semester courses, can be taken in other Washington University departments, including a number of foreign languages, public health, and international affairs. Formal joint degrees are available in law, architecture, social work, and East Asian studies.

While Olin isn't well known for its international curriculum, a couple of offerings in this area are worth your attention. In the experiential learning vein, the Global Management Studies course combines coursework on the history, culture, and business practices of a specific country or region with a consulting project completed during a two-week field research trip. In 1998, a group of 26 students went to Chile and Argentina to explore opportunities in the wine industry for Monsanto and in professional sports for the National Basketball Association. There's also a one-month London study program in which an Olin finance professor teaches classes exclusively to Olin students using the facilities at City University Business School; students also attend a speaker series featuring academics, business leaders, and policy makers. Many participants opt to remain in England for a fall-semester corporate internship coordinated by Olin. (Traditional one-semester exchange programs are available at schools in England, Germany, France, or Venezuela.)

You can also get a bit of a global education just from sitting in class with the large number of international students Olin attracts, more than 32 percent of the MBA population in 2000. In fact, the number of students from overseas had gotten so large—almost 40 percent by 1996—that the school felt it prudent to scale back international admissions to effectively provide the special services many non-U.S. students need in terms of acculturation, socialization, and job placement. At the same time, Olin has been struggling to increase the number of women and minority MBAs it matriculates; Greenbaum's main strategy has been to build visibility among faculty and administration as a sign of Olin's commitment to diversity. Since coming to Olin, the dean has hired two African-American and two Native American faculty members where there previously were none and has recruited several minority students to the school's Ph.D. program.

Olin is situated on the west end of Washington's University campus, its Gothic-style buildings made of red granite, a local resource, that give a cheerier take to the traditional look. The entire university is located on top of a hill overlooking a number of St. Louis suburbs. There are no graduate dorms here, so most students live in apartments and shared homes within five miles of campus in neighborhoods such as Demun, an artsy but somewhat expensive section within walking distance of campus, and the Central West End, a lively area filled with bars and restaurants where you'll find plenty of graduate and medical students catching the shuttle to school. A short walk from campus is Forest Park, the largest park in St. Louis, where MBAs like to chill out by biking, jogging, rollerblading, or playing tennis. You might also find MBAs at the monthly Chuck Berry show, a favorite at the Blueberry Hill Nightclub in the U-City Loop, which is about five blocks from campus. Don't forget all the perks that come from being located in the same city as Budweiser, the world's largest brewery.

PLACEMENT DETAILS

The 80 companies that recruited on campus at Olin in 2000 might be even more impressed next time around with all the changes in the career services office. Salaries here lag behind the top of the list but rose a bit from 1998. On the other hand, at an average of 2.9 job offers per student, Olin stumbled a bit; two years ago, students snagged 3.4 job offers apiece. Despite some obstacles, Olin still had its share of corporate visitors. The school's most important recruiters were Northwest Airlines (5); SBC Communications (5); Bank of America (4); A.G. Edwards (3); Anheuser-Busch (3); Charter Communications (3); Emerson Electric (3); Ernst & Young (3); Goldman Sachs (3); Ralston Purina (3).

Students give the Weston Career Resources Center above average marks for help in the job hunt, especially for those conducting independent searches. That should come as no surprise considering the school's focus on customer service. A series of workshops offers students assistance with résumé and cover letter writing, networking, interviewing skills, and salary negotiations. For recruiters who can't come to campus, the center has a videoconferencing system that allows students to be interviewed by employers long-distance. The center also hosts a number of corporate speakers and panels each year, including Close Encounter Q&A and Lunch with a Pro sessions in which students can get up close and personal with senior executives from firms such as Ernst & Young and A.G. Edwards, and an alumni mentoring program.

OUTSTANDING FACULTY

Mark Soczek (accounting); *Timothy West* (accounting); *Barton H. Hamilton* (economics/management/entrepreneurship); *Guofu Zhou* (finance); *Michael R. Gordinier* (management); *Jeroen Swinkels* (managerial economics/strategy); *V. Padmanabhan* (marketing); *Panos Kouvelis* (operations/manufacturing management); *Stacy Jackson* (organizational behavior).

APPLICANT TIPS

The admissions department is also seeing some changes. Director Pamela K. Wiese is moving into the dean's office and leaving the acceptances to someone else. For now, the administration is still looking for a suitable replacement. But things won't change much for applicants. Like other top schools, Olin looks at objective measures such as GPA and GMAT scores, but also examines your work history, goals, motivation, achievements, and character, not to mention how well you are able to communicate these traits in your application essays and interview. A personal interview is not required, but is strongly encouraged. International applicants may interview by telephone. Those who come to campus will be able to attend first-year classes, tour Simon Hall, and lunch with a student host. The school runs a preview weekend at the beginning of February in which Olin programs are discussed in depth.

Olin has five admissions rounds, one a month from December through April; you can expect a reply five to six weeks later. You would do well to apply early, however, as the school has become more selective in recent years—while nearly half of all applicants were accepted in 1996, just 29 percent made it in 2000. You can apply the old-fashioned way, by requesting a paper application or downloading the form from the school's Web site and mailing it back in, or you can fill it out via computer and submit it electronically.

Contact: Pamela K. Wiese
Director of MBA Admissions and Financial Aid
314-935-7301
Application deadlines: December 14;
January 16; February 12; March 26; April 30

OLIN MBAs SOUND OFF

I just want to add that (admittedly), when I was looking at business schools, I was extremely caught up in the rankings and did not know what to expect from Olin, being out of the top 10 rankings. However, most who have visited in Olin now describe it as a "hidden gem." And I can honestly say, it *is* without a doubt. I think one of the things most students do *not* ask themselves when looking at B-schools is, "Will I be happy here?" Well, I can honestly say that Olin is on the rise, regardless of what the others say. This program has enveloped all of the modern critical attributes that all students are seeking in becoming better managers and entrepreneurs (flexibility, empowerment, experiential learning, and ownership of a community). Olin is on the rise, and I am glad to be part of the momentum.

From an improvement standpoint, I see three main things that are top priorities to improve the school, all of which are currently being attempted: 1) Build the brand name of both Olin and Washington University. 2) Attract more top-quality students. There are currently many outstanding students, but I would say that the overall class is not quite as deep as some other schools I have seen. 3) Strengthen relationships with top companies and get them on campus to interview. As a small school in a slightly out-of-the-way city, it has been very difficult to get top-tier consulting or investment banking firms to campus. The school has done a great job of building relationships that have definitely paid off during the past year but should really begin to have an impact in the next few years.

Olin is an exceptional school in terms of student responsiveness. Before we had an e-commerce class available, six of us were able to craft an independent study course, under the guidance of a professor, to learn what we wanted to know. Furthermore, many of the experiential learning projects are strongly tied to how students would like to experience them. Many of us wanted to increase the school's reputation on the West

Coast and in Silicon Valley, and we were able to obtain school funding and administrative support to arrange the first student-sponsored recruiting trip. If the school sees value in what a student proposes, there is little bureaucracy standing in the way of having it approved. Its small size and close-knit atmosphere help to nurture significant leadership and personal development opportunities. I am leaving Olin smarter, more confident, better connected, and more creative than when I entered.

**24.
UNIVERSITY
OF SOUTHERN
CALIFORNIA**

UNIVERSITY OF SOUTHERN CALIFORNIA

Marshall School of Business
University Park
Los Angeles, California 90089
E-mail address: uscmba@marshall.usc.edu
Web site address: http://www.marshall.usc.edu

Corporate ranking: 25	Graduate ranking: 19
Enrollment: 1498	Annual tuition & fees: $27,060
Women: 31%	Room and board: $11,000
Non-U.S.: 26%	Average GMAT score: 670
Minority: 9%	Average years of work exp.: 4.7
Part-time: 899	Accepted applicants enrolled: 47%
Average age: 28	Intellectual capital: 39
Applicants accepted: 27%	
Median starting pay: $112,500	

Teaching methods: Lecture, 50%   Case study, 30%
Experiential learning, 20%

Contact:
Keith Vaughn
Director of Admissions
213-740-7846
Application deadlines:
December 4
January 8
February 5
April 2

In 1999, the University of Southern California's Marshall School of Business opened the doors to Popovich Hall, a $25 million, three-story, state-of-the-art building that was designed to be a dedicated home to the school's MBA students. The new MBA student home means no longer having to contend with 2000 undergraduate business majors, limited Web connectivity, and other annoying vestiges of the twentieth century. Dennis Draper, vice dean of graduate programs, says the building has done more than give grad students a place to plop their laptops and Palm Pilots. The way Draper tells it—and faculty, grads, students, and recruiters back him up—since Popovich opened its doors, it also opened the doors to a new B-school. And graduates agree. "Because this is their building, and we took their suggestions for what we can do, we gave [students] an opportunity to create something and that has created cohesiveness in the school," says Draper of the transformation effect Popovich has had at Marshall.

Since Popovich opened its classrooms outfitted with traditional VCRs, videoconferencing, and other high-tech perks—not to mention CNN broadcasts and a new first-rate cafeteria—the results have been felt within the curriculum, the culture, and the recruiting at Marshall. Document cameras allow students to download professors' in-class presentations as notes, including those that profs now have the ability to create on the fly, thanks to always-on Internet access. Outdoor and indoor Net plug-ins allow students to get on the Web while enjoying the sunny California climate. And that means the grounds around

Popovich are swarming with would-be MBAs studying, reading, and debating almost 24-7. Thirteen experiential learning centers with computer access also offer opportunities for indoor collaboration. And the tech-aspect of the school has also allowed Marshall to get senior executives from all over the world to give presentations through videoconferencing with real-time Q&As, throughout the building, without taking the time to fly to California and back. Indeed, before Popovich opened, students surveyed by BUSINESSWEEK ranked the school poorly in its ability to bring them into contact with practicing professionals, perhaps because of its location. But graduates in 2000 lauded their new-found real-world connections. "As you might expect, it is much easier to get them for 20 minutes than a whole day. The technology has really enhanced us beyond ways we anticipated," Draper says.

It may seem remarkable that a new building can do all of that, but that's the kind of remarkable lore that makes Marshall the place it is. In the last several decades, the school has been an also-ran in top circles, but respected in its West Coast community. The innovative, entrepreneurial spirit of the school is much in the manner of its benefactor, Gordon S. Marshall. Marshall himself could easily be a character in a Horatio Alger story. A bomber pilot who returned to Los Angeles after World War II with 27 European missions on his flight log, Marshall attacked the fledgling electronics industry with the same ferocity he had unleashed on his military targets. He launched his own company with nothing backing him but a few thousand dollars in the bank and a 1946 diploma from the University of Southern California's business school, and over the next half century built Marshall Industries into a $1 billion electronic components distribution giant.

His alma mater became the Marshall School of Business in 1997 upon receipt of a gift of $35 million from the businessman, and with the check it received a newly galvanized image.

The cash was the first step in moving USC out of the shadows cast by its older, cheaper, and better-known cross-town competitor, UCLA's Anderson School. But Popovich, Draper and many students say, is the edifice that will allow Marshall to cast its own shadows on those who have not yet noticed its impressive entrepreneurship program, international orientation, cadre of high-quality teachers, or its active alumni network. The new facility and funding allowed Marshall to expand its full-time MBA enrollment from 185 a few years ago to about 300 per class, a number Draper says is large enough to offer a wide variety of electives for second-year students and attract a cross-section of recruiters, but small enough to keep the intimate school culture. The Class of 2002 is the school's largest ever, at 296, and the first to have all their classes in Popovich.

More important has been the increase in faculty size to 175, again making those electives possible, Draper says. For years, USC has been home to some of the sharpest and most articulate management thinkers in America, including leadership guru Warren Bennis; Edward Lawler, who runs the school's Center for Effective Organizations; and Morgan McCall, who has developed some of the leading management simulation exercises on the market today. Recent grad Paul Attyah, who now works in mergers and acquisitions at AIG in Los Angeles, supports the argument that Popovich made this all possible. "You can't recruit a professor from the east and then say, 'We have nowhere to put you.'" Attyah, who also has undergrad and post-grad degrees from Duke and Berkeley, says the thing that is making Marshall different is the age of its faculty. He thinks being young makes them more approachable, more accessible, and more aware of the special problems of the New Economy.

Indeed, the faculty's creative streak is certainly one thing that makes a difference at USC. In the last year alone, the school added 14 new courses, or 15 percent of all electives, many of which were born of faculty and student brainstorming. Courses run the gamut from electronic distribution, e-commerce, and corporate finance restructuring to a technological initiatives class and entrepreneurship programs. New electives include: e-Business Supply Chain Optimization, Econometrics of Risk Management, Resource Design, International Management—China, Critical Thinking, and Technology Commercialization. Concentrations include: Business of Entertainment (only at a school this close to Hollywood), Marketing and Finance, General Marketing, Health Care Advisory Services. Marshall students rank their faculty at the top of several important measures, from being aware of what their peers were teaching to offering the best teaching in elective courses to the quality of professors.

However, one gripe from students is that business plans—and how to write and execute them well—were only emphasized to those in entrepreneurship courses, rather than throughout the curriculum. Although students may rank the curriculum lower than those at other top-tier schools when it comes to teaching analytical skills and weaving e-business throughout the non-e-business courses, students give high marks to the outstanding use of technology in the classroom and in the school's many entrepreneurial efforts. Students also praise Marshall for its valuable international experiences. One of the school's chief goals: to be a leader in global business education.

In fact, since his arrival in 1993, Dean Randolph W. Westerfield, a former chairman of Wharton's finance department, has focused on establishing a niche for the school as a management education leader for the entire Pacific Rim and beyond. The most visible sign of Marshall's commitment to overseas study—and what many students say is the most memorable part of the MBA program—is the PRIME program, which stands for Pacific Rim Education. Launched in 1997, this five-week module first concentrates classroom study on Asian and Latin American business practices, then puts teams of six to seven students to work on corporate consulting projects that culminate in a 10-day research trip to one of eight locations in China, Japan, Mexico, and Indonesia, with Chile recently added. In 2001, the school is planning a trip for 30 to 45 students to Cuba. "The international exposure during the PRIME class abroad was a remarkable experience," says one 2000 grad who did his time abroad in Japan. "We had access to knowledge from upper management at the world's leading companies in over seven countries. The exposure to the Japanese culture and working environment could not have been achieved to the same degree by reading case studies or by lectures."

Marshall is the only Top 30 B-school to require all students to complete an overseas study trip in order to graduate (it is mandatory for all first-year MBAs, including part-timers). And while it does cost extra—from a few hundred to more than $1000, depending on the destination—the school estimates 97 percent of students would study overseas even if it were not required. Marshall subsidizes travel costs to minimize expense to students. You'd be hard-pressed to find a participant who didn't think it was worth it. One graduate of the Class of 2000, who describes himself as originally "neutral" about studying abroad, says his time in Japan was one of the highlights of his MBA experience, spawned his research on Asian economic malaise, and made him bullish on Japanese equities when few others are. He is not alone. Increasingly, students enjoy their PRIME experience so much they endeavor to stay longer. In 2000, 50 percent of students arranged their summer internships in the country in which they studied. To accommodate this trend, Marshall revamped the exam and course schedule so that students aren't forced to return to the United States for exams for final coursework.

PRIME is just one of many global offerings that students say are among Marshall's greatest strengths. You can spend an entire semester abroad at 1 of 24 schools with which Marshall has an exchange agreement in Latin America, Asia, Australia, or Europe, or opt for a three- to four-week summer study session at schools in Brazil, Germany, or Austria. Back in L.A., you can take language and cultural classes in Spanish, Mandarin Chinese, or Japanese through the university's College Language Center—or in English, if that's not your native tongue. There's also a dual MBA/M.A. in East Asian Studies and a full-time, 12-month International Business Education and Research program (IBEAR) that gives a select group of 48 experienced middle managers each year the opportunity to participate in an intensive, hands-on international management.

PRIME is part of a newly consolidated, more sharply focused core curriculum introduced in 1997–1998 and refined through 1999–2000 after Marshall switched to a quarter system. The first year consists entirely of required courses, divided up over three 11-week periods. The first quarter concentrates on communication, managerial economics, and an introduction to strategy; the second covers the management functions of accounting control systems, corporate finance, marketing, operations, and organizational behavior; and the third brings everything together through a more advanced look at strategy, a segment on electronic commerce, and a macroeconomics course, in addition to PRIME. The plan was modified in 2000 so that first-years take only three classes at a time, rather than five, to make the workload more manageable.

Teamwork is tantamount to the learning process at USC, starting with your two-day team-building exercise, throughout the first year (it was shortened from five days several years ago). After being trained in team-based management strategies by a corporate consultant from the school's Center for Effective Organizations, the 65-person sections are divided into teams of four to six classmates who stay together across all courses for the first term,

then are shuffled into a fresh mix for each successive quarter. A series of team-based case competitions, in which students examine problems presented by real-life companies and then present their analyses to faculty, peers, and executives, provides a balance of competition and collaboration that students say mirrors what they find at work after graduation. Although some students complain that the caliber of their peers is not top-tier—which can make the group work frustrating—most graduates laud the academic camaraderie. "While competitive, I never felt that my classmates were interested in 'cutting my throat,'" says one typical grad. Indeed, grads say they rarely felt that their classmates put their own interests before that of the group.

As for life in Los Angeles, what's not to love? Sure, there's smog, traffic, and enough plastic surgery devotees to make anyone self-conscious. But at Marshall you are just 20 minutes from the beach, the weather's great, the Pacific Ocean beckons, and you've got a front-row seat to watch the birth of the best of American pop culture. Most Marshall MBAs live away from the campus, which is located about two and a half miles from L.A.'s central business district, next to Exposition Park and the L.A. Coliseum, site of the 1984 Summer Olympics and home of the L.A. Clippers. The neighboring community is pretty rough, although many students choose to live near school because rents are cheaper than the more desirable spots closer to the beach. Others head for the Mid-Wilshire district, a cosmopolitan area known for its many delicatessens and shopping centers, or west to the seaside towns of Santa Monica, Brentwood, Venice, or Redondo.

PLACEMENT DETAILS

The bad news about Marshall is that you're still not going to find the range of Wall Street corporate recruiters beating down the doors to hire grads the way you would at UCLA, Berkeley, or even Stanford—although that may not be the case for long. And depending on your career focus, that may not matter. The median starting post-MBA pay package for USC grads in 2000 was $112,500, an improvement over 1998's $93,000, but still considerably behind the $136,500 pulled down by newly minted MBAs from that other L.A. B-school. Marshall has made significant strides to improve what was once a bleak placement picture. Again, Draper credits the opening of Popovich for an improved placement center, which accounts for 40 percent of the top floor, in part because there are now 12 dedicated rooms for recruiters to come in and conduct interviews and ample space for students to access databases and other resources. In the BUSINESSWEEK survey, recent grads say the school's connections to the business world and to Marshall alums are helpful both in searching for a first job and career development.

The MBA Career Resource Center now employs 18 senior-level staffers, a number the school feels allows them to give students one-on-one career counseling and advice. The center boasts its own server for access to online job banks and application information. Draper says that in the past Marshall was passed over by recruiters for other schools, but in 2000 it heard from some high-profile firms, including Dell Computer, that they skipped UCLA in favor of a trip to USC. "We were shocked," Draper says. "But we've heard a lot of nice things about our facilities and staff."

Kim Cousin, corporate recruiting manager at Wells Fargo, says, "It is the most responsive, organized, thoughtful, and flexible career center that we work with." Wells Fargo hires more grads from USC than any other school (five in 2000), citing their ability to work in cross-functional teams and preparation in finance and accounting as part of the reason the bank has been happy with its USC hires. Perhaps as a result, Marshall's Class of 2000 averaged 3.34

job offers apiece, more than many other higher-ranked schools.

Tom Kozicki, the new executive director of the MBA Career Resource Center, says flexibility has been key in attracting recruiters. His staff is trained to accommodate last-minute changes of companies coming to campus to interview, and has adopted the attitude that "employers are our ultimate customers." Offices away from home allow recruiters to make phone calls, check e-mail, conduct conference calls, and do other tasks that otherwise could stress them out and distract them during the interview process. Recruiters tell tales of Marshall staffers running out to get them lunch when they didn't have time to eat during a heavy interview schedule. Despite the acknowledged strength of Marshall's PRIME program, Kozicki says recruiting international employers remains a challenge. Although U.S. businesses looking for students with international expertise still flock to Marshall, the expense involved in recruiting from overseas has kept foreign firms away.

Some 220 companies recruited on campus in 2000, conducting 3800 interviews with second-year students. Another 1700 jobs were posted electronically, a number Kozicki says is declining because so many firms are now listing job openings on their own Web sites. Because of the school's West Coast location, Wall Street recruiters are still the minority of the employers who come to Marshall and if you have your heart set on a New York I-bank job, Marshall may not be your best bet yet. Kozicki is working on changing that and he has peaked interest in the school from some investment banks. Last year 25 percent of students did internships with I-banks and firms like Goldman Sachs, DLJ, Lehman Brothers, and Merrill Lynch all came to recruit on campus.

The lion's share of Marshall MBAs stay on the West Coast, thanks to that sunny climate. Top employers in 2000 were among some of California's best-known firms, including Hewlett-Packard (which hired 11 grads from the Class of 2000), Intel, and Walt Disney. Other top hires include: Deloitte & Touche (5); Bank of America (5); PricewaterhouseCoopers (5); Clicktemp.com (4); and Dell (3).

OUTSTANDING FACULTY

Mark DeFond (accounting); *Ann Ehringer* (entrepreneurship); *Harry DeAngelo* (finance); *Linda DeAngelo* (finance); *Dennis Draper* (finance); *Suh Pyng Ku* (finance); *Doug Shook* (information systems); *Gary Frazier* (marketing); *Alan Weiss* (marketing).

APPLICANT TIPS

As befits its status as a top B-school, it's no longer easy to get into Marshall. Although 36 percent of applicants were admitted in 1996, only 27 percent got the nod in 2000.

Marshall says it looks for "students with outstanding leadership potential as well as those with the intellectual and interpersonal abilities to contribute to our academic and extracurricular programs." Admissions-speak translation: The whole package counts, from GPA and GMAT scores to work experience, letters of recommendation, and essays. Interviews are only scheduled at the discretion of the admissions office, and you can consider an invitation to interview a good sign: It means you're being considered as a serious candidate. But don't assume the opposite is true as well.

Only about 35 percent of those admitted have face-to-face meetings with admissions. Those who wish to be considered for fellowships or on-campus housing are advised to get their paperwork in by the January deadline, so if you can apply early, just do it. International candidates must apply by February at the latest. You can expect a response four to seven weeks after your particular deadline. Applications may be submitted either on disk or online by accessing the B-school Web site. If you wish to visit campus you can—and are encouraged to—arrange for a student ambassador to take you to a class, a tour of the B-school, and an informal informational session. Call the admissions office to schedule a date.

Contact: Keith Vaughn
Director of Admissions
213-740-7846
Application deadlines: December 4; January 8; February 5; April 2

MARSHALL MBAs SOUND OFF

My professors were very generous with their time outside of class. Anytime I had a question or concern, I was able to make a personal appointment and talk with the professor directly.

Some people blow $75,000 on a BMW, and in a few years the car is in the junkyard. In contrast, I feel like I made a $75,000 investment that will last a lifetime.

My husband went to Kellogg, right before I started Marshall. As a first-year at Marshall, I found myself constantly comparing things to how they did them at Kellogg. Several weeks into my program at Marshall, I found myself really impressed with the resources and instruction. Overall, the program far surpassed my expectations, and I think I truly got more out of my MBA program than my husband did. Perhaps the social aspect of Kellogg was better, but for me and for how I prefer things—smaller program, more potential for networking with corporations—Marshall was, in many ways, quite perfect.

I truly believe that USC is one underrated, underappreciated school. As with any other program, it has some growing pains, but overall, I found that both the curriculum and the student body stood up to any of the other schools in the Top 30. A school chum from undergrad entered another MBA program at the same time as I did, and we found that we were taking the same courses, reading the same cases, and learning the same concepts. Now that we've graduated, we're making the same salary.

My biggest gripe with the program is that I often felt like there were many, to be blunt, dummies in the program. Over and over again I was floored by some of the crap peo-

ple turned in to me when I was assembling group papers. I was floored by how some people have no motivation to learn on their own: they always rely on the smart classmates to take them through any assignment before individually attempting it.

There are many excellent things about the USC Marshall MBA program. I thought I might be at a disadvantage in getting a job since I did not get into a higher-ranked program, but I was able to accomplish everything I wanted, including getting the ideal job for me.

25.
PURDUE
UNIVERSITY

PURDUE UNIVERSITY

Krannert Graduate School of Management
1310 Krannert Building
West Lafayette, Indiana 47907-1310
E-mail address: krannert ms@mgmt.purdue.edu
Web site address: www.mgmt.purdue.edu

Corporate ranking: 19	Graduate ranking: 28
Enrollment: 320	Annual tuition & fees:
Women: 21%	resident—$8972
Non-U.S.: 41%	nonresident—$17,892
Minority: 9%	Room and board: $6658
Part-time: NA	Average GMAT score: 644
Average age: 28	Average years work exp.: 5
Applicants accepted: 23%	Accepted applicants enrolled: 48%
Median starting pay: $101,500	Intellectual capital: 17

Teaching methods: Lecture, 25%   Case study, 50%
                         Experiential learning, 25%

Contact:

Ward D. Snearly
Director of Admissions
765-494-4365
Application deadlines:
Domestic:
November 1
January 1
May 1
International:
February 1

Resting on the soil of the Midwest's farm belt, Purdue University's Krannert Graduate School of Management has consistently churned out grads with down-to-earth values like hard work, self-reliance, and community service. That's much to the continuous delight of recruiters, who shower these MBAs with numerous job offers. The Top 30 B-school has been known to some as "*The* manufacturing school," a concept that incurs both pride and, at times, a certain disdain from students and the administration looking to diversify the program. Its traditional operations management emphasis and a natural foundation in quantitative methods and analytical techniques are a direct reflection of the larger university in many ways. So it follows that Krannert has long attracted a large contingent of Midwesterners and technical types, many with undergraduate degrees in engineering, technology, or science (about 46 percent of this year's class).

But, at this institution in the heartland of America, international students are currently on the rise; nearly half of the program's '02 students, in fact, claim non-U.S. citizenship. Industries like consulting and finance are gaining steam here, too, and the school has finally begun to stretch beyond its hard-skills roots to some of the more modern, "sexier" arenas, like e-business and high-tech management. Lest you forget where you are, however, just consider the Boilermakers—the university's aptly named sports teams. You might also note that the B-school itself is named not for a Wall Street hotshot, but for the founder of a shipping container manufacturer. Even Krannert's tuition smacks of

Midwestern modesty. Last year's out-of-state students paid just under $18,000, making the B-school one of the best values among the Top 30.

The intensifying dichotomy between a solid "meat-and-potatoes" academic menu and the interest in some of the newer, somewhat racier subjects is moderated by the school's recent addition to the administration: new dean Richard A. Cosier. A professor of management, Cosier took over the reins in August 1999 from Dean Dennis Weidenaar, who had held the position since 1990. Cosier's Midwest background includes stints at the University of Oklahoma, Indiana University, and the University of Notre Dame, and graduation from the University of Iowa, where he received his Ph.D. Experience as a planning engineer with The Western Electric Company gives the dean an operations edge, but despite this particular track, Cosier has also established himself as a force behind Krannert's emerging high-tech focus and global initiatives. With support from administrators and faculty, he's been working toward a broader, more integrated education where "you learn in the classroom, outside of class, working with your peers, and understanding and applying concepts." Even the Krannert degree itself can't escape the changing tides; the faculty has approved plans to change the M.S. in Management to the more widely used MBA, and, with approval from the University and the Indiana Higher Education Commission, the change will take place. That should help in the job hunt, making Krannert grads' degree the same as that of grads at other schools.

All Krannert students earn their degree in one of three areas combining the scientific facets of management, like facts and formulas, with more procedural skills (i.e., teamwork and leadership). Although there is some overlap in required courses among the three master's programs, the big difference is that students getting a degree in management (the most popular, drawing about three-fourths of every class) can select nine elective courses during their two years. Students in the human resources sequence choose only six, and those earning the industrial administration degree take just seven during their accelerated study period of 11 months. While students have criticized the teaching quality in Krannert's elective courses, the school has made a concerted effort to bolster its offerings. The slim roster of 65 courses offered in 1998 now contains nearly 80. Students are not required to specialize in an "option"—the equivalent of a major—but most do, selecting from accounting, finance, human resources management, management information systems, marketing, operations, or strategy. A set of three additional, interdisciplinary options—general management, international management, and manufacturing and technology management—has since become four, with the introduction of a new e-business option to rival finance and operations as the most in demand.

There's also room for self-directed entrepreneurs; Krannert students can work with doctoral candidates in the university's engineering school to establish marketing plans for new high-tech products, as well as with small businesses in a Purdue-owned research park near campus. A new Technology Transfer Initiative recently received a $2.49 million grant from the National Science Foundation to establish an Integrative Graduate Education and Research Traineeship, with 30 NSF-funded Ph.D. students and 30 Purdue-funded Master of Science students from Krannert. With faculty from both ends, they'll produce collaborative technical and market research. Interdisciplinary teams also compete in the Burton D. Morgan Entrepreneurship Competition, which is open to the entire university.

On the international end, despite the large number of students hailing from various countries, Krannert had long existed without a foreign exchange program of any kind. The school's first is actually even more than an exchange program; Krannert is a partner with the GISMA (German International Graduate School of Management and Administration) Foundation, a consortium of European businesses and German government officials. Through the GISMA in Hannover, Germany, Krannert offers its one-year MSIA program and its Executive MS program, with courses taught by Krannert faculty and students earning a Purdue degree. The program graduated its premiere set of students in July 2000, and approximately 25 Krannert students and 25 GISMA students are expected to participate during the 2001–2002 school year. In the meantime, Krannert is exploring the possibility of a new exchange program with an institution in France as well as other opportunities for additional exchange relationships. Many of the students coming to West Lafayette from abroad are drawn to Krannert's reputation as a strong "quant" program, and word spreads quickly from satisfied grads throughout their homelands, mobilizing a new batch of international applicants for the following years. The significant number of faculty members from the larger university who are also non-U.S. citizens enhances the diverse community.

Krannert has also begun to emphasize the sheer size of its staff, which has grown, in large part, as a result of the new GISMA partnership. In 2000, the number of full-time professors increased from 75 to 96, and the number of adjuncts tripled. Students had already given the school high marks for the availability of faculty for discussion outside of class. But perhaps this new, higher count of professors will alleviate some of the ongoing criticisms, like poor teaching in core and elective courses. Students also cite a lack of prominent academics in the classroom, the inability of teachers to remain at the leading edge of knowledge in their fields, and the tendency for some professors to compromise their teaching to pursue their own research.

The school's career services office has pulled its own weight, helping to bring in a substantial number of job offers for grads (averaging 3.5 in 2000) and catering to recruiters, who they say are apt to find Krannert students tech-savvy, dependable, teamwork-oriented, and boasting a strong work ethic. But this office, too, has seen its staff grow; in addition to administrators who run the on-campus recruiting process, a new assistant director now handles market intelligence and development, such as making contacts with companies that hadn't recruited on campus before. An associate director specifically advises international students and coordinates career-outreach efforts with Krannert's sister program in Germany. The student body has historically settled en masse in the Midwest, but today's numbers amount to just 39 percent, establishing a greater geographic distribution with Krannert students landing along both coasts, throughout other parts of the country, and abroad. Although there has been more of a focus here on start-ups than in the past, in line with what B-school students everywhere have been experiencing, Krannert grads tend to stick with the more established companies for employment. Of the '00 grads, 30 percent went into finance or accounting, 31 percent took a job in operations or production, and 16 percent went with consulting. Students have recently considered the school's help in connecting with smaller, non-traditional companies almost nonexistent—perhaps a result of the level of student interest as determined by the career services staff.

Krannert students are increasingly better able to understand their value in the marketplace, thanks to an improved educational process covering career-building skills. Seminars on such topics as the comprehensive job search process and salary negotiations take place regularly, and outside speakers often lead workshops in résumé writing and other preparatory practices. A series targeted to international students includes insight on the hiring practices of U.S. firms and processes for securing proper visas and work permission. Krannert students can post their résumés online and search through electronic listings to reach beyond the school's recruiters—an estimated 1.1 for every second-year student seeking a job.

All that is just scratching the surface of Krannert's technology components and modern facilities. The school recently instituted new broadband high-speed wireless technology as well as wireless networking in the Krannert Building, giving students quicker and easier access to online information. Currently on campus are seven computer labs with some 170 individual workstations, including the Enterprise Integration Laboratory, opened in 1997 with the support of Hewlett-Packard and SAP America. Here, students can test out the firms' newest management software. Recently the school's Webmaster has made it easier for recruiters to search the stack of résumés online, by function, location, or other means. Classrooms are equipped with videoconferencing equipment. And, with the school's newest addition to the facilities, the $55 million Rawls Hall (to debut in the fall of 2003), Krannert can maintain its commitment to offering updated resources. In addition to state-of-the-art classrooms, the new building will boast research centers, faculty offices, career services, and distance-learning rooms for the school's executive MBA program—not to mention student breakout rooms, like the one '99 grads supported through their class gift, to foster teamwork and social interaction.

Not that they need the encouragement: Krannert students are already a close-knit, outgoing, and fairly active bunch. (It's a good thing, because social options in the greater Lafayette area are not exactly unlimited, and the Krannert workload doesn't leave a whole lot of time for road trips to Indianapolis, an hour away, or Chicago, a two-and-a-half-hour drive.) From a coffee-and-doughnut break that unites classmates and faculty each morning to boundless other events and activities, there's no shortage of interaction here. The Krannert Graduate Stu-dents Association, the student government and umbrella for clubs and organizations, has control of more than $15,000 a year to spend on social events, speakers, alumni contacts, and placement activities. Happy hours, movie nights, group seating at Big 10 football and basketball games, banquets—you'll find almost every student there, even the married folks with children, since the KGSA provides free babysitting during all social and volunteer activities. Potential employers have even gotten in on the fun, sponsoring tailgate parties at home football games, orientation events, and other crowd-gathering to-dos.

A big part of the social scene here revolves around community service projects. The school runs the national MBA Make a Difference Day Award competition, in which about 80 graduate management programs from across the country compete in charity fund-raising events. (Krannert won first place during its first three years of operation, 1996 to 1998.) Recent community outreach projects of Krannert students include clothing and food drives for a local homeless shelter; cleaning up a stretch of state highway; working with Habitat for Humanity; consulting with local nonprofit organizations; coaching local high school students on interviewing and job search skills; and conducting a charity ball and auction to benefit local organizations like the Kidney Foundation, which received funds from the 2000 ball in honor of a beloved faculty member who had passed away during the school year. Other activities are more career-related, including the Preparing Leaders and Stewards program, in which students commit to 20 hours of leadership skills practice through additional coursework, self-assessment exercises, and self-directed team consulting with local companies. At the same time, a number of master's students defray their already scaled-down tuition costs even further by taking on graduate assistantships or serving as residential advisers to the vast mass of 30,000 Purdue undergraduates.

West Lafayette may be far from the lights of Broadway or the beaches of California, but there's something to be said for the unpretentious, down-home culture of this small, conservative university town; even hard-core city dwellers have found a certain comfort in it for their two-year B-school gig. West Lafayette is the kind of place where you can walk down the street and strangers will say hello and talk about the weather. What the town lacks in excitement it makes up in safety, quality of living, and scenery—it's quaintly situated around a Neoclassical courthouse just across the Wabash River from sister city Lafayette. The B-school is a block away from the Chauncey Village Mall, where grads sometimes meet at the Wabash Yacht Club for drinks or get a cone at Ben & Jerry's. Another favorite spot on campus: Harry's Chocolate Shop, not a candy store but an old, weathered bar with scribbles on the walls, where students migrate after exams. There's a nationally accredited art museum here, as well as a civic orchestra and theater. Every spring, an art fair draws hundreds of exhibits to the sidewalks next to the courthouse, and every summer, bluegrass and mountain musicians gravitate to the city for the Indiana Fiddler's Gathering.

You can easily spot the seven-story Krannert Building on the southeast edge of the university's 1565-acre campus. In a sea of red-brick buildings, it is a massive block of white concrete with narrow strip windows running up and down the sides. It's connected by underground passageways to the Purdue Memorial Union and Stewart Center, which contains TV rooms, bowling lanes, a billiard room, an amusement arcade, a 200-room hotel, two theaters, an auditorium, an art gallery, and student services like automatic teller machines and a newsstand. Although a number of students live on campus in Hawkins Graduate House or one of the university-owned apartments for married couples and families, others find independently owned one-bedroom apartments for as little as $450 within a half-mile of campus (further away, you might find housing within the $375–$400 range, depending on the amenities). Inside Krannert, computer equipment fills the top floor, while the ground floor is home to a French Provincial drawing room that serves as a student lounge soon to be replaced by a newer version, donated by the Class of 1999, in the new Rawls Hall once 2003 rolls around. It's just one more sign of the changing facets of a school simultaneously grounded in tradition and exploring contemporary ways.

PLACEMENT DETAILS

For the most part, Krannert students—many of whom are geared toward technical positions in some of the more established, traditional companies—aren't lacking in the employment department. Class of 2000 grads landed an average of 3.5 job offers, and students appreciate the placement office's enhanced staff, including a new assistant director in charge of making new corporate contacts and an associate director who handles the international end. Compensation took a leap from an $86,500 median starting pay package for '98 grads to $101,500 among the Class of 2000, inching the school closer to peer programs like No. 24 USC ($112,500) and No. 21 Rochester ($110,000), but still on the lower end of the Top 30. The numbers do coincide with a school that sees about 39 percent of its grads settle in the Midwest, where living expenses don't venture anywhere near those of either coast. But more and more Krannert students are staking out positions in higher-paying regions of the country like the Northeast and West Coast, and the administration is looking for pay packages to reflect the trend.

Top employers in 2000 included mainly biggies: Intel (7); Ford (7); IBM (7); Hewlett-Packard (6); Merrill Lynch (5); Owens-Corning (4); PricewaterhouseCoopers (3); Accenture (3);

Thomson Consumer Electronics (3); and TRW (3). Smaller, less traditional firms were hard to come by, according to students, but administrators say that just reflects a lack of interest. The placement office has concentrated more on providing students with job-hunting skills they can use for their own independent searches throughout their entire careers. Much of that training takes place during Forum Days and is augmented by student-initiated activities such as alumni mentoring matchups and an annual Career Assessment Conference, in which professionals in various business functions are invited to campus to share information and advice with students.

OUTSTANDING FACULTY

Jerry Lynch (economics); *Diane Denis* (finance); *John McConnell* (finance); *Charlene Sullivan* (finance); *Mark Kalwani* (marketing); *Ananth Iyer* (operations).

APPLICANT TIPS

Krannert's quant-heavy program places a natural emphasis on undergraduate grades, work experience, and GMAT scores, which averaged about 644 among the Class of 2002 entrants. You might want to schedule an interview if you feel you can't express yourself enough in the essay portion of the application, which consists of little more than 1000 words addressing your education and career goals, your qualifications that could benefit Krannert classmates, and a character-building situation you've encountered. All applicants with less than one year of full-time, post-baccalaureate work experience are automatically interviewed, and the admissions staff likes to meet with others if more information is needed than what was supplied in the application. For everyone else it's optional. To schedule one, you may call the

office, but only after Krannert has received your entire application package. You may also request a campus tour, or get a virtual one through the Krannert Web site, where you can also apply online.

Contact: Ward D. Snearly
Director of Admissions
765-494-4365
Application deadlines: Domestic: November 1, January 1, May 1; International: February 1

KRANNERT MBAs SOUND OFF

Attending the Krannert School of Management is far and away the best decision I have ever made, and has opened doors for me that I never thought possible. Krannert has been exceptionally responsive to students' concerns and holding an eye toward continuous improvement.

Purdue was an excellent experience and well worth the tuition cost and loss of salary—extremely high value. The Lafayette area offers very few distractions from academic life, although it's situated nicely between Indianapolis and Chicago for a short getaway.

I came to Purdue because I wanted to change careers and increase my marketability at a relatively low cost. The result is a job with a leader in IT products and consulting at twice my pre-MBA pay. Along the way I learned much and met some lifelong friends. Given the opportunity, I would again make the choice to attend Purdue.

My experience at Krannert far exceeded my expectations. The people (students and professors) I met were more helpful, intelligent, and dynamic than I anticipated. The classroom discussions were managed well and enabled learning from both the professor and other classmates in good balance. The administration was responsive and attentive, from implementing new and better interview and class registration to supporting the first Krannert Follies.

Without question, my experience at Krannert was well worth the time, energy, and cost. This school has given me opportunities I never would have had had I not come to this school. The professors are always willing to work with you to give you the edge you need to succeed. In many cases, they not only act as professors but become friends and mentors, which is far more valuable in my opinion. I have no regrets about coming to Krannert. In fact, I view it as one of the best decisions I ever made.

Krannert has surpassed all of my expectations about business school. I came from a business background, so I initially viewed the MBA as just a ticket to advancement. However, the depth and breadth of topics that I have been exposed to over the last two years is outstanding. Plus, with the school's comparatively low tuition and an assistantship, the overall cost is very low. I have met lifelong friends here, as well as excellent professional contacts, and am extremely grateful to the program.

My experience at Krannert was more than worth the opportunity cost. Coming from the military, I would have had to take a pay cut if I had gone straight into the job market instead of getting my MBA. My long-term prospects are even better with the Krannert MBA.

26.
GEORGETOWN UNIVERSITY

Contact:
Robert F. Wheeler III
Assistant Dean of
Admissions
202-687-4200
Application deadlines:
February 1
April 15

GEORGETOWN UNIVERSITY

The Robert Emmett McDonough School of Business
Washington, D.C. 20057
E-mail address: mba@gunet.georgetown.edu
Web site address: http://www.gsb.georgetown.edu

Corporate ranking: 21	Graduate ranking: 27
Enrollment: 520	Annual tuition & fees: $26,720
Women: 36%	Room and board: $9126
Non-U.S.: 38%	Average GMAT score: 657
Minority: 8%	Average years of work exp.: 4.8
Part-time: 0	Accepted applicants enrolled: 44%
Average age: 28	Intellectual capital: 26
Applicants accepted: 19%	
Median starting pay: $116,000	

Teaching methods: Lecture, 47%   Case study, 48%
Simulations, 5%

In 2001, Georgetown University's Robert Emmett McDonough School of Business turns 20 years old. And like the turbulent life of any young adult, Georgetown is going through some changes, stretching its wings in a quest for a new level of status and maturity. In 1998 alone, the B-school got a new name, a new dean, and a complete curriculum overhaul; extensively renovated its current building; began planning construction of a new one; expanded career services; and launched a computer-based alumni network. Georgetown reaped the benefits of these efforts and climbed out of the second tier in BUSINESSWEEK's 2000 rankings.

Add these developments to the school's previously established strengths in international and government business, the halo effect of being part of an excellent university, a powerful emphasis on ethics supported by the university's Jesuit tradition, and an unbeatable location amid the hustle and bustle of the nation's capital and—if you don't mind putting up with some growing pains—you've got a B-school well worth consideration. "It's one of the most undervalued brand names in the MBA business," says Lawrence S. Abeln, associate dean and director of MBA Programs. Abeln came to Georgetown in July 1999 after five years at MIT's Sloan School. Georgetown's potential also was enough to lure Dean Christopher Puto away from a nine-year stint at the similarly up-and-coming Eller School at the University of Arizona, where he served as the director of the MBA program before taking the top job at Georgetown in July 1998. "We really do practice the philosophy of continuous improvement," Puto says.

International business is the heart and soul of Georgetown's B-school, a tradition that's been around since the school's inception in 1981. It's a focus you might expect from a university whose Public Policy Institute and School of Foreign Service have long been considered among the finest of their kind in the world. The new MBA curriculum for which students lobbied heavily and which went into effect in the 1998–1999 academic year, aims to further enhance the program's already strong global perspective while injecting large doses of both hands-on experience and technology training.

As of fall 1998, first year is divided into four 6-week modules consisting of four or five functional core courses, encompassing a traditional lineup of accounting, quantitative methods, organizational behavior, marketing, finance, strategy, communication, public policy, and ethics. These modules are interspersed with integrative experiences, or IEs, one-week team-based projects intended to bring together what you've learned in the different areas. IE1 kicks off year one in late August with a live case in which faculty and executives from an international company present students with a current problem or opportunity. The first subject was AES, a global energy company located in Arlington, Virginia. IE2, which follows the first six-week module in October, emphasizes database decision making and provides instruction in quantitative methods, while IE3, which follows the third module, has students working in teams to analyze one or more international industries. In addition, two so-called "thread courses," one in international business and another in technology and knowledge management, meet weekly during parts of the year to weave even more global and IT content into the various disciplines.

The second year starts with a fourth required integrative experience, Virtual Commerce, which examines the ways information and communication technologies affect business functions and operations. In addition, students must take a required course introducing them to advanced decision support models and systems in a functional area of their choice. Also required of all MBAs is a weeklong on-site team project outside of the United States, supported by 12 weeks of classroom work in the Global Experience thread course during the last semester. So far, students have traveled to Hong Kong, London, Buenos Aires, New Dehli, Sao Paulo, and Prague. Finally, a culminating IE called Making a Difference sums up the themes and values of the entire two-year program.

Although the B-school doesn't have formal majors, students can follow school-designed "career tracks" in finance for those headed for investment banking or corporate finance, in marketing for those aiming to work for consumer products companies, or in strategy for consultant wannabes. The new curriculum leaves room for 20 electives, 3 in the first year before your summer internship and the rest in year two. Students can choose from the small menu of 45 electives available through the B-school or from the catalogs of other Georgetown schools and departments offering coursework in international affairs, government, or public policy and law. You can apply to pursue the highly competitive honors certificate in an area of study by passing a foreign language proficiency test and devoting 18 of your elective credits toward classes in the economy, history, language, culture, and governments of the Arab/Middle East, German and European, Latin American, or Eurasian, East European, and Russian areas. For those who aren't yet fluent in another language but would like to add that to their résumés, the MBA Language Learning Program offers intensive classes in French or Spanish during the month of August and the January mid-year break, plus continued instruction during the fall and spring semesters. The program will run you an extra $2500 on top of a hefty B-school tuition topping $26,000 a year. And then there are full dual degrees available in law, public policy, foreign service, and medicine, all four nationally recognized schools of the larger university.

Georgetown's location in the nation's capital obviously provides MBAs with a window on the relationship between business and government, and the B-school capitalizes on that proximity with a vengeance. Its 63 full-time faculty members are supplemented by more than three dozen adjunct and visiting professors who spend most of their days working at places like the U.S. Treasury, the Federal Reserve Board, the Small Business Administration, and the U.S. Senate Banking Committee. Indeed, the D.C. location helps students develop a relationship with government. But it's not just politicos and Beltway insiders; don't write off Georgetown's *business* network just yet. "An often overlooked and integral part of the experience at Georgetown is its strong relationship with the local business community of the Washington, D.C. metro area," says 2000 graduate Tedd Cittadine. "D.C. is the nation's second largest technology area in terms of total tech employment and the nation's largest telecom region. The area is also a leader in optical networking, biotech, and Internet infrastructure firms."

Being situated in Washington, as well as being part of the Georgetown franchise, helps the B-school draw a diverse student body, with a third of the students coming from some three dozen countries outside the United States. Still a relatively small program despite an enrollment expansion during the last couple of years to about 260 per class, Georgetown MBAs tend to be an outgoing bunch who take an active role in the running of the school. It was largely students who first prodded former Dean Parker, then interim dean Kasra Ferdows, into initiating the curriculum revamp. And part of a $245,000 gift from the Class of '98 went toward development of a database on the Web to connect with the school's small but growing alumni network, which now numbers about 2660.

The B-school is in the middle of a $100 million capital campaign, part of which will go toward building a new headquarters. Puto hopes to raise $150 million in a fund-raising campaign scheduled to end in 2003. The effort began in 1998 and, as of 2000, the school is about halfway there. Puto says $90 million in campaign money will go toward hiring additional faculty and maintaining program support. The other $60 million will help finance the new building, which is expected to open in four years.

In the meantime, MBAs are housing their program in the Car Barn, a site made famous for the stairs that appeared in the movie *The Exorcist*. The interim, state-of-the-art facility was renovated a year ago and will be turned over to Georgetown University when the graduate business program finds a permanent home in about four years. The Car Barn is more sufficient than most temporary facilities. Four case-style classrooms, each with tiered seating for 65 students, Ethernet connections at every terminal, and overhead digital projectors are among the highlights. A laboratory and student lounge are also available for Georgetown MBAs as they wait for the new building to be completed.

The Car Barn also features long-distance videoconferencing, an example of how Georgetown is trying to enhance technology on campus. Back in 1998, students gave the school dramatically low marks for being technologically backward. The administrators are slowly climbing out of the dark ages. In the last three years, the McDonough School spent $3.6 million on improving technology. Distance learning is becoming part of executive education options. In addition, full-time MBAs are using Blackboard, an online service that permits classmates and professors to chat with each other and to obtain and turn in assignments. The system gives students greater access to faculty and allows faculty to maintain longer office hours from home. Puto says he's well aware that technology will permeate business education. In an effort to get students up to speed, he's hiring four new IT faculty. Realizing that technology is also a career aspiration of many students, Puto's administration created Cyber Café, an intimate gathering at which a guest from the local technology sector stops by campus to chat with MBAs.

The section of Washington from which Georgetown University takes its name is itself a wonderful, albeit expensive, playground for young adults. Since there's no graduate housing on campus, most MBAs share townhouses in the cosmopolitan neighborhood filled with trendy bars, foreign restaurants, and tiny boutiques. There are cocktail parties in the MBA lounge at the Car Barn, and groups of students often head to The Tombs for thick, crusty pizza and beer after an exam. The MBA crew, of course, frequented legendary hangouts like Garrett's and The Guards. The Class of 2000 held formals at the Kennedy Center, went downtown to places like 1223, 18th Street Lounge, and Xando DuPont. Venturing to the hip Adams Morgan neighborhood and trekking to the White House or the monuments are commonplace occurrences for Georgetown MBAs. Clearly, there's no shortage of things to do in D.C., which is why students tend not to hang around much after class.

PLACEMENT DETAILS

Georgetown's career services office has worked hard in the past couple of years to expand the school's corporate recruiting pool and has seen some progress. In 2000, 60 organizations recruited second-year students on campus, down from 65 in 1998. A total of 767 interviews were conducted, and an additional 550 jobs were posted electronically. Those numbers are still a fraction of the mammoth recruitment machines you'll find at most Top 30 schools, and students say they'd like to see more variety and better quality in companies that visit campus. Nevertheless, they can't complain about

their prospects too much: In 2000, the median starting pay package of $116,000 fell in the middle of the Top 30 and was especially high for the schools rounding out the bottom of the list. And while 16 percent of the Class of '96 had no job offers at the time of graduation, just 4 percent of the Class of 2000 found themselves in that position.

With a keen global perspective, the McDonough School strives for diversity when choosing a student body. The administration holds a special orientation for international students designed to acquaint them with U.S. customs in addition to the usual pre-MBA preparation. Through sponsorship from companies such as Levi Strauss, Texaco, Toyota, and Chase Manhattan, the McDonough School has raised $500,000 for minority student fellowships. Every year, a team from Georgetown heads to the National Black MBA Association case competition with Puto serving as coach. The school has also focused on attracting women. Recently, McDonough hosted the Graduate Women in Business national conference, which brought 500 women MBAs to campus for a few days. Puto calls the school "women friendly" and expects to see rising numbers in the future.

In keeping with the school's global slant, the placement office individualizes job search assistance to find international positions for U.S. graduates as well as for foreign students who want to return to their home countries, other locations overseas, or here in the United States. Among the top employers of Georgetown grads in 2000 were America Online (8); Enron (8); KPMG (7); Chase (7); Pricewaterhouse-Coopers (7); Procter & Gamble (6); Citigroup (5); Deloitte & Touche (5); American Management Systems (4); Arthur Andersen (4).

OUTSTANDING FACULTY

Bardia Kamrad (decision science); *Reena Aggarwal* (finance); *Gary Blemaster* (finance); *Alan*

Eberhart (finance); *Ken Homa* (marketing); *Kasra Ferdows* (operations); *Paul Almeida* (strategy).

APPLICANT TIPS

In addition to academic background, the school places a lot of emphasis on work experience and essay answers. Just 1 percent of the Class of 2002 had worked full-time less than one year; the average experience was five years. Considering the fact that 87 percent of the Class of 2000 was proficient in a second language, and 65 percent lived or studied abroad before entering B-school, you'd be wise to play up any global experiences you've had and how you plan to take advantage of Georgetown's international emphasis in your career.

During the past couple of years, the admissions office has begun conducting evaluative instead of informational interviews; about 25 percent of the admitted applicants in 2002 interviewed with Georgetown. Face-to-face interviews can be scheduled only after your application is submitted in total. Although the final deadline is April 15, the school encourages applicants to get their materials in as soon as possible; the deadline for international students and those applying for financial aid is February 1.

According to admissions materials, Georgetown maintains no minimum GMAT or GPA when accepting students. But make no mistake—the school isn't giving admissions away either. The average GMAT score for the Class of 2002 was 692. As for GPA, admissions officials weigh the numbers based on the institution from which the grades were received. In other words, higher GPAs from the Ivy Leagues have a better shot than those from community schools.

Contact: Robert F. Wheeler III
Assistant Dean of Admissions
202-687-4200
Application deadlines: February 1; April 15

McDONOUGH MBAs SOUND OFF

I was extremely satisfied by my experience at Georgetown. There was a level of cooperation among students in the program that does not exist elsewhere (at least in my discussions with other MBAs from different programs). Additionally, the new curriculum was top-notch. The integrated approach used by Georgetown really gets the faculty to talk about ways to approach teaching in a much more coordinated manner. I give Georgetown my highest recommendation for students looking for a program that will challenge you—yet at the same time support you.

I am starting a company after graduation. By choosing Georgetown, I placed myself in the center of the Washington, D.C. high-tech community, one of the leading centers for technology and entrepreneurship in the country. Other schools to which I applied (and was accepted) would have limited me by their lack of proximity and connections to successful high-tech businesses. These schools may have been ranked better in academic surveys and had more notable professors, but Georgetown gave me the opportunity to succeed in entrepreneurship. Therefore, Georgetown was an excellent experience for my two years as an MBA student.

Although I gave the program a superior rating in "diversity," the program offers just one kind of diversity: international. Gays and people of color are not well represented, in my opinion. In fact, I think the administration does not seek to recruit or support gay people in the program. We seem to have just one gay person in each class of 250 and seem to barely have enough black students for the Black MBA Association. Other than that, I think the program has been excellent. Our global experience was an incredible opportunity. My peers are a compassionate, bright group of people from different business backgrounds including nonprofit work.

Coming to Georgetown MBA was the best career move I could ever have made. I fell in love with the campus and the school as soon as I first set foot on it during the application process. The teamwork and camaraderie among students are unparalleled. Strangers (second-years) literally walked up to me dur-

ing my program to help me prepare for finals. While everyone worked very hard, they seemed to be competing against their own standards—to do and be the best they can—and not against others. The faculty and staff are also visibly dedicated to making this the best MBA program in the world. The school has made tremendous headway since I first came to this school. It is now truly state-of-the-art and is worlds ahead of what I saw two years ago.

27.
UNIVERSITY OF MARYLAND, COLLEGE PARK

UNIVERSITY OF MARYLAND, COLLEGE PARK

Robert H. Smith School of Business
2308 Van Munching Hall
College Park, Maryland 20742-1871
E-mail address: mba_info@rhsmith.umd.edu
Web site address: http://www.rhsmith.umd.edu

Corporate ranking: 28	Graduate ranking: 25
Enrollment: 1100	Annual tuition & fees:
Women: 35%	resident—$11,830
Non-U.S.: 35%	nonresident—$16,888
Minority: 10%	Room and board: $12,650
Part-time: 630	Average GMAT score: 655
Average age: 29	Average years of work exp.: 5.3
Applicants accepted: 23%	Accepted applicants enrolled: 49%
Median starting pay: $105,000	Intellectual capital: 33

Teaching methods: Lecture, 35% Case study, 35%
Group projects, 30%

Contact:
Sabrina White
Director of MBA and
MS Admissions
301-405-2278
Application deadlines:
December 1
February 1
March 15
May 1

Wharton. Kellogg. Tuck. Darden. Smith?

Okay, so maybe Smith isn't among the names that come to mind when you're thinking about top business schools. But the University of Maryland would like to change that. Administrators are making every effort to elevate its B-school: In 1998 the school was renamed the Robert H. Smith School of Business in honor of the real estate developer who donated $15 million to his alma mater. The next step: to turn Smith into one of the handful of household names associated with first-rate management education.

The new moniker is one small step in a larger journey toward establishing a national identity for this up-and-coming school. Another was bringing aboard Howard Frank as dean in 1997. Frank, an information systems expert and entrepreneur, has vowed to distinguish Maryland's B-school by building a strong technological orientation throughout the MBA program. "The world of information technology is revolutionizing business," Frank notes. "I don't want to turn this into an engineering school, but into the nation's leading business school preparing for life in the twenty-first century."

That seemed like a lofty goal for a school just breaking into the upper echelon—1998 marked Maryland's first-ever entry into BUSINESSWEEK's Top 30. But Frank has tackled some pretty grand plans before. Prior to coming to College Park, he oversaw the world's largest information technology budget as director of the IT office at the Defense Advanced Research Projects Agency, the federal entity that played a large part in the development of both the Stealth bomber and the computer mouse. And back in the 1970s, a telecommunications consulting firm he co-founded contracted with the U.S. government to develop "a network that linked computers and human beings, and that allowed computers to interact with one another," Frank remembers. With apologies to Al Gore, that project is now known as the Internet.

Frank says his plans for Smith to become a top-tier school and, with its expansion, one of the largest, aren't overnight efforts, and he's not surprised that the changes he's instituted thus far haven't yet showed up in the rankings. He estimates he's just halfway through "phase one" of his "complete transformation from a very good modern B-school to a leading edge new economy school. We have two to three years to go, but there is just no way of recognizing where we came from," he says. "The school is emerging. It will be one of the greatest. The recognition is coming." True, just three years into Frank's tenure as dean, the info-tech initiative has made its mark in a number of areas on top of what was already a strong and innovative MBA program. Frank says the continued emphases and redesign make sense, despite the fluctuations in the dot-com economy. And prominent tech alumni, like Hewlett-Packard CEO Carly Fiorina, are helping get the word out. "The economy is irrelevant," he says. "This is a fundamental restructuring. We're looking at new ways of reaching markets. There has been no abatement for the demand [for e-business courses] at all."

The school now offers 17 courses in e-commerce as some of its alternatives in studying the new economy and in the last three years added concentrations in supply chain management, entrepreneurship, financial engineering, global business and knowledge, management, business telecommunications, and management of technology in addition to e-commerce. Although a number of the courses listed under these specialties are repackaged versions of previous offerings, a full one-third are brand new to the school's curriculum and look to be popular additions. The first new course in e-commerce filled as soon as it became available, leaving a waiting list of 30 students who were closed out, although in recent semesters the school has made efforts to add more sections to accommodate everyone. The accounting department is mulling a potential concentration in information security for sometime down the road.

Technology isn't the only area that's growing at Smith. Frank hired 13 new faculty members alone in 2000, and posted a net gain of 40 faculty over the last three years. Student enrollment has increased, too, from 925 in 1998 to 1100 in 2000. Frank thinks continued growth in the size of the program is important for meeting his top-tier goals. "A small school with fine faculty is not as prominent as a large school with fine faculty," he says. The Smith gift was a start to help fund this expansion, but the business school also won regents' approval beginning in fall of 1998 to charge market rates for its programs, which Frank says had been significantly undervalued in comparison with the cost of similar schools, both public and private. Better yet, the B-school was allowed to keep the difference between the old and new tuition figures for its own coffers, rather than sharing it with the larger university. Although tuition increased, now $16,888 annually, a Maryland MBA remains one of the best bargains around.

Meanwhile, the state ponied up $6 million and the university another $3 million to enable the school to expand and renovate Van Munching Hall—scheduled to open in mid-2001 to house all B-school student and faculty overflow, as well as research and career centers—without reaching too deeply into its own pockets. In 2002, a second fully wired 103,000-square-foot building will open its doors on campus, making room for Frank's growing classes of MBAs. Unlike many B-schools where undergrads and grad students are never commingled, Van

Munching is home to both, and faculty teach at both levels. Because today's undergrads are so tech-savvy, Frank says they often know things about computers and technology grad students don't, so encouraging exchanges between the two groups has been useful, rather than limiting.

Deeper pockets, a bigger faculty, and a forward-looking technology slant are steps in the right direction, and the school's location doesn't hurt either. The Maryland suburbs just outside of Washington, D.C., are a big draw for many, as are small class sizes, a friendly, team-centered atmosphere, a high level of student involvement in running the school, and a notably diverse student body. (Smith enrolled among the highest proportions of women and international students in the Top 30 in 2000—38 and 37 percent, respectively—but fared less well in attracting minorities, who make up 5 percent of the population.)

Ask Smith graduates what they remember most about the MBA program, and they're likely to mention the Experiential Learning Modules, or ELMs. These are four required one-week mini-courses scattered throughout the two years and designed to expose students to aspects of business that aren't easily taught in a classroom. You'll kick off your first semester at Smith with a Foundations of Business ELM. The Foundations of Business module features a five-day Integrative Simulation Exercise in which you'll be grouped into teams to form a company, and then asked to develop a business plan to secure venture funding. You'll present your plans to a group of venture capitalists. The ISE aims to teach you the value of teams, diversity, and communication in addition to the critical business functions of finance, marketing, human resources, and strategy. MBA core faculty members serve as advisers to each team. In the second semester, everyone heads to nearby Washington for a firsthand look at business-government relations, meeting with congressional staffers, lobbyists, and officials from foreign embassies and regulatory agencies such

as the Federal Reserve and SEC. In the second year, a fall-semester case competition captures campus attention for a week as students teams are put to the test, analyzing complex strategic problems, writing persuasive reports, and honing their presentation skills before a panel of judges who play the role of the company's board of directors. Finally, just before graduation, the class is hauled off to prison. A business ethics module includes a visit with former executives-turned-inmates at Allenwood Federal Prison to discuss the serious consequences of ethical compromises, as well as such topics as environmental issues, product defects, workplace discrimination, whistle-blowing, and "creative" accounting.

In the first year, students complete their entire MBA core coursework, with 45 to 50 students "tracked" to take all their required classes together for the first semester, then reconfigured into new tracks for the second semester. The first half of the year comprises two terms of two-credit courses. A three-credit core course, Data, Models, and Decisions, spans both terms. Fall semester courses include Financial Accounting, Managerial Economics and Public Policy, Business Communications, Leadership and Teamwork, Marketing Management, and Financial Management. In the spring, students take The Global Economic Environment, Managing Human Capital, Managerial Accounting, Strategic Management, Strategic Information Systems, and Supply Chain and Operations Management, plus two electives and the case competition.

In the second year, students focus on their concentrations through chosen electives, plus take a semester-long consulting project that many students say is a highlight of the program. Teams from four to six students, led by a faculty adviser, grapple with real-world work thrown at them by paying client companies. Among them are Sun Microsystems, Proxicom, Hewlett-Packard, Arthur Andersen, Lehman Brothers, and the U.S. Postal Service. The MBA Consulting Program is attracting more clients from the high-tech industry and companies transforming their operations for new economy business practice. MBA projects include development of a desktop management strategy, analyzing current supply chain management processes and identifying e-supply chain improvements, developing an IT infrastructure blueprint, and researching the impact of interactive marketing in business-to-business e-commerce.

Frank is also excited about Smith's participation in testing a new financial trading software with the Reuters news agency. Smith is one of the beta sites for the software, as part of its new Netcentricity Laboratory. The new high-tech teaching, research, and corporate resource facility is devoted exclusively to studying the instantaneous flow of information via the Internet and digital networks. The Laboratory has Sun Microsystems servers, terminals, and software to create a mini-version of the company's Menlo Park supply chain/e-commerce laboratory. The lab is also equipped with applications for real-time supply chain optimization and planning, Oracle's ERP applications, high-speed networks, wireless computing, TIBCO's real-time e-business infrastructure software, a sophisticated multimedia environment, and state-of-the-art flat panel displays and user workstations.

The rest of your time is devoted to electives, selected from among the 66 offered by the B-school. Many students combine two concentrations, usually a traditional, functional discipline such as finance or marketing with a cross-disciplinary area of study, such as e-commerce of information systems. Smith has a strong entrepreneurship program, although entrepreneurship as a concentration is limited to about 25 students a year, all of whom indicated their interest when first applying to the B-school and who are selected on the basis of their entrepreneurial ideas and spirit as well as work experience and previous academic performance. Under the province of the Michael D. Dingman

Center, the program offers students scholarships and the chance to earn stipends, internships, and scholarships by counseling local emerging growth companies, as well as a mentoring network of 200 local attorneys who advise students who are budding start-up artists. (Students from outside the concentration may also sign up to take individual courses in entrepreneurship.) Finance is also a strength here, with a select group of a dozen or so MBAs tapped each year to manage the Terrapin Fund, started in 1993 by three students and an initial $250,000 contribution from the B-school, and now grown to more than $1.2 million.

International offerings at Smith are less limited than they used to be. Students interested in going global may cross-register at the Johns Hopkins University's Nitze School of Advanced International Studies, which provides access to 125 additional courses. Exchange programs are available at eight overseas management schools, in Austria, Denmark, the United Kingdom, France, Italy, Venezuela, Mexico, and Germany through the School's Center for Global Business. Full-time MBAs can do a summer or fall semester second-year exchange. International study trips planned for 2000–2001 include the following courses and destinations: Trade, Technology, and Entrepreneurship in Chile in March and International Technology Policy and Global Internet Economics in Ireland in May.

The school recently signed an agreement with the Asian Technology Information Program (ATIP), a nonprofit organization specializing in Asian science and technology programs, to provide exchange and research opportunities for Smith students and faculty. ATIP is the leading source of English language dissemination of Asian science and technology-related information and analysis, covering Japan, Taiwan, Korea, China, India, Singapore, and Australia, as well as other countries that compromise the Asian region. Back at home, dual degrees are another option, with joint programs available in law, public management, and social work.

All those efforts, though, are for naught if grads feel like they can't find the jobs they want after they finish that coursework. Indeed, the placement center was Smith's Achilles' heel in 2000, with both recruiters and students citing it as the school's weakest link, and one of the worst in the BUSINESSWEEK survey. One 2000 grad sums it up: "Outstanding school and experience. Horrendous Career Placement Center." In the BUSINESSWEEK survey, Smith's placement center ranked near the bottom of the pack in aggressiveness in helping students find summer jobs and internships and middle of the road in connecting students with nontraditional employers and helping them find jobs before graduation. Frank says he's heard the complaints and has done something about them, but the solutions haven't made their way through to a graduating class yet. First up was to elevate the Graduate Career Management Center's (GCMC) leadership position to that of assistant dean. Richard Feldman, who has worked in HR at Johnson & Johnson, Allied Signal, and York, was hired to take the new position. Students still say GCMC drops the ball in a number of ways, not least of which is its inability to attract a large number of high-quality companies for recruiting. Just 84 firms conducted interviews on campus with second-year students in 2000, and 35 for internship jobs. The weak link to the employer community is a big reason Maryland doesn't rate better in BUSINESSWEEK's corporate poll.

In addition to hiring Feldman to aid in placing students, Frank says the new building will have a wing for career services, making the operation higher-tech, with more room for recruiters to interview. Feldman has overhauled the recruiting system, adding two additional career counselors for MBAs and address student concerns that job searches at Smith were "difficult to manage." Feldman is working to improve communication with employers in the Northern Virginia/D.C./Baltimore technology corridor, a community that is growing thanks to the presence of giant America Online. In addition to high-tech, the region is ripe with government jobs, and Frank says a lot of alumni stay in the area as a result. Feldman also plans to launch an MBA mentoring program designed to match incoming students with alumni who have the same career interest.

Frank cites the rapid increase in salaries Smith grads received as evidence that progress is being made. Just a few years ago Smith salaries put the school well below its peers, but today, Smith grads earn salaries similar to grads at peer schools. "I think that the expectations of students change faster than the career center can, but by the end of this year, the perception will catch up with reality," Frank says.

B-school life at Smith centers around Van Munching Hall, a handsome four-story facility built in 1993, with a huge, skylighted roof that floods the cherry-wood interior with sunshine. It's computer labs and comfortable interviewing rooms for recruiters. It's also one of the most attractive buildings on this pretty 1580-acre campus, an incongruously secluded oasis of manicured lawns and trees amidst the suburban sprawl and dizzying network of highways outside Washington. Students are an integral part of the workings of the B-school: The dean breakfasts with 25 MBAs every other week, holds regular town meetings, and includes students on all committees involving curriculum change and facilities planning. A number of student interest clubs connect MBAs with career-focused activities, such as a Visiting Speaker Series; a mentoring program to help incoming students with the transition into the school; a Social Concerns Committee that coordinates charitable efforts such as food drives, literacy programs, home repairs for the needy, and management advice to nonprofit organizations; and a social committee that arranges regular happy hours, tailgate parties when the Terps sports teams are in town, student-faculty picnics, and an annual MBA formal.

Although a small number of apartments for graduate students are available on campus, most students live in surrounding suburban towns that are all well served by metropolitan Washington's extensive bus and subway system. It's also a reasonable commute should you choose to live either in Baltimore or downtown Washington, as both are reachable in under an hour by public transportation.

PLACEMENT DETAILS

Students and recruiters paint a pretty bleak picture of placement services at Smith. While things are actually somewhat better now than they were a few years back, they're not as good as they should be in a strong economy, or as they could be, according to Frank. In 1994, a full 29 percent of graduating students left school without a single job offer. In 1998, every MBA had at least one offer, but in 2000, the number of students who were jobless upon graduation went back up to 13 percent. 2000 grads averaged two job offers each, but even with salaries rising 15 percent, according to Feldman, they weren't the most lucrative offers out there.

While Frank concedes that few Smith grads go to Wall Street—a factor that lowers the school's overall salary figures—some students view that as a plus. Says, one, "I feel empowered after my experience at UMD to explore career paths in a wide range of new industries, and because of this, I believe my investment in an MBA program will yield an attractive return."

Among the employers who often recruit at Smith—Honeywell Inc., Valhalla Capital Management, and America Online—the career center is perceived as being vastly improved in 2000. Some also say analytical skills of students are top-notch, and most agree that the students are well-rounded. Eighty-four firms did recruit second-year students on campus in 2000. Top employers were: Honeywell (4); Deutsche Banc Alex. Brown (4); PricewaterhouseCoopers (4); Marriott International (4); Fannie Mae (4); Johnson & Johnson (4); American Management Systems (3); Goldman Sachs (3); America Online (3); and Barclays (2).

OUTSTANDING FACULTY

Mike Peters (accounting); *Jonathan Palmer* (decision and information technology); *Alex Triantis* (finance); *Meg VanDeWeghe* (finance); *Samir Faraj* (information technology); *Anil Gupta* (management and organization); *Daniel Sheinin* (marketing).

APPLICANT TIPS

Maryland has become a fairly selective school of late, even with its growing class size. Applications for the Class of 2002 hit 1748; only 23 percent of those who applied got in. So you'll need strong GMAT scores and a decent GPA to get in the gate. You'll have an edge if you apply early, by the February deadline at the latest; applications are considered in rounds, and you can expect a reply about eight weeks after each of the first three deadlines, four weeks after the final deadline in April. International candidates should note that they have a different set of dates to consider: Applications from overseas are considered in the November and December rounds, with a final deadline of February. Personal interviews are not required—just one-third of applicants for the Class of 2002 had a face-to-face sit-down—but can help tip the scales in your favor if an admissions decision is in doubt.

Smith prides itself on offering students a wide range of financial aid options, including research assistantships and work-study jobs. If you'd like to be considered for any type of financial aid, you'll have to get your paperwork in by February 1.

Contact: Sabrina White
Director of MBA and MS Admissions
301-405-2278
Application deadlines: December 1; February 1;
March 15; May 1

SMITH MBAs SOUND OFF

The GCMC has had some growing pains. However, they have greatly improved their career counseling team and corporate relations. This can be seen by the types of offers received by my classmates and the increased number of firms recruiting on campus. I see these trends continuing. A number of my colleagues received incredible offers from firms that had not recruited at Smith in the past. Some credit must be given to the GCMC for this. Their weakness lies in the mechanics of the interviewing process and the aggressiveness of the team.

The administration values the opinions of students and incorporates their feedback into all aspects of the program. This has created a greater sense of community and pride.

With a superior faculty and a diverse student body, the University of Maryland has one of the best MBA programs in the country. We continue to be discounted because we do not have the legendary brand names of Duke, Harvard, or Wharton. Fortunately, our momentum is building as applications and salaries increase significantly.

I was pleasantly surprised by the level of cooperation among students at UMD. I cannot think of an instance where students' pursuit of individual goals undercut others' performance, or where it negatively affected class discussions. In fact, I would imagine that the spirit of teamwork at Maryland was greater that most equivalent programs.

As a person moving into the IT field, the Smith School more than met any expectations I may have had. I am very impressed with how information technology, e-business, and e-commerce are woven into almost every single class. I truly feel that the school is churning out the next generation of leaders in the e-business arena.

The Maryland program completely met or exceeded my expectations. I have gotten the job I wanted and had an incredible experience. The academics and camaraderie at the school are above par. I would recommend this program to anyone looking for an MBA with a focus on e-commerce and technology.

The faculty at Smith is very strong, and Dean Howard Frank is extremely responsive to student requests. He is doing everything possible to build the quality and reputation of the school.

28.
EMORY UNIVERSITY

EMORY UNIVERSITY

Goizueta Business School
1300 Clifton Road
Atlanta, Georgia 30322-2710
E-mail address: admissions@bus.emory.edu
Web site address: http://www.bus.emory.edu

Corporate ranking: 34	Graduate ranking: 26
Enrollment: 510	Annual tuition & fees: $26,000
Women: 30%	Room and board: $14,000
Non-U.S.: 33%	Average GMAT score: 650
Minority: 11%	Average years of work exp.: 5
Part-time: 150	Accepted applicants enrolled: 45%
Average age: 27	Intellectual capital: 25
Applicants accepted: 34%	
Median starting pay: $105,000	

Teaching methods: Lecture, 30%   Case study, 50%
                     Group projects, 20%

Contact:
Julie Barefoot
Assistant Dean of
Admissions
404-727-6311
Application deadlines:
November 15
December 15
February 15
March 31

If you ask Kembrel Jones, the student body president of Emory University's Class of 2000 at Goizueta Business School, he'll tell you that the school today bears few similarities to the one he enrolled in two years ago. Indeed, the small program moved into BUSINESSWEEK's Top 30 ranking for the first time, having overhauled both its career placement center and its MBA curriculum. It has opened a fancy new classroom building and is eyeing the same for residences as well as support offices. And all of this followed on the heels of several tumultuous years in which the school said goodbye to its dean of a decade and brought a new top administrator on board; split with one of its most prominent faculty members in a nasty and public dispute; and nearly tripled its endowment.

But Jones isn't a mere alum interested in the ranking of his alma mater and its impact on his résumé. He's emphatic about the changes happening at Goizueta because, well, it's his job. The day after he graduated with an MBA he returned to campus, not to return that last library book or to clean out his student government desk, but to report to work as assistant dean and director of the full-time MBA program. (Jones also is an assistant professor in the practice of marketing.) Jones describes himself as the public face to Dean Thomas S. Robertson's private one. Robertson, previously the deputy principal at London Business School for 4 years and, before that, a 23-year veteran of Wharton and chief architect of its highly successful executive education program, is a consummate fund-raiser. Since he took over in 1998, he's set about adding to the school's coffers—including the original $25 million endowment from the late Roberto C. Goizueta, former CEO of The Coca-Cola Co., and two other $20-something million gifts. Robertson has also used his clout and connections to double the school's faculty.

But it is Jones who is working on the student-side of redesigning Goizueta, with programs from acceptance to graduation designed to make for happy alums. Jones himself says he was "leery" of coming to a B-school. Already armed with two master's degrees from Harvard, he was worried about that every-man-for-himself mentality that seems to stereotype the B-school student. With the goal of eventually holding the title of college president, Jones wanted the MBA so that he could have some finance experience to complement his education background. He chose Goizueta because of its "small, family-like atmosphere" (there were 150 students in his class) and that's one of the qualities he vows not to change as the school gets a fairly complete overhaul. "This is a very supportive community. Students want each other to succeed, because then the school succeeds," he says. "They are the finest human beings."

Recruiters and other alums with less of a vested interest agree. Another 2000 grad says, "In addition to the great learning experience, what I liked was the absence of extreme hyper-competition among students." Others cite times that second-years gave up interview slots to classmates set on working for a particular firm. Recruiters repeatedly describe Goizueta students as "nice": writing thank-you notes, having manners, never accepting offers to later renege, and just plain being decent people. Given the hot economy, it's a welcome relief for oft-snubbed recruiters.

Jones pledges that won't change although much else will as part of the dean's vision—to be a top-tier business school. Says one recent alum: "There is a sense of urgency at GBS to create a top ten business school in Atlanta and the sense around here is that this day is not far off." Jones

and Robertson's first step was one step back, as they called off plans to increase class size to 240 students from 150 a few years ago. After the Class of 2001 came in at an interim 180, the administration re-evaluated, deciding that 175 was the optimum size to keep the community the way it was and also use its new facilities better. This includes the $26.5 million five-story, state-of-the-art facility which opened in 1997, a soaring, columned, light-filled glass-and-concrete structure at the heart of the Emory campus. The building boasts nine case classrooms with comfy swivel chairs and the latest multimedia teaching equipment, a 200-seat auditorium, a student lounge, laptop hookups galore, and a fully loaded fourth-floor computer lab dubbed the Information Center. On the first floor, lining the windows which overlook an open-air courtyard, are high-backed cherry-wood banquettes reminiscent of an English pub that serve as semi-private discussion areas complete with computer ports for up to eight students. The school will soon break ground on a second new building that will house the admissions office, career center, and a conference area.

Despite the plans to slow class growth, the faculty size still doubled, with 26 new faculty over the last two years and plans to hire 12 more in 2001. As a result, Class of 2000 grads ranked the school high in having prominent academics actively involved in teaching in the MBA program, having teachers at the leading edge of knowledge in their fields, and having faculty available for informal discussion when classes were not in session. Young faculty have been lured, in part, Jones believes, by plans to launch a Ph.D. program in the fall of 2002. Jones says younger faculty like the idea of being involved in creating that program. "It will enhance our academic prestige if we do it correctly. It is definitely a risk, but we think it is the right risk because we think it enhances our attractiveness to faculty members," he says.

The team has also overhauled the MBA curriculum and orientation, even though it had been redesigned as recently as 1998. Each of the four 12-week semesters kicks off what's known as Lead Week. The fall program is now more entrepreneurial in focus, with a schoolwide new venture competition. Students are given 48 hours to create a new product, write the business plan, and pitch investors. The spring Lead Week is a study abroad program in China, South America, India, South Africa, or Europe. In 2001, 250 out of 400 students went abroad, while the rest stayed in Atlanta for an intensive two-week course of their choosing.

Fourteen new academic concentrations were created over the last two years, which likely explains why the school ranked near the top of all schools surveyed by BUSINESSWEEK in responsiveness of the faculty and administration to student concerns and opinions. Students also rank the school high in meeting demands for electives. The school has new concentrations in 2000, a mix Jones feels reflects both changes in the economy and student demand. New concentrations include: e-commerce, capital markets, corporate finance, financial analysis, consulting, strategy and analysis, entrepreneurship, innovation and change, marketing consulting, customer relationship marketing, brand management, and global management. Multidisciplinary, cross-functional exploration of how financial, political, environmental, and cultural issues affect the international economy draws an impressive collection of outside speakers. In 2001–2002 former President Jimmy Carter; Warren Buffett; Sam Johnson, CEO of S.C. Johnson; Leonard Lauder, chairman of Estee Lauder; and Steve Forbes were among those who had agreed to offer their experience and viewpoints. Although students surveyed by BUSINESSWEEK rank the quality of teaching electives high, they say that it is lower for core courses. The also say work still needs to be done on faculty integration of coursework from one to the other.

One of Robertson's priorities has been to increase the international component of the MBA experience, not surprising considering his long-standing personal experience as a marketing strategy consultant for companies around the globe. About a third of Goizueta's MBAs come from outside the United States, and the school offers summer and semester study-abroad programs at 31 exchange partner schools in Asia, Eastern and Western Europe, and Latin America. You could also earn an area-studies certificate in Russia and East Europe or Latin America and the Caribbean by taking four electives focused on the region and demonstrating foreign language proficiency (noncredit Emory University language courses are available to B-school students free of charge), or you could spend a fifth semester at one of three business schools in France, Austria, or The Netherlands and earn a dual MBA/international studies degree.

The new yearlong Goizueta Plus program for first-years teaches entrepreneurial leadership and communication skills. "We tried to do something about the overwhelming nature of everything else they have to do," Jones says of the program that is designed to make job searching an organized effort instead of a random activity. The new "bonus" course includes seminars on leading and working in teams and finding your career focus, as well as providing a chance for students to audition their communication skills and receive an evaluation. "It does not matter how smart you are if you cannot communicate your ideas."

Goizueta students are a lively and involved bunch. At any time of the day or night you can find one of the school's 30 groups at the B-school's KO Café (named for Coca-Cola's stock ticker symbol), strategizing and sipping—what else?—cold Cokes. Community coffee breaks are held on Mondays and Wednesday and the dean holds a tea once a month to get feedback from students. To let off steam, students play in the Goizueta Games during orientation, with old-fashioned classics like leapfrog and egg tosses. In the spring, the Follies allows students and faculty to roast one another in a two-hour show sponsored by the school's Jesters Club. Section Feud is a spoof of the Family Feud game show that takes place during finals in December, with questions taken from schoolwide surveys.

A major plus is the school's location in Atlanta, a dynamic community and headquarters to such corporate giants as Coca-Cola, Delta Airlines, and UPS. The university lies within minutes of the laid-back Virginia-Highlands neighborhood, with its casual restaurants and bars; Buckhead, one of the hippest areas of the city, filled with clubs and discos; and Midtown, where you'll find plenty of live music. Most students now live within five miles of campus, but Jones hopes that a new residential graduate building to open on the Emory campus in 2002 will attract many Goizueta students to live on campus and foster a stronger campus feel.

PLACEMENT DETAILS

Four years ago student complaints left Goizueta's placement services near rock-bottom in BUSINESSWEEK's ranking. Today graduates give it higher marks, particularly when it comes to help with independent job searches and connections with nontraditional or smaller recruiters. In August 1999, the school hired Nancy Ortman away from UNC–Chapel Hill's MBA career placement office as its new director of MBA Career Management. Ortman, a former management consultant with Ernst & Young, was brought in to bring higher-profile companies to campus, she says.

Ortman started with a two-day program she likens to "investment banking 101." She brings an associate trainer for a New York firm to campus to cover valuation methods, modeling, and other things first-years might not know but should before they interview for I-bank internships. An annual trip with 40 first-years in tow to New York also helps raise the profile of the school. "New York banks do not like to venture outside of the Northeast," she says. A similar program takes students to the Silicon Valley, Austin, Texas, and Charlotte, N.C. New companies to come to campus in 2001 include Honeywell, Thomson Electronics, Walt Disney, and Accenture.

The next move was a complete restructuring of the career center—increasing the staff by 30 percent—and assigning each staff to 12 to 15 different industries. A separate associate works with international students. That way, when students come in ready to start a sales and marketing job search, they get a counselor who knows what those firms are looking for, what makes one recruiter different from the next, and insider tips from alumni who already work in that industry.

The school now hosts two job fairs—one on traditional MBA jobs and the other on high-tech and e-business. The efforts seem to be a significant start, but it is not an overnight panacea. Seven percent of the Class of 2000 did not have an offer upon graduation. And students still rank the school at the middle of the pack when it comes to the number, diversity, and quality of firms recruiting on campus.

Ortman says recruiters tell her they like Goizueta grads "because our students are willing to roll up their sleeves and do the work. They are not expecting to be CEO right away." Melissa Howard, manager of strategic development for Radiant Systems in Atlanta and herself a '96 Goizueta alum, says Radiant gets so many good hires from the school it has signed on to be a recruiting partner, a new program that gives sponsoring companies priority status for good interview dates and good placement at job fairs. The company is also used in classroom case studies and gives the firm name recognition when students start interviewing.

Radiant is typical, at least in one way, of the majority of Goizueta grad employers: location. Sixty-eight percent of grads stay in the South. One recent grad explains it: "Many students come to Atlanta just to attend Goizueta, but fall in love with the region and often decide to stay in the area after graduation. I think this often hurts the school's recruiting reach in other areas of the country."

Top employers were McKinsey & Co. (6); iXL (5); Gemini Consulting (4); IBM Consulting (4); Bell South (4); IBM (4); Nortel (3); KPMG (3); Coca-Cola (3).

OUTSTANDING FACULTY

Jan Barton (accounting); *Paul Simko* (accounting); *Patrick Noonan* (decision and information analysis); *Shehzad Mian* (finance); *Nicholas Valerio* (finance); *Doug Bowman* (marketing); *Jagdish Sheth* (marketing).

APPLICANT TIPS

Since the school decided to cap the growth on its class size, the percentage of students accepted to the program has dropped slightly from 36 percent to 34 percent. This is due, in part, to what Julie Barefoot, assistant dean of Admissions, calls "significant changes to the application and admissions process."

First among them is that all students have an in-person interview by admissions staff, not alumni, before admittance. The staff travels to four continents to interview prospective international students. Telephone interviews are considered only in the most extreme cases. Barefoot says having her staff conduct interviews lends some consistency to the process, but more important, she says the new policy has changed the tone in the classroom.

"I've been at Emory for 12 years, and I can see a difference in the past two years. Now, before they get a spot in class, we can see a student's passion and leadership and faculty tells us it translates to how engaged they are in the classroom."

The office has worked to admit a higher caliber of student, average GPA eked up from 3.3 to 3.4, and average GMATs rose from 640 to 650. The school is still clear about preferring candidates with significant work experience: Virtually every member of the Class of 2002 has at least two years full-time on the job, with five years the average. There's a greater emphasis on number-crunching and analytical experience than in the past. Barefoot says those who want in at Goizueta should remember that. She reads far too many application essays about things that happened during an applicant's undergraduate education. "It's a real disconnect when someone has been working at Bank of America for five years and they're talking about college. An essay needs to be tied back to their future work," she says.

In the spring of 1999, Jones started a new Goizueta tradition called Welcome Weekend, an event for admitted applicants to meet current students, staff, and faculty for campus tours, social activities, and an introduction to life in Atlanta. The Class of 2001, the first to attend such a weekend, was 180 students and Jones says that is because so many came to campus beforehand and liked what they saw over the weekend.

Contact: Julie Barefoot
Assistant Dean of Admissions
404-727-6311
Application deadlines: November 15; December 15; February 15; March 31

GOIZUETA MBAs SOUND OFF

I truly believe that Emory has a top 10 B-school that is simply not recognized as one. The one thing the school lacks is a large scale, which, although having the advantage of generating a large alumni base, also takes away from a school's intimate setting. For two years

I have watched myself and my peers meet or exceed the performance in interviews and competitions of students from B-schools ranked higher by various sources.

I am pleased with Goizueta's ability to provide a top-quality education/experience that is directed by the student. Whether I wanted hard-core marketing or heavy finance, Goizueta could offer me a fabulous foundation and challenging electives. The partnership between the students, faculty, and staff was a pleasant surprise—and one many outside of the community don't believe. This community allows for a whole new level of learning and improvement—a great benefit of the Goizueta MBA. I chose the school for its upward momentum and am pleased with the "ride" I was given.

Goizueta Business school was a great experience for me and vastly exceeded my MBA expectations. The school has a rare "up and coming" energy throughout that made it a very active and exciting place to be. I saw this attitude nowhere else I considered for an MBA.

For a young, small MBA program, I think the Goizueta School of Business has come a long way and will continue to grow and adjust to the needs of its student body. Goizueta is in a unique position in the Southeast because it is one of the best schools anchored in the area that is able to meet the booming Southern economy's business needs.

I feel that a pillar of the program is its pursuit for excellence and meaning. Business leaders from the old economy like Warren Buffett, Synovus chief Jim Blanchard, and Don Keough, as well as new-economy-savvy execs like Bert Ellis at iXL have placed a premium on working with integrity and meaning, doing what you believe is right. Our beloved professor and friend, former President Jimmy Carter, has shared so much of his vision with us in each of his visits, again imploring students to pursue meaningful endeavors beyond the buck. We also achieve widespread involvement in many charity functions. Events like the Goizueta Gives weekend give students the chance to spend a day working for a charity before the weekend alumni golf tournament which raises money for the annual cause. This year we partnered with Junior Achievement of Georgia to launch JAG (Junior Achievement at Goizueta), a program that sent 10 teams of students into area middle schools and high schools every week to teach international marketing, economics, entrepreneurship, career development skills, and the economics behind staying in school. With each of these efforts, I feel that the program helps keep students and alumni grounded while at the same time seeking new heights.

29.
MICHIGAN STATE UNIVERSITY

MICHIGAN STATE UNIVERSITY

The Eli Broad Graduate School of Management
215 Eppley Center
East Lansing, Michigan 48824-1121
E-mail address: mba@msu.edu
Web site address: http://www.mba.bus.msu.edu

Corporate ranking: 26	Graduate ranking: 29
Enrollment: 246	Annual tuition & fees:
Women: 28%	resident—$11,300
Non-U.S.: 36%	nonresident—$15,300
Minority: 8%	Room and board: $6800
Part-time: N/A	Average GMAT score: 650
Average age: 28	Average years of work exp.: 4.8
Applicants accepted: 26%	Accepted applicants enrolled: 51%
Median starting pay: $93,000	Intellectual capital: 27

Teaching methods: Lecture, 30%   Case study, 35%
Group projects, computer, 35%

Contact:
Randall Dean
Director of MBA
Admissions
517-355-7604
OR 800-4MSU-MBA
Application deadlines:
March 30
June 15 (primary)
December 15
January 31
February 28 (rolling)

The Eli Broad Graduate School of Management at Michigan State University had clearly been on an upswing; after low showings in customer satisfaction areas like teaching quality and computer facilities, the program's most recent dean, James B. Henry, led the school to a complete overhaul of its curriculum. New required courses covered such subjects as ethics, technology, and cross-cultural business practices. Real-world projects came into play, with first-year students working directly with local business execs. A sweeping renovation of the school's facilities boosted the lagging technology amenities and outdated placement office.

The momentum might have pushed the program forward indefinitely, were it not for Dean Henry's resignation in December 2000. The Broad School now finds itself at somewhat of a standstill, with the daunting task of landing a replacement dean at a time when powerhouses like Northwestern University's Kellogg, the University of Chicago's B-school, and the University of Michigan's B-school are also on the prowl for new leadership. "There's definitely some competition," notes Associate Dean John Delaney, who has temporarily assumed Henry's role and says the school hopes to have a new dean in place by the fall of 2001. For now, initiatives like opening a new executive training center, continuing the improvement of the school's technological infrastructure, and creating a trading-room simulation for finance-oriented students are definitely in the works, but the administration could find the goals difficult to accomplish completely until a permanent dean takes over.

Nonetheless, at No. 29 in BUSINESSWEEK's rankings, Michigan State has some strong credentials. Students were so pleased with the Broad School's placement services that they ranked the program second among the 82 B-schools surveyed, in both its efforts to help job-seeking students and its training in such areas as interviewing, negotiating, and developing résumés. Broad MBAs also talk up the school's ability to connect them with nontraditional or smaller recruiters, and to help them secure that all-important summer job. The school gets high marks for placement, in large part because of the popularity of Career Services Director Helen Dashney, who settled into her position in April 1998. "Every school should have someone so friendly, helpful, and well connected," gushes one recent grad. The work of Dashney and her staff was well rewarded in 2000; Broad MBAs accumulated an impressive average of 3.3 job offers each—on-par with schools in the top 10. Biggies like Ford Motor Company, Intel Corporation, and General Motors came to campus to recruit second-years, and each ended up signing students into the double-digits, all from a class of just over 100. But a mere 14 percent of its '00 grads earned more than $100,000, compared with upward of 90 percent at other top schools.

In the curriculum corner, for at least the past 25 years, the school's forte has been supply chain management, an area that combines manufacturing operations, purchasing, transportation, and distribution. Corporate recruiters regularly give high marks to the school's operations department. Also strong is finance, amid a lineup of concentrations that includes business information systems, corporate accounting, hospitality business, human resources management, general management, marketing, and the newest addition—technology marketing—which matches students with industry executives and provides hands-on high-tech experiences for those with their sights set on marketing.

The curriculum, overall, has become more modular in the past two years, and since 1992 the program has followed a semester system, which allows for greater flexibility, since one class can either last the entire semester or be broken up into shorter sections and combined with other shorter classes. Emerging topics, in such areas as entrepreneurship or information technology, can be added more easily, and the faculty can make gentle tweaks and changes continuously—an option they may wish to exercise more regularly, given some students' apparent dissatisfaction with the current teaching quality in elective courses. "The least worthwhile aspect of my MBA education was the classes," notes one disillusioned grad. "Often, they were not structured well, and learning was impeded by 'fluff.'" The school is stepping up its monitoring methods for student satisfaction by establishing new anonymous feedback Web server technology so that Broad MBAs will be able to continually comment on all facets of their courses, and administrators will have a chance to make any necessary changes before it's too late for the same students to experience the results. The scrutiny will extend to critiquing professors, too. "Sometimes there's a mismatch between a faculty member and the MBA students," acknowledges Associate Dean John Delaney, "and this way we can know to put in someone different." In addition to the traditional end-of-semester evaluations, which will continue to hold value, director lunches and a student advisory council consisting of six second-year and six first-year students keep tabs on the program's ebbs and flows. The faculty curriculum committee even encourages student input by calling upon one first-year and one second-year MBA annually to serve and to cast an equal vote on any issues or changes.

The school's team-building practices begin with a weeklong August orientation that has incoming MBAs participating in outdoor team-building exercises at nearby Camp Highlands. They also take in some résumé development advice from the school's placement center before sectioning off into 35- to 40-person cohorts from their larger group of about 110 entering MBAs to tackle their fall semester's required courses. It's no simple feat. The big-picture class is called The Global Organization and the Firm's Strategic Position, and additional courses cover accounting and finance, communications, and ethics and critical thinking. There's also a half-semester class in data analysis followed by another in economics. In the spring, students take a Managing the Workforce class as well as half-semester courses in financial management and cross-cultural business. You're also required to complete a semester-long technology course chosen from a menu of three IT electives.

Early in the first semester, at a dinner at the MSU University Club, your team will meet its corporate adviser, assigned through the Leadership Alliance Program. These execs, from companies like the Big Three carmakers, Ameritech, EDS, and Dow Chemical—many of them alumni of the B-school's executive MBA program—help identify a company issue or problem that will serve as the basis for a team project in the Global Organization course. Students meet regularly with their corporate adviser to apply academic and practical research methods in arriving at analysis. Partly in response to recruiters' concerns regarding Broad students' lack of teamwork skills in the past, last fall the school introduced a new, six-week "lab" exercise that places teams in military situations similar to the ones NATO uses to develop team and leadership skills. Led by Professor John Hollenbeck—the Eli Broad Professor of Management and a psychologist by training—participants indicate their series of decisions by working in multi-person teams responding to a computer simulation. Students are evaluated constantly throughout the simulation based on the conse-

quences of their decisions. The exercises have a value that goes beyond a curriculum consisting solely of lectures and case discussions, according to MBA Program Director Jennifer Chizuk. She explains: "When students see the implications of their decisions, there is a greater understanding of the entire situation."

One final requirement carries over into the fall semester of your second year, when student teams tackle an integrative case study of a current real-world business challenge. The rest of the year is spent sampling some of the program's 55 electives. Students are asked to choose at least one concentration, which requires four courses in a subject area, but many are able to fit in two majors, or to combine one major area of interest with a three-course "subconcentration" in international business or leadership and change management. Global-minded students have the option to partake in a faculty-led international study trip during the brief window between the end of classes and the start of a summer internship. Most recently, the group of 27 students visited Vienna and Budapest to learn about business in both emerging and mature markets. In Budapest, activities included a banking roundtable discussion, visits with representatives from local companies like Audi Hungaria and Gotz Dolls, a boat ride on Lake Balaton, and an evening at the Budapest Opera House. The Vienna part of the trip had students observing a discussion among local executives on Doing Business in Central and Eastern Europe, touring Augarten Porcelain, and indulging in a wine tasting and dinner in the town of Purbach.

MBAs can also extend their international experience by spending a semester in an exchange program with either The International University of Japan in Yamato-Machi, Japan, ITESM-Monterrey in Mexico, The International University in Germany in Bruschal, or The Norwegian School of Management B1 in Sandvika, Norway. The number of Michigan State '02 students who are non-U.S. citizens comes out to 37 percent, an increase from the Class of 2000's 29 percent. Not only that, but the group is considerably more competitive and, as a result, more adaptable to a U.S. program than in the past. "We've been able to select better more recently," says Associate Dean John Delaney. "We have more interviews now, to screen people and examine their communications skills." International topics have become more integrated into the curriculum, too, and the program offers some flexibility for students with more than business, or an extraordinary amount of business, on the mind. Students can complete a combination J.D./MBA degree in four years of full-time study, through Michigan State's Broad School and the Detroit College of Law. There's also a dual-degree program with Thunderbird—The American Graduate School of International Management, which awards graduates with both the Master of International Management from Thunderbird and the Master of Business Administration from Michigan State in four years.

As far as information technology is concerned, the Broad School is just about on track—finally—after first establishing a campuswide computer lab as late as 1991. Not until 1993 was there an MBA-only computer space, which was made possible when the $21.5 million North Business Complex freed up space for renovation in the old Epply Center building. Today, all students are required to bring their own laptops to class, where they can plug in at every seat. A new MBA computer lab opened in Fall 1999, and students can now find state-of-the-art electronic research tools and a substantial selection of team meeting rooms on campus. Students and faculty use MBA Class Link to connect online, converse in chat rooms, and transmit or receive homework help, assignments, and course materials. The school's library also houses laptop outlets at every carrel and table, along with online resources like ABI/Inform, Lexis-Nexis, and Dow Jones Interactive. The new placement center (open to busi-

ness-major undergrads, too) was remodeled from what used to be a business library, and students can also find resources for identifying firms and potential employers there, plus video interviewing capability and interview rooms.

Aside from the latest developments in new facilities, one of the school's biggest assets is its small size. Fewer than 300 students are enrolled, and 50-plus faculty members are on board each year, creating an intimate environment where "cohorts become like a family, and classes naturally develop a sense of camaraderie," according to Associate Dean Delaney. "The program isn't so big that anyone can get lost," he continues, "but with the larger university, students have access to all types of events and resources and still have a chance to get to know the faculty well." The dynamic makes it easier to offer students a degree of attention not found at other peer schools. "From the first day I applied, I was treated as though I was the only applicant to the program," one Broad student remembers. "The program is extremely personal due to its size and the efforts of the administrators and faculty."

The MSU campus boasts 5000 acres of tree-lined grounds and the Red Cedar River, which flows throughout. There are miles of bike paths, rollerblade trails and walkways, and a bus system, plus two golf courses and three intramural athletic facilities. Another entertainment option is the Wharton Center for Performing Arts, which has featured performances by the likes of Bill Cosby, the Hubbard Street Ballet, and Riverdance. The heart of campus sits across the Red Cedar River from the university's more modern additions, which include the law school and Broad's North Business Complex, the 59,000-square-foot building connected by a covered walkway to Eppley Center, the B-school's old brick-and-sandstone home. The tiny MBA program can feel greatly overshadowed by the mammoth undergraduate business program's 4500 students, which in turn seems dwarfed by the 40,000 bodies that converge on campus each academic year. But with management-program-only options, like weekly coffee hours in the MBA Lounge, Broad students can always find a level of comfort.

Housing is plentiful in East Lansing. The majority of MBA students live in nearby apartments starting at about $500 per month for a one-bedroom, and the MBA Office facilitates the housing process by maintaining a notebook that lists information on more than 70 apartment complexes. They'll publish student requests for roommates, too. Still, approximately 30 percent of the students live on campus, and with a student population greater than 43,000, Michigan State does well in offering a variety of apartments and housing options to suit different needs. Many MBAs take spots in the Owen Graduate Center ($2065 per semester) or in University Apartments, where the one-bedroom units start at $418 per month. As long as you reserve early, these are readily available.

As a Big 10 school, Michigan State offers an all-encompassing campus lifestyle for those who want it, with key social events revolving around the Spartans football squad. For pre-game tailgate parties, MBAs get together across the street from the B-school and then walk to Spartan Stadium, where they have a choice block of tickets. There's also the annual MBA picnic at Lake Lansing Park, and every Thursday afternoon business grads pick a local bar in which to quaff and chat; Harper's Restaurant and Brewpub and Beggar's Banquet are some of the favorites. The MBA Association has been active in running a student mentor system, sponsoring community projects such as serving meals at a local soup kitchen and organizing food and clothing drives for the needy, and raising money for Big Brothers and Big Sisters.

PLACEMENT DETAILS

Placement continues to be a strong point for Michigan State, even though only 76 companies recruited second-year students on campus in 2000. MBAs still managed to walk away with an average of 3.3 job offers, and 84 percent were employed by graduation. Recruiters conducted 1121 interviews and posted an additional 450 jobs by correspondence or Internet. Pay packages fell under the common compensation mark gauged by many other Top 30 B-schools in BUSINESSWEEK's Top-30 tier, with just 14 percent of Michigan State's '00 grads earning above $100,000. For the 50 percent or so Broad MBAs who remain in the Midwest after graduation, the difference in pay is not so apparent when comparative costs of living among East- and West-Coasters are factored in. But the school has taken note. Top employers in 2000 included Ford Motor Company (12), Intel Corporation (11), General Motors Corporation (11), Apple Computer (8), U.S. Bancorp (4), Spring (2), Solectron (2), Motorola (2), Cisco Systems (2), and Honeywell International (2).

The new placement center that houses nearly two dozen interviewing rooms; a fully computerized resource center; a recruiters' lounge with its own kitchen, phones, and office equipment; and career services administrative offices unfortunately serves primarily undergrads. But Broad MBAs get the full treatment nonetheless—from a first-semester workshop series on job search skills and videotaped mock interviews with feedback to personal counseling and intensive résumé critiques.

OUTSTANDING FACULTY

William McCarthy (accounting); *Cheri Speier* (accounting); *Naveen Khanna* (finance); *Michael Mazzeo* (finance); *Paul Rubin* (management); *Steven Melnyk* (supply chain management).

APPLICANT TIPS

Michigan State has seen a rise in the level of applicant quality. Average GMAT scores for the

Class of 2002 reached an all-time high of 650, up more than 20 points from two years earlier. The amount of work experience applicants had also increased slightly; those admitted in 2000 averaged 4.8 years of full-time work experience compared with 4 years in 1998. Just 1 percent of the Class of 2000 had less than a year on the job.

Aside from the emphasis on strong scores and experience, personal interviews have also taken on more importance in Broad's admissions processes. A full 100 percent of those admitted to the Class of 2002 were interviewed by admissions officers or trained students, either on campus, by telephone, or during recruiting trips to other states and countries. (In an attempt to diversify the international student mix, the school in 1998 began making recruiting trips to Canada and five European countries.) The school says it is looking for students "who appear well suited for management careers based upon academic ability, maturity, motivation, leadership, and communication skills, as well as personal accomplishments." The priority deadline for fall admission is March 30, when international applicants and those wishing to apply for financial aid must have their paperwork in—but the school continues to accept applications until June 15.

Contact: Randall Dean
Director of MBA Admissions
517-355-7604
OR 800-4MSU-MBA
Application deadlines: March 30; June 15 (primary); December 15; January 31; February 28 (rolling)

MICHIGAN STATE MBAs SOUND OFF

Michigan State offers the complete package: a challenging academic curriculum, entertaining and competitive athletics, and a full and exciting social life. The admissions staff brought in a great mix of students from different cultures, nationalities, backgrounds, and races. The diversity greatly enhanced my learning experience. The faculty and staff were competent, fair, and accessible.

The Michigan State MBA has exceeded my expectations. For the level of investment required, it's the best investment I've ever made. Michigan State also has many assistantships available, which is a financial help. I'm very happy to have attended Michigan State and would gladly do it again.

I believe the Supply Chain Management program at Michigan State is excellent, and I would highly recommend it to students interested in that area. My other concentration, finance, I would consider average.

MSU has a great deal of potential if it begins to focus on teaching, learning, and expectations. When students have a problem with a professor, the administration sometimes eventually addresses the problem, but not until the class is over. Also, the technology marketing concentration will greatly improve the marketing department's standing, but it has actually hampered the ability for current traditional marketing students to secure employment outside of Ford and General Motors.

We are often misjudged as being a regional training ground for the automotive OEM and supplier industries. I contend that this is not the case. Many of us opt to join this industry (in many cases, such as my own, fellowships from the automakers have even paid our way through school). We also send many graduates to the high-tech industry (Intel, Apple, etc.) and the consulting firms (A.T. Kearney, McKinsey, Ernst & Young). MSU should be recognized for what it is: one of the leading business schools in the country.

The professors at MSU have an incredible wealth of knowledge and are always accessible to MBA students. The students are hard-working and willing to help each other out.

There was no cutthroat attitude at MSU. This was a feature I was promised, and it turned out to be true. I was able to really focus on learning and not outscoring my peers or being outscored by them. With only 130 students a year, it's an intimate enough environment that almost every face and name are at least recognizable.

The Career Placement and Planning department was terrific. The staff was deeply committed to helping find internships and jobs, providing terrific advice from their varied and deep experiences, and being friendly and approachable—a feature I've found lacking in other similar departments. Helen Dashney and her supporting staff do a great job and really go out of their way to help you out.

The MSU placement and career counseling office provided outstanding assistance in guiding my career change. MSU MBA administrators are dedicated to being responsive to us and to providing a high level of quality in the program. The combination of student diversity (age, experience, and national origin), great teaching, outstanding placement services, and reasonable tuition (plus a generous merit-based financial aid program) have made my Michigan State MBA experience an excellent value and a most memorable experience.

The MBA program here at Michigan State was excellent, but I felt that the real value was in the Placement Center. In the past, Michigan State and its graduates have relied on a steady stream of jobs in the automotive industry—but things have changed in East Lansing. I was very impressed by the breadth of companies interviewing—and hiring—Broad MBAs.

30.
GEORGIA INSTITUTE OF TECHNOLOGY

GEORGIA INSTITUTE OF TECHNOLOGY

DuPree College of Management
755 Ferst Drive
Atlanta, Georgia 30332-0520
E-mail address: msm@mgt.gatech.edu
Web site address: www.dupree.gatech.edu

Corporate ranking: 15	Graduate ranking: 39
Enrollment: 195	Annual tuition & fees:
Women: 29%	resident—$4196
Non-U.S.: 29%	nonresident—$14,378
Minority: 12%	Room and board: $9500
Part-time: N/A	Average GMAT score: 635
Average age: 27	Average years work exp.: 4.2
Applicants accepted: 35%	Accepted applicants enrolled: 54%
Median starting pay: $95,000	Intellectual capital: 32

Teaching methods: Lecture, 33%   Case study, 34%
                    Group projects, consulting, 33%

Contact:
Ann Scott
Director of Admissions
404-894-8722
Application deadlines:
February 15
April 15
February 15 (int'l)

Much like the DuPree College of Management students who during orientation undertake an outdoor bonding activity in the north Georgia mountains, the rising business program at Georgia Tech is enthusiastically overcoming obstacles. After spending more than a decade in the shadows of the Top 30—worsened most recently by a "temporary mindset," the result of an interim dean's running the show—the small Southern program broke into the Top 30 this year for the first time. Indeed, this is no small feat for a program with just 200 students that has consistently drawn about half its population from the engineering and science fields for a standard quant-heavy education. But with a newer expanding and evolving curriculum, admissions officers are giving more of the "soft skills" applicants (with social sciences and more general liberal arts backgrounds) another look—even as the school continues to hold the mathematically inclined close to its heart. The result: a stronger program with a good mix of students and a more integrated curriculum. "It's sort of a juggling event," explains Admissions Director Ann Scott.

The DuPree program has also morphed from a School to a College in recent years, resulting in higher visibility and status, as well as extended contacts, within the university. DuPree is now aligned with the other five colleges on campus, and the administration interacts directly with the president and provost, rather than reporting to the head of another college, as they used to. Through Georgia Tech's current $148 million multicomplex building initiative, the DuPree College of Management will acquire a significant addition to its growing set of facilities through what is being touted as a "technical showplace." The complex is set to open in 2003. Included in the plans are a new management building with classrooms and administrative offices, a new executive education center, meeting spaces, and breakout areas for teamwork development. To be located in the center of Atlanta's Midtown technology corridor, the new facility will place the program in greater proximity to a number of local tech companies, many of which already have strong connections with DuPree.

Improvements such as these have even led the administration to consider converting the name of the degree from Master of Science in Management to MBA to better represent its content and purposes. "It's just not appropriately named," declares the program's new dean, Terry C. Blum. Since stepping (from a tenured professorship) into her current role in September 1999, Blum has been a driving force behind many of the modifications and has worked to clear a path for the implementation. "Our eyes are huge as to the goals we are setting," she says now. "We're really ready to surge forward."

It's just this sort of high-flying attitude that has boosted the satisfaction level of DuPree students, who mean a great deal to their new dean. "We came from outside the Top 50 all the way to the bottom of the Top 30; in some ways, we see this as, 'We got lucky,'" Blum admits. "But we are customer driven, not ratings driven. We want all our constituencies to be served: recruiters, the business world, faculty, and especially students." These customers have been struck, most recently, by improvements mainly within the career services office and among the faculty. The MSMs are more content with the help they receive in connecting with recruiters and securing summer jobs and permanent positions prior to graduation than they have been in the past. Recent grads gave high marks, also, to the quality of teaching in electives and core courses—and although they didn't quite see their profs at the leading edge of knowledge in their fields, grads are appreciative of their teachers' frequent availability for discussion outside the classroom. Still, Dean Blum is continuing to build on the faculty's strength. Nine new tenure track professors were hired last year, bringing the '00 to '01 school year's total up to 46. Next year she plans to hire 8 to 10 more professors, and, for the long term, to have 75 professors by the time the new building opens. Adjunct professors are also significant to the school; this year there are five, plus two early retirees from Corporate America who speak and teach courses in e-commerce and entrepreneurship. One also lends his time to overseeing the iXL Center for Electronic Commerce, which conducts research and teaching activities in areas like online marketing, information security, and Internet-based ventures. The other oversees the DuPree Center for Entrepreneurship.

The curriculum is evenly split in terms of teaching methods, among lecture (33 percent), case study (34 percent), and other formats like consulting and groupwork (33 percent). First-year students find themselves with a fairly heavy core course load and little room for electives, but most have the opportunity to take one elective during the second semester of the first year. Nevertheless, DuPree's core course array (which includes Financial and Managerial Accounting, Leadership and Organizational Behavior, Managing Human Resources, Financial Management, and Marketing Management) tends to bypass some of the more ho-hum mathematics mainstays by requiring entering students to have a satisfactory grade in a college-level calculus course under their belts. You'll also need a familiarity with probability concepts prior to enrollment.

Having converted from the quarter system, DuPree is currently in its second year of semester conversions, a setup that provides greater opportunity for more in-depth study in specific subject areas. Still, some topics require a shorter segue, and although the administration claims to be careful about eliminating redundancies among the different courses, recent DuPree grads say there is frustrating overlap in the coursework. Some also cited difficulties with conforming to the new schedule. "The change was not very well thought out," says one recent grad. "Most teachers either crammed the old lesson plans from two classes together, or they added a bunch of busy work to the old format, which didn't increase learning at all." No new departments have been added in the past three years, but both e-Commerce and Quantitative and Computational Finance were introduced as concentrations. As a second-year student, you can concentrate in one or more areas, from Accounting and Marketing to International Business and Information Technology Management. You'll take 10 elective courses, plus 1 international management elective, from any of the concentrations. Some of the newer course offerings are trendier or ultraspecific, with titles like Financial Reporting and Analysis of High-Tech Firms, International Accounting, Venture Creation, and Knowledge Management. Other modern classes include Business-to-Business Marketing, Global Strategic Management, and International Information Technology. But, traditionalists fear not: Still prevalent are some of the more typical selections, like Operations Strategy, Advanced Managerial Accounting, and Investments. Most students try to incorporate a variety of fields, which can also include interdisciplinary courses from other Georgia Tech master's programs. While you must complete a total of 10 electives by the end of your second year, up to 30 percent of your coursework can be taken outside the College of Management.

DuPree reciprocates this sharing demonstrated by other programs at the university. About one out of every four students in some of the management courses are Georgia Tech grad students from outside the B-school, including the computing and architecture colleges. The Class of 2000 says they appreciated the mixed bag of academics, and the school seeks to encourage all-around diversity in other ways. About 27 percent of the Class of 2002 is composed of non-U.S. citizens, who are supported by resources like a university international office that provides legal guidance in hiring and visa issues. The fact that minorities, on the other hand, aren't equally visible—with just 14 percent in the Class of 2002—is something administrators attribute to the low numbers of minorities in the engineering and science fields overall. Yet, while women are also underrepresented in these fields, female students at DuPree are still able to make up a respectable 32 percent of the class. "We would like a larger African-American portion of the class," admits Scott, who is hoping to increase the ranks by expanding the school's prospective student outreach efforts among targeted groups, and by encouraging more of Georgia Tech's minority undergrads to enter the graduate management program. "We're serious about managing diversity and making it a positive experience for our classes," she continues. "It's a real direction for us; we're not just working for tokenism."

Although the application count has leveled off at about 500 for the past few years, the level of interest in DuPree could experience a boost from a combination of the school's new Top 30 status and the traditionally reasonable tuition rates. Out-of-state students in the Class of 2002 paid just $14,378 to attend—the lowest among the top-tier programs—placing DuPree in the B-school bargain range. The payoffs, too, are coming fast, though not quite so fruitfully as at competitor schools. DuPree's '00 grads collected a median pay package of $95,000—one of only two schools in the Top 30 falling below the $100,000 mark. Granted, many DuPree grads don't encounter the same steep expenses upon finishing school; about 65 percent of them remain in the South, where a high quality of living is admittedly less pricey than in the heart of a big city like San Francisco or Washington, D.C. But the school has seen a rise in the number of students heading to hotspots like New York City and the West Coast. Eight or nine percent went to each location in 2000, while just six years ago "hardly any" ventured to either coast. The career services staff is preparing to keep up with the trend. Already the school has shown adeptness in attracting recruiters in the investment banking and service industries, who are apt to target students with heavy technical or quantitative backgrounds. The number of on-campus recruiters vying for Class of 2000 second-years numbered 103—or, about one for every student—while 63 potential employers also wooed first-years for summer internship positions. Additionally, for the past two years, the Office of MSM Career Services has organized a DuPree College Career Fair for both permanent and internship positions, which, though open to undergrads also, draws a strong attendance from MSMs. A member of the MBA Consortium, Georgia Tech also encourages its students to participate in the group's recruiting events in such sites as Atlanta, New York, and, as of spring 2001, Silicon Valley.

DuPree '00 grads managed to pull in an average of 2.9 job offers each—a satisfactory showing, but one that administrators are hoping to improve once some new factors kick in. The new facilities, for one, will provide upgrades not only for students and faculty, but also, potentially, for recruiters. A hotel is being planned as part of the complex, albeit as a separate structure not associated only with the new management building. Visitors to both campus and nearby businesses will be accommodated, and they'll find high-tech components as well as videoconferencing capabilities. Training-wise, the career services office has introduced an improved career-building skills curriculum, complete with mock interviews and analysis, résumé workshops, and career seminars on topics from interviewing and networking to dining etiquette and dressing for success. The training begins during orientation for entering students, with discussions led by corporate recruiters and second-year students regarding summer internship options. Ongoing counsel is provided for recruiters regarding the types of sessions to hold, where and when to schedule them, and the best practices, in general, to attract potential employees with particular backgrounds or qualifications.

In addition to the array of campuswide upgrades on the way, including some interdisciplinary and global learning centers, Georgia Tech and the DuPree College are working to secure existing corporate connections with such traditional supporters as Hewlett-Packard, Citibank, and Cox Communications. They're also attempting to seek out and establish new ones. The southern metropolis of Atlanta, home to more than 1200 international businesses and increasingly charged with new high-tech developments, gives MSMs continuous exposure to developing businesses. Students also receive support from the DuPree Center for Entrepreneurship and New Venture Development, as well as the iXL Center for Electronic Commerce, where research and educational activities often come into contact with some of the local startups, like one recently begun by the center's former faculty director. The College's small size is helpful in making such connections, and administrators find it easy to keep track of students' goals, activities, and concerns. "Students can have suggestions, and we're very likely to listen and make changes," says Admissions Director Ann Scott. But in some ways, that's not what the records show. Georgia Tech MSMs gave their school poor reviews of responsiveness from administrators and faculty, a concept that is somewhat surprising given the intimate school setting and inherent sense of Southern hospitality. The school's small size also amounts to a modest alumni base compared with other peer programs; DuPree counts just five alumni clubs in its midst. In a recruiting sense, the College's size affects both students looking for alumni support and connections and potential employers who might find the school's lack of critical mass one reason to knock them off the company's recruiting circuit.

But DuPree students are a resourceful gang who make the most of what they have: high-quality academics with a solid "quant" base; a burgeoning set of top-notch facilities; skilled professors who offer their time and attention within the classroom and beyond; and a diverse, active, and enthusiastic group of classmates. DuPree students have their pick of student-led organizations, from the Financial Management Association and Information Technology Society to the Women in Business and Consulting clubs. A large portion of MBAs take advantage of such activities as intramural sporting events, arts and crafts workshops, and drama and theater productions. Many of the MSM student-led groups, and especially the Graduate Students in Management (GSM), arrange student and faculty mixers, community and public service events, plant visits, and tournaments, in addition to career-focused activities like alumni networking sessions and guest speaker series.

A social bunch, DuPree MSMs often gather upon week's end to venture out into some of Atlanta's more happening areas, like Buckhead and the Virginia Highlands. Favorite foodie spots include Eats, Doc Chey's, Tu Tu Tango, and Vortex, and MSMs can often be found chatting and swigging at popular bars and gathering spots from Park Tavern and the Prince of Whales to Neighbors and Swingers.

Students live all over the metro area, where one-bedroom apartments range from $650 to $1100, and two-bedrooms can cost anywhere from $900 to $1500 per month. Many students get a better value by opting for a multibedroom apartment and dividing the cost. Not surprisingly, prices vary mostly according to their distance from the city. Single students tend to live within the perimeter, in areas such as the Virginia Highlands, Midtown, and Buckhead, while married students gravitate to outside the perimeter in the suburbs. It's best to own a car during your two years here, but if you don't, you'll do fine with an on-campus setup; Georgia Tech operates a shuttle from the Marta station.

PLACEMENT DETAILS

While the majority of Georgia Tech MSMs—about 65 percent—do settle somewhere in the South, typically within one of the more traditional companies or career fields, this is no longer the only heavily traveled path. Career Services Director Mary McRee has seen a change in student interests and geographical preferences, with smaller, less traditional firms growing in popularity and more and more students taking positions in finance centers like New York City or along the high-tech infused West Coast. Still, DuPree's list of top employers continues to feature a larger portion of the more conventional-style companies. But with the school's small lot of students per class (about 100), no one organization can claim much of a significant percentage: Barclays Capital (4); Deloitte Consulting (3); Intel Corporation (3); iXL (3); Cintas (3); Gartner Group (3); Lam Research (3); Delta Airlines (2); HotelTools (2); and Amvescap (2).

Size can be both a benefit and a detriment. The small number of students creates an intimate atmosphere that allows for opportunities to make direct connections with recruiters, especially those that are local and can easily make themselves known on campus. But some companies who see the school as lacking in critical mass of students may find it easier to avoid DuPree altogether. Fortunately for the school, more than 100 companies do see fit to come to campus each year to recruit the soon-to-be grads. Throughout their two years of graduate school, DuPree MSMs have a chance to hone their career-building skills through a curriculum that includes videotaped mock interview sessions with critiques, one-on-one counseling, practice segments of case interviews with guest visitors from Corporate America, and speaking engagements by professionals who cover topics like dressing for success and business etiquette. The new facility, opening in 2003, will feature advanced technology to enhance education and training. On the other end, recruiters, too, will find increased options—from more comfortable accommodations to videoconferencing capabilities—which are expected to give DuPree's placement process, and the school as a whole, yet another welcome boost.

OUTSTANDING FACULTY

Charles Mulford (accounting); *F. Levy* (economics); *N. Jayraman* (finance); *A. Khorana* (finance); *Richard Daniels* (operations management).

APPLICANT TIPS

The DuPree admissions staff has long enjoyed a steady flow of applicants from the engineering and science fields, given Georgia Tech's strong quant reputation. But a greater number of non-techie applicants have shown interest in the school and duly impressed admissions officers, who now look seriously at all types who "are bright and will succeed academically, especially in a teamwork oriented environment like ours." Grades and GMAT scores are important; test scores for the incoming Class of 2002 members averaged around 635. But, as one of about 500 candidates for just 100 spots, you'll also need to stand out in your essays, which, as at most schools, attempt to determine your long-term goals, expectations of the program, and the types of contributions you might make to your class. "We're not looking for traditional responses," warns Director of Admissions Ann Scott. "Appli-

cants should feel comfortable taking a little bit of a risk; there's not one right answer."

You might also want to schedule an interview, which is encouraged but not required (16 percent of the Class of 2002 had one). Even if you don't initiate one, you could hear from the school if an admissions officer wants to learn more than was offered in your application. The admissions staff, in the end, gets to know the stats and background of each and every student, simply because each entering class is so small. If you are not admitted, you can request feedback, and an informed staff member will help point out any weaknesses in your application, for your own knowledge or in case you wish to reapply the following year.

Contact: Ann Scott
Director of Admissions
404-894-8722
Application deadlines: February 15; April 15; February 15 (international)

DuPREE MSMs SOUND OFF

I was extremely satisfied with my time at Georgia Tech. The caliber of students and professors was great and the administration worked hard to make sure everything ran smoothly. The atmosphere was very conducive to learning. There was very little evidence of students putting their own personal desires above those of the teams that they worked on. And all of the students got along well. I think that the small size of the program was a significant factor in my positive experience. The director of the program knew all of the students well, and was aware of any difficulties that arose. The admittedly overburdened Career Services staff was wonderful. I had no difficulties getting interviews and received several job offers even though I did not have the kind of experience that most employers were looking for. The DuPree College of Management does not force students to be successes, but it certainly provides its students the opportunity to succeed in any field they desire.

Georgia Tech's DuPree College of Business is in the process of learning how to emphasize what it does well (operations, quantitative analysis, e-business, and information technology) so as to differentiate itself in the increasingly competitive B-school marketplace. I chose the program because of its quantitative focus, and I learned much that will catapult me forward.

The DuPree College of Management at Georgia Tech just doesn't get it. The professors don't embody what they teach, and the administrators rule the school with their own agenda, subservient only to the administrators of the university as a whole. It is sadly humorous to hear professors laud customer service as a profit strategy, when they fail to treat their students as customers. Although there are several notable exceptions, most of them simply don't make the effort to design classes that add value to the course materials. More focus on faculty, less on building improvements is needed.

Georgia Tech's MBA program is up and coming. The combination of entrepreneurship, the focus on technology, and the fine teachers in the foundational disciplines of Marketing, Operations, and Finance make the MBA program perfect for technology minded managers. The value is outstanding.

Georgia Tech needs to figure out what type of school it is. They should pick a distinct direction (Operations or IT) and focus the curriculum on that. Right now they are trying to be everything to everyone, and with 200 students (both first- and second-years) they don't have the student body to justify a wide variety of classes. We finally got a dean, but there is still much internal strife.

The program expanded my business perspective, analytical skills, creative thinking, and problem solving skills. I worked in teams with talented individuals from a variety of backgrounds, including nontechnical and international students.

The assignment of the dean was a very positive step in terms of leadership. The school is very strong in e-commerce and has started utilizing the potential of other Georgia Tech schools for IT, e-commerce, and entrepreneurship. Access to the incubator on campus is an asset.

THE RUNNERS-UP

> Some Runners-Up schools offer as broad a menu of programs and opportunities as their elite counterparts.

If you're considering getting an MBA, no doubt you'll want a degree from one of the most prestigious and well-known business schools. There's no question that there are some big advantages to having an MBA from a brand name school: Beyond the superior educational benefits, starting pay packages tend to be higher at such schools and many are known for their well-oiled alumni connection machines. But not everyone can pass the rigorous admissions standards set by the most elite schools—and more than this, the most prestigious schools tend to get hundreds, even thousands, more applicants than they could ever admit. Besides, you may not want to spend two years in a location that boasts a Top 30 school. Perhaps you'd rather be in, say, Dallas. There, you could spend two excellent years at Southern Methodist University's Cox School of Business, for example.

Some people mistakenly believe that if you can't manage to gain admission to a Top 30 school, you shouldn't bother going for an MBA at all. That's simply not true. You don't have to go to a first-tier school to get a good graduate business education—or a good job for that matter. The next group of 20 schools, dubbed Runners-Up, generally delivers the same basic body of knowledge as the more prominent institutions, and, in some cases, these schools have floated in and out of the top tier of schools or have begun to catch the eye of top recruiters and students alike. Together, they make up BUSINESSWEEK's Top 50 B-schools. In some cases, the quality of education at Runners-Up schools may even exceed some of the schools on the top list, especially in certain niche areas. Babson College is widely recognized to have the best business school in the world for entrepreneurship. Few schools can ever match the international offerings of Thunderbird. And few schools can best the operations department at Penn State, the accounting department at the University of Illinois, or the ethics emphasis of Notre Dame.

So what's the difference? Overall, these schools sometimes lack the breadth of quality offered at Top 30 schools. Not only will you generally find a smaller percentage of superb teachers and scholars at these schools—many of them tend to stand out in a niche area, but it can be hit or miss on individual subject offerings—you'll also discover that these schools might lack some of the infrastructure needed to support demanding students: the high-tech bells and whistles; the deep-pocketed endowments; and the cohesive, high-powered alumni networks. Graduates of these programs may find it just a little harder to connect with the job market, particularly the prestige employers. That said, these same challenges often present great opportunities for ambitious students to help lead the way to change.

And, some of the Runners-Up schools are just as selective as their elite counterparts. Indeed, some boast even better records of placing their students. And some claim professors in niche areas that are so superior, they might put teachers in the Top 30 to shame.

BUSINESSWEEK lists this group alphabetically, without an actual ranking.

ARIZONA STATE UNIVERSITY

College of Business
Arizona State University Main
Tempe, Arizona 85287
E-mail address: asu.mba@asu.edu
Web site address: http://www.cob.asu.edu/mba

Enrollment: 1100
Women: 29%
Non-U.S.: 33%
Minority: 12%
Part-time: 604
Average age: 29
Applicants accepted: 35%
Median starting pay: $85,000

Annual tuition & fees:
   resident—$7344
   nonresident—$15,800
Room and board: $6950
Average GMAT score: 644
Average years of work exp.: 5
Accepted applicants enrolled: 58%

Teaching methods: Lecture, 30%   Case study, 50%
       Team projects, 20%

Contact:
Judith Heilala
Director, MBA
Recruiting and
Admissions
602-965-3332
Application deadlines:
Domestic—
December 15
March 1
May 1
International—
December 1
March 1

Don't be fooled by the sunshine, the palm trees, and the myriad of majestic golf courses. Though Arizona offers all these things, Arizona State University's College of Business is truly a place to get busy, and your two years here hardly resemble a vacation. Applicants must have an especially clear idea of what they want to accomplish during the program and where they want to land after, not only because those traits appeal to the admissions committee, as at every other B-school, but also because Arizona State doesn't offer a general management program. The curriculum is addressed primarily to niche markets. You will gain a solid base of business fundamentals, but you'll also spend the majority of your second year focusing on one of just a few areas of business the school has developed into a concentration. If you're not interested in supply chain management, finance management and markets, services marketing and management, sports business, information management, or health services management, you'd likely be better off somewhere else. The clearly defined program might seem restricting to some, but MBAs looking for an edge in a particular career track have found it effective. In fact, in just three years after Dean Larry Penley helped launch the new structure in 1995, Arizona State moved into the ranks of BUSINESSWEEK's Top 50 B-schools.

Students are asked in the beginning of their first year to decide on their specialization, and many even name it as early as during the application process. The core of required courses fits snugly within the first year, leaving just enough room for an introductory course in your major before beginning your summer internship. In the second year, you'll take the rest of the courses related to your field of concentration. The school's historical strengths and the directions being taken by the Southwestern business community were strongly considered when Penley and other administrators decided on the specializations Arizona State would offer. Of the six, the supply chain management track could be considered the school's flagship option; after all, Arizona State has been a recognized leader in the field of operations for more than 30 years, and this is the area that draws the most corporate recruiters annually. Instead of focusing solely on operations, students in the supply chain management concentration study the big-picture aspect of customer-responsive processes, including logistical issues like acquisitions and purchasing, plus marketing. They learn to design, develop, manage, and improve the efficiency and effectiveness of these processes, and to transform their ideas into high-quality products and services delivered at competitive prices. Finding ways to achieve superior financial returns within environmental, ethical, and legal constraints is another component.

In the finance management and markets track, topics center on corporate finance to meet the needs of the region's significant high-tech industry (which some have enthusiastically dubbed "Silicon Desert"). Students examine how service, retail, and manufacturing businesses make financial decisions and learn how to identify, analyze, and solve corporate finance problems. Within this area of study, a small number of MBAs also earn the opportunity to gain investment experience through a student-managed securities fund. These Student Investment Management participants interact with an advisory board of portfolio managers and other investment professionals. Implemented in 1999, the sports business concentration is naturally strong, considering that Phoenix boasts four professional athletic teams, is the spring training base for six major-league baseball clubs, and each year hosts the Fiesta Bowl, an intercollegiate football favorite. Another specialization

option is the customer-focused services marketing and management track, which teaches students to market and manage the delivery of products and services to build customer relationships and loyalty. Students can opt instead to complete one of two joint-degree programs: in information management (including e-business) or health services administration, both of which can be completed within the normal two-year MBA time frame with the summer in between spent working.

All Arizona State MBAs, regardless of the area of study, take 11 core courses over three trimesters in their first year. Waivers are not permitted. The relatively large program, with full-timers numbering around 400, is made a more intimate learning environment through these core classes that are limited to 50 students each. Courses range from organizational behavior and managerial economics to accounting, global business, and a requirement in legal, political, and ethical studies. By taking a mandatory introductory course in their chosen track during the third semester, all students gain an extra ounce of preparation for their essential summer internships.

In the second year, in addition to the required and elective courses in your track, you'll take part in a team-based consulting project that lasts two or three trimesters, depending on your area of concentration. Participants in the MBA/M.S. in information management program, for example, work on a 25-week-long field project while getting through eight of nine possible required courses.

A handful of students, provided they can afford to take longer than the typical two years to finish their studies, opt to pursue dual degrees in economics, accounting, taxation, architecture, or law. There's also a joint program with the nearby American Graduate School of International Management (Thunderbird), which rewards its participants with both an MBA from Arizona State and a Master's of International Management from Thunderbird.

Arizona State offers summer programs involving study at either a Washington, D.C., campus or at a business school in France during the months of May and June (leaving time for summer employment). Students might also select a yearlong exchange program with a school in France, Norway, Spain, Mexico, or the most recent option, Peru.

The College of Business is now more closely connected with the College of Engineering through The Manufacturing Institute, a concept that arose from suggestions from Motorola. The semiconductor and cell phone manufacturer, along with Intel, funds this program, which has an emphasis on manufacturing systems and is intended to create opportunities for interdisciplinary research projects. The program also seeks to provide more industry internships for graduate students interested in both engineering and business and the ways in which advanced technology can be used to fuse the two.

During the past year the school saw an influx of some new key administrators. Assistant Dean Carl Harris, a management professional experienced with emerging technologies in applicant recruitment and online application processing, has been working on involving enrolled students in the implementation of certain program services at the school. He has also connected with the alumni services department to help develop a Web-based tool to better connect former MBA students with the college. The school's new career services director, Kitty McGrath, came on board in July 2000 to manage the Arizona State's mix of recruiters (about 50 to 60 percent in the high-tech arena) and match them with students who, in large numbers, have traditionally demonstrated a strong Southwest or West Coast orientation. The former Notre Dame career services director is committed to helping ASU MBAs learn from potential employers how they will be using their degree. She notes that "new corporate faces" or household-name companies that previously had no interest in hiring MBAs are increasingly coming to campus to recruit Arizona State MBAs, and a growing alumni bond is helping perpetuate the process. "We don't have a long tradition of strong alumni relations," says McGrath, "but such contacts are the key to opening doors for our current students." A new director of marketing, additionally, is tasked with highlighting the school's latest initiatives and advancements, which include a planned facilities makeover with renovations beginning in January 2002. The structure will include an admissions and MBA program area, a new career management center, and a new Ford MBA suite with computer labs and a lounge, for which Ford has already pledged at least $3 million. The school's technology structure has been updated to include an Ethernet port at every desk, and students are currently required to begin the fall semester of their first year with a laptop computer selected by and purchased through the ASU MBA program. A wireless network has recently been installed.

Although students have already shown appreciation for the school's new construction and advanced features, it's a safe bet to say they'll continue to reserve some time for the great outdoors. Even when you're focused on your studies, the 300-plus days of sunshine each year in the desert clime are difficult to ignore. Summer daytime temperatures often exceed 100 degrees and the temperature in winter rarely dips as low as freezing. It appears that even the B-school's current, modern window-covered building was designed to take advantage of the seasonal light. All year you'll find MBAs stretched out on the grassy lawns that surround the College of Business. They're also often perched beside the burbling fountain in the center of the plaza in front of the building, reviewing cases or reading in the shade of the numerous semitropical trees that have been imported to campus. Arizona State is one of the biggest universities in the country, and Tempe is a true college town, absorbing the 45,000 students who invade each year. Sandwiched between ever-expanding Phoenix and suburban Scottsdale, it's a haven of bookstores, coffeehouses, and cheap eats. Although MBAs tend to be serious and single-minded here, they do find time to hold a number of golf tournaments annually or to work on community service projects arranged by the Volunteer Council.

PLACEMENT DETAILS

Arizona State draws recruiters mainly from its niche interests, a practice that has resulted in a strong showing from potential employers on campus. In 2000, 176 companies came to the school to recruit second-year students, and more than half the class committed to a position in the Southwest or on the West Coast. Top employers were Integrated Information Systems (10); Hewlett-Packard (6); IBM (5); Honeywell (4); Motorola (4); Apple Computer (4); Cisco Systems (4); Ford Motor Company (3); America West Airlines (3); and Intel (3).

The Career Management Center runs several outreach programs to connect the B-school to the local community of executives. One, Corporate Connection, entails managers rubbing elbows with the school administrators and faculty each fall. Another is the Leadership Roundtable, which matches small groups of students with panels of 10 to 12 professionals in their chosen specialties to discuss each industry and its career paths. Arizona State is sponsoring a three-school internship fair this spring with the University of Arizona and Thunderbird, and the MBA Council's Student Relations Committee regularly arranges tours for students to visit companies firsthand. A student-run nonprofit consulting program also puts MBAs in advisory roles with firms that contract for their services.

OUTSTANDING FACULTY

Steve Golen (accounting); *William Boyes* (economics); *Stuart Lowe* (economics); *Marianne Jennings* (ethics and business law); *George Gallinger* (finance); *Rajiv Sinha* (marketing).

APPLICANT TIPS

Although the majority of each graduating class typically elects to take employment in the country's Southwest or West Coast regions, Arizona State is not definitively a regional school. Only about half of the Class of 2002 came from these parts. Many entering students have a background in business or engineering, or some relation to the high-tech industry, but there are enough liberal arts and social sciences and even arts or music degree-holders to create an interesting mix. Aside from strong academics (an undergrad GPA of at least 3.0 on a 4.0 scale) and competitive test scores, you should have at least two years of work experience prior to applying to the program. You're not required to interview in person, but about one-third of those admitted usually end up doing so. If you'd like to visit the campus and check out the facilities, you can arrange to have a guided tour and an informational interview.

A word of warning: Your work for the admissions process can pile up. You'll have to submit two separate applications, one to the ASU Graduate College and another supplemental application to the MBA program, to be considered for the B-school. For a dual degree, you'll have to put in an additional application to the graduate college as well (without an additional fee, however). The admissions office is looking for candidates who show "evidence of maturity, academic potential, and the ability to communicate clearly and professionally." You have a chance to demonstrate such assets in a personal statement asking you to address why you plan to pursue an ASU MBA and the factors leading to your decision to apply.

Contact: Judith Heilala
Director, MBA Recruiting and Admissions
602-965-3332
Application deadlines: Domestic—December 15; March 1; May 1; International—December 1 or March 1

ARIZONA STATE MBAs SOUND OFF

I gained everything that I set out to gain when I chose to pursue my MBA degree. I wanted to gain a broad understanding of the fundamental concepts of business and how they interrelate with each other. The ASU MBA program did an outstanding job helping me to achieve my goal.

ASU is one of, if not the best, value for the dollar. I have nothing but praise for the state of Arizona, its university system, and the opportunities that have been presented to me as a result of my attendance at ASU.

From a financial standpoint I don't think an individual could make a better investment than going back to business school. From an intellectual standpoint I can look back and am amazed at how much I have learned. I was in a dual-degree program; I am receiving an MBA and an M.S. in economics. I paid a total of $6000 in tuition and fees for both programs. This was the best money I have ever spent, and the best personal decision I have ever made. I am 27 years old and will be making more than my dad does at 58, doing a job in a field I really like. This program opened up doors for me that I never knew were even there. As an alumnus I will support both programs financially and I will

also encourage my company to hire ASU students.

This is the top Services Marketing MBA program in the country. As services become more important to distinguish public and private corporations in the future, students from ASU will be leading the charge to better understand the customer and provide solutions that will enable the corporations to fulfill their own goals.

You might want to check out the MBA in sports Business at ASU. Just as many students enroll to gain experience and knowledge in the technology field, MBA students at ASU are learning how they can differentiate themselves and their organizations in the sports industry. Sports business is no longer a mom-and-pop business; it is becoming big business and needs smart MBAs to lead the organization.

ASU is a good school, but needs to add more academic vigor to its courses. It also suffers because it does not allow students to waive out of courses that they already have extensive experience in. For example, I was an undergrad econ major and had taken several finance courses. Rather than be bored to tears in the four classes I had here at ASU, it would have served my needs much better to take classes in subjects that I had little or no experience in. Everyone gets the same standardized MBA and this is not challenging for many of the students. If the program wants to improve, it needs to be more flexible.

Two schools, two years, two degrees—the ASU MBA and TBird's Master of International Management. It's a well-kept secret, this dual degree program, but incoming business students should learn more about it.

BABSON COLLEGE

F.W. Olin Graduate School of Business
Babson Park, Massachusetts 02457
E-mail address: mbaadmissions@babson.edu
Web site address: http://www.babson.edu/mba

Enrollment: 1497	Annual tuition & fees: $24,370
Women: 36%	Room and board: $10,594
Non-U.S.: 37%	Average GMAT score: 638
Minority: 5%	Average years of work exp.: 5
Part-time: 1160	Accepted applicants enrolled: 45%
Average age: 28	
Applicants accepted: 40%	
Median starting pay: $84,000	

Teaching methods: Lecture, 10%   Case study, 70%
Simulations, site visits, 20%

Contact:
Rita Edmunds
Director of Admissions
781-239-4317
(outside the U.S.)
800-488-4512
Application deadlines:
January 5
February 1
March 1
April 15

Dean Larry Carr, the former professor at Babson College's F.W. Olin Graduate School of Business who was tapped this past August to head the school, is clearly one of its biggest fans. "We're an institution on the rise, doing a lot of the right things," he begins. "We think we've got it right; we try hard." Then he adds, unabashedly: "We're a David among Goliaths," and he seems to pretty much capture the B-school's essence.

Certainly, Carr's words ring true for the 350 or so well-prepared, full-time graduates who each year launch careers within traditional corporations, emerging start-ups, or—as 22 did in 2000, at their own newly created companies. Babson's innovative entrepreneurial focus has attracted the attention not only of ambitious B-school prospective entrants but also of potential employers seeking creative and forward-thinking staff members. More than 200 companies recruit second-years here every year, including biggies like Dow Chemical, Lotus, and Polaroid—even though last year about 45 percent of the class secured employment with a smaller start-up instead. The school's entrepreneurial focus, centered on such areas as the importance of having a global advantage, the value of teamwork, and ethical decision making, can be applied to a range of tasks, from leading an emerging company to helping effect change within a traditional corporation. Potential employers appear to recognize this. The relatively nascent Giant Loop, a fiberoptic and telecom company, for example, signed 11 Babson grads from the Class of 2000 to help expand its operations. Kellogg Cereal's management, on the other hand, has praised Babson MBAs for applying "an entrepreneurial way of thinking toward a brand 100 years old." The overwhelmingly case-study-supported curriculum (70 percent), which includes the much-lauded integrated first-year program and a yearlong team-consulting project, provides a solid business foundation and real-world training to position these students for continuing corporate success.

The unusual first-year curriculum begins with a monthlong module on creative management that's similar to the teamwork exercises used at other schools. Students work together in outdoor challenges and community service projects, and review writing, math, accounting, economics, and computer skills. Teams even tackle creative arts projects in drawing, sculpture, poetry, puppetry, movement, music, and improvisation intended to get the mental juices flowing.

The rest of the fall is spent learning the analytical skills needed to assess business opportunities and companies' competitive positions. In a Business Mentor Program, students have the opportunity to work in groups of five or six with one of two dozen Boston-area companies, ranging from giants in the banking, high-tech, communications, and consumer products industries such as Microsoft Corporation, Reebok, and Fidelity Investments to start-ups and not-for-profit organizations. The team members compile an industry profile gauging their company's competition. During the second half of the year, the students work more closely with executives to analyze a specific part of the company and its fit in the firm's overall strategy. Large chunks of time are set aside during weekdays for students to work on the project.

At the same time, the spring is split between module three, which focuses on operations and teaches students how to design and manage a business delivery system, and module four, which attempts to integrate the entire curriculum in a segment on how to deal with a changing global environment. The first year's themes of teamwork and creative thinking are enhanced by a human resources–style grading system at this point in the program only. In lieu of the classic A, B, and C grades they do earn during their second year, students in the first year are evaluated according to how they measure up to "expectations": Meets, Exceeds, Excels, or Below. There is no grading curve, nor is there any sort of a quota for students to fail, in either the first or second year.

Upgrades in terms of teaching quality and elective offerings (nearly 100 now) have been applied to the program's second year, which Babson students are, inevitably, more apt to criticize after their dynamic first-year run. Elective courses fall into categories among four areas—entrepreneurship, global business environment, strategy, and global strategy—and students must take nine of these, six of which may be in one discipline. To help MBAs prepare themselves to identify and enter the field of their choice upon graduation, many of the electives are organized around five Career Paths: Consulting, Entrepreneurship, Finance, e-Business, and Marketing, each of which contain multiple sub-paths. The Consulting Career Path, for example, offers four sub-paths that include Information Technology and Change Management & Implementation Services. The adherence to a Career Path is optional, but many students do choose to follow one for the extra ounce of guidance it can provide. A student interested in new ventures, for instance, might turn to the Entrepreneurship Career Path to learn about the skills, experiences, and attributes of an entrepreneur, some recommended courses and co-curricular activities, and information on related industries, key companies, and Babson faculty and alumni in the field. (The Entrepreneurship Intensity Track allows students to simultaneously earn an MBA and launch a business.)

The global component of Babson's program has always been strong, but it has become even more so since a "cross-cultural" experience was established a few years ago as a requirement for all MBAs here. One option for American students is a summer overseas internship, which can be arranged by the school as a consulting project in one of more than 35 countries. Students might instead select a semester of study abroad at one of the three schools in Europe with which Babson has formal exchange agreements. There are also several international electives offered during the winter break or summer that send MBAs to various locations in Europe, Asia, or Latin America for three weeks of intensive coursework, company visits, and meetings with executives. (The school's sizable number of international students, who make up some 30 percent of each full-time class, have already fulfilled their requirement by enrolling at Babson, but they can participate in the overseas options as well should they so choose.) An international concentration that combines a major in finance or marketing with a series of global business courses is also available, but it's become somewhat less popular than when it started, since a global aspect has been infused into just about every aspect of the program's curriculum already. Those who demonstrate foreign language proficiency according to diplomatic standards (sorry, but you can't take language courses for credit) get a special designation on their degrees.

Until recently, the B-school program was led by Dean Thomas Moore, who now has his hands full heading Babson's executive education program and serving as CEO for Babson Interactive LLC, a newly launched for-profit venture to develop distance learning programs for executives and graduate students. A new customized MBA setup under the program currently has Babson faculty educating select Intel Corp. employees in person and via online components. Under Moore's leadership, the school saw the dedication of a new building in 1998—the Arthur M. Blank Center for Entrepreneurship, which is named for the Home Depot CEO and president, who is a '63 Babson grad, and which houses the entrepreneurial research cen-

ter. In addition, a number of venture-friendly features took off, and now, under Dean Carr, a 12-year veteran of the Babson faculty, they're operating at full force. A $200,000 seed fund bestows start-up financing upon new grads, and a scholarship program provides tuition support for five entering MBAs each year who show outstanding entrepreneurial experience or promise. Babson's prize money for student business plans now totals about $50,000 a year, and the school also offers free professional workspace in a facility known as The Business Development Hatchery to student start-up artists. More than 10 ventures have marked their beginnings here. Select teams of students who wish to work on their businesses between classes in Olin Hall are awarded space for one Hatchery "term" (fall, spring, and summer) at a time. The space recently underwent a $60,000 renovation as a result of a generous gift from the MBA Class of 1999.

Looking ahead, Dean Carr is committed not only to expanding the distance learning aspects Moore has been pushing, but he is also devoting attention to Babson's evening program, especially by trying to make it "more flexible and responsive to student needs." Already, with cluster and intensity courses, professionals can complete the program by attending just one class one night per week. Babson's alumni base, which currently consists of nearly 12,000 grads in a range of fields, is another item on Dean Carr's agenda. By formalizing the group into a strong network, the dean hopes to increasingly count on alums for help in supporting school initiatives, making greater career connections for students, and finding and screening prospective program applicants.

Those who are admitted and who enroll spend their two years here on a 450-acre campus dotted with hills and wooded areas, nestled among the suburbs some 14 miles west of Boston, which is easily accessible by commuter rail or car. It's about two miles from Wellesley

College and the town that gave the Seven Sisters school its name. Campus life centers around Olin Hall, the glass and red-brick graduate center that opened in 1996, complete with 1200 computer ports wired to the Babson intranet, a 200-seat auditorium, six interactive classrooms, a computer lab, team meeting and study rooms, and administrative offices. It's where MBAs gather for Thursday night socials at Roger's Pub or for lunch breaks at the food-court style dining hall. Housing is available on campus for about 120 graduate students a year in Woodland Hill or Bryant Hall, but most take apartments or houses in pricey Wellesley or other neighboring towns.

PLACEMENT DETAILS

"When Babson students leave, they have had the opportunity to have almost reinvented themselves," says Career Services Director Len Morrison, who points to enhanced résumés from internship and field-based project experiences. As a result, Babson MBAs received an average of three job offers each last year, not to mention the more than 20 who started their own companies. Although they often have steep student loans to face—Class of 2000 grads owed an average of about $37,000 at the time of graduation—the payoff for this enterprising crew often comes a few years down the line.

By partnering with some of the bigger companies for consulting projects, speaking opportunities, and long-term projects—rather than relying solely on traditional hiring transactions—Babson has managed to maintain a steady stream of interested employers. The numbers confirm it: 225 firms conducted interviews with second-years, and 367 jobs were posted electronically in 2000. Top hirers were Giant Loop Networks (11); Polaroid Corporation (5); Fidelity Investments (5); Trueque.com (4); OrderTrust (4); Bricker Keane Consulting (3); Digitas (3); and Smartbride.com (3).

OUTSTANDING FACULTY

John Shank (accounting); *John Marthinsen* (economics/finance); *Leslie Charm* (entrepreneurship); *Steven Spinelli* (entrepreneurship); *Jeff Timmons* (entrepreneurship); *Eric Sirri* (finance); *Anirudh Dhebar* (marketing).

APPLICANT TIPS

Babson is looking for students who can exhibit "leadership, maturity, ethical character, social and civic responsibility, and goal orientation." It's a tall order, but you'll have a chance to demonstrate these qualities in person through an interview, an important part of the admission process here that is not required but is highly recommended. Your best bet is to schedule a trip to campus to attend a general information session (held monthly throughout the year) and a morning visitors program that includes a campus tour and class visit. Interviews are scheduled after attendance at the Visitors Program or upon receiving or completing an application. You can also opt to interview at an MBA Forum or other overseas administrative visit, or by telephone.

In your visits and essays, you'll want to emphasize your appreciation for living and working in a diverse world and how you value differences among people—an important part of the school's culture. Babson requires applicants to have at least two years of work experience before enrolling. You'll also want to get your application in as early as possible—almost all spots are filled by the March deadline, with only extraordinarily qualified applicants considered after that. You can expect a response six to eight weeks after the deadline you meet.

Contact: Rita Edmunds
Director of Admissions
781-239-4317 (outside the U.S.)
OR 800-488-4512

Application deadlines: January 5; February 1; March 1; April 15

OLIN MBAs SOUND OFF

Best Entrepreneurship program in the world! Wrote my business plan, raised money, filled three board seats, found two co-founders in co-MBAs, two profs are board members, one prof an investor, found an outside CTO through prof, found outside CMO through prof, found Web development team through board member which came through prof, found strategic partner in industry through prof. . . . Need I say more? I could go on and on and on!

While focused on Entrepreneurship, Babson's program is phenomenal in creating a holistic view of business. Students understand how entrepreneurial thinking can enhance their chances for success in a start-up environment, but also in a large corporation. Additionally, Babson has been incredible at attracting successful former executives to come back and teach elective courses. Although it is often effective to learn from academics, the opportunity to learn from someone who has already "done it" and "lived it" enhances credibility and the overall learning environment. An example of this is my most recent class in Franchising, taught by Robert Rosenberg—the Dunkin' Donuts CEO who grew the company from 100 franchises into 5000.

Even in a school that graduates nearly all of its students, failure still looms over all assignments. When the faculty says this is the time to try doing the stuff you aren't good at, they haven't got a clue. Teams work because members do what they are already good at. You don't put the team at risk trying to learn statistical analysis. Unfortunately, this environment discourages learning new subjects.

Babson truly deserves its spot as No. 1 in Entrepreneurship, given its strong classes, alumni, faculty, speakers, research, conferences, competitions, pratica in internships and consulting projects, strategic alliances, and the Executive Education Program.

I am a bit disturbed by Babson's conscious efforts to diminish its international perspective (internships, short trips, alumni groups, entire departments and classes). It has a strong presence abroad but has decided to concentrate more and more on technology (the Internet mostly) at the expense of other strengths. The Internet is a wonderful tool, but that is all it is: a tool. It is the not the "be all and end all." This is not a drastic change but a more "creeping" trend.

The MBA experience at Babson College was an awesome experience. The entire team-building aspect was different and produced different and varied skills for working more effectively in groups.

BOSTON UNIVERSITY

School of Management
140 Commonwealth Avenue
Chestnut Hill, Massachusetts 02467
E-mail address: mba@bu.edu
Web site address: http://management.bu.edu

Enrollment: 1122
Women: 35%
Non-U.S.: 41%
Minority: 5%
Part-time: 486
Average age: 27
Applicants accepted: 43%
Median starting pay: $87,000

Annual tuition & fees: $25,467
Room and board: NA
Average GMAT score: 628
Average years of work exp.: 5
Accepted applicants enrolled: 47%

Teaching methods: Lecture, 50% Case study, 30%
Simulation, field projects, 20%

Most MBAs will tell you their program is rigorous enough as it is, with exams, case studies, readings, problem-solving sessions, and group work to manage. Students at Boston University's School of Management are no exception. Their two years here are an intense procession of absorbing lectures, reading and researching, memorizing, and presenting, not to mention facing the high-pressure recruiting process. So what made the school believe it could cram another entire degree—the Master of Science in information systems—along with the MBA into the standard 21 months it takes to finish the regular graduate program? "This may be the redefinition of the MBA going forward," says Dean Louis E. Lataif of the ambitious, as yet unduplicated, new dual-degree program launching in September 2001. A Harvard MBA himself, Lataif has led BU's School of Management for nearly a decade. "It's much more than a mere concentration," he continues. "It's for the savvy student who recognizes that the ability to understand technology will either halt or advance a career."

Certainly the program is doable for the right enterprising MBAs. More significantly, perhaps, it is very much representative of the school's defining cross-functional and "lateral thinking" methods that are increasingly being used to produce graduates who operate uniquely in the business world, whether building systems or working in groups. By lateral thinking, the school means understanding that decisions you make in one area of business affect the other areas, regardless of your function within the organization. MBA courses developed by teams of faculty from different academic disciplines, such as The Global Man-

Contact:
Peter Kelly
Graduate Admissions
617-353-2670
Application deadlines:
Domestic—
December 15
February 1
March 1
April 15
International—
December 15
February 1
March 1

ager, combine business elements like organizational behavior, strategy, and information systems to illustrate the concept. Various projects also link courses in different areas, like marketing and operations management.

Additionally, through a trademarked Team Learning™ concept, the school differentiates its practice of having "individuals learning collectively" from the more mainstream "group work" found in many other B-school programs. In some projects here, this idea manifests itself as grades that are weighted against each other to make up each teammate's final performance value. The students, therefore, have a measurable stake in the performance and knowledge acquired by the members of their team—all have to pull their own weight. In business, the school reasons, it's difficult to create measurement systems that hold you accountable if your entire team fails; your marketing prowess, for instance, may remain untainted even if your team doesn't reach its profit goals. BU's Team Learning™ concept, therefore, seeks to prepare their MBAs to inspire themselves and the other members of a team to operate at their highest, most effective levels to help ensure group success in addition to the individual achievement that might come more easily. The response has been positive. Recruiters, the school says, have noted a change in the way BU MBAs approach business problems. "Their minds are wired differently—horizontally," Dean Lataif explains. General Electric has such faith in Team Learning™ methods, in fact, that the company has given the program grant funds of more than $1 million—one of the highest amounts GE has ever given to any school.

A strong emphasis on information systems—throughout the entire program, not just within the M.S./MBA—is another of BU's priorities. Courses such as Competing in the Knowledge Economy, Network Security, and Strategies and Technology for B2B e-Commerce—open to all MBAs—are just some of the school's up-to-date offerings. And the faculty is constantly growing to keep up with student interest and demands; four teaching slots, the most in any department, were added to management information systems within the past three years. "We want to strengthen the IS department," confirms Dean Lataif, "and sprinkle the mentality throughout the school." Additionally, students and faculty are well connected, through any of the school's 4000 dataports located throughout the campus. As far as facilities go, the Hariri Building is more than up to speed in this area. When it opened in 1996, it was considered among the most technologically focused structures ever built for management education. In addition to a 375-seat lecture hall and 25 classrooms with multimedia and distance learning capabilities, the building houses five computer labs, an in-house management library with more than 80,000 volumes, and a fourth floor devoted to the school's executive education programs. (Just an aside: In a testament to the school's cross-disciplinary emphasis, faculty members don't even sit according to their discipline here; every other office represents a different subject area.)

But let's get back to that challenging dual-degree program—and the academics here in general. B-school students can follow the M.S./MBA, MSIS, or MBA program with concentrations in areas like finance, marketing, health care, and public and nonprofit management. The first M.S./MBA cohorts begin study in September 2001, and this group will number no more than 100, although the program may grow with time. Most MBAs follow the same first-half sequence, with the year split into two semesters with 18 credits of coursework in each. The fall is booked for five required courses: Managing Organizations and People, Financial Management, Marketing Management, Financial Reporting and Control, and Data Analysis for Managerial Decision-Making. In the spring, MBAs and M.S./MBAs have room to take one elective in addition to their four required courses, which include IT Strategies for a Networked Economy and Creating Value through Operations and Technology. The summer between the first and second years is when paths begin to differ. MBA students generally work at an internship for the duration of the summer break, while M.S./MBAs enroll in one intensive eight-credit course and have the option of taking on an internship plus an online course or completing four courses instead, one of which is conducted online.

In the second year, M.S./MBAs focus heavily on the information sciences aspect of their degree through both coursework and a seven-month IS team consulting project at a client company. Such projects, which entail a defined deliverable at the end, have already existed as a component of the MSIS program at BU, and most recently involved client companies like Bain & Co., Deloitte Consulting, Parametric Technologies, and Putnam Investments. Courses for M.S./MBAs during their second year include Technology Tools for e-Business, Database Management, Systems Analysis and Design, and Information Systems Strategy and Organization.

The tech focus and rigorous requirements are intended to draw heaps of attention from a more ambitious group of prospective students—plus faculty and potential employers—to a school that, until now, often fell short in BUSINESSWEEK's B-school survey. Dean Lataif and other administrators believe the new dual-degree program, as well as additional improvements and initiatives like the Team Learning™ concept and the infiltration of information sciences content, are finally positioning BU as a real competitor among some of the biggies who have consistently landed in the Top 50. "There's a lot of good going on here, a lot of momentum behind this place," one administrator says. "We're just glad the world is catching on."

The elective course offerings are another boon, despite the fact that BU MBAs have traditionally rated elective course teaching below average. In your second year, you can choose from 101 electives, among them some newer offerings like Auditing, Corporate Financial Management, Intellectual Property and Business Strategy, and Competing in High Technology. Your electives can center on one area of study, like entrepreneurship, finance, or hospitality management, but a concentration is not required. Some students devise an elective cluster, with courses grouped around a management function or an industry sector, like organizational behavior or human relations. For added flexibility, you can shape 34 percent of your curriculum (24 of 64 credits) with courses in other schools and colleges at Boston University, including the College of Engineering, the School of Public Health, and the Graduate School of Arts and Sciences.

The school has shown burgeoning strength in some of these concentrated areas of study, like entrepreneurship, with the help of complementary facilities. Within the Bronner e-Business Center and Hatchery, for example, selected students with ideas for new businesses have the opportunity to develop their plans with guidance from faculty members and can receive access to venture capital firms such as Bessmer Venture Partners, Charles River Ventures, General Catalyst, and Softbank Capital Partners. No Hatchery companies have launched just yet, but several are working their way through the development stages, the school reports. Students can also participate in an annual business plan competition and a semi-annual Business Plan Boot Camp. More than 10 new companies have been launched by Class of 2000 grads, under their own initiative or with faculty support.

Aside from the innovations in academics and career direction, BU's program demonstrates a relatively solid global component that may also experience new growth. Overseas management programs are currently available in China, Japan, and Korea, with the possibility of additions in South America and Europe for coming years, and administrators say they are increasing the international component in the mix of cases taught in various classes. But more significantly, perhaps, is the vast array of international students: 41 percent of the Class of 2002 are non-U.S. citizens, putting BU, along with Purdue's Krannert School, at the top of the charts in this area. The number of female students, too, falls above average, at about 25 percent, although minority students make up a paltry 5 percent of the class—a figure the school is working to improve with ideas and assistance from students, including the MBA student body president, who is African-American. The significant global showing among the student body has traditionally been a result of the university's strong ties in Asia and prominent presence in Europe. But recently BU has also made investments in Latin America, and that group is now the largest international group represented in the MBA program.

International students, as well as students from all over the United States, find comfort in BU's prime location within the charming and scholarly city of Boston, home to more than 50 universities and colleges and more than 200,000 students. Not only is Boston a giant in New England commerce, with strong showings in the fields of finance, health care, high technology, manufacturing, and biotechnology—but there's more than enough in the way of diversion. The Red Sox's Fenway Park is just two blocks from the School of Management, for starters. Students also enjoy venturing into the city to listen to music at clubs or to dine at authentic Italian restaurants in the North End or at some of the ritzier spots along Newbury Street. And with cultural attractions such as the Museum of Fine Arts, the Boston Symphony Orchestra, and the Boston Ballet, BU MBAs have a busy time juggling studies and social events.

PLACEMENT DETAILS

BU MBAs fare just fine in the recruiting process, which last year resulted in 94 percent of grads receiving at least one job offer by the time they

had finished the program. Finance and consulting positions are the big draw, although "we try to get students to broaden their thinking—to look at brand management, for example," says Assistant Dean Jennifer Lawrence. Indeed, 12 companies were launched by Class of 2000 grads. The biggest hirers: Pricewaterhouse-Coopers (5); Chase (4); C-Bridge Internet Solutions (3); Deloitte Consulting (3); FleetBoston Financial Corp. (3); State Street Bank & Trust (3); and Benchmarking Partners (3).

Career training is taken seriously. Students must complete Career Lab, a full semester course covering interviewing techniques, résumé and cover letter writing, and detailed job search plans, is required for students before they can begin the recruiting process. MBAs also have access to international business forums, consulting workshops, peer networking groups by industry, an e-Day event, and "Company of Friends," a partnership with *Fast Company* magazine that allows BU students and faculty to connect in a chat room community.

OUTSTANDING FACULTY

K. Menon (accounting); *Rebecca Todd* (accounting); *Allen Michel* (finance); *Israel Shaked* (finance); *Patrick Kaufmann* (marketing); *Janelle Heineke* (operations); *Andrew Hoffman* (organizational behavior).

APPLICANT TIPS

To get a spot in BU's full-time program, which is up to about 630 students now, you'll need the requisite advanced degree credentials—strong test scores (average GMAT for the Class of 2002 was 628) and work experience, plus glowing recommendations. You'll also want to show in your essay how your application to business school makes sense at this point in your career. Be sure to explain how your work experiences and personal and professional characteristics make you a good fit for BU's program. You should note that if you've had fewer than two years of work experience you will have a considerably more difficult time getting accepted.

The school encourages prospective students to "do a lot of investigation and make the process a personal experience as much as possible." That means visiting BU and speaking with a current student or alum, which can be arranged through the admissions office. You can also schedule an interview, which is encouraged but not required.

Contact: Peter Kelly
Graduate Admissions
617-353-2670
Application deadlines: Domestic—December 15, February 1, March 1, April 15; International—December 15, February 1, March 1

BU MBAs SOUND OFF

The quality of instruction and quality of fellow students in the classroom exceeded my expectations. I was thrilled with the value of my education at Boston University. The career center has been an immense help to me personally in my career development plans and my current job search. I am confident that with the skills I have gained here and with the help of the career services I will have no trouble finding a full-time position in my field. I have had several offers in terms of employment, but have not yet settled on one. Boston University is making great strides to become a leading business school. The MBA building houses some of the latest technology, and it is fully utilized.

Boston University Graduate School of Management was a wonderful experience, particularly the cross-functional learning and

management as a system philosophy. I was impressed with the responsiveness to student feedback: quickly making adjustments, updating and adding courses, and creating an improved student community.

BU would be one of the best schools in the United States if there were a better social atmosphere in the school. It is far too easy to go through the two years of the MBA and come out with no real friends—only lots of acquaintances. The clubs are poor and because of the workload nobody is keen to initiate any social, charity, or other events. Sports and other student activities are almost nonexistent. At BU, it's a life of going to class, then rushing home to get the next paper ready. Most people rarely hang out on campus.

I thought the BU MBA was a great experience. I only wish that the school got more recognition, so that better firms (consulting, VC, and investment banks) would recruit at the school. The program is top notch.

The School of Management at Boston University is a solid MBA program. The professors (for the most part) are top notch in their field, the building is new, and the quality of students is getting better each year. I really feel that this school is moving up fast.

BU's MBA program is definitely up-and-coming. It has some issues to work out, relevant to its current curriculum, but the talent of professors is definitely there and growing. Based on the school's name/reputation, its new School of Management facility, and ability to attract top-name professors, BU stands to compete with many of the higher-ranked MBA programs.

Academically, BU is an excellent school. The quality of my classmates and the professors exceeded my expectations. Unfortunately, the BU MBA alumni network is not as strong as it should be, even in Boston. This is slowly changing, however. The new director of the career center seems to understand the importance of this and is taking steps to address this gap. I fully expect to participate vigorously in the BU MBA alumni network with the hope of substantially improving it.

I have no doubt that BU deserves a high ranking based on the talents of the students enrolled. Unfortunately the school has inadequate networking and alumni support. In spite of their efforts, until we can get alumni support and more students who receive offers from top employers, there is little they can do to change the situation, especially with Harvard and Sloan in the same market.

THE COLLEGE OF WILLIAM & MARY

THE COLLEGE OF WILLIAM & MARY

Graduate School of Business
P.O. Box 8795
Williamsburg, Virginia 23187-8795
E-mail address: Amy.Hughes@business.wm.edu
Web site address: http://business.wm.edu

Enrollment: 355
Women: 36%
Non-U.S.: 33%
Minority: 5%
Part-time: 159
Average age: 28
Applicants accepted: 49%
Median starting pay: $88,000

Annual tuition & fees:
  resident—$7301
  nonresident—$16,647
Room and board: $8330
Average GMAT score: 629
Average years of work exp.: 5.5
Accepted applicants enrolled: 45%

Teaching methods: Lecture, 40%   Case study, 45%
                      Simulation, field studies, 15%

Contact:
Kathy Pattison
Director of Admissions
757-221-2944
Application deadline:
March 1

Although most business schools focus more on the future than the past, it would be hard not to get a healthy dose of both at the College of William & Mary's Graduate School of Business. Located in the heart of Colonial Williamsburg, a place thousands of tourists visit each year, you can hardly spend two years in the MBA program without getting a strong sense of early American history. After all, the college is one of the oldest in the country, and its Colonial red brick buildings have been the site of the education of such prominent historical figures as Thomas Jefferson, James Monroe, and John Tyler. "Colonial Williamsburg is a beautiful place," says Lawrence Pulley, the B-school dean. "For us it's a reminder of the tremendous tradition of educational accomplishment that keeps us focused and whets our appetite to continue that focus."

That focus is primarily on preparing students for the wild unknown of the twenty-first century, but MBAs still benefit from the ubiquitous sense of tradition on the meticulously maintained campus and its surrounding environment. "The College of William & Mary has been known for teaching and accessible faculty, and we're committed to that process and experience," says Pulley. "When we hire faculty members, we tell them not to come to William & Mary unless they are interested in teaching." Pulley says he spends about 250 hours reading every single student evaluation on every single faculty member, and it shows. MBAs gave the school high marks in teaching, especially in the rigorous core courses, where they ranked the school's efforts in the top 10 out of the 82 schools surveyed by BUSINESSWEEK.

Pulley, an alumnus of the college and a B-school professor for a dozen years before taking on the deanship in August 1997, is now in the midst of developing a new strategy for the school. Although the blueprint for moving the school forward is not completed, he hopes to further expand the curriculum, attract high-quality students, and increase the size of the program so the school can offer a wider variety of courses and attract more companies to recruit on campus. He also wants to hire more faculty members and get business leaders involved in teaching a fuller range of electives in marketing and finance, as well as exploring such areas as entrepreneurship and ethics. "We are focused on continuing to improve the quality of our curriculum and our students," says Pulley.

So far, the dean has devoted a lot of his time to public relations. He's traveling around the country meeting with alumni and Corporate America to convey the message that William & Mary is more than just a good regional school. As he tries to catapult the B-school into the national arena, he's managed to fill a major hole in the placement office, where there hadn't been a stable director since July 1997. The most recent hire stayed for less than a year. In the meantime, Pulley picked up the slack by marketing the quality of his students when he's out visiting companies, but it hasn't been enough; Class of 2000 grads say there were too few companies coming to campus and complained that the ones that did visit were strictly regional. MBAs ranked the number and quality of firms coming to campus in the bottom 10 of 82 schools. The school was looking for a new placement director and found one in Tony Somers late in 1999. But improving quality will be an uphill battle.

If you decide to enter the MBA program here, be prepared for an intense first-year curriculum. You'll take 12 courses in subjects like accounting, finance, and management four or five mornings a week. However, the class schedule changes weekly because all courses are taught in modules and don't have an equal number of sessions or the same start and finish dates. There is no room for choice in the first year, and MBAs say they work very hard, with all-night study sessions a common occurrence.

In the second year, students are free to pick their own electives, but there is not a great variety of subjects to choose from relative to other schools. You can major in one of four areas—accounting, finance and economics, marketing, or operations and information technology—or a combination. One major component of the second year is a required field studies project. Students earn three credits consulting in groups for a local company such as Nextel Communications under the supervision of a faculty member. The program receives mixed reviews from MBAs. Some find the experience extremely valuable. Others, especially those who don't get one of their top-choice projects or who have a significant amount of previous work experience, say they could have lived without it.

Because the program is so small (about 100 students per class) and so rigorous, students get to know one another and the faculty very well. They spend a lot of time together both inside and outside the classroom, attending most of their classes in one building, Blow Memorial Hall, on the older section of campus adjacent to the restored area of Colonial Williamsburg.

There are plenty of outdoor recreational activities in the area. In their free time, MBAs boat on the York River, hike in nearby parks, and bike along Colonial Parkway, a 28-mile loop from Jamestown to Yorktown. Those who crave city life can drive two hours to Washington, D.C. The weather is mild enough for MBAs to take in the occasional round of golf or trip to the beach. Since there's not much of a nightlife in town, students spend most of their time at three local hangouts a short walk from Blow Hall. Paul's Deli and College Delly serve sandwiches, pizza, and beer, while the Greanleafe is a slightly more upscale pub. For those who want to travel back in time, you can still get mint juleps and cider in the area's many taverns.

PLACEMENT DETAILS

The turnover in William & Mary's placement office did not make things easier for the Class of 2000 MBAs, but the economy did; there were plenty of jobs available, with each graduate averaging about 2.5 job offers—but, fewer than 75 percent of students seeking jobs had one by graduation, a big lag compared to most other schools. That's not bad, considering that only about 45 companies conducted interviews on campus. The biggest 2000 hirers: Dell (4); Nortel Networks (4); Bristol-Myers Squibb (3); Accenture (3); PricewaterhouseCoopers (3); Nextel (3); IBM (2); American Management Systems (2); Free Markets (2); 3M (2).

OUTSTANDING FACULTY

Kim Smith (accounting); *Bud Robeson* (economics); *Deborah Hewitt* (finance); *George Oldfield* (finance); *John Strong* (finance); *Larry Ring* (marketing).

APPLICANT TIPS

The admissions process at William & Mary is a rolling one, so get your application in as early as possible to get a crack at one of the 100 open spots. The school reviews applications and makes decisions at the beginning of each month. The B-school is trying to diversify its population (about 50 percent of MBAs are Virginians, compared with about 80 percent five years ago) and attract even brighter students to the program, so there are plenty of research assistantships and scholarships available. The school grants about 65 research assistantships a year, but only about 5 are awarded to first-year students because of the tough workload. Most of the 65 scholarships, ranging from $1500 to full tuition, go to first-year MBAs. The school aggressively recruits women and minorities and has had a lot of success with women, in part

because of the visibility of the Women in Business Organization; at 42 percent, William & Mary boasts the highest percentage of female students of all of BUSINESSWEEK's Top 50 schools. The school has been less successful on the minority front but says it offers all qualified minority students some financial assistance.

Work experience is the most important criterion the admissions office uses to assess applicants. The school is unlikely to waive its two-year minimum work experience requirement unless you are an exceptional student and had good internships during college. Personal interviews are mandatory. "We want people who will jump right in here and not be shy and fit in well with the team environment," says Susan Rivera, who recently resigned her position as director of admissions. Rivera prefers that candidates come to campus, but if that's not possible, alums can interview the student and she can follow up with a phone interview.

Contact: Kathy Pattison
Director of Admissions
757-221-2944
Application deadline: March 1

WILLIAM & MARY MBAs SOUND OFF

An aspect of the W&M program that is worth mentioning is the intense dedication of the new Director of Career and Employer Development (CED). He has been an excellent addition to our program and has shown that he has good ideas, the right contacts, and the motivation to build our CED into what it should be. He made great strides with the internship program this year, which will only spill over into the full-time hiring season next year.

The first year of W&M's MBA program is extremely challenging and rigorous with an emphasis on team/group projects and a yearlong communications course. W&M students can be described as very easy to work with, very competitive but in a friendly way, very involved in the direction of the MBA program, very intelligent, and very driven for success. W&M's MBA program provides the same or better skill set and overall business education as the top-ranked programs.

Despite the fact that there are many areas that could be improved in the William & Mary MBA program, I still believe it was two years well spent. In addition, the school was very generous with financial aid.

The core curriculum at the school was tremendous. I learned a once unthinkable amount of information, which I feel I have retained for the most part. The second year was nearly a complete washout as the program has virtually nothing to offer elective-wise. The employment office was a total embarrassment. I was offended at their obvious lack of interest in being proactive in any manner. More than half of my classmates were without positions on May 1, and I am placing this blame solely on the employment office as these unemployed classmates are, for the most part, solid candidates.

OHIO STATE UNIVERSITY

OHIO STATE UNIVERSITY

Max M. Fisher College of Business

Gerlach Hall

2108 Neil Avenue

Columbus, Ohio 43210

E-mail address: cobgrd@cob.ohio-state.edu

Web site address: http://www.fisher.osu.edu

Enrollment: 507

Women: 30%

Non-U.S.: 29%

Minority: 12%

Part-time: 221

Average age: 28

Applicants accepted: 29%

Median starting pay: $85,000

Annual tuition & fees:

   resident—$9384

   nonresident—$18,975

Room and board: $7000

Average GMAT score: 645

Average years of work exp.: 5

Accepted applicants enrolled: 49%

Teaching methods: Lecture, 40%   Case study, 40%
                        Teamwork, 20%

Contact:

Laura Lembo

Associate Director of

Admissions

614-292-8511

Application deadlines:

November 15

December 12

January 15

March 15

April 30

There's nothing like a $120 million construction project to cause a stir. This, the largest multi-building project ever undertaken in Ohio State's history, was formerly a source of frustration to MBAs wrapped up in the resulting on-campus confusion two years ago. But, near to completion now, the project has simultaneously drawn positive attention to the 68-year-old Max M. Fisher College of Business and made it possible for some long-awaited comfort. "The environment now finally matches what we've been doing all along," MBA Program Director Michelle Jacobson says happily, and not without a sign of relief. "It's much more pleasant to host people here, and we've been attracting a higher caliber of staff and students."

One of the first new structures to open its doors to great fanfare in 1998—in addition to the Fisher Hall administrative building—was Gerlach Hall, the MBA program's "home." The facility houses tiered and flat classrooms with extensive audiovisual capabilities and also offers Nasdaq and Bridge terminals in its Batten Investment Management Laboratory. A new Career Services center within contains the usual résumé and job listing banks, but also greater video-on-demand features for students who want to prepare for interviews by watching recruiting videos. Services for potential employers coming to campus have been updated here as well to include private interviewing rooms that are a "virtual office," with Internet access, telephone, and fax. A year later, in 1999, the complex became even more substantial with the emergence of three new buildings: Schoenbaum Hall, the undergraduate program facility; Mason Hall, the library and computing center; and Pfahl Hall, the executive education and conference center. The final structure-in-progress—The Inn at Fisher College, a much needed on-campus hotel with 151 rooms for visiting executives—is scheduled to debut in 2002.

Such improvements, which are providing the school with nearly 400,000 square feet of new, modern space, have not come without a price, of course. The resident tuition rate has gone from $5898 to $9024 over a two-year period, and nonresidents have also seen an approximate $4000 increase. But the rewards are clear. "The brand-new facilities have encouraged everyone, from the students and faculty to the administration, to want to make this school a top 10 success," cheers one student.

Another element earning kudos from MBAs here is the program's teamwork focus. "It's not a new thing," insists Jacobson, who notes the B-school's long-term emphasis on group projects and consensus building in its curriculum. From the start, each incoming class of just under 150 students is divided into four cohort groups, with consideration given to diversity in terms of ethnicity, gender, and professional background. For every quarter of the program's first year, each cohort is paired with another, rotating so that all cohorts have a chance to work with each other at some point. Most students favor the setup, although some find it a bit tedious. One dissident says, "Every single one of my classes required me to work on a team. I understand the importance of teamwork, but I believe too much of an emphasis was placed on it at the expense of individual work." Others say the system encourages cooperation and camaraderie by "organizing the core classes so that you can be on a first-name basis with everyone." Students are also grouped within their cohorts into small work teams with which they tackle class assignments and hold study sessions throughout the year.

For many, the MBA program starts in early September with optional pre-enrollment classes that allow incoming students to bone up on their skills in accounting, economics, and statistics. These classes immediately precede what the school calls "Super September Start-Up," an orientation segment designed to jump-start the MBA program. Not merely a feast of social events, Start-Up puts newbies through case simulations, case studies, tours of local businesses, and lectures from senior executives. There's also a community service project in which students have built a Habitat for Humanity home or have gone into local elementary schools to read books, plant trees, paint classrooms, and build playgrounds.

In your first year of studies, Fisher gives you the business basics, providing flexibility for two electives or courses in a major area. A key feature of the program is Business Solutions Teams, in which small groups of students spend 20 weeks working on a consulting project for a local corporation. At the project's end, each team presents its recommendations to the client firm's senior executives. In recent years, BSTs, as they are called, have worked with Emery Worldwide, Nationwide Insurance, and California Fitness Centers.

During year two, students must choose a major and can pick up a minor as well. Fisher offers six majors—corporate financial management, investment management, marketing management, operations and logistics management, consulting, and interdisciplinary studies (in which you combine three minor areas to form a major)—plus a new concentration, e-Commerce. "We are more aggressively developing expertise in the area of electronic commerce while monitoring the field to understand what has worked and what has failed," the school's dean of about 10 years, Joseph Alutto, has said. Overall, the school offers a menu of 67 elective courses, the most popular of which are Emerging Technologies and Electronic Commerce, Principles of Electronic Marketing, The Stock Market, Emerging Markets, Managerial Negotiations, Entrepreneurship and Business

Plan Development, and Implementing and Managing Lean Processes. The required 13 core courses and 14 electives can be completed in six quarters.

In addition to newer subject areas like e-commerce, operations and logistics are a key focus of the school, along with accounting and finance. Fisher puts more than $22 million of endowment money into the hands of selected MBA students so they can manage a real investment portfolio. The risk has produced big profits for the university and hands-on experience for students; in recent years, MBAs participating in the Student Investment Management Program (SIM) have consistently outperformed the Standard & Poor's 500 index.

The internationally oriented find plenty of global learning options at Ohio State. All MBAs have the chance to hear lectures by executives from around the world through the B-school's Distinguished International Speaker Series and The Fisher Council on Global Trade and Technology, an organization established by The Limited, Inc. chairman Leslie Wexner. (Recent guests have included NAFTA expert Sidney Weintraub and former President Gerald Ford.) Study abroad programs for second-year MBAs are conducted with B-schools in Italy, Chile, South Korea, Germany, and Mexico. If you prefer to spend just a week or so traveling, enroll in one of the quarter-long student-planned emerging markets courses that cover the business, economic, and cultural environment of 1 of 13 countries, including Turkey, Egypt, Hong Kong, Argentina, Hungary, and Brazil. The group conducts site visits during spring break at multinational companies like Accenture, IBM, and Wal-Mart in its particular country of study. Participants also write relevant case studies upon their return. A new partnership with the Peace Corps allows selected Fisher MBA candidates to take on a two-year business assignment abroad after their first year at Ohio State, with a final year of study at the B-school upon their return. In addition, Ohio State offers MBAs a series of business-oriented language classes in Japanese, Chinese, Russian, Spanish, French, and more.

Columbus is not exactly a major business or financial center, even though The Limited, Wendy's, and Worthington Industries had their starts as small companies here. Nevertheless, the city is a fairly hospitable place for Fisher MBAs to spend two years. The sprawling campus is just two miles from downtown, which boasts a major art museum and a new convention center. Nearby are restaurants, nightspots, galleries, and shops in Short North, Brewery District, and German Village. The city also cheers on its own major league soccer team and will soon sport a new arena for its major league hockey franchise.

For a campus with 55,000 students, the MBA class size is minuscule—about 145 full-time graduates each year. This dynamic creates a lot of room for students to lead or at least become involved in some of the school's student organizations, from the Business Law Society and High Tech Club to Net Impact and the Black MBA Association. Case and business plan competitions also command a large portion of many students' time. Although the small number of MBAs here helps to provide an intimate and active learning experience, it has historically hurt Ohio State in the placement area. Some companies are just not willing to make the trip to Columbus because they can't fill more than a day of interviews. "Not enough firms from the East or West Coasts came to campus," one recent grad confirms. Another cites a "lack of effort on the part of the career services staff" as one of the program's biggest drawbacks. "Most students were dissatisfied with the amount of help they received, particularly the international students," he asserts. Even so, and with the new facilities as added incentive, Class of 2000 Fisher grads did all right for themselves: A full 93 percent were employed by graduation. And who knows what will happen once recruiters can start getting comfy in the new inn after it opens in 2002.

PLACEMENT DETAILS

MBAs have traditionally complained that the placement office is too Midwest oriented, and even with new facilities and an enhanced career services staff, there's just no getting around the challenges of the B-school's small size and non–financial center location. Nonetheless, Class of 2000 Ohio State MBAs managed to pull in an average of three job offers each, and nearly all had accepted a position by the end of their two years.

To increase the geographic diversity of recruiters, in addition to continuously attempting to draw more and more companies to campus, Ohio State is concentrating on having a greater number of firms reach Fisher MBAs "virtually," through such means as online job postings and videoconferencing techniques. Administrators are also working on building up the school's database of alumni and executive contacts. Adding opportunities for internships will help with placement, too, as more than half of last year's summer stints resulted in job offers for Class of 2000 grads. The biggest recruiters: Accenture (7); IBM (4); Procter & Gamble (4); Dell (3); Ford (3); International Paper (3); Kimberly-Clark (3); 3M (3); Cinergy (2); CSC Consulting (2); Hyperion (2); Intel (2); Motorola (2); National City Bank (2); and SGI (2).

OUTSTANDING FACULTY

Peter Easton (accounting); *Anil Makhija* (finance); *John Persons* (finance); *Arnon Reichers* (human resources); *Neeli Bendapudi* (marketing); *J. Dix* (marketing).

APPLICANT TIPS

Work experience is one of the most important factors in admissions decisions at Ohio State. "We want the people who have the most to contribute," says MBA Program Director Michelle Jacobson, who advises applicants to demonstrate how they may have worked through conflict, their leadership skills, and what they can incorporate into the academic experience. Students in the Class of 2002 have an average of 5 years of experience. Applicants who are "fresh out of the undergrad experience" are considered if they excel in other areas, but few tend to be accepted. GMAT scores, another important admissions factor, have leveled off in recent years at an average of about 645, which is what Class of 2002 MBAs registered.

In the past, Ohio State did not encourage applicants to come to campus to interview because the building was in such bad shape. But now that the B-school has a new home, interviews are not only encouraged but are required of those whose applications are viewed favorably. Current students will call or e-mail about 400 such applicants and invite them to interview on campus with both student ambassadors and an admissions officer. This trip also offers an opportunity to meet with a group of students over lunch and attend a class if you prearrange it through the admissions office. Prospective students who have not yet applied can request a short informational interview as well.

Contact: Laura Lembo
Associate Director of Admissions
614-292-8511
Application deadlines: November 15; December 12; January 15; March 15; April 30

FISHER MBAs SOUND OFF

I think that Fisher has done a superb job of being responsive to student initiatives. In the three years that I have attended Fisher (I am a dual-degree student), I saw the creation or implementation of virtually dozens of student-suggested changes. New electives, new minors, dismissing core faculty who were not performing, going above and beyond to retain top professors, new student organizations, and creating an interview component to the admissions process were wholeheartedly supported (financially and otherwise) by the administration.

I believe strongly that the new facilities contributed significantly to the success and strength of the program. Having gone to Ohio State for my undergraduate degree (and studying business in the old business school) I can appreciate the impact our building has had on many areas. With classes all in one building (which includes a large computer lab) interaction with fellow classmates has been enhanced, as well as the quality of speakers and the general atmosphere.

I found the opportunities to cultivate leadership to be excellent in quality and many in quantity—it would be very difficult for one to justify not having grown while in the program. I found the environment 100 percent conducive to personal and professional growth and the staff very willingly engaged in the cycle of continuous improvement. The facilities were state of the art!

The people here are incredible, both students and faculty. There is absolutely no "cutthroat" attitude. Everyone helps each other. Through social interaction as well as interaction in the classroom, we have become a close-knit group. The faculty and staff are so responsive. They added nine new electives this year alone in response to student demand. We have regular town meetings that are nearly standing-room-only where students can express their concerns. Student initiatives are encouraged and supported.

The quality of the teaching was mostly very good, but in some areas it was average to poor, especially in the first-year core courses. Fisher was responsive to student concerns in this area, and made a number of teaching changes

in the core classes this year, which appear to have been well received. Also, there was a sense of genuine camaraderie among my classmates, and they were very supportive of each other. Students did not try to compete with each other, and overall there was a friendly atmosphere in classes and social events.

I believe that Fisher's lenient grading system (very rarely were grades below a B– given) made it easy for many students to take advantage by not contributing as much to groupwork. Often, a particular course's total point percentage for midterms and exams were worth as much (or more) than the group projects in the course, even though the group projects were much more time-consuming. I think this caused many to neglect their roles on teams. If so much emphasis is placed on teams, more needs to be done to punish those who don't contribute.

Fisher needs to do a better job at attracting a diverse student body. Too many students seemed "cut from the same mold," with little to no relevant work (or life) experiences. Too much emphasis was placed on getting people with high GMAT scores rather than with diverse and well-rounded work experiences. As a result, I don't think I learned as much about business from my fellow classmates as I thought I would before business school.

I really believe that the administration and the school are heading in the right direction. The new classroom and office buildings help to attract higher-quality professors and higher-quality students. The administration has made an effort to listen to students' needs.

The school needs the most work in recruiting, especially in getting blue-chip companies from outside the Midwest. Each year a few grads get placed at companies where there are no Fisher alums. This year, students are going to Dell, Intel, and 3M for the first time. This should lead to more favorable impressions of Fisher among non-Midwest companies that have traditionally recruited at more established schools with national reputations. As this snowballs, I think the Fisher name will have more "juice" with employers.

The program needs a lot of work on the placement service front. Most international students barely get any service from this office. The school needs to enroll a diverse variety of American students since the majority of the American students are either from Ohio or the Midwest region.

PENNSYLVANIA
STATE
UNIVERSITY

PENNSYLVANIA STATE UNIVERSITY

The Mary Jean and Frank P. Smeal College of Business Administration
106 University Administration Building
University Park, Pennsylvania 16802-3000
E-mail address: szm6@psu.edu
Web site address: http://www.smeal.psu.edu/mba

Enrollment: 209
Women: 25%
Non-U.S.: 35%
Minority: 11%
Part-time: 0
Average age: 28
Applicants accepted: 15%
Median starting pay: $87,000

Annual tuition & fees:
   resident—$8422
   nonresident—$16,086
Room and board: $6100
Average GMAT score: 616
Average years of work exp.: 5
Accepted applicants enrolled: 59%

Teaching methods: Lecture, 30%   Case study, 40%
                 Problem-based learning, 30%

Contact:
Gerry R. Browder
Director of Admissions
814-863-0474
Application deadlines:
December 15 (early admission)
February 15 (int'l)
May 15 (domestic)

In the past few years, Penn State's MBA program has found itself in a rebuilding process intended to integrate and streamline everything from the curriculum to the very heart of the program: its mission. The somewhat vague-sounding mottoes from brochures and promotional materials for The Mary Jean and Frank P. Smeal College of Business Administration—such as "We learn to compete by cooperating"—are now overshadowed by four bolder buzzwords that hold significant and timely meaning: *convergence, communications, customization, community.*

Behind the freshly hatched catchphrase is a newly installed dean—Judy Olian, the former second-in-command at the University of Maryland's Robert H. Smith School of Business. Arriving in July 2000, Dean Olian came spirited and determined to boost the B-school upward in its reputation and rankings, and with the support and assistance of such key faculty as the highly popular among students MBA Program Director Rocki DeWitt, the mission is underway. Dean Olian declares: "Our focus is on having students understand how the world is changing and how this affects business."

Although the current incompleteness of the project has the B-school in a state of flux—at press time, there was no determination of a definite number of core course requirements—you can rest assured that the renewal is steadily taking shape. About 7 to 10 new faculty members are being hired each year to teach across disciplines, a strategy designed to better integrate topics throughout the curriculum and improve overall teaching quality. The latter has been a legitimate concern here; Smeal rated below average on student satisfaction measures of teaching in both core courses and electives. After a comprehensive visionary exercise that took place last summer, the B-school began revising the curriculum, which formerly had students traveling through 27 credits of required courses of varying lengths in fits and starts as needed. The new structure is a 7-1-7 model applied, for now, only to electives. Each course is broken up into two blocks of seven-week study periods, with an "Immersion Week" in between. The interim one-week period either builds on the material learned in the first half of the course or preps students for what will come in the second half. MBAs can use the time to take courses from the executive program roster, participate in an intensive educational experience from the Smeal Research Center network, or work through a business project on-site at a corporation.

Elective courses are also now grouped into portfolios in eight subject areas—Corporate Financial Analysis and Planning, e-Business, Information Technologies for Management, Investment Management and Portfolio Analysis, Product and Market Development, Entrepreneurship, Strategic Consulting, and Supply Chain Management—to provide students with "domain expertise." MBAs can opt to complete at least two portfolios, which have coursework beginning in the first year. Of the subject areas, one of Smeal's strongest is supply chain management, the procurement of raw materials and the distribution of products after they are manufactured. Corporate recruiters ranked the school's operations skills training well in 2000. Corporate Financial Analysis and Planning, another popular area of study, has been enhanced with a new trading room that opened last spring and gives MBAs access to live market data feeds and software programs that simulate such processes as trading and portfolio management. Also renowned is Smeal's expertise in business-to-business marketing, driven by the

school's Institute for the Study of Business Markets. The concepts taught here synergize nicely with those behind another new research center on electronic commerce established in 1999. The school has developed several programs in conjunction with other schools in the university, too, including a one-year Quality and Manufacturing Management degree that connects MBAs with the College of Engineering. There's a five-year MBA/B.S. in science and dual degrees in law and health administration, too. For MBAs interested in a global experience, Smeal offers exchange partnerships with B-schools in Europe, Asia, Mexico, and New Zealand.

Smeal's MBAs, additionally, train hard their entire first year for a friendly but grueling contest, the Executive Panel Competition, which has taken place for the past 25 years. Each April, the first-year class is divided into teams of five and then presented with a complex business case that they have 48 hours to analyze. (In 2000, the subject was American Education Corporation, an educational software provider.) In just two days' time, each team must not only come up with its recommendations in the case but also prepare a concise written report and a sparkling oral presentation, complete with high-tech visual aids, which are delivered to a mock management board made up of faculty and alumni. The three judged best by the board then make their presentations again, this time in front of a panel of visiting executives, including some from the company under scrutiny, and the rest of their classmates.

The competition wraps up Smeal's yearlong Management Communications course, one of the country's oldest and strongest B-school communications programs. It's a feature of the MBA program that draws raves from students for teaching them how to write polished business memos, letters, and reports, and make individual and group proposals. But the course is even more than that: It's also an exercise in bringing together the skills in strategy, finance, marketing, and the other business basics that are interwoven throughout the first year. The other course that integrates and spans the B-school program is the new Strategy for Converging Economies, which has students studying business cases throughout both years to learn principles and perspectives of operating within the old and new economies.

Tuition here is a bit higher than you'll find at a number of the public schools in the Top 50. Students at a number of public schools paid less in 2000–2001 than Smeal's in-state fee of $8422 a year. There is some tuition relief with the help of graduate assistantships and scholarships. But payback is relatively quick; Penn State was ranked ninth of the 82 B-schools surveyed by BUSINESSWEEK in terms of the fastest returns for students on their MBA investments. Administrators have also made it a priority to increase funding for scholarships and assistantships, not only to alleviate tuition concerns for a greater number of selected students in coming years but also to help to attract a more competitive crop of MBAs.

Smeal is hoping to woo more top candidates, additionally, by offering updated facilities along with the program's renewed components. One attraction, certainly, is the new William and Joan Schreyer Business Library, which opened in 1999 on the third floor of the Paterno (that's right, the coach put up the money) Wing of the university's main Pattee Library. The expansion has doubled space for the business collection and also includes group study areas, computer ports for Internet access, and an arsenal of electronic research resources. At the same time, four classrooms in the "BAB"—the Business Administration Building, which houses both MBAs and 5600 business undergrads—were remodeled to provide computer hookups at every seat and the latest videoconferencing and multimedia presentation technology used by MBAs with their required laptops. Smeal students now enjoy access to a new electronic auction lab that, launched in 2001, provides an "eBay-like" laboratory environment. There's also a new eIncuba-

tor lab for MBAs who want to cultivate new business ideas. But the biggest boon will be an improved home for Smeal, which is currently in the works. The school is slated for a new building that will make its mark as the largest academic building on campus, but it probably will not open until the 2003–2004 school year.

With some 79,000 students in 24 locations across Pennsylvania, Penn State doesn't exactly bring to mind the idea of intimacy. But it's the right word for describing the MBA program: The 120 students per class are divided into cohorts of 60 for core courses, while the average class size for electives shrinks to 20. Students are accepted only in the fall and are able to complete their coursework by spring break of their second year, so they can return to permanent employment earlier than most MBAs or extend their stays abroad following a spring break study tour. Not surprisingly, the operative mode for the close-knit program is teamwork, which starts with Orientation Week and continues into classes. Trained second-year facilitators and an outside conflict consultant coach first-year teams as they work their way through assignments and inevitably encounter tension and challenges. It doesn't take long before everyone, faculty included, is known on a first-name basis, and students say they quickly forge bonds that carry over into a strong alumni network.

Alums volunteer as mentors to work with students with similar career interests on job hunting strategies and industry networking; recent graduates come back each year for the Simulated Interview Program and Career Exploration, an evening question-and-answer session that gives current students a reality check on their career plans. Alumni have also been instrumental to Smeal in building a strong corporate network. A speaker series brings in executives from a variety of businesses for formal presentations and informal talks over a meal, and the Corporate Associates Program involves more than two dozen firms in more intensive student interactions such as simulated interviews and on-site visits. Companies on the roster include IBM, Cap Gemini Ernst & Young, Accenture, Pfizer Inc., Johnson & Johnson, and PNC Bank, all major employers of Smeal MBAs; one active associate firm, Air Products & Chemicals, currently employs more than 500 alums of Penn State's B-school and other departments.

All of this activity led the Class of '00 to praise Smeal for providing students with numerous contacts with professionals in the community. The success is made all the more remarkable by Penn State's location smack dab in the middle of Pennsylvania, which the school likes to characterize as equidistant from everywhere, but which is actually more like the middle of nowhere. (It's 120 miles east of Pittsburgh and 150 miles west of Philadelphia, with the sprawling 5032-acre University Park campus and its 40,000 students the most exciting attraction in between.) Although the location makes independent job searches more difficult and limits the number of companies willing to come to campus to recruit employees, it isn't necessarily a turnoff. Students give favorable reviews to the lifestyle in what is known as "Happy Valley." The campus, surrounded by mountains, is great for biking, hiking, and other outdoor activities; the community is safe and relatively inexpensive. Most MBAs live within five miles of the school, making it easy for them to participate in the many social events, sports, and community service activities that fill students' spare time.

PLACEMENT DETAILS

A few years ago Smeal's career services department made improvements by adding new features like databases that link MBAs with alumni and inviting corporate recruiters to conduct practice "dry runs" with students through the Simulated Interview Program. These days, the department also boasts a new career coach who offers students one-on-one advisory sessions and a new Director of MBA Marketing who has

a mandate to strengthen corporate relationships. The career services office is devoted to assisting students to land internships, particularly now that they are a required part of the curriculum. (It's a good thing: in 2000, about 60 percent of students' summer internships led to job offers.) Executive advisory boards created for each portfolio also provide students and faculty with greater access to professionals and successful alums. And even though not being located near a major metropolitan area can be a challenge, drawing recruiters to campus doesn't appear to be: About 150 interviewed second-years here last year. But even so, just 82 percent were employed by graduation, leaving some Smeal students to bemoan the selection of employers. "Certain companies heavily recruit here year after year," says one recent grad. "I feel like the administration relies on these companies for a majority of the class, and individuals seeking careers outside these 'mainstays' must rely on their own efforts to secure employment—without help from career services."

In 2000, the majority of Smeal students headed for jobs in finance (38 percent), while roughly equal numbers took jobs in logistics and supply chain management (21 percent) and marketing and sales (20 percent). Just 12 percent went into consulting and 9 percent landed in general management positions. Top employers were IBM (8); Hewlett-Packard/Agilent (6); Cap Gemini Ernst & Young (3); Air Products & Chemicals (2); Apple Computer (2); AT&T (2); Citigroup (2); Delta Airlines (2); Eastman Kodak (2); Honeywell (2); ICF Consulting (2); Johnson & Johnson (2); Liberty Mutual (2); and Lucent Technologies (2).

OUTSTANDING FACULTY

David Butt (communications); *Fariborz Ghadar* (finance); *Chris Muscarella* (finance); *Dennis Sheehan* (finance); *Timothy Murphy* (marketing); *Wayne DeSarbo* (marketing).

APPLICANT TIPS

For the next few years, Smeal will be working on gradually growing its MBA numbers from about 200 to 300 per class while shrinking its massive undergraduate classes and instituting a new executive MBA program. For the Class of 2002, just 15 percent of its 1000-plus pool of applicants were admitted, making the B-school more selective than 23 of BUSINESSWEEK's Top 30. But for a school with all this selectivity, the average GMAT score of 616 for Class of 2002 students was surprisingly low. Class of '02 students also registered an average five years of work experience (a one-year increase from 2000); the school recommends you have at least two years on the job before applying. You should also be computer literate, mathematically competent, and have a working knowledge of statistics, basic economics, and basic accounting. Because the school is on a rolling admissions system and the class size is small, it's advisable to get your paperwork in before the June 1 deadline if possible. Those seeking scholarships and fellowships should aim for February 15, and international applicants must submit completed materials by March 1.

Contact: Gerry R. Browder
Director of Admissions
814-863-0474
Application deadlines: December 15 (early admission); February 15 (international); May 15 (domestic)

SMEAL MBAs SOUND OFF

Penn State's program is academically solid. The faculty is top notch. The social experience, however, leaves a lot to be desired. Penn State's MBA program provides all the snobbishness of an Ivy League school, without all the brains. Many of the students are wealthy suburbanites from the Philadelphia area. If you do not have sufficient money or the right type of social background it is very difficult to fit in socially in the Smeal College MBA environment.

The small program enabled me to meet and get to personally know all of my classmates; however, I feel the small size caused a lack of proactive recruiting on the administration's part. This is the area Penn State needs to work on the most. The staff tries hard, but they're stretched too thin.

I think the key advantage to the Smeal MBA is the size of the program. With only 120 people in three sections, you get personal attention that is not available at the larger programs. Your professors know you by your first name and are readily available outside of class. Many of the elective classes are as small as 15 to 20 students, which is an excellent learning environment.

The marketing engineering concepts are cutting edge, and the communications program is second to none. I can put together a top-notch presentation in a matter of hours. My business partner and I used these skills to put together a presentation over a weekend to request investment in our business from a local economic development agency. After the presentation, we were high on the list to receive funding (which came through at the requested level).

Penn State has the advantage of the low cost of living and high quality of life in the State College area. I saved to attend school and focus on entrepreneurship. And now I can actually afford to put my degree to use right away, as I am not facing huge loans that require immediate income to pay down.

I feel that the education provided by the Smeal program was the equivalent of one of the higher-ranked schools, but with a smaller group in a very supportive atmosphere. I learned the same information without the huge debt.

The size of Penn State's MBA program is one of its strengths. The small size enables a more "community" atmosphere within the larger Penn State world. Additionally, the type of student here is not only focused on individual achievement, but on that of the group as well. There are always faculty, staff, and other students who are willing to help and assist.

In my opinion, the Smeal MBA combines a great learning experience in a small personal environment. There are not too many schools out there where students go out for a mountain-bike ride with their professors.

Because of the small size of the program, it is impossible for Penn State to offer majors in every business field. If Penn State is to break into the Top 30 tier of MBA programs it must focus its resources on two or three key programs instead. Also, Penn State is located in the middle of Pennsylvania and, as such, it is difficult to just pop in on a company that one may want to work for. Thus, either the recruiters come here, there is a phone interview, or students must make a long trip to a major city. It can be inconvenient with a full courseload.

I was very impressed by the level of alumni participation in the MBA program. Past graduates were involved in everything from in-class projects to recruitment to professional mentoring. The Penn State alumni network is not only large and pervasive, but also supportive of its members.

RICE UNIVERSITY

RICE UNIVERSITY

Jesse H. Jones Graduate School of Management

P.O. Box 1892

Houston, Texas 777251

E-mail address: enterjgs@rice.edu

Web site address: http://www.jonesgsm.rice.edu

Enrollment: 308	Annual tuition & fees: $21,500
Women: 30%	Room and board: $7500
Non-U.S.: 20%	Average GMAT score: 640
Minority: 12%	Average years of work exp.: 5
Part-time: 0	Accepted applicants enrolled: 58%
Average age: 28	
Applicants accepted: 39%	
Median starting pay: $96,000	

Teaching methods: Lecture, 33%   Case study, 33%
Team projects, group work, 34%

Contact:
Rachel Seff
Assistant Director of
Admissions and
Marketing
713-348-5347
Application deadlines:
December 1
February 1
April 6

The man for whom the Jesse H. Jones Graduate School of Management was named in 1974 has long been gone from Houston, but his legacy lives on. The Houston entrepreneur and financier Jesse H. Jones chaired the Reconstruction Finance Corp. and was U.S. Secretary of Commerce under Franklin D. Roosevelt. He is credited with helping to pull the nation though the Great Depression, and now the benefactor seems to be an inspiration for doing the same for the B-school that bears his name.

Instead of quietly and solemnly preserving the past, the B-school has, over the last couple of years, been a hotbed of change, much of it initiated by its dean, Gilbert R. Whitaker. Having served as provost of the University of Michigan from 1990 to 1995 and, for the 12 years before that, as dean of Michigan's B-school, Whitaker's move to Houston is something of a homecoming (he got his B.A. in economics from Rice back in 1953).

Since taking over as dean in 1997, Whitaker moved swiftly to transform the Jones School from a strong regional institution to one well regarded on a national scale. Indeed, Whitaker says that when fellow members of the Jones board of directors tapped him to lead the B-school, which they considered lagging far behind the widely recognized quality of the rest of the university, their mandate was either to "fix it or close it." One of his first initiatives was to clinch official accreditation for the school by the AACSB, something Jones had lacked for many years because of a technicality involving control of an undergraduate "managerial studies" major. He has also overhauled the MBA curriculum, borrowing a few ideas from the highly ranked Michigan program, to highlight action learning and leadership skills and instituted an ambitious program "second to none among the world's business schools."

Both Whitaker and Jones have a long way to go in that regard; the B-school hasn't jumped into the Top 30 yet, although Whitaker wants it to be "top ten in ten years." But Whitaker does have a plan in place. He wants to raise $24 million for endowed chairs to increase the number of faculty from 45 to 60; $60 million for the new technologically advanced B-school building; and $7.5 million to increase financial aid to MBA students, a group he hopes to expand from 308 to 360.

The plan broke ground—literally and figuratively—in May 2000 for the new 167,000-square-foot building, tentatively slated to open in 2002. And not a moment too soon. Students say the new building, three times the size of the current one, is desperately needed: the old one is so overcrowded that students often race each other to class in order to grab a rare available seat. Whitaker also established the school's first international exchange partnership and an executive MBA weekend program, from which the first graduates received their degrees in 2000.

Under his new, integrated curriculum, introduced in 1998–1999, each semester has been divided into three 5-week modules, with courses varying from 5 to 10 weeks in length. The schedule packs in a lot of material—you hit the ground running with an orientation expanded to 2 weeks to include a communication skills assessment; math and computing camps; workshops on time management, leadership, and team building; and an introduction to case study methodology. The fall semester alone covers accounting, data analysis, strategy, managerial economics, organizational behavior, ethics, information technology, marketing and finance, plus a semester-long management communication course and the start of a new three-module Leadership and Managerial Skills

sequence, which addresses such issues as corporate politics, effective negotiation, and partnership building.

The spring brings coursework in the world economy, globalization, cost management, operations, business, government relations, and change management; you'll also finish up Leadership and Managerial Skills and work in one 10-week or two 5-week electives. But the centerpiece, launched in spring of 1999, is the Action Learning Project, modeled after Michigan's highly successful Multidisciplinary Action Projects. Mid-semester, you'll meet your four teammates, find out what company you'll be working with, and begin background work on a real-time, real-world consulting project. Then you'll spend the last 5 weeks of the year on-site at your sponsoring firm, with no other classwork to distract you. Possible ALP work can run the gamut. Perhaps a company needs to develop or distribute a new product, streamline its purchasing processes, build an annual sales forecasting tool, or examine its capital appropriation process. Sponsors vary from year to year, but are companies that must submit proposals to the school in order to participate. Recent ALP sponsors have included Chase Bank of Texas, Continental Airlines, IBM, Reliant Energy, The Sabre Group, Solvay Polymers, and WorldOil.com Inc.

Although students say they like the new flexibility and the quality of teaching—Jones students put their professors near the top of all schools surveyed by BUSINESSWEEK when it comes to availability outside the classroom, and say they're tops at helping them develop interpersonal skills, too—the workload with the new curriculum is thought to be excessive by many. During your second year, you'll be required to take a 5-week strategy course and a 10-week entrepreneurship module. In 1996, Rice became one of the only top-ranked schools that won't let you graduate without some entrepreneurial studies under your belt. The rest of the year can be devoted to electives chosen from the B-school's catalog of 101 courses. One of

Whitaker's priorities has been to expand the full-time faculty, which has traditionally been outnumbered by adjunct and visiting professors. For the start of the 2000–2001 school year, tenure-track professors numbered 38, up from 25 in 1996, but still fewer than his goal of 60. Whitaker has already plucked professors from the staffs of top schools like Michigan, Cornell, and North Carolina and plans to make five additional hires in 2001.

While second-year students now have 11 elective areas from which to choose—accounting, organizational behavior and human resource management, entrepreneurship, information technology, finance, international business, strategy, operations, legal, marketing, and health care—Jones has no departments or requirements for concentrations. Whitaker describes the program as "designed to prepare students for new ways to work within established companies." Students rate the international business department at Jones in the top 10 of all schools ranked by BUSINESSWEEK, a dramatic change from 1998, when it was among the worst. It was after that 1998 rank that Whitaker set out to change things, launching the school's first overseas exchange program in 1998 with a business school in Costa Rica and proposing to put in place five more partner schools in Europe and Latin America during 1999. Rice now also offers dual degrees in engineering, medicine, and a Ph.D. focused on the biotech, pharmaceuticals, and health-care industries.

This is still a fairly small but growing program—with about 150 students per class in 2000, it's 15 percent bigger than it was in 1996 and will expand to a still-cozy 360, which Whitaker thinks is the smallest size a top-tier school can be. And with the faculty expansion, Jones will maintain its low student/professor ratio. The small B-school enrollment and relative youth of the MBA program, founded in 1974, does limit the size of an alumni network that numbers just 1750—smaller than two grad-uating classes from Harvard, Wharton, or Northwestern. But that's balanced by the active involvement of Houston's sizable corporate community—the second largest concentration of Fortune 500 headquarters—with a Council of Overseers made up of 32 local executives who advise the dean on school strategy and curriculum, and speakers of national prominence drawn not only to the B-school but to Rice's numerous research centers, such as the James A. Baker III Institute for Public Policy.

Students here aren't the most diverse group of MBAs around, because Jones attracts just 20 percent of its enrollment from outside the United States. The school fares better with women, who make up about 30 percent of the MBAs, and underrepresented U.S. minorities, who make up about 12 percent of the population. Whatever their backgrounds, Jones students tend to be a hard-working and somewhat competitive bunch who take an active role in enriching the school. In fact, two administrative posts are now held by recent grads—the MBA program director, Carrie Chamberlain, was a member of the Class of 1997, and Deanna Sheaffer, of the Class of 1996, is director of alumni affairs and finances and marketing. The student-run Leadership Development Program provides an array of experiences for strengthening leadership skills, running a high-adventure ropes course, participating in charity projects benefiting The Texas Children's Hospital or Habitat for Humanity, or organizing a corporate golf tournament.

Herring Hall sits in the middle of the 300-acre Rice campus, an oasis of tranquility—with more trees than students—just a few miles from the infamously smog-ridden business district. Across the street is the enormous Texas Medical Center; within walking distance are several museums, the Houston Zoo, Hermann Park, and Rice Village, a collection of shops and restaurants. Students like to hang out in the nearby Montrose neighborhood, filled with art film houses, ethnic restaurants, boutiques, and coffeehouses. Most MBAs live off campus, although a deluxe graduate housing facility completed in 1999 now gives students more on-campus options.

PLACEMENT DETAILS

After grads in 1998 reported that they were not very enthusiastic about the Jones placement operation, Whitaker cleaned house, and in 2000 the entire staff was new. He upped the office from two to five staffers, including Director of Career Planning and Admissions Peter Veruki, who came from Vanderbilt and is the author of *The 250 Job Interview Questions You'll Most Likely Be Asked . . . and the Answers That Will Get You Hired!*

Monika Drake and the other second assistant directors have been assigned by class and industry, and the restructuring has already paid off. Nearly 7 percent of 1998 grads had no job offers at graduation. That number was down to 5 percent in 2000. And of the 95 percent with job offers, students had an impressive 3 offers each. Of that class, 26 percent accepted jobs outside of Texas, compared to 5 percent in 1999. The average starting salary was $96,000, including bonus.

The Career Planning Center's program focuses on personalized career planning, meeting individually with first-year students to discuss career goals and strategy, then requires each student to be videotaped in a mock interview. The CPC also brings in outside firms to run employment skills workshops and on Thursday afternoons holds corporate-sponsored "partios" on the Herring Hall patio to give students and faculty a chance to share pizza and beer with potential employers in an informal setting.

Only 66 companies recruited on campus in 2000, but the school has improved its efforts to get out to recruiters who don't make it all the way to Houston. That includes trips to both New York and the Silicon Valley. Hires by AOL,

Hewlett-Packard, and Intel are among the evidence the CPC counts as progress in this area. For the Class of 2001 there is a greater emphasis on entrepreneurship and jobs at start-ups. The center expects the Class of 2001 to exceed the Class of 2000's 13 percent of students who went to work for a start-up and 4 percent who started their own companies.

Top employers were Enron (9), Compaq (8), Chase (6), Deloitte Consulting (5), Intel (4), Dell (3), Continental (3), Pricewaterhouse-Coopers (3), Reliant Energy (3), and Campbell Soup (2).

OUTSTANDING FACULTY

Ed Williams (entrepreneurship); *Jeff Fleming* (finance); *David Ikenberry* (finance); *Barbara Ostdiek* (finance); *Piyush Kumar* (marketing); *Sanjay Sood* (marketing).

APPLICANT TIPS

Jones accepted 32 percent of applicants to the Class of 1994. It accepted 48 percent to the Class of 2000. But applicant acceptance dropped back to 30 percent for 2001. What does all the flip-flopping mean? You have an excellent opportunity to get into an up-and-coming program, but it is by no means a shoo-in.

How do you get an edge? Your GMAT and GPA matter, of course, but Rice also takes into account your choice of major, electives, course load, and grade patterns in evaluating your academic background. Leadership potential ranks high on the list of criteria for admission, so you should stress your experiences leading others and utilizing management skills on the job and in extracurricular and community activities, both in the three application essays and an interview—which the school requires. About 9 percent of the Class of 2000 had less than a year's work experience, but five years was the average time on the job and the school says it looks for at least two.

You're also encouraged to apply early—those who apply by the December or January deadlines can expect a response in six weeks; if you wait until February or April to apply, you won't hear for two months.

Contact: Rachel Seff
Assistant Director of Admissions and Marketing
713-348-5347
Application deadlines: December 1; February 1; April 6

JONES MBAs SOUND OFF

I would like to highlight that the teaching at the Jones School of Business is exceptional, and I learned a tremendous amount from both the professors and visitors that taught there. I have been very impressed with the influx of quality new professors to the school and believe that they are changing the dynamics and environment there.

My years at Jones were years of great change in the program during which the school implemented a new curriculum and teaching structure and underwent significant turnover in the career placement department. Although some of the changes were not effective as implemented, I commend the administration for its readiness to listen to student concerns and its responsiveness in making the necessary changes.

The courses are demanding and the workload is intensive, but the interaction between students and teachers creates an environment that allows everyone to grow. The culture is such that students actually challenge professors to push harder.

I came into the Rice program when it was going through a transition. The curriculum changed drastically, and classes were added that focused on the human side of business, such as Negotiation, Leadership, and Change Management. Although some students moaned about the "soft" classes during their first year, many were able to cite specific instances when those classes came in handy during their summer internship.

The curriculum and faculty are outstanding at the Jones School; they surpassed all of my expectations. However, the Career Center has been through three directors in the past year, and it's been difficult to appreciate the last two years when I'm coming upon graduation with no job prospects. Unfortunately, I share this situation with many other graduates.

More than anything, the administration at Rice was responsive to the students' desires to upgrade the curriculum. Due to the many students taking employment in the energy industry, we asked the administration to add courses in this field that would assist us upon graduation. They responded by adding two courses, Business Strategy in the Energy Industry and Energy Derivatives, Trading, and Risk Management.

SOUTHERN
METHODIST
UNIVERSITY

SOUTHERN METHODIST UNIVERSITY

Edwin L. Cox School of Business
Dallas, Texas 75275-0333
E-mail address: mbainfo@mail.cox.smu.edu
Web site address: http://www.cox.smu.edu

Enrollment: 908	Annual tuition & fees: $24,680
Women: 36%	Room and board: $7885
Non-U.S.: 30%	Average GMAT score: 644
Minority: 13%	Average years of work exp.: 4.5
Part-time: 672	Accepted applicants enrolled: 55%
Average age: 27	
Applicants accepted: 33%	
Median starting pay: $93,000	

Teaching methods: Lecture, 40%   Case study, 40%
Group projects, 20%

Contact:
Brenda Hernandez
Interim Director of
Admissions
800-472-3622
Application deadlines:
November 30
January 8
February 12
March 30
May 15

Although Southern Methodist University's Edwin L. Cox School of Business is an 81-year-old program, the school today is functioning much more like a shiny newcomer. When you ask Cox students and graduates what they like about their program, the answers are enthusiastic: small classes; a smart but accessible and caring faculty; an extremely active mentoring program that pairs MBAs with Dallas business executives and Cox alumni; an administration that listens to their requests. But when you ask corporate recruiters from outside Texas or the Southwest region what they like about Cox, their answer might sometimes be, "Who?"

And that's the dilemma Dean Albert W. Niemi, Jr., who came to SMU from the University of Georgia in 1997, has been facing. Few other Top 50 B-schools exhibit such a large gap in the perceptions of its two main constituents, the MBAs who attend the school and the companies who hire them. And that's been one motivating factor behind a number of changes to the program being implemented by Niemi. He's tried to overhaul Cox's curriculum by adding both more global and technological emphases for the program, expanding the faculty and career services staffing, and developing a national recruiting network that makes better use of the school's 7800 enthusiastic alumni.

The completely new curriculum was put in place in the fall of 2000, so there are no Cox graduates yet who have come out on the other side and can evaluate its real-word value. But among the Class of 2000—the students who were influential in helping Niemi shape the changes—enthusiasm is high. In fact, says one recent alum: "I am so jealous that I will not be here next year to take the new courses."

Students describe the 2000–2001 curriculum as "dramatically improved," with a module system that focuses on team building in the first year and offers a remarkable 93 percent of new electives in the second year, without requiring a concentration. Among SMU's growing strengths are international programs, entrepreneurship, and off-campus, hands-on business leadership. In December 2000, for example, the Business's Business Leadership Center sent 54 MBAs to the Disney Institute in Orlando for a three-day intensive course in Disney leadership theories and their actual application within Epcot Center, Disney World, and MGM Studios; Cox is the only MBA program invited to study at the Disney. In October Cox expanded its Information Technologies and Operations Management department, adding four faculty members, including former Vanderbilt University professor Bezalel Gavish, an expert in telecommunications research and education.

But while it seems that Niemi's objective of "great things" may, indeed, come to Cox, there is still a great deal in flux in the interim. Of course, Cox is no stranger to upheaval—as recently as 1992, the school skipped an entire graduating class of MBAs as it transformed its compressed one-year MBA format into the more traditional two-year program. And although the latest changes aren't on that scale, students who entered SMU after 2000 have opportunities that are very different from those of their predecessors.

Most noticeable is the modular system. If you choose to go to SMU, you'll have a first-year courseload that includes Financial Accounting, Marketing Management or Financial Management, Managerial Statistics and Forecasting, and Economics for Business Decisions in the first semester and Operations and Technology Management, Marketing Management or Financial Management, Organizational Behavior and Diversity, Global Leadership Program, and two electives in the second semester. After your summer internship, your second year is almost all

yours, with Managing Your Career, Strategic Analysis in a Global Era, and 16 electives.

The centerpiece of the new schedule is the American Airlines Global Leadership Program, now required of all first-year students during the final three weeks before you head off for your summer internships. The class is divided into three groups, each focused on a different region: Latin America, Europe, or Asia. After a three-day on-campus orientation, the faculty-led groups will spend two weeks abroad in May, meeting with business and government leaders and visiting manufacturing facilities.

On the global itinerary are Beijing, Shanghai, Tokyo, and Taipei in Asia; London, Paris, and Munich in Europe; and Buenos Aires, Rio de Janeiro, Sao Paulo, and Santiago in Latin America. Once back on U.S. soil, you'll participate in a three-day on-campus symposium to share your observations with both the school and members of the Dallas business community. Overseas participating firms include Shanghai Bell, Banco Central de Chile, and DaimlerChrysler, among others.

Niemi visited Japan 15 years ago, and he says that two-week trip still sticks with him today. So he's confident that the experiences of all SMU's MBAs will stay with them at least until second year, where the international experiences are included in class discussion across disciplines. "This kind of global experience will give our students the knowledge and perspective employers look for and leaders need. The dynamics of globalization can only be comprehended through experience," he says. And unlike the international components of most MBA programs, the Global Leadership Program doesn't cost anything extra . . . it's covered entirely by the regular MBA tuition, thanks to a three-year gift from American Airlines (based in Dallas), which covers about $1 million in airfare.

Strengthening programs abroad isn't Niemi's only emphasis. This fall Cox added 30 different e-commerce courses (not all of which are always available simultaneously); the Information Systems and Operations Management was renamed Information Technologies and Operations Management as it welcomed its four new faculty members. The B-school's once limited catalog of 58 electives now numbers 107. Among the most popular current offerings are those related to the energy industry, not surprising considering the Texas locale and the backing of Cox's Maguire Energy Institute research center, renamed in 1999 to reach an even broader audience.

To handle the increased number of courses in the modular schedule, Niemi has already boosted the number of full-time faculty from 65 to 80, with e-commerce, technology, and real estate/insurance/business law among the departments that most benefited from the expansion. The new hires further enhance what students call one of the finest teaching faculties anywhere. The Class of 2000 reported that prominent academics were active in teaching and were almost always accessible for informal discussion. And students agreed that professors were knowledgeable about the latest issues in their fields. Almost one-third—29 percent of Cox faculty—have more than five years' experience working for corporations in their fields. Coupled with a cozy class size of about 130 full-time MBAs a year, this means students get the personal touch: "Because it was a small community, the faculty was on a first-name basis with every student, which helped facilitate learning in and out of the classroom," says one 2000 grad. "I cannot imagine a better professor lineup anywhere: the teaching was awesome," effuses another.

Also providing plenty of individual attention are 200 local managers and executives who act as mentors for Cox MBAs. Indeed, in the BUSINESSWEEK survey, students ranked SMU in the top 20 in providing connections that will be useful throughout one's career. Drawn from the large cadre of corporations that call fast-growing Dallas home, including EDS, American Airlines, Frito-Lay, and JCPenney, as well as the ranks of entrepreneurs and venture capitalists, mentors are matched by occupational interest with first-years soon after they arrive on campus. Throughout the two-year program, mentors meet with their designated students regularly, inviting them to their organizations for tours and sharing advice on business and careers, not to mention breakfasts and cocktail parties.

With the curriculum revision, Cox's leadership development program—a series of seminars on communication, team building, and other practical skills used on the job—has become a for-credit requirement. Topics range from stress management and creative thinking to presentation techniques and negotiating skills. Several of the sessions take the form of outdoor team exercises and computer simulations, and a series of skill and personality tests to assess your individual strengths and weaknesses, given over the course of your two years at SMU, helps to gauge how effective the training has been. Also required for credit will be a series of workshops, sponsored by the Career Management Office and led by alums and second-years, on field-specific career opportunities. The office holds workshops on résumé writing, job-search strategy, salary negotiation, and interviewing as well. Alums and outside consultants are also available to conduct and critique mock interviews.

When you're not in the classroom, the grassy campus invites you to study outdoors. Cox is near the center of the university's tree-lined 160 acres, set in University Park, an affluent residential neighborhood five miles from downtown Dallas. The B-school is made up of three attached, classically styled, red-brick buildings arranged in a horseshoe shape around a courtyard; one wing is designated as MBA headquarters. Few SMU grads live on campus, most making their homes in "the village," a maze of apartment complexes about a half-mile from campus. The university's affiliation with the Methodist Church means that virtually all drinking must be done off campus, so on Thursday nights (there are no classes on Fridays), MBAs gather at the Old Monk. An increase in the number of minority students—from 5 percent in 1998 to 13 percent in 2000—has helped make the school somewhat less provincial.

The familial feel of SMU doesn't stop with those connections with alums and local business execs. Students here say everyone goes out of their way to make SMU feel like home, even if you're not a Southerner by birth. "The truly great thing about Cox is the support that everyone gives you. When a class is 'full,' they figure out a way to get you in," says Jason Kirkpatrick, a Class of 2000 graduate who is working on his own start-up. "I also made a valuable contact for my business through the dean's secretary. I had spoken with her about a week before a social event with the Cox Mentor Board. At the event she remembered our conversation and introduced me to the person I described."

Visiting and exchange students are often welcome to stay with the director of student service until they find a place to live, and Niemi buys pizza during study breaks before all final exams.

PLACEMENT DETAILS

The one area in most need of improvement at Cox is the Career Management Office. While most students are happy with the results of their job search—90 percent had offers at graduation and the average graduate in 2000 had two offers—the school is still an unknown to recruiters outside the South. An increasing number of students say that doesn't bother them much.

"My experience is that when SMU students have gone head-to-head for the same job with students from 'top 10' schools, in many, many cases, we have gotten the offers," says one. Others say that the cost of living in Dallas is so low, they've realized it would be "ridiculous" not to consider the offers they're getting to stay in town from the city's 6000 employers. And while salaries may be low, the overwhelming majority of Cox grads are offered substantial signing bonuses and stock options.

But for those with an eye toward I-banks or other traditional MBA jobs on the coasts, SMU still has work to do. Just 54 companies interviewed second-years on campus in 2000, and most of those were regional firms. Like many schools in the center of the country, administrators are working on building interview opportunities in a number of cities. Because Cox alumni are particularly loyal and schooled in the mentoring philosophy, the strategy may work faster here than elsewhere.

Alumni also like Niemi's newest creation, a comprehensive package of online services for alumni that includes a searchable directory, career links, lifetime e-mail, instructions for building individual home pages, and bulletin boards around various topics of interest. Top employers of the Class of 2000 were American Airlines (4), Nortel Networks (4), Sabre (4), Akili Systems (3), Associates First Capital (3), Donaldson, Lufkin & Jenrette (3), Exxon Mobil (3), A.T. Kearney (2), Chase Bank (2), Cisco (2).

OUTSTANDING FACULTY

Randy Beatty (accounting/finance); *James Smith* (economics); *David Mauer* (finance); *Mike Vetsuypens* (finance); *Robin Pinkley* (negotiations/organizational behavior).

APPLICANT TIPS

Cox has pushed hard over the last couple of years to increase student quality, which means it's now much harder to get into this school than it once was. While the B-school accepted a majority—62 percent—of applicants to the

Class of 1998, just 32 percent of those who applied to the Class of 2000 were admitted, a number that remained steady at 33 percent for the Class of 2002. Over that same four-year period, the average GMAT score increased from 601 to 636 to 644; and the number of entering students with less than a year's work experience plunged from 13 percent to 2 percent. Meanwhile, the number of applications the school received jumped from 491 in 1997 to 595 in 1998 to 650 in 2000.

One way you can distinguish yourself from the growing pack is through a personal interview, not required but strongly recommended. After the office receives your application materials they'll contact you about scheduling an interview, either on campus or off campus, with a designated admissions representative, or via telephone with an admissions representative. Of the prospective students applying to the Class of 2002, 62 percent interviewed. On-campus candidates are invited to meet with a current MBA student host. Off-campus interviews are also frequently conducted when the admissions staff travels with the MBA Tour in Latin America, and at the GMAC Forums in North America.

The admissions office says selection criteria focus not only on one's academic record but also on "distinctive achievements, commitments, and motivation for a graduate business education." Among the qualities the school seeks in candidates: "leadership ability, international experience, initiative, management potential, communication skills, and interpersonal skills," plus "an entrepreneurial spirit." So, you should look to play up those aspects of your background in your interview and essays. Those who apply by November 30 will receive a response by January 12; if you wait until the May 15 deadline, you won't hear until June 15. A new application process allows you to choose to apply—either on the Web or on paper—in two phases, completing an information page first and submitting other materials as you have them ready.

Contact: Brenda Hernandez
Interim Director of Admissions
800-472-3622
Application deadlines: November 30; January 8; February 12; March 30; May 15

COX MBAs SOUND OFF

Cox is an extremely responsive, student-driven school. The students are so empowered and take such ownership of the program it is truly amazing.

Student Services at Cox were unsurpassed. The staff and faculty are extremely responsive to the needs of the students and every effort was made to encourage us to take ownership of the program. Leadership opportunities for students were also abundant, which I think is important for an MBA program. I appreciated the fact that my classmates had work experience—nobody came straight through from undergraduate.

The relationship with the business community allowed for an unprecedented amount of personal interaction between the students and businesspeople. Since we were encouraged to develop ties with the mentors/business leaders, there were many opportunities for career planning, job hunting, and general success strategies.

The faculty at SMU was outstanding. While the range of electives offered wasn't as deep as other schools, the quality of the teaching was outstanding. Also, as the students realized holes in the education, the admin and faculty did everything possible to fill the gaps and offer the students the electives they sought.

The smaller class size allowed for more interaction between students and teachers both in and out of the classroom. The faculty were also very receptive to adjusting electives to match our expectations and needs.

The SMU MBA program is excellent and perhaps underrated. The relatively small size of the program is a major asset, though it may reduce the visibility of the program. I believe a number of new initiatives, in e-commerce, career management, and the new Global Leadership program, will help the school stand out and be recognized as the solid program that it is.

While at the school I also enjoyed the opportunity to meet (at a one-on-one level) with numerous industry leaders. I toured facilities across the country and was privileged to have been given the opportunity to debate corporate policy with those individuals upon whom the case studies were based. Additionally, the size of the school afforded the students the opportunity to form close friendships with a majority of the program. Two years after starting I now have 120 new friends.

THUNDERBIRD, THE AMERICAN GRADUATE SCHOOL OF INTERNATIONAL MANAGEMENT

THUNDERBIRD, THE AMERICAN GRADUATE SCHOOL OF INTERNATIONAL MANAGEMENT

15249 North 59th Avenue
Glendale, Arizona 85306-6000
E-mail address: tbird@t-bird.edu
Web site address: http://www.t-bird.edu

Enrollment: 1400	Annual tuition & fees: $24,950
Women: 26%	Room and board: $7200
Non-U.S.: 47%	Average GMAT score: 611
Minority: 10%	Average years of work exp.: 5
Part-time: 0	Accepted applicants enrolled: 47%
Average age: 28	
Applicants accepted: 76%	
Median starting pay: $82,000	

Teaching methods: Lecture, 25%   Case study, 50%
Group projects, simulations, 25%

Contact:
Judy Johnson
Director of Admissions
800-848-9084
OR 602-978-7596
Application deadlines:
January 30 (fall)
July 30 (spring)
November 30
(summer)

The problem with being ahead of the curve is that at some point the masses catch up with you. That's been the conundrum facing Thunderbird, The American Graduate School of International Management in recent years. When Thunderbird was founded in 1946 on a deactivated Army air training base outside Phoenix—and for the 30 years that followed—it was the only business program in the United States with a serious orientation toward international business. But in the last decade, schools from Ivy Leaguers all the way down to tiny, local junior colleges have jumped on the bandwagon, offering a global slant to their business programs. Where Thunderbird once had a clear arena for excellence in its specialty, it's now being challenged by the likes of Wharton, Michigan, and even Marshall and Cox, which both now have highly regarded overseas initiatives. Students still rank Thunderbird No. 1 among U.S. schools for its international business efforts and third worldwide, but recruiters often cite the programs at Top 30 schools as being more well-rounded in global economics.

To be sure, Thunderbird's got plenty that those other programs don't, because here internationalism is a way of life, not just a concentration. In fact, if you were to try to imagine a business version of the United Nations, you'd probably come up with something very much like Thunderbird. Indeed, the U.N. flag flies each day outside the school's administration building. In addition, a "flag of the day" from one of the 80 different home countries of Thunderbird's students flaps in the dry Arizona breeze near the main entrance to the 87-acre campus, next to a wall bearing the word "welcome" written in 10 different languages.

"Being at Thunderbird is like being in an Olympic Village," says Naji El-Khalil, a member of the Class of 2000. "You don't even remember that you are in the States until you go out the gate." And it doesn't stop with flag-waving. The student newspaper is called *Das Tor* ("The Gate" in German). At graduation every year, grads do more than don mortarboards and gowns: Many carry the flags of their homelands in a colorful parade of bright reds, whites, yellows, blues, and greens.

The uniqueness of the program goes well beyond these symbols. It is the only B-school in the United States devoted exclusively to the study of international business, a freestanding graduate institution unattached to a general university. Students in the BUSINESSWEEK survey ranked the school first of all B-schools surveyed in fostering interaction between various ethnic and national groups, so the multiculturalism isn't just lip service. And the school's grads also say Thunderbird is tops in stressing interpersonal skills.

Thunderbird awards not an MBA degree, but an MIM—Master's in International Management. The curriculum encompasses three areas of study (called the three-discipline or tripartite here), all accenting the global nature of the program: international politics, language, and world business. Every graduate leaves the program fluent in two, if not more, languages. During any given fall or spring, one-sixth of the more than 1400 full-time students are overseas in internships and exchange or study-abroad programs; half the school's 32,000 alumni are located abroad.

However, nearly three dozen schools ranked higher than Thunderbird—including SMU's Cox—in student opinion of the overseas program in BUSINESSWEEK's 2000 graduate survey, meaning Thunderbird has a lot of work to do to climb back to the top of the world. Or at least back into the Top 30 B-schools, where it sat just four years ago.

Thunderbird president Roy A. Herberger, Jr. is addressing those issues. In 2000 his team unveiled a brand new curriculum designed to offer you more choices, but retaining the school's historical strengths. Students still meet international studies, modern languages, and world business requirements. However, courses are more sequenced and integrated to build upon each other and maximize learning, a concern of some alums in the past. Coursework now emphasizes case studies significantly more than in the past, up from 36 percent in 1998 to 50 percent in 2000. Thunderbird now offers 214 different electives, 71 of which were new in 2000.

In addition those required core courses (called Flexi-Core), you'll now choose a regional focus and begin foreign language study if you're not already fluent in two or more languages. Language classes continue throughout your tenure at Thunderbird, based on your proficiency level. After completing the Flexi-Core, you'll complete one of six specialization tracks offered beginning fall 2000: country risk and business intelligence, entrepreneurship, finance, global management, marketing, and technology management. And in the new curriculum, e-business is now better integrated throughout the coursework, another area students had pegged as in need of help.

At the same time, Thunderbird students continue to complain that the placement office simply isn't up to the task of connecting a mammoth graduating class of some 750 a year with the specialized jobs at a wide cross-section of multinational corporations and trade agencies for which they've been somewhat narrowly trained. As one Class of 2000 graduate quips: "Great experience. Worth every dollar. Now, if I only had a job. . . ."

Indeed, when asked, "If the organizations you targeted for employment did not recruit on your campus, how would you assess your school's assistance in supporting your independent search for a job?" students ranked the school 13th from bottom in the BUSINESSWEEK survey. They then ranked Thunderbird one slot lower in the school's aggressiveness in helping them find summer jobs and internship and several more slots further down the list on performance in helping them find jobs on graduation.

The school has been refining its five-year-old intranet, known as My Thunderbird, which now links professors, alumni, and staff as well as students. Current MIMs can now search out alumni in the fields in which they are interested, a move that may allow alumni to boost the placement situation and aid students with their new regional focus. The new-and-improved intranet serves as a cradle-to-grave communications tool from the time you submit your application right on through your years as an alum. Web pages are constructed for every incoming student, with links to faculty, classmates, assignments, instructional materials, and discussion groups. These pages serve as a placement tool, connecting students to career services' corporate database and interview scheduling and allowing companies to view students' electronic résumés online.

What Thunderbird lacks in innovation or placement acumen, it makes up for in spades with flexibility. You can enter the program at one of three different points during the year. Whenever you arrive, you'll begin with a mandatory two-week orientation called Foundations of International Management, which focuses on bringing everyone up to speed on team-building and leadership skills, ethics, cross-cultural communication, self-assessment and career planning, and presentation and computer skills.

Among Thunderbird's other unique features is Winterim, a three-week period each January in which the school serves up an unusual menu of courses taught by prominent international experts who travel from around the globe to Arizona to teach. You might take a course such as Marketing to U.S. Hispanics, attend a conference on insurance and risk management, or study global conflict-resolution techniques. Or you could travel to Washington, D.C., Wall Street, or one of several overseas locations— including Cuba, India, and Austria—chosen each year depending on student interest and faculty availability and expertise.

The school also has traditional exchange partnerships with 16 schools in Latin America, Europe, Asia, and Africa, including Brazil, Chile, Costa Rica, Egypt, Finland, France, Germany, Lebanon, Mexico, Norway, South Korea, Spain, and Taiwan. In addition to the MIM, Thunderbird has master's degree programs in international health management and international management of technology, as well as dual MBA/MIM degree programs in conjunction with 10 different B-schools around the United States.

Thunderbird has pushed hard over the last few years to shake the nonacademic image some snobby professorial types still scorn. The faculty, now 98 strong, with 8 new faculty in 2000, has been drawn from well-regarded B-schools around the world; you'll also find some novelty acts on the professorial roster, like visiting prof and former vice president Dan Quayle. Approximately 50 percent of the faculty are of non-U.S. nationalities. Students rank the school at the middle of the pack in terms of their faculty being at the leading edge of their fields. However, Thunderbird is ranked fifth from the top for student gripes that faculty pursued their own research to the detriment of teaching.

It's the rare B-school whose central quadrangle boasts a swimming pool, but getting your master's in the sunny Southwest does have its advantages. Located smack in the middle of Arizona in Glendale, winter temperatures at an elevation of 1100 feet are mild and pleasant, while summer is hot and dry—this is, after all, the desert. A three- to four-hour drive takes you to the Grand Canyon or the ski resorts in the northern part of the state; a half-day's drive south and you're in Mexico.

Even with the ever-changing population on campus that results from overseas sojourns and varying admissions points during the year, the

Student Government provides a smorgasbord of clubs and organizations satisfying almost any interest and reflecting the wide-world view that epitomizes Thunderbird. You'll find cricket, yoga, and kendo clubs along with soccer, skiing, and football; salsa and merengue as well as aerobics; and regional clubs for students from around the globe. There's room for about 500 students to live on campus, but there are no on-campus accommodations for married couples. And while the school is tops for having a mix of students from different cultures, the percentage of female students dropped from 37 percent in 1998 to 26 percent in 2000.

PLACEMENT DETAILS

In 2000, 178 companies recruited second-year students on campus at Thunderbird. But students say it's not the number but the quality of recruiters that's lacking. Just 58 percent of the Class of 2000 had a job upon receiving their diplomas, although the school says that because of the way the program is structured, the job search often begins at or after graduation because that's the first time students are freed up for the global travel which this search often requires.

To address these issues, career services now uses a program on the My Thunderbird intranet called ProFit, which lets students upload and recruiters view résumés, as well as linking students with alumni.

Unlike most B-schools, Thunderbird gives credit for company internships, which can be undertaken not only in the summer but also during the academic year, with sponsoring companies such as Accenture, Chrysler, Ernst & Young, IBM, Merck, and Motorola or with firms contacted by the students themselves. Ninety percent of the internships net a company paycheck as well. Students can spend anywhere from 14 to 42 weeks with a single firm, or even take two separate internships with different companies. Before heading off to work, you must have completed at least one trimester on campus and have completed or waived all your basic-level course requirements. To receive school credit for an internship, you must write an academic paper about your experience and maintain regular contact with a faculty adviser during your time away from campus.

Top hirers in 2000 were Ford Motor Company (7); Hershey International (5); Motorola (5); Citibank (4); General Motors (4); Enron (3); IBM (3); Intel (3); Johnson & Johnson (3); Accenture (2).

OUTSTANDING FACULTY

Roy Nelson (international studies); *Guiomar Borras* (modern languages); *K. Ferris* (world business); *Christopher Miller* (world business); *W. Nie* (world business); *Graham Rankine* (world business); *Anant Sundaram* (world business).

APPLICANT TIPS

Thunderbird's high number of acceptances—the school admitted 76 percent of applicants to the Class of 2002—is somewhat deceptive, because the school's unique focus and requirements create a pool of candidates that is already somewhat weeded out by individual global experience and goals. And even though the average GMAT of 611 might make acceptance seem a shoo-in for those with higher scores, you'll have an advantage if you can also demonstrate international exposure and genuine interest.

The Thunderbird admissions profile is different from traditional B-schools because of the international curriculum and factors like the language proficiency requirement. "We are very up-front about our admissions requirements, second language requirement, and preferences for people who have some international experience, which means we have a lot of people self-selecting for T-bird in the application process," says James Grant, associate vice president.

In addition to work experience, you should demonstrate that you have a clear direction, and have thought about how an MIM, rather than a MBA, supports your career objectives. Thunderbird accepts new students at every semester and on a rolling basis, so it's always an appropriate time to apply. Applications for financial aid, however, are due by February 15.

Walking tours of the campus, led by student "ambassadors," are scheduled three times a week during the school year beginning at noon. You'll also get a complimentary lunch in the dining hall and an information session with the admissions office. Personal interviews are not required, but about two-thirds of admitted applicants do interview, either with admissions officers on campus or at recruiting events around the world, or with one of the school's far-flung alums. What other American B-school can set you up to speak with a graduate in Burkina Faso or Kyrgyzstan?

Contact: Judy Johnson
Director of Admissions
800-848-9084
OR 602-978-7596
Application deadlines: January 30 (fall); July 30 (spring); November 30 (summer)

THUNDERBIRD GRADS SOUND OFF

The core competency of Thunderbird is being a fully international school. At the graduation ceremony can you find students from more than 80 countries, most of whom you know personally and whom you are more than sure are willing to help you anytime, anywhere?

That is the T-bird spirit that I believe no other school has yet.

I think Thunderbird has the opportunity to do some great things, but administrators are not building loyalty to the school, but loyalty between students, kind of a "prisoners' syndrome." The current administration needs to take some of its own courses and use the students' abilities to become more dynamic.

Ten percent of the Thunderbird experience takes place in class. The other 90 percent involve interactions with people, students, faculty, alumni, and campus activities. Those are the things that really light you up and make you invaluable. The first time you meet with your small group for most classes, the first negotiation point isn't how to divide up work. It's what language you're going to conduct the group meetings in.

The administration at Thunderbird lacks strategic direction and the ability to maintain a high standard of ethics in their operation. They are guided by political infighting between the various departments but do a great job at pretending all is well while painting a pretty picture.

Thunderbird is not a school for everyone, and it requires you to have the right mind-set in respect to international business. The folks here are of a different breed than the average MBA student, because the students accepted here have had international exposure that is hard to beat. This exposure not only makes the average student at Thunderbird interesting and a valuable source of information, but it also supports academic progress without fostering excessive competitive behavior.

UNIVERSITY OF
CALIFORNIA
AT DAVIS

UNIVERSITY OF CALIFORNIA AT DAVIS

Graduate School of Management
Davis, CA 95616-8609
E-mail address: gsm@ucdavis.edu
Web site address: http://www.gsm.ucdavis.edu

Enrollment: 431
Women: 37%
Non-U.S.: 22%
Minority: 6%
Part-time: 292
Average age: 29
Applicants accepted: 31%
Median starting pay: $103,000

Annual tuition & fees:
   resident—$10,504
   nonresident—$20,308
Room and board: $9000
Average GMAT score: 673
Average years of work exp.: 5
Accepted applicants enrolled: 57%

Teaching methods: Lecture, 45%   Case study, 37%
                         Projects, presentation, discussions, 18%

Contact:
Donald Blodger
Assistant Dean of
Admissions and
Student Services
530-752-7399
Application deadlines:
February 1
April 1

Compared to the start-up-studded communities in nearby Silicon Valley, the Graduate School of Management at the University of California at Davis is a cozy, intimate spot as far as business schools go, just like its location—the college town–ish Davis. The young B-school with—surprise, surprise—a technology management emphasis was established in 1981 and is steadily grooming its full-scale program to match the other stalwarts among BUSINESSWEEK's Top 50. For now, though, with graduating classes of 69 full-time students, Davis is at a uniquely stirring growth phase. "The technology slant draws students and allows us to place them well when they leave," says the school's dean of nearly 12 years, Robert Smiley. "They're often so talented technically, we have to scramble to keep up." Assistant Dean Don Blodger recalls the day he asked a group of students to tell him why they had chosen UC Davis specifically. "One of them especially left an impression on me," Blodger remembers. "He said, 'You looked like you had something to prove, and I wanted to be a part of that.'"

Sure enough, UC Davis has been angling to make its mark. To bolster its already accomplished set of faculty, administrators have hired away profs and Ph.D.s from B-school stars like Michigan, Duke, Wharton, and Northwestern—so MBAs who've currently been enjoying a 10 to 1 student–faculty ratio now have even more to grin about. A new e-commerce concentration has enhanced the technology management focus, and the program has become better connected with leaders from local companies. (An Executive-in-Residence program and the Dean's Advisory Council add to the mix.) Since about 80 percent of each class typically remain on the West Coast after graduation, the improvement should certainly serve the school well. As it is, 70-plus companies make UC Davis a stop on their Stanford–Berkeley second-year-student recruiting tours—amounting to nearly one employer per Davis MBA. Still, there are some who impatiently grouse about a "lack of a vast alumni network," a charge that can only be corrected by an increasing graduate base—which takes time.

For the most part, Davis MBAs are satisfied with the program and especially the advanced tech focus, with an emphasis on innovation in a global economy. The two years begin with a 10-day orientation and optional GSM Boot Camps that help shaky students solidify their accounting, math, and computer software skills. Then it's on to a first year that incorporates six of seven required core courses: Financial Accounting, The Individual and Group Dynamics, Markets and the Firm, Data Analysis for Managers, Marketing Management, Financial Theory and Policy. In your winter and spring quarters, you'll have room for a few electives, which you can choose from a 47-item menu that includes New Product Development, Management of International Firms, and Business Design for e-Commerce. Before embarking on 1 or more of 11 "standing" concentrations (or self-designed versions) in their second year, Davis MBAs complete three breadth courses in the area(s) on which they are planning to focus their studies. The courses—such as Auditing, Internal Control and Public Accounting, and Managing Professionals: Budget Controls and Ethics for a student interested in Not-for-Profit Management—are designed to allow MBAs to draw on the initial required topics of study and to apply what they've learned to their chosen concentrations.

The school's required capstone course, Management Policy and Strategy, which is taken during the second year, also has students applying newly honed skills in analysis and synthesis, human relations, communications, and strategic business planning. Davis MBAs can gain real-world experience through business analysis proj-

ects, in which they help executives from local companies with actual corporate assignments, from building a Web site to creating an annual economic report. Others gain their experience by providing consulting services to organizations that otherwise could not afford them through the student-organized Community Consulting Group. The school's Business Partnership Program also provides opportunities for groups of students to devise strategic plans and offer suggestions for improvements for such successful companies as Intel Corporation, Del Monte Foods, PricewaterhouseCoopers, and The Sacramento Bee. These students may also find themselves with invitations to network with some of the company execs at their breakfast meetings.

Davis MBAs who want to sharpen their global marketplace perspectives can participate in one of the school's nine exchange programs—with universities in Europe, Asia, or Latin America—during the fall quarter of their second year. Study tours are another option for students seeking exposure to foreign business practices beyond what they learn in lectures or class assignments. On these one- to two-week trips, professors introduce their students to non-U.S. companies with which they have developed professional relationships. The career services office is also in the process of establishing an array of international finance and marketing summer internships in Germany, the United Kingdom, Chile, and Brazil for credit, with a small stipend for expenses (Mercedes and Deutsche Bank are among the first takers).

The second-year concentration areas include finance, e-commerce, marketing, and general management, along with some more uncommon selections like agricultural management and environmental and natural resource management, the latter of which entails courses in engineering, environmental science, and law offered elsewhere on campus. In all, students can fulfill up to 10 percent of their curriculum through courses in other schools or departments at the university. Four joint degrees—the MBA/J.D.,

MBA/Master of Engineering, MBA/Master in Agricultural and Resource Economics, and MBA/M.D.—are also offered, along with a corporate environmental management program that entails study at UC Davis and sister UC campuses in Santa Barbara, Berkeley, Irvine, and Los Angeles.

Students here enjoy use of a wireless local area network that provides high-speed access to the Internet as well as the GSM intranet, where you can learn about recruiters coming to campus, course information, and upcoming lectures or events. There is no laptop requirement, but most students do come equipped with one, even though the school offers a computing lab exclusively for MBAs, with updated equipment and technology. Finance-minded scholars take full advantage of the array of online research tools—from ABI and Lexis-Nexis to the UC system–wide Melvyl database—to access articles, case studies, and trade journals in business, management, finance, and economics.

The technological facilities appear to be up to speed, but the school is most certainly behind the times in terms of size and space. Plans for a new building are in the works, and administrators are simultaneously chipping away at a proposal to expand the size of the program—especially since funding is already in place. Starting this year, class size has increased from about 65 to 85 students, and administrators would like the momentum to continue. Another, more unusual, priority is a new worldwide wine executive MBA program in which UC Davis has partnered with a university in Bordeaux that grants the degree. Participants complete a portion of their degree at UC Davis and also undertake periods of visitation at locations in France, South Africa, Japan, Australia, and Chile. Just as this new UC Davis program is taking off, already under consideration is another: an online MBA to Central California.

MBA students, no doubt, will be supportive of the continuous change; they tend to be a cohesive, cooperative bunch that thrives in the program's tight-knit, team-oriented structure. The examples are numerous and telling. Last year's graduating class voted to start a student-supported endowment; the gift's total came to $35,000, with 100 percent class participation. "At UC Davis, there were people who were as bright as at any other school, but they also seemed to care if their peers were succeeding and getting the most out of the program," says one recent grad. Another remembers a particularly difficult statistics course. "I was struggling the night before the final, after my regular study group had disbanded, and the two students who were setting the curve in the class showed up unannounced at my doorstep to help me study. Where else," he asks, "does that kind of B-school camaraderie exist?"

Given the students' enthusiasm here, and the school's small size, it's impossible for anyone to be anonymous. Students put time and energy into all kinds of activities, from student–faculty intramural sporting events and executive–student golf tournaments to informal networking functions and community or nonprofit volunteer work. Many student organizations are organized around career plans, such as the Internet Working Group for techie types and the Finance Association for would-be Wall Streeters and others with an interest in the field. Colorful schoolwide events planned by the Associated Students of Management are held often. One that shouldn't be missed is UC Davis Picnic Day, with its parade through campus featuring the MBAs marching in a "briefcase brigade."

Students here also find time to explore the city of Davis and its surroundings. The state capital of Sacramento is just 12 miles to the east, and an hour-and-a-half to the southwest is the San Francisco Bay Area, where, not surprisingly, a significant portion of Davis MBAs make their home upon graduation. While at Davis, though, they delight in trips to Lake Tahoe in the north for downhill skiing in the mountains. Escapes to the wine country of nearby Napa and Sonoma are a treat, and most students don't finish the program without at least one trip to the wondrous Yosemite, a short drive to the southeast.

PLACEMENT DETAILS

Given UC Davis's hot West Coast location and high-tech focus, naturally, the school's recruiters are heavily weighted in this area. Lately, this has come to mean more traditional companies with tech-oriented departments or positions, rather than an onslaught of start-ups. "Dotcoms aren't answering their phones, let alone recruiting now," remarks Assistant Dean Blodger. Class of 2000 grads' average number of job offers, 2.5, was on the low end among Runners-Up B-schools. But the prospect of guaranteed international summer internships abroad bodes well, as do the school's increased efforts to hold events like a high-tech career fair to lure recruiters (as it was, 70-plus companies came to campus to interview second-year students last year). Five new companies were launched by students in the Class of 2000. For everyone else, top hirers were Intel (8); Wells Fargo (4); Lam Research (4); Hewlett-Packard (3); Deloitte & Touche (3); Agilent (2); GATX Capital (2); and Dayton-Hudson (2).

Career services training for Davis MBAs starts before they even arrive on campus, with information provided by the office on writing a résumé and instructions for taking a business interest test online. Curriculum during the two years of B-school includes interviewing techniques (with videotaped mock interviews conducted by an actual executive), an assessment appointment with a counselor, negotiations workshops, and advice on everything from conducting an interview over lunch to reviewing job offers.

OUTSTANDING FACULTY

Michael Maher (accounting); *Brad Barber* (finance); *R. Castanias* (finance); *Eyal Biyalo-*
gorski (marketing); *Prasad Naik* (marketing); *Chi-Ling Tsai* (statistics).

APPLICANT TIPS

UC Davis admissions officers ask applicants to be sure they are looking for a rigorous, tech-oriented MBA at a small school that emphasizes speaking skills and teamwork, and friendly, not cutthroat, competition. These are some of the characteristics that will unite admitted applicants. But, that said, you should focus on differentiating yourself in your application—the school is continuously looking for a mixed bag. "We conduct admissions as though we're casting a play," says Assistant Dean Don Blodger. "We look at what each one can bring to the table, and we don't want clones of people here." In your essays, indicating international exposure or work experience in a particular industry can help. The school will also look closely at GMAT scores (the Class of 2002's average was 673) and transcripts; strengths in accounting, economics, calculus, and statistics are extremely beneficial, although the admissions staff insists it "balances all the variables" to determine a candidate's potential.

Interviews are also strongly encouraged. About 70 percent of the applicant pool normally has one, with either a staff member or an alum, to present a more complete picture of themselves to the admissions committee. "We take admissions very seriously," warns Blodger. "A larger school can afford to make a few mistakes here and there. We're a young, ambitious school—we really want the right students to advance our program."

Contact: Donald Blodger
Assistant Dean of Admissions and Student
Services
530-752-7399
Application deadlines: February 1; April 1

DAVIS MBAs SOUND OFF

UC Davis is a young and small program and this is seen by some as a negative feature. This factor was actually an important selling point in my selection of this school. UC Davis had people that were as bright as anywhere but they also seemed to care if their peers were succeeding and getting the most out of the program.

The MBA program at UC Davis has the advantages and disadvantages of being one of the smallest and youngest nationally ranked schools. Disadvantages include a small alumni pool, small student body, difficulty enticing recruiters, and a low-key reputation. Among the advantages are the program's flexibility, the way the school listens to students, the great team and interpersonal dynamics, and the excellent teacher–student ratio.

Judging from the discussions I have had with my friends and family at other B-schools, the sense of community at Davis is unparalleled. The initial collaboration, teamwork, and familiarity developed into genuine concern for classmates. Competition is good-natured and never cutthroat. The amount of diversity within such a small number of people is exceptional and very rewarding.

The size of the class is small and the size of the alumni pool is small. While on the surface this might seem to be a negative in light of larger, older schools, in reality it is not a big factor. The quality of the alumni pool and their commitment to the school after graduation make this group very effective and useful to the current students. I was able to call many alumni and speak to them at any time, both at home and at work. They were very happy to help and worked very hard to aid me in any way needed. I am extremely satisfied with my experience at UC Davis and will work tirelessly to help future students in every way I can.

UC Davis is a very young but incredible school, now regularly attracting top faculty. Any weaknesses that it may have stem from the fact that the school is so small and so young. The caliber of students is amazing, and the faculty (in general) is incredible. I was initially disappointed that I wasn't accepted into my first choice school, but now I wouldn't trade my experience at UC Davis Graduate School of Management for anything.

UC Davis was a fabulous school that combined all the advantages of a Top 30 school with the intimacy and personal attention you get at a small school. I got in to UCLA and UC Berkeley but decided to go to UC Davis and I am happy I did so.

Our faculty and staff are always available and know us personally. Our concerns and feedback about the curriculum were immediately addressed and revisions were made for the subsequent class. The flexibility of the electives is great and allowed me to do a marketing project for an automotive firm (my personal area of interest) that will hopefully lead to a job in the industry.

UNIVERSITY OF CALIFORNIA AT IRVINE

UNIVERSITY OF
CALIFORNIA
AT IRVINE

Graduate School of Management
University of California
Irvine, California 92697-3125
E-mail address: gsm-mba@uci.edu
Web site address: http://www.gsm.uci.edu

Enrollment: 651
Women: 23%
Non-U.S.: 31%
Minority: 2%
Part-time: 367
Average age: 29
Applicants accepted: 33%
Median starting pay: $79,000

Annual tuition & fees:
   resident—$11,498
   nonresident—$21,742
Room and board: $7520
Average GMAT score: 670
Average years of work exp.: 5.5
Accepted applicants enrolled: 64%

Teaching methods: Lecture, 40%   Case study, 40%
                      Other, 20%

Contact:
Kathy Hildebrand
Associate Director,
Admissions &
Marketing
Full-Time MBA
Program
949-824-4207
Application deadlines:
January 8
March 2
May 1

Among the youngest of the MBA programs surveyed by BUSINESSWEEK, UC Irvine is making a name for itself through a fresh approach to MBA education that's matched only by the innovation of its California environs. Touted by some as a southern version of Silicon Valley, or, at the very least, one part of the developing "Technology Coast," the area is dense with high-tech companies and inventive organizations in a range of areas, from entertainment to real estate. But even though UC Irvine's graduate management program wasn't launched until 1981, administrators have had enough time and the foresight to develop a wider-ranging focus than just the ephemeral e-business arena.

Students, instead, are immersed in a two-year examination of how information technology drives and transforms all aspects of business—from marketing to finance, and even human resources. Leading the charge to achieve this and keep the school from becoming solely a "techno-MBA" program is Dean David Blake, who headed the B-schools at Southern Methodist University, Rutgers, and Northeastern University before arriving at Irvine in October 1997. Sure, you'll find the usual au courant courses in new venture development or Internet marketing, and there *is* an e-business specialization. But what was, until recently, a divisive two-track program—with one section for regular MBAs and another for students on an information technology management path—has since been molded into one cohesive experience that integrates ITM throughout the entire curriculum. The change recognizes the unavoidable importance of a technological background for all would-be business leaders, and UC Irvine students say they're highly satisfied with the techie emphasis, even if they're not as happy in other areas of the program, like the teaching quality or career networking opportunities.

From the start, Irvine MBAs are required to come equipped with their own laptops. (The school provides a $500 rebate for the laptop price for full-time students and actually covers the cost for executive MBA students.) It's not long before you'll learn to do everything from registering for classes to communicating about various social events to signing up for job interviews on Catalyst, the progressive student-created intranet. All classrooms and public spaces in the school's main building are wired, and an extensive high-speed wireless network was recently installed. But even with such timesaving technological facilities, there's no escaping the rigors of the 23-quarter-courses-over-two-years workload, made extra strenuous by four required ITM labs in which you must use commercially available software to solve problems. If you take the Operations Management Lab, for instance, you might design the logistical support for a business using SAP R/3 to assess the relationship of such factors as in-store sales, inventory, and distribution centers. In the Marketing Lab, you'd be using Claritas software to determine the best locations for stores. A new Lincoln Mercury ITM Lab in Marketing, introduced in fall 2000, has Irvine MBAs using geographical information systems (GIS) like MapInfo, census data, and other database applications to conduct market analyses and sales forecasts for products and services.

During the first year, Irvine MBAs are assigned to a section of students with whom they'll take their 12 required core courses, which range from Statistics for Management and Financial Accounting to Principles of Marketing and Organizational Analysis. In the spring quarter students have room for one elective course (the other eight are taken in the second year). If you have completed substantial undergraduate work in a particular area, you can petition to waive a related required course, provided you replace that one with another. Irvine also requires all MBAs to undertake an international experience. This can take the form of either an international elective; participation in one of the school's seven exchange programs in Europe, Asia, or Latin America; or enrollment in an upper- or graduate-level international course in another school at UC Irvine or at another UC campus, pending approval.

One of Irvine's burgeoning strengths is in new venture development and innovation, as evidenced by some of the tantalizing electives in this area, including Business Planning for Entrepreneurs and New Venture Management. "This place is hopping in terms of new business development," enthuses Dean Blake. "We're rapidly growing companies in spite of what the markets are doing." Indeed, the list of business endeavors recently launched by UC Irvine MBAs is steadily growing; in the past year, at least four such firms emerged, including MyDrugRep.com, a pharmaceutical Internet marketing service; Intelligent Horizon, a B2B business intelligence service provider; and AntiqueParlor.com, an Internet marketplace for antiques. But most significant for enterprising MBAs is the "garage"-style facility for new venture development that is housed, for the time being, in a small trailer on campus. Open 24 hours a day, seven days a week, the Irvine Innovation Initiative (I^3) was established in January 2001 with seed funding from Safi Qureshey, one of the founders of AST Research and a strong supporter of Southern California start-ups in general. Students who are selected to participate, based on their business plans, can use the space to create their new concepts with guidance from faculty and other professionals. Currently, Irvine is in the process of assigning trailer space to six teams (20-plus individuals), which include students from other schools within the university, such as the Engineering and Medical schools. The university hopes to offer more elaborate digs by next year, but for now, the "garage" will function fine.

All MBAs are also encouraged to participate in the ThinkTank/Graduate School of Management New Venture Business Plan Competition, which, supported jointly by the school and entrepreneur and alum Scott Blum, currently awards a total of $30,000 in prize money to the top two most viable business ideas. Students from other schools at the university are welcome to join MBAs on competing teams. The school is also in the process of arranging a possible campuswide business plan competition that would involve students from a mixture of disciplines—including the biological and computer sciences, engineering, medical, and digital arts—in the quest for a yet to be determined grand prize.

Business skills are further honed with help from the GSM Center for Leadership Development, which focuses on creating programs outside the classroom that will help students learn to "create, manage, and lead change within an organization." Among the offerings is a Corporate Partners Mentoring Program that puts students in contact with professionals who can dispense advice on such topics as career paths and corporate expectations. The Center also runs a speaker series, as well as workshops and seminars to further develop students' management perspectives.

The school offers electives in e-commerce, information systems, finance, economics, organization and strategy, and health care, among other areas—plus opportunities to attend lectures, seminars, and conferences in many of the subjects or industries. All MBA students can also fulfill up to four elective courses, or 16 out of a total of 92 credits, by taking "appropriate" classes at other UC campuses. The school's only joint-degree program, the M.D./MBA, is for students who not only seek a career as a physician but also hope to have administrative and management responsibilities in health-care organizations.

Even with the array of study areas, UC Irvine faces the constant challenge of distancing itself from a too-heavy tech branding—especially when student interest in start-ups and high-tech ventures, as well as the school's proximity to numerous functioning examples—can be overwhelming. About 83 percent of Irvine MBAs remain in the West upon graduation, making their homes in California, Seattle, Phoenix, or other high-tech hotspots. About 30 percent of Class of 2000 grads did take a job in marketing, last year's top functional area, and those marketing jobs were distributed across a variety of industries, from biotechnology to entertainment. But consulting jobs, which drew 45 percent of Irvine MBAs as hires in 1999, attracted a mere 23.5 percent in 2000. Even with the tech sector serving as the major source of employment here, Irvine students have at least found a greater show of diversity in the types of companies recruiting, which fall anywhere along the traditional-to-atypical spectrum. More international opportunities are unfolding, additionally, and the school says that students overall have been happier with their placement than before. About 80 percent located their job through internships, the direct efforts of the career services office, or other activities facilitated by the school.

One area that is facing a major overhaul is the school's facilities. For now, you'll take all your classes at the technologically enhanced Graduate School of Management building, where MBAs hang out at the blue tables right outside of the building. But the B-school is most certainly outgrowing its current setup, and by the beginning of 2002, the school will add about 50 percent more space, including classrooms, student study areas, and room for the 24/7 business-building facility. Plans are underway for a new multibuilding complex to accommodate intended enrollment increases over the next 10 years, but this facility won't open until at least 2006. In the meantime, Irvine is increasing the size of its program gradually over the next two to three years (current class size is about 160). Officials say there will be somewhat of a greater focus on increasing minority representation, which is at an almost nonexistent 2 percent. Prohibited by California law from using race, ethnicity, and gender in making admissions decisions, administrators say they've been attending more minority-targeted events and they're "hoping for larger interest, to create the best possible array of people in the program." Numbers for international and female students currently come in at a rather average 31 percent and 23 percent, respectively.

In all, the MBAs here are a tight-knit group. They gather every Thursday for happy hour, which is usually held in the Multi-Purpose Room (MPR) of the B-school or the on-campus pub. Students can participate in a wide variety of extracurricular activities, including clubs that highlight a range of interests from consulting to golf. Irvine is halfway between Los Angeles and San Diego (about 45 minutes away from each city), and there are plenty of restaurants, bars, movie theaters, and shopping malls near the school. The Steelhead Brewery, with its high ceilings and wingback chairs, is the local favorite among the B-school students. When not in class, MBAs take advantage of Southern California's sunny climate to participate in a host of outdoor sports, including rollerblading, hiking, and mountain biking. The school's proximity to beaches makes it a great place for those who love surfing, diving, and swimming.

PLACEMENT DETAILS

With Irvine's strong high-tech focus, more than three-fourths of graduating MBA classes tend to land along the West Coast. But there is still some degree of diversification among corporate suitors, who range from the big consulting firms and marketing outfits to media and entertainment giants. Smaller start-ups also have a presence, and among the Class of 2000 grads were MBAs responsible for launching four companies within the digital marketplace. Irvine's top employers in

2000 included Deloitte Consulting (7); Deloitte & Touche ERS (6); Gateway (6); Intel (4); Ford (3); Conexant (3); Disney (2); Silicon Graphics (2); Experian (2); WFS Financial (2).

Students receive career services training mainly in the form of a series of mandatory workshops and seminars on conducting the job search, negotiating a salary, assessing leadership skills, résumé writing, and interviewing. The school is especially helpful in connecting students with local internship opportunities; the multi-billion-dollar Newport Beach start-up Conexant ended up with 16 Irvine interns last summer, and Sun Microsystems and Disney are also known to hire enthusiastically here.

OUTSTANDING FACULTY

James Wallace (accounting); *Mark Freeman* (finance); *Connie Pechmann* (marketing); *Marta Elvira* (organizational behavior); *Thomas Eppel* (statistics); *Steven Postrel* (strategy).

APPLICANT TIPS

Irvine has a rolling admissions policy, so you should apply early. Although you don't need to have a strong technology background to gain admittance to Irvine, the school wants to see that you have good quantitative skills. Work experience is not required, but about 97 percent of MBAs have at least one year of professional experience. If you're a member of an underrepresented minority, you should note that African-Americans, Hispanic-Americans, and Native Americans make up just 2 percent of Irvine's enrollment—lowest of the Runners-Up. While that may give qualified minority applicants an edge as the school seeks to increase that population, it can also make attendance here a lonely proposition for some.

Irvine strongly encourages applicants to interview, and it is also possible to set up an informational interview at an early stage in your application process. The admissions office interviews almost everybody on campus, but you can schedule an appointment by phone if you can't make it. Letters of recommendation are also extremely important. Assistant Dean Joanne Starr suggests applicants conduct as much research as possible on the school before applying. "Our hope is to be grounded in what is important to the candidate," she says. "We look carefully at how they plan to play out the experience once they're here."

Contact: Kathy Hildebrand
Associate Director, Admissions & Marketing
Full-Time MBA Program
949-824-4207
Application deadlines: January 8; March 2; May 1

IRVINE MBAs SOUND OFF

One of the best things about UCI is that it is the only major business school in the heart of the high-tech hotbed of Orange County/San Diego, and local companies are very eager to work with the students. As a result, during the course of my MBA, I was able to participate in projects with eight different high-tech companies of all sizes—ranging from Fortune 500 to pre-IPO. I gained invaluable experience working on these projects and this served me extremely well in my interviews during my second year. I encourage anybody who is interested in both a first-rate academic experience and an incredibly exciting laboratory of real companies to consider UCI very seriously.

I feel that UCI's greatest value added for its students is its small size and flexibility. Size gives the program flexibility in interweaving classic B-school curriculum with skills. Further, the financial aid offered by the school made the ROI presented by the program a no-brainer. However, the small size of the school is clearly a negative in terms of an existing alumni network. At the same time, the school's existing network, which is focused heavily in "new economy"/high-tech companies as well as in IT/e-commerce, helped me to develop a network targeted to my areas of preference.

I think that, overall, I had a great experience at UCI and learned a lot. I feel like the school is small and growing, and maybe the growth is causing some growing pains and difficulty. Facility resources are short and elective demand is starting to exceed supply. That said, I think the program is moving in the right direction as they try to get a larger building and a more diverse group of recruiters to the school. If I were to classify the program, I would say it is a very good program that is very valuable but that it could be a great program with additional recruiters and finance and marketing electives.

While my school was not perfect, I learned a lot and enjoyed every minute of it. To me, the friendships and networks forged at GSM are far more significant than the schoolwork itself. Whether intentional or not, GSM was able to bring together a diverse group of people to create a noncompetitive, helpful student body that made it fun to learn. In my estimation, this puts it above schools that are ranked higher.

After "discovering" UCI's GSM, with its positive and dynamic atmosphere, I made a decision that five years earlier I would have resisted: relocating to Southern California from the San Francisco area. In the end, the move was incredibly worthwhile, as the GSM program delivered more than I expected in most aspects outside of the typical MBA experience. The courses were updated constantly to incorporate the latest information, which left all of us feeling that we have received the most current education available. The school is building its community in a progressive, positive, and professional nature that is being well accepted and recognized. The social interaction is open, allowing students to network with virtually every individual at the school, not to mention all the industry and alumni contacts. Finally, the location is practically ideal: central to the burgeoning "Tech Coast" and wealthy Orange County. Likewise, UCI is in a beautiful locale with excellent weather.

UCI GSM is a small school; I liken it to a start-up company. The small size makes the school environment quick paced and continually changing, just like the Internet economy. It offers tremendous opportunity to those who are willing to put forth the effort to build the organization. A more established school would not have given me the opportunity to "seize the reins" and take charge of building a program from the ground up.

UNIVERSITY
OF FLORIDA

UNIVERSITY OF FLORIDA

Warrington College of Business
Gainesville, Florida 32611-7152
E-mail address: floridamba@notes.cba.ufl.edu
Web site address: http://www.floridamba.ufl.edu

Enrollment: 468	Annual tuition & fees:
Women: 12%	resident—$4430
Non-U.S.: 22%	nonresident—$14,518
Minority: 2%	Room and board: $6230
Part-time: 112	Average GMAT score: 645
Average age: 27	Average years of work exp.: 5.5
Applicants accepted: 22%	Accepted applicants enrolled: 46%
Median starting pay: $71,000	

Teaching methods: Lecture, 60%   Case study, 40%

"You can't come here with the idea that you've gotten into an MBA program and that was the hard part," says the Warrington College of Business's Dean John Kraft, who has headed the University of Florida's B-school program for more than a decade. "You have to perform." Sure enough, even though they might wear shorts and T-shirts around campus most days of the year, Warrington MBAs are no slouchers. With lots of drive and keen technical skills, they're dedicated to their studies and to the B-school's opportunities—something you'll have to be if you're eyeing this Gainesville institution as an MBA destination.

Thanks in part to the College of Business's array of specialized master's programs, the MBA program offers 7 joint degree options, 16 international exchange opportunities, and 15 concentrations, including such specific subject areas as Arts Administration, Latin American Business, Human Resources Management, and Sports Administration. Students can add a certificate to their MBA degree by focusing the majority of their electives in one of six disciplines deemed the school's functional strengths: e-Commerce, Entrepreneurship and Technology Management, Financial Services, Supply Chain Management, Decision and Information Sciences, and Global Management.

All this choice goes to a relatively small group of MBAs—about 200 full-timers—especially considering that the University of Florida, one of the nation's oldest and largest universities, has a total of 46,000 enrolled students each year. Currently there are just 50 or so full-time MBAs in their first year; the drop from last year's 136 is a result of the B-school's current initiative to boost program quality. (Already, average GMAT scores have increased from 615 to 645, and work experience from three years to five-and-a-half.) Joining these 50 students next

Contact:
Laura Parks
Director of Admissions
352-392-7992
Application deadlines:
Domestic—
December 15
February 15
April 15
International—
December 15
February 15

year, in the second year of their program, will be about 40 more MBAs holding undergraduate business degrees. Those students will be completing the B-school's accelerated one-year program.

Even with the different options for areas of study and the more than 100 electives, MBAs in the traditional two-year program follow a pretty rigid program their first year. The fall and spring semesters are spent completing core courses in finance, management, marketing, operations, international business, quantitative methods, accounting, and business law. One last required course, Strategic Management, must be fit into the second year, while the rest of the time is spent exploring different industries and issues through elective classes within the program or in other schools or departments at the university. Most students choose to complete two concentrations, and some end up designing their own with related electives from various fields. If you need to brush up on your quantitative skills, count yourself in for the optional math and accounting camp before beginning the program; about 40 percent of your classmates are arriving with an engineering degree or other technical background. (One-fourth of the Class of 2002 has an undergraduate engineering degree from the University of Florida itself.) After the camp, you'll join the rest of your class in a week's worth of team-building and leadership orientation activities, including a "challenge" course that takes up a full day.

Students in the one-year option begin their studies in May with their own one-week orientation, followed by curriculum focusing on basic concepts so that this group can be caught up with the two-year program participants they will join in the fall. After a Foundations Review, some writing and communications courses, and other case-based courses in accounting and management, the one-year MBAs take mostly electives during their fall and spring semesters.

International studies is one of the 15 concentrations offered here, but all MBAs in the two-year program are eligible to participate in one of various international exchange programs in Europe, Asia, and Latin America. Florida will soon launch a new exchange program that reverses the usual order of study: Students will first complete half their program at the international location (in France, England, Japan, Hong Kong, Germany, Turkey, or Chile). Then they'll finish the other half at UF, where they will take electives and get to participate in the recruiting process. A dual degree option with Thunderbird is also offered for students who want to receive a Master of International Management from that school as well as their MBA from Florida in two-and-a-half to three years. Students spend the first part of the program at the Warrington College of Business, then transfer to Thunderbird for the rest.

What Florida's MBAs appear to appreciate most are the B-school's manageable size, cooperative environment, and tuition value. State residents pay just $4430, while out-of-state students still fare well among the Runners-Up with a tuition of $14,518. Lectures make up 60 percent of the teaching here, but students also take required courses, such as leadership and oral and written communication, in groups and teams. Throughout the program they complete an array of team-building exercises and group projects. "I was constantly impressed by my classmates," says one recent grad who benefited from the teamwork element. "The student body is both talented and resourceful, and work groups were, overall, a wonderful experience. Students are eager to share ideas for learning, as well as contacts for employers."

It's a good thing Warrington MBAs are on top of the networking process because the career services department, lately, has fallen short. Grumbles one of the B-school's recent grads: "The CSO is an embarrassment to the Florida MBA programs. They offered virtually no support in my career search and left me and many of my colleagues completely on our own to find gainful employment." He's certainly not alone in his dissatisfaction; more than a fourth of the Class of 2000 was unemployed upon graduation. But new classes may achieve better results in their recruitment experiences at UF, with the addition of both a new Director and Associate Director of Career Services who arrived in 2000. Both come from industry (one has worked in consumer goods and the other in banking) and they've been targeting the expansion of the program's industry relations. Historically Florida's MBA program has achieved the greatest placement success with finance and technology firms like IBM, and also biotech companies. Entrepreneurial and advanced manufacturing companies like Ford are regular employers as well, but the B-school is "underweighted in the McKinseys and brand management opportunities," admits Director of the MBA Program Erik Gordon. A revitalized focus on the power of Florida alums is one of the program's strategies for improving placement. "We've been running at about 50 percent efficiency of tapping into these Gators," Gordon explains, adding that the B-school is formalizing its approach to connecting with graduates who have been successful and are in a position to help current students. Many of these alums who agree to serve as mentors or contacts are joining the MBA program's growing Advisory Council database. The B-school also enjoys access to senior execs through a Distinguished Speaker Series that has yielded such high-profile presenters as Warren Buffett and Outback Steakhouse founder Tim Gannon.

Another area in flux is the college's facilities. The college is located on the northeast corner of campus (which happens to be listed as a historic district on the National Registry of Historic Places). Three adjacent buildings with wired classrooms and a variety of electronic and audiovisual equipment serve as the B-school's center; the MBA program administration is housed on two floors of the same building that contains the B-school student lounge facility.

Within two years, however, the MBA program will be able to expand somewhat into a fourth building. Although participants of other grad schools at the university will share the new facility, the additional building will help advance such subject areas as information systems and supply chain management especially, by providing not only extra space but also upgraded technological features. Warrington MBAs currently use information technology in many forms, starting with the laptop computers they're required to show up with. Courses in fields like Decision Information Sciences call on students to utilize popular software programs like SAP R/3, the enterprise resource planning package. And all MBAs are in constant communication online through Lotus Notes, which also allows for Internet research, submission of class assignments, and chat sessions with professors and classmates.

The majority of communication, though, takes place in person among Warrington MBAs in their classes, on project teams, and at social events. Since the program is small, students bond quickly and find it easy to take on a leadership role in any one of the college's student organizations, from the MBA Association and MBA Ambassadors—who often plan student activities—to career-specific groups like the Consulting or Sports Business Clubs. It's impossible not to want to take advantage of the weather here, and sun-struck MBAs are often found on the university's outdoor tennis courts, in the swimming pools, or on the golf course that's part of the 2000-acre campus. There's even an 81-acre wildlife sanctuary area surrounding Lake Alice. Off campus, MBAs frequent Gainesville's casual college-town coffee shops, bars, and restaurants, including one favorite MBA haunt known as "The Swamp." Weekends not spent catching up on schoolwork often include road trips to historic St. Augustine or other attractions like Disney World, Universal Studios, Busch Gardens, and Sea World.

PLACEMENT DETAILS

Challenged by both the B-school's small size and its nonurban, southeastern location, the Career Services office, not surprisingly, has found it somewhat difficult to satisfy students, who have lodged some of their biggest complaints concerning the recruitment experience. The average number of job offers for last year's grads was just two, among the lowest of the Runners-Up. And not even three-fourths of the Class of 2002 were employed by graduation.

To redirect the office's strategies, a new director and an associate director—both with industry experience—have recently taken the helm, and administrators are hoping they'll help the school capitalize on its strong ties with businesses in the Southeast and create new ones to give students more options. A recent increase in the quality of enrolled MBAs should also help draw added corporate interest, along with stepped-up efforts to connect with alums. In 2000, top employers were Ford Motor Company (5); Program Planning Professionals (5); Johnson & Johnson (3); ZTEL Communications (3); Jabil Circuit (2); Renaissance Worldwide (2); Xcelerate (2); Renaissance Cruise Lines (2); Exactech (2); and Intermedia Communications (2).

OUTSTANDING FACULTY

Hadley Schaefer (accounting); *Asoo Vakharia* (decision and information science); *Jay Ritter* (finance); *Michael Ryngaert* (finance); *Joe Alba* (marketing); *Barton Weitz* (marketing).

APPLICANT TIPS

Like most schools, "academic ability, managerial promise, and personal character" are among the main factors in admissions decisions regarding Florida's MBAs. The B-school also looks for strong interpersonal skills, motivation and maturity, leadership potential, the ability to communicate, and career focus. Even if you possess these qualities but haven't worked for at least two years prior to the time of enrollment, though, it's unlikely you'll be admitted. The school is making an effort to increase the quality of each class, and five-and-a-half years of work experience is the latest average, along with an average GMAT score that's recently jumped from 615 to 645. Essays are important; you should try to express any aspect of your background that may be unique and might suggest how you can contribute to the program's diversity.

Apply early, as admission is rolling, although there are three suggested deadlines in December, February, and April. You'll normally receive word within two months after the deadline you've chosen. Interviews are granted by invitation only to those who have a significant chance of being accepted. Any applicants can arrange to tour the campus and sit in on some classes by calling the admissions office.

Contact: Laura Parks
Director of Admissions
352-392-7992
Application deadlines: Domestic—December 15, February 15, April 15; International—December 15, February 15

WARRINGTON MBAs SOUND OFF

Overall, my MBA experience at UF was a positive one. As soon as I raised a concern, Student Services would get on it right away. They would not only assist me but also try to issue some general policy statement to make it easier for others in the future. I often felt as though I was running into walls, but that was because UF allowed me to create my own path through the program. As soon as I ran into any obstacles, they were there to help me through.

Sure, Florida's MBA program has its share of problems . . . but this environment is ideal for developing the "leaders of tomorrow." It gave me numerous opportunities to display and hone my leadership skills . . . and I feel as though I have had a positive impact on this program. I'm sure that I, along with all of my classmates from the Class of 2000, will long be remembered by the MBA Program staff. Together, we helped rejuvenate a program that had lost its character and, with the support of the faculty and staff, brought it back to life.

Choosing to attend the University of Florida MBA program is the best decision and investment I've ever made. The students are very friendly and social. The program has a family atmosphere—everyone is usually willing to help other classmates. The faculty is very strong. Many of our professors are leaders in their respective fields of study. Several of the professors attend student activities. Most of the faculty members show a genuine concern for the students.

I thoroughly enjoyed my academic experiences at Florida. The quality of the faculty and students is truly outstanding. The facilities and technological resources were quite acceptable for a state institution. The friendships I have made here will last throughout my life. Unfortunately, our Career Services Office is a completely disorganized disaster.

Yes, it is obvious that the salaries for MBAs are lower in the southeastern United States, but so is the cost of living. I'd rather have my $75,000 salary and live in sunny West Palm Beach than $100,000 in good old Boston or New York, two cities where I have previously worked.

The Florida MBA was one of the best experiences I could have had. It made me feel confident, prepared, and knowledgeable going out to pursue the career that I wanted. The faculty is one of its biggest assets. They are very involved in the program and really take an interest in helping the students both in and outside the classroom. The Marketing faculty is a jewel in the rough at Florida.

UF MBA faculty members are very talented and the program is small enough to allow students to form relationships with professors. In addition, the MBA program staff is extremely responsive to student concerns and ideas for improving the program.

Gainesville is a great place to live and the university is very spirited, with diversity in a casual atmosphere. I found that the rigors and stress of the MBA program were often offset by the great students, administrators, and faculty. I am so pleased that I invested in my education at UF. The business community will see many great leaders and "doers" who are graduates of the program.

The general staff, professors, and fellow students were of the highest quality at this MBA program. The classes were challenging, stimulating, and highly educational. They provided not only theoretical knowledge but also practical applications that will help in my future career. However, the Career Services Office was severely lacking in quality personnel. They failed to attract quality companies for recruiting purposes and did little to help students make contact with the companies on their own. This department is an embarrassment to a program that is otherwise top notch in all regards.

UNIVERSITY
OF GEORGIA

UNIVERSITY OF GEORGIA

Terry College of Business
Athens, Georgia 30602-6264
E-mail address: ndodson@terry.uga.edu
Web site address: http://www.terry.uga.edu

Enrollment: 271
Women: 26%
Non-U.S.: 21%
Minority: 5%
Part-time: 15
Average age: 27
Applicants accepted: 28%
Median starting pay: $82,000

Annual tuition & fees:
  resident—$3776
  nonresident—$12,794
Room and board: $5870
Average GMAT score: 645
Average years of work exp.: 4.5
Accepted applicants enrolled: 53%

Teaching methods: Lecture, 30%   Case study, 30%   Projects, 40%

Contact:
Donald R. Perry Jr.
Director of MBA
Admissions
706-542-5621
*Application deadlines
for two-year program:*
April 1 (international)
May 1 (domestic)

About half of each Terry College of Business MBA class at the University of Georgia comes from the Southeast—and nearly all of those who apply do so perhaps partly because they have Georgia on their minds, judging from the high number of students who stay and work in the Southeast after graduation. Close to 60 percent of Class of 2000 MBAs made their homes there at the program's end. Little wonder: The B-school and the college town of Athens—which has dubbed itself Georgia's Classic City because people joke that there are probably more Greek columns here than anyplace else except Athens, Greece—practically ooze a Southern charm that's easy to get used to. From as early as the admissions process, administrators dole out an extra helping of personal attention that applicants would be hard pressed to find elsewhere. Says Admissions Director Don Perry, "We want everyone leaving the process feeling like they're important, because they are to us."

The curriculum instills a similar sense of personal service. Although the majority of students come with some kind of technical background (which helps with employment success, Perry notes), the school, led by Dean P. George Benson since July 1998, also emphasizes "soft skills," or nonquantitative qualities. Whether on the regular two-year program or 11-month accelerated MBA for students with undergraduate business degrees from AACSB-accredited schools (about 20 percent of each class), Terry MBAs are all required to participate in MBA P.L.U.S., which stands for "pathways," "leadership," "unity," and "service." Student-driven and redesigned by each new class, the program highlights these soft skills with workshops on topics such as effective work habits, problem solving, and negotiation and presentation techniques, plus a series of lectures by business executives. There's also an outdoor adventure segment, which sends MBAs to bond in the nearby Oconce Forest by negotiating a high ropes course or river rafting on one of North Georgia's wild and woolly waterways. In addition, each MBA is expected to complete at least one community service project a year, with the university coordinating its "Volunteer Dawgs" to clean up local highways, build housing for the homeless, read to the blind, or mentor local youngsters.

The program's intimate size, with about 250 full-time students and a total of 116 faculty members, breeds a level of friendliness most participants find both impressive and important. "I walked into Brooks Hall on my first day at the school and a professor I hadn't met yet greeted me by name," one recent grad remembers. "It turned out he had had all our pictures and profiles sent to him before the start of the program so that he would know every one of us. This experience was indicative of my time at Terry."

That down-home Southern hospitality is reinforced by the school's more-than-generous tuition rates: Each year, about half of all Terry MBAs get a Top 50 business education for well under $1000 a year. Graduate students who are selected on a competitive basis for merit-based assistantships (13 hours a week of work for a professor or a B-school office or department) receive a $5000 annual stipend, a waiver of non-resident status, and a reduction of tuition and fees to about $850 per academic year. Add in some scholarship money, which about 50 percent of MBAs here also receive, and you could actually end up making money from your education here. "I more than doubled my salary while getting paid $10,000 per year to go to school," gushes one satisfied grad. "You can't beat the Terry MBA."

Even students who don't want to have to hold down a job while going to school get a pretty remarkable deal here—the 2000–2001 tuition for Georgia residents of $3776 is the lowest of BUSINESSWEEK's Top 50, and MBAs leave here with the least average debt, just $13,700. An added bonus is the opportunity to spend two years in Athens, which, about 70 miles northeast of Atlanta, is a fun and lively community with a progressive music scene that has spawned such nationally recognized bands as REM, the B-52s, and Widespread Panic. On campus, Old South meets the New; Rhett and Scarlett would have felt right at home on this 532-acre campus, which could have been a setting for *Gone With the Wind,* with its antebellum architecture, tree-lined walkways, and fiery-colored azalea bushes. At the same time, MBAs delve into the nuances of finance, marketing, real estate, insurance, and information systems.

The program runs on a semester system, with two-year students entering together in late July to take three-week pre-term classes in negotiations, business ethics, and team development. Then they're divided into teams to spend the first year covering a pretty typical schedule of core courses: accounting, micro- and macroeconomics, statistics, leadership, and MIS in the fall; finance, marketing, business law, accounting, operations, and a capstone course in strategy and communication in the spring.

Students in the 11-month program enter in late May to spend the summer covering an abbreviated version of the core, then join the second-years in choosing two or more specializations. Georgia calls its concentrations "sequences," and there are 14, which range from corporate finance and marketing to real estate analysis and risk management and insurance. Each sequence is made up of two or three required courses plus several option-related electives listed in a catalog totaling 65 offerings. New in 2000–2001 is a sequence in e-commerce, but finance, MIS (which features e-commerce as a component), and marketing are the most popular. Also in demand, the school notes, is the entrepreneurship sequence, even though among the Class of 2000 grads none actually launched their own businesses (and hardly any went to work for start-ups). "This year, students have just become more cautious," comments Mel Crask, director of the MBA Program.

In fact, the majority of Terry MBAs tend to take jobs in the finance and consulting fields. Just three-fourths of the Class of 2000 were employed by graduation, so even though students do receive extensive training in terms of interviewing practice, résumé writing, and salary negotiation strategies, the career services office—with a new director and two assistant directors—has been targeted for improvement. The B-school is also planning to devote greater attention to its network of gung-ho alums.

Although all MBAs here are required to take at least one international elective in order to graduate, Georgia's B-school isn't known for its international offerings. What was once the sole program—in the Netherlands—has been dormant for several years because of logistical problems. But Georgia is now eager to add some study abroad opportunities to the mix, just as soon as the school can complete its search for a candidate to fill the newly created position of director of International Programs. Administrators are looking into a joint course offering with schools in Brazil, Norway, and Singapore, which would utilize distance learning methods by faculty from each of the participating schools.

Students interested in law can earn a dual degree in a joint program with Georgia's law school that nets both the MBA and a J.D. in four years' time. There's also a new Master of Internet Technology program in which MBAs can take the 32 hours' worth of courses as a concentration during their last two semesters to earn an MBA with a concentration in Internet Technology. Two other offerings are helping the school expand its size and reputation: a custom-made program for PricewaterhouseCoopers made up of both on-campus and distance-learning components and a new part-time program in the metro Atlanta suburb of Gwinnett County. "We're constantly looking at new ways to deliver the MBA," says Mel Crask.

Partly in response to complaints from past grads who said they weren't thrilled with the teaching quality at Georgia (a lack of integration in core courses, in particular), the school has undertaken the task of revising the curriculum. The MBA Committee is currently considering incorporating into existing coursework three main areas of focus for the college—enterprise risk management, leadership, and management of technology—to ensure that the technical-oriented students here receive well-rounded management training. Three new centers revolving around leadership advancement, information systems leadership, and enterprise risk management studies will help; the centers already received major outside funding for the development of research and teaching techniques in these areas to bolster the program.

Students do appreciate the fact that a majority of professors tend to make themselves available to students outside class, many in spite of being swamped by their responsibilities for teaching the B-school's huge contingent of 5200 undergraduates as well. As far as facilities go, the MBA's main classroom building is Sanford Hall (named for Charles S. Sanford Jr., former CEO of Bankers Trust in New York), where most of the third floor is designated for MBAs only. There are fully wired classrooms, a student lounge, and a computer lab separate from the larger computer center shared with undergrads. But Crask says the program is outgrowing this facility, which opened as recently as 1997. The school is making plans for a new facility, as well as an increase in the entire amount of space for the program. But so far no commitments have been made.

Housing, on the other hand, is readily available on campus for both singles and married couples, but many MBAs choose to take nearby apartments instead. The social life here is coordinated by the Graduate Business Association, which plans tailgate parties for Bulldogs football games, an alumni-MBA golf tournament, and the end-of-year MBA Follies show. The downtown district, adjacent to the university's north campus, is the shopping, dining, and nightlife hub of the city. Be sure not to miss (not that you'll be able to) the annual Twilight Criterium, one of the nation's largest bicycle races, which draws Olympic-level riders from around the world every May for a high-speed competition at dusk through the downtown streets.

PLACEMENT DETAILS

When Dean P. George Benson took over a few years ago, one initiative was to aid the school's ailing career services office, but recent graduates are still smarting from some disappointing experiences with the office, from difficulty in finding internships and permanent jobs to problems obtaining networking opportunities. Benson did add a new director and two associate directors to the staff, though, and Terry MBAs now have a more positive outlook for the future here. "With the new director," predicts one, "the program will attract more firms and improve its reputation among recruiters." So far, it hasn't been easy attracting recruiters to a school with so few students to interview. The paltry 45 companies who came to campus in 2000 to interview second-years lacked breadth both in terms of types of employment offerings and geographic range (granted, many Georgia MBAs prefer to remain in the area). But the worst part is that 25 percent of Class of 2000 grads had no job offers at all when they got their diplomas—and 1998's figure of 13 percent had been considered disappointing.

The Class of 2000 pulled down a median starting pay package of $82,000—which sounds even better when you consider how inexpensively most were educated. Top employers were UPS (5); Wachovia Bank (3); Arthur Andersen (2); PricewaterhouseCoopers (2); Eli Lilly (2); Prudential Securities (2); Bell South (2); Sun-

trust Bank (2); Cintas (2); Accenture (2); and Capital One (2).

OUTSTANDING FACULTY

Dennis Beresford (accounting); *Marc Lipson* (finance); *Peter Shedd* (legal studies); *Bob Vandenberg* (management); *Srinivas Reddy* (marketing); *H. Munneke* (real estate).

APPLICANT TIPS

Georgia happens to boast a high level of selectivity, admitting only 28 percent of those who applied—making this B-school one of the most selective of the Runners-Up. One reason is the small size of the program. Student quality has also leveled off at a satisfactory range in recent years, with the average GMAT of 645 for the Class of 2002 approximating those of such higher-ranked schools as Purdue University and Indiana University.

Apply early. The final deadline is in May, and most applications are received by February 1 for the 11-month program and March 1 for the two-year program. Applications sent in after those dates are likely to be at a competitive disadvantage, not only for admission but for those highly sought-after scholarships and assistantships; if you want financial aid, get your paperwork in by February 1.

Although on-campus interviews are not mandatory, they are strongly encouraged. About 70 percent of those admitted to the Class of 2002 were interviewed. About 7 percent of the class had less than a year's work experience. Applicants should be able to demonstrate both a knowledge of calculus and computer proficiency prior to enrollment.

Contact: Donald R. Perry Jr.
Director of MBA Admissions
706-542-5621

Application deadlines for two-year program: April 1 (international); May 1 (domestic) **Deadlines for the 11-month program:** 15–60 days earlier than two-year deadlines for domestic and international students, respectively

TERRY MBAs SOUND OFF

It's hard to find a more beautiful campus and a more pleasant and friendly city than Athens, and the people at Terry made me feel at home from day one (even though I was thousands of miles from where I grew up and lived all my life). The program does an outstanding job of forming a truly collaborative team atmosphere, and teachers are committed to helping you learn. I will always count the two years at Terry among the best experiences of my life. The friendships I formed, the things I learned, and the personal and professional growth resulting from such an intense leadership-oriented program, with constant interaction with bright people from around the world, are invaluable. I know I will miss Athens, my classmates, and the University of Georgia a great deal.

A few positive points about the University of Georgia Terry MBA Program: (1) Best program for the money: almost all of the students receive in-state tuition, graduate assistantships, and/or scholarships. (2) Teamwork is highly encouraged. The students develop great relationships and learn a lot from each other. Students challenge themselves instead of feeling competitive with their classmates. (3) We are far from perfect—but the professors, administration, and students realize this weakness. There is constant change and effort for improvement on behalf of the students and faculty. This year, we struggled in the career services department, but by the end of the year, we had brought on two new, out-

standing directors. I think next year's class will greatly benefit from these changes.

Terry College of Business is an up-and-coming institution. The students here are of the same caliber as those at any of the top schools. The best aspect of the program here is that the students, staff, faculty, and administration all work together in a collegial, cooperative way. This has added tremendously to the value of my degree.

The Career Services office was largely atrocious. However, at the end of the year, new people were brought in and there will certainly be a huge improvement. The people (fellow students) in the program were top notch and contributed more value than anything else in the MBA experience. This university has a lot going for it.

Our program is very small, and this dramatically reduces the resources that we are given by the school. All in all, they do a great job with what they have to work with at the Terry College.

Athens is a wonderful and relatively inexpensive city and the state of Georgia is a rising star with plenty of opportunities. Terry's faculty do a poor job of reaching out to the business community to take advantage of these opportunities and in staying current with topics from the business world.

Excellent experience. The low marks I gave for career services are a known issue at the school and recent changes should improve the situation immediately for the next classes. The Terry MBA is an outstanding value. My total tuition/fee bill for the one-year MBA was $10,000, less a $5000 scholarship they gave me. Many students received work-study grants, which reduced their tuition bills to near zero.

UNIVERSITY OF ILLINOIS AT URBANA-CHAMPAIGN

UNIVERSITY OF ILLINOIS AT URBANA-CHAMPAIGN

College of Commerce and Business Administration
1407 West Gregory Avenue
Urbana, Illinois 61801
E-mail address: mba@uiuc.edu
Web site address: http://www.mba.uiuc.edu

Enrollment: 415
Women: 35%
Non-U.S.: 52%
Minority: 12%
Part-time: 0
Average age: 27
Applicants accepted: 41%
Median starting pay: $83,000

Annual tuition & fees:
   resident—$12,410
   nonresident—$20,136
Room and board: $7510
Average GMAT score: 621
Average years of work exp.: 4
Accepted applicants enrolled: 60%

Teaching methods: Lecture, 40%   Case study, 40%
   Projects and simulations, 20%

Contact:
Camille Gilmore
Director of Admissions
and Recruitment
217-244-4275
OR 800-MBA-UIUC
Application deadlines:
Domestic—
December 15
April 1
International—
December 15
February 1
Financial aid—
May 1

As recently as four years ago, graduate students at the University of Illinois at Urbana-Champaign's College of Commerce and Business Administration were grousing that the MBA program was nothing more than a loosely related collection of courses on various business topics. In fact, they blasted the curriculum as one of the 10 least integrated among BusinessWeek's Top 50 schools. Show us how everything fits together, they pleaded. We want more connection! More teamwork! Make the program more practical!

Bring the Class of 1996 back to campus in the fall of 2000, and they'll likely not recognize the place. They'd probably be shocked to learn just how radically Dean Howard Thomas reworked the curriculum. Under his watch, first-year students no longer take a list of required courses in the various management functions; instead, they find themselves assigned to student teams even before they arrive on campus to tackle a lockstep schedule of just one team-taught, cross-functional course per seven-week module. The emphasis on intermingling everything that you're learning doesn't end with the first year, either—a required capstone course focusing on international corporate strategy brings everyone back together for the program's final semester. Add to that the hands-on experience of an intensive week-long case study, another week spent in an international management simulation, and a menu of consulting projects that send as many as half the graduate students out to work with real-world companies, and you've got an MBA program that now showcases practicality and integration: The Class of 2000 rated Illinois one of the most well-integrated programs of the B-schools surveyed by BUSINESSWEEK.

Unfortunately, the momentum that Thomas began may be grinding to a halt. In August 2000, Thomas left Illinois to become dean of the Warwick Business School in England's MBA Program. He left aware that the transformative process he had begun had some "difficulties." And even before then, the transition had been something less than smooth. Some recent alums complained of being disoriented by a shifting lineup of courses each year as the program moved gradually toward the final product being rolled out for the 1999–2000 school year. Student dissatisfaction with various aspects of the curriculum-in-progress was the topic for a continual stream of venting on an open forum chat line via FirstClass, the B-school's internal computer network. Then, in December 2000, William R. Bryan, the former associate dean who had been named to serve as interim dean while Thomas's permanent replacement was chosen, passed away.

Accounting Professor Frederick L. Neumann was picked to hold the reins in the interim spot, a move that may help leverage the school's top accounting reputation. But the musical chairs have had an effect on morale and confidence in the direction the school is taking. "The professors that I had were incredible and the curriculum truly is integrated. There were numerous opportunities to build leadership skills that I didn't feel would be possible at other schools I visited," says one 2000 grad. "The only thing holding this school back is the need for a stronger administration."

In 2000, alums at Illinois were less likely to recommend the program to friends than alums at nearly every other B-school surveyed, a signal that changes are still needed. The school is trying to emphasize its strong suits during this period. Technology has a lofty tradition at the university, where Mosaic, the precursor of Netscape, and Eudora, a prototypical e-mail application, were developed. Illinois was recently ranked sixth nationwide among "Techno-MBA" and MBA "Best Buys" programs by *Computer World* magazine.

And the B-school has spent more than $7 million on technology upgrades in Commerce West (soon to be officially renamed Wohlers Hall), the MBA headquarters, since 1995, wiring classrooms and the student lounge, installing multimedia presentation and videoconferencing equipment, upgrading Web and groupware servers. Class notes are available by computer for virtually every course, and students can post questions for faculty and classmates 24 hours a day. As of 1999, career services went completely online as well, with Web-accessible student résumé and interview schedules.

Despite their administration woes, recent alums are generally impressed with the faculty across the board. They say Illinois's professors are generally at the leading edge of their fields; however, they say some of the school's top academics were not as involved in teaching as students would like.

As for placement, you can think of the school as a farm team for Chicago's business community, with students following a well-worn path north along Interstate 57 to work for such prestige firms as Arthur Andersen, Leo Burnett, Kraft, or PricewaterhouseCoopers. The only more direct route to a job in the Windy City is to attend Kellogg or the University of Chicago—and, let's face it, those two B-schools are a lot harder to get into and, for Illinois residents, a much more significant financial investment.

A three-day orientation kicks off the Illinois program, when incoming MBAs meet the team of four or five classmates with whom they'll work during the first three modules. During the first year, you'll take five to seven classes per module (there are two modules each semester). The administration says to plan on spending at least 20 hours per week on studying, and recent grads say the workload is a fair one. The first half of the second semester focuses on understanding how to identify and interact with a company's shareholders, followed by a one-week Applying Business Perspectives Seminar. This pits student teams against one another in the competitive Global Tycoon computer simulation, as their make-believe companies negotiate contracts to try to meet delivery schedules and production deadlines while still achieving their strategic objectives. A panel of executives and professors judges each team's performance at week's end.

Finally, the fourth module, Managing Change, brings in a parade of corporate executives, entrepreneurs, and faculty members who speak about the effects of such issues as technological development, environmental protection, globalization, and workforce diversification on an organization. During the second semester, students also choose 5 seven-week Topics in Management from a list of 15 or so that are updated annually, transitioning into more advanced, specialized study in such areas as decision analysis, Internet strategy, cross-cultural communication, IT, marketing, and finance.

During the second year, you'll take four classes per semester in your chosen area of concentration. The first seven weeks are spent studying Foundations of Business with seven professors from seven different disciplines synthesizing accounting, computing skills, strategy, and economics, among other topics. Then your team and another one join up for the Applying Business Perspectives Seminar, a weeklong case study in which each expanded team must develop and present a business plan, strategy, and marketing objective. The course for the next seven weeks, Designing and Managing Business Processes, covers operations, corporate finance, data analysis, organizational structure, and management communications.

New concentrations added in the last three years include: Manufacturing Management, Real Estate Management, Public Administration, Marketing with Advertising Focus, Food and Agribusiness Management, Technology Management, Entrepreneurship, New Venture Creation, and Electronic Commerce.

The second year also offers students three options: studying abroad at one of a dozen business schools in Europe, Asia, or Latin America; adopting a "professional track" in accounting, finance, information systems, marketing, or choosing a self-designed track that usually leads to a consulting career; or, as 50 MBAs a year do, pursuing a joint degree in architecture, computer science, engineering, journalism, law, or medicine. Besides taking electives from the catalog of 200 offered by the B-school, 50 percent of students participate in one, or even two, consulting projects arranged by the B-school's Office for Strategic Business Initiatives, which was launched in 1996. Through the OSBI, student teams have conducted "due diligence" for a possible acquisition by Kohlberg Kravis Roberts; performed a pricing analysis for Walt Disney Records; developed a global services plan for Lucent Technologies; assisted in technology transfer for Mayo Medical Ventures; and evaluated privatization of a next-generation space shuttle for Lockheed Martin. There are also projects involving accounting, marketing, or production for small start-ups through the Kaufmann Foundation for Entrepreneurial Leadership, as well as market analyses for emerging technologies being developed by university researchers in engineering and agribusiness. OSBI is a big push on the side of attending Illinois's MBA program over other schools, grads say.

MBAs currently share space in Commerce West and David Kinley Hall with Illinois's large undergraduate business program. There, too, the school increased technology recently, adding improved Internet connectivity access points in the MBA student lounge as well as in the MBA student computer lab to maximize use of laptops, which you'll have to have as part of your required equipment should you decide to enroll. A third building is in the offing, with dedicated MBA space, a technology center, and placement offices. Planning began in 2000, before the originally scheduled 2002 date, but groundbreaking is still far off, particularly now that administration leadership is in flux. Before he left, Thomas lamented, "All the years I have served as dean have been beset by inadequate budgets. Private funding has certainly helped us maintain our competitive edge. But it is recurring state funds that are required for everyday operations."

The campus is an oasis of culture surrounded by miles of farmland (hence the agribusiness concentration). The Krannert Center for the Performing Arts pulls in big-name classical and rock musicians alike. Across from the center is Espresso Royale, which has become an after-concert institution for coffee lovers. The campus also is home to the World Heritage Museum's extensive collection of ancient art, but you'll find far more sports lovers than museum goers in these parts. The MBA Association sponsors tailgate barbecues before football games that bring the faithful out to watch the Fightin' Illini and their now—thanks to the age of political correctness—quite controversial mascot, Chief Illiniwek. And an annual event is the MBA trip to Evanston for the Northwestern/Illinois basketball game, an outing that invariably includes sessions with the B-school's loyal alums, tours of the Chicago futures and options exchanges, shopping along Michigan Avenue's Miracle Mile, and drinking and dancing at jazz bars and rock clubs until the wee hours. Even the tech firms get into the sports mind-set at Illinois, with several dot-coms joining forces to sponsor one football tailgating event. If you're not into pigskin, you can learn that one skill essential to success in business: golf. The MBA school sponsors an annual golf scramble.

With almost half—48 percent—of the class from outside the United States, the school tries to develop events for its international students. Among those is a Thanksgiving dinner that introduces them to the Pilgrim tradition and gives them something to do while other students head out of town.

PLACEMENT DETAILS

Those same international students are among the ones who most loudly lament the state of career placement at Illinois, because they claim the school isn't much of a help when it comes to finding jobs outside the United States. Overall, graduates ranked the school in the middle of the pack when it came to career help.

Gripes one graduate from the Class of 2000: "I didn't receive help in finding an internship. I got one on-campus interview and that is because I did networking on my own the prior semester. I received my internship on my own merit. They are going to include my finding a job with their placement rate. This will boost their placement rate even though they were of absolutely no help."

True, just 68 companies recruited on campus in 2000, and most of the school's recruiting efforts are Midwest focused. However, another 2000 alum had the opposite experience: "Great network for the future. Incredible learning experience (I now know what really makes businesses work)."

Recruiters seem content, if not overwhelmed, with career placement at Illinois. "What we like best about [Illinois] graduates is . . . their ability to think in the gray areas and combine theory and practical knowledge to solve real-world problems," says a recruiter from Dow Chemical. Others mentioned the amount and quality of data available on each student as a plus.

Among the top employers of the Class of 2000 were Honeywell (9); Ford Motor Company (8); Deloitte & Touche (6); Pricewaterhouse-Coopers (5); Intel (4); Dynegy (3); General Electric (3); KPMG (3); Samsung (3); Agilent Technologies (2).

OUTSTANDING FACULTY

Donald Kleinmuntz (business administration); *Larry DeBrock* (economics); *James Gentry* (finance); *Josef Lakonishok* (finance); *Neil Pearson* (finance); *Brian Wansink* (marketing).

APPLICANT TIPS

Although a small percentage of graduate students enter Illinois's B-school with less than a year's work experience, the admissions office points out that most of them enroll in the joint degree programs (for which the GRE rather than the GMAT may be sufficient for admission), and Illinois MBAs on average work full-time for four years before returning to school. Officially, the school recommends a minimum of two years' work experience, still less than most programs. Students are admitted only for the fall semester on a rolling admissions schedule that begins making decisions in January; international students must apply by February 1 and domestic students by April 1.

Personal interviews are not required; in fact, fewer than half of applicants are interviewed. However, the school would like to make the interview more of a key part of the admissions process. In an attempt to increase the quality of the applicant pool, Illinois hosts four Preview Weekends between December and April when the B-school flies in, at the school's expense, a total of some 200 promising candidates from around the United States and Mexico to check out the campus. If you're interested in visiting—even if you have to foot the bill yourself—call the admissions office or check out the revamped Web site to arrange for a tour, meetings with current students, and class attendance. You can expect to hear from Illinois four to six weeks after you submit your application.

Contact: Camille Gilmore
Director of Admissions and Recruitment
217-244-4275
OR 800-MBA-UIUC
Application deadlines: Domestic—December 15, April 1; International—December 15, February 1; Financial aid—May 1

ILLINOIS MBAs SOUND OFF

I love FirstClass (FC), an intercommunication tool for MBA students. Professors respond to us through FC promptly and FC has been used extensively throughout our MBA life. It is more effective to communicate with each other via FC than by e-mail. FC helps us become a community.

Although the Illinois MBA is not one of the Top 30 business schools, I feel that the curriculum at Illinois is top notch. My expectations entering the program were far exceeded. I am very happy with the quality of education that I received at Illinois.

The University of Illinois has an excellent reputation with outstanding faculty. The educational experience that can be realized at this school is incredible. The campus is your playground as an MBA student. You have the opportunity to take courses and pursue interests wherever you desire. I would recommend it to all of my friends.

The Illinois MBA program is at the cutting edge of technology and that is emphasized extensively in their curriculum. Moreover, the National Center for Supercomputing Applications and other research centers provide the students access to, perhaps, some of the most brilliant minds in the world. The Food and Brand Lab run by Professor Brian Wansink is conducting incredible research in practical areas and allowing MBA students to learn and gain exposure to new as well as established practices in the marketing field.

The MBA experience was a great boost for my career in terms of salary and position held. Besides that, the learning experience was tremendous. Moreover, Urbana-Champaign is a perfect place for those who prefer a more quiet place where one can really focus on studies. Living expenses are much lower than in big cities.

The Illinois MBA program is an outstanding program that not only helps students grow professionally, but personally as well. The camaraderie between students is incomparable. Students sincerely want to help each other succeed. The faculty is always available for consultation and assistance. We push each other and ourselves to become the best we can be.

THE UNIVERSITY OF IOWA

Henry B. Tippie School of Management
108 Pappajohn Business Administration Building
Iowa City, Iowa 52242-1000
E-mail address: iowamba@uiowa.edu
Web site address: http://www.biz.uiowa.edu/mba

Enrollment: 867
Women: 28%
Non-U.S.: 47%
Minority: 3%
Part-time: 702
Average age: 28
Applicants accepted: 38%
Median starting pay: $87,000

Annual tuition & fees:
   resident—$5866
   nonresident—$13,620
Room and board: $11,230
Average GMAT score: 638
Average years of work exp.: 4.3
Accepted applicants enrolled: 56%

Teaching methods: Lecture, 40%   Case study, 40%
   Team projects, panel discussions, outside
   speakers, 20%

Contact:
Mary Spreen
Director of MBA
Admissions and
Financial Aid
319-335-3604
OR 800-622-4692
Application deadlines:
April 15
July 15

"If you build it, they will come."

In the movie *Field of Dreams,* an Iowa farmer, played by Kevin Costner, hears a voice urging him over and over again to construct a baseball diamond amidst his acres of corn—which he does, in hopes of materializing the ghost of his hero, legendary player Shoeless Joe Jackson.

Dean Gary Fethke may not resemble Costner, but it could be that he's heard that same call. Under Fethke's watch, the University of Iowa's Henry B. Tippie School of Management is gradually building its MBA program into an undiscovered diamond in the Hawkeye State.

It's fair to call Iowa's B-school a good place that's getting better. A responsive administration has acted on student requests for better teaching, a more flexible curriculum, and improved career services, without forgetting its analytical strengths, which were ranking sixth from the top in BUSINESSWEEK's student survey. The school has made excellent use of a new state-of-the-art building that opened in 1993, parlaying its technological bells and whistles into a giant leap forward in the quality of the information systems program long before most of its top-tier competitors did the same. Combined with a small full-time program of just 100 new MBAs a year, low tuition, and a vibrant college-town setting, it's a business education package well worth a second look.

That said, Iowa is not Michigan or Stanford—nor does it have ambitions to be. The long list of coastal high-powered recruiters who make the rounds of top-tier schools are not going to make the trek to

Iowa City, although those in between rarely miss the stop. The breadth of course offerings is less expansive than you'd find at a bigger, richer school, and some areas of study, such as international business, are still in their infancy. But given Iowa's limitations, students here appear to be a more satisfied bunch than ever before, in part because they're not saddled with huge loans once they leave. At B-school they've been taught to look at ROI, and when seeing their salaries and the outstanding loans, the numbers add up. "In addition to receiving a great education, I more than doubled my salary and landed a job working in e-commerce with Sprint Corp. I could not have wished for better results," says one graduate from the Class of 2000. And another: "The Tippie MBA is a hidden gem waiting to be unearthed. Top faculty and excellent students in a personalized program made for an outstanding return on my investment."

That class was the first to go all the way through the program with a curriculum overhaul instituted in 1998. The result was a streamlined core that allows room for electives before the first year is over. Now, first-years take six required credits in the fall, including marketing, managerial economics, corporate finance, managerial finance, and quantitative analysis. In spring, there are nine credits, divided between required courses and electives. Students can launch into their concentrations and get three advanced courses under their belts before heading off for their summer internships. When they return for the second year, the only remaining requirement is a capstone, team-taught integrative course in strategic management and business policy, in which student teams analyze live cases involving companies such as Deere & Co., Cargill, Pier One Imports, The Bravo Networks, and Baxter International, whose visiting executives lead discussions.

MBAs can choose from among nine concentration tracks, ranging from accounting and finance to marketing and product development and management; many major in two disciplines, combining marketing or finance with information systems, for example. The newest tracks are e-commerce and entrepreneurship. About 2 percent of Iowa MBAs started their own businesses last year, but some grads say they're inspired by the fact that the Center now owns 207 different companies.

Gaining more attention is the management information systems concentration, which is well supported by the seven-year-old, $36 million Pappajohn Business Administration Building. The facility also serves the 1300 undergraduates, 80 Executive MBA students, and executive education participants that make up the rest of the business school, but has a wing dedicated to MBAs. In this bright, cheerfully colored environment, you'll find an impressive library, a well-equipped computer lab, classrooms with videoconferencing capabilities, and a real-time trading room, linked by high-speed phone lines to more than 130 exchanges around the world.

In 2000 the school added 200 computers and upgraded computer/video projection units in laboratories and classrooms. The Stead Advanced Learning Technologies Center has been developed to assist faculty in developing course materials and Web-based learning sites, a new program designed to encourage students to develop personal professional portfolios. If you don't have your own laptop you can now check one out from the library and then check your e-mail from a wireless LAN throughout building. Wondering how that 401(k) you put on hold for two years is doing? Check stock quotes from Bridge Telerate and Bloomberg software in the library and Advanced Real-time Information Center. A dedicated marketing lab now allows students to focus on scanned data and geographic information systems.

Those who want to take further advantage of Iowa's MIS program and who have highly technical leanings can now take a dual-degree program, first offered in 1998, that nets both an MBA and master's in information systems in just five semesters. About a dozen students annually enroll in joint-degree programs in law, hospital and health administration, nursing, and library and information science. Students say the programs aren't as integrated as they should be, complaining that they often had to leave one class early in order to get across the expansive campus to get to the next on time. "This does not help to foster good feelings between the professors and students," one joint law/MBA quipped. Others say the dual workload was "brutal," but worth the extra effort in the end.

The B-school also encourages those pursuing traditional MBAs to look to the larger university to supplement the catalog of 80 business electives. If you don't find a concentration to meet your needs, you can design your own, with administrative approval—for example, a student interested in international business could come up with her own combination of finance, language, and area studies courses. Among the more interesting new B-school offerings is a course during spring break in which students head for an Iowa-based national manufacturing company to work a 50- to 60-hour week on-site learning about rapid continuous improvement. The school also started to beef up its international coursework, developing a joint program with the University of Wisconsin that sends students and faculty from both schools to London. The Wisconsin and Iowa professors teach three-week classes—students can choose either finance or marketing—as well as arranging for outside speakers and tours.

Back in Iowa City, you'll find a campus whose students participate to an unusual degree in the school's workings. There's at least one student on every faculty committee, save the one that handles promotions and tenure, including a new strategic planning committee. Associate Dean Gary Gaeth, who began directing the MBA program four years ago, says that committee's first meetings focused on how Iowa can better connect with the corporate world, which has never been one of the B-school's strongest

features. But that's changing somewhat. In November 1998, a newly formed management advisory council, made up of 17 business executives, convened for the first of what will be quarterly meetings. To get a handle on where to direct their efforts, the execs talked with student focus groups—without Iowa faculty or staff being present.

One thing students have no complaints about is the campus environment. Unless you've visited Iowa City, it's hard to imagine how active this town is. With a population approaching 80,000, including 30,000 students, Iowa City is the state's answer to Wisconsin's Madison or Colorado's Boulder. It's also home to one of the premier writing programs in the nation, the Iowa Writers Workshop, which means you're surrounded by one of the country's best selections of used and new bookstores, not to mention great authors reading on campus, often for free. By Iowa standards, housing here is pricey, about $500 for a one-bedroom apartment. Ninety percent of MBAs live off campus, in either apartment complexes or Victorian homes that have been divided into apartments. One thing to keep in mind: The student body has a good number of international students but is otherwise rather homogeneous, with women making up about a quarter of the enrollment. American minority students are dealt an even worse hand, with a dismal 3 percent enrollment figure.

You might think the local restaurant fare was all meat and potatoes—and there is plenty of that—but Iowa City boasts great ethnic cuisine, including one of the best vegetarian Indian meals you'll have this side of Bombay.

The campus sits on a bluff overlooking the Iowa River and intermingles with the downtown area. During fall and spring evenings, musicians play guitars and portable keyboards along a pedestrian mall, a favorite place for MBAs to gather. On Thursday nights they stop by the Airliner, a local pub owned by former NBA player Brad Lohaus. The MBA Association sponsors a number of community service activities that get students involved with local residents, including participation in hospice, free lunch, and public school literacy programs. Throughout the year, Iowa students experience a good quality of life that's safe and down-to-earth. Some students claim Shoeless Joe Jackson was given the right answer when he finally showed up on Kevin Costner's field of dreams and asked "Is this heaven?" The answer: "No. It's Iowa!"

PLACEMENT DETAILS

Career services, once a regular target of student criticism, have become a priority in recent years. There have been some major improvements. Just 2 percent of the Class of 2000 had no job offers at graduation, compared with 20 percent of the Class of 1996. The median starting package of salary, bonus, and other compensation in 2000 was $87,000, up significantly from $52,950 four years before. Iowa's placement staff has been expanded from two to four positions, including three associate directors who specialize in new business development, internships, and career management, respectively. As part of an earlier curriculum overhaul, a not-for-credit course is required of all first-year students. Called MBA Competitive Prep, it includes weekly sessions for the first 9 or 10 weeks of the school year, covering the basics of professionalism, personal and career assessment, writing résumés and cover letters, interviewing, and negotiating salaries. The Class of 2000 ranked the school at the middle of the BUSINESSWEEK pack in covering this kind of skill building.

However, some students still call career services "a disaster," because few I-banks and tech firms from the coasts recruit on campus. The career staff is well aware of just how isolated Tippie is from the nation's business hubs and supports student efforts to reach out, underwriting recruiting trips for some exceptional

students and thinking of ways for recruiters to reach students without making the plane flight. The on-campus recruiting system went online in fall of 1998, and the placement office now regularly uses videoconferencing equipment so candidates can interview with companies that can't make it to campus.

In 2000, 66 companies came to Iowa City to recruit second-year students. An additional 96 participated in off-campus job fairs, with another 485 jobs posted online and through videoconferencing. Most of the firms that recruit on campus continue to be from the Midwest, although they're not no-name firms. Arthur Andersen, Kraft, McDonald's, Fed-Ex, Kimberly-Clark, and Procter & Gamble are among the regulars. Top employers were top 10 companies: HON Industries Inc. (6); Deere & Co. (5); Sprint Corp. (4); U.S. Bancorp (4); The Pillsbury Co. (3); Northwest Airlines (3); Scotia Capital (2); Kraft Foods (2); National City Corp. (2); PricewaterhouseCoopers (2).

OUTSTANDING FACULTY

D. Collins (accounting); *Bruce Johnson* (accounting); *Matt Billett* (finance); *Kurt Anstreicher* (management science); *Thomas Gruca* (marketing); *Baba Shiv* (marketing).

APPLICANT TIPS

Over the past couple of years, Iowa has been much more selective in its admissions as part of a strategic decision to emphasize student quality. Whereas 47 percent of those who applied in 1996 were admitted, just 27 percent got in in 1998. That number rose to 38 percent in 2000, possibly due to the overall decline in MBA applicants in that year's strong economy. As a result, enrollment has shrunk almost 25 percent, with core class sizes now numbering 40 instead of 70. The strategy appears to have been successful: The average GMAT has increased, from 589 for the Class of '98 to 638 for the Class of 2000, as has average work experience—while 20 percent of the Class of '98 had less than a year of previous full-time work before entering the program, just 5 percent of the Class of 2000 falls into that category. You'll also find that admissions interviews, once a rare occurrence, are now required, either on campus or by telephone with admissions staff, or with an Iowa alum in your local area. Interviews—focusing on communication skills as much as anything else—now count as one of the five admission criteria.

The school says it places a good deal of emphasis on essays, so you'll want to spend some time crafting your answers to the questions on the application that have to do with how an Iowa education fits into your career plans and how you've demonstrated potential for success. Although the school's final deadline for fall admission isn't until July 15, you'd be well advised to apply earlier, seeing as how class size is limited. If you want to be considered for fellowships or graduate assistantships, your paperwork must be in by the priority deadline of April 15, and admissions and financial aid decisions are made on a rolling basis beginning in December.

Contact: Mary Spreen
Director of MBA Admissions and Financial Aid
319-335-3604
OR 800-622-4692
Application deadlines: April 15; July 15

IOWA MBAs SOUND OFF

The best part of my experience was the small-sized classes and ability to interact with faculty. I also valued the ability to design my program around my interests, including tak-

ing classes outside the business school. Another strength is the ability of the students to give back to the program and make it what we want it to be. International consulting projects, finance and marketing forums, case competitions, the *MBA Journal,* cultural festivals and other programs are developed by and for students to further our business education. The workload is tremendous, but pays off in the end.

I had never even been to the state of Iowa prior to coming to school here. My move from the East Coast to the Midwest was the best decision I have ever made. The small size of the program and personal interaction with the faculty have made these two years the most productive of my life.

After being accepted here I still had the opportunity to look at/visit other MBA programs for benchmarking purposes and found that the technology access at Iowa is equal to or superior to virtually all others. It is obvious that the Iowa program has put emphasis on allowing MBAs access to technology.

Bottom line, I really am very satisfied with the program. It exceeded virtually all of my expectations, especially considering the very reasonable cost of the program in relation to other programs of similar quality.

My educational experience here at the University of Iowa has been outstanding. The quality of my classmates, the faculty, and the administrators and staff are exceptional. While I learned much from the professors, I learned even more from my classmates. When considering the cost and the quality of the program, I could not have made a better choice than to come here.

UNIVERSITY OF MINNESOTA

UNIVERSITY OF MINNESOTA

Carlson School of Management

321 19th Avenue South

Minneapolis, Minnesota 55455

E-mail address: mbaoffice@csom.umn.edu

Web site address: http://www.csom.umn.edu

Enrollment: 1150	Annual tuition & fees:
Women: 25%	resident—$14,124
Non-U.S.: 22%	nonresident—$18,230
Minority: 9%	Room and board: $5,340
Part-time: 900	Average GMAT score: 640
Average age: 29	Average years of work exp.: 5.6
Applicants accepted: 33%	Accepted applicants enrolled: 41%
Median starting pay: $83,000	

Teaching methods: Lecture, 25% Case study, 40%
Group projects, 35%

Contact:

Tracy Keeling

Admissions

Coordinator

800-926-9431

OR 612-625-5555

Application deadlines:

January 1

February 15 (int'l)

March 1

April 1

Until four years ago, if MBA students at the Carlson School of Management at the University of Minnesota wanted to hang out and discuss class materials they would have to sit on the floor in the hallway. "Either that or go home," remembers Dean David S. Kidwell. That's not much of an environment for a program that prides itself—almost obsessively—on its strong sense of community. Carlson is a school where the admissions staff says it weighs candidates' willingness to be team players as much as GMAT scores. And the school sells itself on its interactive relationships between students, faculty, and members of the Twin Cities' business community. Yet classes were scattered in a number of different buildings across the U of M campus and there were no common areas for students to sit and chat.

The irony was not lost on Kidwell, who is also a professor of finance. Since taking the top office in 1991 he started aggressively fund raising. He built a development office of 17 and, as a result, radically swelled the school's coffers. When Kidwell was named dean, Carlson typically raised about $500,000 from annual giving and had a $25 million endowment. Today Kidwell brings in about $10 million in annual giving and the school has a $150 million endowment.

Thanks to this financial acumen, by January 1998, the school moved into a new $45 million building, $8 million of which came from the state of Minnesota—solving that little problem of students having nowhere to sit. The new 243,000-square-foot building has plenty of space, including a 250-seat lecture hall, 33 meeting rooms, 2 cafeterias (one's called a private dining room), and a student lounge for MBAs only. Better yet, faculty offices are clustered together to reflect the school's new integrated curriculum.

Kidwell thinks the building speaks volumes about the direction he is (and plans to continue) taking Carlson. "It is a statement to all that when you see our building that it is a powerful business school, like a bank building gives security. This is a dramatic building." In the old facilities, faculty complained that they were locked in the proverbial ivory tower and could go weeks without bumping into a student outside of class, says Gary Lindblad, assistant dean and director of MBA programs. "Now, faculty can't run to the bathroom without running into a student. It is not an isolated experience."

Indeed, the connection between professors and students was one of the most significant problems at Carlson and one that caused it to drop into the third tier of B-schools in BUSINESS-WEEK's 1998 ranking. The program moved back into the second tier in 2000, after a concerted effort on the part of Kidwell, Lindblad, and Tim Nantell, faculty director, to revamp the teaching quality at Carlson. Today the school has 112 faculty members, which is an increase of 34 faculty members over the last three years, an improvement that could not have been made in the old facility, as there was no room to add another desk. "The physical space has forced interaction. Everyone now eats together," Kidwell says.

Although the school has long been recognized as a strong research institution, students in the past griped that they felt left out. "We weren't sure that it translated into quality of teaching for students. We made substantial strides in the student services side of things," Kidwell claims. He launched a blue-ribbon committee to look at MBA teaching and that, combined with the new building, has resulted in a culture change. Faculty are more focused on programs and students, they attend annual teaching seminars, pay attention to extensive surveys of students, and "those who do not teach well do not get promoted," the dean says. "Outstanding teaching is expected here."

"The faculty here are very connected to the business community," adds Michael Agnew, assistant dean and director of the Graduate Business Career Center. "They are very attuned to career needs that students have." Students now say that the school's most prominent academics tend to be more heavily involved in teaching and they seem satisfied with the availability of faculty for informal discussions. Of course, all the enthusiastic faculty in the world aren't of much use if they don't have anything innovative to teach. So, the Carlson curriculum was completely overhauled and unveiled in the fall of 1999, with the core courses cut in half, allowing you to get to the stuff in which you are interested more quickly. Nantell says some MBAs now even manage to swing a double concentration. "It is integrated. I think we do this as well as any other school in the country," Nantell effuses. The objective is to get to electives earlier so that you have that experience before you start your internship. "The characteristics of MBA students have changed. They have gotten older and more experienced, and we wanted to give them something that will be of the most value to them," says Lindblad.

New concentrations added in the last three years include e-business, supply chain management, entrepreneurial studies, health-care management, and international business. Students give the school low marks in weaving e-commerce throughout curriculum, but rank Carlson high when it comes to using other tech tools as part of the curriculum.

With the new curriculum, you'll start with business basics, including financial accounting and quantitative statistics and then apply those skills in the Carlson Integrated Management Simulation (CIMS), a team project of running your own business, which is followed by an opportunity to present your plan to a panel of faculty. Spring semester is your chance to begin to specialize. You'll take on strategy as well as those electives and benefit from having a mentor from the large Minneapolis business community—by some counts it is the fifth largest corporate market in the United States—to give you some hands-on experience. Options for specialization include accounting, e-business, entrepreneurship, finance, health-care management, information sciences, international business, marketing, operations management, strategic management, supply chain management, and self-designed programs. Other requirements for study include a field consulting project with an area business, for which they'll pay the school for your thoughts. Executives from General Mills, Bristol-Myers Squibb, Medtronic, and others also lecture in the second-year Top Management Perspectives course.

One of Carlson's most innovative—and popular—additions is the Financial Markets Lab. The local business community donated $3.5 million in assets for students to manage, and those with a finance concentration can opt to work as investment managers for the Golden Gopher Growth Fund as their field consulting requirement.

In addition to the new international business concentration, the school sponsors 10-week study abroad programs in Europe, the Pacific Rim, and Latin America. The jaunts cost extra, but additional financial aid is available. "We believe that in the future top business schools will have to have an international presence," Kidwell says. "Everyone does exchange programs. What we want is a global network in key geographic areas."

Another "hot button" for the school, says Lindblad, is the "double-edged sword" of the allure of the Twin Cities. Many students come expecting the pace to be frozen tundra (which it is several months of the year), but then they end up staying. With job offers from the likes of General Mills and 3M, a community that is welcoming to newcomers, and a low cost of living, there's reason to stay put. But that means that for many years it has been hard for students to get jobs elsewhere as recruiters outside the Mid-

west shied away, thinking Carlson grads wouldn't move across the country. "We have made a huge effort to help students who want to go outside Twin Cities," Lindblad says, and according to the Class of 2000, it's true. Those students surveyed by BUSINESSWEEK ranked the school toward the top end of aggressiveness in helping them find summer jobs and internships.

Looking around off campus, it is easy to see why many grads are hesitant to leave. St. Paul and Minneapolis—dubbed the Twin Cities—afford the amenities of living in a big city but with a much more human face. Winter here is harsh, for sure, but with more than 105 theater companies, the most per capita of any American city, there is plenty to do. There are 136 art galleries, 15 museums, and 9 dance companies. In fact, some call the area "Mini-apple." And contrary to popular belief, there's more up north to eat than fried fish, with an impressive array of ethnic restaurants. The cities are some of the fastest growing in the states, making it a great place for start-ups. And if the great outdoors is more your style, there are 15,291 lakes, 25 ski areas, and 4000 miles of trails for biking and hiking. And while you are stocking up on trivia, don't forget that the Twin Cities are home to Mall of America.

All that activity means housing is not small-town cheap. Most students live off campus in apartments that typically range from $700 to $900. A new graduate student housing opened in 2000 across the street from the B-school and law school. But this isn't for a student budget. Rent at the GrandMarc starts at $760 for a studio apartment. Two bedrooms start at $823 per month, per bedroom.

PLACEMENT DETAILS

After Carlson fell into the third-tier of BUSINESS-WEEK's rankings in 1998, in large part because of gripes about the Midwest-focused placement efforts, the school hired Mike Agnew to head the Graduate Business Career Center. Having worked at both Wharton and Michigan State, he says he was brought here to bring a broader focus to the office. "The commission I had was to nationalize placement. We have a great corporate community but it was nationally perceived that students wouldn't leave."

Since Agnew joined the Carlson team, more grads have gone outside Minnesota to work: from 20 percent in 1998 to 27 percent in 1999 to 30 percent in 2000. In 2000 alone 10 percent of students went to each coast. Agnew attributes that to his "take the mountain to Mohammed" approach to interviewing. While 111 firms interviewed on campus in 2000, more significant, he says, were the trips he and 20 to 25 students each made to New York, Silicon Valley, Chicago, Denver, and other cities. Using the network of 38,000 alumni, Agnew gained entrance into Goldman Sachs, Alex Brown, and a number of other I-banks for Carlson students.

Such trips would not have been possible without a $1 million reorganization of the career services center, with six people now doing the job one used to do. Four MBA relationship directors work with companies to recruit Carlson grads, and grads and undergrads no longer have to wait in the same line at GBCC to get advice. Derrick Brown, a staffing specialist at Thermo King, says the new crew is good at the job, making recruiters feel welcome and comfortable while being organized and offering quality candidates.

Of the Class of 2000, 95 percent had received a job offer by graduation, with an average of 2.5 offers each, and they seem optimistic about GBCC's turnaround. They rated it solidly middle of the pack in BUSINESSWEEK's survey when asked how helpful the school was in job searches with firms that did not come to campus. And the class made a $20,000 donation to the office. Average starting pay package was $82,000. Top hirers in 2000 were U.S. Bancorp (7); Piper Jaffray (5); Intel (4); General Mills (4); IBM (4); Medtronic (4); Deloitte Consulting (4); Ecolab (3); CBS MarketWatch (3); Alliance Capital (3).

OUTSTANDING FACULTY

Ari Mukherji (accounting); *Scott Gibson* (finance); *Tim Nantell* (finance); *Rick Nelson* (finance); *Raj Singh* (finance); *Andrew Winton* (finance); *Mark Bergen* (marketing); *Ken Roering* (marketing); *M. Peteraf* (strategy).

APPLICANT TIPS

Even as Carlson expands its class size—applications are up about 50 percent—it is becoming more selective, with GMAT scores increasing 40 points in the last decade. That said, in addition to good GPAs and GMATs and "all the similar things other schools want," Sandra Kelzenberg, director of MBA marketing and admissions, says Carlson looks for MBA candidates who are active and like hands-on approaches rather than a more lecture-based curriculum. "That's what makes us different. You know by what people say they liked in previous jobs. If they say they don't like teamwork, then this is not the place for them."

Kelzenberg and her staff interview about 50 percent of prospective students from 18 domestic sites, including campus, as well as overseas. The school doesn't use peer reviews except when absolutely necessary, because it doesn't feel it gets an accurate assessment on a candidate. Overseas in particular, Kelzenberg says, culture obligations make it difficult for an alumni to turn in a fair review of a prospective student. Although not a requirement, Kelzenberg highly recommends the interview, as long as you're prepared.

When writing your essay, Kelzenberg asks you to remember that she often reads 20 to 50 applications in a day and at this point can pretty much spot a generic essay from one tailored for Carlson. "I know that there are a lot of essays to write. We are sensitive to that. But make sure your application to us doesn't say 'Emory' on it."

In 2000 Carlson changed its application process from a batch system to rolling admissions, the opposite of what many schools are doing. Now, whenever you apply, you can expect to hear within six weeks. International students can expect a respond within two months. Kelzenberg says the system "makes it easier for candidates." If you're interested in financial aid or scholarships, Kelzenberg says the sooner you apply the better. "By the third deadline there are not as many dollars left."

Contact: Tracy Keeling
Admissions Coordinator
800-926-9431
OR 612-625-5555
Application deadlines: January 1; February 15 (international); March 1; April 1

CARLSON MBAs SOUND OFF

The resources for entrepreneurial students at the Carlson School are outstanding. This is helped by the small class size, high-quality students, and terrific local business atmosphere. My education far outstripped even my highest expectations.

I'm walking away from my MBA experience with no debt, my dream job, and an entire new network of friends. Looking back, I believe the risk that I took two years ago—quitting a well-paying job—was great. The rewards have been worth it. I feel very strongly that there's a positive momentum going on at Carlson School and that there is quite a bit of positive change. Even over the two years that I have spent there, the amount

of listening being done by both administration and faculty has improved, and the school has benefited tremendously.

I've accomplished all my goals at the Carlson MBA Program. . . . However, there's still room for improvement. One particular area is in the information and decision sciences (IDS) concentration. For many years, the needs of MBA students in the IDS concentration were not satisfactorily met.

The Minneapolis business community is very underrated; you have the diversity of firms much like a big city, but because of the city's size you are able to interact with the local firms on a much more intimate basis. I can't imagine such interaction in New York or Chicago, with the same level of attention. The school should continue to improve in the future, and it is a program I would highly recommend. Based on my experience and in looking at other programs, I think the school matches up well with several Top 30 programs.

Higher expectations are helping the school. The increasing scores, and so forth, of students are raising standards toward private school quality, pulling forward the public school inertia. The school has not concentrated on the social aspects of business school. They hold some events, but there is not a strategy to increase the value of the MBA experience by engaging the students with each other.

Most of my education in elective coursework has revolved around investment finance and the Golden Gopher Growth Fund, where I worked as a telecommunications student equity analyst. That experience put me in front of senior management at the companies I was researching and covering. The growth fund provided an educational medium that is not available at most other schools around the world. Where else can future investment professionals have the training grounds to learn and grow, where students are provided the room to make mistakes and grow from them without jeopardizing their careers on Wall Street? More than not jeopardizing their careers, the Growth Fund opened doors into the investment community that would not have otherwise been available.

UNIVERSITY OF NOTRE DAME

UNIVERSITY OF NOTRE DAME

Mendoza College of Business
MBA Program Suite 276
P.O. Box 399
Notre Dame, Indiana 46556-0399
E-mail address: mba.1@nd.edu
Web site address: http://www.nd.edu/~mba

Enrollment: 325	Annual tuition & fees: $23,780
Women: 33%	Room and board: $5285
Non-U.S.: 35%	Average GMAT score: 659
Minority: 10%	Average years of work exp.: 4.1
Part-time: N/A	Accepted applicants enrolled: 53%
Average age: 26	
Applicants accepted: 29%	
Median starting pay: $84,000	

Teaching methods: Lecture, 25%   Case study, 35%
                   Experiential learning, 40%

Contact:

Hayden F. Estrada
Director of Admissions
219-631-8488
Application deadlines:
November 15
January 15
March 15

When people hear the words, "the University of Notre Dame," all sorts of images run through their heads. Green and gold. Do-gooders. Football. Enthusiastic fans. Faith. More football. Likely absent from that list are money and the Silicon Valley. Indeed, Notre Dame's Roman Catholic heritage dominates the school. Founded by the congregation of the Holy Cross in 1842, the campus still retains its religious identity today. That doesn't mean MBAs are required to start their days with Mass, but you're not apt to ever forget you're attending a Catholic school. There is a chapel in every dorm. The university's elaborate cathedral is situated in the center of the campus. Adjacent to the church is Notre Dame's administration building, its legendary golden dome topped by a statue of the Virgin Mary.

But in April 2000, 1973 graduate Tom Mendoza and his wife, Kathy, gave the B-school $35 million. And with that, many of those associations are likely to change. The Mendozas are both executives at Network Appliance Inc., a Sunnyvale, California–based data storage firm. He's president and she's director of worldwide strategic alliances. Faculty, administration, and alumni think the school, now renamed the Mendoza College of Business in honor of the gift, which was the largest in the university's history, will benefit from the Silicon Valley connection. Thanks to Net App's impressive client list—Intel, Dell, Earthlink, and Oracle, just to name a few—the University of Notre Dame name may now come up on the high-tech radar that previously didn't reach to South Bend, Indiana.

Tom Mendoza is happy to have the school use the endowment to raise its profile, but he says he doesn't have an agenda to make ND's B-school into something it's not. As he told the *Observer,* Notre Dame's student newspaper, "We don't want any control [over the college]. All we're trying to do is give them resources to make the right decisions. We're just happy to give them the money to help them compete. The business school world is very competitive." Indeed, those funds will come in handy for Carolyn Y. Woo, the B-school's dean. When the former Purdue administrator and management professor arrived at Notre Dame in July 1997, she intended to bring the school into national focus, hoping to move it from its also-ran status into a top-tier school, without changing its mission or focus. While already on her way before the Mendoza gift, Woo says the funds will help continue on that track, with none of the funds going toward bricks-and-mortar projects. Woo, who is the rare female B-school dean, still has a long way to go to reach her ambitious goal. Her main priority now is getting the word out, a move the name change and Mendoza gift may assist with. Behind the scenes, she says, her main focus has been improving the quality of students through scholarships and fellowships and recruiting top-notch junior faculty.

One thing she hasn't changed is the basic structure of the program. You'll find a fairly nuts-and-bolts MBA that comes in two flavors: a regular two-year program and a one-year version for students with undergraduate degrees in business, which is lauded by those who enroll. "My experience was improved significantly by my participation in a one-year accelerated program," says one 2000 graduate. "Because I already had an undergraduate degree in business I was able to avoid repetition and skip many of the basic courses. I would never have returned to school if it required the full two years."

For the majority who do the two-year program, the first year you'll take the usual array of core courses and have time for two electives. In year two, MBAs must choose an ethics elective and an international business elective. Students can apply some of their other seven electives to 1 of 14 concentrations, but they are not required to pick one. Woo has added several new majors, including management consulting, corporate finance, management information systems, entrepreneurship, and e-commerce. The administration has also bolstered elective offerings in response to student complaints that there weren't enough and that the corporate finance choices, in particular, were lacking.

Woo appointed Leo Burke (ND '70 and a third generation "Domer") as associate dean and director of the Executive Programs. Before being wooed away by Woo, Burke was director of strategy for Motorola University, global education and development arm of Motorola Inc., yet another connection the dean feels will help leverage the school's reputation outside its current circles.

Given the program's basic structure, Notre Dame differentiates itself through ethics, a tie-in that makes sense with the underlying mission of the Catholic school and the beliefs of its alumni. The B-school's ethics program is one of the oldest in the country. Second-year MBAs examine such things as labor relations, environmental issues, and equal opportunities for women and minorities. But Woo is not satisfied with this already successful ethics program, she's aiming to make it more a part of the school culture than merely an academic concentration. "This is a place where we strive to be faithful to Catholic ideals. We have to prepare our students for success, to understand their impact as a citizen of society, not just a resident of the world," she says. "We need them to be a citizen." There are now five professor chairs dedicated to ethics and 60 faculty who volunteer—from both the undergraduate and graduate sides—to participate in some form of the program. Says Woo: "Ethics is just a critical part of leadership. If people cannot trust you, you cannot lead."

Community service is a critical element of the school's culture; if you're not interested in doing your fair share of charity work, don't apply to Mendoza. In all likelihood, you won't be admitted and if you are, you won't like it once you're there. Virtually all MBAs participate in some form of volunteering thanks to the Community Service Committee, which organizes activities for three local charities. Students are aware of this focus from the moment they step on campus, since a community service event is part of the two-week-long orientation program.

The school's small size provides a family-like atmosphere, and that's remained the case, even as Woo has increased school size from 280 students to 325. Students run into familiar faces all the time at the Huddle, the campus food court where teams often study. Increasing the MBA enrollment is designed to attract more corporate recruiters, support more international programs and course offerings, and make better use of the school's facilities, Woo says.

The increase in the number of students, along with the Mendoza money, has helped fund additional international exchange programs. Currently, students can study in London, England, or Santiago, Chile, for a semester and programs in East Africa and Asia are in the works. Woo, a Hong Kong native, is particularly excited about a new trip for eight students (about 40 applied) to South Africa to study entrepreneurship and ethical issues there. The London Program is located in its own Law/MBA Centre in the heart of the city's financial district. A Notre Dame professor acts as resident director, teaching one course, and professors from British schools teach the remainder of the coursework.

Located 90 miles east of Chicago, Notre Dame's hometown of South Bend has a population of about 250,000. The campus is located on the northern edge of the town, and students tend not to stray too far. There's a slew of school-sponsored gatherings, ranging from the annual Halloween Costume Party to the Spring Formal, where students mix with faculty and administrators. The Senior Bar on campus is a hangout on Thursday nights. Popular spots include Coach's and The Linebacker, both just a few blocks off campus. With names like Coach's and The Linebacker, it's easy to guess that football is popular here . . . in fact when some say Notre Dame is a religious school, they're not talking about Catholicism; they're talking football. "There is nothing quite like seeing a Notre Dame football game," says one grad from the Class of 2000, likely overwhelmed by the caravans of cars that come to South Bend on Saturdays, weather notwithstanding, to tailgate in the parking lots hours before each game.

Football mania helps for the job search, too, since recruiters and alums travel to South Bend on fall weekends for the spectacular festivities. MBAs say it's a great way to tap into Notre Dame's powerful alumni network and one the administration plans to use more in the future.

PLACEMENT DETAILS

Notre Dame's placement office may finally be showing signs of improvement, after several false starts. For years, grads said it was one of the worst at any of the Top 50 schools. And after most of the career staff left in 1998–1999, leaving the Class of 2000 directionless for their first-year placement, those same grads ranked the school at the very low end when it came to helping with independent job searches and helping students find a job before graduation. One uses the word "horrible" to describe the center. Others use: "unimaginative, unmotivated, and somewhat clueless." They also said the school doesn't cut it when it comes to helping students find summer jobs or internships, and complain about the lack of diversity of firms recruiting on campus.

And in that Notre Dame the-glass-is-always-half-full way, one alum says the transition was part of what made Mendoza a good experience for him: "The difference between

Notre Dame and other schools is that when we were without a career services staff, the students banded together and we independently helped each other find internships. We used our student network to get everyone placed. I don't think you would find that level of teamwork and selflessness at any other schools."

But all hope is not lost. A new senior director of MBA programs, Lee Junkans, has started an aggressive new program to address all aspects of career planning and placement at Mendoza. It starts with a new pass/fail class required for all first-years, which includes workshops on cover letter and résumé writing and interviewing skills. "If our students are going to represent the University of Notre Dame, they are going to impact the perception of the school every time [they are] in front of a company," Junkans says.

Junkans added staffers who specialize in overseas recruiting and career advising, and is in the process of hiring another, who can hold down the fort as he goes out to recruit recruiters. "I arrived in April 1999, and before then there had been little or no marketing done," says Junkans, who came to Notre Dame after working at both Fuqua at Duke and Simon at Rochester. For now, placement continues to have a Midwest focus, but he is working to change that, organizing the school's first-ever trip to Silicon Valley—the area which he says is now his No. 2 priority—as well as Chicago, New York, and Boston. On Junkans's side the unusually strong network of Notre Dame alums— these are folks who come back for football games and have ND license plates—are more than happy to hire one of their own. In fact, putting students in contact with practicing professionals is one of the placement areas in which Mendoza grads seem satisfied. Junkans plans to use that loyalty to get more interviews for students from firms that don't want to make the trip to Indiana.

Still, with all those obstacles, the Class of 2000 fared well. On average each grad had 2.6 job offers by graduation. Interviews were con-ducted by 113 companies, not bad for such a small class. The big hirers of the Class of 2000: Ford Motor Company (8); Accenture (5); Dell Computer Corporation (4); IBM Corporation (4); Corning Inc. (3); Intel Corporation (3); PricewaterhouseCoopers (3); Procter & Gamble (3); C-Bridge Internet Solutions (2).

OUTSTANDING FACULTY

Ramachandran Ramanan (accounting); *John Affleck-Greaves* (finance); *Jerry Langley* (finance); *Frank Reilly* (finance); *Paul Schulz* (finance); *Matt Bloom* (management); *Edward Conlon* (management); *Joe Urbany* (marketing).

APPLICANT TIPS

Woo has long said that one of her major priorities is improving the quality of students entering the program, even as she boosts its size. And she's proven that she wasn't kidding. In 1998, 57 percent of applicants who applied were accepted. In 2000 that number dropped to 29 percent and that number is one both the admissions staff and dean's office would like to see even lower.

As a result, work experience is becoming ever more important at Notre Dame. Students entering in 2000 averaged more than four-and-a-half years of work experience, up from three years for those entering in 1996. But it's not just longevity on the job, says Brian T. Lohr, assistant director of MBA admissions. The admissions office likes to see professional experience with leadership and management experience on a number of projects. Of course, your GPA and GMAT will play a major role in the admissions process, even more than they once did. The average GMAT score of a Mendoza MBA was below 600 in 1996, was 613 in 1998, by 2000 it was 659, an "incredible" jump in Woo's opinion.

But it is the essays, recommendations, and personal interview where you can differentiate yourself. While not required, Lohr describes the interview as "almost imperative." About 80 percent of candidates do interview with a member of the admissions staff—no alumni interviews—and that's the best way for the office to learn if you've got the mix they're looking for. An interest in community service is a real plus. "Our task is to get the finest candidates who are in tune with the ethos at Notre Dame," Lohr says. "Of course, we train MBA candidates, but we want people who are in tune with our ethics, as well as having academic excellence."

Mendoza is one of the few MBA programs that still has rolling admissions, but, of course, the sooner you can apply, the better. Expect to hear back about a month after you apply. Deadlines are the same for domestic and international candidates. You can apply online, through GradAdvantage or with old-fashioned paper and ink.

Contact: Hayden F. Estrada
Director of Admissions
219-631-8488
Application deadlines: November 15;
January 15; March 15

NOTRE DAME MBAs SOUND OFF

The University of Notre Dame's MBA Program gave me exactly what I needed to complete such a rigorous program successfully. The school's reputation, tremendous network, necessary resources, accessible faculty, and the outstanding new management of our Mendoza College of Business have given me the preparation required to be successful in a business career.

The academic training was world class. The professors were attuned to the needs of the students and were available for advice and counsel. The student body was also a source of inspiration and teamwork. They created a cohesive unit that banded together to help everyone achieve their potential. I feel the admissions office did a wonderful job of selecting students who not only possessed superior intellect but also had the integrity, character, and attitude that embodied the Notre Dame tradition.

Much of the disappointment I had was in the administrative functions. The MBA administrative office was not in touch with the students. There seemed to be a lack of leadership vital to developing a compelling vision for the program. It feels like the students were a hindrance to the organization rather than their reason for existence.

The MBA program at Notre Dame has been extremely beneficial for me, not only because of the career opportunities available, but also due to the high amount of interaction between the students, professors, and administration. The students in this program have an excellent sense of community/community service, are willing to support each other, and are extremely involved in the program. I have learned a great amount from my teams throughout the past two years in addition to information provided in the classroom.

UNIVERSITY OF PITTSBURGH

Katz Graduate School of Business
276 Mervis Hall
Pittsburgh, Pennsylvania 15260
E-mail address: mba-admissions@katz.business.pitt.edu
Web site address: http://www.katz.pitt.edu

Enrollment: 807
Women: 30%
Non-U.S.: N/A
Minority: N/A
Part-time: 637
Average age: 27
Applicants accepted: 43%
Median starting pay: $68,000

Annual tuition & fees:
   resident—$17,460
   nonresident—$29,742
Room and board: $13,100
Average GMAT score: 620
Average years of work exp.: 4
Accepted applicants enrolled: 43%

Teaching methods: Lecture, 40%   Case study, 40%
   Experiential learning, 20%

Contact:
Kelly R. Wilson
Director of Admissions
412-648-1700
Application deadlines:
December 1
February 1

In the late 1950s, executives from western Pennsylvania's old industrial powerhouses approached the University of Pittsburgh's business school with a novel proposal: Create an MBA program to train our workforce, they said, and we'll guarantee that all your graduates are employed. But because of the Steel City's tight labor market, the corporations demanded one more thing to make the deal iron clad: Pitt's MBA program could last just one year.

Turns out, the University of Pittsburgh's Katz School of Business's Old Economy mission is playing right into the New Economy's hand. With just a few months being the difference between millionaire and may-have-been in the high-tech start-up game, Dean Frederick W. Winter claims the B-school's shorter time-span gives Katz grads an edge. "Two years is just too long to keep students out of the economy," he argues. "In today's economy, faster is much better."

There's no doubt Katz is fast. Although many B-schools offer accelerated master's degrees, Katz is the only first-rate U.S. school that requires all students to complete their MBAs in just 11 months. It's also intense. With two years of coursework packed into less than a year's time, this is no experience for the meek or mild. As one recent grad puts it, the workload is such that you "sometimes feel as if you're trying to take a sip from a fire hose."

Still, the 11-month schedule certainly has its advantages. Grads say that the heavy workload, rapid-fire deadlines, and teamwork-based curriculum force them to optimize their time and work more productively. It also makes B-school more affordable: For one thing, you're paying only one year's tuition and losing only one year's wages, so you're guaranteed a quicker payback on your investment than with a two-year program. If you have strong ideas about where your career is heading, you may be more than happy to cut your sojourn away from the working world in half; if your graduate education is being sponsored by your employer, the company will likely be thrilled to lose you from the workplace for just a year, instead of two. Katz is also particularly attractive to international students, who are often eager to save on tuition and return to their families, friends, and familiar cultures back home. Its students hail from 45 countries outside the United States, but many recent grads complained that the school didn't do enough to ease their adjustment to life in the United States.

Still, there are some drawbacks. In the first months of school, students find themselves meeting with prospective employers at the same time that they are meeting their new classmates, and nearly everyone complains about the pressure and the difficulty of managing their time. Moreover, there's not much room to fit in the traditional extracurricular activities that students at other B-schools find so enriching. Career switchers or those with little or no work experience lose the opportunity for a summer internship, which can be a considerable negative—it can be a lot easier to sell your finance-heavy résumé to the corporate marketing department you your eye on if you've spent a few months as an intern on the job, say, at a consumer products company. "Students don't come to Katz to find themselves," says 2000 grad Geoff Owen. "They come to Katz to better themselves and rejoin the marketplace."

However, with the fast-paced "real-world" less than a year away, an MBA program that requires its students to, what Winter calls "work at the pace of business," can be an effective tool for preparing students for the road ahead. It's a mentality that Winter brought to Katz in 1997, after heading the B-school at the State University of New York at Buffalo. As dean, Winter constantly assesses all aspects of the MBA experience, and to help him benchmark the school's progress, he instituted a new system called "Katz, Inc." Using part of a $300,000 alumni donation, Winter issued shares of $20 "phantom" stock to give incentive to the Katz faculty and staff to work toward the school's strategic priorities. The stock's "value" fluctuates according to a formula based on a weighted average of 15 key inputs, ranging from GMAT scores to teaching evaluations and rankings' positions. The results are posted in the B-school's hallways for everyone to see. Although B-school staff can cash out their shares at any time, they may not want to just yet: Since 1999, Katz stock has been on a steady upward track, raking in gains of almost 24 percent.

It's just one sign that Winter's initiatives are on track. But certainly there are others. When Winter came to Katz, for example, he vowed to shrink enrollment considerably while increasing the number of faculty as a way of improving teacher quality and classroom interaction. Whereas the Class of '98 had 240 full-time students, the school expects to enroll just 145 MBAs in 2000. Meantime, Winter has made 15 new faculty appointments, and that number could rise to as many as 21. And while students still say that teaching quality varies, Katz officials are quick to point out that if they hear enough complaints about a professor in a core class, the next class of students will no longer see that person in front of the blackboard.

Moreover, Winter has spearheaded a number of curriculum reforms. Unlike many other B-schools that rushed to offer e-commerce and other New Economy tracks, the dean stressed bolstering the fundamentals. Now, virtually every one of Katz's core classes is linked with a high-powered corporate partner, ensuring that students learn what's being practiced in the real world. Started in 1999, the "Best Practice Partners" program has attracted companies—including Alcoa, Cisco, IBM, Intel, Heinz,

Motorola, PNC Bank, and GlaxoSmithKline—to "adopt-a-class" in a key business area in which the firm excels. (For example, IBM sponsors the information technology course while PNC Bank lends its name to accounting class.) As part of the program, the corporate partners send a senior executive into the classroom to teach alongside a regular Katz professor. Not only do the execs pepper a basic principles lecture with practical insight and relevant client examples, they sometimes even review internal company documents with the class to show how the theory is applied. Participating firms also award an internship to a Katz MBA during the year.

But that's not the only new initiative Winter has launched. In the summer of 2000, he established the Katz Tech Fellowship program, which provides a year's worth of financial support for grads who want to work in New Economy start-ups—and stay in Pittsburgh. About a half-dozen newly minted Katz MBAs spent their first summer after graduating in new positions at local high-technology, bio-tech, and venture capital firms, such as Zlingshot!, Mobot, and Pro-Tech. Besides providing graduates with hands-on experience, Winter believes these programs have the potential to pay off in other ways. Establishing ongoing relationships with these companies, he says, will help increase awareness of Katz—and the chances that these highly coveted firms will recruit more heavily from the B-school in the future.

Katz MBAs start their whirlwind year in mid-July, when their friends are still tanning themselves on the beach, with a two-week orientation that focuses on self-assessment and time-management skills. Entering students also meet their Management Learning Organizations, or MLOs. These are teams of about five students, each of whom comes from a different background and work experience, who are assigned to study and work together on projects throughout the program. "The first couple months, [the MLO program] builds you up so you get to know each other," explains Brett Schweikle, whose team project involved writing a market analysis for an industrial shipping company. "Halfway through the year, you were familiar with each other's strengths and weaknesses so that you could delegate responsibilities to get the project done quickly." By the end of July, you've embarked on the first of six 7-week modules.

You're required to complete 12 core courses before graduation. Five of them, Introduction to Decision Technologies in Manufacturing and Operations, Finance, Human Resources, Information Systems, and Marketing, can be taken during any of the six modules. You'll also take two-module sequences in accounting and statistics during the first two modules and a two-module sequence in economics and organizational behavior during the second and third modules. The requirements are rounded out by an ethics course in module three and a two-course project sequence in the fourth and fifth modules that focuses on competing in a global environment and managing strategic performance. In conjunction with that sequence, the MLOs work on consulting projects for such firms as Bayer, Deloitte & Touche, PNC Bank, PPG, and Rubbermaid, presenting their results to corporate heads at a formal briefing.

The rest of your 22 credits are devoted to the school's 80 electives, most of which are one-module, 1½-credit courses but some of which last for two modules and net you three credits. MBAs are also encouraged to use their electives to complete a Signature Program track. So far, students can adopt a cross-functional focus in one of five key areas including valuation, emerging market strategy, engineered product marketing, process management, and organizational behavior. While Katz does not offer a formal entrepreneurship or e-commerce program, Katz students tailor their electives to those fields. Moreover, Pitt recently established an e-business incubator called Pantherworks that has attracted a number of MBAs.

Overall, employers give Katz the highest marks for its technology program, which utilizes the school's impressive computer lab filled with $6 million worth of hardware and software; electives in management information systems outnumber those in any other department. The school is also recognized for its programs in operations, management, and finance. With regard to the latter, every MBA, regardless of specialty, is paired with a floor broker or market specialist at the New York Stock Exchange for an insider's look at the workings of Wall Street during his or her time at Pitt. Some of the most rewarding electives are project courses that allow students to consult with firms in Pittsburgh's sizable corporate community on actual problems. Katz MBAs have helped to forecast trends in entertainment behavior for Eastman Kodak and helped build a computer-simulated model of an operating room for a local hospital.

Winter also has been working to enhance Katz's international offerings, and the school now offers students the opportunity to spend a module abroad in Central Europe, Latin and South America, Western Europe, or Asia; a minimum of 15 students must sign up for a region in order for a trip to take place. While overseas, participants take four courses plus a group project at a partner school. There's also an international field study elective in which 30 to 40 students choose a region of the world to explore, tailor their classwork to the business and environmental issues in that area, and develop research hypotheses regarding a local enterprise. They then spend 10 days traveling in the region under study—recent classes have visited Austria and the Czech and Slovak Republics—to gather information and tour financial and marketing institutions. And although it is still possible to earn a dual degree that combines an MBA with a master's in international business, Katz officials say they are phasing out that formal program over the next two years. Meanwhile, Katz still offers a number of popular double-degree programs in MIS,

public and international affairs, area studies, health administration, law, and divinity. And expect to see one merging business with biotechnology soon. With the chance to earn two degrees in the time most MBAs take to earn one, it's no wonder that more than 27 percent of Katz MBAs opt to stay an extra year.

Most students, of course, find the one 11-month degree program tough enough to handle. But there is at least a little relief from the grueling pace: On Wednesday between classes, the dean and other faculty members join students for doughnuts, coffee, and conversation. And "Ed the Guard," who has worked the B-school's evening security shift for the past 13 years, is around to brighten those finance-filled days. Every year, he makes sure to learn the names of each MBA, teaches students snippets of Polish, and even sends them get well cards when they're sick. Also, the B-school doesn't schedule classes on Fridays; instead, Katz loads up that day with optional workshops and presentations by outside executives. The school also boasts an extremely active speakers' program. Each week, it brings in corporate honchos such as the CEOs of Mellon Bank, Heinz, PPG, and PNC Bank to lead lunchtime Executive Briefings with students. And during the spring, a daylong American Assembly Dialogue brings execs from companies like Lucent Technologies, Hershey Foods, USX, and Accenture to discuss issues involving the economy, public policies, and the changing face of Corporate America. The B-school also has an executive speaker series on leadership and ethics and puts on a number of "international night" ethnic celebrations.

In the limited amount of time Katz students have outside of classwork and career-focused activities, MBAs tend to gravitate to the café in the basement of Mervis Hall, the B-school's striking glass and steel building. Located nearby, a new $1.3 million "PNC Team Technology Center" will create team rooms for MLO meetings as well as a business information area that will accommodate both student and faculty research needs.

The University of Pittsburgh is located in the hilly Oakland section of Pittsburgh, alongside Carnegie Mellon University. The city of Pittsburgh—no longer a steel town, but a modern, attractive mecca for some two dozen major corporate headquarters—offers a number of convenient housing options in culturally diverse Oakland or the nearby, more upscale Shadyside or Squirrel Hill neighborhoods.

PLACEMENT DETAILS

Students have continued to give mixed reviews to Katz's Career Services Center. But, in general, those MBAs who had focused career plans and were using the B-school as a stepping stone to corporate jobs were more likely to have positive experiences. "Start-ups were not their forte," explains Katz 2000 grad Cathy Bibel-Byham. "People who wanted a job with a larger company were very happy, but if you wanted a job with a smaller firm, it is more a self-directed search." Other MBAs complained of a "take-what-you-can-get" mentality among the staff when it came to helping students in the bottom tier of the class. "Rather than try to understand my career aspirations, they told me to return to my previous field of work because my chances for employment were better," one student complained. Students say the Career Services Center has attempted to reach out to more national firms, but some feel that it could do more to help grads find jobs outside the Pittsburgh region, where more than 39 percent of the Class of 2000 decided to stay. Unlike other B-schools, just a handful of Katz grads headed to the West Coast.

Moreover, day-to-day operations have shown improvement. A career counseling assessment instrument went on line in 1998, as did scheduling for recruitment interviews, and a placement officer has been hired to deal solely with computer-based activities. Another placement officer has been dedicated exclusively to working with the school's large international contingent, who have complained in the past that they've been shortchanged in help with their job searches. And the career services division has been providing assistance, ranging from reviewing résumés to setting career objectives to Katz MBAs even before they arrive on campus.

Some 100 companies recruited Katz MBAs in 2000. Top hirers were Ford Motor Co. (7); IBM (6); Deloitte Consulting (5); PricewaterhouseCoopers(5); Deloitte & Touche (4); Freemarkets (4); Heinz USA (4); PNC Bank (4).

OUTSTANDING FACULTY

Donald Moser (accounting); *Dung Nguyen* (economics); *Kenneth Lehn* (finance); *Tim Heath* (marketing); *Vikas Mittal* (marketing); *Prakash Mirchandani* (operations).

APPLICANT TIPS

Unlike many accelerated MBA programs, Katz does not require applicants to have an undergraduate business degree, although it wouldn't hurt in coping with the heavy workload. The program draws a few applicants each year from professions such as law and medicine who intend to stick with those careers but feel some business acumen would be helpful. The school encourages candidates to apply, even waiving application fees for anyone who applies online. That, combined with the number of places per class being slashed, means that getting your application in early is even more essential. Full-time applications are reviewed every four to six weeks from November through May. Those who'd like an early answer should try to meet one of the school's priority deadlines in January, February, or March; international applicants must have their paperwork in by February 15.

Katz says it seeks applicants who are highly motivated and have demonstrated leadership in work, extracurricular activities, community service, and their personal lives. Considering the rigor of the program, you'll also want to emphasize your ability to handle pressure, motivate yourself, and manage your time well. Personal interviews are encouraged, but only 41 percent of those admitted to the Class of 2002 had face-to-face meetings with admissions officers. Group information sessions are held regularly throughout the year, and Katz suggests that prospective students attend one of their "MBA for a Day" sessions during the fall. You can call the admissions office for a schedule and to set up an interview, class observation, and student-led tour.

Contact: Kelly R. Wilson
Director of Admissions
412-648-1700
Application deadlines: December 1; February 1

KATZ MBAs SOUND OFF

Students don't come to Katz to find themselves. They come to Katz to better themselves and rejoin the marketplace. There are certainly downsides to a one-year program, but they are far outweighed by the positives. The only true negative is that the school suffers in donations and endowment money because students do not spend enough time there to become attached to the school and the community.

The one-year MBA program simulates a working environment in that an academic concept is learned and then you are expected to apply that knowledge in projects and classroom assignments. Katz gave me the skills and toughness to successfully operate in today's fast-paced workplace. I could not be more satisfied with the knowledge I gained and the quick return on my investment. It should be noted that this program is not for the faint of heart and you'd better be ready to *work!* The payoffs are well worth the grueling workload.

Three or four times I asked for appointments with the director of career services only to never get a response from her. There was only one person in the career services office that knew me by name. The typical response of career services to people seeking employment outside of the Pittsburgh–Middle Atlantic [region] was that they were on their own. As one of four or five students seeking employment in the West, they pretty much told me that they couldn't help me. Nothing about the program was negative except for career services.

I was impressed by the high level of personal attention received from faculty and staff. The coursework presented challenge and drive, yet the environment added support and encouragement. My experience at Katz furnished me with many valuable skills that I can carry into the workforce.

UNIVERSITY OF WISCONSIN— MADISON

UNIVERSITY OF WISCONSIN—MADISON

School of Business
Grainger Hall
975 University Avenue
Madison, Wisconsin 53706
E-mail address: uwmadmba@bus.wisc.edu
Web site address: http://www.bus.wisc.edu/

Enrollment: 583
Women: 30%
Non-U.S.: 38%
Minority: 9%
Part-time: 116
Average age: 28
Applicants accepted: 26%
Median starting pay: $86,000

Annual tuition & fees:
   resident—$7130
   nonresident—$19,958
Room and board: $8040
Average GMAT score: 635
Average years of work exp.: 4.25
Accepted applicants enrolled: 53%

Teaching methods: Lecture, 50%   Case study, 30%   Other, 20%

Contact:
Lisa K. Urban
Director of Admissions
and Financial Aid
608-262-4610
Application deadlines:
January 15
February 15
March 15
April 15

Sometimes what makes you strong also highlights your weaknesses. That's the difficult situation of the School of Business at the University of Wisconsin—Madison. Looking for a great place to live? A city with good schools, little crime, and ready access to excellent health care? A progressive government and low unemployment rates? Plenty of clean air and miles of waterfront for year-round recreation? A thriving intellectual community? Cities like San Diego, California, and Seattle, Washington, may come to mind first, but Madison is often ranked as one of the best cities in which to live. So put location in the school's "pro" column.

But a three-hour drive from Chicago and centrally located near, well, not much except a 40-foot fiberglass cow in nearby Janesville, and Madison's oasis in the middle of the Midwest makes it a long trek for recruiters from each coast. While the school is making efforts to expand its reach, the B-school is still not No. 1 on many recruiters' itineraries. So, put location in the school's "con" column. UW—Madison has a lot that makes it different from the other MBA programs you're considering: several niche programs that are among the best around in their specialties (if you can even find similar programs elsewhere); a newly compressed core curriculum with small class sizes so MBA students can take full advantage of those specialties; and an administration dead set on becoming more open and responsive to student concerns. So, put diversity of academics in the school's "pro" column.

But with its specialties across the board—both M.S. and MBA degree programs—including the Applied Security Analysis Program, the Weinert Entrepreneurship program, the AC Nielsen Marketing Research Program, and the Applied Corporate Finance Program, not to mention degrees in arts management and other esoteric leadership niches, the curriculum, faculty, and administration are pulled in many directions. That means teaching can run the gamut from good to bad. The same goes for career planning efforts and personal attention. So, put diversity of academics in the school's "con" column.

And so it goes for the UW—Madison. The B-school's package of assets pushed Wisconsin into the Top 25 in BUSINESSWEEK's 1996 rankings, when the positives outweighed the negatives. But UW—Madison moved back into the second tier in 2000, when both recruiters and students sensed a lack of focus, and students griped of too much interaction with undergrads, a spotty faculty, and average career center. In fact, the complaints of recent graduates are as unfocused as they claim the program is. No one says anything is really awful. In the survey of recent alums by BUSINESSWEEK, UW—Madison ranked in the middle of the pack in almost every meaningful measure from satisfaction with the overall experience to meeting their expectations to having access to faculty for informal discussions. On the curriculum side, students say the B-school doesn't do enough to stress interpersonal skills, but does a good job of teaching analytical skills.

UW—Madison's ratings seesaw does not come as a result of lack of focus or effort on the part of the administration. Over the last decade Dean Andrew J. Policano has been a tireless champion for a program he feels is oft overlooked. He's tried to get salary information on UW—Madison to be taken into consideration with the lower cost of living in the Midwest. He's stressed that the types of fields that some grads go into, like the aforementioned arts management, don't pull the same paychecks as I-banking. And he's been obsessive about learning what it is that students want. He jokes that he's shared so many meals during conversations

about school improvement—weekly lunches with students, Tuesday morning breakfasts with faculty and staff, periodic whole-school "town meetings" over pizza—that he "ought to be headed to Weight Watchers."

In 1996 Policano began a major overhaul to the curriculum that made the coursework more modular, designed to give students more flexibility. But now students say that the coursework is not particularly well integrated, and what they learn in one class may or may not apply to the next. When he decided to scrap the entire MBA program, he began building a new one from scratch, based on feedback from corporate recruiters, extensive exit surveys of new graduates, and benchmarking against the schools to which he aspired. Nine external advisory boards were created, bringing 220 executives to campus twice a year to provide input from the business community. Among the initiatives that helped put Wisconsin on the national B-school map: a weekend executive MBA program; a part-time evening MBA program; and a large menu of 300 two- to five-day executive education courses that now draw some 16,000 business people to the B-school each year.

The more flexible curriculum for the 460 or so full-time master's students just completed its three-year phase-in period. In order to allow students to tailor their studies as precisely as possible to their individual levels of experience and specific interests, Wisconsin offers four different degrees: the MBA, a master of science in business, a master of accountancy, and a master of arts in business. Within the MBA and M.S. programs (the latter is for students with an undergraduate business degree already in hand) you can choose from 16 different specialties, each of which has its own prerequisites and requirements for graduation. While it may seem and feel confusing—and is part of what contributes to that lack of cohesion—40 percent of master's students come to Wisconsin precisely to enroll in special programs they could never find elsewhere.

Policano has announced that he will step down as dean in August 2001, although he plans to remain on the faculty of the school's finance department. When he took the helm of the B-school in 1991 (he came to Madison from the State University of New York at Stony Brook), he intended for it to be a 10-year stint and that time is up, although the mission he began is still a work in progress. The school was still conducting a search for a new dean at press time. But as the search for a new leader continues, UW—Madison is not standing still. New concentrations for MBAs include applied corporate finance, applied real estate security analysis, and supply chain management, all of which are thought to be tops in their field. Students say their experience in these areas has put them ahead of MBAs from higher-ranking schools. Indeed, several of the B-school's niches are top-notch. The school's risk management and insurance program and its real estate and urban land economics program are nationally recognized. Says one Class of 2000 M.S. graduate who liked the real estate–centric courseload: "The UW—Madison offers more real estate courses than any other university and is respected in the industry accordingly."

In the arts administration program, students work during the school year at paid assistantships at local arts institutions, such as Wisconsin Public Radio and the Elvehjem Museum of Art, then spend summers elsewhere interning with organizations such as the Metropolitan Opera or the National Endowment for the Arts in Washington, D.C. Most niches are small. The Grainger Center for Supply Chain Management, for example, accepts just 12 grad students a year. But even core courses typically average just 30 students. Among the most popular is the Applied Security Analysis Program, which even has its own placement professionals.

In 2000 Ford Motor Company announced a $1 million gift, over five years, to fund a Ford Motor Company Distinguished Chair in Management and Human Resources. The gift will also enable the school to give scholarships to students in the areas of supply chain management and manufacturing and technology.

But even if you don't know what you want to be when you grow up, UW—Madison has a track for you. More than 50 percent of Wisconsin's students end up with the garden-variety MBA upon graduation. True, it's not one of the school's strengths. But Policano's module system has won raves thus far, allowing students to learn in seven-week bites. The school now offers 106 different electives, 12 percent of which are new in the past three years.

Eight new faculty slots were also added in the last three years; two each in accounting, finance, management and human resources, and information systems. After nine years working as an investment banker, Roger A. Formisano has rejoined the faculty to teach strategy and leadership. And in 2000 Michael Lehman, vice president and CFO of Sun Microsystems and David Grainger, senior chairman of W.W. Grainger Inc. (for whom the school's hall is named), gave $5 million to UW—Madison to assist in recruiting and retaining top faculty, a move that will help the school keep on top of research but recruit faculty interested in day-to-day interaction with students.

Global studies aren't overlooked either. With the University of Iowa, Wisconsin now offers a short-term program in Paris and London during winter break to graduate business students. First introduced in 1999–2000, you can earn three credits toward your master's degree in the three-week global brand management course. Regardless of the direction you choose, you'll find state-of-the-art technology support for your studies. The $40 million Grainger Hall houses a library, computer lab, and even the aptly named Blue Chip Deli. In the last three years the B-school has invested $975,000 in technology, adding new projection units to classrooms and updating Internet connections. Course materials, reserved readings, and support services are now all available online.

While Madison is surrounded by farmland, the city itself is a surprisingly liberal, cosmopolitan, progressive place with parks, quirky cafés, and state government. Sure, people here are a little nutty about the Badgers, football, brats, and beer, but you've got to give them credit for getting out and doing stuff during the long, cold winters. The rest of the year is idyllic, with plenty of opportunities to rock climb, hike, fish, and enjoy other outdoor sports.

Few B-school students live on the 933-acre campus, which looks like a textbook example of a brick and ivy oasis if ever there was one. Private apartments are relatively inexpensive; you may be lucky enough to find one for $500 a month. Some students commute the hour from Milwaukee or other nearby towns by train, but even if they do, they stick around after hours. A town square–like area near campus is home to lots of coffee shops, pubs, and, of course, places to eat brats, providing the locale for a great social life. Year-round special events, from a GBA ball and a retro party help raise money for charity and keep MBAs enrolled in disparate niches in touch with one another.

PLACEMENT DETAILS

Like much of Wisconsin's B-school, its placement office suffers from trying to be all things to all people. The Business Career Center serves both undergrads and graduate students in all the school's different specializations and tracks, meaning some students and recruiters have a great experience, while others feel their needs aren't being met.

"My only disappointment has been the career center's contacts for anything other than the standard MBA job titles in accounting, finance, and marketing," says one Class of 2000 graduate. But another says, "The real estate alumni network (about 1200 members) is unparalleled and extremely helpful in students' job searches." Derrick Brown, a staffing specialist at Thermo King, particularly likes the quality of UW—M's manufacturing and mechanical engineers who have joint degrees in business.

Because of the niche nature of many of the fields in which Madison grads seek jobs, the school has started calling on its 9800 MBA alumni to help. Alumni have access to a free password-protected online community, which includes an alumni directory, job postings, message boards, permanent e-mail forwarding, and personal home pages. In addition, many are involved with current students each year by offering career advice, speaking in classes, and to student groups, not to mention hiring students.

According to Karen Stauffacher, assistant dean and director of the BCC, in 2000 229 firms recruited on campus, with another 450 job openings posted on the Web site. Eighty-seven percent of the class had at least one job offer by graduation. Top employers in 2000 were Accenture (3); DaimlerChrysler Inc. (2); Epic Systems (2); Ford Motor Company (2); GTE (2): Guidant Corporation (2); General Mills Inc. (3); Intel Corporation (3); Arthur Andersen LLP (2); Cambridge Technology Partners (2).

OUTSTANDING FACULTY

Robert Pricer (entrepreneurship); *Jim Seward* (finance); *Mason Carpenter* (management/human resources); *J. Inman* (marketing); *James Rappold* (operations); *Kerry Vandell* (real estate); *John R. Nevin* (supply chain management).

APPLICANT TIPS

If you have no prior business experience, but if you still want to go to B-school now, Wisconsin may be your best bet. Of students admitted to the Class of 2002, 10 percent had less than a year of experience. Officially the policy is that two years' business experience is required, except for "exceptional candidates" in the M.S. programs in finance/applied security analysis, actuarial science and risk management, and insurance. Policano says that these niche programs are so specialized that prior experience is often irrelevant, and that the programs build in plenty of hands-on work to put on your résumé.

Application requirements and processes vary from program to program, so be sure to check out the specifics for the one in which you're interested. In addition to the standard good GPA and GMAT scores, Wisconsin says it looks for candidates with "a lively curiosity about the world around them, a demonstrated record of achievement in their chosen career, a well-conceived plan for their future, excellent communication skills, and leadership potential." And just because work experience may or may not affect whether or not you get in, don't fool yourself into thinking that UW—Madison is a safety school. In 2000 just 26 percent of applicants were accepted, compared with 47 percent in 1998 and 33 percent in 1996.

The school no longer accepts MBAs for the spring semester, although some M.S. programs do have openings in the spring. Completed applications received in the first four months of the year will be responded to by the fifteenth day of the following month.

Personal interviews are not required; about 60 percent of admitted applicants in 2000 were interviewed on campus and 30 percent of all applicants met with admissions staff. The admissions office will arrange a tour of Grainger Hall, attendance in a B-school class, and meetings with current students if you decide to visit. About 40 percent of UW—Madison students receive merit-based financial aid. Aid decisions are typically made by April 15.

Contact: Lisa K. Urban
Director of Admissions and Financial Aid
608-262-4610

Application deadlines: January 15; February 15; March 15; April 15

MADISON MBAs SOUND OFF

I believe that the general MBA program at UW—M is average; however, there are many niche programs, (such as the Applied Security Analysis Program that I was involved with, and the Distribution Management Program and the Weinert Entrepreneurship program), that are top-notch programs.

There really is no better program for security analysts and portfolio managers in the country. The ASAP program provides real-world investment experience by allowing the students to manage $13.5 million of endowment money in equity and fixed income portfolios.

A huge problem with this school is the fact that there are many courses that have both graduate and undergraduate students. The result is a class with 5–10 graduate students and 25–30 undergraduate students. Basically, a graduate level course has been turned into an undergraduate course. There are many more examples of cross-listed courses. I did not come to graduate school to sit in a class with undergraduates who have very little more to add to class discussion than the latest frat party.

My experience at The Graduate School of Business at UW—Madison was extremely enjoyable and provided me with many useful skills. I was a member of the Applied Security Analysis Program (ASAP) and felt it was the best learning experience of my life. It allowed me to compete in the job market with graduates of other better-known programs such as Wharton, Kellogg, and the University of Chicago. During my summer internship I worked alongside students from Wharton and the University of Chicago and my experience at ASAP provided me with an advantage over those students. I felt that I knew more about the financial markets and had better analytical skills.

The strength of UW—Madison is its niche programs such as ASAP, the Weinert Applied Ventures Program, the AC Nielsen Marketing Research Program, and the Applied Corporate Finance Program. The graduates of these programs are as talented and skilled as the graduates from the "top" schools and spend much less money in tuition (I have no student loans!).

I believe the tremendous diversity (ethnicity, international aspect, and work experience) of the students in my school is a great strength to the program. Almost all the faculty are available to discuss professional and personal issues in informal settings and help students tailor the program for maximum benefit.

**WAKE FOREST
UNIVERSITY**

Contact:
Mary C. Goss
Assistant Dean of
Admissions
336-758-5422
OR 800-722-1622
Application deadlines:
December 1 (early)
April 1

WAKE FOREST UNIVERSITY

Babcock Graduate School of Management
Winston-Salem, North Carolina 37109
E-mail address: admissions@mail.mba.wfu.edu
Web site address: http://www.mba.wfu.edu

Enrollment: 654	Annual tuition & fees: $22,225
Women: 23%	Room and board: $5600
Non-U.S.: 29%	Average GMAT score: 645
Minority: 9%	Average years of work exp.: 4.1
Part-time: 433	Accepted applicants enrolled: 49%
Average age: 27	
Applicants accepted: 51%	
Median starting pay: $89,000	

Teaching methods: Lecture, 25%   Case study, 50%
Integrative exercises and field study consulting,
25%

Nestled in the gently rolling hills of North Carolina's Piedmont region, Wake Forest University's Babcock Graduate School of Management is like little David surrounded by a pack of B-school Goliaths. With Top 30 schools like Duke and the University of North Carolina just a stone's throw away, and the University of Virginia also relatively close at hand, why should students choose Babcock for their MBA education?

That's exactly the question R. Charles Moyer, a longtime professor of finance at Babcock, asked himself upon taking over as dean in 1997. The answer he came up with: Provide Babcock's cozy cadre of about 114 full-time students a year with personal attention—already a hallmark of the school—at a level that other, bigger B-schools just can't match. While Babcock had previously divided each class into two sections of 57, comparable to the sections of 60 to 65 at its competitors, Moyer has now shrunk core sections to fewer than 40 participants each in what is marketed as the "3/38 Plan"—three first-year sections a year with 38 students apiece, give or take a few. He's also brought on board 12 additional professors, bringing the tenure-track faculty total to 42 and lowering the student–faculty ratio to 6 to 1. "That gives students at least 50 percent more air time" to voice their opinions in class, Moyer explains. "You have that many more opportunities to do presentations, to stand up and defend yourself, and the faculty has that much more time to deal with you."

Many students say that it was the small class size, along with the highly integrated curriculum and heavy use of group study and team-based learning, that brought them to Babcock in the first place, and that the school delivers on its promise of an intimate learning environment. Of the 82 schools surveyed by BUSINESSWEEK in 2000, students ranked Babcock sixth in terms of faculty availability outside class and eighth for emphasizing teaching over research. "Wake [Forest]'s small size is what attracted me to the program," one grad says. "Although it doesn't have a reputation as a great research institute, having quality professors focused on teaching significantly enhanced the learning process." At the same time, recent graduates warn that the same small class size that's such an advantage for learning can be a major drawback when it comes to the job hunt, making it difficult during recruiting season to draw a large number of big-name corporations to a small school that's a little off the beaten path. In fact, the Class of 2000 placed Babcock in the bottom half-dozen schools among the Top 50 for the number and quality of recruiters it brought on campus—a problem that has existed for nearly a decade.

Small B-schools with tightly interwoven curricula tend to work their students hard—witness Dartmouth, Virginia, or Purdue—and Babcock is no exception. For one thing, the 3/38 Plan means you can't hide in the crowd if you aren't prepared to carry your weight in in-class discussions. The first year begins with a 10-week Business Foundations module that has you taking courses in accounting, analysis and communications, law and ethics, management information systems, managerial economics, organizational behavior, and quantitative methods. In the second module, which lasts 20 weeks, you explore the major functional areas of finance, marketing, and operations and their interconnection while delving further into accounting, law and ethics, managerial economics, organizational behavior, and quantitative methods. The third module focuses for 10 weeks on globalization, with courses in International Business Management and International Competitive Policy, along with more work in law and ethics, macroeconomics, and info systems. Assigned teams of five to seven students tackle numerous group projects in all courses throughout the year, starting with the Babcock Business Games during orientation week.

During year two, you're required to take two half-semester capstone courses, one on international strategy and another on management control systems. If you have less than three years' work experience—as do many Babcock students, since the average time on the job is four years and 9 percent have less than a year of full-time work under their belts upon entering the program—you'll also be required to do a field study project in which student teams work as project consultants to real-world corporations or nonprofits such as Pilot Biotechnologies, Lowe's Foods, Fortis Homes, and Northern Telecom. (About half the students with more than three years' experience opt for the field study anyway.)

In 1998, for the first time second-year students were asked to declare a concentration from a menu of 13 possibilities, including finance, operations, marketing, consulting, entrepreneurship, information technology, e-business, or a student-designed independent track if none of the others suits your fancy. The concentrations are fairly specific—you might choose commercial finance and lending, for example, or business-to-business marketing—and require 10 to 12 half-semester courses in that specialty out of a total of 16 elective slots available (18 if you exempt out of the field study). Corporate recruiters consider accounting and general management to be Babcock's forte. You also have the option of earning a joint degree in law or medicine.

This is not a B-school that has always rated well in terms of cultural diversity—but the times are changing. While just 19 percent of students in 1998 were from countries outside the United States, 31 percent of the student body hailed from international locations in 2000; but women still number fewer than one-quarter of MBAs, and African-Americans, Hispanic-Americans, and Native Americans together make up only 7 percent of enrollment—up 2 percent from 1998. It doesn't help that half the students are from the South (a third are from North Carolina alone).

You can stretch your wings a bit by participating in one of Babcock's international study or work programs. The school sponsors two-week-long summer study trips to China, Japan, and Austria or through the European Business Studies Program at Oxford University in England; there are also semester-long exchange partnerships the administration arranges on a case-by-case basis with schools in Europe and Latin America. Or Babcock will assist you in lining up an international summer internship. Back on campus, the student-run International Business Association coordinates an annual Global Forum seminar series on international business issues, organizes an International Food Festival, and compiles a résumé book for students, foreign or American, who'd like to work overseas after graduation.

Babcock works hard at integrating information technology into its MBA program, and the effort shows. Purchase of a laptop computer package is included in the tuition price. In 1993, the B-school moved into a modern, 178,000-square-foot professional building shared with Wake Forest's law school; the three-story center, U-shaped with separate wings and distinctive entrances for each school but joined by a common library, is chock full of technology. Every learning space, from classroom seats to team meeting rooms to study carrels, is wired for hookup to the Internet and Babcock's own internal computer network. Lifetime e-mail for alums has been expanded into the Babcock On Call service, which allows current and former students with questions related to coursework or jobs to connect with an appropriately expert faculty member for advice. At the same time, however, students say the information technology curriculum is getting better, but is perhaps not the best choice if you're looking for a high-tech career.

The Wake Forest campus is a picture-postcard-perfect prototype of a small liberal arts college, a beautiful oasis of manicured green lawns and gorgeous trees punctuated by classically styled red-brick buildings. Each spring, the school hosts a golf tournament with students, faculty, staff, and alumni. Every Wednesday is doughnut day—a time for students and faculty to get together informally for treats and coffee. The university is located in Winston-Salem, which may not be Boston or Los Angeles but is North Carolina's fourth largest city. Halfway between Washington, D.C. and Atlanta, it's a comfortable place to spend two years. Just 90 minutes away by car are the majestic Blue Ridge Mountains; Carolina's sandy beaches are close enough for weekend trips when the weather's warm. A number of student groups keep folks hopping when they're not slaving over their classwork, most of them career-oriented clubs such as the Marketing Club or Babcock Entrepreneurs organizations. Most students live off campus but close by, and every June, the admissions office hosts an annual house hunt in which current students escort members of the incoming class around Winston-Salem to search for apartments. The day ends with a schoolwide cookout—just the kind of personal touch Dean Moyer wants his school to provide.

PLACEMENT DETAILS

Winston-Salem is no business metropolis, and Babcock's placement record reflects both that and the fact that more than a few companies don't want to trek to North Carolina for the opportunity to interview just a handful of students. But, given the competitive environment of the last two years, Babcock has benefited from companies' desire to see more grads from a variety of new schools. Because of that, more big name firms are recruiting on campus now, and 96 percent of the Class of 2000 had a job by graduation. A mentor program matches students with executives in businesses and career specialties they'd like to explore. And three major speakers series bring high-ranking officials from such companies and organizations as USX, AT&T, General Motors, and the Federal Reserve Board to campus not only to lecture but to network with students.

Jobs weren't too hard to find at most Top 50 B-schools in 2000, including at Babcock—grads averaged nearly three employment offers at graduation. Pay packages are also on the rise: The median starting pay package of $89,000 was about average for the Top 50 and up about $8000 from 1998. Arguably, it wasn't higher because of Babcock grads' preference for remaining in the South. Corporate investment banking and marketing drew a little over a quarter of the Class of 2000 apiece, while consulting and finance attracted about 17 percent and 12 percent, respectively. Meanwhile, the school's nontraditional employer connections have beefed up, with about 27 percent of students who graduated in 2000 joining a start-up company. The 55 companies that recruited on campus conducted about 700 interviews. Top employers were First Union (6); Wachovia (5); Bank of America (2); Sara Lee Corp. (2); Nabisco (2); Deloitte & Touche (2); Johnson & Johnson (2); American Express (2); Capital One (2); Daymon Associates (2); Daleen Technologies (2).

OUTSTANDING FACULTY

Ken Middaugh (accounting); *Rick Harris* (economics); *Rob Nash* (finance); *Ajay Patel* (finance); *B. R. Baliga* (marketing); *Aniel Mishra* (organizational behavior); *Jon Pinder* (quantitative methods).

APPLICANT TIPS

Babcock is one of the very few B-schools that actually invite applicants to call up its very top administrators and ask questions about the program. As the school puts it, "Every applicant has access to the directors of admissions and financial aid, career services, and the dean through our toll-free number. . . . Personal attention in the admissions process distinguishes Wake Forest from other MBA programs and is indicative of students' experiences here." The school says it seeks candidates who "have demonstrated potential for management careers through academic achievement, professional experience, and extracurricular activities. . . . We also look for evidence of leadership ability, teamwork skills, and a strong sense of values." On-campus interviews are strongly recommended—about 47 percent of those admitted to the Class of 2000 interviewed with admissions officers in Winston-Salem. Mondays, Wednesdays, and Fridays are set aside for interviews, campus tours, and lunch with a current student; after January 1, you must have your application in before making an appointment. Call the admissions office to arrange your visit. If you submit your application by the early-decision deadline of December 1, you'll have an answer by Christmas; those seeking financial aid should have paperwork in by March 1, with the deadline for applying for 10 full-tuition scholarships February 15.

Contact: Mary C. Goss
Assistant Dean of Admissions
336-758-5422 OR 800-722-1622
Application deadlines: December 1 (early); April 1

BABCOCK MBAs SOUND OFF

The interactive nature of the school and the personal interaction with other students was as much a part of my education as the classroom studies. With a small class size such as ours (114), you really learn to get along and work in groups to get things done. The teamwork atmosphere that the school espouses instills in the students the ability to work in teams, much like many companies are now requiring employees to do.

The top faculty at Babcock are as good as you will find anywhere in the country. The small size allowed you to really learn from them, but that small size also hurt in recruiting new faculty and in getting companies to come on campus.

I enjoyed my time at Babcock and would definitely repeat my choice. It was a mind expanding journey and the camaraderie the students share is wonderful. I have enjoyed the small classroom settings, the ability to interact freely with the professors and the visitors they bring, and gaining a wide breadth of knowledge. Although there are many students going outside Babcock's traditional geographic boundaries, the reach of the career services office is insufficient for students who wish to work outside the Eastern Seaboard. The new director of career services seems to be working very diligently toward correcting this. Babcock is on the path toward becoming a national school, but some areas still have a regional feel.

For the most part, Babcock's faculty members demonstrate a genuine concern for the students. The professors' "approachability," combined with an extensive knowledge of their subject matter, make them Babcock's greatest asset. I am certain that I can return to them for guidance in the future, but I am also certain that the time I spent with them in classes and individual conversations will provide me with a solid foundation for my business career.

Having pursued an undergraduate degree in biology, the MBA degree from Babcock is indispensable to my career development. Babcock's 3/38 Plan, Mentor Program, and the school's obvious commitment to technology were especially appealing. Its innovative and refined curriculum helped me develop an integrated understanding of business functions and strengthened managerial competencies, while encouraging interaction with business leaders and top students. At Babcock, I combined my practical business skills with the theoretical depth provided by an MBA degree. This winning combination helped me obtain a career combining finance with management and strategy.

THE BEST BUSINESS SCHOOLS OUTSIDE THE UNITED STATES

Global reach. Global strategies. Global village. And, lately, global financial crisis. You've heard all of these terms ad nauseum by now, whether you're interested in getting an MBA or not. And in the business school world, the word *global* is now being attached to nearly every degree program in the United States—whether it offers one internationally oriented course or 100—as companies expanding beyond their home markets scramble for cross-cultural managers.

As U.S. business schools try to rethink their curricula in a less provincial way—adding study trips, Chinese cooking lessons, cultural weeks to help international and American students better understand one another, and team-based consulting projects in foreign lands—they also face growing competition from non-U.S. institutions that are doing the same thing. And although the U.S. B-school population is diversifying every year, there are still schools located abroad that are more global, with no dominant culture present inside or outside of the classroom. As a prospective business school student trying to find your dream school, you might ask: Should I consider getting my MBA outside of the United States?

It's certainly worth considering. Although the U.S.-based programs remain the most widely known throughout the world, carrying large networks and muscular brand names, many non-American schools are gaining more attention than ever and attracting foreigners who once flocked exclusively to the United States. They're also attracting North Americans interested in a global career. At London Business School, for example, some 80 percent of the Class of 2000 is from outside of the United Kingdom. Although most of the schools receiving attention—such as INSEAD, the London Business School (LBS), IMD, the Rotterdam School of Management, IESE, the Ivey School, and Toronto—are in Europe or Canada, there is a staggering range of business schools from which to choose all over the globe. Some of the best known outside Europe include Chulalongkorn University's Sasin Graduate Institute of Business Administration in Bangkok, or the

> Many non-U.S. B-schools are beginning to attract a bigger cross-section of students.

> An international B-school can offer the kind of experiences and contacts you will only get from extended time abroad.

Indian School of Management in Ahmedabad. That said, those not wishing to commit to a career in Asia might think twice before passing up American schools, says Sally Lannin of consulting firm MBA Strategies. "I do not see any programs [in the Pacific Rim] that will be internationally competitive in the next 5 to 10 years," she says, "especially for U.S. applicants."

Nonetheless, new additions are popping up everywhere, many of which have been cultivated by U.S. B-schools eager to gain better access to foreign brainpower. The deans of American schools now spend a good chunk of their time jet-setting around the world, signing alliances and cooperative pacts to get new institutions off the ground. One example: The October 1998 announcement that The Wharton School and Northwestern's Kellogg School would team up to create the Indian School of Business, which opened a campus in Hyderabad in 2000. Particularly in Asia, joint programs with Western B-schools are proliferating, from the China Europe International Business School (a venture between the European Union and China) to the Sasin B-school's links to Wharton and Kellogg. Duke has opened a cross-content MBA program in Germany. University of Chicago now has a Singapore campus. Another new entrant is the Duxx Graduate School of Business Leadership, a one-year program based in Monterrey, Mexico. Hundreds of institutions outside the United States now offer a master's degree in business. Most of them continue to be located in Europe, and as Europeans abandon their traditional disdain for the MBA as crass and unsophisticated, they're opening up the floodgates and increasing enrollment. INSEAD, for example, now boasts an enrollment of nearly 700 at its two campuses in Fountainbleau, France, and Singapore—up 200 students in the last two years alone.

As American schools push for globalization and international schools begin to emphasize such hot topics as entrepreneurship, the curricula of most elite B-schools—no matter where they are in the world—are beginning to look more alike. Yet there still are many significant differences beyond the obvious geographic and cultural ones. U.S. business schools have traditionally been stronger in number-crunching skills, while European counterparts have tended to emphasize broader management concepts. "The tendency in the United States is to emphasize the quantitative skills and significant business experience as part of the prerequisite to receive an MBA," says Hoyle Jones, Citibank's director of global management associate recruiting.

And while schools such as INSEAD, LBS, and Nijenrode in the Netherlands have moved to inject more teamwork into their curricula, many foreign schools tend to rely more heavily on lectures as the primary delivery system for education. "In Europe, social consensus is much more important than [in the United States]," says Marc Boheim, a University of Chicago grad who spent a quarter at IESE in Barcelona. "Maximizing shareholder value is not every company's primary concern." But, that doesn't mean the U.S. schools aren't importing their ideals—whether through their joint programs, or through the non-U.S. schools' adoption of U.S. management education teachings.

With the rapid pace of change in both U.S. and, particularly, European B-schools, there seems to be more of a consensus than ever before on what makes a good B-school. Says Citibank's Jones: "The European schools have shown significant progress in strengthening the analytic aspects of the curriculum, while continuing to stress general management." That union of skills is starting to hold greater appeal for U.S. and multinational recruiters, who, while still filling most of their quota for elite MBAs in the States, are venturing abroad more often. "When we look at global talent, we look at both U.S. schools and international [schools]," says Mary Lou Rinaldi, manager of global staffing at GE Capital. "Anyone who comes here has to understand the global aspect of the company." Of the 247 top recruiters responding to BUSINESSWEEK's 2000 survey, about 20 percent said they recruited at INSEAD; just under 20 percent go to LBS; and about 8 percent go to IMD, IESE in Barcelona, and Canada's Ivey B-school.

Clearly, a one- or two-year sojourn in France, England, or Mexico has obvious appeal for those interested in setting foot on foreign soil. Yet going abroad for your MBA is right for some—and not so right for others. With companies both in the United States and abroad clamoring for people who are comfortable in a variety of environments, the chance to fully immerse yourself in another culture should work to your advantage, particularly if you're up against another candidate from your home country without such experience for a job later on. You'll learn to communicate better with people who might not understand your slang or nuances; you may improve your ability to speak a different language or learn a new one altogether; and you'll learn to approach new ideas with an open mind, rather than assuming the way it's done at home is always the best way.

> You'll quickly discover how to conduct yourself socially and professionally in a different culture.

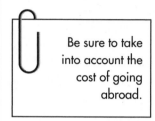

Be sure to take into account the cost of going abroad.

Some of this exposure to foreign cultures can be found at U.S. schools, which are working hard to create a carefully selected melting pot of ethnicities, genders, and backgrounds in each class. At the Top 30 schools, an average 30 percent of the students in the Class of 2000 came from outside the United States, up from 15 percent in 1988. Still, the dominant culture is clearly American; those who aren't familiar with baseball, barbecues, or speaking out in the classroom must adjust quickly—or find themselves marginalized. Although things are improving, most U.S. schools still have a distance to go when it comes to creating a truly global culture. It's different when Americans are the minority, says Ira Gaberman, an American student at INSEAD, where just 11 percent of the students are his compatriots. "It's not like an American business school where by and large the foreign students hang out together. There is no one predominant culture."

If your goal is to build a career abroad, an international B-school will help you build networks of people with similar interests. Although many U.S. and large multinational companies do recruit actively at such schools as INSEAD, London Business School, Ivey (Canada), IESE (Barcelona), and the International Institute for Management Development—IMD (Lausanne), most of them are looking for people to remain overseas, whatever their nationality. Many elite firms that hire hundreds of MBAs—GE Capital and McKinsey & Co., to name two—love what they get at those schools and have expanded recruiting there. Keep in mind, however, that if you're not a member of the European Community, your employer must get you a work permit before you begin a job in Europe, and similar restrictions hold in other parts of the world. By contrast, an MBA from a non-U.S. school is probably not ideal if you intend to spend your entire career in the States.

Although alumni networks are growing at virtually all international schools, you're not likely to find many from Rotterdam's B-school at a reception in Denver. Cost, too, is something to consider; add on the price of international plane tickets for trips home and the high cost of living in such places as London, and your cost–benefit analysis may not look so great, even though salaries for graduates of INSEAD and LBS, at least, are comparable to those of the top U.S. schools.

What you gain in the "international" diversity of the student population at a non-U.S. business school you may lose in the paucity of underrepresented American minorities and economi-

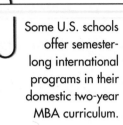

Some U.S. schools offer semester-long international programs in their domestic two-year MBA curriculum.

cally underprivileged students in these schools. Many of the prestigious foreign institutions are far more class-conscious and overtly elitist than their U.S. rivals. And, certainly, U.S. B-schools are working harder than ever to provide a better global experience, particularly because the greatest growth in the MBA market is coming from overseas. At USC's Marshall School of Business, all students are now required to travel abroad as part of the popular PRIME program, a five-week module that culminates in a project-oriented trip to Asia or Latin America. At such schools as Thunderbird, Carnegie Mellon, and Rochester, the international contingent is nearing 50 percent, and efforts are being made to move the faculties to similar percentages.

More and more American and international students are choosing to attend a U.S. B-school—but spending a semester or a quarter in an exchange program abroad. With this option, you get the clout and brand recognition of an American MBA as well as a taste of living overseas. You won't get the chance to truly comprehend another culture, but it will certainly give you a new perspective, not to mention a sense for whether you'd truly be happy spending your life in a faraway land. Says Marc Boheim, the Chicago grad who studied at IESE in Barcelona: "One of the reasons I went was because I wanted to be able to conduct business in Spanish. Being able to speak Spanish not only gives me access to Spain but to almost the entire continent of South America."

Chicago offers more than 25 programs around the world, and nearly every elite U.S. B-school allows students to pick from a variety of international exchange programs, with the exception of Harvard, Stanford, and Yale, which require that the B-school coursework be completed at home. UCLA leads the Top 30 with nearly 40 options. Sure, such exchange programs are expensive— often between $5000 and $6000—but not nearly as pricey as spending two years abroad. Although it can disrupt interview schedules for some students, the added experience can only help in the job market.

Still want to take the plunge? Then it's time to do a little homework. Factors to consider include the language requirements, the additional cost, the program's length, and the types of recruiters that come to each school—not to mention, of course, the overall quality of the institution. INSEAD requires fluency in two languages before entering, as well as another one by the time you leave, and LBS requires two, including English. Says Klein, the LBS student: "The best thing an American can do before coming here is to get started or refreshed on a language."

Whatever you decide to do, you're likely to have an unforgettable experience. You'll learn as much about business as you will about local foods, customs, and musical traditions. But you'll probably learn the most about yourself and how you react when home turf is thousands of miles away.

Following are the profiles of schools from BUSINESSWEEK's first-ever ranking of non-U.S. business schools.

1.

INSEAD

INSEAD

Boulevard de Constance

77305 Fontainebleau, Cedex, France

1 Ayer Rajah Avenue
Singapore 138676
E-mail: mbainfor@insead.fr
Web site: http://www.insead.fr/MBA

Corporate ranking: 1	Graduate ranking: 1
Enrollment: 679	Annual tuition & fees: $32,095
Women: 24%	Room and board: N/A
International: 90%	Average GMAT score: 688
Part-time: 0	Average years work exp.: 5
Average age: 28	Accepted applicants enrolled: N/A
Applicants accepted: N/A	Intellectual capital: 2
Median starting pay: $124,000	

Teaching methods: Lecture, 25% Case study, 35% Other, 40%

Business schools have sometimes had a reputation of being a place for white males, investment bankers, or anyone infatuated with the odd spreadsheet. But step onto the campuses of INSEAD in Fontainebleau, France, or its newest building in Singapore, and you'll see that the face of business education—and business—in Europe is well on its way to a change.

The 43-year-old global program at INSEAD brings people in from all over the world—and sets them loose at a frantic pace from day one. The MBA program is an intensive 10½-month ordeal that takes place among an extremely bright and diverse group of students. And this year, capped off with the No. 1 ranking among BUSINESSWEEK's non-U.S. B-schools, new leadership under Dean Gabriel Hawawini, and a year-old campus in the Buena Vista section of Singapore (a 5- to 10-minute drive from the center of the city), INSEAD is hotter than ever. The school's total faculty has grown 50 percent since 1995. The endowment swelled to $40 million, from "next to nothing" in 1994, the school's development director says. Women make up 24 percent of the student body, up from 18 percent in 1998. And now, the school offers its MBA degree on two continents, with students and faculty free to move between campuses. Fifty did just that in 2000, and the school expects that figure to double in 2001.

The Singapore campus, with a permanent faculty of 14 professors of its own, as well as its own placement office, has the ability to link its classrooms with ones in France, or elsewhere. With a focus on attracting

Contact:

Myriam J. Perignon
Director of MBA
Programs
33-1-60-72-40-05
Application deadlines:
February for
September
(France only)
July for January
(France and
Singapore)

MBAs from around the world who are interested in Asian business as well as folks already in the region and in the market for executive education courses, INSEAD Singapore is already hot.

Despite its locations in France and Singapore, the B-school is anything but a French or Asian school. An alliance forged in March 2001 with the University of Pennsylvania's Wharton School makes that clear. The alliance lets INSEAD's MBAs spend about seven weeks taking classes on Wharton's campuses in the United States. Students can also expect more interaction between INSEAD and Wharton classes. INSEAD'S classes are held in English, and students come after an average 5.2 years of work experience. Over half of the students hail from non-Western countries, and the school manages to attract the top business students from areas of the world that other B-schools can't seem to snag, such as Lebanon, Iran, Uzbekistan, and Peru. Singapore students come from 36 different nationalities, while the French campus hosts students from 46 countries. "What makes this school really international isn't the percentage of foreign students, but what's different here is that we don't have a concept of foreign or non-foreign," says H. Landis Gabel, director of the MBA program. "There's no dominant culture. Students often grew up in one country, studied in another, and worked in another," he adds.

INSEAD's Fontainebleau MBAs can start in September, graduating the following June, or they can start in January, take a seven-week summer break, and finish up in December. Singapore MBAs start in January only. The program is divided into five 8-week periods, the first two of which are made up almost entirely of core courses. As at many U.S. B-schools, incoming students are assigned to diverse study groups of five to seven people for most of the first four months. INSEAD requires 15 core courses along with at least seven electives in order to complete the degree. Most of the core courses are considered "business fundamentals," including such basics as Financial Accounting, Applied Statis-

tics, and Managerial Behavior. But there are four required courses that look at the "big picture": Economic Analysis, Strategic Management, Industrial Policy and International Competitiveness, and International Policy Analysis. In the third period, you can begin taking such electives as Bank Management, Strategies for Pacific Asia, and Management of Environmental Resources.

INSEAD's breathless pace applies to the administration as well, which has moved to increase MBA enrollment in both of its two campuses. (France has 620 and Singapore has 115, up from 53 in 2000.) The school says that its Singapore campus will accept 160 MBAs by 2002 and aims to have another cohort of students start every year. Hawawini, a former faculty member, who took the reins of the school in September 2000, says that Singapore will soon be the same size as the Fontainebleau campus, and that the school will consider adding a third campus down the road.

No matter what campus an MBA chooses, once an applicant is accepted, he or she is guaranteed a loan—upon passing a basic credit check and regardless of nationality or needing a co-signer—through ABN AMRO bank.

On the career placement front, INSEAD's graduates have both advantages and disadvantages. Although the shortened program allows you to save some money and get out into the workforce earlier, there is no time allotted for internships—unless you start INSEAD in January and work during the seven-week summer break. The list of recruiters visiting INSEAD mirrors that of many of the top U.S. business schools. Over 100 companies trekked to the school's campuses in the spring and autumn of 2000. Students in Singapore or France that wanted to interview at companies that only visited the other campus could do so via videoconferencing. And the school added some tech to the recruiting process with its Web-based system called CMS Online. Ultimately, close to 200 companies made presentations to the students, and the MBAs ended up with an average 2.7 job offers.

Top hiring companies in 2000: McKinsey & Co. (56); Boston Consulting Group (26); Bain & Co. (18); A.T. Kearney (11); Accenture (11); Goldman Sachs (10); Booz-Allen & Hamilton (8); Cluster Consulting (7); L'Oreal (7); Salomon Smith Barney (7).

Contact: Myriam J. Perignon
Director of MBA Programs
33-1-60-72-40-05
Application deadlines: February for September (France only); July for January (France and Singapore)

2.
LONDON BUSINESS SCHOOL

LONDON BUSINESS SCHOOL

Regent's Park
London NW14SA
E-mail address: mbainfo@london.edu
Web site address: http://www.lbs.edu

Corporate ranking: 3	Graduate ranking: 2
Enrollment: 851	Annual tuition & fees: $27,000
Women: 22%	Room and board: N/A
International: 80%	Average GMAT score: 690
Part-time: 315	Average years work exp.: 5
Average age: 30	Accepted applicants enrolled: 73%
Applicants accepted: 32%	Intellectual capital: 1
Median starting pay: $137,000	

Teaching methods: Lecture, 33%   Case study, 33%   Other, 34%

Contact:
Julia Tyler
Admissions Director
jtyler@london.edu
Application deadlines:
December 8
January 5
March 2
May 4

There are plenty of places to get an MBA. But of all the pickings—New York City; San Francisco; Hanover, New Hampshire; Miami; Fontainebleau, France; Monterrey, Mexico; or Rotterdam—few are as intoxicating as London. It's a city that is increasingly becoming a hub of international commerce and that served as the center of the dot-com craze as it swept the continent last year. The city has it all—film, theatre, history, Parliament, pubs, and even jobs. So it's little surprise that a B-school in its center would reap the benefits as more people around the world decide to pursue business education in hot urban centers.

Walk from the Baker Street underground station north and you might miss the London Business School sign along a brick wall on the right-hand side of the road. You won't miss the student café, Fresh, or the business bookstore. Once you find the entrance, you're transported into a world that is half academic, half trendy. A courtyard centers itself among the Sainsbury Wing, with the MBAR (that stands for MBA bar) on the left, Bizz restaurant, and the Bite sandwich shop on the right. A two-minute walk from the main campus is two-year-old Taunton Place, worth $18 million, that includes a gym, computer lab, library, reading room, and swimming pool.

The picturesque lawn that spills onto Regents Park—the Queen's Calvary still parades through once a week—casts the impression that the B-school's academic, pensive side rules, but it's not the case. There's a buzz in the air since this B-school of 536 full-time MBAs has been rising in international prominence to BUSINESSWEEK's rating of No. 2 outside of the United States. Still, things are changing at the 35-year-old B-school. In January, the school's dean of three years, John Quelch, announced he planned to leave the school in July of 2001. Quelch, a former marketing professor from Harvard Business School, gave LBS a wake-up call when he arrived. He set up 34 alumni associations in 29 countries (the school had none before). He increased revenues by 50 percent and brought the number of faculty to 90. It's no doubt that London's next dean will have to work diligently to keep those numbers up. And students have to hope the transition is a quick one if the momentum is to continue.

The school's flagship offering is its full-time, 21-month MBA. (The school also offers a five-year-old master's in finance program that streams 120 graduates into banks around the world.) The school's MBA program mirrors an American approach, but it's anything but a simple outpost for U.S.—or British—culture. LBS is swollen with people and practices from other coasts, cultures, and creeds: 80 percent of the Class of 2002 hails from outside of the United Kingdom and from over 50 countries. Although Americans don't face a language barrier on this campus, all LBS students must show competence in at least one language other than English by the time they graduate.

The MBA program is divided into six terms, with 15 required core courses packed into the first nine months. In the second year, students choose 12 electives from a catalog of 80 courses. LBS revised the core curriculum in 1999 to focus on interpersonal skills alongside concentrations in information management and entrepreneurship, with ethics and e-business concentrations introduced since 1997. The MBAs have time for a summer internship as well as an optional semester abroad in one of the largest MBA exchange programs in the world. Nearly one-third of second-year MBAs take advantage of London's partnerships with 35 other schools, many of them in the United States as well as in the rest of Europe, Asia, and South America.

As in the United States, entrepreneurship is a popular elective option. Over 700 Executive MBAs, Sloan Fellows, and MBAs are taking such courses in 2001. Every year, LBS, together with INSEAD, organizes the European Business Plan competition. Just a few months after the 2000 competition, two participating teams had set up shop. The school created the Foundation for Entrepreneurial Management in 1996 to help launch start-up businesses and to fund graduating students and alums involved in new ventures for LBSers. The school also raised £20 million to finance such start-ups.

The 245-person class is kept deliberately small to create a sense of intimacy in the midst of a very urban environment. Students live scattered throughout London and get to campus by bus or the underground (subway) but often grab a pint and some traditional English fish and chips at the Windsor Castle Pub, attached to the school. LBS also boasts some 30 sports and subject-related clubs. Joseph Nahhas, a second-year MBA, says that LBS isn't "quite as competitive as some of the U.S. schools. You don't have to get a good grade at the expense of someone else." Like other European B-schools, London competes in the MBA games, and in 2000 traveled to France to share its beer (students say that after competing schools ran out, LBS came to the rescue) and play sports.

The school is packed with more technology than ever. Over the past three years, the school invested $1.6 million to create new online courses and to build an advanced computing facility.

Landing a spot in London's MBA class in increasingly competitive, with 32 percent of applicants snagging seats in 2000. Applications for the Class of 2003 are up as much as 25 percent, making it more important than ever to apply to the school in the fall, rather than at the last deadline in May when the class is more likely to be full. An interview is mandatory at LBS, and it's the time that the school focuses on an applicant's international outlook, says Julia Tyler, director of admissions at the school. Self-reflection shows a candidate's potential as a leader, too, she says. "One of the things that we're looking for both when we review the paper application and also when we're meeting [an applicant] is the degree of self-awareness and self-reflection [they have]." GMAT scores average 690, and the average age is 30.

The career management center is ever-improving at LBS. Under the guidance of a former Royal Navy specialist, Chris Bristow, the office is becoming more professional and is focusing on attracting a wider variety of firms. One 2000 graduate says, "Come here if you have an interest in working outside the United States—the opportunities are many and quite remunerative." LBS hosted 120 recruiters on campus in 2000 for internship positions, and another 162 for full-time jobs. Top recruiters for the class included McKinsey & Co. (11); Bain & Co. (7); Booz-Allen & Hamilton (7); Goldman Sachs International (7); Deloitte Consulting (6); and Donaldson, Lufkin & Jenrette (6).

Contact: Julia Tyler
Admissions Director
jtyler@london.edu
Application deadlines: December 8; January 5; March 2; May 4

3.

IESE

IESE—INTERNATIONAL GRADUATE SCHOOL OF MANAGEMENT

The University of Navarra
Avenida Pearson 21
08034 Barcelona
Spain
E-mail address: mbainfo@iese.edu
Web site address: http://www.iese.edu

Corporate ranking: 2	Graduate ranking: 3
Enrollment: 440	Annual tuition & fees: $16,765
Women: 24%	Room and board: N/A
International: 63%	Average GMAT score: 655
Part-time: 0	Average years work experience: 4.3
Average age: 28	Applicants accepted enrolled: 72%
Applicants accepted: 31%	Intellectual capital: 7
Average starting pay: $77,000	

Teaching Methods: Lecture, 20%   Case study, 70%
                     Simulations, presentations, 10%

Contact:
Alberto Arribas
Director of Admissions
(34) 93-253-4200
Application deadline:
April 27—domestic
and international

It's the afternoon, and a TV set mounted above the bar is tuned to CNBC—the U.S. markets are open. Students at the International Graduate School of Management, IESE, in Spain's second-largest city, Barcelona, are nearly done with their day. In between courses, the MBAs at IESE often stop at el bar for café con leche or una cerveza. The students come from 55 countries—many are Europeans; others are from the Americas; a small cluster hail from Asia.

The school was founded with help from Harvard Business School and has links to Opus Dei, a Catholic organization of laymen and priests who strive for a Christian way of life. That's one reason that the school has emphasized ethics in its curriculum since the days before ethics became trendy, thanks to protests against sweatshops, deforestation, and scandals on Wall Street broke.

The program is ideal for anyone looking to master Spanish—the language can't be avoided in the two years you'll spend here. The program is bilingual, and students, split into two groups during the first year, can elect to take their 15 core classes in English or Spanish. Nonnative, first-year MBAs can take a one-month intensive Spanish course before the program starts in October. "What more can you ask for," says 31-year-old Jonathon Fleming from Scotland. "It's a school where you can get an MBA and learn another language," he says. The second year includes one final core class and 14 elective classes chosen from a catalog of 70. (Note: some elective classes are taught only in Spanish.) The school says that entrepreneurship is its forte, having begun its entrepreneurial classes in

1974. In 2000, the school was given approval to form its own Entrepreneurship Foundation, which awards money to student and alumni groups with business plans that appear solid.

Academics aside, IESE is a fun place to study. The fun starts at the end of November, when the school hosts a Thanksgiving Gala Dinner for the entire school. They serve turkey and put on a host of shows and student skits. During a long weekend in February, close to 100 students hit the slopes in the Pyrenees Mountains. In April, the students travel to France to compete in the annual sports tournament against European rivals London Business School, INSEAD, IMD, Rotterdam, and others. IESE's strength? Rowing, students say. Although most of that travel is for pleasure, it's one example of how the school opens doors across the continent for its MBAs. "I want to be involved in the European and South American markets," says Gabriel Salaverry, who will graduate this spring. "Schools in the United States wouldn't have had these connections."

When they aren't on holiday, IESE MBAs can be found in a number of student clubs, such as the Media and Communications Club, finance, and e-business groups, among others. However, the school doesn't currently have any women in the business club.

In an effort to increase the numbers and types of firms recruiting on campus, IESE started an E-biz Forum in 2000. After a day of presentations, panel discussions, and other events, about 50 of the companies interview job-hungry IESE MBAs. The school is focusing on the kinds of MBAs they produce for the job market, however, so the career development office now works hand-in-hand with the admissions team to screen candidates. "We want to be

a good match with their [job] expectations," says Placement Director Mireia Rius. That could make IESE more selective. The admissions director, Alberto Arribas, adds that in 2001 the school has seen a 40 percent increase in applications. What counts most? The GMAT, in which IESE students average scores of 655, and the interview carry the most weight in admissions these days. Not all applicants, however, are interviewed. If the school likes the look of an applicant on paper, that person is invited to interview, and, ultimately, all admitted MBAs complete interviews.

For all of its momentum, with a January 2001 announcement that the school's dean of 14 years, Carlos Cavalle, is leaving, the No. 3 ranked school can't avoid change. Cavalle's goals were to increase the school's visibility around the world, and he did that. He wanted to revise the curriculum, and he did that in 2000 when he shortened the program to 19 months from 21 and added new requirements such as entrepreneurship and e-business. He brought five new faculty members to the school in 2000, for a total of 78 from 16 countries in all. But the possibilities for who could take the top seat at IESE are wide, and some say it could be someone on the inside.

An MBA program is much more than its politics, though. And if you're someone that hits the business books seriously, but requires time to relax, you can't do much better than Barcelona.

Contact: Alberto Arribas
Director of Admissions
(34) 93-253-4200
Application deadline: April 27—domestic and international

4.

IMD—INTERNATIONAL INSTITUTE OF MANAGEMENT DEVELOPMENT

IMD—INTERNATIONAL INSTITUTE OF MANAGEMENT DEVELOPMENT

Ch. de Bellerive 23
CH-1001 Lausanne, Switzerland
E-mail address: mbainfo@imd.ch
Web site address: http://www.imd.ch

Corporate ranking: 4	Graduate ranking: 4
Enrollment: 86	Annual tuition & fees: $28,000
Women: 20%	Room and board: N/A
International: 95%	Average GMAT score: 650
Part-time: 0	Average years of work exp.: 7
Average age: 31	Accepted applicants enrolled: 83%
Applicants accepted: 13%	Intellectual capital: 3
Median starting pay: $124,000	

Teaching methods: Lecture, 10%   Case study, 65%
Team consulting projects, 25%

Contact:
Joann Pitteloud
MBA Admissions
Joann.Pitteloud@imd.ch
Application deadlines:
February 1
April 1
June 1
August 1
September 1

Set in a pristine Swiss landscape along the shores of Lake Geneva, the attractiveness of the physical locale in Lausanne of the International Institute of Management Development (IMD) is nearly matched by its MBA program. The school has the reputation around the world for being a place that's tough to gain access to. Indeed, with just 80 seats for MBAs from 40 nations, just 13 percent make the cut, making it one of the most selective schools worldwide. (Wharton accepted 14 percent of its applicants in 2000 and Stanford accepted 8 percent.)

Because it is a small program that demands focus, it's considered best suited for a professional with more work experience than the average four years that U.S. B-schoolers wield. That keeps the crowd elite and lets the school mix its executive MBAs and regular MBAs in elective classes toward the end of the 11-month program. IMD students average seven years of experience, so "any [class] discussion was pretty rowdy, and the opinions were generally strong," says James Craig, 33, who graduated from IMD in December 2000 and now works in the Netherlands. About 60 percent come from hard-core industries, such as manufacturing, oil, gas, consumer goods, and, of course, 12 percent are from consulting.

Classes start in January and end in December, and in that time, the school says you'll be ready to run your own business. From day one, students have access to over 50 full-time faculty members from 20 different nationalities—that's a student-to-teacher ratio that is tough to beat. Craig adds that students "could get information from teachers they weren't even working with at the moment," the community was so close.

Of course, getting to know professors isn't the only perk at IMD. Students say they walk away from campus knowing a good deal about most of their classmates. That's certainly aided by the fact that they spend over 1700 hours in classes that begin at 8:00 a.m. on Monday mornings and run through 1:00 p.m. on Saturdays. After each module, students change their small teams so that they get to know more people, too.

Once you're in, the MBA program is no easy ticket. Students say that the amount of required reading is daunting, and in small classes being silent isn't to your advantage. And with so much work to do, having a social life is difficult. "Officially, we don't have one," says Roland Siebelink, a Dutch 31-year-old who began the program in 2001. "But we've forced it in," in one case, by way of a fondue party at the start of the semester.

That's something to consider for the 40 percent of students who bring families to school. The school says that it admits, along with its students, about 12 to 20 MBA kids. Of course, some are born during the program, too. Although the school doesn't offer residences, it says that finding housing is easy. The cost is about 900 Swiss francs ($525).

Siebelink chose IMD because it was everything but American. In fact, the school says that U.S. applicants often fare poorly in admissions, despite the number that are interested, because they lack the right mix of international experience. "A lot haven't lived and worked outside of the United States," says Joann Pitteloud, director of admissions for IMD. And if IMD is looking for any Americans, it is the Latin American students it hopes to attract more of.

Despite being an international program, English is the only language spoken in class. The program is also the least flexible of the MBA programs. Students read three cases per night, or about 100 pages. Broken into eight 4- to 6-week modules from "dealing with complexity," to "taking charge," the set schedule leaves just one module for electives. The program is like "clockwork," Pitteloud says, with little sympathy for those who hope to skip classes from time to time. Still, one-third of the curriculum, the school says, is altered annually.

Consulting projects let students branch out, too. In February, just one month into the program, students form teams to work on new business ideas that can contribute to a community. When students present in July, the best six-person team is awarded a cash prize of about 5000 to 6000 Swiss francs to split (approximately $3000 to $3500). During the last two modules, students work on international consulting projects that send them around the world to deal with current issues in companies. The companies pick up the expenses.

IMD graduates fare well at graduation, too. Reporting median starting salaries of $100,000, they top rivals INSEAD and London Business School, where graduates report $90,000 starting base salaries. That's probably because of the work experience IMD students bring to the program.

The only drawback to IMD could be its relatively small alumni community. Compared to Wharton's 30,500 living alumni, just 1500 at IMD seems paltry. But compare Philly (heck, anywhere) to Switzerland, where you can study next to a lake that harbors inspiration, and you might be better off while you face the grind of one of the most demanding B-schools. And the elite community of insiders may be one of the best networks out there.

Contact: Joann Pitteloud
MBA Admissions
Joann.Pitteloud@imd.ch
Application deadlines: February 1; April 1; June 1; August 1; September 1

5.
THE UNIVERSITY OF WESTERN ONTARIO

THE UNIVERSITY OF WESTERN ONTARIO

Richard Ivey School of Business
1151 Richmond Street North
London, Ontario, Canada N6A 3K6
E-mail address: mba@ivey.uwo.ca
Web site address: http://www.ivey.uwo.ca/mba

Corporate ranking: 5	Graduate ranking: 5
Enrollment: 600	Annual tuition & fees: $14,000
Women: 25%	Room and board: $4200
International: 40%	Average GMAT score: 661
Part-time: 0	Average years of work exp.: 5
Average age: 28	Accepted applicants enrolled: 70%
Applicants accepted: 40%	Intellectual capital: 5
Median starting pay: $70,700	

Teaching methods: Lecture, 10%   Case study, 80%   Other, 10%

Contact:
Larysa Gamula
Director of Admissions
519-661-3419
Application deadline:
April 1

If you want the kind of MBA that builds on the case study method employed at such schools as Harvard, but don't want to pay Harvard prices, go to London, Ontario, located two hours from both Detroit and Toronto. That's where you'll find the Richard Ivey School of Business, part of the University of Western Ontario. Pay with U.S. dollars and you'll find that the exchange rate allows you a first-rate education—for a lot less than most elite U.S. schools. Though tuition is on the rise, it hit just $14,000 a year in 2000.

This year, the school has the ability to tag itself "elite," too. That's because in BUSINESSWEEK's first-ever ranking of B-schools outside of the United States, the Ivey school ranked No. 5. That will make it easier for the school's dean, Larry G. Tapp, to continue with his crusade to bring more revenues to the 79-year-old B-school as he removes the public school tuition caps.

The school is considered Canada's best, and it now attracts 280 MBAs to its campus every fall. The school has continued to make a big effort to attract non-Canadians, moving from 10 percent in the mid-1990s, to 36 percent in 1999, and 45 percent in 2000. Best known for finance and general management training, the two-year, full-time program focuses primarily on the case study method—the same employed at Harvard. The school is also the second-largest writer of cases in the world, after Harvard, and boasts a world-class faculty to teach them. That means a tough workload, but an experience to help young managers think on their feet.

The first year of the program is devoted to the core curriculum, offering such basics such as marketing and operations, as well as the global environment of business, business statistics, and management information systems. The mandatory classes lean heavily on the case method and run daily from 8:00 a.m. to 1:00 p.m. "We've had to come up with tough answers for tough problems using the case method," says Andrea Lekushoff, 30, who will graduate into a job at Deloitte Consulting in Toronto in 2001. In December, many first-years also participate in case competitions—sponsored by Accenture in 2000. To slip into the second year of the program, tagged MBA II, students need to meet basic requirements. But don't think that means that students are competitive in class. "This is not a competitive school," says Lekushoff. "[My classmates] are supportive and cooperative. Last year, when people got an exam framework [outline] they e-mailed it to the entire section of 70 students."

In the second year, students create their own schedule based on a selection of elective courses and have the option to choose concentrations or "streams" in consulting, entrepreneurship, or any other relevant subject area. In the winter of 2001, the school introduced a new stream called "e-leadership," focusing on developing leaders who have skills in e-business. Students have to bid, however, to get into the 70-person streams. Students can also choose courses outside of the business school, such as languages or law, or opt to spend a term at exchange partner schools in 1 of 16 international locations. Learning a second language is encouraged, but not required.

Like other B-schools, Ivey is working hard to expand its ties with Asia and Asia's rising demand for MBA skills. Ivey has a dedicated campus in Hong Kong, thanks to a $3.75 million gift from Dr. Henry Cheng of New World Development Cp., Ltd. And the school offers an executive MBA program in Hong Kong. Every May, four Ivey MBA students are selected to teach a four-week business class of business students at the School of Economics and Management at Tsinghua University in Beijing. Fifty other students travel to Eastern Europe as part of the LEADER (Students Leading Education and Development in Eastern Europe) program. LEADER participants teach three-week classes at selected host institutions.

On the home front, Ivey's MBAs spend most of their time in the school's handsome sandstone building, set on the University of Western Ontario's 100-year-old campus. London, Ontario, is a pleasant, if sleepy, university town, and most students live off campus in reasonably priced apartments or houses. There's plenty to get involved with on campus, too. In the fall of 2000, students began LeaderLab, a student-led forum that invites such leaders as Alan Webber, the co-founder of *FastCompany Magazine*, a former U.S. naval commander, and Toben Anderson, a Canadian adventurer and cancer survivor, to campus. About 500 people come to the events, with about 100 alumni and business execs tuned into live Webcasts. Next year, the students expect to double the number of speakers.

One weakness shared by most Canadian B-schools is attracting top-name recruiters to its campus. But at Ivey, 96 recruiters came on campus to hire summer interns, and 240 recruiters came to hire full-time employees in 2000. In 1999, top recruiting companies included Ernst & Young, General Motors, Scotia Bank, CIBC Bank (Canada), and Salomon Smith Barney. Graduates reported to BUSINESSWEEK median starting salaries of $70,700 after incurring about $92,000 in debt for the two years of study. Since non-Canadian and non-U.S. Ivey MBAs tend to have a hard time being placed in North America for summer internships, the career office offers the MBA Step-Up Program, which places them in local companies to get job skills, as well as a course for credit over the summer. Once they're on the job, the school keeps in touch with its 8500 alumni through 20 alumni clubs worldwide and through the lifetime e-mail addresses given to students in their first year.

Becoming part of the 600-strong MBA community remains relatively easy, with 40 percent of applicants making the cut in 2000. Students have, on average, five years of work experience. Some 5 to 10 percent of the MBAs are admitted without undergraduate degrees, an allowance the school makes because such students have about 13 years of work experience behind them.

Contact: Larysa Gamula
Director of Admissions
519-661-3419
Application deadline: April 1

**6.
ROTTERDAM
SCHOOL OF
MANAGEMENT**

Contact:
Connie Tai
Director of Admissions
+31 (0) 10-408 22 22
Application deadline:
June 15

ROTTERDAM SCHOOL OF MANAGEMENT

P.O. Box 1738
3000 DR Rotterdam
The Netherlands
E-mail address: rsm@rsm.nl
Web site address: http://www.rsm.nl

Corporate ranking: 7	Graduate ranking: 6
Enrollment: 496	Annual tuition & fees: $12,000
Women: 21%	Room and board: $10,550
International: 92%	Average GMAT score: 622
Part-time: 222	Average years of work exp.: 5.6
Average age: 29	Accepted applicants enrolled: 65%
Applicants accepted: 40%	Intellectual capital: 6
Median starting salary: $76,000	

Teaching methods: Lecture, 40%   Case study, 40%
Simulations/games, 20%

In the cultural capital of Europe for 2001, as tagged by the Ministers of Culture of the European Union, is a B-school that's young but feisty. Rotterdam School of Management, part of Erasmus University, only began offering an MBA program in English in 1985, but since graduating some 2500 students has made its way onto many prospective MBAs' and recruiters' top-choice lists.

In September 2000, the school enrolled its largest class yet, with 148 students, a 28 percent increase, into its two-year MBA program. Students hail from 47 countries, and 95 percent of them are fluent in another language. About 25 percent of the MBAs come from Asia, about half come from Europe, and another 20 percent hail from North and South America. Just 6 percent from the Middle East and Africa study at Rotterdam. Once they sit down in their English-taught classes, more than half of their professors are from outside of the Netherlands.

That's the right mix in the eyes of Canadian-born Kai Peters, the school's dean since March 2000. He's focused on enhancing the school's international focus even more, by linking students on global consulting projects with students at B-schools around the world.

The school has just about every program a prospective MBA could ask for. Its part-time MBA program, with 222 students, began in 1996. Showing the school's commitment to technology, RSM also offers a full-time MBA/MBI program in general management and information technology. And in the fall of 2001, the school will launch a 12-month, full-time Master's in Financial Management program for those who want an even firmer grasp of finance. In 2000 the school moved into a new building on the Erasmus University campus. The building is fitted with state-of-the-art facilities, including a simulated trading room—the school claims it's the only trading room in a B-school on continental Europe—and is packed with technology.

But the full-time MBA is the school's hallmark program, as well as its oldest, after over a decade of offering Dutch programs. In the first-year core, you can expect to focus on the basics: business methods, organizational behavior, and managerial economics. The second semester homes in on the functional areas such as human resources management and marketing management. Throughout, the school holds various mandatory workshops on everything from business communications to self-assessment, writing a CV, interviewing, project management, and consulting.

Just as in other 18-month programs, Rotterdam MBAs are required to snag real-world experience during the summer between their first and second years. All are required to do a project within a company. In the past, some students have focused on such things as building brands via wireless technology for the European interactive marketing division at Procter & Gamble, or researching the factors affecting new moves into markets in the agricultural commodities sector. At the end of the summer, students have to present a structured report to Rotterdam. Most present the same report to the company as well.

Back on campus for year two, Rotterdam MBAs get to hand pick their electives from a book of 70 courses. This is the time, the school says, for the MBAs to develop an expertise—one that will help them market themselves to companies—in such subject clusters as finance, information systems, marketing, or a specific grouping of electives that follow their career goals. (The school offers the same electives to its part-time MBAs, so full-timers have a chance to

interact with students with more work experience who are still on the job.)

Between classes, students say that Rotterdam is a great gateway to just about any activity in Europe. There's a women's weekend trip to Edinburgh, for example. And for MBAs living in continental Europe for the first time, the weekends are the time to pack a duffel bag and do some light traveling. Rotterdam participates in the MBA Olympics every year in Paris, and also sends a team of rugby players down to Barcelona to compete. For those with more of a knack for drinking, there's the carnival in Maastricht, a Dutch town that juts south into Europe between Belgium and Germany. Students cook together a lot, too. After all, what better excuse to have a glass of wine during a study group?

Margaret Gold, an MBA who graduated in March 2001, says that students don't rest on Sundays either. "You'll find a good sized group playing outdoor soccer at the Fina station, another group playing basketball, and another group enjoying Belgian beer with live jazz at Hoofdstuck II." On weeknights, you'll be sure to find plenty of classmates at local pubs Locus Publicus, O'Connel's, O'Shea's, and Concordia.

When it comes to living, it's just like going back to college. Ninety-two percent of the class hails from outside of the Netherlands, so the school has a housing office that can link MBAs to about 200 accommodations around Rotterdam. Of the 80 percent of the non-Dutch MBAs using the office, all are placed, the school says. Most are single-occupancy rooms with a shared bathroom; some also have private kitchens for about 850 guilders (approximately $340) a month. Students who come to campus with partners or families can rent fully furnished apartments for about 2400 guilders (approximately $975), including utilities, through a rental agency the school works with. Indeed, the school is exploring ways to increase this type of housing as more MBAs bring families to school. But one thing is a must no matter where you live and that's a bicycle, Holland's main mode of transportation. Just make sure you have a sturdy lock, as bike theft is a common, albeit comical, occurrence.

After a hefty investment in an MBA—2000 grads say they invested a median $132,000 in their MBAs—students want to feel as if their time and effort were well spent at B-school. And while the graduates from 2000 said that was the case, they do graduate with lower salaries—median starting base salaries of $76,000—than students at other B-schools in Europe, such as IMD, London, and INSEAD.

The good news is that getting accepted to RSM isn't as competitive as at other schools. The school gave the thumbs up to 40 percent of applicants last year. Rotterdam does require that its admitted students complete an interview. "About 75 percent of the candidates who apply get an interview," says Connie Tai, director of admis-

sions. "Out of those students, about 80 percent were offered a place [in 2000]." What students does the school want? Tai says that the more fun the student is, the better an applicant's chances of being seen as the right fit for Rotterdam.

To pay for a Rotterdam MBA, it helps to be from Turkey, Germany, Taiwan, or South Africa, countries where Rotterdam has set up full scholarships for deserving MBAs. The school does have an extensive list of resources on its financial aid Web site, listed by country. Dutch students, for instance, are guaranteed a loan through ABN AMRO and can go straight to the banks without filing any sort of application to the school for financial aid.

Contact: Connie Tai
Director of Admissions
+31 (0) 10-408 22 22
Application deadline: June 15

7.

UNIVERSITY OF TORONTO

UNIVERSITY OF TORONTO
Joseph L. Rotman School of Management
105 St. George Street
Toronto, Ontario M5S 3E6
Canada
E-mail address: mbaprog@mgmt.utoronto.ca
Web site address: http://www.mgmt.utoronto.ca

Corporate ranking: 6
Enrollment: 415
Women: 26%
International: 14%
Part-time: 152
Average age: 27
Applicants accepted: 31%
Median starting pay: $59,700

Graduate ranking: 7
Annual tuition & fees:
   resident—$11,700
   nonresident—$14,992
Room and board: N/A
Average GMAT score: 674
Average years of work exp.: 4.4
Accepted applicants enrolled: 46%
Intellectual capital: 4

Teaching methods: Lecture, 60%   Case study, 30%   Other, 10%

Contact:
Cheryl Millington
Director of Recruitment
and Admissions
416-978-3499
Application deadlines:
November 30
January 30
April 30

Toronto, Canada is one of the most diverse cities in North America. It's also the fifth largest city in North America by population. It's got symphony, theater, and a Wall Street of its own called Bay Street, where Canadian and U.S. banks have set up shop next door to one another. After work, there are plenty of sports to watch to release some tension, such as hockey and basketball. The one sport that Toronto lacks is football.

And just around the corner from one of Toronto's four Chinatowns is an increasingly popular B-school. That's the business school BUSINESSWEEK recently ranked No. 2 in Canada and No. 7 worldwide, University of Toronto's Joseph L. Rotman School of Management.

Many attribute the recent attention attracted by the school to its new dean, Roger L. Martin. Before coming to Rotman, the Canadian-born dean—a 1981 Harvard Business School alum—was a director of Monitor Company, a strategy-consulting firm based in Cambridge, Massachusetts. Once he settled into his campus office in 1998, he began insisting that the school "break down the silos" that business education revolves around, such as finance and marketing faculties. "Functional areas create narrow subjects and narrow faculty," Martin says.

His vision is to graduate future CEOs rather than functionally specific managers. The move caused a bit of commotion—some professors have left the school since his arrival. But overall, the reaction is good. Martin says he'll double the size of the MBA class to about 500 students by 2003. The endowment, if he has his way, will grow to $100 million

(Canadian), from the $52 million the school has now. Compare that to Wharton's nearly $340 million endowment, and it's clear that Martin has his work cut out for him.

On campus, Martin can't be avoided. In the first year, Martin leads a weeklong course on thinking skills to help MBAs process all of the information hitting them. The real core starts thereafter with 14 core courses in the first year, among them Business Ethics, Economics of Enterprise, Marketing, and Financial Accounting. The second year includes 2 compulsory courses—Advanced Strategic Management and Management Skills Development—and then opens the door for students to choose 9 elective courses from a book of over 50.

In the second year, Dean Martin enters the fray again to teach an increasingly sold-out class called Learning to Lead, where Martin says students learn "how to deal with clashing models," which he admits "is not a very MBAish process." The second year is also the time that MBAs choose which "streams" of concentration they want to pursue. Consulting, financial engineering, and investment banking remain the most popular, with e-business and new ventures (entrepreneurship) attracting a fair crowd as well, though only 2 percent of grads in 2000 went to companies with fewer than 100 people.

In between classes, life is pretty relaxed in the busy city. The university has increased the amount of living space on campus so that anyone who wants an on-campus residence can get one. But most MBAs rent condos on Bay Street or live in "the Annex," a progressive neighborhood near campus packed with writers, actors, and, yes, MBA students. There's a subway stop up the street from Rotman's main building, but many MBAs drive thanks to a 700-car garage under the school.

Toronto's students say that the community at Rotman is strong. Indeed, a common complaint among students is that "the school's identity still needs to catch up to the ever-improving caliber of its student body," says Joanna Roten-berg, who will graduate in 2001 with a J.D./MBA. "Not only are students bright and inspiring to one another from an educational standpoint, but they make the time to have fun as well. This breeds a lot of camaraderie, and makes otherwise painful moments during 'crunch' times seem more enjoyable."

It helps that group tickets are cheaper to see the Raptors play basketball, but you'll also find the MBA students together once a week for Thirsty Thursdays at popular hangouts including the Bedford Academy and The Madison. But these MBAs bond before classes start, thanks to a weeklong orientation put on by second-year MBAs in the woods three hours north of Toronto. The soon-to-matriculate MBAs spend a week on courses, in mini-lectures, swimming, and dancing at 1970s-themed parties and square dances. The MBA Games are an annual classic, too. The most popular sport? Probably drinking, some quip, but Rotman did manage an overall win in 2000, only to lose the title in 2001. By the springtime—you'll come to appreciate the word *thaw*—students are planning for talent shows and suiting up for formal dances.

Around the same time, students are scrambling for their promised MBA jobs and internships, too. And that's where the school struggles. Until recently, the B-school's career development office served both graduate and undergraduate students—the school has 50,000 students in total. In fact, only 18 companies recruited on campus for first-year internships and 35 recruited for second-years. By graduation, many students were earning good salaries for Canada—a median of $52,500—but mediocre compared to B-schools in the United States and Europe. That's after a median total investment of $99,000.

The good news is that tuition is paltry compared to U.S. B-schools. Tuition across Canada is on the rise, reaching $14,992 in 2000 for non-residents, but compared to a $21,110 annual bill at a school such as University of North Carolina–Chapel Hill, it's a clear bargain.

Snagging money to help pay for the program isn't easy at Toronto unless you're Canadian. While the school has an interest-free tuition loan program with Scotia Bank, nondomestics aren't eligible. The average aid package is $10,000 Canadian. "One of the things that's on my 'to-do' list is to lobby the banks to see if they will consider offering loans to non–Canadian citizens or residents," says Cheryl Millington, director of recruitment and admissions at Rotman.

Applicants will probably find it more difficult to be accepted by the school in coming years. Millington says that Rotman has benefited from its recent ranking by BUSINESSWEEK, noting an increase in applications. In 2000, 31 percent of applicants made the cut, and in 2001 even fewer will. The school is marketing to U.S. students, who would probably help boost its job placement results if they returned to the United States to take their post-MBA jobs.

Contact: Cheryl Millington
Director of Recruitment and Admissions
416-978-3499
Application deadlines: November 30; January 30; April 30

INDEX